Comprehensive Handbook of
Clinical Health Psychology

Comprehensive Handbook of Clinical Health Psychology

Edited by
Bret A. Boyer and M. Indira Paharia

WILEY

John Wiley & Sons, Inc.

Library of Congress Cataloging-in-Publication Data:
Comprehensive handbook of clinical health psychology / [edited] by Bret A. Boyer, M. Indira Paharia.
     p. : cm.
Includes bibliographical references.
ISBN 978-0-471-78386-2 (cloth : alk. paper)
1. Clinical health psychology—Handbooks, manuals, etc. I. Boyer, Bret A. II. Paharia, M. Indira.
[DNLM: 1. Behavioral Medicine—methods. 2. Disease—psychology. 3. Health Behavior. WB 103 C737 2008]
R726.7.C64 2008
616.001'9—dc22
                                    2007008876
Printed in the United States of America

10 9 8 7 6 5 4 3 2 1

To Sonia, Julia, and Noah, who together are the legs that hold up my table,
as well as the wine and flowers atop.
—Bret

To my mother, who fought for her health with courage and dignity until the end.
To my father, whose caregiving of so many is an inspiration.
To my husband, who lifts me up to life's potential.
— Indira

Contents

Editor Biographies

Bret A. Boyer, PhD, is a licensed psychologist who has devoted the past 20 years to therapy, teaching, and research regarding clinical health psychology. He is an assistant professor and director of the Health Psychology Concentration at Widener University's Institute for Graduate Clinical Psychology. He is also the founder and director of The Family Health Psychology Center (www.familyhealthpsychology.com), a clinical practice providing therapy to a diverse clientele since the mid-1990s, and serves as Director of Behavioral Medicine for the Mercy Catholic Medical Center. He actively consults with Integrated Diabetes Services and with the Practice Based Research Network of Crozer-Keystone Health System. Dr. Boyer has conducted and published empirical research on diabetes, pediatric spinal cord injury, cancer, and the application of clinical interventions. He completed an MA in behavior analysis and therapy at Southern Illinois University, a PhD in clinical psychology from Temple University, as well as a postdoctoral fellowship in pediatric psychology in the oncology division of The Children's Hospital of Philadelphia.

M. Indira Paharia, PsyD, MBA, MS, is a licensed clinical psychologist with specialties in health psychology and disease prevention. Dr. Paharia has lectured both nationally and internationally on topics of health care finance, disease management, and health promotion. She currently serves as the Assistant Director of Behavioral Health and Wellness for Regence Blue Cross Blue Shield, where she is responsible for clinical and financial operations, disease management and health promotion programs, integrated primary care, corporate strategy, and quality improvement for a carve-in managed behavioral health organization serving 3 million members in four states of the Pacific Northwest. Former positions held include Assistant Director of the Institute for Graduate Clinical Psychology and Assistant Professor of Health Psychology at Widener University and Assistant Professor and Director of the Behavioral Medicine Division at Temple University School of Dentistry. She has conducted grant-funded research and training programs in health psychology and served as Co-Director of the Coalition for the Advancement of Community Health Psychology. Dr. Paharia has specialized clinical experience in providing tobacco cessation, treatment for obesity, pre/post-bariatric surgery assessment and management, as well as disease management for chronic conditions. She received her doctorate in clinical psychology from the University of Denver.

Foreword

THE DEVELOPMENT of this book reflects the growing recognition of the interrelationships between personal beliefs and behaviors and mental and physical health problems. Individuals' beliefs about themselves, their health problems, and their behaviors can effect both the development of mental and physical health problems as well as their outcomes. Mental health problems are more common among patients with chronic disease and can contribute to the development and course of these diseases. It is not surprising, therefore, that the likelihood of depression increases two to three fold among those suffering from common chronic medical conditions such as coronary artery disease, diabetes, cardiovascular disease, and arthritis. We also know that depression is associated with a 40 to 60% increased risk of morbidity associated with arthritis (Egberts, Leufkens, Hofman, & Hoes, July 1997) and a three-fold increased risk of morbidity associated with hypertension (Rabkin, Charles, & Kass, 1983). Depression is also associated with a 40% increased risk of cardiac events in patients with coronary artery disease (Carney, Rich, & Freedland et al., 1988) and, following a myocardial infarction, depression increases the risk of coronary fatalities from 3 to 16.5% at 6 months and from 6 to 20% at 18 months. (Frasure-Smith, Lesperance, & Talajic, 1995; Frasure-Smith, Lesperance & Talajic 1993). Diabetic patients who are depressed have worse treatment adherence and glucose control, more symptoms, and an elevated rate of complications compared to nondepressed diabetic patients. (DiMatteo, Lepper, & Croghan, 2000; Lustman, Griffith, Freedland, & Clouse, 1997; Van der Does, De Neeling, & Snoek et al., 1996; Lustman, Clouse, & Carney 1988; Goodnick, Henry, & Buki 1995; Leedom, Meehan, Procci & Zeidler, 1991; deGroot, Anderson, & Freedland, et al., 2001). Anxiety disorders are also more common among patients seen in the primary care setting, and are associated with high levels of somatic symptoms, functional impairment, health care utilization, and adverse health behaviors such as cigarette smoking and sedentary lifestyle (Kroenke, Spitzer, Williams, Monahan, & Lowe, 2007).

The issues addressed in this book are of critical importance in preventing and controlling a wide variety of chronic diseases. Mental health professionals with expertise in health psychology are needed to help patients modify maladaptive behaviors and beliefs, cope with chronic disease, and integrate mental health care into the medical care setting.

During the past decade the field of health psychology has demonstrated an increased presence in the health care arena through both clinical and empirical contributions. It is likely that this presence will continue to grow in the coming decades. Currently more than 50% of patients with mental health problems are seen only in the general medical sector. New models of care have been developed that have effectively integrated mental health clinicians into the primary care setting. These models will provide health psychologists with unprecedented opportunities to participate in the management of patients with chronic medical conditions. This opportunity cannot be fully realized, however without the guidance and training of future generations of clinicians. To this end, Drs. Boyer and Paharia present a timely and outstanding contribution to the field of health psychology through the *Comprehensive Handbook of Clinical Health Psychology*.

This *Handbook* provides a modern approach to the clinical practice of the biopsychosocial model for both mental health and medical professionals, built on sound theoretical principles and empirical evidence. An impressive array of authors present knowledge of the most prevalent chronic diseases of our time, including cardiovascular disease, cancer, AIDS, diabetes mellitus, and obesity, and other relevant issues such as substance abuse in medical settings. The *Handbook* offers essential and practical information to guide the reader clinically and uses illustrative case examples to demonstrate assessment and intervention. This text is rife with valuable clinical and empirical information and emphasizes burgeoning roles for health psychologists, such as in chronic disease prevention, integrated primary care, presurgical evaluations, transplant service, and treatment of psychological factors and improvement of self-regulation to maximize medical outcomes in chronic disease management. It provides students, teachers, and practitioners with an armamentarium of sound clinical tools for working in interdisciplinary settings. The *Handbook* bridges the proverbial gap between medical and mental health, thereby providing the reader a map for treating the patient in his or her entirety through mind, body, and spirit.

David Brody

REFERENCES

Carney, R. M., Rich, M.W., & Freedland, K. E. (1988). Major depressive disorder predicts cardiac events in patients with coronary artery disease. *Psychosomatic Medicine, 50,* 627–633.

De Groot, M., Anderson, R., Freedland, K. E., Clouse, R. E., & Lustman, P. J. (2001). Association of depression and diabetes complications; a meta-analysis. *Psychosomatic Medicine, 63,* 619–630.

DiMatteo, M. R., Lepper, H. S., & Croghan, T.W. (2000). Depression is a risk factor for noncompliance with medical treatment: meta-analysis of the effects of anxiety and depression on patient adherence. *Archives of Internal Medicine, 160,* 2101–2107.

Egberts, A. C., Leufkens, H. G., Hofman, A., & Hoes, A.W. (1997). Incidence of antidepressant drug use in older adults and association with chronic diseases: the Rotterdam Study. *Int Clinical Psychopharmacology,12,* 217–223.

Frasure-Smith, N., Lesperance, R., & Talajic, M. (1993). Depression following myocardial infarction. Impact on 6-month survival. *JAMA, 270,* 1819–1825.

Frasure-Smith, N., Lesperance, R., & Talajic, M. (1995). Depression and 18-month prognosis after myocardial infarction. *Circulation, 91,* 999–1005.

Goodnick, P. J., Henry, J. H., & Buki, V. M. (1995). Treatment of depression in patients with diabetes mellitus. *Journal of Clinical Psychiatry, 56,* 128–136.

Kroenke, K., Spitzer, R. L., Williams, J. B. W., Monahan, P. O., and Löwe, B. (2007). Anxiety disorders in primary care: Prevalence, impairment, comorbidity, and detection. *Annals of Internal Medicine, 146,* 317–324.

Leedom, L., Meehan, W. P., Procci, W., & Zeidler, A. (1991). Symptoms of depression in patients with type II diabetes mellitus. *Psychosomatics, 32,* 280–286.

Lustman, P. J., Clouse, R. E., & Carney, R. M. (1988). Depression and the reporting of diabetes symptoms. *Int Journal of Psychiatry Medicine, 18,* 295–303.

Lustman, P. J., Griffith, L. S., Freedland, K. E , & Clouse, R. E. (1997). The course of major depression in diabetes. *Gen Hosp Psychiatry, 19,* 138–143.

Rabkin, J. G., Charles, E., & Kass, F. (1983). Hypertension and *DSM-III* depression in psychiatric outpatients. *American Journal of Psychiatry, 140,* 1072–1074.

Van der Does, F. E., De Neeling, J. N, & Snock, F. J. (1996). Symptoms and well-being in relation to glycemic control in type II diabetes. *Diabetes Care, 19,* 204–210.

Preface

HEALTH PSYCHOLOGY has matured over the past several decades into a consolidated subspecialty of psychology, integrating theory, empirical research, clinical practice, and public policy endeavors. Multiple books have addressed this field for undergraduate education, graduate study in various disciplines, and continued education for practicing clinicians and investigators. In coming to author this book, our own education was augmented by not only our own empirical research and clinical experience, but indeed by these previous health psychology texts. As the old dictum states, this book clearly "stands on the shoulders of giants."

Our goal was to write a text that was clear and yet addressed each topic in its full complexity, detailed and yet accessible to readers from multiple professional disciplines. We wanted to create a comprehensive coverage of health psychology, and to write adequately about every health condition that a health psychologist might encounter, in every body system, including special topics relevant to health psychology. Such breadth would indeed require a multiple-volume endeavor, so our decision was, instead, to write comprehensively about fewer topics in order to not sacrifice depth for breadth. Each of us may notice the absence of a topic that we feel passionate about; however, we chose our topics by considering those conditions and trends that have become most prevalent in the field of health psychology today, and for which health psychology endeavors offer important contributions to medical and psychological outcomes.

While this text is designed predominantly for the psychology graduate student, it may also serve other purposes. It is suitable for graduate level psychology courses in health psychology, behavioral medicine, adjustment to chronic health conditions, and disease prevention. In addition, this text may be especially useful for courses about behavioral health and psychological factors for students of medicine, nursing, and social work, by bridging the gap between the pathophysiology and the experience and response of patients. Finally, the text offers comprehensive, current, and readily accessible information for practicing professionals, as an up-to-date reference guide regarding empirical research about conditions and interventions.

This text is unique in several aspects. We have included a chapter on insurance and managed care issues and a chapter on substance abuse in medical settings, topics that are seldom covered in graduate health psychology texts but are frequently asked about by graduate students. We also devoted a section of the text to chronic disease prevention, a growing focus in today's health care environment. Additionally, we present a new model for guiding the clinician through the application of the biopsychosocial model, as it has been our experience that students may comprehend the theory but feel uncertain of its application. This model, the Model for Integrating Medicine and Psychology (MI-MAP), is a practical tool to guide assessment and treatment planning. After developing and applying this model for over ten years with clinical psychologists training in health psychology as well as with internal medicine residents and interns, MI-MAP serves as a bridge between the existing conceptual models for the adaptation to health conditions and applied clinical interventions. It thereby guides the application of the biopsychosocial model "where the rubber meets the road." MI-MAP is presented in Chapter 1 and is consistently used throughout the chapters in Part 3 of the text, thereby utilizing a parallel construction. That is, the reader can find the same sections in each of these chapters, allowing for quick reference, comparison, and contrast regarding the research on different health conditions.

The text is organized in four parts. Part 1 includes a description of theoretical models in health psychology and the relevant insurance and managed care issues. Part 2 is devoted to health psychology's role in chronic disease prevention, highlighting tobacco cessation and obesity treatment. Part 3 is subdivided into the most common medical disease states (cardiovascular diseases, HIV/AIDS, cancer, etc.) that health psychologists face in practice. Part 4 covers special topics in health psychology, such as chronic pain and pediatrics. Each clinical chapter includes a detailed case that illustrates health psychology treatment approaches. Our contributing authors were chosen for their expertise in respective subspecialties of health psychology and for their skill and experience as researchers and clinicians. It is our fervent hope that the *Comprehensive Handbook of Clinical Health Psychology* will prove to be an invaluable tool in your clinical development.

We have many individuals to thank for their assistance in making this book possible. We would like to thank Kristin Van Doren, Nicholas Wood, Rebecca Rothbaum, and Xiaolu Jiang for help with literature searches and Isabel Pratt for help with manuscript preparation. Dr. Boyer would like to thank Geoffery Marczyk and Virginia Brabender for their advice regarding authorship/editorship endeavors; Frank Masterpasqua; Tamar Chansky-Stern, Phillip and Meredith Stern; Sandra Kosmin; Joanne, David, Jonathan, and Georges Buzaglo for support; and Roseanne Cantor, Erica Henninger, and Jennifer de Moose for their support and patience. Dr. Paharia would like to thank Shelly Smith-Acuna, Tony Bandele, Pam Haglund, Clydette Stulp, William Aaronson, Barbara Manaka, Arnold Raphaelson, and Tom Getzen for their mentorship and support in shaping her career.

—Bret A. Boyer and M. Indira Paharia

Author Biographies

Lamia P. Barakat, PhD, is an Associate Professor of Psychology at Drexel University, where she also serves as training director for the PhD program in clinical psychology. She received her PhD in clinical-community psychology from the University of South Carolina. Following pre- and postdoctoral training at the University of Medicine and Dentistry of New Jersey (Newark), she moved to the Children's Hospital of Philadelphia, where she undertook research focused on childhood cancer survival. Currently, her clinical and research endeavors comprise risk-and-resistance models for understanding quality of life and psychosocial adaptation for children with chronic illness as well as application of the model to empirically supported interventions, particularly for children with sickle cell disease, childhood cancer survivors, and youth with HIV/AIDS.

Albert J. Bellg, PhD, is a Clinical Health Psychologist at the Appleton Heart Institute in Appleton, Wisconsin. He is also a lecturer in psychology at Lawrence University. Dr. Bellg received his PhD in clinical psychology from the University of Rochester in New York and did his internship at Rush Medical Center in Chicago. He was a Fellow in Consultation-Liaison Psychiatry (Psychology) at Henry Ford Hospital in Detroit and in the Advanced Clinical Educators Fellowship in the Department of Medicine at the University of Rochester School of Medicine and Dentistry. Prior to coming to the Appleton Heart Institute, he was Director of Cardiac Psychology at the Rush Heart Institute in Chicago and Assistant Professor of Psychology and Medicine at Rush Medical College. He developed the Health Behavior Internalization Model (*Behavior Modification*, October, 2002) to understand and predict long-term health behavior maintenance. Among his other publications is *Listening to Life Stories: A New Approach to Stress Intervention in Health Care* (New York: Springer, 1997).

Anu Bodetti, MD, has recently finished her nephrology fellowship at Georgetown University in Washington, DC. She now practices nephrology in private practice.

Adam C. Brooks, PhD, is a research scientist at the Treatment Research Institute in Philadelphia. He has a PhD in clinical psychology with a specialization in marital and family therapy from St. John's University. For the past 5 years, he has treated substance abusing patients at the Columbia University Division on Substance Abuse, using a variety of empirically validated treatments, and is an expert supervisor in Motivational Interviewing.

Allan Goody, MD, is a graduate of Georgetown University School of Medicine. After medical school, he completed a residency in internal medicine and a nephrology fellowship at Georgetown University in Washington, DC. Dr. Goody is currently in nephrology private practice at the Virginia Hospital Center in Arlington, Virginia. He is also a Clinical Associate Professor of Medicine (Nephrology and Hypertension) at Georgetown University.

Jeff M. Greenblatt, MD, FACP, MBA, received his MD from Hahnemann University in 1987 and completed a residency in Internal Medicine at Jefferson University in 1990. He is board certified in internal medicine and has been involved in several medical education leadership positions since 1996. He earned his MBA from Widener University in 2001 and is currently Director of Internal Medical Education and Program Director for the Internal Medicine Residency at Hurley Medical Center. His interests include medical education, quality improvement, patient safety, and health literacy.

Reverend Debra W. Haffner is the Executive Director of the Religious Institute on Sexual Morality, Justice and Healing. She is the former CEO and President of the Sexuality Information and Education Council of the United States (SIECUS). She has been a sexologist for 30 years and was ordained as a Unitarian Universalist minister in 2003. She is the author of five books, including two books for parents, *From Diapers to Dating* and *Beyond the Big Talk,* as well as several books for congregations on sexuality issues.

Melanie S. Harris, PhD, received her PhD in clinical psychology from the University of Miami, Coral Gables, Florida. She completed a postdoctoral fellowship in psychosocial oncology in the Complementary Medicine Program of Albert Einstein College of Medicine, Bronx, New York. She is currently an Assistant Professor of Psychology at Touro College in New York City. She has published and presented at national conferences regarding spiritual-existential and psychoeducational interventions for underserved, advanced-stage cancer patients, stress-related growth, and quality of life following cancer.

Kevin A. Hommel, PhD, is Assistant Professor of Clinical Psychology, University of Pennsylvania School of Medicine, Department of Psychiatry; The Children's Hospital of Philadelphia, Division of Gastroenterology, Hepatology, and Nutrition. Dr. Hommel received his doctorate in clinical psychology at Oklahoma State University, and completed his residency in pediatric psychology and postdoctoral fellowship at Cincinnati Children's Hospital Medical Center in the Division of Psychology. He has published in the areas of adherence to medical regimens and psychological adjustment to pediatric chronic illness, particularly inflammatory bowel disease.

Aparna Kalbag-Buddhikot, PhD, graduated from the University of Colorado at Boulder with a doctorate in clinical psychology in 2001. Until 2005, she served as research scientist in the Columbia University Division on Substance Abuse. She served as co-investigator and co-principal investigator on two National Institute of Drug Abuse grants, testing the effects of medication and cognitive-behavioral therapy in the treatment of substance abuse disorders.

Larina Kase, PsyD, MBA, received her doctorate in clinical psychology and her masters in business administration from Wright State University, Dayton, Ohio. She served as psychologist and faculty member at the Center for the Treatment and Study of Anxiety, University of Pennsylvania, until 2005. Dr. Kase is currently in private practice in the Philadelphia area and the President of *Strength Weight Loss & Wellness* (www.StrengthWeightLoss.com), a national consultancy. Dr. Kase is the author or coauthor of six books, including the self-help book, *Joining the Thin Club: Tips for Toning Your Mind After You've Trimmed Your Body*, as well as many electronic books, including *4 Steps to Ending Emotional Eating* (www.EndingEmotionalEating.com).

Elizabeth McQuaid, PhD, is an Associate Professor in the Brown Medical School Department of Psychiatry and Human Behavior, and Staff Psychologist at Rhode Island Hospital. Her early research assessed adherence to pediatric asthma regimens across the adolescent transition, and individual and family characteristics that influence pediatric asthma outcomes. More recently, her work has involved designing and implementing interventions to promote adherence to long-term controller medications in pediatric asthma, through funding from the National Institute of Child Health and Human Development (NICHD), the National Institute for Nursing Research (NINR) and a Career Investigator Award from the American Lung Association. Currently, she directs or collaborates on several projects that assess psychological and family characteristics that influence asthma management and outcomes in pediatric asthma.

Daphne Koinis Mitchell, PhD, is an Assistant Professor at the Department of Psychiatry and Human Behavior at Brown Medical School. She is also a clinical psychologist specializing in pediatric psychology at Rhode Island Hospital. She received her PhD in clinical psychology from the University of Massachusetts, Boston, and completed her predoctoral clinical internship and postdoctoral fellowship training at Brown University. Dr. Koinis Mitchell's research interests are in the area of urban poverty and child development, with a particular interest in pediatric asthma health disparities.

Alyson Moadel, PhD, received her PhD from Yeshiva University and completed a postdoctoral fellowship at Memorial Sloan Kettering Cancer Center in New York City. She is now Assistant Professor at Albert Einstein College of Medicine and Cancer Center, in the Department of Epidemiology and Population Health, and serves as Director of the Psychosocial Oncology Program and the Quality of Life Cancer Research Program Division of Behavioral and Nutritional Research. Over the past several years she has published multiple articles regarding cancer survivorship, seeking meaning and hope, yoga, and other studies of underserved and ethnically diverse populations with cancer.

Nicole Monserrate, MD, is a graduate of Georgetown University School of Medicine. She went on to complete her residency in internal medicine at Georgetown. Dr. Monserrate is currently an Associate Program Director for the Georgetown Internal Medicine Residency program and practices at the Virginia Hospital Center, where she serves as the Medical Director of the hospital's outpatient clinic. Dr. Monserrate's interests include medical education and health care for the underserved.

John D. Otis, PhD, is an Assistant Professor of Psychology and Psychiatry at Boston University and the Director of Pain Management Psychology Services at the VA Boston Healthcare System. Dr. Otis has conducted research and produced scholarly writing about pain throughout the lifespan. He has focused his clinical research career on the development of innovative approaches to pain management, tailored to specialized patient populations.

Allison Dorlen Pastor, PhD, graduated from Fordham University in 2001 with a doctorate in clinical psychology. She served as Research Scientist in the Columbia University Division on Substance Abuse until 2004, providing psychotherapy for drug-dependent and dually-diagnosed participants in clinical trials. She also trained and supervised psychology interns and medical residents from Columbia-Presbyterian Medical Center on diagnostic assessment, relapse-prevention therapy, and motivational enhancement therapy for substance abusing patients. Currently she is in private practice, specializing in substance abuse, women's issues, and couples therapy. Her offices are located in New York City and northern New Jersey.

Donna B. Pincus, PhD, is an Associate Professor at Boston University and the Director of the Child and Adolescent Fear and Anxiety Treatment Program at the Center for Anxiety and Related Disorders. Dr. Pincus has focused her clinical research career on developing new, evidence-based treatments for children and adolescents with anxiety disorders. Dr. Pincus created the Child Anxiety Network (www.childanxiety.net), which presents state-of-the-art information on child anxiety to the public and to health care professionals.

J. Scott Richards, PhD, ABPP, is a clinical psychologist who has worked in the rehabilitation field his entire career. He is a graduate of Kent State University and is a tenured professor and Vice Chair of the Department of Physical Medicine and Rehabilitation, University of Alabama at Birmingham. He has been engaged in the provision of clinical services, teaching, and research, with the latter focused on adjustment to spinal cord injury and chronic pain.

Elizabeth J. Richardson, MA, is a medical (clinical) psychology doctoral student at the University of Alabama at Birmingham. She obtained her BA in psychology at Birmingham-Southern College and her MA in clinical psychology at the University of Alabama at Birmingham. Her current research endeavors in rehabilitation psychology include post-spinal cord injury adjustment and chronic pain.

Amy Rogers, PhD, is an Associate Professor of Psychology at Delaware State University. She completed her MA in social psychology at Arizona State University and her PhD in applied experimental psychology at Southern Illinois University in Carbondale. She has engaged in research, publishing, and professional presentations in the area of HIV/AIDS.

Lynda M. Sagrestano, PhD, earned a PhD in social psychology from the University of California at Berkeley and held NIMH-funded postdoctoral fellowships at UCLA and the University of Illinois at Chicago. She is now the Director of the Center for Research on Women at the University of Memphis. Her research interests include maternal and prenatal health, adolescent sexual behavior, HIV prevention, domestic violence, and gender and work stress.

Susan Schaming McNiff, EdD, earned a Doctorate in Counselor Education and Supervision from Duquesne University in Pittsburgh. She is a Licensed Professional Counselor and is Nationally Board Certified as an education and human-service professional with more than 22 years experience in a variety of behavioral health, educational, and counseling settings. Dr. McNiff facilitates the Elementary and Secondary School Counseling Programs at Widener University, and serves as the advisor to graduate students in those programs.

Arron Service, PhD, earned his PhD in applied psychology from Southern Illinois' University at Carbondale in 2006. His graduate research focused on HIV/AIDS and models of behavior change. He is currently working in the Research and Evaluation Department of the David Thompson Health Region in central Alberta. In this role he consults and provides education to clinicians on conducting research in applied health settings.

William R. Stayton, MDiv, ThD, PhD. After graduating from seminary, Bill went on to get his doctorate in theology in the field of psychology from Boston University. Bill is an ordained American Baptist clergyperson. He has a PhD from the Institute for the Advanced Study of Human Sexuality (IASHS) in San Francisco, where he also serves on the adjunct faculty. For 30 years, Bill was on the faculty of the Human Sexuality Program at the University of Pennsylvania. Eight years ago he, along with the other faculty members, moved the program to Widener University in Chester, Pennsylvania. He was Professor and Director of the Program until July 2006, when he retired from that position and was designated as Scholar in Residence. In November, 2006, Bill became the Executive Director of the Center for Sexuality and Religion. Bill is a former president of the Sexuality Information and Education Council of the United States (SIECUS) as well as the American Association of Sex Educators, Counselors and Therapists (AASECT). He has over 55 publications.

Kirk Stucky, PsyD, ABPP, received his doctoral degree in clinical psychology from Florida Tech, in Melbourne, Florida, in 1995 and completed fellowship training in clinical health psychology within the Consortium for Advanced Psychology Practice (CAPT) in 1997. He has earned board certification in Rehabilitation Psychology and Clinical Neuropsychology. Currently, Dr. Stucky works at Hurley Medical Center, where he is the program director for an APA-approved postdoctoral fellowship in clinical health psychology (CAPT). He is also the acting Director of Rehabilitation Psychology and Neuropsychology and an Assistant Adjunct Professor for the Michigan State University College of Human Medicine.

PART I

FOUNDATIONS

CHAPTER 1

Theoretical Models in Health Psychology and the Model for Integrating Medicine and Psychology

BRET A. BOYER

HISTORY AND DEVELOPMENT OF HEALTH PSYCHOLOGY

Although health psychology is a rather recent focus of behavioral science, interest in the interplay between humans' psychological and physical well-being dates back throughout history and spans many cultures, with written discussion as far back as the fourth century BC (Hippocrates, trans. 1923). Of particular historical significance was the conceptual separation of the *mind* from the *body* by René Descartes in the seventeenth century (Cummings, O'Donohue, Hayes, & Follette, 2001). However, regarding health psychology as a subspecialty of psychology and medicine, it is useful to revisit its development over the past 30 years. If we start slightly earlier in the historical timeline, early attention was paid to the effects of the psyche upon physical functioning and physical symptoms as early as Stanley Hall (1904), who emphasized the role of psychology in physical healing. William James (1922) discussed the role of people's individual processes in approaching work and life stresses, an idea that foreshadowed the current conceptualization of "coping" (Lazarus & Folkman, 1984). Psychoanalytic attention to physical health generated the terms *psychosomatic* and *psychosomatic medicine*, indicating that the "psyche," or mind, interacted with the "soma," or body. Although not specifically determined by this term, *psychosomatic* acquired a connotation that implied a directionality of influence. That is, the *psyche* affected the *soma*, as in somatoform disorders (*DSM-IV-TR*, 2000). Medical symptoms were conceived of as physical symptoms representing the expression of psychological distress, albeit unintentional and unconscious (Freud, 1916–1917, trans. Strachey, 2000). Indeed, the individual remained partly or wholly unconscious of the psychological etiology that created the physical symptoms. During the early twentieth century, psychodynamic investigations sought to identify particular personality organizations that would be prone to the development of physical disease (Alexander, 1950; Dunbar, 1943). While some research has continued on the "cancer-prone personality" (Eysenck, 2000; Katz & Epstein, 2005), for example, research to support it as an etiological factor in the disease is not very convincing (Amelang, Schmidt-Rathjens, &

Matthews, 1996; O'Leary, 2006). Most modern conceptualizations have changed; now, they investigate individual factors such as the impact of genetics or lifestyle on health (e.g., tendency to smoke cigarettes, drink alcohol excessively, or eat a particular diet), and stress, or coping dispositions that put individuals at risk for a poorer adjustment once health changes occur. After a reduction in professional investigation of the topic during the mid-twentieth century, focus on the interaction of psychological and physical health was renewed by findings that humans could intentionally control physiological activity that was previously considered involuntary (Miller, 1969). These findings became the foundation for the creation of *biofeedback* (Miller, 1978).

The consolidated rebirth of modern health psychology and behavioral medicine occurred in the 1970s. After renewed interest in the 1960s and 1970s, Gary Schwartz and Stephen Weiss organized a meeting of scientists interested in defining *behavioral medicine* in 1977, and Neal Miller chaired a subsequent meeting to organize clinical and research interests relating to these topics, resulting in a meeting of interested professionals at the National Academy of Science's Institute of Medicine. These efforts to define behavioral medicine as a field of clinical study and treatment as well as a professional endeavor yielded several articles summarizing these defining events and concepts (Schwartz & Weiss, 1977, 1978). Behavioral medicine was defined as "the field concerned with the development of behavioral science knowledge and techniques relevant to the understanding of physical health and illness and the application of this knowledge and techniques to prevention, diagnosis, treatment, and rehabilitation. Psychosis, neurosis, and substance abuse are included only insofar as they contribute to physical disorders as an end point." (Schwartz & Weiss, 1978, p. 3). The Society of Behavioral Medicine was subsequently formed, first within the confines of the Association for the Advancement of Behavior Therapy, then as a separate and independent organization (Weiss, 2003, as interviewed in Albright, 2003). This was followed by disagreement regarding the most appropriate terminology for this pursuit of study and treatment.

Health Psychology has "made substantial contributions to the understanding of healthy behaviors and to the comprehension of the myriad factors that undermine health and often lead to illness" (Taylor, p. 40). The term *Health* Psychology has been defined as "the aggregate of the specific educational, scientific, and professional contributions of the discipline of psychology to the promotion and maintenance of health, the prevention and treatment of illness, the identification of etiologic and diagnostic correlates of health and illness and related dysfunctions, and the analysis and improvement of the health care system and health policy." (Matarazzo, 1982, p. 4). This latter definition has been criticized for being too broad and encompassing, and subdefinitions will be needed to characterize the specialties regarding particular domains of academic, clinical, and policy endeavors (Marks, Sykes, & McKinley, 2003). Other definitions, however, have emphasized four differing approaches within health psychology: a clinical focus, a public health focus, a community focus, and the approach of critical health psychology (Marks, Murray, Evans, & Willig, 2000).

To briefly summarize the consensus, or lack of consensus, about these terms, we here present all of the titles currently used in the professional context:

The term *behavioral medicine* is preferred by those who view this context as growing from the field of behavioral science or applied behavior analysis; however, this implied theoretical bias has engendered some professionals to use the term *health psychology*. Those who favor the term health psychology perceive it as depicting the application of psychological principles to the study and treatment of physical health without evoking the theoretical position of behaviorism. Coming full circle, however, those who favor the term behavioral medicine feel that this implies a nonpharmaco-logical/nonsurgical focus on physical health by any discipline of study (including such disciplines as medicine, nursing, physical therapy, occupational therapy, nutri-tion, exercise physiology, epidemiology, public health, and social work), and not just psychology (Weiss, 2003, as interviewed in Albright, 2003).

In turn, some clinicians and theorists have criticized health psychology and behav-ioral medicine regarding their inattention to the larger social context and social fac-tors. Family therapists communicated that behavioral medicine and health psychol-ogy pursuits were successful in contributing the "psycho" to the "bio," as dictated by the biopsychosocial model, but were failing to adequately address the "socio" aspect of the biopsychosocial model. This concern generated the term *medical family therapy* (Doherty, McDaniel, & Hepworth, 1994; Rolland, 1987), and is consistent with other models within pediatric psychology, such as the social ecological model of health (Bronfenbrenner, 1975; Kazak, 1986), which emphasizes the impact of illness on the social circles surrounding the patient as well as the impact of social family/support on patient adjustment. In the interest of fairness, however, we note that significant at-tention is paid within the health psychology and behavioral medicine literature to so-cial support factors, prevention issues in at-risk populations, and sociopolitical factors (Marks et al., 2000).

For the purpose of clarity throughout this book, we will allow the terms *health psy-chology* and *behavioral medicine* to be rather parallel and synonymous, and that these will include the study and treatment of environmental and social factors, as empha-sized by medical family therapy. We concede that there exist different emphases among the use of these terms, but here we emphasize their commonalities: the appli-cations of psychological, family, social, spiritual, and other nonpharmacological fac-tors in the role of physical health, and we use these terms with emphasis on their shared definitions and goals rather than on their differences. It is also important to note that the field of health psychology investigates the role of psychosocial factors in the development of disease, the stressors posed by disease for subsequent psycho-logical adjustment, and the ongoing reciprocal influence of physical and psychosocial factors over time, consistent with the biopsychosocial model.

THE BIOPSYCHOSOCIAL MODEL

The traditional biological model of medicine is primarily focused on the assessment and treatment of pathology in biological structure and function, or pathophysiology (Van Egeren & Striepe, 1998). In response, Engel (1977) criticized the over-focus of medicine on biological factors, and proposed the *biopsychosocial model*. Because the biopsychosocial model incorporates multifactorial explanations for health and bi-directional or reciprocal influences between these factors, and allows for complex direct and indirect effects of biological, psychological, and social factors on health outcomes, it has become the predominant model within health psychology (Belar & Deardorff, 1995; Smith & Nicassio, 1995). It is also progressively becoming accepted among allopathic and osteopathic medical training, nursing, and other therapies.

MODELS OF THE INTERACTION OF PSYCHOSOCIAL AND PHYSICAL FACTORS

As the biopsychosocial model has become widely accepted as an overarching model with great utility for engendering more comprehensive and effective health care services, multiple models have been created to conceptualize the exact manner in which these biopsychosocial factors interrelate. Although we will not here review all models, we will briefly overview the main ones and present a new model for assessment and treatment planning. Some models have been characterized as more categorical, suggesting that different diseases pose different stressors, and that the difficulties the patient and his or her family face will be predictable by particular aspects of the disease state (Rolland, 1987). In addition, the *social ecological model* (Bronfenbrenner, 1977; Kazak, 1986) emphasizes that the health condition affects individuals in the patient's social structure, including family, extended family, friends, community, and society in general, as well as the effect of these social circles on the support and adjustment of the patient directly experiencing the disease. Other models have emphasized that, regardless of the specific disease state, there are individual-specific or family-specific factors that impact the individual's reaction and adjustment to the diagnosis and treatment of the disease. Among these are the *disability-stress-coping model* (Wallander & Varni, 1992), and the *transactional stress and coping model* (Thompson, Gustafson, Hamlett, & Spock, 1992). These models have been characterized as *risk and resistance* models, or *integrative theoretical models* (Wallander, Thompson, & Alriksson-Schmidt, 2003). An additional model, similar to the risk and resistance models, is the *resiliency model of family stress, adjustment, and adaptation* (McCubbin & McCubbin, 1993), which emphasizes that chronic health conditions demand ongoing adjustment over time, and that a patient's and family's adjustment is affected by changes in symptomatology, representing a process rather than a single adaptation.

We will then present a new model, the Model for Integrating Medicine and Psychology (MI-MAP), which integrates the categorical and risk-resistance models into a guide for sequential assessment and treatment planning regarding comprehensive health psychology factors.

CATEGORICAL MODELS

Much of medical training involves the description of symptom clusters as diagnoses. The dangerous implication that may result, of categorically diagnostic conceptualizations, is that "everyone with this diagnosis is experiencing the same symptoms and etiological factors," and the diagnosis informs the clinician about the individual's or family's experience. The application of the biopsychosocial model has great utility to debunk the all-too-common "all cases of [diagnosis] are the same" approach to clinical understanding.

In an attempt to understand the experience and challenges posed to those facing physical health problems, Rolland (1987) developed the *psychosocial typology model*, theorizing that different diseases would have somewhat predictable differences in the stresses that they will pose to patients and their families. The descriptive characteristics of different diseases include *onset, course, outcome,* and *incapacitation.* Rolland categorized the onset of illnesses as either *acute* or *gradual* in the patient's development of symptoms. The course of the disease was categorized as either *constant, progressive,* or *relapsing/episodic.* As such, Rolland made the distinction between disease states that were either constantly symptomatic but stable in severity (constant), constant in symptomatology but steadily worsening in severity (progressive), or characterized by periods of improvement or remission and periods of worsening or relapsing of symptoms (relapsing/episodic). Rolland (1987) defined three categories of outcome: fatal, life shortening, and nonfatal. Incapacitation was defined as the degree of impairment

Table 1.1
Risk and Resistance Factors to Predict Adjustment to Health Conditions

Risk Factors	Resistance Factors
Disease factors:	*Intrapersonal factors:*
Specific diagnosis	Temperament
Severity of condition	Competencies
Visibility of condition	Motivation for self-management
Brain involvement (i.e., cognitive impairment)	Problem-solving skills
Impaired functional independence	*Social-Ecological factors:*
	Family environment
	Social support
	Parental (or other family members') adjustment
	Resources in community/culture
Psychosocial stressors:	*Stress processing:*
Disability-related problems	Appraisal
Major life events	Coping
Daily hassles	

Source: Adapted from Wallander and Varni (1992).

the disease induced in either physical capabilities, cognitive capabilities, or motor functioning. By considering these factors as dimensions on which diseases can vary, Rolland offered a schemata to characterize the types of experience and stresses likely to accompany particular illnesses. These differences will be more fully discussed in the Disease Factors section of the Model for Integrating Medicine and Psychology (MI-MAP).

RISK-RESISTANCE MODELS

The risk-resistance models, considered integrative theoretical models (Wallander, Thompson, & Alriksson-Schmidt, 2003), organize the factors affecting adjustment into factors that pose risk for poorer adjustment (risk factors), and factors that serve as resources that benefit adjustment to the risk factors (resistance factors). Wallander and Varni's (1992) disability-stress-coping model of adjustment, for example, considers several variables to be risk and resistance factors (see Table 1.1).

MODEL FOR INTEGRATING MEDICINE AND PSYCHOLOGY

The Model for Integrating Medicine and Psychology (MI-MAP) was developed over 10 years of training physicians both about behavioral health and psychological factors and training psychologists about physical health and pathophysiology. Just as models such as the categorical and risk-resistance models have hypothesized how all the biopsychosocial factors may relate to one another to predict patient and family adjustment, MI-MAP attempts to utilize these models' collective factors and predictions to achieve two related goals: (1) to combine the categorical and individual aspects of other models and create a more integrated depiction of the factors to be assessed, and (2) to organize a sequential process by which the clinician can perform a comprehensive yet expedient inquiry regarding symptomatology relevant to the biopsychosocial model. In doing so, MI-MAP serves as a guide to answer the question, "How do

I clinically employ the concepts of the biopsychosocial model, and apply these concepts consistently in the process of clinical evaluation, treatment planning, and clinical intervention?"

The agenda for developing the MI-MAP stemmed from several observations in the clinical training setting. Physicians and nurses often struggle with the psychosocial components of biopsychosocial practice. In the medical setting, patients present with their physical symptomatology, and physicians often over-focus on the assessment of pathophysiological etiology. At least six factors may contribute to this phenomenon. It is important for health psychologists, nurses, and physicians to be aware of these factors, since health psychologists and medical educators may be crucial in consulting to overcome these barriers.

1. Despite the expanding acceptance of the biopsychosocial model in medical training, allopathic and osteopathic medical training continues to be primarily a biological science. As such, less training is geared to behavioral health than the assessment and intervention with pathophysiology. As a result, many physicians and nurses feel less prepared to assess and respond to the psychosocial aspects of biopsychosocial care.

2. The acuity of risk related to certain pathophysiological dysfunction requires the immediate "work-up" and "rule-out" of potentially lethal disorders. For example, for a patient accessing emergency services for shortness of breath and chest pain, myocardial infarction (heart attack) and pulmonary embolism (a blood clot occluding vessels in the lungs) can be acutely fatal, and requires immediate assessment. A panic attack, however, is not an acutely fatal condition, and will therefore be lower in priority on the physician's differential diagnosis. Due to this prioritizing of etiology by lethality, however, many clinicians conclude their assessment after ruling out the potentially lethal medical conditions before assessing the psychosocial phenomena, which may be seen by critical care clinicians as either superfluous or outside the role of acute critical care. As a result, individuals experiencing panic disorder often do not get diagnosed in the critical care context and continue to seek and utilize irrelevant and unnecessary medical resources because diagnosis and treatment of panic disorder are not offered (Grudzinski, 2001; Rief, Martin, Klaiberg, & Brähler, 2005).

3. The very real issue of time pressures in the scheduling of physicians' clinical practice creates further barriers to the comprehensive assessment of biopsychosocial issues, which are not primary to the traditional history and physical examination of the patient. Most traditional history and physical examinations will inquire about smoking and alcohol consumption as social history factors, and will inquire about little else.

4. In addition, although physicians may have less experience, less training, and lack adequate time regarding assessment of psychosocial factors, they may also perceive patients as wanting to avoid these disclosures (Brody et al., 1995), and have less familiarity with the diagnostic criteria for psychological diagnoses than for physical disease states. In contrast, empirical research has documented that major depressive disorders are present in about 5 to 40% of patients seeking services in the outpatient primary care setting (Niles, Mori, Lambert, & Wolf, 2005), and that 66% of patients in outpatient ambulatory care feel that physician attention to their emotional needs is "somewhat" to "extremely" important (Brody, Khaliq, & Thompson, 1997).

5. Even if a medical practitioner is (a) well trained regarding psychosocial factors, (b) facile yet comprehensive regarding careful assessment of more-to-less acutely lethal conditions, (c) expedient regarding use of practice time, and (d) aware of the startling prevalence of psychological disorders among those presenting for medical care, they may be emotionally uncomfortable assessing these clinical components.
6. More debilitating may be the phenomenon that, even if a physician or nurse has mastered the skills to overcome these barriers, they may feel they have a paucity of clinical resources to provide intervention for the psychosocial aspects of disease management.

Paralleling the discipline-specific process for physicians and nurses, clinical psychologists are often ill-equipped regarding information about physical symptomatology and pathophysiology. Multiple factors contribute to psychologists' discomfort with pathophysiology, similar to that experienced by physicians regarding psychosocial factors.

1. Many psychologists have not studied physiology, may have actively avoided biological focus in their education, and may identify this domain of study to be beyond the scope of their discipline.
2. Psychologists, as well as many other professionals, may have internalized the mind/body duality, and truly do not understand the role that factors ascribed to each of these domains play in affecting comprehensive health.
3. Some psychologists may actually be intimidated by the biological sciences and the medical setting, and may have low perceived self-efficacy about understanding physical sciences.
4. Some psychologists may feel uncomfortable with the "blood and guts" aspects of medical sciences.
5. Some psychologists may be uncertain about the boundaries of their legitimate professional expertise, and fear being accused of practicing medicine without appropriate training. Indeed, much care must be paid to the legal and ethical issues, as well as the clinical issues surrounding appropriate interdisciplinary collaboration.

To the degree that health psychologists often function in an explicitly medical setting, it appears appropriate to orient the psychological practitioner to the physical health starting point of patients' presentation in medical services. Therefore, the rationale for MI-MAP grew from the purpose of making attention to psychosocial factors *easier* yet *more comprehensive* for physicians, nurses, health psychologists, generalist psychologists, and social workers, and starting from the patients' (as clientele) starting point: the presenting complaint of physical symptomatology.

For these reasons, the MI-MAP begins with factors related to the *physical condition (disease factors)*, proceeds sequentially to factors related to the *medical treatment regimen (regimen factors)*, then proceeds to the *individual factors* that will interact with the demands of the condition and its treatment (*individual factors*), and finally to the consideration of *comorbid psychopathology* (see Figure 1.1). This offers clinicians of any discipline an organizational sequence by which to investigate the health condition and treatment factors from a stress and coping perspective, then proceed to the individual factors that will determine how the patient will adapt to these health stresses and coping demands.

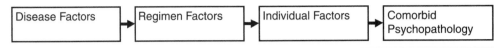

Figure 1.1 Model for Integrating Medicine and Psychology Assessment Sequence

DISEASE FACTORS

We could start with the dictum, "All diseases are not created equal!" Some health conditions or disease states are more homogeneous than others, from one individual's case to the next, and others are more heterogeneous. Similarly, one individual may process and cope with these disease factors differently than others. We can, however, assess particular factors that differentiate the onset and progression of each disease or health condition. If we conceptualize these factors as identifiable stresses posed by each specific health condition, and the demands that this health condition poses for an individual's or family's coping, we can characterize these stress and coping situations from one disease to the next. This process, in most respects, utilizes many elements of Rolland's psychosocial typology model (1987). The following section (see Figure 1.2) highlights several factors that can be used to conceptualize differences among different diseases and health conditions.

DISEASE ONSET

"Is the onset of the disease symptomatic or not?" Some diseases may begin with clear symptoms that are discernable by the patient. In contrast, other disease processes may begin without any noticeable symptoms. This distinction is important for several reasons. First, the presence of symptoms usually prompts the patient to seek medical services, and serves as a motivation to alleviate these symptoms. For this reason, conditions with a symptomatic onset are likely to be diagnosed sooner, and patients are likely to feel that treatment is useful to alleviate discomfort and to feel better. Health conditions that produce no discernable symptoms, however, may start and begin to progress before the disease is detected. As such, the diseases with an asymptomatic onset may go undiagnosed until the disease has advanced to a more serious stage of disease progression. In addition, health conditions with no perceptible or discomforting symptoms may engender a patient's perception that he or she need not pursue treatment, even after the disease is diagnosed. At the very least, when symptoms are absent, there is less impetus to continue treatment activities (e.g., take medication,

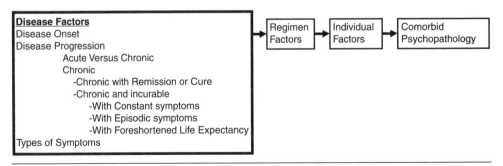

Figure 1.2 Disease Factors

avoid particular foodstuffs) in order to relieve symptoms. In operant behavioral terms, the symptoms serve as discriminative stimuli to seek and continue treatment, and the relief of these symptoms provides negative reinforcement that promotes the continuation and consistency of treatment. For symptomatic disease onset, as discussed by Rolland (1987), the rate in which symptoms develop is also important. Acute development of symptoms may be experienced as more threatening than those that develop gradually over an extended time.

"Is the onset of the disease traumatic or not?" Another important consideration regarding disease onset is whether the onset involves trauma. There are at least two ways in which the disease onset may be experienced as traumatic. First, the cause of the health condition may be a traumatic event. Examples of this may include burns (DiFede and Barocas, 1999; DuHamel, Difede, Foley, & Greenleaf, 2002; Van Loey, Maas, Faber, & Taal, 2003; Stoddard et al., 2006), spinal cord injuries (see Chapter 10), or traumatic amputations (Cheung, Alvaro, & Colotla, 2003; Cavanagh, Shin, Karamouz, & Rauch, 2006). In these examples, the event causing the injury may induce posttraumatic stress symptoms, even if the person had not sustained the injury. The injury, however, may increase risk for the development of posttraumatic stress. Second, the disease onset may involve symptoms or diagnostic information that many individuals perceive to be potentially life-threatening, or treatment side effects that are aversive and stressful, such as myocardial infarction (heart attack; see Chapter 7) or cancer (see Chapter 6). Such diagnoses may pose risk for posttraumatic stress symptoms related to the diagnosis and/or treatment of the disease. It is also important to consider that public appreciation or knowledge about diseases and disease-related threat may be different than the current medical consensus about prognosis. For example, while a stage-one presentation of many cancers may be considered less risky and more likely to result in a cure than Hepatitis C, most individuals without medical training may be more frightened by a cancer diagnosis than by the diagnosis of hepatitis. For this reason, the clinician must consider the patient's and the patient's family's appraisal of the disease-relevant threat.

DISEASE PROGRESSION

The next consideration is the disease progression, or what Rolland (1987) referred to as *course of disease*. The way in which a particular health condition persists over time, or changes over time, will affect the course of the stresses and demand for adaptation by the patient and his or her family. Although the exact course of disease progression may be uncertain, there is often some predictability to how specific diseases will progress, and how they will respond to particular treatments. Here is a categorization of the factors that may be predictable regarding disease progression:

Chronicity: "Is this health condition acute or chronic?" In many instances, it may be predictable whether the health condition will be acute or chronic. For acute conditions, the stress is more short-term and the demand to cope with these stressors will be time limited. In contrast, chronic conditions will pose stressors and the demand to cope with these stressors over an extended period of time. While acute conditions may affect the patient for a shorter time, the intensity of the symptoms, or risk that the patient perceives from the symptoms may still be high. On the other hand, chronic conditions may have lower severity at particular stages of disease progression, but the demand to cope with these symptoms will persist for an extended period. In the clinical setting, providers will often hear very different comments from patients who are frustrated with their health problems. Individuals with acute conditions often remark that "I can't wait until this is over," or "I don't know if I can get through this." Those faced with chronic conditions often make comments such as "I can't keep this up," "I am getting so weary of all this," "I used to be on top of this, but now I'm losing my patience," "I need a vacation from this disease," or "I'm worn out!"

Furthermore, the disease progression for each chronic condition will not be the same. Several categorical types of chronic disease progression are overviewed in the following sections.

Pattern of disease progression: "How will this disease change over time?" The progression of a specific disease may depend on many factors, such as the particular pathophysiology of each case, an individual's response to treatment, the patient's success or difficulty with self-management aspects of treatment, availability of particular treatments, presence of other comorbid health problems, or exposure to and coping with environmental stressors. However, there may be some predictability as to whether and how particular health conditions will progress. Several categories are listed in the following sections.

Chronic Conditions That Will Remit or Be Cured   Many health conditions may pose long-term stressors, challenges, and demands for an individual or family to cope with, but may either remit or be cured by appropriate treatment. Among these are certain cancers, or cancers at particular stages at the time of diagnosis. Despite the fact that 90.5% of cases of Acute Lymphocytic Leukemia (ALL) in children 5 years old or younger will attain remission and never recur, constituting a cure, the process of treatment toward that cure consists of 3 years of intense and stressful endeavors (Leukemia & Lymphoma Society, 2007). Many cases of idiopathic partial epilepsy in children will spontaneously remit as children grow older (Berg et al., 2004; Shinnar & Pellock, 2002). Such diseases pose lengthy and stressful demands to adjust, despite the expectation of eventual cure or remission. In addition, even when cure rates are extremely high, the uncertainty of whether each individual will be in the "high percent that get cured" or the "unlucky few who do not" still exists. This, however, is different from diseases that offer no hope of eventual cure or permanent remission.

Chronic Incurable Conditions   For many common diseases, there is no known cure and/or no impending progress toward a cure. In these cases, the stresses pose an ongoing demand for self-management. In other words, the goal of treatment is the ongoing management of symptoms rather than the elimination of the disease. Such conditions present individuals and families with a difficult paradox: *If I accept the need to manage the disease/symptoms on an ongoing basis, I will not suffer the discomfort and limitations of those symptoms, and the disease will cease to intrude on my quality of life. However, if I try to ignore the disease and its symptoms, the symptoms will persist and impair my functioning and comfort.* As such, chronic, ongoing diseases constitute a long-term, persisting stress and demand for coping.

The actual disease progression, or the pattern of symptoms over time and potential for progression of symptoms over time, varies among diseases. In order to understand the stressors and coping demands related to each pattern of disease progression, we need to consider the various ways in which symptoms and illness express themselves over time for different health conditions (Rolland, 1987). Examples are given here for each pattern of disease progression.

Chronic and Constant Conditions   Some diseases present the patient, and the patient's family, with continuous symptoms that vary very little over time. The steady stress of the constant symptoms poses the patient with a constant need for self-treatment, as discussed in the Regimen Factors section. Examples of such conditions include diabetes, hypertension, or some types of chronic pain. One could summarize, for example, that if someone coped well with their diabetes or hypertension, or optimally managed their diabetes or hypertension about 60% of the time, they were not coping with or managing well their disease, due to the constancy of the disease state.

The constant and continuous need to cope with symptoms and exert self-management activities to the self-treatment of such diseases results in fatigue or burnout, frustration at the need for such consistency, and results in patients reporting experiences such as:

> I used to be doing such a great job. I'm so tired of keeping all this up, and I need a break. I wish I could get a vacation from all this. I don't know what's wrong with me that I can't do as good of a job as I used to with this.

Patients with chronic and constant conditions report feeling weary and beleaguered. In contrast, individuals with chronic and episodic conditions struggle with the repetitive and recurrent nature of an ever-changing level of symptoms.

Chronic and Episodic Conditions   Many conditions are characterized by periodic, alternately worsening and reduction of symptoms over time. Individuals experiencing such conditions often communicate:

> I never know what to expect. I can't plan anything. Every time I think things are better, this comes back again and again. I feel like I should be able to prevent these episodes, but they keep recurring. Every time I plan something, I don't know if the symptoms are going to flare up and ruin my plans.

Furthermore, the exact pattern of recurrent, episodic conditions vary, as described next.

Episodic conditions with full remission of symptoms between episodes. Some health conditions create episodes of exacerbated symptoms, and these symptoms may entirely remit between these episodes of exacerbation. An example of this is, for many patients, sickle cell disease. Some patients experience no pain or symptoms over time, except during discrete sickle-cell crises. Even in the absence of symptoms, however, patients may need to keep well hydrated and be watchful for fever, and bear the ongoing threat of possible crises. As such, the manner by which patients cope with this abstract threat during remission periods will have great impact on overall adjustment (See discussion in Chapter 16).

Episodic conditions with reduction (but not full remission) of symptoms between episodes. More common than full remission of symptoms between exacerbations is the lessening of symptom severity without full remission of symptoms between episodes. Many individuals experience presentations of asthma that fit this description. Irritable bowel syndrome may exhibit this pattern for some individuals. In these conditions, some very mild and unobtrusive symptoms may persist at baseline, but periodically exacerbate to much more severe level of symptoms. As discussed in the Regimen Factors section, this presents patients with the experience that, if they do a more consistent and careful job of managing the baseline symptoms, they may avert the development of an episode of extreme symptoms.

Despite the persistence of a lower severity of symptoms during between-episode baselines, the patient continues to experience the frustration of the recurrent fluctuation of symptoms.

Episodic conditions with a worsening of baseline symptoms between each subsequent episode. Some diseases tend to progress in a pattern characterized by an episodic worsening, and continuation at a new plateau of a worsened between-episode baseline. Among examples of this are chronic obstructive pulmonary disorders (COPD, such as emphysema), or multiple sclerosis (MS). For individuals experiencing these types of conditions, the pattern becomes rather apparent over time. That is, patients soon realize that, when they experience an episode of exacerbation and get admitted to the hospital, they will not return to their previous between-episode baseline upon returning home. Patients begin to understand that each serious episode may constitute a progression to a worsened ongoing health status.

Patients with these types of conditions report:

> Every time I go in the hospital, everything gets worse. Each exacerbation is another nail in my coffin. I have to prevent these episodes, because each one takes years off my life and renders me less functional than before.

Individuals with such conditions begin to experience the pressure that each exacerbation permanently worsens their condition and functioning. Even if they are better after discharge from the hospital after the exacerbation than when they were admitted, they are worse than the baseline before they were admitted for the exacerbation of symptoms. Such experiences may foster a sense of impending doom and desperation.

Episodic conditions with a foreshortened life expectancy. Many chronic health conditions are accompanied, even at the point of diagnosis, with the threat of a foreshortened lifespan. Among such conditions are cystic fibrosis, HIV infection, or cirrhosis. Such conditions may engender desperation and hopelessness and thereby decrease the quality of life for individuals and their families.

TYPE OF SYMPTOMS

Regardless of the pattern of, or progression of, symptoms over time, providers also need to consider the type of symptoms. That is, to what degree do these symptoms impact functional independence? To what degree do they interfere with quality of life? Some important differences in types of symptoms involve the following questions. Are the symptoms of the disorder visible or not? For example, cerebral palsy may be very visible to others in a social setting, as observers will notice a difference in an individual's gait and motor movements, whereas those who are HIV positive may not look any different to anyone else in a social context. Does the condition involve pain? Pain is an intensely intrusive symptom, especially when chronic or severe (see Chapter 15). Are the symptoms contagious, or even perceived by others to be contagious? Are the symptoms, or the presence of the condition itself, stigmatizing? For instance, there is evidence that those with Hepatitis C, a chronic liver disease, experience higher depression and anxiety, poorer quality of life, and more difficulty coping when they feel stigmatized by others in social contexts (Zickmund et al., 2003).

Many of these factors are included in the risk and resistance models (Wallander, Thompson, & Alriksson-Schmidt, 2003).

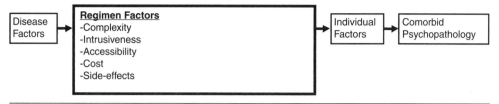

Figure 1.3 Regimen Factors

REGIMEN FACTORS

In the same manner that disease factors may vary yet offer some predictability, the range of treatments available for specific diseases is usually known at the point of diagnosis. By considering the exact treatment regimen that will be used to treat each patient's condition, providers can anticipate the types of stressors and difficulties that may ensue. Many of the regimen factors involve the degree to which patients and their families can tolerate the treatment, and the degree to which they can and will participate actively in the treatment process. An overview of factors that are important to consider is displayed in Figure 1.3.

Throughout the 1980s, many professionals took issue with the idea of *compliance,* which implied that patients were following authoritarian dictates of their physicians. The reconceptualization of medical service provision, from a paternalistic practice (in which the knowledgeable doctor instructs the patient in the treatment process) to a collaborative practice (in which the doctor and patient collaborate in defining, prioritizing, and executing the treatment plan), led to a reconceptualization of *noncompliance.* The patient's participation was no longer conceptualized as the patient's complying with the doctor's wisdom, but as an active collaboration with the physician toward treatment planning and medical outcomes. Regarding diabetes, Schilling, Grey, and Knafl (2002) defined *self-management* as an active, proactive patient-driven *process* that involves specific *activities* toward disease management *goals.* As health professionals conceptualize patients' follow-through on medical activities, it appears useful to conceptualize these as successes and/or failures regarding self-management of their disease process. Health professionals of all disciplines need to resist the temptation to conceive of noncompliance or nonadherence as a condition that "a patient *has.*" More instrumentally useful is the investigation of the factors that facilitate a patient's *success with self-management* or follow-through with the medical regimen, and factors that increase a patient's *difficulties or failures with self-management* or follow-through with the medical regimen. By identifying the factors that contribute to either success or difficulties with self-management, the medical team can identify the means to help a patient, or the patient's family, succeed with the demands of that particular treatment regimen.

Following are factors that have been identified in empirical studies of adherence that explain elements of medical treatment regimens that predict difficulty in self-management or follow-through by patients and their families.

COMPLEXITY

It makes intuitive sense that a more simple treatment will be easier to manage than a more complex regimen. Complexity, however, can manifest in several different ways.

First, the number of treatment-related behaviors may be more or less (e.g., taking more rather than fewer pills). Second, the scheduling and/or timing of particular treatment-related behaviors may be more or less complex (e.g., taking pills at four different times a day, rather than all pills at one or two times per day). These two factors may often interact. One example is that it is easier to take azithromycin once a day for 5 days than it is to successfully take Amoxicillin three times a day for 10 days. Another example is the multimedication, multitime schedule for many regimens of highly active antiretroviral therapies for HIV/AIDS. Coordinating the multiple drugs, with different dosages, and different timing for medication-taking can be far more difficult than simpler plans (Dilorio, McDonnell, McCarty, & Yeager, 2006).

INTRUSIVENESS

Another important consideration involves the intrusiveness of the disease or the treatment to manage the disease. Put simply, how much do the symptoms or the activities necessary to manage the disease get in the way of desired life pursuits? Investigations by Gerald Devins and colleagues suggest that *intrusiveness*, as a construct, is stable across the 15 diagnoses that they evaluated (i.e., rheumatoid arthritis, osteoarthritis, systemic lupus erythematosus, multiple sclerosis, end-stage renal disease, kidney transplantation, heart/liver/lung transplantation, and insomnia), and that both exploratory and confirmatory factor analysis identified three underlying factors: (1) Relationships and personal development, (2) intimacy, and (3) instrumental life domains (Devins et al., 2001). It appears that, for a varied patient population, the health condition and treatment regimen may interfere with interpersonal and intimate life activities, as well as the accomplishment in activities of daily living. When assessing how an individual or family may respond to an illness, it may be imperative to consider both the demands of the particular self-management process for that particular health condition, as well as consider the lifestyle and life activities that may become disrupted for this particular individual and family.

ACCESSIBILITY

The issue of accessibility of treatment is a crucial consideration. Accessibility may represent a geographical barrier to treatment. If an individual resides near a major metropolitan area, especially one with many university medical schools such as Boston, New York, Philadelphia, Chicago or Los Angeles, there may be many more treatment and service provider options available than if a patient lives in a remote rural area. Accessibility also dovetails with the issue of intrusiveness, when the demands of treatment require attendance to long and involved office visits. For example, an individual with insulin-dependent diabetes may find that the complexity of monitoring blood sugar, assessing grams of carbohydrates in meals and snacks, and using a unit of insulin:grams of carbohydrate ratio to properly dose his or her insulin all constitute an intrusive process throughout each day. In contrast, however, the patient with diabetes mellitus (DM) can use small, readily available blood glucose monitoring devices and insulin pumps or pens to accomplish these tasks without greatly deviating from daily plans, whereas an individual with end stage renal disease may need to attend a dialysis center three times a week for several hours to access hemodialysis. The accessibility of mobile technology may, for most patients, make DM-management much less intrusive than the need to sacrifice three half-days a week at a clinic with hemodialysis. These different tasks, specific to their treatments, highlight the different ways in which accessibility and intrusiveness impact ongoing quality of life.

COST

The national direct and indirect costs of health care are discussed in detail in Chapter 2, and costs specific to each disease are discussed in the following chapters that address these health conditions. The cost of treatment to each individual patient or family is, however, another matter. For any costs that are not covered by medical insurance for medication, supplies, travel to appointments, or particular foodstuffs for dietary needs, the burden falls on the patient and his or her family. The unitary nature of use for such items as pills and syringes means very simply that the more consistently the patient uses them, the greater the cost. As described in Chapter 8, the strips for someone with diabetes to test his or her blood glucose (BG) may cost approximately $1.00 per strip. If a patient is experiencing difficulty being consistent and active in monitoring his or her BG, the fact that it costs a dollar for each episode may operantly punish the behavior, encouraging him or her to test fewer times in order to save money.

Even when patients enjoy insurance prescription plans that cover the cost of medication, supplies, and medical appointments, the co-pays or coinsurance may pose barriers for those who are either stressed financially or have other priorities for monetary expenditure. Patients may perceive that "if I go fewer times to the doctor" or "go more slowly through my prescription," they will limit costs of co-pays/coinsurance, and thereby reduce the effectiveness of their medical treatment. Clinicians should also consider the nonmedical costs of treatment regimen. For someone with celiac disease, for example, most gluten-free foods are more costly than their standard counterparts. Clinicians may play an important role by understanding and assisting patients to problem-solve such difficulties in order to prevent these cost issues from rendering treatment ineffective.

SIDE EFFECTS

Side effects of any treatment regimen may become a primary barrier to patients' ongoing participation in treatment. The type or degree of side effects of medication or self-treatment activities may be painful or disruptive of quality of life. Some examples of intolerable regimen side effects may include medications that interrupt sexual functioning; activities, such as intramuscular injections for muscular sclerosis, may deter individuals from carrying out those activities; or treatments that increase the risks of health problems other than those it treats. For example, some chemotherapy protocols for active cancer may pose the increased risk of other cancers. This author has known patients for whom this information regarding increased cancer risk in the future, discussed during the informed consent for treatment, made them almost unwilling to accept the chemotherapy. The clinician plays an important role by helping the patient explore, understand, and problem-solve this daunting dilemma: The therapy that is likely to cure the cancer you *already have* may increase your risk of other cancers in the future.

INDIVIDUAL FACTORS

As we consider the specific demands placed on the individual and family by the condition factors and the regimen factors to treat or manage the disease process, we have

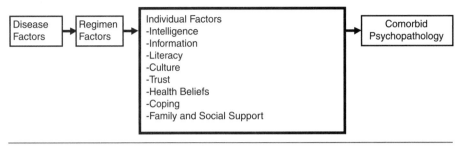

Figure 1.4 Individual Factors

not yet considered how *this person* will interact with these demands, how *this individual* will cope with the challenges and changes in lifestyle, functional independence, and expectations for the future. We must next consider the individual factors and how these will interact with the challenges posed to the individual and family. Even though we have been considering the condition factors and the regimen factors very carefully, considering the demands that are specific to *this* individual's disease presentation and treatment plan, we have been considering these factors rather categorically. We have been considering the stress and coping demands predicted by the disease and treatment in a rather categorical manner. We must now consider how the individual characteristics of *each patient* and *each patient's family* will appraise these stressors and coping demands, how they will adjust and adapt to these challenges, and how identifiable individual characteristics will become strengths or risk factors in dealing with the health condition and treatment.

We will start with a reasonable list of these factors, as indicated in Figure 1.4.

INTELLIGENCE

Intelligence is usually considered to be a rather stable factor, especially among adults. For that reason, and since it is not particularly amenable to interventions that may alter or increase intelligence (except among developing children), it has not received much research attention. Nonetheless, it is obvious that the understanding of disease progression, of treatment regimens, or self-management activities will be greatly affected by an individual's cognitive skills. More importantly, some treatment regimens are more difficult to understand and master than others, and more likely to pose difficulties for someone with low intelligence. For example, taking a single pill each day may not be greatly affected by a patient's intelligence, whereas an insulin regimen for diabetes, or issues related to transmission of viral diseases like HIV or Hepatitis C may pose enough complexity to render those with lower intelligence less capable of managing their condition.

INFORMATION

Having considered a patient's intelligence, we must next consider the amount and type of information a patient acquires. Given the common dictum "knowledge is power," the amount of useful information provided to patients may vary from one health condition to the next, or from one clinical setting to the next. A quick case example may help make this point. A 48-year-old man with type II diabetes had progressed to needing insulin to manage his blood glucose. He was quite intelligent, but received very little information about his insulin regimen in the primary care setting. He understood that Regular insulin (a fast-acting insulin) had a greater impact, per unit of insulin, on blood glucose than the NPH insulin (an intermediate-action insulin). However, he did not understand that each had a different response time. That is, he wasn't adequately informed that Regular insulin began acting within .5 hour and peaked and abated its action within a few hours, and that NPH insulin began acting at about 4 hours, and peaked at about 6 hours. So, he would awaken and test his blood glucose. It was 320, rather than the goal of 70–130. He would take only the NPH, because he didn't want to take the "stronger" Regular insulin, because he feared it would dangerously lower his blood glucose, inducing hypoglycemia (low blood glucose). He would test his blood glucose again at about 11 AM, finding that it was still about 320. This would not surprise the diabetologists of the world, as the NPH had not yet begun to act to lower his blood glucose. He would then become frustrated and acquiesce to taking some Regular insulin. As such, he was taking additional short-acting insulin, just at the time when his NPH was about to initiate its peak. Within an hour or two, his blood sugar would be about 30 (dangerously low), and he found himself shaking and sweating. He would then overeat, to compensate for the low blood glucose, not take any more insulin, and wake up with his blood glucose at 250. Now, anyone who is adequately informed about the response time of the insulins would realize that he was almost killing himself every afternoon, yet taking no insulin to properly manage his morning, evening, or nighttime blood glucose. Once this was explained to him, he quickly initiated a new, more appropriately timed insulin delivery (see Chapter 8 for a full discussion of diabetes regimen factors).

LITERACY

In many situations, information about new diagnoses or treatment options are provided in the form of written material. This ignores the fact that many individuals cannot read, or cannot read well. Inadequate health literacy may relate to poorer understanding and follow-through on treatment (Kripalani et al., 2006). Most individuals who cannot read are very protective of this fact and will not readily admit to their reading difficulties. Although the average reading level in the United States is at the eighth grade, almost no information about medical issues is at that level of reading comprehension.

CULTURE

Culture has become a more critical consideration in the provision of health services as the U.S. population becomes steadily more diverse (Whitfield, Weidner, Clark, & Anderson, 2003). It is important to consider culture from multiple perspectives, including the following factors: race, ethnicity, gender, sexual orientation, nation of origin, religion, socioeconomic status, and residential geography. Although there is not an opportunity to overview cultural factors in detail here, the following are important parameters for consideration in health psychology research and treatment endeavors:

1. How each of these factors affect risk for particular health problems.
2. How each of these factors affect access to health services.
3. How each of these factors affect an individual's approach to and utilization of available health services.

   4. How each of these factors affect patient interest, trust, acceptance, and follow-through regarding treatment options.

See chapters 2 and 3 regarding disparities in access, risk factors, and prevention issues regarding culture.

TRUST

As medical providers and caregivers, we assume that patients understand that we are attempting to help them, and have their best interest in mind. This makes it difficult to conceive that some individuals do not trust us. Even beyond issues related to culture, as described, other experiences may result in substantial mistrust among our patients.

Some individuals have, in the past, not felt heard by their providers. They have been told that "there's no reason to be experiencing the reported pain," or "the medication should be making that better," even when the symptoms persist and it appears that their providers do not wish to hear these experiences. At the extreme, individuals may experience events related to medical treatment as traumatic. Several examples may highlight this. First, a 59-year-old woman was raped by a physician in the physician's office in 1965, at age 18. In the year 2006, she is extremely hesitant and distrusting of her new primary care physician, 41 years later. Indeed, this woman was experiencing post-traumatic stress symptoms, triggered by meeting a new, unfamiliar male physician. While this had nothing to do with the actual approach or medical services of this new physician, the traumatic event was not something that this woman was going to disclose unless the physician and the medical team directly addressed her apprehension.

Another example involves a young African American woman with sickle-cell disease (SCD). In multiple previous admissions to the hospital with SCD crises, she observed that the physicians would start analgesic medication with meperidine HCl, which would make her feel agitated and not reduce the pain. After several hours on meperidene HCl, the physicians would switch her to IV morphine, and usually need to add hydromorphone to alleviate the pain. After multiple admissions, in which the patient observed that morphine and hydromorphone would remit both the pain and the episode more quickly, in about 12 hours, allowing her to return home with no narcotic prescription, she attempted to inform her emergency and hospital providers about this pattern. When the providers accosted her for "drug seeking," because she was asking for a particular medication and at particular doses, she would recoil and stop her disclosure of the pattern of analgesic efficacy in previous admissions. She developed the expectation that the medical team would attack her unjustly, and often presented in a preemptively hostile and defensive manner. However, when practitioners listened to her report of previous analgesic responses and assessed that she did not show any pattern of between-crisis narcotic usage, they would hear her self-observation, respond appropriately, and often save an entire day of inpatient services.

HEALTH BELIEFS

The *health beliefs model* was developed with the observation that patients have their own beliefs about disease risks and treatment benefits. Individuals often develop their own naive beliefs about the causes of disease, the significant signs and symptoms of disease, and the remission of disease (Leventhal & Nerenz, 1982), and construct their own theories about disease factors. The health beliefs model (Becker, 1991; Rosenstock, 2000) posits that patients' beliefs about their disease states may be more influential to their disease-related activity than medically determined disease information. The health beliefs model identifies several factors for which patients' beliefs may affect their treatment participation: (1) patient beliefs about the *severity* of their condition, (2) patient beliefs about their *susceptibility* of acquiring the disease or complications of the disease, (3) patient beliefs about *cost* of treatment adherence (including costs in inconvenience, effort, time, and money), (4) patient beliefs about *benefits* of treatment adherence, and (5) patient beliefs regarding the environmental and social *cues to action* that may assist in their treatment adherence. Simply stated, a patient who believes that the *severity* of his or her disease is great, the *susceptibility* to future complications is high, but the *benefit* of self-management is high and the *cost* of self-management is low, and that the *cues* in his or her environment will help him or her to adhere to treatment will likely engage more successfully in self-treatment than someone who perceives the *severity* of his or her disease to be low, the *susceptibility* to future complications to be low, the *cost* of self-management to be high and the *benefit* of self-treatment to be low, and that there will be few *cues* in his or her environment to help remember to adhere to treatment. Research into the role of health beliefs and disease management and prevention has yielded mixed results, depending on the type and the complexity of the health-related behavior (Ironson, Balbin, & Schneiderman, 2002). Studies have indicated that individuals' cancer screening behavior was affected by their perceived severity of cancer and benefits of cancer screening (for a review, see Fertig, Hayes, DiPlacido, Zauber, & Redd, 1998), as well as perceived barriers and inconvenience of screening (Rimer et al., 1991) and perceived risk of getting cancer (Diefenbach, Miller, & Daly, 1999; Epstein & Lerman, 1997; Farley, Minkoff, & Barkan, 2001; Hailey, Carter, & Burnett, 2000; Lerman et al., 1993; Lindberg & Wellisch, 2001 McCaul, Branstetter, Schroeder, & Glasgow, 1996).

Coping

Coping refers to the actions or strategies employed to manage or reduce stressful experience. The most widely applied model of coping is the cognitive-mediation model (Lazarus, 1999). The model emphasizes the role of cognitive appraisal in the processing of stimulus conditions, explaining why different individuals respond differently to the same types of stressors, and why the same individual may respond differently to a similar stressor at different times. The model articulates three essential stages in the coping process. The first is *primary appraisal,* in which the individual evaluates the stressor. In the second stage, *secondary appraisal,* the individual evaluates what options are available to manage the stressful situation or reduce its impact. Third, in the *coping* stage, the individual chooses and uses a strategy to cope with the stressor (Lazarus, 1999; Lazarus & Folkman, 1984). The model emphasizes that there is no universally best strategy for effective coping, that most individuals employ a variety of coping strategies over time and in different stressful situations, and it respects the fluid complexity of most stressful conditions (Folkman & Lazarus, 1985). Coping strategies are conceptualized to function as either *problem-focused coping,* strategies that attempt to change the stressful situation or the relationship between the individual and the stressful context, or *emotion-focused coping,* in which the individual alters his or her appraisal or emotional reaction to the stressful situation (Lazarus, 1999). Factor analyses have identified factors that constitute problem-focused coping, emotion-focused coping, and at times a third category, such as escape/avoidance (Ingledew,

Hardy, Cooper, & Jemal, 1996; Rosberger, Edgar, Collet, & Kournier, 2002), or social support (Aldwin & Revenson, 1987; Rosberger et al., 2002). Research suggests that coping is most effective when the individual's appraisal of the stressor matches well with the demand characteristics of the situation, and the individual chooses a coping strategy that matches this appraisal of the stressor. That is, if an individual accurately assesses that the stressor is controllable and chooses a problem-focused coping, or accurately appraises the situation to be uncontrollable and chooses an emotion-focused coping, there exists a reasonable match between the coping strategy and the characteristics of the stressor. Spiegel and Classen (2000) emphasize, however, that *active coping*, rather than resignation or avoidance, is imperative, and can serve both problem-focused and emotion-focused functions in controllable and largely uncontrollable stressors. Indeed, finding means to actively accept and address controllable aspects of chronic and potentially life-threatening disease is important, and active, problem-focused coping is often most helpful in these situations (Fawzy et al., 1990). Studies have indicated that, for many health stressors, active coping results in better psychological adjustment and quality of life and in better medical outcomes (see Manne, 2003, for a full review).

SOCIAL SUPPORT

The beneficial role of positive social and family support has been studied extensively, although a full discussion of the topic is beyond the scope of this chapter. It will be discussed regarding separate diseases in almost each chapter in Part 3. It is worth mentioning here, however, that the degree of social support has been associated with the development of coronary heart disease, endocrine reactions to stress, immunocompetence, and disease recovery and adjustment (see Manne, 2003, for full review).

COMORBID PSYCHOPATHOLOGY

Up to this point in the chapter, all the factors that have been discussed are relevant to any and all patients and families. That is, the role of these factors in adjusting to and self-managing disease and health conditions does not always constitute psychopathology. In addition to the influence of these factors on adjustment to illness, however, the presence of psychological disorders poses difficulties that can significantly impact adjustment to health conditions, self-management of chronic conditions, response to medical treatment, and the resulting medical outcomes.

Since these factors will be discussed with regard to each of the diseases covered in Part 3, and chapters 14 to 17 in Part 4, I will here generally overview the particular difficulties that prevalent psychological disorders may pose for diagnosis and treatment of acute and chronic health problems (see Figure 1.5).

DEPRESSION

Depending upon study methodology and sample, the prevalence of major depression is approximately 4.9% and 17% for current and lifetime depression, respectively among the general public (Blazer, Kessler, McDonagle, & Swartz, 1994), 4% to 40% among patients attending outpatient medical visits (Katon & Schulberg, 1992; Cavanaugh & Zalski, 1998; Niles et al., 2005), and 10% to 14% among nonpsychiatric medical inpatients (Katon & Schulberg, 1992). Depression is twice as prevalent among

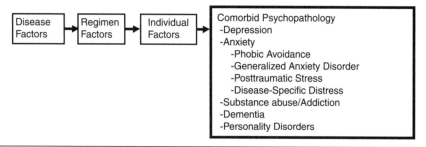

Figure 1.5 Comorbid Psychopathology

women as men (Kessler, 2003). Individuals with depression are more likely to have a chronic disease (Cavanaugh & Zalski, 1998), and those with a comorbid medical disease exhibit poorer recovery from their depression (Katon & Schulberg, 1992). In general, individuals experiencing depression report more physical symptoms, poorer self-appraised health, seek medical attention at two to ten times the rate (Cavanaugh & Zalski, 1998; Von Korff, Katon, & Lin, 1990), and are 25% more likely to be obese (Simon et al., 2006) than individuals without depression.

Higher rates of depression have been detected among individuals with particular diseases, such as diabetes and cardiac conditions, and depression is associated with poorer medical outcomes among these patients (see chapters 6 and 8 for full review). In addition, underdiagnosis and inadequate treatment of depression persists. A study of depression and anxiety among patients on an inpatient cardiac unit found that providers identified only 15% of the patients with major depressive disorder following myocardial infarction (heart attack; Huffman et al., 2006).

Given the fatigue, difficulty with motivation, hopelessness, and dysphoria that constitute the typical experience of depression, it is understandable that these symptoms can hinder consistent self-management of health problems. Furthermore, the assessment of depression symptoms among those with a physical health condition can be complicated by overlapping symptomatology, requiring careful consideration of the respective somatic, affective, and cognitive symptoms of depression. Given the relationship between comorbid depression and poorer outcomes in medical treatments, assessment and treatment of depression is imperative for optimal medical outcomes.

ANXIETY

Studies indicate that generalized anxiety disorder (GAD) is nearly as prevalent as major depression, in the range of 2.8% to 8.5% (Roy-Byrne & Wagner, 2004). Panic disorder prevalence has been reported at 4% in primary care populations, but may be 20% to 50% among patients with cardiac conditions, and 28% to 40% among patients with gastrointestinal conditions (Roy-Byrne, Wagner, & Schraufnagel, 2005). Partial diagnosis of full posttraumatic stress disorder (PTSD) was found in 11.8% of primary care patients (Stein, McQuaid, Pedrelli, Lenox, & McCahill, 2000), but at higher rates among populations treated after injuries (Zatzick, Russo, & Katon, 2003). Similar to depression, greater disability and higher utilization of health care have been observed among individuals with GAD (Wittchen et al., 2002), PTSD (Stein et al., 2000), and panic disorder (Roy-Byrne, Wagner, & Schraufnagel, 2005). Individuals with undiagnosed panic disorder often present in the emergency medical service, fearing they are experiencing a heart attack.

Considering the elevated arousal of the sympathetic nervous system that may accompany anxiety disorders, anxiety may interact directly with the pathophysiology of particular diseases. For example, the increased heart rate, vasoconstriction, and blood pressure that may accompany anxiety states pose a risk for someone with cardiac ischemia (Fleet et al., 2005), while neuroendocrine changes may increase blood glucose for individuals with diabetes (Cox & Gonder-Frederick, 1991).

As described earlier, regarding the stresses posed by *disease factors* and *regimen factors* of medical illness, the individual may become anxious regarding his or her disease and treatment. Anxious reactivity to these stresses and demands may generate disease-specific distress that constitutes an adjustment disorder. In some instances, this reactive anxiety may constitute posttraumatic stress, as has been found following diagnosis and treatment of cancer, myocardial infarction, or diabetes (see chapters 7, 6, and 8, respectively).

SUBSTANCE ABUSE AND ADDICTION

A full coverage of substance abuse issues is provided in Chapter 17. In general, however, substance abuse can exacerbate health problems in at least four different ways:

1. The effect of excessive substance usage can act as the primary etiology for a health condition, such as cirrhosis caused by alcohol or a myocardial infarction induced by the vasoconstrictive effects of cocaine or methamphetamine.
2. The drug may increase the same risk factors as a co-occurring disease, such as alcohol increasing the risk for cardiovascular diseases similar to diabetes.
3. Intoxication may decrease consistency of self-management or treatment adherence, or recreational drugs may interact to decrease medication efficacy, thereby diminishing treatment outcomes.
4. Administration of recreational drugs may relate to transmission of infectious diseases, as described in Chapter 17.

DEMENTIA AND OTHER COGNITIVE IMPAIRMENT

Individuals with cognitive impairments will be unlikely to independently make health-related life changes or manage their treatment regimen. For this reason, assistance from family, friends, or supportive services may be imperative for treatment success. Furthermore, ongoing observation and assessment for the development of neurocognitive dysfunction is important in conditions that may induce cognitive changes. For example, if an individual with AIDS develops AIDS dementia, it will become greatly difficult for him or her to manage the complex treatment regimen (see Chapter 9).

PSYCHOSIS

As with cognitive dysfunction due to dementia, psychosis will pose severe difficulties for an individual to self-manage his or her regimen for a chronic health problem. Further complicating this observation is that some antipsychotic medications may pose increased risk for health problems. Atypical antipsychotics, for example, have been linked to the development of diabetes (Ananth & Kolli, 2005; Gianfrancesco, Wang, & Nasrallah, 2006), and those with psychotic disorders have particular difficulty managing their diabetes (El-Mallakh, 2006).

PERSONALITY DISORDERS

Whereas the relationships between personality disorders and health conditions have received much less empirical research investigation than depression and anxiety, it is important to consider personality disorders in several respects. First, individuals with personality disorders may experience difficulties in their relationships with their medical providers. Second, personality disorders that involve risk taking, greater substance abuse, or poor social support may all pose greater exposure to risk factors for acquisition of disease and poorer adjustment following diagnosis.

COMPREHENSIVE ASSESSMENT AND TREATMENT PLANNING

The utility of MI-MAP is the coordination of a comprehensive and consistent process for assessment and treatment planning. By organizing the inquiry about the impact of a specific disease, treatment, and life situation on a patient and family's adjustment, the health psychology intervention may be tailored to the exact stressors, demands for coping, and individual factors that serve as risks or resources for each patient's adjustment. The MI-MAP can also be useful if a clinician is called on to help a client with a disease the clinician is not already proficient with or knowledgeable about. By identifying which of this rather exhaustive set of factors are relevant to a patient's health or adjustment difficulties, treatment strategies can be individualized to the needs of each particular patient. In order to quickly yet responsibly educate oneself about a disease state, its treatment, and organize the inquiry regarding the patient's response, MI-MAP offers a ready map.

REFERENCES

Albright, C. (2003). Reflections and projections: Interviews with the founders of the Society of Behavioral Medicine. *Outlook,* (Summer): 4–5.

Alexander, F. (1950). *Psyhosomatic medicine.* New York: Norton.

Alwin, C. C., & Revenson, T. A. (1987). Does coping help? A reexamination of the relation between coping and mental health. *Journal of Personality and Social Psychology, 53,* 337–348.

Amelang, M., Schmidt-Rathjens, C., & Matthews, G. (1996). Personality, cancer, and coronary heart disease: Further evidence on a controversial issue. *British Journal of Health Psychology, 1,* 191–205.

American Psychiatric Association (2000). *Diagnostic and statistical manual of mental disorders* (4th ed.) Washington, DC: Author.

Ananth, J., & Kolli, S. (2005). Atypical antipsychotic agents and increased risk of diabetes: Class action or differential action? *Expert Opinion on Drug Safety, 4,* 55–68.

Becker, M. H. (1990). Theoretical models of adherence and strategies for improving adherence. In S. A. Shumaker, E. B. Schron, J. K. Ockene, C. T. Parker, & J. L. Probstfield (Eds.), *The handbook of health behavior change* (pp. 5–43). New York: Springer.

Belar, C. D., & Deardorff, W. W. (1995). *Clinical health psychology in medical settings: A practitioner's guidebook.* Washington, DC: American Psychological Association.

Berg, A. T., Jianxin Lin, Ebrahimi, N., Testa, F. M., Levy, S. R., & Shinnar, S. (2004). Modeling remission and relapse in pediatric epilepsy: Application of a Markov process. *Epilepsy Research, 60,* 31–40.

Blazer, D. G., Kessler, R. C., McDonagle, K. A., & Swarcz, M. S. (1994). The prevalence and distribution of major depression in a national community sample: The national comorbidity survey. *The American Journal of Psychiatry, 151,* 979–986.

Brody, D. S., Khaliq, A. A., & Thompson, T. L. (1997). Patients' perspectives on the management of emotional distress in primary care settings. *Journal of General Internal Medicine, 12,* 403–406.

Brody, D. S., Thompson, T. L., Larson, D. B., Ford, D. E., Katon, W. J., & Magruder, K. M. (1995). Recognizing and managing depression in primary care. *General Hospital Psychiatry, 17,* 93–107.

Bronfenbrenner, U. (1977). Toward an experimental ecology of human development. *American Psychologist, 32,* 513–531.

Cavanagh, S. R., Shin, L. M., Karamouz, N., & Rauch, S. L. (2006). Psychiatric and emotional sequelae of surgical amputation. *Psychosomatics, 47,* 459–464.

Cavanaugh, S., & Zalski, A. (1998). Psychiatric diagnosis. In L. S. Goldman, T. N. Wise, & D. S. Brody (Eds.), *Psychiatry for primary care physicians* (pp. 19–40). Chicago: American Medical Association.

Cheung, E., Alvaro, R., & Colotla, V. A. (2003). Psychological distress in workers with traumatic upper or lower limb amputations following industrial injuries. *Rehabilitation Psychology, 48,* 109–112.

Cox, D. J., & Gonder-Frederick, L. A. (1991). The role of stress in diabetes mellitus. In P. M. McCabe & N. Schneiderman (Eds.), *Stress, coping, and disease* (pp. 119–134). Hillsdale, NJ: Erlbaum.

Cummings, N. A., O'Donohue, W., Hayes, S. C., & Follette, V. (2001). *Integrated behavioral healthcare: Positioning mental health practice with medical surgical practice.* San Diego, CA: Academic.

Devins, G. M., Dion, R., Pelletier, L. G., Shapiro, C. M., Abby, S., Raiz, L. R., Binik, Y. M., & Dunbar, F. (1943). *Psychosomatic diagnosis.* New York: Hoeber.

Diefenbach, M. A., Miller, S. M., & Daly, M. B. (1999). Specific worry about breast cancer predicts mammography use in women at risk for breast and ovarian cancer. *Health Psychology, 18,* 532–536.

Difede, J., & Barocas, D. (1999). Acute intrusive and avoidant PTSD symptoms as predictors of chronic PTSD following burn injury. *Journal of Traumatic Stress, 12,* 363–369.

Dilorio, C., McDonnell, M., McCarty, F., & Yeager, F. (2006). Initial testing of the Antiretroviral Medication Complexity Index. *Journal of the Association of Nurses AIDS Care, 17,* 26–36.

Doherty, W. J., McDaniel, S. H., & Hepworth, J. (1985). Medical family therapy: An emerging arena for family therapy. *Journal of Family Therapy, 16,* 31–46. Special issue: Developments in family therapy in the USA.

DuHamel, K. N., Difede, J., Foley, F., & Greenleaf, M. (2002). Hypnotizability and trauma symptoms after burn injury. *International Journal of Clinical and Experimental Hypnosis, 50,* 33–50.

Dunbar, F. (1943). *Psychosomatic diagnosis.* Oxford: Hoeber.

El-Mallakh, P. (2006). Evolving self-care in individuals with schizophrenia and diabetes mellitus. *Archives of Psychiatric Nursing, 20,* 55–64.

Engel, G. L. (1977). The need for a new medical model: A challenge for biomedicine. *Science, 196,* 129–136.

Epstein, S. A., & Lerman, C. (1997). Excessive health behaviors in those at risk for physical disorder. *Journal of Psychosomatic Research, 43,* 223–225.

Eysenck, H. J. (2002). Personality as a risk factor in cancer and coronary heart disease. In D. T. Kenny, J. G. Carlson, F. J. McGuigan, & J. L Sheppard (Eds.), *Stress and health: Research and clinical applications* (pp. 291–318). Amsterdam: Harwood Academic.

Farley, M., Minkoff, J. R., & Barkan, H. (2001). Breast cancer screening and trauma history. *Women & Health, 34,* 15–27.

Fawzy, F. I., Cousins, N., Fawzy, N. W., Kemeny, M. E., Elashoff, R., & Morton, D. (1990). A structured psychiatric intervention for cancer patients. I. Changes over time in methods of coping and affective disturbance. *Archives of General Psychiatry, 47,* 720–725.

Fertig, D. L., Hayes, D. F., DiPlacido, J., Zauber, A., & Redd, W. J. (1998). Psychological issues in cancer screening. In J. C. Holland (Ed.), *Psycho-oncology* (pp. 147–172). New York: Oxford University Press.

Fleet, R., Lespérance, F., Arsenault, A., Grégoire, J., Lavoie, K., Laurin, C., et al. (2005). Myocardial perfusion study of panic attacks in patients with coronary artery disease. *The American Journal of Cardiology, 96,* 1064–1068.

Folkman, S., & Lazarus, R. S. (1985). If it changes it must be a process: Study of emotion and coping during three stages of a college examination. *Journal of Personality and Social Psychology, 48,* 150–170.

Gianfrancesco, F., Wang, R. H., & Nasrallah, H. A. (2006). The influence of study design on the results of pharmacoepidemiologic studies of diabetes risk with antipsychotic therapy. *Annals of Clinical Psychiatry, 18,* 9–17.

Grudzinski, A. N. (2001). Considerations in the treatment of anxiety disorders: A pharmacoeconomic review. *Expert Opinion on Pharmacotherapy, 2,* 1557–1569.

Hailey, B. J., Carter, C. L., & Burnett, D. R. (2000). Breast cancer attitudes, knowledge, and screening behavior in women with and without a family history of breast cancer. *Health Care for Women International, 21,* 701–715.

Hall, G. (1904). *Health, growth, and heredity.* New York: Teachers College Press.

Hippocrates. (1923). *Volume II: On decorum and the physician.* (W. H. S. Jones, Trans.). London: Heinemann.

Huffman, J. C., Smith, F. A., Blais, M. A., Beiser, M. E., Januzzi, J. L., & Fricchione, G. L. (2006). Recognition and treatment of depression and anxiety in patients with acute myocardial infarction. *The American Journal of Cardiology, 98,* 319–324.

Ingeldew, D. K., Hardy, L., Cooper, C. L., & Jemal, H. (1996). Health behaviours reported as coping strategies: A factor analytical study. *British Journal of Health Psychology, 1,* 263–281.

Ironson, G., Balbin, E., & Schneiderman, M. (2002). Health psychology and infectious diseases. In T. J. Boll, S. B. Johnson, N. W. Perry, Jr., & R. H. Rozensky (Eds.), *Handbook of clinical health psychology: Vol 1, Medical disorders and behavioral applications* (pp. 5–36). Washington, DC: American Psychological Association.

James, H. (1922). *On vital reserves: The energies of men.* Cambridge, MA: Harvard University Press.

Katon, W., & Schulberg, H. C. (1992) Epidemiology of depression in primary care. *General Hospital Psychiatry, 14,* 237–247.

Katz, L. S., & Epstein, S. (2005). The relation of cancer-prone personality to exceptional recovery from cancer: A preliminary study. *Advances in Mind-Body Medicine, 21,* 3–4.

Kazak, A. E. (1986). Families with physically handicapped children: Social ecology and family systems. *Family Process, 25,* 265–281.

Kessler, R. C. (2003). Epidemiology of women and depression. *Journal of Affective Disorders, 74,* 5–13. Special issue: Women and depression.

Kripalani, S., Henderson, L. E., Chiu, E. Y., Robertson, R., Kolm, P., & Jacobson, T. A. (2006). Predictors of medication self-management skill in a low-literacy population. *Journal of General Internal Medicine, 21,* 825–856.

Lazarus, R. S. (1999). *Stress and emotion: A new synthesis.* New York: Springer.

Lazarus, R. S., & Folkman, S. (1984). *Stress, appraisal, and coping.* New York: Springer.

Lerman, C., Daly, M., Sands, C., Balshem, A., Lustbader, E., Heggan, T., Goldstein, L., James, J., & Engstrom, P. (1993). Mammography adherence and psychological distress among women at risk for breast cancer. *Journal of the National Cancer Institute, 85,* 1074–1080.

Leukemia & Lymphoma Society. (2007). Retrieved January 15, 2007, from http://www .leukemia-lymphoma.org/all_page?item_id=7026#treatment

Leventhal, H., & Nerenz, D. R. (1982). A model for stress research and some implications for the control of stress disorders. In D. Meichenbaum & M. Jaremko (Eds.), *Stress prevention and management: A cognitive behavioral approach* (pp. 5–38). New York: Plenum Press.

Lindberg, N. M., & Wellisch, D. (2001). Anxiety and compliance among women at high risk for breast cancer. *Annals of Behavioral Medicine, 23,* 298–303.

Manne, S. (2003). Coping and social support. In A. M. Nezu, C. M. Nezu, & P. A. Geller (Eds.), Handbook of psychology: Health psychology (Vol. 9, pp. 51–74). Hoboken, NJ: Wiley.

Marks, D. F., Murray, M., Evans, B., & Willig, C. (2000). *Health psychology: Theory, research, and practice.* London: Sage.

Marks, D. F., Sykes, C. M., & McKinley, J. M. (2003). Health psychology: Overview and professional issues. In A. M. Nezu, C. M. Nezu, & P. A. Geller (Eds.), *Handbook of psychology: Volume 9: Health psychology.* Hoboken, NJ: Wiley.

Matarazzo, J. D. (1982). Behavioral health's challenge to academic, scientific, and professional psychology. *American Psychologist, 37,* 1–14.

McCaul, K. D., Branstetter, A. D., Schroeder, D. M., & Glasgow, R. E. (1996). What is the relationship between breast cancer risk and mammography screening? A meta-analytic review. *Health Psychology, 15,* 423–429.

McCubbin, M. A., & McCubbin, H. I. (1993). Families coping with illness: The resiliency model of family stress, adjustment, and adaptation. In C. Danielson, B. Hamel-Bissell, & P. Winstead-Fry (Eds.), *Families, health and illness.* New York: Mosby.

McGowan, P., Kutner, N. G., Beanlands, H., & Edworthy, S. M. (2001). Structure of lifestyle disruptions in chronic disease: A confirmatory factor analysis of the Illness Intrusiveness Ratings Scale. *Medical Care, 39,* 1097–1104.

Miller, N. E. (1969). Learning of visceral and glandular responses. *Science, 163,* 434–445.

Miller, N. E. (1978). Biofeedback and visceral learning. *Annual Review of Psychology, 29,* 373–404.

Niles, B. L., Mori, D. L., Lambert, J. F., & Wolf, E. J. (2005). Depression in primary care: Comorbid disorders and related problems. *Journal of Clinical Psychology in Medical Settings, 12,* 71–77.

O'Leary, A. (2006). np. Emotions and breast cancer: Health consequences of women's coping. *PsycCRITIQUES.*

Rief, W., Martin, A., Klaiberg, A., & Brähler, E. (2005). Specific effects of depression, panic, and somatic symptoms on illness behavior. *Psychosomatic Medicine, 67,* 596–601.

Rimer, B. K., Lerman, C., Trock, B., King, E., & Engstrom, P. F. (1991). Why do some women get regular mammograms? *American Journal of Preventive Medicine, 7,* 69–74.

Rolland, J. S. (1987). Family illness paradigms: Evolution and significance. *Family Systems Medicine, 5,* 482–503.

Rosberger, Z., Edgar, J., Collet, J. P., & Fournier, M. A. (2002). Patterns of coping in women completing treatment for breast cancer: A randomized controlled trial of Nucare, a brief psychoeducation workshop. *Journal of Psychosocial Oncology, 20,* 19–37.

Rosenstock, L. M. (2000). Health belief model. In A. E. Kazdin (Ed.), *Encyclopedia of psychology* (Vol. 4., pp. 78–80). Washington, DC: American Psychological Association.

Roy-Byrne, P. P., Wagner, A. W., & Schraufnagel, T. J. (2005). Understanding and treating panic disorder in the primary care setting. *Journal of Clinical Psychiatry, 66*(Suppl. 4), 16–22.

Schilling, L. S., Grey, M., & Knafl, K. A. (2002). The concept of self-management of Type 1 diabetes in children and adolescents: An evolutionary concept analysis. *Journal of Advanced Nursing, 37*, 87–99.

Schwartz, G. E., & Weiss, S. M. (1977). What is behavioral medicine? *Psychosomatic Medicine, 39*, 377–381.

Schwartz, G. E., & Weiss, S. M. (1978). Yale Conference on Behavioral Medicine: A proposed definition and statement of goals. *Journal of Behavioral Medicine*, 1:3–12.

Shinnar, S., & Pellock, J. M. (2002). Update of the epidemiology and prognosis of pediatric epilepsy. *Journal of Child Neurology, 17*, S4–S17.

Simon, G. E., Von Korff, M., Saunders, K., Miglioretti, D. L., Crane. P. K., van Belle, G., et al. (2006). Association between obesity and psychiatric disorders in the US adult population. *Archives of General Psychiatry, 63*, 824–830.

Smith, T. W., & Nicassio, P. M. (1995). Psychological practice: Clinical application of the biopsychosocial model. In P. M. Nicassio and T. W. Smith (Eds.), *Managing chronic illness: A biopsychosocial perspective* (pp. 1–31). Washington, DC: American Psychological Association.

Spiegel, D., & Classen, C. (2000). *Group therapy for cancer patients: A research-based handbook of psychosocial care*. New York: Basic Books.

Stein, M. B., McQuaid, J. R., Pedrelli, P., Lenox, R., & McCahill, M. E. (2000). Posttraumatic stress disorder in the primary care medical care setting. *General Hospital Psychiatry, 22*, 261–269.

Stoddard, F. J., Saxe, G., Ronfeldt, H., Drake, J. E., Burns, J., Edgren, C., & Sheridan, R. (2006). Acute stress symptoms in young children with burns. *Journal of the American Academy of Child & Adolescent Psychiatry, 45*, 87–93.

Strachey, J. (2000). *The standard edition of the complete psychological works of Sigmund Freud*. New York: W. W. Norton.

Taylor, S. E. (1990). Health psychology. *American Psychologist, 45*, 40–50.

Thompson, R. J., Jr., Gustafson, K. E., Hamlett, K. W., & Spock, A. (1992). Stress, coping and family functioning in the psychological adjustment of mothers of children with cystic fibrosis. *Journal of Pediatric Psychology, 17*, 573–585.

Van Egeren, L., & Striepe, M. I. (1998). Assessment approaches in health psychology: Issues and practical considerations. In P. M. Camac & S. J. Knight (Eds.), *Clinical handbook of health psychology: A practical guide to effective interventions* (pp. 17–50). Ashland, OH: Hogrefe & Huber.

Van Loey, N. E. E., Maas, C. J. M., Faber, A. W., & Taal, L. A. (2003). Predictors of chronic posttraumatic stress symptoms following burn injury: Results of a longitudinal study. *Journal of Traumatic Stress, 16*, 361–369.

Von Korff, M., Katon, W., & Lin, E. (1990). Psychological distress, physical symptoms, utilization and the cost-offset effect. In N. Sartorius, D. Goldberg, G. de Girolamo, J. Cost e Silva, Y. Lecrubier, & V. Wittchen (Eds.), *Psychological disorders in medical settings* (pp. 159–169). Toronto: Hogrefe & Huber.

Wallander, J. L., Thompson, R. J., & Alriksson-Schmidt, A. (2003). Psychosocial adjustment of children with chronic physical conditions. In M. C. Roberts (Ed.), *Handbook of pediatric psychology*. New York: Guilford.

Wallander, J. L., & Varni, J. W. (1992). Adjustment in children with chronic physical disorders: Programmatic research on a disability-stress-coping model. In A. M. LaGreca, L. Siegel, J. L. Wallander, & C. E. Walker (Eds.), *Stress and coping in child health* (pp. 279–298). New York: Guilford.

Whitfield, K. E., Weidner, G., Clark, R., & Anderson, N. B. (2003). Sociodemographic diversity and behavioral medicine. *Journal of Consulting and Clinical Psychology, 70,* 463–481. Special Issue: Behavioral medicine and clinical health psychology.

Wittchen, H. U., Kessler, R. C., Beesdo, K., Krause, P., Höfler, M., & Hoyer, J. (2002). Generalized anxiety and depression in primary care: Prevalence, recognition, and management. *The Journal of Clinical Psychiatry, 63*(Suppl. 8), 24–34.

Zatzick, D. (2003). Posttraumatic stress, functional impairment, and service utilization after injury: A public health approach. *Seminars in Clincal Neuropsychiatry, 8,* 149–157.

Zickmund, S., Ho, E. Y., Masuda, M., Ippolito, L., & LaBrecque, D. R. (2003). "They treated me like a leper": Stigmatization and the quality of life of patients with Hepatitis C. *Journal of General Internal Medicine, 18,* 835–844.

CHAPTER 2

Insurance, Managed Care, and Integrated Primary Care

M. INDIRA PAHARIA

INTRODUCTION

Health psychologists, perhaps more than any other specialists within the discipline of psychology, find themselves working within managed care settings (e.g., acute care hospitals, outpatient medical clinics) that survive in a third-party payment system. This system is often a source of confusion and frustration for clinicians as they try to navigate the complexities of third-party payment, both for their patients and for themselves. It is ever-evolving, constantly in flux, and composed of myriad entities that differ in policy, procedure, structure, network, and reimbursement. It can be exhausting to keep pace with such a quickly changing system. However, those clinicians that lack an understanding of the system in which they work may find themselves at a disadvantage, especially those just entering the field of health psychology. It is humbling to realize that psychology is but one facet of behavioral health, which additionally encompasses psychiatry and social work, and that behavioral health is but one facet of the health care delivery system, which further encompasses medicine, dentistry, pharmacy, and numerous other specialties (i.e., ancillary providers). Given that health psychologists work closely with medical professionals and are often housed within medical settings, they will inevitably face issues of insurance and managed care.

This chapter is written to demystify the health insurance and managed care industry for the clinician, and strives to provide historical fact and current information, shed light on potentially confusing concepts, and emphasize health psychology's increasingly prominent role in managed behavioral health. To aid the reader, the chapter is divided into five sections. Section One provides an overview of the main private and public insurance plans, the differences between them, and the uninsured. Section Two presents the major types of managed care plans, utilization management, and current trends. Section Three provides information on insurance concepts, financial structures, and reimbursement. Section Four provides a recent history of behavioral managed care and current trends in this industry that impact the health psychologist. Finally, Section Five discusses the development of integrated primary care and the health psychologist's related roles and opportunities.

Given the multitude of mergers and acquisitions since the inception of the health insurance and managed care industry, it is impossible to present every existing amalgamation. Instead, essential information is provided that allows the reader to grasp key concepts. While this is a slight oversimplification of this industry, it gives the reader a manageable format and a strong foundation on which to build. The goal of this chapter is to leave clinicians more empowered and informed advocates for both themselves and their patients.

SECTION 1: PRIVATE AND PUBLIC INSURANCE

Health insurance provides a third-party payment system, meaning that payment for services rendered by the provider to the patient is not directly exchanged, but rather paid by the patient's insurance (the third party). The insurance not only covers the patient but may cover his or her dependents (spouse, children) as well. In general, the insurance may be subsidized by the patient's employer (private) or by the government (public).

PRIVATE INSURANCE

The earliest private health insurance is Blue Cross (inpatient) and Blue Shield (outpatient). Today there are 40 Blue Cross/Shield member organizations (similar to franchises, organized as independent corporations and licensed under the national association), that cover over 80 million people in all U.S. states, making it the largest private health insurer (Gapenski, 2003). Private health insurance also includes commercial insurance that is issued by investor-owned insurance companies (health, life, casualty) and self-funded employer plans (i.e., a large employer provides its own health insurance to its employees). In 2005, approximately 68% of the U.S. population was covered by private insurance (U.S. Census Bureau, 2006).

PUBLIC INSURANCE

There are numerous public insurance programs, including TRICARE (health care for uniformed services) and the State Children's Health Insurance Program (SCHIP), and direct government health care services through the Department of Veterans Affairs and Department of Defense. The two major government insurance programs are Medicare and Medicaid. In 2005, approximately 27% of the population was covered by government insurance, with Medicare (13.7%) and Medicaid (13%) representing the majority (U.S. Census Bureau, 2006). The Social Security Act of 1965 established Medicare and Medicaid and significantly changed the landscape of the U.S. health care system.

Medicare   Given that the majority of the U.S. population receives health insurance through employers, the retired elderly may be left without insurance because of adverse selection (see Section Three for more detail). Medicare was conceived as the solution to this problem. Medicare is administered by the federal government under the Department of Health and Human Services through the Centers for Medicare and Medicaid Services (CMS). Medicare was established for U.S. citizens or permanent residents age 65 and older and now consists of four parts (A, B, C, D).

Part A provides hospital and some skilled nursing home coverage, and is free (no premium required because it was already paid for through payroll taxes while working) to all people eligible for Social Security benefits. People younger than 65 who receive social security income for disability are eligible for Medicare after 2 years, and those with end-stage renal disease are entitled to Part A regardless of their age.

Part B (supplemental medical insurance) provides coverage for outpatient and physician services. Although Part B is optional and requires a monthly premium, 98% of Part A beneficiaries enroll in part B (Getzen, 2004). About 29% of Medicare beneficiaries have poor health and nearly half have incomes below poverty level. For those who do not also qualify for Medicaid but whose incomes fall below 135% of the federal poverty level, subsidies such as Medicare savings programs are available (Center for Medicare Advocacy, 2006a).

Part C, formerly known as "Medicare+Choice" is now known as "Medicare Advantage." If a person is entitled to Part A and is enrolled in Part B, he or she can elect to switch to a Medicare Advantage plan that is provided through private managed care plans (CMS, 2006b). Because there are significant gaps in coverage with Part A (large hospital deductibles and coinsurance [daily inpatient copay]), Part C has the advantage of covering all of Parts A and B and the gaps in Part A. Therefore, a person with Part C does not require Medigap insurance. Medigap policies are sold by private insurance companies to fill the gaps in Parts A and B. There are 12 different Medigap policies to choose from, all of which must meet federal and state laws (CMS, 2006b).

Part D was added by the Medicare Prescription Drug, Improvement, and Modernization Act of 2003. Given that the elderly are the highest utilizers of prescription drugs, and that parts A, B, and C did not cover medications outside of hospitalization, this placed the elderly at a serious disadvantage, where many were choosing between paying rent and groceries versus their medications. While some were able to purchase Medigap policies that covered a portion of prescription costs, most were paying cash out of pocket. Part D was instituted in 2006 and pays for outpatient prescription medications, but it has been a source of confusion for many, given its significant gaps in coverage. Known as the "doughnut hole," Part D covers prescription drugs after a $250 deductible is paid by the patient, then covers 75% of the next $2,000 spent, then covers *nothing* for the next $2,850 spent (i.e., coverage gap, second deductible), and then covers 95% for medication bills over $5,100 (Center for Medicare Advocacy, 2006b). However, "dual eligibles" (those who qualify for both Medicare and Medicaid) have no gap in coverage and pay no deductible or premium (CMS, 2006b). Dual eligibles are automatically enrolled in Part D and no longer receive their medications through Medicaid. Unfortunately, many dual eligibles are finding themselves with less drug coverage than they had under Medicaid (Center for Medicare Advocacy, 2006b). Of those whose incomes fall below the poverty level, only half qualify for Medicaid. For those who do not qualify for Medicaid, a full drug subsidy is available for those with incomes below 135% of the federal poverty level, and partial subsidies are also available for those at 150% (Center for Medicare Advocacy, 2006b). These prescription drug plans (PDPs) are provided through private insurance companies and are only available to those enrolled either in Part A or Part B. Those enrolled in Part C must get their drug coverage through a Medicare Advantage Plan if one is available; otherwise they may purchase a PDP through Part D. Depending on the formulary (list of medications covered by the plan), patients can determine which options best suit their prescription needs. The formulary is important because those drugs that are not listed do not count toward Part D deductibles (Center for Medicare Advocacy, 2006b).

Medicaid   Medicaid is funded jointly by the federal government and the states, and the percentage of federal subsidy depends on the wealth of the state (Getzen, 2004). It provides coverage for low-income pregnant women, mothers and children, and for elderly, blind, and disabled persons receiving benefits from supplemental security income (SSI; Gapenski, 2003). Half of all Medicaid beneficiaries are children, with SCHIP covering the remainder of low-income children (Kaiser Commission on Medicaid and the Uninsured, 2006b). Over 50% of those covered by Medicaid are in fair or poor health (Kaiser Commission on Medicaid and the Uninsured, 2006b). Medicaid covers hospital and physician services and prescription drugs, and in 1972, a mandatory nursing home benefit was added, making it the dominant funding source for nursing homes (Getzen, 2004). Eligibility to enroll in Medicaid is set by the state within federal guidelines (visit www.cms.gov for more information).

The Uninsured   Low income does not ensure eligibility for Medicaid, leaving many low-income families uninsured. Over a third of the poor (below 200% of the poverty level) and nearly a third of the near-poor (100 to 199% of the poverty level) are uninsured, and most adults without dependent children are ineligible for Medicaid (Kaiser Commission on Medicaid and the Uninsured, 2006b). In 2005, approximately 21% (46 million) of non-elderly adults in the United States were uninsured, with the majority being under age 35 (~60%; Kaiser Commission on Medicaid and the Uninsured, 2006a). Of those uninsured, the majority were part-time workers (~30%), minorities (34% Hispanic; 32% American India/Alaska Native), and non-U.S. citizens (Kaiser Commission on Medicaid and the Uninsured, 2006a). Many of the uninsured are the working poor, or those who work full- or part-time for employers who do not provide health insurance and who cannot afford to purchase it independently. Eighty-one percent of the uninsured are in working families, with 69% having at least one full-time worker (Kaiser Commission on Medicaid and the Uninsured, 2006b). Lack of insurance increases the risk for poor health status and accrual of health-related debt. Up to a 15% reduction in mortality could be achieved if the uninsured gained health coverage. Most of the uninsured do not receive health services at a reduced charge, with hospitals frequently charging uninsured patients several times more than what insurance pays (Kaiser Commission on Medicaid and the Uninsured, 2006b). In 2004, the $41 billion in uncompensated care was covered by the federal government (58%), state funding (27%), and private money (15%; Kaiser Commission on Medicaid and the Uninsured, 2006b).

SECTION 2: TYPES OF MANAGED CARE PLANS

In 1929, indemnity health insurance was introduced (U.S. Department of Health and Human Services, 1999). Prior to this, most health care was paid for "out of pocket" (i.e., direct cash payment for services rendered). Early indemnity insurance simply secured the policyholder (i.e., the patient) against loss, but was not involved in treatment planning decisions (i.e., utilization review). With indemnity insurance, the policyholder was responsible for paying a deductible (i.e., a predetermined percentage of the policy) before coverage for that year would begin. After the deductible was met, the insurer would pay 80% and the insured was responsible for 20%. Almost all charges were covered, and originally there were no lifetime maximum or other restrictions on reimbursement. Later changes to the indemnity insurance plan included setting a lifetime maximum (i.e., the maximum the insurer would pay for the life of the policy), no coverage for preexisting conditions (exceptions to this could be made after a certain time period), certain exclusions (i.e., cosmetic surgery), and maximum fee schedules, meaning that common health care procedures had customary, regional charges. Until the late 1960s mental health coverage was excluded (Cummings, 2001a). As benefit structures expanded, so did costs. Because of this, in the 1980s, indemnity insurers began to violate the doctor-patient relationship by changing their role to include decision making about the medical necessity of services.

Around this time, in the 1970s, health maintenance organizations (HMOs) were emerging. The first HMO (not named so at the time) was founded by Dr. Sidney Garfield and the industrialist, Henry J. Kaiser, as prepaid medical service provided by Garfield and his team for Kaiser's employees (Getzen, 2004). Today, Kaiser Permanente is the largest HMO in the United States and remains a nonprofit foundation (Getzen, 2004). The term *HMO* was established by Dr. Paul Ellwood, who observed that hospitals were being financially rewarded for increasing length of stay (LOS) and extending outpatient treatment, thereby creating a lack of financial incentive to restore health (Cummings, 2001a). The HMO Act of 1973 ensued, which established the requirements of HMOs and eventually gave way to the proliferation of this model throughout the country.

Given the multitude of mergers and acquisitions in managed care, it is impossible to present every possible current configuration. Getzen (2004) provides a useful framework in which to understand the differences between the major managed care models (see Figure 2.1). On this spectrum, the HMOs exist on one end (tight management controls), whereas indemnity insurance sits at the other end (no management controls). In a closed-group HMO, the HMO employs its own providers, owns the hospitals, purchases the drugs, enrolls members, and so on (e.g., Kaiser Permanente). In a closed-group HMO, the patient can only see in-network providers and must have a referral from the selected primary care physician (PCP) in order to see a specialist. The only major difference between a closed and open HMO is that with an open-access HMO, the patient can self-refer to a specialist but pays a higher copay to do so. Under either type of HMO, the patient generally has no deductible and low out-of-pocket expenses. The Preferred Provider Organization (PPO) and Point of Service (POS) exist between the two ends of the spectrum.

Unlike indemnity insurance, HMOs employ many tactics to restrict utilization, thus the term *managed care*. These management controls include, but are not limited to, preauthorization, reauthorization, and gatekeeping. Preauthorization means that care may not be rendered until it is approved by the HMO, and payment can thereby be denied for unauthorized services. Reauthorization means that the HMO must approve the continuation of care, which can also be denied. Gatekeeping means that the patient must choose one PCP who coordinates his or her care and, except with an open-access HMO, must authorize any referrals to specialists. In choosing a PCP, the patient is restricted to the HMO's network of credentialed providers and can only receive care from hospitals that participate with the HMO. HMOs were initially created

Figure 2.1   Spectrum for Managed Care Models
Source: Adapted from Getzen (2004).

to address the rapidly increasing cost of health care under indemnity insurance. From 1980 to 1990, the total cost of private health insurance increased at an average annual rate of over 12%, thereby leading employers to switch from indemnity to managed care plans (Shi & Singh, 2004). However, as health care inflation began to slow, many consumers wanted less restrictive coverage.

Private insurers developed other less restrictive (i.e., less limited network, less utilization controls) forms of managed care (PPO, POS) to compete with HMOs, and now offer any combination of these to their members. The insurers contract with physicians (i.e., Independent Practice Associations [IPAs]) and hospitals to create a network of providers. A PPO allows members to use providers outside of its network by charging the member a higher copay for non-subcontracted providers. Therefore, the PCP does not act as a gatekeeper. The preferred providers who are contracted in the PPO's network agree to provide service at a reduced fee in exchange for a consistent referral base. The POS is a hybrid HMO that allows the patient to opt out of the HMO at the point of service to see an out-of-network provider by paying a higher out-of-pocket expense (Shi & Singh, 2004).

In 2005, 97% of workers covered by health insurance through their employer were enrolled in a managed care plan, with the majority in a PPO (61% in PPO, 21% in HMO, 15% in POS; Kaiser Family Foundation, 2006). In 2005, 12% of Medicare, and in 2000, 56% of Medicaid beneficiaries were enrolled in a managed care plan (Kaiser Family Foundation, 2005, 2001). The insurance industry and employers continue to find ways to decrease health care costs. Some of the latest trends include the use of physician-incentive plans (i.e., pay-for-performance programs) by the insurance industry, and consumer-driven health care by employers. Pay-for-performance (PFP) programs provide financial incentives for the use of evidence-based performance measures to improve quality and outcomes, but such programs also have the potential for misuse (rewarding cost savings rather than quality), thereby having the opposite effect. To allow for fair and ethical use of these programs, the American Medical Association (AMA) has established five principles for PFPs to follow: (1) ensure quality of care, (2) foster the patient/physician relationship, (3) offer voluntary physician participation, (4) use accurate data and fair reporting, and (5) provide fair and equitable program incentives (American Medical Association, 2005). Consumer driven health care includes the flexible spending account (FSA), medical savings account (MSA), health reimbursement arrangement (HRA), and the health savings account (HSA). For more information, the interested reader is referred to www .consumerdrivenhealthcare.us. These trends are still in their infancy and have yet to be widely adopted.

SECTION 3: FINANCIAL STRUCTURES AND REIMBURSEMENT

Insurance companies adopted and employers embraced models of managed care because of the associated cost savings. In 2005, national health expenditures were $2 trillion, with 16% from Medicaid and SCHIP, 17% from Medicare, and 35% from private insurance (Centers for Medicare and Medicaid Services, 2006a). At 16% of the gross domestic product (GDP) for 2005, the health care industry is considered the largest single industry in the U.S. Although there has been a slowdown of health care inflation in the last few years, prescription drug costs continue to rise at a higher percentage than other sectors of the health care industry (Centers for Disease Control and Prevention [CDC], 2006). This slowdown has been attributed to managed care (U.S.

Department of Health and Human Services, 1999). However, there is insufficient data available to conclude how this has impacted the quality of care provided. Health care cost continues to rise faster than the gross domestic product (GDP), and reasons for this may include medical technology, an aging society, fraud, administrative costs, the practice of defensive medicine (more tests/procedures conducted to protect against liability), and the dramatic rise in chronic disease. In fact, chronic disease accounts for approximately three-fourths of U.S. health care expenditures (Pruitt, Klapow, Epping-Jordan, & Dresselhaus, 1998).

The overarching purpose of health insurance is to protect the patient from catastrophic financial loss (U.S. Department of Health and Human Services, 1999). However, health insurers employ techniques to reduce payments and their own financial risk. Such strategies include moral hazard, adverse selection, and risk transfer. Moral hazard means that if the cost of being ill is entirely covered by a third party, there is less incentive for the patient to decrease unnecessary utilization of medical services or to engage in preventive care. Insurance companies use deductibles and copayments to minimize moral hazard. Adverse selection means that if an insurance company offers generous coverage, it will attract the sickest members with the highest utilization of services. To address adverse selection, insurance companies will restrict coverage and avoid enrolling those people with the highest morbidity rates. Risk transfer is a fundamental principle of the insurance industry. The third party payment system is based on the transfer of risk associated with losing money, whereby the insured (patient) passes the financial risk of getting sick onto the insurer, and the insurer then transfers some of the financial risk onto the provider. Depending on the reimbursement structure, the provider will assume more or less risk.

A full review of all inpatient and outpatient hospital and provider reimbursement procedures is beyond the scope of this chapter. Therefore, the focus is on the most widely adopted payment systems that reimburse hospital inpatient services and provider outpatient services.

In 1983, Medicare adopted a prospective payment system (PPS) for Part A that established criteria for inpatient hospital reimbursement in advance (Shi & Singh, 2004). This was done to slow its continued growth in spending. Today, Medicare uses the PPS to reimburse all acute care hospitals, and most specialty hospitals that were previously exempt are now adopting this system (e.g., psychiatric hospitals began phasing in PPS in 2005; U.S. Department of Health and Human Services, 2004). Many other payers have now adopted this system as well (Getzen, 2004).

Under the PPS, predetermined reimbursement amounts are based on diagnosis-related groups (DRGs) to determine inpatient payment. Over 500 DRGs are divided into diagnostic categories that correspond to the major organ systems (Gapenski, 2003). The DRG coding is then weighted based on the type of hospital, location, teaching, and other factors to determine the amount of reimbursement to the hospital (U.S. Department of Health and Human Services, 2005). Although DRGs have significantly slowed expenditures, hospitals were losing money on Medicare patients and new opportunities for fraud were introduced, such as upcoding (assigning an unsubstantiated, higher-paying diagnosis).

In general, there are two major reimbursement methods for providers: (1) the resource-based relative value scale, and (2) capitation. In terms of the financial risk transfer from insurer to provider, the provider incurs the greatest financial risk with capitation (Gapenski, 2003).

Capitation means that a fixed payment is made to the provider (usually based on a per member-per month basis [PMPM]), regardless of the amount of services rendered (Gapenski, 2003). This leaves the provider with the financial risk of caring for the members with a fixed payment. HMOs predominantly use capitation with providers. As a financial incentive, an HMO may keep a portion of the total capitated amount in reserve (i.e., the withhold pool) and will distribute it at the end of the year to individual physicians who meet certain financial goals; if goals are not met, the HMO keeps the withhold pool (Gapenski, 2003). More than two-thirds of HMOs are for-profit corporations (Zelman, 1996), and take 15–20% of premiums for administration, marketing, and profit, with profit margins around 5% (Getzen, 2004).

Under the Omnibus Budget Reconciliation Act of 1989, Medicare developed a reimbursement method under Part B for physician outpatient services (Shi & Singh, 2004). This method, instituted in 1992, was termed the *resource-based relative value scale* (RBRVS); it reimburses physicians based on a value assigned to each physician service (Shi & Singh, 2004). Part of the calculation for the RBRVS is based on the International Classification of Diseases, ninth revision, Clinical Modification (ICD-9-CM) medical diagnosis assigned, and (if a procedure is performed) coding from the Current Procedural Terminology, fourth edition (CPT-4; Getzen, 2004). The ICD-9-CM contains approximately 13,000 diagnostic codes and is copyrighted and updated annually by the American Hospital Association (AHA). There are approximately 7,500 CPT-4 codes that are paid under the RBRVS (Getzen, 2004). CPT codes describe the procedure or service rendered and are copyrighted and updated annually by the AMA. The RBRVS has been widely adopted, and Medicaid, Blue Cross, and commercial insurance use a modified form of this system (Getzen, 2004).

Psychologists use both CPT codes and diagnoses from the *Diagnostic and Statistical Manual of Mental Disorders, Fourth Edition, Text Revision* (DSM-IV-TR; American Psychiatric Association, 2000) to submit claims for outpatient services (see Table 2.1). Medicare has spearheaded the use of a new set of Health and Behavior CPT codes (bottom half of Table 2.1) that allows psychologists to provide behavioral medicine/ health psychology interventions to patients whose primary diagnosis is physical in nature without having to unnecessarily stigmatize patients with psychiatric diagnoses. This allows psychologists to more accurately bill for services that include health-promotion, adherence to medical treatment regiment, symptom management,

Table 2.1
Sample Behavioral Health CPT Codes

CPT CODE	Type of Service
90801	Diagnostic Interview
90806	Individual Psychotherapy (45–50 minutes)
90846	Family Psychotherapy without patient
90847	Family Psychotherapy with patient
90853	Group Psychotherapy
96117	Neuropsychological testing with report
96150	Health and Behavior Assessment (1 unit = 15 minutes)
96152	Health and Behavior Intervention (1 unit = 15 minutes)
96153	Health and Behavior Group Intervention (1 unit = 15 min)
96154	Health and Behavior Family Session (1 unit = 15 minutes)

Source: Adapted from AMA (2006).

and overall adjustment to physical illness. Because of this, they are billed at 15-minute increments rather than the standard 45–50 minute therapist hour. Additionally, these codes must be accompanied by an ICD-9-CM medical diagnosis rather than a DSM-IV-TR diagnosis, because a previously diagnosed medical disorder is required. With these health and behavior codes, Medicare reimburses the provider at a higher rate (80% of the claim versus the standard 50% with mental health codes), thereby requiring a smaller copay from the patient (American Psychological Association [APA], 2005). It remains to be seen whether other insurers will accept these codes as well in the future.

SECTION 4: MANAGED BEHAVIORAL HEALTH CARE

MENTAL HEALTH CARE PRIOR TO THE CARVE-OUT

In the 1980s, the cost of behavioral health services was increasing at about twice the rate of medical care costs and four times that of general inflation (Feldman, 1998). As previously discussed, the PPS was successful in curtailing increasing inpatient costs in acute care hospitals. However, at that time, psychiatric units and hospitals were exempt from this system, largely due to difficulty in establishing DRG coding for mental health diagnoses. During this period, state government certificate-of-need requirements that had previously limited construction of new hospitals were less restrictive (Feldman, 1998). The combination of decreased restrictions for construction and reimbursement led to rapid expansion of psychiatric services. Construction of psychiatric hospitals increased by 70% and psychiatric units in acute care hospitals grew by 56% (Feldman, 1998). In 2 years, the rate of growth in behavioral health care expenditures increased from 2% to 16% (Cummings, 2001b). Behavioral health inpatient costs and length of stay (LOS) were high while utilization of outpatient treatment was low. Inpatient treatment was covered at between 80 to 100%, with little restriction on LOS, whereas outpatient treatment was only covered at 50% with a reimbursement limit (Shaffer, 2001). Inpatient services accounted for 75% of total behavioral health costs (Feldman, 1998), and employers incurred 15-20% annual increases in behavioral health expenditures (Shaffer, 2001). To contain these costs, employers began to limit behavioral health care benefits. Some have argued that employers would have dropped the behavioral benefit completely if not for the introduction of the managed behavioral health carve-out.

THE CARVE-OUT INCEPTION

Managed behavioral health care decreased hospital admissions and LOS, thereby forcing behavioral health care to shift to outpatient, residential, and partial hospitalization treatment modalities. Utilization management policies such as preauthorization and concurrent review became popular among administrators but not among providers. Cost savings were also achieved by paying lower fees to clinicians, at least 20% below usually customary rates (UCR; Feldman, 1998). Employers, however, began to see a 25 to 40% cost decrease in the first year of implementing a managed behavioral health care program (Feldman, 1998; Shaffer, 2001). During that first year, access to behavioral health care rose by at least 15%; however, related impact on quality was not assessed (Shaffer, 2001). Inpatient costs dropped from 50% of overall behavioral health costs in 1988 to 22% of costs in 1995 (Shaffer, 2001). Spending for mental health care declined as a percentage of total health expenditures during 1986–1996 (U.S. Department of Health and Human Services, 1999).

Behavioral health is largely managed through a carve-out structure. According to Grazier and Eselius (1999), a carve-out strategy is one in which insurance benefits for a specific service category are separated from other insurance benefits and managed under a different contract. By this definition, behavioral health and pharmacy are examples of carved-out services.

When behavioral health is carved out, the employer or health plan (i.e., client company) contracts to have its behavioral health care administered separately by a managed behavioral health organization (MBHO). The MBHO is considered a carve-out company with its own network of providers, separate budget, and contracts with facilities and programs (U.S. Department of Health and Human Services, 1999). Care may be provided from within or outside of the network, with a differential in benefits, as described previously, regarding HMOs, PPOs, and POSs. Utilization management through preauthorization and treatment review for reauthorization (or denial) of care is frequently used. It is worth noting that utilization reviewers typically have less knowledge and education than providers (Miller, 1996). Almost all MBHOs are investor-owned (i.e., for profit; Hodgkin, Morgan, Garnick, & Merrick, 2002), and currently the largest MBHO in the United States is Magellan Health Services (Gray, Brody, & Johnson, 2005).

Depending on the financial risk arrangement, client companies generally contract with MBHOs under one of two conditions. In the first condition, the contract is for administrative services only (ASO). This means that the MBHO provides all the administrative functions of delivering and monitoring behavioral health care, such as the network, care management, and claims processing, but does not assume any of the financial risk involved in the delivery of that care. Therefore, the client company is at risk for the health care costs. Under this condition, the MBHO is reimbursed by the client company on a per employee-per month basis, and any cost savings or loss is a direct benefit or risk to the client company (Shaffer, 2001). This condition is typically seen when the contract is between the MBHO and a self-insured employer (Feldman, 1998). In the second condition, the MBHO not only provides the administrative functions but assumes the financial risk as well. The MBHO must manage the risk as part of the overall contract and is reimbursed by the client company on a per member–per month (PMPM; i.e., capitation) basis (Shaffer, 2001). Therefore, there is greater incentive for the MBHO to effectively manage cost of care. This condition is typically seen between an HMO and the MBHO (Feldman, 1998). In between capitation and ASO lie many contract variations of financial risk sharing, and there is evidence that as the contracting moves from ASO to capitation, utilization rates drop (Hodgkin et al., 2002).

Many client companies have made employee assistance programs (EAPs) the front end of their behavioral health care benefits by using their own internal EAP or by contracting for this service with the MBHO (Shaffer, 2001). This creates additional cost savings, because some issues can be resolved within the EAP before a patient needs to access his or her behavioral health care benefit. There are, of course, multiple variations within contracts, further adding to the complexity of the carve-out system, that are beyond the scope of this chapter.

The proliferation of managed behavioral health carve-outs is nationwide. It has been estimated that 88% of the insured managed care population is enrolled in a managed behavioral health carve-out program (Kiesler, 2000; Sanchez & Turner, 2003), which is approximately 176 million Americans (Melek, 2001).

The Downside of the Carve-Out

Although it has been argued that the carve-out saved the behavioral health benefit, it has done so at the possible expense of quality care. In 1999, the landmark report on mental health from U.S. Surgeon General Satcher concluded that managed behavioral health plans varied significantly in access and quality and that there is little incentive in these plans to improve quality (USDHHS, 1999). Furthermore, services are at a minimum, and the majority of cost savings has already been realized. In fact, increases in mental health costs observed in the late 1990s were the result of the overprescribing of psychotropic medications, predominantly SSRIs, by primary care physicians (PCPs) who were not subject to control by carve-outs (Gray, Brody, & Johnson, 2005). Moreover, high administrative costs continue for the management of carve-outs, which are estimated to range from 8 to 15% of claims costs (Frank & McGuire, 1998). Carve-out systems also require the client company and the MBHO to maintain separate data systems, thereby exacerbating fragmented and uncoordinated care. Because care is provided to persons—not conditions—the carve-out system works against the development of an integrated system (Grazier & Eselius, 1999). The overall costs of care will only increase if comorbid conditions are treated in a nonintegrated fashion on both the behavioral and medical sides.

Perhaps the most damaging impact of the carve-out system has been the lack of parity, or equality, granted to mental health coverage as compared to medical coverage. While some insurers refused to cover any mental health care, those that did would impose financial restrictions, such as lower annual and lifetime limits on care and higher deductibles and co-payments, placing the patient at greater risk of suffering from catastrophic loss in addition to untreated mental illness (USDHHS, 1999). For instance, whereas limits on medical coverage could extend to $1 million, limits on mental health coverage were typically $25,000, but went as low as $5,000 (USDHHS, 1999). Further, although higher co-pays for outpatient mental health services may have reduced inappropriate use, this may have also discouraged appropriate and needed services as well (USDHHS, 1999). Parity legislation has sought to bring mental health financing to the same level as general health financing. The Mental Health Parity Act was passed in 1996 and enforced equal lifetime limits on coverage for mental and physical health, but did not address other restrictions, such as higher co-pays and deductibles (USDHHS, 1999). Moreover, those insurers with a greater than 1% increase in premiums as a result of implementing the parity act could apply for an exemption (USDHHS, 1999). In 1999, legislation was passed that instituted parity regarding co-pays and deductibles for federal employees (Goldman et al., 2006). Research has shown that parity generally results in less than a 1% increase in total health care costs (USDHHS, 1999). Recent research conducted by Goldman and colleagues (2006) further supports these earlier findings. They compared seven federal employee health benefits (FEHB) plans that included parity benefits with a matched set of health plans that did not include parity benefits, and reported that increases in mental health benefits used under the FEHB plans were comparable to increases in the nonparity plans, and concluded that implementation of parity coupled with management of care does not increase total costs.

According to Gray, Brody and Johnson (2005), carve-outs have "fallen out of favor" as insurance and managed care are carving mental health back into general medical benefits. They postulate several reasons for the growing disfavor with carve-outs, including incentives to shift mental health care to primary care (because the MBHO financial risk is only for specialty mental health), duplicated administrative functions, not addressing pharmacy costs, and lack of integration with primary care. For instance, lower co-payments for medication versus psychotherapy lead to greater reliance on medication for treatment of psychological disorders (Gray et al., 2005). Health plan administrators are now adopting a carve-in structure that has the potential to integrate medical and behavioral health (Gray et al.).

CARVE-IN SYSTEM OF INTEGRATION

A carve-in system of integration exists when a health insurance or managed care organization owns and operates its behavioral health organization as a subsidiary and therefore retains the risk for the mental health services (Gray et al., 2005). In this system, management focuses on the whole person as well as a combination of medical and psychological services (Gray et al.). Integration occurs on two levels: administrative and clinical. At the administrative level, there is decreased overlap in management and increased use of common datasets. At the clinical level, behavioral health is provided alongside medical care. The most recent example of a carve-in behavioral health plan is Aetna Behavioral Health.

A carve-in more fully addresses parity issues and allows for improved access to care, quality of care, and cost savings. Achieving parity and increasing access are essential, given that the World Health Organization has ranked psychological disorders second only to cardiovascular disease as a leading cause of worldwide disability (Murray & Lopez, 1996). At the clinical level, mental health providers would have greater access to patients in need of services who may not seek a mental health provider on their own. When physicians and mental health providers can collaborate more freely, the quality of the care provided to the patient improves. This structure may have the added benefit of destigmatizing mental health care, as patients come to see mental health providers as part of the medical team. At the administrative level, less money is spent on management and the financing of care is essentially coming from the same source, meaning that there is a greater potential to achieve parity for mental health benefits. Furthermore, administrative integration allows for a single data system where behavioral and medical care can be accurately tracked. This common dataset allows for actuarial analysis of medical cost offset, which is where the potential for tremendous cost savings lie. Of course, this offset is not possible with a carve-out structure, because it results from integration at the clinical level and is calculated by integration at the administrative level.

MEDICAL COST OFFSET

The *medical cost offset* occurs when the savings in medical costs derived from behavioral health services are greater than the cost of providing the behavioral services (Dana, Connor, & Allen, 1996). Not only can the behavioral health care pay for itself in a carve-in system, but it can result in significant medical savings as well. A modest 10% reduction in medical/surgical costs resulting from integrated behavioral health care interventions would exceed the entire behavioral health budget (Cummings, 2001b), and this offset has been calculated in the range of 20 to 40% (Strosahl, 2001). In fact, HMOs save between 20 to 30% by replacing a carve-out structure with a carve-in (Gray et al., 2005). There are two types of medical cost offset: direct and indirect (Strosahl, 2001). *Direct cost offset* results from the behavioral services used in place of more expensive medical services. *Indirect cost offset* results from a more efficient system, because physicians have more time to treat acute medical problems. Cost offsets have been demonstrated with many types of medical and psychological disorders, including asthma, coronary artery disease, obesity, depression, anxiety, somatization, and chronic pain (Strosahl & Sobel, 1996). According to a meta-analytic review of medical cost offset research, the offset has been found to be greater for older than younger patients and for behavioral medicine rather than traditional psychotherapy (Chiles, Lambert, & Hatch, 1999). The largest cost offsets have been seen with behavioral medicine interventions for presurgical preparation and primary care (Strosahl, 2001).

As previously mentioned, $2 trillion was spent in 2005 on health care in the United States. The opportunity for behavioral health services to impact health care expenditures is significant, particularly in primary care. Although behavioral health impacts almost all specialties of medicine, as has been discussed in detail throughout this text, the opportunity to influence utilization patterns related to mental health issues is greatest in primary care. Therefore, primary care holds special relevance to integration at the clinical level in realizing the medical cost offset. Primary care includes family and internal medicine, obstetrics-gynecology, and pediatrics, and is composed of physicians, physician assistants, nurses, and other providers who may collaborate.

It is important to note that a focus on financial offset for justification of expanding mental health coverage comes out of a history of rapidly rising mental health expenditures that resulted in discrimination against such coverage. Other sectors of the health care system are seldom forced to justify their existence, and money is spent simply because it improves quality of life (Strosahl & Sobel, 1996). However, a financial argument may improve access to and quality of mental health services. As Cummings (1999, p. 223) has written, "the value of psychological services increases in importance to the buyers [employers, insurers, government] to the degree that they can impact the billions of dollars in unnecessary medical/surgical costs that plague the health system."

Barriers to Integration

While a carve-in system of integration has many benefits to the overall health care system, there remain barriers to adopting a carve-in model. Physicians may not want to decrease high utilization behavior if they believe it increases their revenues. Currently, managed care has not provided financial incentives for adopting an integrated model of care (USDHHS, 2001), which could lead to the marginalization of behavioral services within medicine. Also, a lack of integrated technologies makes administrative integration difficult (Melek, 2001). Furthermore, most medical settings are not structurally designed to accommodate behavioral health providers and are therefore prohibitive of colocation (i.e., mental health providers and medical providers located in the same office; Melek). There is no financial incentive for carve-outs to participate in integrated treatment because they cannot recoup cost offsets (USDHHS, 2001), and, given that carve-out companies have the majority of the insured behavioral health care market, they will strongly oppose the carve-in movement. However, if client companies decide to adopt a carve-in structure they can terminate contracts with MBHOs.

One of the biggest challenges to integration remains the lack of adequate reimbursement policies. Coding for mental health remains largely separate from that of physical health. As discussed previously, CPT coding for integrated services is limited, and Medicare is the only payer reimbursing these services (Gray et al., 2005).

Funding for these codes does not come out of behavioral health carve-outs with limited mental health dollars that are subject to higher co-pay; instead, they come out of funding for general medical services, which allows for a lower co-pay (APA, 2005). However, without the expansion of such codes, it will be difficult to track the medical cost offset (Newman, 1999).

SECTION 5: INTEGRATED PRIMARY CARE

Integrated primary care and the carve-in structure exist in a codependent relationship in which one is not fully sustainable without the other. Primary care is considered the de facto mental health system in the United States (Reiger, Narrow, Rae, Manderschied et al., 1993). Equally as many people receive mental health care through primary medical care as those who receive mental health care through specialty mental health services (USDHHS, 1999). In fact, 60 to 70% of all medical visits primarily have a psychosocial basis (Fries, Koop, & Beadle, 1993; Garcia-Shelton & Vogel, 2002) and approximately 25% of primary care patients have a diagnosable psychological disorder, with anxiety and depression being the most common (Olfson et al., 1997). In addition, more than 50% of patients with mental health problems are seen only in primary care, and almost 70% of all psychotropic medications are prescribed by nonpsychiatric physicians (Beardsley, Gardocki, Larson, & Hidalgo, 1988; Pincus et al., 1998). Even so, detection of behavioral disorders is missed up to 50% of the time in primary care. Less than a third of adults with a diagnosable mental disorder receive treatment each year, leaving the majority without care (USDHHS, 1999). By integrating behavioral health care with primary care, accurate identification of patients in need of mental health services and access to those services should increase. In former Surgeon General Satcher's report on the integration of mental health services and primary care (USDHHS, 2001), he identifies primary care as one of the "prime portals of entry" for mental health treatment and emphasized that this partnership is "crucial for overall balanced health." Given the aforementioned statistics, there is significant need for mental health providers to be situated in primary care.

Behavioral health care in primary care takes on more of a health psychology model, which includes such interventions as improving patient self-management skill, detecting and treating undiagnosed mental illness, implementing prevention programs, and decreasing overutilization from somatization, all of which improve medical treatment outcomes. These psychological interventions are best implemented onsite, because only 10% of patients ever follow through on their physicians' referrals to psychologists (Cummings, 1999). When behavioral health specialists are onsite, however, this results in an 80% acceptance rate by patients (Cummings).

This type of model represents a "reunification of mind and body" (Blount, 1998) by challenging the mind/body dualism that began with the philosophy of Descartes during the seventeenth century (Cummings, O'Donohue, Hayes, & Follette, 2001). Since then, it has been accepted practice that medical and mental disease should be diagnosed and treated separately. However, many conditions are not clearly delineated as either medical or mental in nature. Research has supported that there is a reciprocal causal relationship between physical and psychological conditions. Chronic anxiety and stress can lead to hypertension, eventually causing cardiac conditions. For instance, anxiety can cause sympathetic nervous system arousal, leading to increased heart rate, vasoconstriction, and high blood pressure, which can be risk factors for cardiac conditions. Rates of anxiety can also be higher among cardiac and other medical patients. Panic disorder may be identified in up to 50% of cardiac patients and up to 40% of patients with gastrointestinal conditions (Roy-Byrne, Wagner, & Schraufnagel, 2005). Additionally, depression increases the risk of heart disease, stroke, and hypertension (Davidson, Jonas, Dixon, & Markovitz, 2000; Jonas & Lando, 2000; Jonas & Mussolino, 2000).

For the last several decades, behavioral scientists have demonstrated improved clinical outcomes as well as cost savings resulting from targeted psychological interventions that have been integrated within primary and specialty medical care (Katon et al., 1995; Lorig, Mazonson, & Holman,1993; Pallak, Cummings, Dorken, & Henke 1995; Robinson, Schwartz, Magwene, Krengel, & Tamburello, 1989; Smith, Rost, & Kashner, 1995). Many chronic diseases, such as diabetes, pulmonary disease, hepatitis, and asthma can be prevented or managed more effectively with behavioral interventions targeted at diet, exercise, smoking, chronic pain, sexual practices, and adherence to medical regimens to improve medical treatment outcomes.

PSYCHOLOGICAL INTERVENTIONS IN PRIMARY CARE

As previously mentioned, the opportunity to influence utilization patterns related to mental health issues is greatest in primary care. According to Friedman, Sobel, Myers, Caudill, and Benson (1995), there are several "psychosocial drivers" of medical utilization and cost. Some of the more significant psychosocial drivers that they and others have identified include (1) patient lack of information and self-management, (2) somatization, and (3) undiagnosed and misdiagnosed mental illness. By intervening in these important areas, not only does unnecessary utilization and associated costs decrease, but more importantly, clinical outcomes improve.

Patient Lack of Information and Self-Management   When patients lack appropriate information, skill, and self-efficacy in self-management, this leads to patient suffering, unnecessary physician visits, and overuse of the health care system. It is estimated that a significant number of physician office visits are for problems that patients can treat themselves, such as the common cold or low-grade fever (Friedman et al., 1995). Interventions can include teaching patients how to effectively distinguish those symptoms and circumstances that require professional attention from those that can be self-managed. For instance, when parents, as part of a controlled study, were given a self-care guide on managing a child with a fever, medical visits for fever decreased by 35% and visits for all acute illnesses decreased by 25% (Robinson, Schwartz, Magwene, & Krengel et al., 1989). Another example is seen in a study conducted by Lorig, Mazonson, and Holman (1993) at the Stanford Arthritis Center, in which an arthritis self-management course was taught. Those patients who attended the class reported experiencing a significant increase in self-efficacy for managing their arthritis, a 20% reduction in pain, and a 43% decrease in physician visits as compared to pretreatment levels.

Somatization   Somatization not only leads to increased physician time but also leads to increased use of expensive testing. Patients who somatisize underlying emotional problems often present with an unusual constellation of symptoms that leads to extensive testing to find a medical diagnosis. The most common complaints seen by PCPs are chest pain, fatigue, dizziness, headache, edema, back pain, dyspnea, insomnia, abdominal pain, numbness, impotence, cough, and constipation (Cummings, 2001).

On average, only 15% of these symptoms end up with a diagnosable organic etiology, meaning that they are most often the result of underlying psychosocial issues (Kroenke & Mangelsdorff, 1989). In one study of patients presenting with acute chest pain, 17.5% met criteria for panic disorder and 23.1% met criteria for depression (Yingling, Wulsin, Arnold, & Rouan, 1993). Of patients presenting with fatigue in primary care, 20 to 40% suffer from depression (Walker, Katon, & Jelka, 1993). When physicians were taught a behavioral medicine intervention for handling somatizing patients, this resulted in a 33% reduction of annual median cost for the patients' medical care (Smith, Rost, & Kashner, 1995). In addition, Pallak and colleagues (1995) used a behavioral medicine intervention with a group of high utilizers of Medicaid services and found that this intervention reduced medical costs by up to 36% for those patients enrolled in the intervention for 12 months, as compared to a rise of 22% for those who did not receive the intervention. Having mental health providers on site can help decrease these costs by addressing somatization before repeating expensive medical testing or beginning inappropriate medical interventions. These studies also found improved physical and mental health among patients receiving behavioral medicine interventions, because the true underlying psychological causes of their distress were more likely to be identified and addressed.

Undiagnosed and Misdiagnosed Mental Illness   Those with poor psychosocial functioning are more likely to have poor general health status, functional disability, and higher morbidity and mortality, all of which lead to decreased quality of life and increased utilization of health services. Many mental illnesses go undetected and therefore untreated in primary care. Detection of mental disorders is missed up to 50% of the time in primary care (Melek, 2001). For instance, PCPs fail to recognize depression in 30 to 50% of their patients (Brody, 2003), which is of concern, given that half of all depression is treated exclusively in primary care (Thomas & Brantley, 2004). This may be attributed to time constraints and the lack of behavioral medicine training that PCPs receive (USDHHS, 2001). Untreated, depressed primary care patients use two to three times more health services that their nondepressed counterparts (Simon, Von Korff, & Barlow, 1995). Less than 50% of primary care patients who are prescribed antidepressant medications meet diagnostic criteria warranting treatment for depression (Katon et al., 1996), which not only further escalates pharmacy costs but also interferes with the patient attaining an appropriate level of care. By having mental health providers on site, screenings leading to more detailed diagnostic procedures can take place to provide a more accurate clinical picture and appropriate treatment services. Katon and colleagues (1995) demonstrated superior clinical outcomes for the treatment of depression in an integrated primary care setting with colocated mental health providers, (74% of patients showed symptom reduction) as compared to standard treatment with the PCP and referral to a mental health provider (44% of patients showed symptom reduction). This study further revealed that 80% of participating physicians expressed that the collaboration with mental health providers greatly increased their satisfaction in treating depression.

Health psychologists are uniquely trained to lead a movement toward integrated primary care at the clinical level. They possess the requisite behavioral medicine knowledge and the skills to implement targeted interventions designed for specific populations, to conduct outcomes research, and to effectively collaborate with physicians and other medical providers. Furthermore, as previously mentioned, targeted behavioral medicine interventions are more effective in achieving cost offset than traditional psychotherapy. A push toward carve-in financial structures would allow the health psychologist to be a true member of the primary care team, thereby opening up new opportunities for practice and reimbursement. According to Blount (1998), this is the structural realization of the biopsychosocial model. Integrated primary care is best achieved when the mental health provider is colocated, has a consistent presence, provides consultation to PCPs, and comanages patients (Strosahl, 1998). If on-site first-line interventions are not effective, then the patient can be referred for outside mental health services, which would likely improve the appropriateness and frequency of referrals to mental health private practitioners and other mental health agencies. This model provides further opportunities for disease prevention and for assisting PCPs in learning how to apply behavioral interventions (Strosahl). If integration is ever realized and proliferates, in order to preserve the mental health system and protect the interests of mental health providers (i.e., not replacing them with less-trained workers from other disciplines), health psychology will need to assert a dominant role in this model. The Model for Integrating Medicine and Psychology, described in Chapter 1, provides an expedient assessment sequence to assist psychologists in understanding the stresses and coping demands of various physical illnesses as well as to orient physicians and nurses to the psychosocial factors that may interfere with important medical outcomes.

CONCLUSION

As can be gleaned from this chapter, the U.S. health care system is quite intricate. Managed care, originally thought to be a passing phase, appears to be here to stay, at least for the foreseeable future. However, it is anyone's guess as to how the health insurance and managed care industry will continue to morph. Trends indicate that we are headed toward outcomes-based payment structures (e.g., PFPs), but the continuing rise in health care expenditures, which outpace general inflation, will not be solved without a complex and multidisciplinary approach. Of great concern is the growing number of uninsured persons and the lack of reasonable mental health coverage, even for those who are insured. Proponents of universal health care (i.e., health insurance for all Americans) believe this to be the answer, yet opponents argue that it is too costly and results in lengthy waits for certain types of medical care. Moreover, health insurance companies would strongly oppose it. Yet, even though for-profit, investor-owned companies play a major role, true market forces do not exist in health care. Regardless, mental health parity has yet to be realized, and perhaps the answer lies in moving from a carve-out to a carve-in structure of managed behavioral health. The mental health industry may then become a major vehicle for achieving medical cost offset through integrated primary care, with health psychology leading the way.

REFERENCES

American Medical Association. (2005). *Principles for pay for performance programs.* Retrieved January 10, 2007, from: http://www.ama-assn.org/ama1/pub/upload/mm/368/principles4 pay62705.pdf

American Medical Association. (2006). *CPT 2006 standard edition.* New York: Thomson Delmar Learning.

American Psychiatric Association. (2000). *Diagnostic and statistical manual of mental disorders, text revision* (4th ed.). Washington, DC: Author.

American Psychological Association. (2005). *APA Practice Directorate announces new health and behavior CPT codes.* Retrieved February 5, 2006, from http://www.apa.org/practice/cpt_2002.html

Beardsley, R., Gardocki, G., Larson, D., & Hidalgo, J. (1988). Prescribing of psychotropic medication by primary care physicians and psychiatrists. *Archives of General Psychiatry, 45,* 1117–1119.

Blount, A. (1998). Introduction to integrated primary care. In A. Blount (Ed.), *Integrated primary care: The future of medical and mental health collaboration,* (pp. 1–43). New York: W. W. Norton.

Brody, D. S. (2003). Improving the management of depression in primary care: Recent accomplishments and ongoing challenges. *Disease Management Health Outcomes, 11,* 21–31.

Centers for Disease Control and Prevention. (2006). *Health expenditures.* Retrieved January 10, 2007, from http://www.cdc.gov/nchs/fastats/hexpense.htm

Center for Medicare Advocacy. (2006a). *Medicare Part B matters.* Retrieved January 10, 2007, from http://www.medicareadvocacy.org/PartB_PartBMatters.htm

Center for Medicare Advocacy (2006b). *Medicare prescription drug coverage.* Retrieved January 10, 2007, from http://www.medicareadvocacy.org/FAQ_PartD_Info.htm#whatIsD

Centers for Medicare and Medicaid Services. (2006a). *The nation's healthcare dollar, calendar year 2005: Where it came from.* Retrieved January 10, 2007, from http://www.cms.hhs.gov/NationalHealthExpendData/downloads/PieChartSourcesExpenditures2005.pdf

Centers for Medicare and Medicaid Services. (2006b). *Want to learn more about the new Medicare prescription drug coverage?* Retrieved January 10, 2007, from http://www.medicare.gov/medicarereform/drugbenefit.asp

Chiles, J. A., Lambert, M. J., & Hatch, A. L. (1999). The impact of psychological interventions on medical cost offset: A meta-analytic review. *Clinical Psychology: Science and Practice, 6 (2),* 204–220.

Cummings, N. A. (1999). Medical cost offset, meta-analysis, and implications for future research and practice. *Clinical Psychology: Science and Practice, 6 (2),* 221–223.

Cummings, N. A. (2001a). A history of behavioral healthcare: A perspective from a lifetime of involvement. In N. A. Cummings, W. O'Donohue, S. C. Hays, & V. F. Follette (Eds.), *Integrated behavioral healthcare: Positioning mental health practice with medical/surgical practice* (pp. 1–18). San Diego, CA: Academic Press.

Cummings, N. A. (2001b). A new vision of healthcare for America. In N. A. Cummings, W. O'Donohue, S. C. Hays, & V. F. Follette (Eds.), *Integrated behavioral healthcare: Positioning mental health practice with medical/surgical practice* (pp.19–37). San Diego, CA: Academic Press.

Cummings, N. A., O'Donohue, W., Hayes, S. C., & Follette, V. (2001). Preface. In N. A. Cummings, W. O'Donohue, S. C. Hayes, & V. Follette (Eds.), *Integrated behavioral healthcare: Positioning mental health practice with medical/surgical practice,* (pp. xi–xvi). San Diego, CA: Academic Press.

Dana, R. H., Conner, M. G., & Allen, J. (1996). Quality of care and cost containment in managed mental health: Policy, education, research, advocacy. *Psychological Reports, 79,* 1395–1422.

Davidson, K., Jonas, B., Dixon, K., & Markovitz, J. (2000). Do depression symptoms predict early hypertension incidence in young adults from the CARDIA study? *Archives of Internal Medicine, 160,* 1495–1500.

Feldman, S. (1998). Behavioral health services: Carved out and managed. *The American Journal of Managed Care, 4,* SP59–SP67.

Frank, R. G., & McGuire, T. G. (1998). The economic functions of carve-outs in managed care. *The American Journal of Managed Care, 4,* SP31–SP39.

Friedman, R., Sobel, D., Myers, P., Caudill, M., & Benson, H. (1995). Behavioral medicine, clinical health psychology, and cost offset. *Health Psychology, 14* (6), 509–518.

Fries, J., Koop, C., & Beadle, C. (1993). Reducing health care costs by reducing the need and demand for medical services. *The New England Journal of Medicine, 329,* 321–325.

Gapenski, L. C. (2003). *Understanding healthcare financial management* (4th ed.). Washington, DC: Health Administration Press.

Garcia-Shelton, L., & Vogel, M. E. (2002). Primary care health psychology training: A collaborative model with family practice. *Professional Psychology: Research and Practice, 33*(6), 546–556.

Getzen, T. E. (2004). *Health economics: Fundamentals and flow of funds* (2nd ed.). Danvers, MA: Wiley.

Goldman, H. H., Frank, R. G., Burnam, M. A., Huskamp, H. A., Ridgely, M. S., & Normand, S. T. (2006). Behavioral health insurance parity for federal employees. *The New England Journal of Medicine, 354,* 1378–1386.

Gray, G. V., Brody, D. S., & Johnson, D. (2005). The evolution of behavioral primary care. *Professional Psychology: Research and Practice, 36* (2), 123–129.

Grazier, K. L., & Eselius, L. L. (1999). Mental health carve-outs: Effects and implications. *Medical Care Research and Review, 56* (2), 37–59.

Hodgkin, D., Morgan, C. M., Garnick, D. W., & Merrick, E. L. (2002). Quality standards and incentives in managed care organizations' specialty contracts for behavioral health. *The Journal of Mental Health Policy and Economics, 5,* 61–69.

Jonas, B. S., & Lando, J. F. (2000). Negative affect as a prospective risk factor for hypertension. *Psychosomatic Medicine, 62,* 188–196.

Jonas, B. S., & Mussolino, M. E. (2000). Symptoms of depression as a prospective risk factor for stroke. *Psychosomatic Medicine, 62,* 463–471.

Kaiser Commission on Medicaid and the Uninsured. (2006a). *Health insurance coverage in America, 2005 data update.* Washington, DC: The Henry J. Kaiser Family Foundation.

Kaiser Commission on Medicaid and the Uninsured. (2006b). *The uninsured: A primer.* Washington, DC: The Henry J. Kaiser Family Foundation.

Kaiser Family Foundation. (2001). *Medicaid and managed care.* Retrieved January 10, 2007, from http://www.kff.org/medicaid/loader.cfm?url=/commonspot/security/getfile.cfm&PageID=13724

Kaiser Family Foundation. (2005). *Medicare advantage fact sheet.* Retrieved January 10, 2007, from http://www.kff.org/medicare/upload/Medicare-Advantage-April-2005-Fact-Sheet.pdf

Kaiser Family Foundation. (2006). *Kaiser/HRET survey of employer-sponsored health benefits, 1999–2005.* Retrieved January 10, 2007, from http://www.kff.org/insurance/7315/sections/ehbs05-5-1.cfm

Katon, W., Robinson, P. vonKorff, M., Lin, E., Bush, T., Simon, G., et al. (1996). A multifaceted intervention to improve treatment of depression in primary care. *Archives of General Psychiatry, 53,* 924–932.

Katon, W., von Korff, M., Lin, E., Walker, E., Simon, G., Bush, T., et al. (1995). Collaborative management to achieve treatment guidelines: Impact on depression in primary care. *Journal of the American Medical Association, 273,* 1026–1031.

Kiesler, C. A. (2000). The next wave of change for psychology and mental health services in the health care revolution. *American Psychologist, 55* (5), 481–487.

Kroenke, K., & Mangelsdorff, A. (1989). Common symptoms on primary care: Incidence, evaluation, therapy and outcome. *American Journal of Medicine, 86,* 262–266.

Lorig, K., Mazonson, P. D., & Holman, H. R. (1993). Evidence suggesting that health education for self-management in patients with chronic arthritis has sustained health benefits while reducing health care costs. *Arthritis and Rheumatism, 36,* 439–446.

Melek, S. P. (2001). Financial risk and structural issues. In N. A. Cummings, W. O'Donohue, S. C. Hays, & V. F. Follette (Eds.), *Integrated behavioral healthcare: Positioning mental health practice with medical/surgical practice* (pp. 257–272). San Diego, CA: Academic Press.

Miller, I. J. (1996). Managed care is harmful to outpatient mental health services: A call for accountability. *Professional Psychology: Research and Practice, 27,* 349–363.

Murray, C. J. L., & Lopez, A. D. (Eds.). (1996). *The global burden of disease. Comprehensive assessment of mortality and disability from diseases, injuries, and risk factors in 1990 and projected to 2020.* Cambridge, MA: Harvard School of Public Health.

Newman, R. (1999). Comment on Chiles et al. *Clinical Psychology Science and Practice, 6,* 225–227.

Olfson, M., Fireman, B., Weissman, M. M., Leon, A. C., Sheehan, D. V., Kathol, R. G., et al. (1997). Mental disorders and disability among patients in a primary care group practice. *American Journal of Psychiatry, 154*(12), 1734–1740.

Pallak, M. S., Cummings, N. A., Dorken, H., & Henke, C. J. (1995). Effect of mental health treatment on medical costs. *Mind/Body Medicine, 1,* 7–12.

Pincus, H. A., Tanelian, T. L., Marcus, S. C., Olfson, M., Zarin, D. A., Thompson, J., & Zito, J. M. (1998). Prescribing trends in psychotropic medications: Primary care, psychiatry, and other medical specialties. *Journal of the American Medical Association, 279,* 526–531.

Pruitt, S. D., Klapow, J. C., Epping-Jordan, J. E., & Dresselhaus, T. R. (1998). Moving behavioral medicine to the front line: A model for the integration of behavioral and medical sciences in primary care. *Professional Psychology: Research and Practice, 29* (3), 230–236.

Reiger, D., Narrow, W., Rae, D., Manderschied, R., Locke, B., & Goodwin, F. (1993). The de facto U.S. mental and addictive disorders service system: Epidemiologic Catchment Area prospective 1 year prevalence rates of disorders and services. *Archives of General Psychiatry, 50,* 85–94.

Robinson, J. S., Schwartz, M. M., Magwene, K. S., Krengel, S. A., & Tamburello, D. (1989). The impact of fever health education on clinic utilization. *American Journal of Diseases of Children, 143,* 698–704.

Roy-Byrne, P. P., Wagner, A. W., & Schraufnagel, T. J. (2005). Understanding and treating panic disorder in the primary care setting. *The Journal of Clinical Psychiatry, 66* (Supplement 4), 16–22.

Sanchez, L. M., & Turner, S. M. (2003). Practicing psychology in the era of managed care. *American Psychologist, 58* (2), 116–129.

Shaffer, I. A. (2001). Managed care: Cost and effectiveness. In N. A. Cummings, W. O'Donohue, S. C. Hays, & V. F. Follette (Eds.), *Integrated behavioral healthcare: Positioning mental health practice with medical/surgical practice* (pp.187–206). San Diego, CA: Academic Press.

Shi, L., & Singh, D. A. (2004). *Delivering healthcare in America: A systems approach* (3rd ed.). Sudbury, MA: Jones & Bartlett.

Simon, G., Von Korff, M., & Barlow, W. (1995). Health care costs of primary care patients with recognized depression. *Archives of General Psychiatry, 52,* 850–856.

Smith, G. R., Rost, K., & Kashner, T. M. (1995). A trial of the effect of a standardized psychiatric consultation on health outcomes and costs in somatizing patients. *Archives of General Psychiatry, 52,* 238–243.

Strosahl, K. (1998). Integrating behavioral health and primary care services: The primary mental health care model. In A. Blount (Ed.), *Integrated primary care: The future of medical and mental health collaboration,* (pp. 1–43). New York: W. W. Norton.

Strosahl, K. (2001). The integration of primary care and behavioral health: Type II change in the era of managed care. In N. A. Cummings, W. O'Donohue, S. C. Hays, & V. F. Follette (Eds.), *Integrated behavioral healthcare: Positioning mental health practice with medical/surgical practice* (pp. 45–69). San Diego, CA: Academic Press.

Strosahl, K. D., & Sobel, D. (1996). Behavioral health and the medical cost offset effect: Current status, key concepts and future applications. *HMO Practice, 10*(4), 156–162.

Thomas, J. L., & Brantley, P. J. (2004). Factor structure of the Center for Epidemiologic Studies Depression Scale in low-income women attending primary care clinics. *European Journal of Psychological Assessment,* 20 (2), 106–115.

United States Census Bureau. (2006). *Current population survey, 2005 and 2006 annual social and economic supplements.* Retrieved January 10, 2007, from http://www.census.gov/hhes/www/hlthins/hlthin05/fig06.pdf

United States Department of Health and Human Services. (1999). *Mental health: A report of the Surgeon General.* Rockville, MD: USDHHS, SAMHSA, NIH, NIMH.

United States Department of Health and Human Services. (2001). *Report on a Surgeon General's working meeting on the integration of mental health services and primary care; 2000, Nov. 30–Dec. 1; Atlanta.* Rockville, MD: Office of the Surgeon General.

United States Department of Health and Human Services. (2004). *Medicare program; prospective payment system for inpatient psychiatric facilities; final rule.* Rockville, MD: CMS.

United States Department of Health and Human Services. (2005). *Medicare program: Changes to the hospital inpatient prospective payment systems and fiscal year 2006 rates; final rule.* Rockville, MD: CMS.

Walker, E. A., Katon, W. J., & Jelka, P. R. (1993). Psychiatric disorders and medical care utilization among people in the general population who report fatigue. *Journal of General International Medicine, 8,* 436–440.

Yingling, K. W., Wulsin, L. R., Arnold, L. M., & Rouan, G. W. (1993). Estimated prevalences of panic disorder and depression among consecutive patients seen in an emergency department with acute chest pain. *Journal of General Internal Medicine, 8,* 2315.

Zelman, W. A. (1996). *The changing healthcare marketplace: Private ventures, public interests.* San Francisco: Jossey-Bass.

PART II

PREVENTION

CHAPTER 3

Chronic Disease Prevention

M. INDIRA PAHARIA

INTRODUCTION

Prior to the twentieth century most people died from acute infections, and life expectancy was too short to develop chronic disease. Today, although we enjoy a longer life expectancy, this also increases the likelihood of developing chronic disease. In general, *chronic diseases* are defined as those that persist indefinitely, cannot be prevented by vaccines, and cannot be cured by medication. Such prolonged illness leads to ongoing pain, suffering, disability, and diminished quality of life. In 2000, about 125 million Americans, or 45% of the population, had a chronic disease, and 61 million (21% of the population) had multiple chronic diseases (Anderson & Horvath, 2004). Over 70% of deaths in the United States are attributed to chronic diseases (U.S. Department of Health and Human Services [USDHHS], 2003). These trends are seen outside the United States as well. Globally, 60% of all deaths in 2005 were due to chronic diseases (heart disease, stroke, cancer, chronic respiratory diseases, and diabetes), with 80% of these deaths occurring in low- and middle-income countries (World Health Organization [WHO], 2006). The chronic diseases that are the leading causes of death in the United States, in order from higher to lower mortality rates, are heart disease, cancer, stroke, chronic respiratory diseases, and diabetes (National Center for Health Statistics [NCHS], 2006a). There are many contributing factors to the rise in chronic diseases, including tobacco use, pervasive obesity, sedentary lifestyle, poor diet, larger food portion sizes, longer life expectancy, fast-paced lifestyle, increased pollution, and the proliferation of fast food and tobacco industries. Although it is likely the result of a complex interaction of genetic, behavioral, and environmental influences, the rate at which chronic diseases have risen may suggest that behavioral and environmental influences have played a larger role than biological changes. In response to these growing trends, the field of chronic disease prevention, spearheaded by public health, has continued to evolve and now includes many other disciplines, such as medicine, psychology, and business, all with the same focus on preventing the onset and progression of chronic disease. Never has there been a more relevant time for the field of chronic disease prevention, as new prevention technologies are being created, more prevention efforts are being funded, and new environmental policies are being instituted.

PREVENTION LEVELS

Disease prevention involves three levels: primary, secondary, and tertiary. *Primary* prevention directly addresses the mediating causes of diseases and is carried out before the onset of disease, thereby preventing its occurrence. Examples of primary prevention include lifestyle changes (i.e., weight loss, tobacco cessation) and patient education programs. *Secondary* prevention involves early detection and treatment of a disease before a full-blown illness develops. Examples of secondary prevention include screenings (i.e., mammography, pap test) and treatment regimen adherence (i.e., glycemic control for those with diabetes). See Chapter 1 under "Regimen Factors" for more information regarding treatment regimen adherence. *Tertiary* prevention attempts to prevent recurrence or progression of a disease that has already occurred. Examples of tertiary prevention include chemotherapy to prevent the spread of cancer, early screening for diabetes complications (i.e., eye, foot, and kidney abnormalities), and smoking cessation for patients with chronic obstructive pulmonary disease (COPD). There are obvious benefits in reaching people at a primary or secondary level of prevention, as the majority of chronic diseases could be prevented or delayed by changing lifestyle behavior and obtaining screening services (Clarke & Meiris, 2006). Most patients, however, are not seen until the disease has progressed, when treatment is most expensive and outcomes are limited (Clarke & Meiris). This chapter primarily focuses on primary and secondary levels of prevention, as tertiary interventions for common disease states are described in detail throughout this text.

Table 3.1 presents empirically supported interventions at each level of prevention for those chronic diseases that are not only leading causes of death but are also potentially preventable: cardiovascular disease (CVD; includes heart disease and stroke), cancer, COPD, and type 2 diabetes mellitus (T2DM). Major areas of primary, secondary, and tertiary prevention can be seen for each disease condition.

While chronic diseases have both genetic and modifiable risk factors, Table 3.1 and this chapter focus on modifiable risk factors. Modifiable risk factors become even more important when genetic risk factors are already present (i.e., family history). Each modifiable risk factor individually increases the risk of disease. Multiple risk factors for the same condition, when in combination, increase risk dramatically. It is very common for people to have these multiple risk factors simultaneously.

FOUR PILLARS OF PRIMARY PREVENTION

As seen in Table 3.1, there are four primary prevention interventions that significantly impact the diseases presented. These are tobacco cessation, weight loss, healthy diet, and regular exercise, which are referred to here as the Four Pillars of Primary Prevention (4Ps), because they form the basis of primary prevention, are also useful in secondary and tertiary prevention, and support an overall healthy lifestyle (see Figure 3.1). Given the significance of the 4Ps, they are fully covered in chapters 4 and 5.

Figure 3.1 displays both the direct and indirect effects of the 4Ps on chronic disease prevention. For example, the 4Ps can directly prevent the onset of T2DM, thereby indirectly preventing a later, diabetes-related onset of CVD. Weight loss, healthy diet, and regular exercise are presented as separate pillars because none alone necessitates the others. For instance, regular exercise does not necessarily lead to dietary changes or weight loss, dietary changes do not necessarily lead to regular exercise or weight

Table 3.1
Levels of Prevention for Leading Causes of Death

	Primary Prevention	Secondary Prevention	Tertiary Prevention
CVD	1. tobacco cessation 2. healthy diet 3. regular exercise 4. weight loss 5. hypertension control 6. hyperlipidemia control 7. diabetes management	1. treatment regimen adherence (Rx, rehab, etc.) & primary prevention	1. treatment regimen adherence (Rx, rehab, etc.) & primary prevention
Cancer	1. tobacco cessation 2. healthy diet 3. regular exercise 4. weight loss 5. reduced exposure to UV light	1. Screenings (e.g., mammogram, pap-test, endoscopy)	1. chemotherapy 2. radiation 3. surgery 4. hormonal therapy
COPD	1. tobacco cessation	1. tobacco cessation 2. treatment regimen adherence (Rx, rehab, etc.)	1. tobacco cessation 2. treatment regimen adherence (Rx, rehab, etc.)
T2DM	1. tobacco cessation 2. healthy diet 3. regular exercise 4. weight loss	1. hypertension control 2. hyperlipidemia control 3. glycemic control & primary prevention	Prevent complications through glycemic control: heart disease, stroke, blindness, kidney failure, amputation

loss, and weight loss does not necessarily lead to (or result from) dietary changes or regular exercise. In fact, weight loss from bariatric surgery or prescription medications can still prevent or even reverse disease (see Chapter 4). Each of the four pillars has its own impact on the prevention of disease, and in concert may have added benefits. Even so, a recent survey of over 150,000 U.S. citizens concluded that less than 3% adhere to not smoking, maintaining a healthy weight, eating a healthy diet, and exercising regularly, and almost 10% do not adhere to any of them (Clarke & Meiris, 2006). Three of the 4Ps (weight loss, regular exercise, and healthy diet) can further prevent hyperlipidemia (high blood cholesterol) and hypertension (high blood pressure) from developing, both of which are risk factors for CVD and T2DM. Although tobacco use does not directly contribute to the development of hyperlipidemia and hypertension, it can exacerbate their impact (Hankinson, Colditz, Manson, & Speizer, 2001). It is important to note that adoption of the 4Ps does not completely preclude the onset of chronic disease. Even those who live a healthy lifestyle can still develop chronic disease, because genetic factors also play a significant role. Therefore it is more accurate to consider the 4Ps as a strategy to reduce the *probability* of developing chronic disease.

Tobacco Use

More than 430,000 Americans die each year as a result of cigarette smoking (Centers for Disease Control and Prevention [CDC], 1997). Nearly 21% of adult Americans and

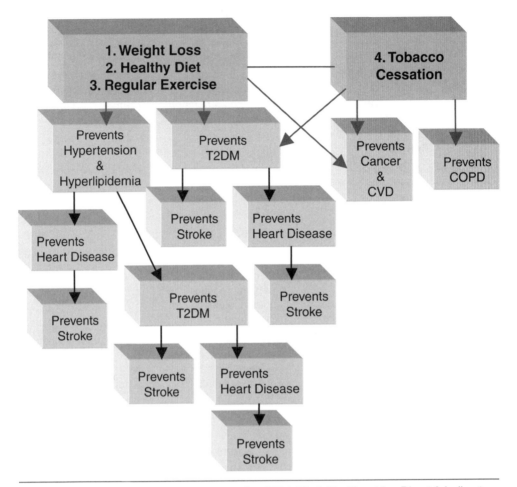

Figure 3.1 The 4 Pillars of Primary Prevention (4Ps): Their Far-Reaching Direct & Indirect Effects in Chronic Disease Prevention
Note: Gray arrows represent the 4Ps direct effect whereas black arrows represent their indirect effect.

nearly one-quarter of high school students smoke today (NCHS, 2006b). Cigarette smoking causes several types of cancer (lung, oral, bladder, larynx, esophagus, and pharynx), heart disease, and COPD, and significantly contributes to stroke and other cancers (cervical, pancreatic, and kidney) (USDHHS, 2000e, 2004). Smoking is responsible for 80 to 90% of COPD deaths and approximately 90% of lung cancer deaths (CDC, 2004). The benefits of smoking cessation are almost immediate. After only 20 minutes of cessation blood pressure and heart rate drop to normal, after 3 months lung function improves by up to 30%, after 9 months respiratory symptoms decrease, after 1 year risk of coronary heart disease decreases by 50%, after 10 years precancerous cells are replaced by normal cells, thereby decreasing cancer risk, and after 15 years death rates are nearly the same for ex-smokers as they are for those who never smoked (USDHHS, 1990). See Chapter 5 for a full review of tobacco cessation.

WEIGHT

Approximately 300,000 deaths per year are attributable to obesity, making it a leading cause of death in the country (National Institutes of Health [NIH] & National Heart, Lung and Blood Institute [NHLBI], 1998). Of Americans age 20 and over, 66% are classified as either overweight or obese. In addition, 18% of American children (ages 6–11 years) and 17% of adolescents (ages 12–19 years) are overweight (NCHS, 2006b). Obesity increases the risk of type 2 diabetes, heart disease, stroke, hypertension, osteoarthritis, colon and breast cancer, sleep apnea, and depression (USDHHS, 2001). Approximately 20 to 30% of coronary heart disease mortality can be attributed to excess body weight (Seidell, Verschuren, van Leer, & Kromhout, 1996). Further, obese women are nearly six times more likely to develop hypertension (Witteman et al., 1989), and obese persons have almost 10 times the risk of diabetes as compared to nonobese peers (Colditz, Willet, Rotnitzky, & Manson, 1995). Research supports that losing as little as 5 to 10% of body weight can significantly reduce obesity-related conditions (NIH & NHLBI, 1998; USDHHS, 2001). For instance, sustained weight loss of 7 to 10 lbs through diet and exercise over a 4-year period was found to reduce the incidence of type 2 diabetes in high-risk subjects in randomized controlled trials by 40 to 60% (Knowler et al., 2002). See Chapter 4 for a comprehensive review of obesity.

EXERCISE

It is recommended that patients gradually build up to 30 to 45 minutes of moderate exercise three to five times per week (NIH & NHLBI, 1998). Exercise need not be strenuous and may include walking, weight lifting (anaerobic), and other aerobic activities (swimming, running, bicycling, etc.). The benefits of regular exercise are far reaching and include weight loss (by expending calories), improved mood (by releasing endorphins), lowered blood pressure (by dilating blood vessels), improved cholesterol levels (by removing low-density lipoprotein [LDL] from artery walls), lowered risk of CVD, lowered risk of type 2 diabetes (by improving physical response to insulin), lowered risk of osteoporosis (by promoting bone development), and decreased risk of certain cancers (colon, breast; Hankinson et al., 2001). Despite these numerous benefits, approximately 40% of adults do not participate in any regular exercise (USDHHS, 2001). Those who are physically inactive are twice as likely to develop CHD as those who exercise regularly (USDHHS, 2000c). Regular exercise is associated with fewer outpatient and inpatient services and needing less medication (CDC, 2006). See Chapter 4 under *Exercise* for more related information.

DIET

Poor dietary choices have been implicated in hyperlipidemia, hypertension, CVD, certain cancers, and type 2 diabetes (NCHS, 1997). Only 36% of Americans get less than 10% of their calories from saturated fat, meaning that 64% have too much saturated fat in their diet (USDHHS, 2000b). Saturated fats are implicated in heart disease because they increase LDL ("bad cholesterol") levels. Saturated fats come from natural sources, such as red meat, whereas trans fats (i.e., partially hydrogenated vegetable oil) are vegetable fats that have hydrogen added to them to improve taste and lengthen storage capacity. Trans fats are heavily implicated in heart disease and are widely used in commercial baking and frying. In fact, New York City recently issued a ban on the use of all trans fats in its restaurants, including fast food chains that will be enforced in 2008 (Adamy, 2006).

The AMA recommends following the food guide pyramid (at least 2 servings of low-fat dairy, 2 servings meat, 3 servings vegetables, 2 servings fruit, and 6 servings grains per day) with these additional guidelines: Three meals plus two snacks per day consisting of 45 to 65% from carbohydrate, 20 to 35% from fat, 10 to 35% from protein, one-third of vegetable servings from dark green or orange vegetables, and 25–30 grams of fiber (Kushner, 2003). In general, Americans do not follow these guidelines, and eat too many grains, sugars, red meat, and fat, and not enough fruits, vegetables, fiber, and low fat dairy. Fruits and vegetables have been found to have a protective effect against CVD and certain cancers (Hankinson et al., 2001). Of Americans age 2 and older, only 28% consumed at least two daily servings of fruit, and only 3% met daily intake requirements for vegetables (USDHHS, 2000b). Healthy foods are usually less calorie dense and may therefore lead to weight loss, further reducing health risk. See Chapter 4 under the subheadings *Diets* and *Nutritional Guidelines* for more related information.

LEADING CAUSES OF DEATH

The chronic diseases that are the leading causes of death in the United States, in order from higher to lower mortality rates, are heart disease, cancer, stroke, chronic respiratory diseases, and diabetes (National Center for Health Statistics [NCHS], 2006a). These, in addition to hyperlipidemia and hypertension are discussed in this section.

CARDIOVASCULAR DISEASE

Cardiovascular disease (CVD) encompasses both heart disease, the leading cause of death, and stroke, the third leading cause of death. Heart disease accounts for approximately 30% of all deaths in the United States (CDC, 2005b). Coronary heart disease (CHD) accounts for the majority of heart disease, and it is estimated that one out of every two males and one out of every three females in the United States over the age of 40 will develop CHD in their lifetime (USDHHS, 2000a). A stroke, or cerebrovascular accident, is caused by disrupted blood flow to the brain, usually from a blocked or ruptured vessel. For a comprehensive discussion of cardiovascular disease, see Chapter 6 of this text.

Major modifiable risk factors for CVD include the 4Ps, hyperlipidemia, hypertension, and diabetes. For instance, smoking has been linked to CHD because tobacco smoke can cause buildup of cholesterol on artery walls and can promote the formation of blood clots (Hankinson et al., 2001), and smokers have twice the risk of having a myocardial infarction (heart attack) and three times the risk of having a stroke as compared to nonsmokers (USDHHS, 1997). Furthermore, as weight increases, so does CVD risk, which is likely attributed to the fact that weight gain increases other associated CVD risk factors. Regarding hyperlipidemia, a meta-analysis of over 20 studies found that high total cholesterol, high LDL cholesterol, or low high-density lipoprotein (HDL; "good") cholesterol doubled the risk of heart disease among middle-aged women (Hankinson et al., 2001). Hypertension increases the risk of CHD and stroke by putting increased pressure on the artery walls, and those with hypertension have about three times the risk of CHD as compared to their nonhypertensive counterparts.

Diabetes increases the risk of CVD because it contributes to the development of atherosclerosis (hardening of the arteries) and increases blood pressure and cholesterol levels. Compared to nondiabetics, diabetic men and women have up to four and seven times the risk of CHD, respectively, and also have an elevated risk for stroke. Risk of stroke is also increased by heart disease. For instance, a myocardial infarction can cause a clot formation from irregular heartbeat that can then travel to the brain, and a transient ischemic attack (TIA) increases the risk of stroke by five times (Hankinson et al., 2001). Therefore, preventing heart disease also prevents stroke.

The good news is that an estimated 80% of heart attacks can be prevented or delayed through lifestyle changes (Hankinson et al., 2001). After 1 year of quitting smoking, the risk of CHD decreases by 50% (USDHHS, 1990), and physical activity has also been found to reduce the risk of CHD by up to 50% by lowering associated risk factors, such as being overweight (Hankinson et al.). Additionally, the risk of CHD drops by 2 to 3% for every 1% decrease in total blood cholesterol level (Hankinson et al.).

CANCER

Cancer is the second leading cause of death in the United States, and more than 50% of cancers can be prevented through tobacco cessation and healthier diet (USDHHS, 1990; Willet, 1996). In addition, exercise and weight control also contribute to cancer prevention, especially for breast cancer (Greenwald, Kramer, & Weed, 1995; USDHHS, 2000c). For instance, postmenopausal women who are overweight are at increased risk of developing breast cancer (Henderson, Pike, Bernstein, & Ross, 1996). Cigarette smoking causes several types of cancer (lung, oral, bladder, larynx, esophagus, and pharynx), and significantly contributes to other cancers (cervical, pancreatic, and kidney) (USDHHS, 2000e, 2004). Furthermore, the most common cause of cancer death is lung cancer, and smoking is responsible for approximately 90% of lung cancer deaths (CDC, 2004). Moreover, tobacco use, including smokeless tobacco, is responsible for 75% of deaths from oral and pharyngeal cancer (CDC, 2000). Therefore, the 4Ps play a crucial role in primary cancer prevention, with an emphasis on tobacco cessation. For a comprehensive review of cancer, see Chapter 7.

The importance of secondary prevention through cancer screening cannot be overstated, given that greater use of screenings could prevent at least half of the deaths from cancer (American Cancer Society [ACS], 2006). Screenings such as mammograms and papanicolaou (pap) tests can detect breast and cervical cancer early enough to aggressively and effectively limit, cure, or prevent the disease. Recent declines in deaths from breast and cervical cancer can be attributed to increased use of screening and improved treatment technologies. Mammography, for example, will detect 80 to 90% of breast cancers, the most common cancer among women, and can reduce related deaths by up to 39% in women over 50 and up to 17% in women ages 40–49 (ACS, 2007). However, in 2004, only 58% of women over 40 had a mammogram in the past year (ACS, 2006). Cervical cancer is most commonly caused by the human papillomavirus (HPV; NIH, 1996). Annual pap tests and vaccination with the new HPV vaccine (i.e., Gardasil) could prevent almost all cervical cancer deaths and significantly limit its development. Gardasil is approved for girls and women ages 9 to 26, protects against HPV Types 6, 11, 16, and 18 (known causes of cervical cancer), and is best administered before exposure to HPV (Merck, 2007). In 2004, approximately 85% of women over 18 had a pap test in the past 3 years. Colorectal cancer, the third most common cancer among men and women, can be screened for using a fecal occult blood test or an endoscopy. Similar to cervical cancer, colorectal cancer can actually be prevented through screening because of detection and removal of precancerous cells. Even so, in 2004, only 52% of adults over 50 were screened for colorectal cancer (ACS, 2006). Unfortunately, for many types of cancers, early detection screenings either do not exist, are not covered by insurance, or have not been empirically substantiated as best practice. For more information on cancer screening guidelines, visit the American Cancer Society's web site at www.cancer.org.

CHRONIC OBSTRUCTIVE PULMONARY DISEASE

One of the most common forms of chronic respiratory diseases is COPD, a leading cause of death in the United States. An estimated 10 million Americans are diagnosed with COPD, but as many as 24 million may be affected (CDC, 2003). COPD death rates for women are increasing at a higher rate than for men, which is likely attributed to increases in women smoking prior to 1960 (CDC, 2003). Smoking tobacco (cigarette, cigar, and pipe) and secondhand smoke are the leading causes of COPD. Given that smoking is responsible for 80 to 90% of COPD deaths (CDC, 2004), tobacco cessation is the most effective intervention for preventing COPD from developing or progressing. Moreover, the effectiveness of interventions such as pulmonary rehabilitation and other treatment regimens for COPD are dependent on abstinence from tobacco use. For a full review of COPD, see Chapter 12.

TYPE II DIABETES MELLITUS

Diabetes is the sixth leading cause of death in the United States and the leading cause of nontraumatic amputations, blindness in persons ages 20–64, and end-stage renal disease (i.e., kidney failure; CDC, 2005c). Together, type 1 (insulin-dependent) and type 2 (non-insulin-dependent) diabetes affect approximately 7% of the population, with type 2 diabetes accounting for 90 to 95% of all diabetes diagnosed. For a comprehensive discussion on diabetes, see Chapter 8. While T2DM was previously called *adult-onset diabetes*, it is now being diagnosed in children and adolescents more frequently, which has been attributed to the rise in pediatric obesity. Diabetes causes high blood glucose levels from insufficient insulin production or action, which can lead to additional serious health problems. For instance, over 70% of diabetics have blood pressure in the prehypertensive range, and adults with diabetes have up to four times the rate of death from heart disease and up to four times the risk of stroke as compared to those without diabetes (CDC, 2005c). Modifiable risk factors for T2DM include the 4Ps and control of blood pressure and cholesterol levels. Of these, weight is considered the greatest modifiable risk factor for diabetes onset, given that approximately 80% of those diagnosed with T2DM are obese (Hankinson et al., 2001; Herald, 2004). Further, smokers are at increased risk of developing diabetes because smoking lowers insulin levels while increasing blood glucose levels (Hankinson et al., 2001). Diabetics who smoke are also at increased risk of CHD and diabetic neuropathy, a condition involving numbness and pain in the feet and legs.

Primary prevention of T2DM must include lifestyle changes that address the 4Ps, and is especially crucial for those with pre-diabetes, or impaired glucose tolerance that has not reached diabetic levels. Pre-diabetes is typically diagnosed with two different blood tests, the fasting plasma glucose (FPG) test and the oral glucose tolerance test (OGTT). Intervention at this stage can prevent the onset of diabetes. In the Land-

Table 3.2
Guide to Lipid Levels

Category	LDL Cholesterol	HDL Cholesterol	Total Cholesterol
Optimal	< 100	≥ 60	< 200
Near Optimal	100–129		
Borderline High	130–159		200–239
High	160–189		≥ 240
Very High	≥ 190		
Low		< 40	

Adapted from the American Heart Association (2007).

mark Nurses' Health Study, those women who lost up to 18 pounds decreased their risk of diabetes by 50%, and those who lost more than 18 pounds reduced their risk even further (Hankinson et al., 2001). In this same study, women who exercised moderately for 3 hours per week and who exercised vigorously for 1.5 hours per week lowered their risk of diabetes by 40%. Exercise, diet, and weight loss are not only essential in preventing diabetes, but are also important in managing blood glucose for those who already have the disease, because glucose control can prevent progression and later complications (Herald, 2004). Effective glucose control requires daily monitoring of blood glucose levels, and only 60% of adult diabetics do so (CDC, 2005c). Control of blood pressure and cholesterol levels are also important secondary prevention strategies. By controlling blood pressure or cholesterol, diabetics can reduce their risk of CVD by up to 50% (CDC, 2005c). Finally, yearly eye and foot exams are also needed.

Hyperlipidemia

High blood cholesterol can increase risk of hypertension, CHD, and stroke because it causes atherosclerosis. Optimal LDL cholesterol is below 100 mg/dL, optimal HDL cholesterol is above 60 mg/dL, and total cholesterol should be below 200 mg/dL (see Table 3.2). HDL cholesterol helps protect against heart disease by removing LDL cholesterol from the blood. Three of the 4Ps (weight loss, regular exercise, and dietary changes) are modifiable risk factors for hyperlipidemia.

Hypertension

Hypertension, or high blood pressure, can cause atherosclerosis, forcing the heart to work harder to pump blood through the arteries, thereby increasing the risk of CVD. In fact, hypertension is the leading cause of congestive heart failure, hemorrhagic stroke, ischemic coronary disease, and cerebrovascular disease (NIH, 1997). Hypertension is known as the "silent killer" because there are usually no symptoms and nearly one-third of those who have hypertension do not know it. In the United States, 30% of adults over 20 years old have hypertension, with a slightly higher rate for women (31%) than men (28%; NCHS, 2006b). Of those who are aware that they have hypertension, only 50% are receiving treatment and only 32% are actively controlling it (CDC, 2005d), meaning that half of all people who have hypertension are not being treated.

Blood pressure is the force in the arteries when the heart beats (systolic) and when the heart is at rest (diastolic). As can be seen from Table 3.3, optimal blood pressure is less than 120/80 and hypertension begins at 140/90, with three stages. Hypertension

Table 3.3
Adult Blood Pressure Classification

Category	Systolic BP (mmHg)	Diastolic BP (mmHg)
Optimal	less than 120	less than 80
Normal	less than 130	less than 85
Pre-hypertension	130–139	85–89
Hypertension		
Stage 1	140–159	90–99
Stage 2	160–179	100–109
Stage 3	180 and above	110 and above

Adapted from National Institutes of Health (1997).

is further classified as primary or secondary, where primary hypertension is caused by a combination of genetic and environmental factors and secondary hypertension is the result of another medical condition or medications. There are numerous antihypertensive medications available to lower blood pressure (i.e., beta-blockers, calcium channel blockers), but adherence to prescription regimens is often a barrier to reducing blood pressure. However, even a slight decrease in blood pressure can reduce the risk of CVD (Hankinson et al., 2001).

While the exact cause of hypertension is unknown, modifiable risk factors include three of the 4Ps: weight loss, exercise, and diet with limited salt intake. Although tobacco use does not directly contribute to the development of hypertension, it can exacerbate its effects (Hankinson et al., 2001). A meta-analysis on the effects of exercise on blood pressure showed that exercise consistently lowers blood pressure (Kelley & Kelley, 2000). Further, a positive correlation exists between body mass index and blood pressure (i.e., as weight increases so does blood pressure; Trials of Hypertension Prevention Collaborative Research Group [TOHP], 1997). The TOHP demonstrated that weight loss led to the greatest reduction in blood pressure, followed by dietary sodium reduction.

In this study, stress management had little to no effect on reducing blood pressure, and the role of stress in hypertension remains unclear, given numerous contradictory studies (e.g., Beilin, Puddey, & Burke, 1999; Patel et al., 1985). Nevertheless, stress management programs that address both cognitive and physiological responses to stress through a variety of techniques such as progressive muscle relaxation, diaphragmatic breathing, problem solving, and cognitive restructuring, are important adjuncts to any lifestyle changes (i.e., smoking cessation, weight loss) because many people adopt unhealthy behaviors as coping mechanisms. Furthermore, negative interpretations of stressful events and personality characteristics, such as hostility, can increase the level of stress experienced. Stress activates the sympathetic nervous system, thereby causing physiological arousal, such as increased heart rate, peripheral vasoconstriction, and blood pressure. Prolonged and chronic stress may therefore negatively impact the heart and blood vessels.

DISPARITIES

Minority groups and those with lower socioeconomic circumstances are at greater disadvantage for chronic disease risk factors and are overrepresented in chronic disease populations. These disparities are in part attributed to lack of insurance, poverty, language barriers, and racial discrimination. Minority populations have higher rates of poverty and of being uninsured (ACS, 2007). In general, those without health insurance cannot access preventive services, especially screenings. Poverty is also correlated with tobacco use and obesity, major risk factors for chronic diseases. Even in comparable circumstances regarding insurance coverage, income, and health status, minorities still receive lower-quality health care than Caucasians, which is likely due to racial discrimination and language barriers (ACS, 2007). Distrust of the health care system also affects minority use of preventive services. The numerous accounts of historical and present-day maltreatment of African Americans and other minorities in the health care system are well documented (Bhopal, 1998; Randall, 2006), the most disquieting of which was the Tuskegee syphilis study.

SMOKING

Among minority groups, smoking rates are highest for American Indian and Alaska Native men (34%) and women (29%). Smoking is also three times more likely among adults with less than a high school education as compared to those with education at the bachelor's level or higher (NCHS, 2006b).

WEIGHT

Percentages for overweight and obesity are highest among African American women (80% overweight; 52% obese) and Mexican Americans (over 70% of men and women are overweight; 40% are obese). Among Americans below the poverty level, over 60% are considered overweight, with over 30% as obese. Percentages for overweight children and adolescents are also higher among African Americans and Mexican Americans. Approximately 26% of Mexican American boys and 25% of African American girls are overweight; 20% of Mexican American male adolescents and 24% of African American female adolescents are overweight. (NCHS, 2006b).

CARDIOVASCULAR DISEASE

The prevalence of CVD is 20% higher among African American males and 38% higher among African American females than their Caucasian counterparts (AHA, 2006). Risk of death from CVD is also higher for African Americans, in part because they are at higher risk for stroke and have higher prevalence of hypertension (USDHHS, 2003). African Americans are also at higher risk for many other modifiable CVD risk factors.

CANCER

Overall, the cancer mortality rate is about one-third higher among African Americans than among Caucasians, and African Americans have higher incidence rates of many types of cancers than other ethnic or racial groups (USDHHS, 2003). For example, the annual incidence of cervical cancer is higher among African American women than among Caucasian women. Additionally, the incidence of cervical cancer among Vietnamese women in the United States is five times greater than among Caucasian women (CDC, 2006). African American mortality rates are higher than any other group for breast, colon, lung, and prostate cancers. For instance, African American men have a 40% higher death rate from lung cancer than Caucasian men. Furthermore, although overall breast cancer mortality rates have declined, African American women continue to be more likely to die from breast cancer than Caucasian women because of low utilization of mammography (USDHHS, 2003).

TYPE II DIABETES MELLITUS

American Indians and Alaska Natives have the highest prevalence of diabetes of any ethnic or racial group (18%), followed by African Americans (15%), Hispanic Americans (14%), and Caucasians (8%; CDC, 2005c). African Americans also have twice the death rate from diabetes as compared to Caucasians (CDC, 2005c). Much of this can be attributed to aforementioned disparities in diabetes-related risk factors.

HYPERTENSION

African American women (45%) and men (42%) over the age of 20 have the highest rates of hypertension (NCHS, 2006b). Some research supports a relationship between the stress of constant racial discrimination and elevated blood pressure (Jonas & Lando, 2000; Krieger & Sidney, 1996; Krieger, Sidney, & Coakley, 1998). Of African Americans who are aware that they have hypertension, only 30% actively control it. Although Mexican Americans have slightly lower hypertension rates (25%) than Caucasians (28%), their rates of control over hypertension are much lower (17% Mexican Americans; 30% Caucasians; CDC, 2005d).

ECONOMIC RELEVANCE

Increased focus on chronic disease prevention stems, in large part, from the associated financial burden. A major reason for continuously increasing U.S. health care expenditures is that chronic diseases account for more than 60% of those expenditures (Clarke & Meiris, 2006), with some estimates as high as 76% (Pruitt, Klapow, Epping-Jordan, & Dresselhaus, 1998). In 2005, national health expenditures were $2 trillion, or 16% of the gross domestic product (GDP; Centers for Medicare and Medicaid Services, 2006), meaning that chronic disease accounted for more than $1.2 trillion (~10% of GDP) and as much as $1.5 trillion (~12% of GDP). As a reference for comparison, total health care expenditures in 1980 were $255 billion and only 9% of the GDP (Stanton, 2006).

The leading causes of death are also the most expensive chronic diseases. By disease condition (with the most recent available annual cost data), CVD cost the United States $300 billion (2001 total costs; CDC, 2006), cancer cost $210 billion (2005 total costs; Mackay, Jemal, Lee, & Parkin, 2006), diabetes cost $132 billion (2002 total costs; CDC, 2005c), and COPD cost $32 billion (2000 total costs; Clarke & Meiris, 2006). Total costs are composed of both direct costs, which are health care expenditures, and indirect costs, which are those related to lost productivity from disability, unemployment, and premature death. When these chronic disease figures are separated into direct and indirect costs, direct costs accounted for 60% of CVD, 35% of cancer, 70% of diabetes, and 50% of COPD expenditures. Therefore, CVD and diabetes are the most costly diseases for the health care system, while cancer leads to the greatest costs in lost productivity. Health care expenditures have also been reported in terms of lifestyle behaviors. Annual direct medical costs from physical inactivity were $77 billion (2000; CDC, 2006), from obesity-related diseases were $75 billion (2003; Finkelstein, Fiebelkorn, & Wang, 2004), and from tobacco-related diseases were $76 billion (2001; CDC, 2005a).

These statistics are staggering, but the potential for cost saving to the health care system and society as a whole through primary and secondary chronic disease prevention is tremendous. These cost savings are most often measured through cost-effectiveness analysis (CEA) studies. Cost-effectiveness analysis is a measure of economic outcome that is suitable for application in health care programs and interventions because it is not purely a financial calculation. Contrary to a measure such as cost-benefit analysis (CBA), where all aspects of the calculation are converted to dollar units, CEA evaluates the relationship between the financial investment of a program and its clinical outcomes. Those clinical outcomes are not measured in financial units, as in CBA, but rather in quality adjusted life years (QALYs). Cost-benefit analysis outcomes are therefore reported as dollars per QALYs gained, and both direct and indirect costs are factored into the calculation. Cost-effectiveness analysis is the preferred method of economic evaluation in health care because it evaluates both the financial benefit of the intervention, but most importantly, the clinical effectiveness as well. Moreover, the evaluation is conducted from a societal perspective, meaning that all costs borne are considered (i.e., costs to patient, health organization, clinicians), as opposed to one entity's cost perspective, such as the managed care company. Quality of life years are generated from subjective patient assessments regarding their experience of their own health status. Quality of life years are a significant measure for patients suffering from chronic disease because quality of life and disability are major concerns for these patients.

In prevention studies, CEA has most often been applied to tobacco cessation, and has demonstrated excellent outcomes for these interventions. For this reason, tobacco cessation is considered to be the gold standard of cost-effective interventions (CDC, 2006). For instance, smoking cessation programs ranging from $1,100 to $4,500 in cost have saved one QALY (CDC, 2006). Even when the results are presented in purely financial CBA terms, the outcomes are still impressive, where tobacco cessation programs have demonstrated a benefit-to-cost ratio of 3:1 (i.e., for every dollar invested in the program, three dollars is saved; USDHHS, 2000d). These cost savings come from reduced utilization of medical services, meaning that the interventions not only pay for themselves but also produce a future cost offset. Many other areas of chronic disease prevention are also now being analyzed using CEA, such as obesity treatment and diabetes management, which are showing promising results. Some have argued that these savings will eventually be cancelled out because as those who may have prematurely died instead live longer, their lifetime medical costs will likely increase. The evidence for this has not borne out (Fries, Koop, & Beadle, 1993), largely because today premature death is not usually a result of acute illness, but rather chronic illness with high accumulated health care expenditures. Moreover, this type of argument is fundamentally flawed, as it neglects the mission of health care, which is to decrease human suffering and improve quality of life. Furthermore, those who have improved quality of life with increased life expectancy will likely contribute to society in more productive ways, thereby decreasing indirect costs such as from disability and unemployment.

Even though prevention interventions have demonstrated solid economic outcomes, barriers to reimbursement from insurance companies still exist. In fact, lack of insurance coverage has been found to be the single greatest barrier to the delivery of preventive services (Amonkar, Madhavan, Rosenbluth, & Simon, 1999; Davis, Bialek, Parkinson, Smith, & Vellozzi, 1990). Overall, medical laboratory tests and screening procedures are more often reimbursed than counseling interventions (Parkinson & Lurie, 1996). In the early 1990s, only 40% of health maintenance organizations (HMOs) covered smoking cessation (Group Health Association of America, 1992), largely because managed care organizations did not have evidence to support that preventive interventions would provide short-term cost savings. An additional barrier was the lack of consensus from the scientific community regarding best practices for certain prevention interventions. Today, this is somewhat improved by greater use of CEA, more clinical outcomes research on preventive interventions, and the inclusion of prevention services on quality measures such as the Health Plan Employer Data and Information Set (HEDIS). For instance, Medicare and Medicaid now cover limited counseling sessions and pharmacy for tobacco cessation, but only a small percentage of private insurers have followed suit (Bjornson & White, 2006). However, in general, most public and private insurers offer minimal coverage of preventive services (Clarke & Meiris, 2006). Other preventive interventions, such as behavioral therapy for weight loss, are unlikely to be covered if payers do not see financial benefits from coverage of tobacco cessation. Ironically, the initial concept of the HMO was founded on the maintenance of health through prevention. Over 30 years later, this goal of the model has yet to be realized, as we find ourselves in a chronic-disease-ridden country ineptly managed by an acute care health system.

Another major barrier to access is lack of insurance for so many Americans who could benefit from preventive services. As previously discussed in the *Disparities* section, minorities and the poor, who have higher rates of chronic diseases and associated risk factors, also have higher rates of being uninsured. In fact, 19% of Asian Americans, 21% of African Americans and 33% of Hispanics/Latinos are uninsured, compared to 13% of Caucasians (Kaiser Commission on Medicaid and the Uninsured, 2006). Furthermore, over a third of the poor (below 200% of the poverty level) and nearly a third of the near-poor (100 to 199% of the poverty level) are uninsured (Kaiser Commission on Medicaid and the Uninsured). Lack of insurance increases the risk for developing chronic disease, and up to a 15% reduction in mortality could be achieved if the uninsured gained health coverage (Kaiser Commission on Medicaid and the Uninsured). Lack of insurance therefore contributes to overrepresentation of chronic diseases in minority populations and the poor. For instance, the uninsured are less likely to receive preventive care and more likely to be hospitalized with avoidable conditions than those with insurance (Kaiser Commission on Medicaid and the Uninsured). It is difficult to reach the uninsured population for primary prevention, which increases the likelihood of disease onset and inadequate treatment to manage or slow disease progression. Consequently, the uninsured are more likely to be diagnosed at later stages of disease, with subsequently higher death rates (ACS, 2007).

HEALTH PSYCHOLOGY'S ROLE

Given the clinical evidence, it begs the question of why so few people engage in preventive care. Assuming adequate insurance coverage, the reasons are numerous, including lack of awareness, high co-payments for services, fear of positive screening results, prior experiences with false positive test results, time constraints, and lack of motivation. Even those who can find the time and are aware may not value a healthy lifestyle or the prevention of disease. Those who already have chronic diseases may feel overwhelmed or even hopeless to prevent their health from deteriorating further. Some may suffer from clinical or sub-clinical levels of depression in addition to chronic disease, further complicating treatment.

Unhealthy behaviors, such as eating too much of what we know is bad for us, lying on the couch instead of exercising, and smoking, can actually be quite enjoyable. It can be difficult to help someone who has yet to experience any negatively related health consequences to give up such pleasurable indulgences. While a healthy lifestyle may sound like a good thing, it requires consistent hard work, dedication, and comfort with delayed gratification. Delayed gratification is a particularly challenging concept for many in our "get it now" society. Moreover, adopting a healthy lifestyle and engaging in preventive health care requires consideration of and value for one's future health. According to Beck's cognitive triad (Beck, 1976), a person suffering from depression will experience negative thoughts about the self, the world, and the future. Depression may therefore have a deleterious impact on a person's consideration of the future, and the fatigue, hopelessness, lack of motivation, and dysphoria that typically constitute depression undermine a person's ability to engage in healthy behaviors. Depression will also have a negative impact on a person's perceived self-efficacy (Bandura, 2000). Depression is associated with higher rates of smoking and lower levels of physical activity (Anda, Williamson, Escobedo, Mast, Giovino, & Remington, 1990; Camacho, Roberts, Lazarus, Kaplan, & Cohen, 1991), and those with depression are more likely to have chronic disease (Cavanaugh & Zalski, 1998). In fact, depression increases the risk of obesity, hypertension, heart disease, and stroke (Davidson, Jonas, Dixon, & Markovitz, 2000; Jonas, Eberhardt, & Lando, 1998; Jonas & Lando, 2000; Jonas & Mussolino, 2000).

Health psychologists are uniquely trained to address many of the aforementioned barriers because most of them are psychological in nature. As Bandura (2005, p. 250) states, "biomedical approaches are ill-suited for chronic diseases because they are devised mainly for acute illness." While other disciplines are involved in chronic disease prevention (e.g., public health, preventive medicine), only health psychology brings the tools and knowledge of applied behavioral theory to medical populations, and the required qualifications to treat comorbid psychological disorders such as depression. Furthermore, health psychologists typically work in medical settings where they can gain access to patients with chronic diseases, such as primary care. In fact, integrated primary care provides an excellent model by which clinical and financial outcomes may be realized in preventing chronic disease onset and progression (for more information about integrated primary care, see Chapter 2).

Certain psychological models and theories lend themselves well to preventive care and have been mentioned throughout this text. The following theories will be elaborated here, with an emphasis on their application to behavioral prevention: the Transtheoretical Model (Prochaska & DiClemente, 1982), Motivational Interviewing (Miller & Rollnick, 1991), Social Cognitive Theory (Bandura, 1999), and the Preventive Health Model (Myers & Wolf, 1990).

TRANSTHEORETICAL MODEL

The Transtheoretical Model (TTM) was developed by Prochaska and DiClemente (1982) in response to what they identified as an increasing divergence in the practice of psychotherapy that could lead to fragmentation without some synthesis among the various therapeutic systems. They identified five common processes of change from analyzing 18 leading therapeutic systems. These processes were (1) consciousness raising, (2) choosing, (3) catharsis, (4) conditional stimuli, and (5) contingency control (Prochaska & DiClemente). Consciousness raising includes helping the patient gather information about oneself and the problem, such as through verbal clinician feedback or printed informational materials. Choosing includes increased awareness that there are healthy alternatives to the unhealthy behavior. Catharsis includes emotional expression of the problem behavior and the process of change. Conditional stimuli includes both stimulus control and counterconditioning. Stimulus control is avoidance of stimuli associated with the problem behavior and the operant extinction of that stimulus' effect to cue the problem behavior, while counterconditioning is training an alternative, healthier response to those stimuli. Finally, contingency control includes the use of positive reinforcement from oneself and others and reevaluation of how the problem behavior has impacted one's self-image and the environment. The TTM has been termed atheoretical by some (Bandura, 2000; Davidson, 1992).

From these five processes of change, Prochaska and DiClemente eventually identified six stages of change (SOC). These are (1) precontemplation, (2) contemplation, (3) preparation, (4) action, (5) maintenance, and (6) relapse. Precontemplation is the stage at which the person is not even considering changing his or her behavior, does not see the behavior as a problem, minimizes associated risks, and avoids information to the contrary. In the contemplation stage, the person has become aware of why the behavior is a problem but is ambivalent about changing, and likely sees as many benefits as costs to his or her behavior. During preparation, the person has made a decision to change, and is planning his or her strategy for change, but has not yet taken action. In action, the person has implemented a plan and is changing the behavior. In maintenance, the person has been able to sustain new behaviors and avoid reverting to old patterns of behavior for a significant period of time. In relapse, the person does revert to old patterns of behavior, thus placing him or her back to an earlier stage of change to begin the change process again. These stages have been criticized for not providing etiological knowledge (Bandura, 2000) and Prochaska and DiClemente concede that this was not their primary focus in the development of the TTM and SOC (Prochaska, DiClemente, Velicer, & Rossi, 1992).

The SOC are not thought to be linear in sequence but rather cyclical, in that a person can relapse and reenter at a later stage such as preparation. Given this, according to Bandura (2000), the SOC is not a true stage theory, such as Piaget's stages of cognitive development, because the SOC stages do not operate in an invariant sequence, each stage is not moved through only once (nonreversibility), and there are not qualitative changes through the stages. Prochaska and DiClemente have also operationalized the stages of change by duration as follows: precontemplators are not thinking of changing in the next 6 months; contemplators are thinking of changing in the next 6 months; those in preparation are thinking of changing in the next month; those in action are in the process of changing behaviors; and those in maintenance have sustained behavior change for at least 6 months (Prochaska, DiClemente, & Norcross, 1992). However, these subdivisions of duration have been criticized as arbitrary (Bandura, 2000).

Prochaska and DiClemente identified a relationship between the five processes of change and the six stages of change, whereby the processes of change were matched to appropriate stages to motivate the person to move through the SOC. Consciousness raising, choosing, and catharsis were seen as psychodynamic processes occurring primarily within the person, whereas conditional stimuli and contingency control were viewed as behavioral processes that focused on external environmental forces (Prochaska & DiClemente, 1982). It was found that the psychodynamic processes were best suited for the earlier stages of change during precontemplation and contemplation, while the behavioral processes were best suited for the later stages of change during preparation, action, and maintenance. This makes intuitive sense in that behavioral processes will not be used until a person is committed to acting. At the time, Prochaska and DiClemente presented a novel approach to treatment. Their model suggested that change moves along a continuum and interventions should be matched to the stage the person is in. Instead of viewing resistance as something existing within the patient, they viewed this as a mismatch between the clinician's intervention strategies and the patient's readiness to change.

The transtheoretical model and SOC have proliferated throughout addictions treatment and have utility in most other areas of behavior change. In its early inception, TTM and SOC were criticized for lacking empirical support for matching stages to interventions (Davidson, 1992). However, Prochaska and DiClemente (1983) have conducted studies on the application of their model with many populations, including smokers, and have demonstrated empirical support for matching the processes of change with the stages of change. For instance, smokers in the contemplation stage use more consciousness-raising and choosing processes, while those in action and maintenance stages benefit more from conditional stimuli and contingency control processes (Prochaska & DiClemente). Many other researchers have also successfully applied the model to substance abuse, smoking cessation, condom use, weight loss, dietary changes, adoption of regular exercise, and use of mammography.

Motivational Interviewing

Motivational Interviewing (MI; Miller & Rollnick, 1991), another therapeutic model, has frequently been used with the SOC. Influenced by Carl Rogers, MI is a client-centered approach to treatment that came out of Miller and Rollnick's extensive work with substance-abusing patients. They found that it was more effective to work collaboratively with patients rather than directly challenge them to change their behavior. Motivational interviewing is particularly useful in helping patients resolve ambivalence toward changing by increasing intrinsic motivation (Miller & Rollnick). They purport that arguments for change coming from the patient are more powerful than those that come from the therapist. They further propose that MI is different from more directive cognitive behavioral approaches because such approaches assume that the patient is already in an action stage of change. Although MI is not directly confrontational, it *is* goal directed, with the goal of increasing the patient's motivation to move further along the continuum of change.

There are five general principles of MI: (1) express empathy, (2) develop discrepancy, (3) avoid argumentation, (4) roll with resistance, and (5) support self-efficacy. Expressing empathy on the part of the therapist requires an attitude of acceptance without judgment through reflective listening and normalizing of ambivalence to change. Such accurate empathy, which meets the patient where he or she is, is thought to give the client the freedom to consider the possibility of embracing change rather than being put on the defensive. Developing discrepancy is akin to Festinger's concept of cognitive dissonance, in that the therapist is working to help the patient identify a discrepancy between present behavior and future goals. Once this discrepancy is identified, the therapist works to amplify the differences between personal values and present behavior in order to increase the patient's motivation to change. In this vein, the patient, and not the therapist, is presenting reasons for change. Avoiding argumentation and rolling with resistance are skills used to prevent resistance from the patient, which is likely if the therapist becomes too adamant. Instead, it is preferred that the therapist work to actively engage the patient in problem solving by treating him or her as a valuable resource to solutions (Miller & Rollnick, 1991). Finally, supporting self-efficacy (Bandura, 1977) is central to increasing the patient's belief in his or her ability to succeed in change, even among obstacles. Motivational interviewing is not a comprehensive theory that explains the etiology of behavior. Rather, it is a counseling style that has borrowed aspects of its model from Rogers (client-centered), Festinger (cognitive dissonance), and Bandura (self-efficacy).

Rollnick, Butler, and Stott (1997) developed a quick assessment and intervention for motivation and confidence to change unhealthy behavior (in this case, smoking) that was found to be clinically effective in primary care settings. To assess motivation and confidence, they used a 10-point self-rating scale and then elicited reasons from patients for why they had assigned themselves those numbers. This was followed up with problem solving and a discussion of the pros and cons of not changing. In 2005, Hettema, Steele, and Miller conducted a meta-analysis on 72 studies of motivational interviewing, almost half of which were for alcohol use (31) but also included smoking (6) and diet and exercise (4). They found that overall, MI increases treatment adherence and retention (average short-term between-group effect size of MI was 0.77), but with varying effect sizes across providers, populations, and target problems (i.e., short-term effect size was only 0.04 for tobacco use). Interestingly, a "sleeper effect" was observed with diet and exercise, as the initial 3-month effect size was 0.42 and jumped to 0.78 at 1-year follow-up.

As health professionals, we may see very clearly why someone ought to change their behavior. We cannot, however, assume that people either want to change or that their health is a prime motivation for change. The SOC and MI recognize that ambivalence is at the core of change and that without addressing this ambivalence, the patient will likely remain overly attached to what he or she perceives as the benefits of his or her current behavior. As mentioned previously, SOC and MI are frequently used in conjunction. For example, MI strategies with a precontemplator may include expressing empathy and avoiding argumentation in order to help him or her consider that change is even an option. Developing discrepancy is a useful strategy with contemplators whose ambivalence toward change is high. The therapist can help the patient explore the pros and cons of the behavior while highlighting where the behavior does not mesh with the patient's personal values and future goals. During the action stage of change, the MI principle of supporting self-efficacy is important in helping the patient build confidence to sustain behavior change. During relapse, expressing empathy and supporting self-efficacy are crucial. Knowing which stage of change the patient is in can help the therapist to employ strategies and techniques that are best suited to the situation and most beneficial to the patient. The principles of MI have been found to be most useful in the earlier stages of change, such as precontemplation, contemplation, and preparation (Miller & Rollnick, 1991).

PREVENTIVE HEALTH MODEL

Decision making in preventive care has been a focus of attention, particularly for cancer prevention screening. The Preventive Health Model (PHM) is a "conceptual framework that integrates behavioral and decision-making theory" (Myers, 2005, p. S71). Because patients are often educated about various cancer screenings in their doctor's office, PHM is ideally used during these encounters. Therefore, health psychologists in integrated primary care settings are well situated to provide such counseling if the physician is under time constraints, as is often the case. Although many decision aids are available that present patients with factual information, little attention is paid to identifying and addressing the patient's cognitive and affective responses to decision making (Myers, 2005). In making decisions about preventive care, a person is influenced by his or her sociocultural background (including medical and preventive history) and his or her cognitive and emotional representations of health (Myers, 2005). For example, when considering a cancer screening procedure, such as a pap test, a patient may have emotional reactions such as fear of the results or concern about pain during the procedure. She may also have cognitive representations of what it could mean to have cervical cancer (e.g., "I won't be able to handle the treatment; I will get sick and die"). Such considerations will influence the patient's decision about whether to undergo the screening (Myers, 2005).

The PHM involves helping the patient to clarify preferences related to available options, and this preference clarification process is seen as central to decision making. This approach gives the patient an opportunity to consider his or her personal values in relation to preventive care. Through preference clarification, the patient expresses his or her cognitive and emotional representations to a preventive intervention (e.g., endoscopy), determines how those representations fit with his or her personal values, and then uses this information to select a preferred alternative that is in line with personal values. By using this process, and assuming thorough patient education regarding the procedure, the patient should be able to make a well-informed choice among the available options (i.e., having/not having a mammogram). The PHM has been useful in predicting outcomes such as cancer screening utilization (Myers et al., 1994, 1999).

SOCIAL COGNITIVE THEORY

Social Cognitive Theory (SCT; Bandura, 1999) is a comprehensive theory that has been successfully applied to the field of chronic disease prevention and health promotion. SCT provides both etiologic explanation of poor health management and clinical application of health promotion. It is beyond the scope of this chapter to provide a comprehensive overview of SCT. This section will, however, highlight key aspects of the theory and focus on its utility in health promotion. Social cognitive theory includes three processes of personal change: the adoption of new behaviors, generalized use of those behaviors under different circumstances, and maintenance of them over time (Bandura, 1997). Social cognitive theory further "specifies a core set of determinants, the mechanisms through which they work, and the optimal ways of translating this knowledge into effective health practices" (Bandura, 2004, p. 114).

The core determinants are cognitive in nature and include: (1) *knowledge* of health risks and benefits of preventive interventions, (2) *perceived self-efficacy*, (3) *outcome expectations* about the costs and benefits of adopting a healthy lifestyle, (4) *health goals*, (5) *perceived facilitators* to attaining goals, and (6) *impediments* to attaining goals (Bandura, 2004). The *knowledge* of health risks and benefits of preventive interventions is a precondition for change, in that a person has little reason to change if he or she does not understand why it is necessary. *Self-efficacy*, the core principle of SCT, is a person's belief in his or her ability to use skills possessed and is the foundation of motivation (Bandura, 1977). If a person does not believe that his or her actions can produce the desired outcome, there is little incentive to act or persevere when faced with obstacles (Bandura, 2004). In health promotion, self-efficacy is then the belief that one can exercise control over one's health habits to produce the desired health results, and those with low self-efficacy will likely not engage in preventive care. *Outcome expectancies* include both the costs (e.g., hard work, giving up pleasurable things, conflicts with friends) that are experienced as disincentives to change, and the benefits (feel healthier, look better, receive recognition from others) that are experienced as incentives to change. Short-term *goals* should be set to meet long-term ones, and self-regulation is essential to achieving these health goals. *Impediments* and *facilitators* will have an impact on self-efficacy by either challenging one's belief or enhancing it, respectively. Self-efficacy is strengthened by facilitators and by surmounting obstacles to goals, such as continuing a regular exercise routine in the face of fatigue or inclement weather (Bandura, 2004).

Self-efficacy is considered the core principle of SCT because it directly affects health behavior and the other cognitive determinants (Bandura, 2004). For instance, those with stronger self-efficacy will set higher goals, expect favorable outcomes, and view impediments as surmountable challenges. There are four sources of influence over self-efficacy. The most significant is through mastery experiences, meaning that a person's self-efficacy becomes more robust as he or she sees himself or herself succeeding, especially in the face of obstacles. The second is by vicarious experiences observed through valued social models. Seeing others similar to oneself succeed enhances a person's belief that he or she, too, can succeed. The third is through social persuasion from valued others. Having others believe in us helps us to believe that we are capable, and those with strong self-efficacy tend to surround themselves with supportive others who believe in them (Bandura, 2000). Finally, the fourth source of influence stems from the person's physical and emotional states when judging his or her capabilities. For instance, if a person judges his or her stress reactions as a sign of inefficacy, this will lead to self-doubt (Bandura, 2000). Therefore, cognitive restructuring in interpreting these physiological and emotional states can bolster self-efficacy. This is especially crucial during the early phase of abstinence from a substance (e.g., nicotine) when physiological withdrawal will weaken self-efficacy to remain abstinent. Those with stronger perceived self-efficacy will be better able to adopt and maintain health-promoting behavior; research has supported this with changing diet (Desmond & Price, 1988), reducing cholesterol through diet (McCann et al., 1995), adopting a regular exercise program (McAuley, 1992), managing diabetes (Hurley & Shea, 1992), and quitting smoking (Shadel & Mermelstein, 1993).

Self-regulation, another central tenet of SCT, is also influenced by cognitive determinants. Self-regulation depends on how well a person can observe and monitor his or her behavior and how he or she judges and reacts to it (Bandura, 2000). Perceived self-efficacy will also affect how one judges his or her own behavior. For instance, those with strong self-efficacy will tend to judge failures as resulting from insufficient effort or strategy, whereas those with low self-efficacy will likely attribute failures to a lack of ability (Bandura, 2000). Therefore, self-regulatory efficacy is needed to maintain health habits, and health changes will have little consequence if they do not endure (Bandura, 1997). Health promotion research on self-regulatory mechanisms of SCT has shown that these mechanisms helped patients make significant reductions in several risk factors for coronary artery disease, including smoking. Specifically, patients were able to lower their LDL cholesterol, raise HDL cholesterol, lose weight, and increase exercise (Haskell et al., 1994). In a study by DeBusk and colleagues (1994), this self-regulatory system was found to be more effective in reducing cardiovascular risk factors than standard medical care.

CONCLUSION

Our chronic disease epidemic requires a multifaceted solution, with the four pillars of primary prevention at its core. The keystone of behavior change for this population is health psychology. Social cognitive theory provides a comprehensive explanation for the etiology of unhealthy behaviors and a detailed framework for health-promotion interventions. Integrated primary care provides health psychologists with access to the chronic disease population. In this fast-paced environment, psychological models such as motivational interviewing, the transtheoretical model, and the preventive health model would be well utilized. Unlike most biomedical interventions, such as expensive testing and pharmacy, health psychology interventions tailored to the chronic disease population and delivered in primary care settings are inexpensive and have demonstrated superior outcomes. In order to slow the soaring health care expenditures of chronic disease and reduce disparities, health psychology should be seen as a major facet of the solution.

REFERENCES

Adamy, J. (2006, December 6). New York trans fat ban could spread. *The Wall Street Journal*, p. D8.

American Cancer Society. (2006). *Cancer prevention and early detection facts and figures 2006.* Retrieved January 10, 2007, from http://www.cancer.org/downloads/STT/CPED2006PWSecured.pdf

American Cancer Society. (2007). *Cancer facts and figures 2007.* Retrieved January 10, 2007, from http://www.cancer.org/downloads/STT/CAFF2007PWSecured.pdf

American Heart Association. (2006). Heart and stroke statistics–2006 update. *Circulation, 113,* e85–e151.

American Heart Association. (2007). *What are healthy levels of cholesterol?* Retrieved January 10, 2007, from http://www.americanheart.org/presenter.jhtml?identifier=183

Amonkar, M., Madhavan, S., Rosenbluth, S., & Simon, K. (1999). Barriers and facilitators to providing common preventive screening services in managed care settings. *Journal of Community Health, 24*(3), 229–247.

Anda, R., Williamson, D., Escobedo, L., Mast, E., Giovino, G., & Remington, P. (1990). Depression and the dynamics of smoking: A national perspective. *Journal of the American Medical Association, 264,* 1541–1545.

Anderson, G., & Horvath, J. (2004). The growing burden of chronic disease in America. *Public Health Reports, 119,* 263–270.

Bandura, A. (1977). Self-efficacy: Toward a unifying theory of behavioral change. *Psychological Review, 84,* 191–215.

Bandura, A. (1997). *Self-efficacy: The exercise of control.* New York: W. H. Freeman.

Bandura, A. (1999). Social cognitive theory of personality. In L. A. Pervin & O. P. John (Eds.), *Handbook of personality: Theory and research* (2nd ed., pp. 154–196). New York: Guilford.

Bandura, A. (2000). Health promotion from the perspective of social cognitive theory. In P. Norman, C. Abraham, & M. Conner (Eds.), *Understanding and changing health behavior* (pp. 299–339). Amsterdam: Harwood Academic.

Bandura, A. (2004). Health promotion by social cognitive means. *Health Education and Behavior, 31*(2), 143–164.

Bandura, A. (2005). The primacy of self-regulation in health promotion. *Applied Psychology: An International Review, 54*(2), 245–254.

Beck, A. (1976). *Cognitive therapy and the emotional disorders.* New York: International Universities Press.

Beilin, L. J., Puddey, I. B., & Burke, V. (1999). Lifestyle and hypertension. *American Journal of Hypertension, 12*(9), 934–945.

Bhopal, R. (1998). Spectre of racism in health and health care: Lessons from history and the United States. *British Medical Journal, 316*(7149), 1970–1973.

Bjornson, & White (2006). *Trends in the delivery and reimbursement of tobacco dependence treatment.* Tobacco Cessation Leadership Network. Retrieved January 10, 2006, from http://www .tcln.org/resources/pdfs/Trends_in_Delivery_and_Reimbursement_final.pdf

Camacho, T., Roberts, R., Lazarus, N., Kaplan, G., & Cohen, R. (1991). Physical activity and depression: Evidence from the Alameda County Study. *American Journal of Epidemiology, 134,* 220–231.

Cavanaugh, S., & Zalski, A. (1998). Psychiatric diagnosis. In L. S. Goldman, T. N. Wise, & D. S. Brody (Eds.), *Psychiatry for primary care physicians* (pp. 19–40). Chicago: American Medical Association.

Centers for Disease Control and Prevention. (1997). Cigarette smoking-attributable mortality and years of potential life lost. *Morbidity and Mortality Weekly Report, 46*(20), 444–451.

Centers for Disease Control and Prevention. (2000). Oral health in America: A report of the Surgeon General. *Morbidity and Mortality Weekly Report, 41,* 325–327.

Centers for Disease Control and Prevention. (2003). Facts about COPD. Retrieved January 10, 2007, from http://www.cdc.gov/nceh/airpollution/copd/pdfs/copdfaq.pdf

Centers for Disease Control and Prevention. (2004). *Tobacco use in the United States.* Washington, DC: National Center for Chronic Disease Prevention and Health Promotion. Tobacco Information and Prevention Source.

Centers for Disease Control and Prevention. (2005a). Annual smoking-attributable mortality, years of potential life lost, and productivity losses–U.S., 1997–2001. *Morbidity and Mortality Weekly Report, 54*(25), 625–628.

Centers for Disease Control and Prevention. (2005b). Deaths: Leading causes for 2002. *National Vital Statistics Reports, 53,* 17.

Centers for Disease Control and Prevention. (2005c). *National diabetes fact sheet, United States, 2005.* Retrieved January 10, 2007, from http://www.cdc.gov/diabetes/pubs/pdf/ndfs_2005.pdf

Centers for Disease Control and Prevention. (2005d). Racial/ethnic disparities in prevalence, treatment, and control of hypertension, United States, 1999–2002. *Morbidity and Mortality Weekly Report, 54*(1), 7–9.

Centers for Disease Control and Prevention. (2006). *Chronic disease overview.* Retrieved January 10, 2007, from http://apps.nccd.cdc.gov/EmailForm/print_table.asp

Centers for Medicare and Medicaid Services. (2006). *The nation's healthcare dollar, calendar year 2005: Where it came from.* Retrieved January 10, 2007, from http://www.cms.hhs.gov/ NationalHealthExpendData/downloads/PieChartSourcesExpenditures2005.pdf

Clarke, J. L., & Meiris, D. C. (2006). Preventive medicine: A "cure" for the healthcare crisis. *Disease Management, 9*(suppl. 1), S1–S16.

Colditz, G. A., Willet, W. C., Rotnitzky, A., & Manson, J. E. (1995). Weight gain as a risk factor for clinical diabetes mellitus in women. *Annals of Internal Medicine, 122*(7), 481–486.

Davidson, K., Jonas, B., Dixon, K., & Markovitz, J. (2000). Do depression symptoms predict early hypertension incidence in young adults from the CARDIA study? *Archives of Internal Medicine, 160,* 1495–1500.

Davidson, R. (1992). Prochaska and DiClemente's model of change: A case study? *British Journal of Addiction, 87,* 821–822.

Davis, K., Bialek, R., Parkinson, M., Smith, J., & Vellozzi, C. (1990). Paying for preventive care: Moving the debate forward. *American Journal of Preventive Medicine, 6*(suppl.), 7–32.

DeBusk, R., Miller, N., Superko, H., Dennis, C., Thomas, R., Lew, H., et al. (1994). A case management system for coronary risk factor modification. *Annals of Internal Medicine, 120,* 721–729.

Desmond, S. M., & Price, J. H. (1988). Self-effacing and weight control. *Health Education, 19,* 12–18.

Finkelstein, E. A., Fiebelkorn, I. C., & Wang, G. (2004). State-level estimates of annual medical expenditures attributable to obesity. *Obesity Research, 12*(1), 18–24.

Fries, J., Koop, C., & Beadle, C. (1993). Reducing health care costs by reducing the need and demand for medical services. *The New England Journal of Medicine, 329,* 321–325.

Greenwald, P., Kramer, B., & Weed, D. (Eds.). (1995). *Cancer prevention and control.* New York: Marcel Dekker.

Group Health Association of America. (1992). *GHAA's annual HMO industry survey.* Washington, DC: Group Health Association of America.

Hankinson, S., Colditz, G., Manson, J., & Speizer, F. (Eds.). (2001). *Healthy women, healthy lives: A guide to preventing disease, from the Landmark Nurses' Health Study.* New York: Simon & Schuster.

Haskell, W., Alderman, E., Fair, J., Maron, D., Mackey, S., Superko, H., et al. (1994). Effects of intensive multiple risk factor reduction on coronary atherosclerosis and clinical cardiac events in men and women with coronary artery disease. *Circulation, 89,* 975–990.

Henderson, B. E., Pike, M. C., Bernstein, L., & Ross, R. K. (1996). Breast cancer. In D. Schottenfeld and J. F. Fraumeni, Jr. (Eds.), *Cancer epidemiology and prevention,* 2nd ed., 1022–1039. New York: Oxford University Press.

Herald, K. C. (2004). Achieving antigen specific immune regulation. *Journal of Clinical Investigation, 113,* 346–349.

Hettema, J., Steele, J., & Miller, W. (2005). A meta-analysis of research on motivational interviewing treatment effectiveness. *Annual Review of Clinical Psychology, 1,* 91–111.

Hurley, C., & Shea, C. (1992). Self-efficacy: Strategy for enhancing diabetes self-care. *The Diabetes Educator, 18,* 146–150.

Jonas, B., Eberhardt, M., & Lando, J. (1998). Symptoms of anxiety or depression as risk factors for incidence of obesity. *Annals of Behavioral Medicine, 20,* 140–145.

Jonas, B. S., & Lando, J. F. (2000). Negative affect as a prospective risk factor for hypertension. *Psychosomatic Medicine, 62,* 188–196.

Jonas, B. S., & Mussolino, M. E. (2000). Symptoms of depression as a prospective risk factor for stroke. *Psychosomatic Medicine, 62,* 463–471.

Kaiser Commission on Medicaid and the Uninsured (2006). *The uninsured: A primer.* Washington, DC: The Henry J. Kaiser Family Foundation.

Kelley, G. A., & Kelley, K. S. (2000). Progressive resistance exercise and resting blood pressure: a meta-analysis of randomized controlled trials. *Hypertension, 35,* 838–843.

Knowler, W. C., Barrett-Connor, E., Fowler, S. E., Hamman, R. F., Lachin, J. M., Walker, E. A., et al. (2002). Reduction in the incidence of type 2 diabetes with lifestyle intervention or metformin. *New England Journal of Medicine, 346,* 393–403.

Krieger, N., & Sidney, S. (1996). Racial discrimination and blood pressure: The CARDIA study of young black and white adults. *American Journal of Public Health, 86*, 1370–1378.

Krieger, N., Sidney, S., & Coakley, E. (1998). Racial discrimination and skin color in the CARDIA study: Implications for public health research. *American Journal of Public Health, 88*, 1308–1313.

Kushner, R. F. (2003). *Roadmaps for clinical practice: Case studies in disease prevention and health promotion—assessment and management of adult obesity: A primer for physicians.* Chicago: American Medical Association.

Mackay, J., Jemal, A., Lee, N. C., & Parkin, D. M. (2006). *The cancer atlas.* Atlanta: American Cancer Society.

McAuley, E. (1992). Understanding exercise behavior: A self-efficacy perspective. In G. C. Roberts (Ed.), *Motivation in sport and exercise,* (pp. 107–127). Champaign, IL: Human Kinetics.

McCann, B., Bovbjerg, V., Brief, D., Turner, C., Follette, W., Fitzpatrick, V., et al. (1995). Relationship of self-efficacy to cholesterol lowering and dietary change in hyperlipidemia. *Annals of Behavioral Medicine, 17*, 221–226.

Merck. (2007). *Who should receive Gardasil?* Retrieved January 10, 2007, from http://www.gardasil.com/who-should-receive-gardasil.html

Miller, W. R., & Rollnick, S. (1991). *Motivational interviewing: Preparing people to change addictive behavior.* New York: Guilford.

Myers, R. E. (2005). Decision counseling in cancer prevention and control. *Health Psychology, 24*(4), S71–S77.

Myers, R., Chodak, G., Wolf, T., Burgh, D., McGrory, G., Marcus, S., et al. (1999). Adherence by African American men to prostate cancer education and early detection. *Cancer, 86*(1), 88–104.

Myers, R., Ross, E., Jepson, C., Wolf, T., Balshem, A., Millner, L., et al. (1994). Modeling adherence to colorectal cancer screening. *Preventive Medicine, 23*(2), 142–151.

Myers, R., & Wolf, T. (1990). Instrument development for a colorectal cancer screening survey. In E. C. Travaglini (Ed.), *Fox Chase Cancer Center scientific report, 1988–1989* (pp. 231–232). Philadelphia: Fox Chase Cancer Center.

National Center for Health Statistics. (1997). Report of final mortality statistics, 1995. *Monthly Vital Statistics Report, 45*(11), Suppl.2.

National Center for Health Statistics. (2006a). Deaths-leading causes. Retrieved January 10, 2007, from http://www.cdc.gov/nchs/fastats/lcod.htm

National Center for Health Statistics. (2006b). *Health, United States, 2006.* (Library of Congress Catalog no. 76-641496). Washington, DC: U.S. Government Printing Office.

National Institutes of Health. (1996). Cervical cancer. *NIH Consensus Statement, 14*(1), 1–38.

National Institutes of Health. (1997). The sixth report of the Joint National Committee on prevention, detection, evaluation, and treatment of high blood pressure. *Archives of Internal Medicine, 157*, 2413–2446.

National Institutes of Health and National Heart, Lung and Blood Institute. (1998). *Obesity education initiative: Clinical guidelines on the identification, evaluation, and treatment of overweight and obesity in adults.* Bethesda, MD: U.S. Department of Health and Human Services.

Parkinson, M., & Lurie, P. (1996). Reimbursement for preventive services. In S. Woolf, S. Jonas, & R. Lawrence (Eds.), *Health promotion and disease prevention in clinical practice.* 525–542. New York: Lippincott, Williams & Wilkins.

Patel, C., Marmot, M., Terry, D., Carruthers, M., Hunt, B., & Patel, M. (1985). Trial of relaxation in reducing coronary risk: Four year follow-up. *American Journal of Public Health, 290*, 1103–1106.

Prochaska, J., & DiClemente, C. (1982). Transtheoretical therapy: Toward a more integrative model of change. *Psychotherapy: Theory, Research and Practice, 19*(3), 276–288.

Prochaska, J., & DiClemente, C. (1983). Stages and processes of self change of smoking: Toward an integrative model of change. *Journal of Consulting and Clinical Psychology, 51*(3), 390–395.

Prochaska, J., DiClemente, C., & Norcross, J. (1992). In search of how people change. Applications to addictive behaviors. *American Journal of Psychology, 47,* 1102–1114.

Prochaska, J., DiClemente, C., Velicer, W., & Rossi, J. (1992). Criticisms and concerns of the transtheoretical model in light of recent research. *British Journal of Addiction, 87,* 825–835.

Pruitt, S. D., Klapow, J. C., Epping-Jordan, J. E., & Dresselhaus, T. R. (1998). Moving behavioral medicine to the front line: A model for the integration of behavioral and medical sciences in primary care. *Professional Psychology: Research and Practice, 29,* (3), 230–236.

Randall, V. R. (2006). *Dying while black.* Dayton, OH: Seven Principles Press.

Rollnick, S., Butler, C., & Stott, N. (1997). Helping smokers make decisions: The enhancement of brief intervention for general medical practice. *Patient Education and Counseling, 31,* 191–203.

Seidell, J. C., Verschuren, W. M., van Leer, E. M., & Kromhout, D. (1996). Overweight, underweight, and mortality: A prospective study of 48,287 men and women. *Archives of Internal Medicine, 1569,* 958–963.

Shadel, W., & Mermelstein, R. (1993). Cigarette smoking under stress: The role of coping expectancies among smokers in a clinic-based smoking cessation program. *Health Psychology, 12,* 443–450.

Stanton, M. (2006). The high concentration of US healthcare expenditures. *Agency for Healthcare Research and Quality Research in Action, 19,* 1–12.

Trials of Hypertension Prevention Collaborative Research Group. (1997). Effects of weight loss and sodium reduction intervention on blood pressure and hypertension incidence in overweight people with high-normal blood pressure. The Trials of Hypertension Prevention, Phase II. *Annals of Internal Medicine, 157,* 657–667.

U.S. Department of Health and Human Services. (1990). *The health benefits of smoking cessation: A report of the Surgeon General* (DHHS Publication No. CDC 90-8416). Washington, DC: U.S. Government Printing Office.

U.S. Department of Health and Human Services. (1997). *Changes in cigarette-related disease risk and their implication for prevention and control* (Rep. No. NIH 97-4213). Rockville, MD: USDHHS, PHS, NIH, NCI.

U.S. Department of Health and Human Services. (2000a). Heart disease and stroke. In *Healthy People 2010:* Vol. 2. *Understanding and improving health and objectives for improving health* (2nd ed., pp. 12-3–12-36). Washington, DC: U.S. Government Printing Office.

U.S. Department of Health and Human Services. (2000b). Nutrition and overweight. In *Healthy People 2010:* Vol. 2. *Understanding and improving health and objectives for improving health* (2nd ed., pp. 19-3–19-53). Washington, DC: U.S. Government Printing Office.

U.S. Department of Health and Human Services. (2000c). Physical activity and fitness. In *Healthy People 2010:* Vol. 2. *Understanding and improving health and objectives for improving health* (2nd ed., pp. 22-3–22-39). Washington, DC: U.S. Government Printing Office.

U.S. Department of Health and Human Services. (2000d). *Reducing tobacco use: A report of the Surgeon General.* Atlanta, GA: Author.

U.S. Department of Health and Human Services. (2000e). Tobacco use. In *Healthy People 2010:* Vol. 2. *Understanding and improving health and objectives for improving health* (2nd ed., pp. 27-3–27-40). Washington, DC: U.S. Government Printing Office.

U.S. Department of Health and Human Services. (2001). *The Surgeon General's call to action to prevent and decrease overweight and obesity.* Rockville, MD: U.S. Department of Health and Human Services, Public Health Service, Office of the Surgeon General.

U.S. Department of Health and Human Services (2003). *Promising practices in chronic disease prevention and control: A public health framework for action.* Washington, DC: Author.

U. S. Department of Health and Human Services (2004). *The health consequences of smoking: A report of the Surgeon General.* Atlanta, GA: Centers for Disease Control and Prevention.

Willet, W. (1996). Diet and nutrition. In D. Schottenfeld & J. Fraumeni (Eds.), *Cancer epidemiology and prevention,* 2nd edition. New York: Oxford University Press.

Witteman, J. C., Willet, W. C., Stampfer, M. J., Colditz, G. A., Sacks, F. M., Speizer, F. E., et al. (1989). A prospective study of nutritional factors and hypertension among U. S. women. *Circulation, 80*(5), 1320–1327.

World Health Organization. (2006). *Chronic diseases and health promotion.* Retrieved January 10, 2007, from http://www.who.int/chp/en/

CHAPTER 4

Obesity

M. INDIRA PAHARIA and LARINA KASE

INTRODUCTION

There has been a dramatic rise in the prevalence of obesity in the last 30 years. In fact, since 1976, the percentage has more than doubled (National Center for Health Statistics [NCHS], 2006). According to the American Medical Association (AMA), in order to be considered overweight, a person must have a body mass index (BMI) of 25 to 29.9 (Kushner, 2003). Obesity is divided into mild (BMI of 30 to 34.9), moderate (BMI of 35 to 39.9), and severe/extreme (BMI $\geq$ 40) classifications (Kushner). The cutoff begins at a BMI of 25 because chronic disease risk increases at this weight status and over (Kushner; U.S. Department of Health and Human Services [USDHHS], 2001). Body mass index is calculated as weight in pounds divided by height in inches squared, multiplied by 703. When working in the field of obesity treatment, it is simpler to have BMI charts handy (see Chart 4.1). The calculation of BMI is not a perfect measure, as it does not distinguish between body fat, bone density, and muscle mass.

The Centers for Disease Control and Prevention (CDC) report the following 2004 statistics (NCHS, 2006):

Sixty-six percent of all Americans age 20 and over are overweight or obese. This includes 71% of males and 61% of females. Percentages for overweight and obesity are higher in certain minority populations (e.g., African American, Mexican American). Of greatest concern is that 80% of African American women and over 70% of Mexican American men and women are overweight or obese. Regarding socioeconomic status, over 60% of those below poverty level are also overweight or obese.

Obesity alone accounts for 32% of all Americans age 20 and over. This includes 30% of males and 34% of females. Of greatest concern is that 52% of African American women and 40% of Mexican American women are obese. Regarding socioeconomic status, over 30% of those below poverty level are also obese.

Eighteen percent of American children (ages 6 to11 yr) and 17% of adolescents (ages 12 to 19 yr) are overweight. A slightly higher percentage of males in both age groups are overweight as compared to their female counterparts (~18% > 16%). Percentages for overweight children and adolescents are also higher in certain minority groups (e.g., African American, Mexican American). Approximately 26% of Mexican American boys and 25% of African American girls are overweight; 20% of Mexican American male adolescents and 24% of African American female adolescents are overweight.

81

Body Mass Index Table

	Normal						Overweight					Obese										Extreme Obesity															
BMI	19	20	21	22	23	24	25	26	27	28	29	30	31	32	33	34	35	36	37	38	39	40	41	42	43	44	45	46	47	48	49	50	51	52	53	54
Height (inches)												Body Weight (pounds)																								
58	91	96	100	105	110	115	119	124	129	134	138	143	148	153	158	162	167	172	177	181	186	191	196	201	205	210	215	220	224	229	234	239	244	248	253	258
59	94	99	104	109	114	119	124	128	133	138	143	148	153	158	163	168	173	178	183	188	193	198	203	208	212	217	222	227	232	237	242	247	252	257	262	267
60	97	102	107	112	118	123	128	133	138	143	148	153	158	163	168	174	179	184	189	194	199	204	209	215	220	225	230	235	240	245	250	255	261	266	271	276
61	100	106	111	116	122	127	132	137	143	148	153	158	164	169	174	180	185	190	195	201	206	211	217	222	227	232	238	243	248	254	259	264	269	275	280	285
62	104	109	115	120	126	131	136	142	147	153	158	164	169	175	180	186	191	196	202	207	213	218	224	229	235	240	246	251	256	262	267	273	278	284	289	295
63	107	113	118	124	130	135	141	146	152	158	163	169	175	180	186	191	197	203	208	214	220	225	231	237	242	248	254	259	265	270	278	282	287	293	299	304
64	110	116	122	128	134	140	145	151	156	162	168	174	180	186	192	197	204	209	215	221	227	232	238	244	250	256	262	267	273	279	285	291	296	302	308	314
65	114	120	126	132	138	144	150	156	162	168	174	180	186	192	198	204	210	216	222	228	234	240	246	252	258	264	270	276	282	288	294	300	306	312	318	324
66	118	124	130	136	142	148	155	161	167	173	179	186	192	198	204	210	216	223	229	235	241	247	253	260	266	272	278	284	291	297	303	309	315	322	328	334
67	121	127	134	140	146	153	159	166	172	178	185	191	198	204	211	217	223	230	236	242	249	255	261	268	274	280	287	293	299	306	312	319	325	331	338	344
68	125	131	138	144	151	158	164	171	177	184	190	197	203	210	216	223	230	236	243	249	256	262	269	276	282	289	295	302	308	315	322	328	335	341	348	354
69	128	135	142	149	155	162	169	176	182	189	196	203	209	216	223	230	236	243	250	257	263	270	277	284	291	297	304	311	318	324	331	338	345	351	358	365
70	132	139	146	153	160	167	174	181	188	195	202	209	216	222	229	236	243	250	257	264	271	278	285	292	299	306	313	320	327	334	341	348	355	362	369	376
71	136	143	150	157	165	172	179	186	193	200	208	215	222	229	236	243	250	257	265	272	279	286	293	301	308	315	322	329	338	343	351	358	365	372	379	386
72	140	147	154	162	169	177	184	191	199	206	213	221	228	235	242	250	258	265	272	279	287	294	302	309	316	324	331	338	346	353	361	368	375	383	390	397
73	144	151	159	166	174	182	189	197	204	212	219	227	235	242	250	257	265	272	280	288	295	302	310	318	325	333	340	348	355	363	371	378	386	393	401	408
74	148	155	163	171	179	186	194	202	210	218	225	233	241	249	256	264	272	280	287	295	303	311	319	326	334	342	350	358	365	373	381	389	396	404	412	420
75	152	160	168	176	184	192	200	208	216	224	232	240	248	256	264	272	279	287	295	303	311	319	327	335	343	351	359	367	375	383	391	399	407	415	423	431
76	156	164	172	180	189	197	205	213	221	230	238	246	254	263	271	279	287	295	304	312	320	328	336	344	353	361	369	377	385	394	402	410	418	426	435	443

Chart 4.1 Adult BMI

Source: Adapted from Clinical Guidelines on the Identification, Evaluation, and Treatment of Overweight and Obesity in Adults: The Evidence Report.

The relevance of these statistics in terms of health status, quality of life, and economic burden is staggering. Approximately 300,000 deaths per year are attributable to obesity, making it a leading cause of death in the country (National Institutes of Health [NIH] & National Heart, Lung and Blood Institute [NHLBI], 1998), and the total cost of obesity-related diseases is over $100 billion annually (USDHHS, 2001). Obesity increases the risk of type 2 diabetes, heart disease, stroke, hypertension, osteoarthritis, colon and breast cancer, sleep apnea, and depression (USDHHS, 2001). Approximately 20 to 30% of coronary heart disease mortality can be attributed to excess body weight (Seidell, Verschuren, van Leer, & Kromhout, 1996). Further, obese women are nearly six times more likely to develop hypertension (Witteman et al., 1989), and obese persons have almost 10 times the risk of diabetes as compared to non-obese peers (Colditz, Willet, Rotnitzky, & Manson, 1995). As alarming as these statistics are, research supports that losing as little as 5 to 10% of body weight can significantly reduce obesity-related conditions (NIH & NHLBI, 1998; USDHHS, 2001). For instance, sustained weight loss of 7 to 10 lb through diet and exercise over a 4-year period was found to reduce the incidence of type 2 diabetes in high-risk subjects in randomized controlled trials by 40 to 60% (Knowler et al., 2002).

There are numerous theories as to why the prevalence of obesity is so high in the United States. Lack of exercise, large food portions, poor food choices, a fast-paced society, and increased technology have all been implicated. Approximately 40% of adults do not participate in any regular exercise (USDHHS, 2001). Some blame the proliferation of the fast food industry (National Alliance for Nutrition and Activity, 2002; Newman, 2004). After all, according to Brownell and Nestle (2004), 25% of all vegetables eaten in the United States are french fries, most likely because energy-dense foods tend to be cheaper, as these foods are made with less expensive ingredients, such as hydrogenated vegetable oil, which is an inexpensive substitute for butter and cream and the main dietary source of trans fat. Americans also tend to eat more when portion sizes are larger. A study conducted at Penn State University demonstrated that people ate 27% more food on average when given bigger portions, but did not report feeling any fuller (Glaeser, Shapiro, & Cutler, 2003). In addition, genetics (i.e., resting metabolic rate [RMR], appetite) plays a significant role in mediating the development of obesity. A study conducted by Stunkard, Harris, Pederson, and McClearn (1990) examined body weights in identical twins raised apart compared to those raised together and found that genetic factors accounted for approximately two-thirds of the differences in weight between the two groups. According to Stein and Colditz (2005) however, the rapid increase of obesity suggests that behavioral and environmental influences have played a larger role than biological changes. Nevertheless, no single theory has proven to fully account for our current obesity epidemic and, regardless of etiology, many treatment options are available. Obesity is the result of a complex interaction of genetic, behavioral, and environmental influences, indicating that a multidisciplinary approach to treatment is necessary.

MEDICAL TREATMENTS

This section reviews the most widely adopted medical treatments for weight loss, including prescription medications and surgical interventions.

PHARMACOTHERAPY

Of the prescription medications used for weight loss, only two are approved by the Food and Drug Administration (FDA) for long-term use (Aronne, 2002; Kushner, 2003). These are Sibutramine (Meridia) and Orlistat (Xenical). Sibutramine is a serotonin norepinephrine reuptake inhibitor (SNRI) and acts as an appetite suppressant by increasing satiation (Kushner). Therapeutic dosage begins at 10 mg per day, with maximum dosage at 15 mg per day (Aronne). In randomized controlled trials, within 6 to 12 months, subjects on Sibutramine lost 6 to 8% of body weight compared to 1 to 2% on placebo (Finer, 2002). Adverse effects of Sibutramine include an increase in blood pressure and heart rate (Aronne).

Orlistat blocks the digestion and absorption of about 30% of dietary fat consumed and works as an inhibitor of lipases, which are required for the hydrolysis of dietary fat (Kushner, 2003). Therapeutic and maximum dosage of Orlistat begins at 120 mg three times per day (Aronne, 2002). In randomized controlled trials, subjects on Orlistat lost 9 to 10% of body weight compared to 4 to 6% on placebo (Lucas & Kaplin-Machlis, 2001). Additionally, it has demonstrated a reduction in serum and low-density lipoprotein (LDL) cholesterol levels (Kushner). Adverse effects of Orlistat include decreased absorption of fat-soluble vitamins and gastrointestinal symptoms (Aronne).

Guidelines for the prescription of Sibutramine and Orlistat include nonpregnant patients with a BMI > 30, or BMI > 27 when obesity-related risk factors or diseases are present (Kushner, 2003). In further clinical trials of up to 2 years' duration, both Sibutramine and Orlistat demonstrated superior weight loss compared to placebo (Leung, Thomas, Chan, & Tomlinson, 2003; Padwal, Li, & Lau, 2004). An early response to these medications is predictive of longer-term effect, and maximum weight loss is typically achieved by 6 months (Kushner, 2003). Studies have shown, however, that discontinuation of weight loss medications results in weight regain, indicating that patients may need to use such medicines indefinitely to maintain their weight loss, and the long-term effects of these medications remains uncertain (Baron, 1997).

BARIATRIC SURGERY

As demand for obesity surgery continues to grow, there has been a substantial increase in bariatric surgeries performed in the United States. From 2001 to 2003, the number of these surgeries performed more than doubled (47,000 to ~100,000; Mitka, 2003). According to the NIH, eligibility for bariatric surgery includes BMI > 40 or BMI > 35 with high risk comorbid conditions (Mitka, 2003). These criteria have actually motivated patients to gain weight in order to qualify for the surgery (Mitka, 2003). On average, bariatric surgery, which may or may not be covered by insurance, costs $25,000 (Freudenheim, 2003). There are two major classifications for bariatric surgery: restrictive and malabsorptive-restrictive.

Restrictive surgery limits the amount of food the stomach can hold and slows the rate of digestion. The two main restrictive operations are vertical-banded gastroplasty (VBG) and laparoscopic adjustable gastric banding (LAGB). During VBG, a 30 mL gastric pouch is created by the use of vertical linear stapling. The outlet of the pouch is constricted and reinforced by a polypropylene or silicone band. Vertical-banded gastroplasty is not as commonly used today. Unlike VBG, LAGB is reversible and does not require stapling. Instead, LAGB uses a silicone band to compartmentalize the stomach into a smaller pouch (see Figure 4.1). Otherwise known as the LAP-BAND

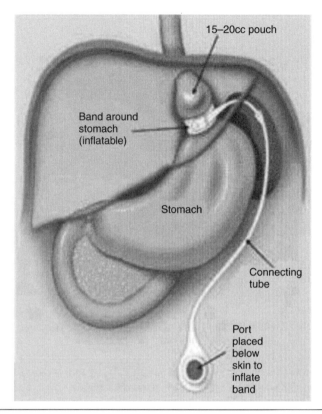

15–20cc pouch

Band around
stomach
(inflatable)

Stomach

Connecting
tube

Port
placed
below
skin to
inflate
band

Figure 4.1   Laparascopic Adjustable Gastric Band

system, this less invasive procedure is performed laporascopically. The silicone band is filled with saline and is adjustable through a reservoir that is implanted under the skin. Therefore, the band can be tightened or relaxed by injecting saline into or removing saline from the reservoir (Kushner, 2003).

Malabsorptive-restrictive surgery produces a smaller gastric pouch and leads to malabsorption of food and the "dumping syndrome." The dumping syndrome is a negative response to the consumption of simple sugars that results in the rapid emptying of food, causing nausea, cramping, diarrhea, and other symptoms. Although this syndrome is a powerful reinforcer for avoiding carbohydrates, it tends to disappear within 2 years post surgery. The most common malabsorptive-restrictive surgery is the Roux-en-Y gastric bypass (RYGB). This surgery is performed by dividing the stomach into two parts so as to create a smaller pouch. The lower part of the small intestine, the Roux limb, is then attached to the small pouch, thereby allowing food to bypass the larger stomach. The small intestine attached to the larger stomach is also then attached to the other end of the Roux limb, creating a Y-shape, so that the smaller stomach still has access to the large intestine (see Figure 4.2; Kushner, 2003).

In general, 60 to 80% of excess weight loss is achieved with maximum weight loss reached within 2 years post surgery (Aronne, 2002). More weight is lost after RYGB than after VBG and LAGB, but with greater associated risk. Mean excess weight loss at 5 years ranged from 48 to 74% after RYGB and 50 to 60% after VBG (Mitka, 2003). Mean excess weight loss was also found to be higher after RYGB than after LAGB at

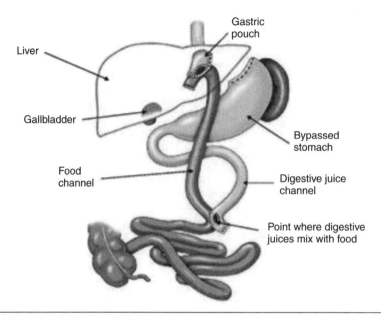

Figure 4.2 Roux-En-Y Gastric Bypass

years one and two (67 vs. 42; 67 vs. 53) but not in subsequent years (O'Brien, McPhail, Chaston, & Dixon, 2006). Other benefits of bariatric surgery include improvement or reversal of type 2 diabetes, sleep apnea, gastroesophageal reflux disease (GERD), and peripheral edema (Mitka; Sjostrom, Lissner, Wedel, & Sjostrom, 1999).

There are numerous risks associated with bariatric surgery. Up to 20% of patients eventually regain all weight lost (Aronne, 2002). Nonlaparoscopic procedures require a greater length of hospital stay and have a 20% associated risk of incisional hernia (Latifi, Kellum, De Maria, & Sugerman, 2002). Rapid weight loss is also associated with a high incidence of gallstone formation (Latifi et al.), and dietary deficiencies are common after RYGB, such as vitamin B12 and iron deficiencies, reported to occur in more than 30% of patients (Kushner, 2003). Although patients who have undergone bariatric surgery tend to maintain more weight loss as compared to diet and exercise, adverse affects are significant and the long-term consequences of bariatric surgery have yet to be determined.

In addition to the weight requirements to qualify as a candidate for surgery, a number of other criteria must be met. These include motivation and ability to follow complex pre- and post-surgical treatment regimens, adequate social support, absence of substance abuse or other psychopathology, and previous adherence to medical treatment plans (Kushner, 2003). Given these criteria, most bariatric centers and insurance companies require a psychological evaluation before the patient will be cleared or covered for surgery. In a recent survey by Bauchowitz and colleagues (2005), it was found that 88% of bariatric surgery programs across the country required patients to undergo a psychological evaluation. While it is beyond the scope of this chapter to provide a comprehensive discussion on psychological reports for bariatric surgery, some of the more relevant controversies and recommendations are highlighted.

Standardized guidelines or best practices for conducting such an evaluation are not currently available, thereby allowing for significant variability in quality and content

(Bauchowitz et al., 2005; Fabricatore, Crerand, Wadden, Sarwer, & Krasucki, 2006). Fabricatore and colleagues found that of mental health professionals surveyed who conduct these evaluations, the majority use clinical interviews, symptom inventories, and objective personality/psychopathology measures. Psychological contraindications to surgery include depression, substance abuse, bulimia nervosa, binge-eating disorder (BED), and night eating syndrome. Of these, BED is associated with greater weight regain resulting from less dietary restraint, and may therefore require pre- or post-surgical intervention (Kalarchian & Marcus, 2003). A study of psychological evaluation recommendations for bariatric surgery found that over 80% of applicants had no psychological contraindication (Powlow, O'Neil, White, & Byrne, 2005). As clinical anecdote, the authors have noted a potential confound during this type of assessment in that the patient's motivation for surgery can negatively influence the accuracy of information he or she provides during the evaluation. In conducting a presurgical psychological evaluation for bariatric surgery, the mental health provider should include a clinical assessment of aforementioned contraindicated diagnoses, an assessment of the patient's medical compliance and psychiatric history, an assessment of the patient's motivation and support for aftercare, mental status and comprehension of surgical risks involved, a detailed history of prior weight loss attempts, and diagnostic conclusions and summary recommendations. For those interested in learning more about conducting these assessments, the reader is referred to Wadden and Sarwer (2006). Because changes in diet and exercise are expected with the postsurgical bariatric patient, many of the following psychological interventions can be used with this population of weight loss patients as well.

PSYCHOLOGICAL TREATMENT

This section covers empirically supported assessment and intervention factors of psychological treatment for obesity.

Assessment

The assessment phase of treatment may take several sessions. In addition to a standard psychological intake, the following five areas of assessment should be included: (1) weight history; (2) weight loss history; (3) medical history; (4) comorbid psychological conditions; and (5) motivation, self-efficacy, and readiness to change.

Weight History   Weight history includes whether the patient was overweight as a child as well as the weight history of his or her parents and siblings. This information may indicate a biological predisposition to obesity. Children with two obese parents have an 80% chance of being overweight, compared to 40% with one obese parent and 20% when neither parent is obese (Brownwell & Stunkard, 1980). This is also an opportunity to inquire about attitudes toward weight and eating in the family, and cultural issues. For instance, if a patient is the only overweight member of his or her family, and being overweight is viewed negatively within the family, this dynamic can impact the patient's confidence and self-image. The patient should be asked about his or her highest and lowest weights as a child and as an adult. Often the patient is at his or her highest weight at the start of treatment. It is also useful to obtain a detailed weight history as an adult. The clinician can walk the patient through his or her adult years by decade to obtain average weights in the 20s, 30s, 40s, and so on. This may shed light on how major events in the patient's life have affected his or her weight. For instance, a common experience among women is weight gain related to childbirth. Other life events that can impact weight include marriage, job loss, injury, family illness, and deaths.

Weight Loss History   Obtaining a detailed weight loss history is essential. For each major weight loss effort, patients should be asked to report the methods used, their age at the time of the effort, the duration of the effort, the amount of weight lost, weight attained, length of time the patient was able to maintain this weight, and triggers to weight regain. This provides the clinician with valuable information regarding what weight loss successes and failures the patient has experienced, and which triggers are most likely to undermine success. In addition, if the patient's weight history included significant fluctuations as opposed to consistently increasing, this can indicate that resting metabolic rate has been lowered, which will be an added barrier to weight loss and may require introducing exercise at an earlier stage in the treatment. Patients should be asked about how much weight they would like to lose and why. Clinicians can then calculate the patient's current BMI and goal BMI and discuss how realistic this is. For instance, if the patient's current BMI is 38 and their goal BMI is 30, this is not a realistic initial goal, and may not even be a realistic long-term goal, depending on the patient's weight history. The clinician can also inquire about eating and exercise habits, although these will be revealed in more detail during the initial monitoring phase of treatment. For instance, the clinician can ask the patient to describe a typical day. Finally, patients can be asked about how their weight has affected other areas of their life (e.g., relationships, intimacy, employment, discrimination).

Medical History   A detailed medical history should be obtained, including any recent surgeries (i.e., bariatric) and current medications being taken. Certain medications can contribute to weight gain, such as psychiatric (e.g., Paxil) and hormone (e.g., Prednisone) medications. Clinicians should ask about cardiac, respiratory, hypertensive, or diabetic conditions that may impact treatment. Other common conditions among obese patients include sleep apnea and joint pain. This is also an opportune time to obtain releases of information from the patient to consult with his or her primary care physician and/or specialists.

Comorbid Psychological Conditions   Patients should be asked if they are currently smoking or using alcohol. Alcohol can significantly contribute to weight gain—even minimal drinking should be reduced or eliminated during weight loss treatment. If alcohol use is found to be excessive or abusive, a referral for substance abuse treatment should be provided. If the patient is currently smoking, it is not advised that they quit during the weight loss program, as this introduces too many changes at once, which can overwhelm the patient and reduce motivation. The clinician can discuss strategies for quitting during the maintenance phase of treatment (for more detail on smoking cessation, see Chapter 5). Patients may be asked about their coping skills and about current stressors that could interfere with weight loss. Many patients cope with stress by using food, so a stress management plan can be worked into the treatment. Screening for abuse history and psychological disorders such as depression and eating disorders is essential. If not directly related to obesity, treatment of these disorders may take precedence over weight loss. The prevalence of BED among obese patients seeking treatment has been estimated at 8%, and is associated with more severe obesity and an earlier onset of overweight (Stunkard, Berkowitz, Wadden, Tanrikut, Reiss, & Young, 1996). It is recommended that binge eating be brought under control before attempting weight loss (Fairburn, 1995).

Motivation, Self-Efficacy, and Readiness to Change   Finally, an assessment of how ready the patient feels to begin weight loss treatment, his or her motivation to proceed, and his or her confidence about weight loss should be conducted. A simple way to assess motivation and self-efficacy is to use a 10-point rating scale followed by a discussion of why the patient assigned him- or herself that number. This rating scale can be used throughout treatment. A discussion of barriers to change and pros and cons of treatment usually ensues, each of which should be explored in detail. For a detailed discussion of theories of behavior change (e.g., motivational interviewing, stages of change, social cognitive theory), the interested reader is referred to Chapter 3.

TREATMENT FACTORS

A crucial aspect of treatment is a comprehensive introduction and explanation of the treatment protocol. The patient should be informed that treatment factors emphasize lifestyle changes requiring commitment, time, and dedication. Moreover, the patient should be informed at the beginning of treatment that he or she will be asked to monitor and change thoughts and behaviors, and that he or she will learn new skills, such as stress management. Patients should also be instructed not to weigh themselves at home and should be weighed at each session, thereby requiring the clinician to have access to a reliable scale. This is an opportunity for the patient and clinician to discuss reactions about the weight, so as to prevent the patient from sabotaging efforts and to reinforce success. In addition, providing a time frame for the patient is helpful. Typically, behaviorally oriented weight loss programs focus on active weight loss for about 6 months (Jeffrey et al., 2000) with 3 to 6 additional months for maintenance therapy at progressively less frequent intervals (Cooper, Fairburn, & Hawker, 2003).

Clinicians can improve the quality of the services provided through interdisciplinary collaboration. When the clinician is a behavioral health provider, it is imperative that he or she consult with a supervising physician or that the patient is under the care of a medical provider during the course of treatment. The use of multiple treatment modalities to maximize outcomes requires the behavioral health clinician to become familiar with treatment approaches used by professionals in other disciplines (e.g., bariatric surgeons, registered dieticians, exercise physiologists).

Goal Setting   Discussing the patient's weight loss goals will provide valuable information regarding his or her motivations. To assess what drives the patient to adhere to the weight loss program, the clinician can ask open-ended questions, such as, "How do you see your life improved when you meet your weight loss goal?" Common sources of motivation include improved health, enhanced appearance and self-confidence, greater physical stamina and capabilities, serving as a role model for children, inspiring others (spouses, other family members) to lose weight, reduction of stress or anxiety, and improved mood. Other sources of motivation include being able to shop in regular stores, feeling younger and more energetic, reducing weight discrimination and prejudice, and decreasing physical discomfort. Knowing the patient's specific sources of motivation will help the clinician to recognize and reinforce the patient's accomplishments, thereby increasing motivation throughout the treatment process.

Many patients have unrealistic goals for weight loss, such as 30% of body weight (Foster, Wadden, Vogt, & Brewer, 1997). Most experts recommend an initial weight loss goal of 5 to 10% of body weight, and a weight loss rate of one to two pounds per week. (Rossner, 1992; Serdula, Khan, & Dietz, 2003) When client expectations exceed reasonable outcomes, they are likely to set themselves up for perceived failure, decreased motivation, and reduced adherence to their weight loss plan. As previously mentioned, even a modest weight loss of 5 to 10% of body weight can have a significant impact on health status. Goals should be established that are specific, measurable, achievable, and time limited, and clinicians should address overly ambitious expectations early in treatment to help the patient identify more realistic goals.

Self-Monitoring   Once weight loss goals and specific sources of motivation are established, the patient can begin with self-monitoring. Food records are helpful in assisting patients in seeing what they are eating and how their eating changes over time, but they are often inaccurate. Normal-weight people tend to underreport what they eat by 10 to 30%, and overweight people underreport by 30% or more (Champagne et al., 2002). While food records are often inaccurate, patients can increase their awareness of eating behaviors with self-monitoring. In addition, clinicians can assess a patient's eating and adherence to his or her weight loss program and track changes over time. Self-monitoring is, therefore, a key component to an effective weight loss program and will help identify triggers in the environment that lead to overeating or less-healthy food choices. Accuracy of self-monitoring may be improved by addressing the shame that obese patients can experience when recording their eating behaviors. The clinician can share with the patient his or her nonjudgmental stance and the value of accurate monitoring.

Self-Efficacy   Many patients have been unsuccessful in previous attempts at weight loss. Many have also lost weight but then regained it. It follows that patients are often unsure about their ability to lose weight and doubt whether they will be successful in their new attempts. An unfortunate self-fulfilling prophecy can be created, in which patients doubt their abilities and do not expect success and therefore do not work as hard as necessary to achieve success.

Expectations are closely linked with results, so some preliminary work to help patients build a sense of self-efficacy can be very useful. Clinicians can inquire about other areas in the patient's life where he or she has been successful, and reinforce all of the patient's initial efforts on his or her new weight loss program to help build confidence. For instance, the patient may have made another significant lifestyle change in the past, such as quitting smoking, or may have a successful career, and the skills used in these achievements can be identified and applied to the weight loss effort as well.

Self-Regulation   Effective treatment approaches help patients to regulate their environments such that food intake is optimal. Using stimulus control, patients can learn to keep food that triggers overeating out of their environment and eat in a way that promotes reduced food consumption. For example, patients can be advised to eat only while sitting down, so as to gain awareness and enjoyment of food ingestion. People often benefit from learning to eat more slowly and not eating in situations where they are unaware of food consumption, such as in front of the television.

Portion control is a key component of weight loss treatment. Patients are advised to not eat directly out of bags or containers and instead to measure food to appropriate servings. Behavioral treatment providers have found success with providing patients with structured meal plans. Studies have shown that providing patients with specific meal plans or boxed food led to superior outcome over patients that were given a daily caloric goal (Wing et al., 1996).

Diets Diets tend to fall into one of four groups: Low-fat diets, low-carbohydrate diets, portion-controlled diets, and fad diets. The key differences between these diets are as follows.

Low-fat diets have been popular, in part, because patients can learn to count fat grams as an alternative to counting calories. Daily fat intake of 20 to 35 percent or less is recommended (Kushner, 2003), which means eating between 20 and 35 grams of fat for each 1,000 calories in the diet. Low-fat diets however, may not be more effective than other types of weight loss diets. A meta-analysis of six clinical trials comparing advice on low-fat versus other types of weight-reducing diets concluded that low-fat diets were no better or worse than other weight-reducing diets for achieving sustained weight loss (Pirozzo, Summerbell, Cameron, & Glasziou, 2002).

There has been a recent trend toward low-carbohydrate diets, in which carbohydrate intake is restricted to 20 to 30 grams per day. Advocates of low-carbohydrate diets claim that they prevent hunger, but opponents caution that they are high in protein and fat and that they are ketogenic (the body burns its own fat for fuel, possibly leading to health consequences such as osteoporosis). Patients often experience rapid weight loss with low-carbohydrate, high-protein diets, much of which is associated with water loss. Some randomized trials have shown that low-carbohydrate diets are more effective for weight loss than a low-fat diet (Foster et al., 2003; Samaha, Iqbal, Seshadri, & Chicano, 2003). It is possible that the weight loss seen with low-carbohydrate diets is related to smaller portion sizes, leading to decreased caloric intake, which appears to be mediated by greater satiation from protein. Serdula and colleagues (2003) emphasize calorie reduction as the most significant dietary aspect of weight loss. A systematic review of 107 articles stated that there is insufficient evidence to conclude that low-carbohydrate diets are more or less effective than other diets (Bravata, Sanders, Huang, & Krumholz, 2003). Many patients find it hard to maintain a carbohydrate-restricted diet because of cravings for carbohydrates, and also report difficulty preparing and accessing low-carbohydrate food with their lifestyles.

Another common weight loss plan includes portion-controlled diets, which also result in decreased caloric intake. One of the simplest ways that portion-controlled diets are implemented is by using prepackaged foods, including drinks, frozen food, powders or formulas, and diet bars. In one study, a meal plan consisting of breakfast bars for breakfast, formula diets or a frozen lunch entree for lunch, and a frozen, calorie-controlled entree with additional vegetables for dinner resulted in weight loss which then was maintained (Flechtner-Mors et al., 2000).

The number of fad diets is endless. Evaluating all of them is beyond the scope of this text. Some diets utilize starvation and are termed "very low-calorie diets," often with caloric intake of just 200–800 calories. There are numerous side effects of very low-calorie diets, such as hair loss, thinning of the skin, coldness, increased risk of gallstones, and weight regain when the diet ends. They are, therefore, not typically sustainable approaches. Many diets that restrict food intake to a single group of food, such as grapefruit, result in a very low-calorie diet, and patients do not receive adequate nutrition. Fad diets should, therefore, be evaluated and implemented with caution. For more information regarding fad and commercial diets, the interested reader is referred to the American Dietetic Association (ADA; 2004, 2006) and Womble, Wang, and Wadden (2002).

Nutrition Guidelines   A 500 to 1000 calorie daily reduction produces weight loss of 1.25 to 2.5 lb per week (NIH & NHLBI, 1998). The AMA recommends following the food guide pyramid, with these additional guidelines: Three meals plus two snacks per day consisting of 45 to 65% from carbohydrate, 20 to 35% from fat, 10 to 35% from protein, 5 to 9 servings of fruits/vegetables, 25 to 30 grams of fiber, and two servings of low-fat dairy (Kushner, 2003).

Many obese patients lack nutritional information, such as what constitutes healthy eating, how to read food labels, caloric content, and portion sizes, and may therefore benefit from working with a registered dietician (RD). Patients may work with an RD for ongoing sessions or they may elect to see an RD for an initial consultation to create meal plans to follow. An area where RDs can be particularly helpful is in helping patients to understand and use the glycemic index (GI) to their advantage. Food that has a strong effect on blood glucose levels has a high GI (e.g., simple carbohydrates), whereas food that has a small effect on blood glucose has a low GI (e.g., complex carbohydrates). Foods with a high GI can leave a person feeling hungry even after eating a full meal. Registered dieticians can be found through the ADA. In addition to the patient working with the RD, the clinician can collaborate and communicate with the RD to be sure that consistent messages are given to the patient. If patients cannot afford or are not able to work with an RD directly, clinicians can request specific information from RDs to be sure that any information or advice they give to their patients reflects optimal standards of practice.

Cognitive-Behavioral Techniques   Cognitive-behavioral techniques focus on how thoughts influence attitude and behaviors about eating and exercise. Behavioral interventions address avoidance and ritualistic types of behaviors, which are generally discouraged. The literature supports the use of cognitive-behavioral therapy (CBT) for obesity as an effective treatment approach (Blackburn, 2002; Cooper, Fairburn, & Hawker, 2003; Wilson & Brownell, 2002).

Clinicians who use cognitive interventions help patients to monitor and challenge thoughts that interfere with weight loss. A common thinking pattern that interferes with weight loss is all-or-none thinking, such as believing that foods are either "bad" or "good" and that one needs to exercise for long periods of time in order for it to be helpful. Other cognitive distortions to address include fortune telling ("I'll never change, so why try?"), mind reading, ("I'm sure he doesn't like me because I'm fat"), overgeneralization ("My whole life stinks because I'm overweight," or "All my problems will go away once I lose weight"), and minimization of one's coping abilities or strengths ("There must be something wrong with me because I can't lose weight").

After clinicians assist patients in spotting maladaptive thought patterns, they can help them to challenge their thoughts by asking, "What's the evidence?" If, for example, a patient is working on challenging the belief that "Fat is bad," the clinician can ask, "What's the evidence that all fats are bad? Is there any evidence that some fats are healthy?" In evaluating the evidence, the patient may conclude that nothing in moderation is horrible and, in fact, that some fats (such as olive oil, nuts, and avocados) are healthy. The goal is to help patients think critically about their thoughts rather than to accept them at face value. Many patients will learn that challenging and changing their thought patterns leads to an improvement in mood (hence less risk of emotional eating) and a change in behaviors.

There are things that people who are overweight get into the habit of avoiding. Some common areas of avoidance are: weighing oneself (especially at the doctor's office), being photographed, wearing tight-fitting clothes like bathing suits or exercise apparel, engaging in sexual activity, shopping, being around attractive people, standing in certain poses, and looking in the mirror. In addition, ritualistic behaviors are often present. Rituals include activities such as checking and fixing aspects of appearance, weighing oneself frequently, or asking others for reassurance. Fixing rituals are done throughout the day, such as fixing one's shirt to hide his or her stomach.

Avoidance and ritualistic behaviors may increase anxiety, distress, and self-consciousness, and reinforce a negative body image, even after weight reduction. The solution is to reduce the avoidances and rituals and to purposefully expose oneself to the situations that feel uncomfortable. This can be accomplished with exposure therapy. When patients learn that they can experience those things that they have been avoiding, they will become more comfortable and confident. When the situations that patients avoid are initially too intimidating to face, clinicians can help patients to break these down into more manageable steps. For instance, if wearing a swimming suit at a public pool feels unbearable for a male patient, he can begin by wearing shorts and a tee shirt out in public. The next step may include a sleeveless shirt or shorter pair of shorts. Then the patient could go to the pool and keep his tee shirt on. Next he could wear only his swimming trunks in the lounge chair without getting up. Finally, he could wear only swimming trunks to the pool, and walk around and swim. Ending avoidance leads patients to feel less self-conscious and uncomfortable, and allows them to experience enjoyable activities that would otherwise have been avoided. These pleasurable activities improve mood and energy and motivation to keep up with the weight loss program. Such an intervention also teaches the patient that engaging in these types of activities is not dependent on first reaching an ideal weight, as many overweight individuals deny themselves these pleasures.

Understanding hunger cues is another useful technique. Because patients may be eating for reasons other than hunger (e.g., response to emotions or environmental cues), they can often benefit from relearning their internal cues for hunger. Patients can be taught how to rate their physical hunger before they decide to eat. Additionally, mindful eating can be employed. Many people mindlessly eat while watching television, working on the computer, or talking on the phone, and therefore are not connected to the activity of eating. Patients can be directed to eat more slowly, without distraction, to fully enjoy the food and feel more satisfied.

Patients can also be taught how to manage cravings effectively, as they are usually short lived. Active distraction techniques, such as going for a walk or telephoning a friend, can be used to get through cravings until they pass (Cooper, Fairburn, & Hawker, 2003). Further, it is important that the clinician provide extra guidance and support to help the patient manage eating at restaurants and during holidays.

Support   Support groups can be helpful for patients to be around people who face similar issues, stresses, fears, struggles, joys, celebrations, and ideas. Many people find support groups run by organizations such as Weight Watchers to be helpful. Support groups work very well when a professional is present as a facilitator, so that patients do not rely on misinformation from other group members.

Patients should also be encouraged to utilize their natural support network. A study by Wing and Jeffrey (1999) found that social support improved long-term weight maintenance. The "support by friends" group was the most effective of the various groups in the study, showing a long-term maintenance of 66% over 6 months. In contrast, people who were recruited for the study without the support of friends (but did receive behavioral treatment maintenance) showed a 24% maintenance rate.

Exercise If the patient is not already actively exercising, it is not recommended that an exercise program be initiated at the beginning of treatment. Implementing too many goals and changes at once can be a setup for failure. Cooper, Fairburn, and Hawker (2003) recommend that a focus on exercise be delayed until consistent weight loss has been established. However, the patient can be instructed early in the treatment to gradually structure his or her lifestyle to increase activity levels, such as walking instead of driving or using the stairs instead of the elevator. Once the weight loss program is under way, including dietary and cognitive-behavioral changes, a more formal exercise program can be introduced. It is recommended that patients gradually build up to 30 to 45 minutes of moderate exercise three to five times per week (NIH & NHLBI, 1998). Consulting with the patient's physician at this point is crucial, especially for those with cardiac or respiratory conditions. It may also be necessary to address any anxiety or shame the patient may feel about being in a gym and/or wearing tight-fitting exercise clothes.

Exercise is not sufficient for weight loss when eating habits are not also addressed. Research by the NIH and the NHLBI (1998) indicates that diet or diet plus exercise generally produces greater weight loss than does exercise alone. One study showed minimal effects of exercise alone (approximately 0.1 kg/week) except in military recruits (1.8 kg/week) who exercised very rigorously (Lee, Kumar, & Leong, 1994). Typically exercise plus nutritional changes produce the most effective weight loss.

General activity level and physical exercise, however, are perhaps the most important components of long-term weight loss (Jakicic, Winters, Lang, & Wing, 1999). The National Weight Control Registry tracked people who successfully maintained their weight loss over 5.5 years. They found that only 9% reported maintaining their weight *without* regular physical activity. This means that 91% of those who were able to keep their weight off engaged in regular activity that was typically a combination of lifestyle and programmed exercise. Another study showed that the maintenance of weight loss was directly related to the amount of exercise that individuals continued after their initial treatment (Schoeller, Shay, & Kushner, 1997).

Patients can benefit greatly from working with a personal trainer or exercise physiologist. A trainer will oversee the exercise plan and ensure that the regimen is designed to burn an optimal number of calories and provide strength or resistance training. Personal training can be particularly helpful at the beginning of a patient's exercise program to ensure that the program is designed effectively and to prevent injury. Clinicians can collaborate with personal trainers to be sure that each professional communicates a consistent message to the patient.

Body Image Body image is one's relationship with his or her body. Body image is not the objective view of the patient's body, but rather the mental image and associated feelings that he or she holds about his or her body. Some of what patients see is based on the objective physical reality of their appearance. However, a patient can look in a mirror and experience a distorted view of him- or herself (Cash, 1995). This can result from too much focus on one physical feature that the patient perceives negatively and then overgeneralizes as representative of his or her entire body. Body image can be a major obstacle in moving from the weight loss phase of treatment to the maintenance phase if patients feel dissatisfied with their appearance after losing a realistic amount of weight (Cooper et al., 2003). Therefore, it is advisable to address body image concerns after significant weight loss has been achieved but before moving into maintenance. Addressing behavior that maintains a negative body image, such as body avoidance, was discussed previously with exposure as an intervention. Patients can also be challenged to consider how realistic their ideal body shape is and whether they unfairly compare themselves to society's stereotypes of beauty. Cognitive therapy regarding a patient's changing body and body image can be a useful adjunct (Rosen, Orosan, & Reiter, 1995).

Many obese patients have a negative body image, and there may not be a direct relationship between body image and weight or weight loss. While studies show that body image typically does improve with weight loss, additional weight loss is not associated with greater improvements in body image. It is hypothesized that small amounts of weight loss leads to improved body image; however, further improvement does not occur with further weight loss (Brown, Cash, & Mikulka, 1990). A study by Adami, Gandolfo, Bauer, and Scopinaro (1995) examined people's body image after they lost weight. Findings revealed that those who became obese early in life had a negative body image after weight loss. Their body image had solidified during their teens and continued even after losing weight. On the other hand, those who became obese later in life had body image satisfaction following weight loss similar to people of normal weight who had no history of obesity.

Discrimination and Multicultural Issues   A change motivator for many patients is to reduce the discrimination they experience as an obese person. While this motivator can help patients adhere to their treatment program, it can also create difficulties. A treatment success (considered to be 5 to 10% of initial weight) may involve the patient remaining overweight and a target for prejudice and discrimination even after his or her weight loss goals have been achieved. This is especially true for morbidly obese patients, who have a significant amount of weight to lose. Clinicians should be cognizant of this and discuss issues of weight discrimination with their patients. Moreover, clinicians should be sensitive to the patient's associations to terms such as "obese" or "overweight."

Additionally, patients experience various multicultural issues that can either improve or reduce the effectiveness of their weight loss program, in part dependent on the multicultural sensitivity of the clinician. For example, a clinician may recommend an eating program that does not feature foods consistent with the patient's cultural norms and tastes. Instead, patients can be taught how to prepare foods that are part of their culture in more healthful ways, for example, by baking instead of frying food items. As well as differences in diet, minority cultures have varying ideal body shapes and sizes that may conflict with the average American ideal. This could have an impact on minority patients' weight loss goals.

Clinicians should be aware of the patient's socioeconomic situation and take the costs of food and exercise programs into account when helping patients create and adhere to a weight loss program. If patients are concerned about ongoing financial investments to lose or maintain their weight, they are less likely to be successful. Clinicians can spend some time brainstorming low- or no-cost eating and exercise plans with patients, and help patients learn how to overcome their own concerns. For example, if a patient is concerned that she cannot afford a gym membership, her clinician can help her plan to walk outside in a safe area or up and down stairs in her apartment building, and do push-ups and sit-ups at home. Patients can purchase a set of free weights to lift at home, along with an inexpensive exercise video. It is important that clinicians inquire about the patient's cultural and individual backgrounds and experiences, and problem-solve with patients as they confront obstacles to long-term weight loss.

Maintenance   Although behavioral treatments for obesity have been proven effective, most weight lost is regained over the succeeding 3 years (Jeffrey et al., 2000; Perri, 1998, 2002). To prevent this, researchers have focused on the importance of the maintenance phase of treatment (Cooper, Fairburn, & Hawker, 2003; Perri, 1998, 2002). Because most patients will reach their maximum weight loss at the 6-month mark of active treatment (Jeffrey et al., 2000), it is recommended that maintenance therapy begin around this time, meaning that a focus on active weight loss will be replaced with a focus on keeping the weight off. Patients may continue to lose weight, but the focus should shift to how the patient can reasonably and comfortably maintain the current weight. If the patient is on a restrictive low-calorie diet or an intense exercise regimen, these will need to be adjusted to a more realistic long-term level at which weight gain can still be prevented. Furthermore, it is not sufficient to spend only a few sessions on maintenance. The maintenance phase is now seen as a central component of weight loss therapy and may require up to 6 months (Cooper, Fairburn, and Hawker, 2003). As the patient becomes skilled at maintaining the current weight and ingraining the many behavioral and cognitive changes into his or her lifestyle, the clinician can begin tapering the sessions from once per week to once every 2 weeks to once per month to prepare for termination.

It is helpful to address cognitive barriers to long-term weight maintenance and to emphasize the differences between weight loss and weight maintenance, some of which include lack of ongoing reinforcement of weight loss (the numbers on the scale going down), and potentially the need to accept a goal weight that was not the patient's original goal (Cooper, Fairburn, and Hawker, 2003). Additionally, while weight loss elicits reinforcement such as praise from others, maintaining the weight loss may not (Anderson & Wadden, 1999). During the maintenance phase, the clinician should also focus on preventing and managing relapse to old eating habits.

As previously mentioned, ongoing exercise is a key component to weight maintenance. A meta-analysis of 493 studies involving aerobic exercise in moderately overweight subjects found that those who participated in exercise alone lost 2.9 kg, the diet-only group lost 10.7 k, and those who combined diet and exercise lost 11.0 kg. Importantly, 6.6 kg weight loss was maintained in the diet-only group, whereas the diet and exercise group maintained 8.6 kg of weight loss after 1 year (Miller, Koceja, & Hamilton, 1997). One research team found that formerly obese women who were successful at maintaining their weight loss for 1 year participated in approximately 80 minutes per day of moderate-intensity activity or 35 minutes per day of vigorous activity (Schoeller et al., 1997).

Weight loss coaching is another strategy that can be used during the maintenance phase. Coaching can be seen as a method to help patients adhere to a treatment protocol created by a behaviorist or other weight loss clinician. This approach can help patients to stay on track, have ongoing support and accountability, remain motivated, and successfully achieve goals. Coaching can therefore be particularly useful after treatment terminates to help patients continue with their new lifestyle.

CHILDREN AND ADOLESCENTS

While it is beyond the scope of this chapter to provide a comprehensive discussion of obesity in childhood and adolescence, issues distinct to this younger patient population will be reviewed. Readers interested in learning more about this topic are referred to *Pediatric Obesity: Prevention, Intervention, and Treatment Strategies for Primary Care*, published by the American Academy of Pediatrics.

Parallel to the rise in adult obesity, there has been a similar trend among American children and adolescents, and obese children are at greater risk of becoming obese adults. Seventy to 80% of obese children and adolescents are likely to remain obese into adulthood (Moran, 1999). Associated health risks among obese adults, such as type 2 diabetes, and psychological problems, such as depression, are similar among obese children and teens. The 95th percentile and higher is considered overweight for children and adolescents (USDHHS, 2001). Pharmacotherapy and bariatric surgery are not recommended for use with this population. However, psychological treatment, detailed previously, can be age adjusted and implemented, with some added considerations. In fact, evidence suggests that behavioral treatments for obesity may be more effective for children and adolescents than adults (Epstein, Valoski, Kalarchian, & McCurley, 1995).

Adopting a systems approach to treatment is useful when working with children and adolescents. Because changes in diet and activity level for children must be age appropriate, it is worthwhile for clinicians to collaborate with the patient's pediatrician. The school and family environment should also be factored into treatment. Many school systems allow vending machines that dispense unhealthy food options, thereby undermining healthy eating efforts (Center for Science in the Public Interest, 2004). During teen years, fast food and junk food are the norm, and it may mean going against peer values to make dietary changes. Furthermore, the discrimination that obese teenagers experience is more overt. Because the peer group is so relevant during adolescence, taunting about weight can be especially detrimental to self-esteem and can lead to social isolation.

Families have a highly influential role in eating and activity habits with children, more so than with teens. In treatment, the clinician can make use of modeling by helping parents to recognize that their children will tend to like foods that they see around the home and that they see their parents eat. This may require having parents meet with an RD to discover what constitutes healthy eating. Further, children will get their cues regarding activity levels from what they see their parents doing, what parents' expectations are, and what is reinforced (Epstein, 1986). Clinicians can model positive reinforcement for parents during family sessions. Parents should also be discouraged from using food as reinforcement for desired behaviors. Many obese children and adolescents also have one or more overweight or obese parent. In addition, overweight and obesity in children and adolescents may be symptomatic of family discord, similar to that seen in families of anorexic and bulimic patients. Therefore, a family approach to addressing dynamics, increasing activity, and changing diet may be more effective than focusing solely on the young patient. Parents who adopt a healthy lifestyle will be more effective at encouraging and reinforcing such behavior with their children.

CASE ILLUSTRATION

Jen, a 43-year-old Caucasian female, was referred for treatment by her bariatric surgeon. She had undergone RYGB two years prior. Before the surgery, the patient had weighed 322 lb (BMI = 53.6; severe/extreme obesity), and her lowest weight after the surgery was 195 lb (BMI = 32.4; mild obesity). At the time of evaluation, her current weight was 216 (BMI = 35.9; moderate obesity), with a goal weight of 160 lb (BMI = 26.6; overweight). Jen had not experienced the dumping syndrome post surgery and was frustrated and concerned by her recent weight regain of approximately 20 lb. She had met with her surgeon to discuss the possibility that the surgery had failed and to explore revision surgery. Her surgeon suggested that she first pursue behavioral strategies.

Although Jen had undergone a presurgical psychological evaluation with another provider, her history of binge eating was not addressed. As Jen reported during initial sessions, she had a significant history of binge eating beginning at the age of six. She reported eating to the point of involuntary vomiting several times per week for most of her life. She was overweight as a child as early as she could remember and reported that her parents and her brother were of a "normal" weight. Before opting for surgery, she had made multiple attempts at weight loss, including Weight Watchers, liquid diets, and low-carbohydrate diets. Although she had some success with these approaches, she was not able to maintain the weight loss for more than 6 months. The patient was single, had a sparse recent dating history, and felt that her obesity had contributed to her social isolation. Her medical history included type 2 diabetes, and a myocardial infarction that had lead to quadruple coronary artery bypass graft surgery. Since the RYGB, her diabetes had reversed and she no longer required related medications. Her current medications included prescriptions for hypertension and high LDL cholesterol.

The patient denied any history of emotional, physical, or sexual abuse, and denied any history or current use of drugs, alcohol, or tobacco. She did not meet criteria for depression and denied any psychiatric history. The patient did not meet criteria for an eating disorder, with the exception of her binge-eating history. Jen reported using food as a way to cope with stress, boredom, and other emotions. On a 10-point scale, she reported her motivation for treatment as 9 and her confidence regarding weight loss as 5, stating that past failures were impacting this confidence.

Initial treatment sessions focused on how realistic her ideal BMI was, her fears that the surgery had failed, and the self-blame associated with this. The patient was of above average intelligence, had obtained a graduate degree, worked as a professional and felt successful in most other areas of her life. However, as it pertained to her weight, the patient classified herself as "a total failure" and suffered with a negative body image. It was discussed with the patient how BED can impact the outcome of bariatric surgery and how the surgery itself does not address this problem. Although the patient was not currently binge eating to the point of vomiting, for fear of "stomach rupture," she did continue to snack continuously throughout the day, mostly on carbohydrates. The patient expressed extreme frustration that she had not experienced the dumping syndrome as a result of the surgery, as she had been counting on this to dissuade her from her "addiction" to carbohydrates. The patient was referred to a nutritionist to begin monitoring her diet.

Over the course of 6 months, the patient learned many cognitive-behavioral strategies. These included stress management, mindful eating, changing her environment by substituting high-carbohydrate with low-carbohydrate snacks, managing cravings with distraction, and identifying emotions that triggered binge eating. Stress management included diaphragmatic breathing and progressive muscle relaxation. The patient was taught these skills and instructed to practice using them before making food choices. Jen felt overwhelmed by the abundance of food choices in the work setting and often impulsively reacted by overeating. By using relaxation skills, she had time to scan her environment and make a more controlled and healthy food choice. Jen was also taught mindful eating. This consisted of two steps. The first was relearning signs of hunger by identifying and rating her physiological symptoms of hunger (stomach feeling empty, stomach growling, fatigue) and to distinguish these from environmental or emotional triggers to eating. Jen noted that she ate to "fill emptiness" in her life more often than to fill emptiness in her stomach. She was able to gain some control over these triggers and more often eat as a response to physiological hunger. Because Jen would frequently become anxious before rating her physiological hunger, she was encouraged to use relaxation skills before rating, which she found helpful. The second step in mindful eating focused on eating more slowly while increasing awareness of the food. Given Jen's extensive binge-eating history, she tended to dissociate while eating and to eat very quickly. This step was therefore challenging for Jen, and she reported finding it to be psychologically painful to be more aware of the food she was eating. She was instructed to progressively lengthen the period of time it took her to eat a meal, to eat at the dining room table instead of in front of the television, to chew slowly and focus on the tastes and textures of the food, and to take breaks in between bites. She revealed that this was painful for her because eating was not something she fully enjoyed, but was rather a great source of conflict and emotional avoidance. Through this exercise, we were able to begin to identify her emotions and thoughts that had triggered binges in the past and continued to currently undermine her control over eating.

Jen was consistently exercising three times per week; however, she was only able to exercise at a moderate level, given her cardiac history. Exercise, particularly walking, was useful for Jen as a distraction technique to manage cravings. She was weighed weekly in the psychologist's office and was instructed to avoid the scale at home. Because Jen was not losing but rather maintaining weight, weekly weighing was a source of frustration that often required time to process in order to prevent her from undermining her progress at gaining more control over her eating patterns. Because the number on the scale was not moving down, Jen's sense of being a failure felt reinforced. Given that Jen had little support in her life, we worked on increasing her support system. She also had some difficulty asserting herself with others, so assertiveness skills were role-played in session, although she was reluctant to use these. Later in treatment she shared that she had joined a popular dating service and was giving it a try. At that point, body image work became the focus of treatment, as she had concerns regarding intimacy with her current weight. She had been putting many things on hold until after she had reached her ideal weight, and we discussed how much pressure this placed on her. Jen engaged in body avoidance frequently (avoiding mirrors, shopping for clothes, physical intimacy). Body image work therefore focused on reducing avoidance and increasing acceptance of her current shape and weight through exposure.

Although Jen had successfully implemented many of the change strategies learned, her weight remained around 220 lb. After 6 months of treatment, we discussed the reality that she may not be able to lose any more weight and that her focus may need to shift to maintaining this weight. Jen shared that she felt like a failure, and we focused on reframing this experience. In fact, Jen had still lost over 100 lb from the surgery, had minimized binge eating, and had employed many new skills to increase control of her eating. In addition, she had tackled difficult subjects, such as intimacy and body image, related to her weight. Jen was able to spend the last 3 months of treatment focused on maintenance but continued to feel disappointed and frustrated by her surgical outcome. Toward the end of treatment she revisited her bariatric surgeon to discuss once again the possibility of revision surgery. The surgeon was reluctant to pursue this as it was his opinion that the risks of surgery at that point far outweighed the benefits.

CONCLUSION

Obesity poses serious health risk, decreased quality of life, and increased health care expenditures. While obesity has reached epidemic proportions, treatment options have expanded. These include psychological treatments, pharmacotherapy, and bariatric surgery. Research continues to investigate the efficacy and risks associated with these interventions. A multifaceted approach to the reduction of obesity in the United States is needed, which may include changes in environment, policy, and priorities as a society.

REFERENCES

Adami, G. F., Gandolfo, P., Bauer, B., & Scopinaro, N. (1995). Binge eating in massively obese patients undergoing bariatric surgery. *International Journal of Eating Disorders, 17,* 45–50.

American Dietetic Association. (2004). *Nutrition fact sheet: Popular diets reviewed.* Retrieved January 5, 2007, from http://www.eatright.org/ada/files/popdiets_fact_2-04.pdf

American Dietetic Association. (2006). *Nutrition fact sheet: Popular diets reviewed, part 2.* Retrieved January 5, 2007, from http://www.eatright.org/ada/files/0106_Pop_Diets_Reviewed_(2)_1_5_05.pdf

Anderson, D. A., & Wadden, T. A. (1999). Treating the obese patient: Suggestions for primary care practice. *Archives of Family Medicine, 8,* 156–167.

Aronne, L. J. (2002). Treatment of obesity in the primary care setting. In T. A. Wadden & A. J. Stunkard (Eds.), *Handbook of obesity treatment* (pp. 383–394). New York: Guilford.

Baron, R. B. (1997). Obesity. In M. D. Feldman & J. F. Christensen (Eds.), *Behavioral medicine in primary care: A practical guide* (pp. 150–156). Stamford, CT: Appleton & Lange.

Bauchowitz, A. U., Gonder-Frederick, L. A., Olbrisch, M. E., Azarbad, L., Ryee, M. Y., Woodson, M., et al. (2005). Psychosocial evaluation of bariatric surgery candidates: A survey of present practices. *Psychosomatic Medicine, 67*(5), 825–832.

Blackburn, G. L. (2002). Weight loss and risk factors. In C. G. Fairburn & K. D. Brownell (Eds.), *Eating disorders and obesity: A comprehensive handbook* (2nd ed., 484–489). New York: Guilford.

Bravata, D. M., Sanders, L., Huang, J., & Krumholz, H. M. (2003). Efficacy and safety of low-carbohydrate diets: A systematic review. *Journal of the American Medical Association, 289,* 1837.

Brown, T. A., Cash, T. F., & Mikulka, P. J. (1990.) Attitudinal body image assessment: Factor analysis of the Body-Self Relations Questionnaire. *Journal of Personality Assessment, 55,* 135–144.

Brownell, K., & Nestle, M. (2004, June 7). Are you responsible for your own weight? *Time, 163,* 113.

Brownwell, K. D., & Stunkard, A. J. (1980). Childhood obesity. In A. J. Stunkard (Ed.), *Obesity.* Philadelphia: Saunders.

Cash, T. (1995). *What do you see when you look in the mirror? Helping yourself to a positive body image.* New York: Bantam.

Center for Science in the Public Interest. (2004). *Dispensing junk: How school vending undermines efforts to feed children well.* Retrieved January 5, 2007, from http://www.cspinet.org/new/pdf/dispensing_junk.pdf

Champagne, C. M., Bray, G. A., Kurtz, A. A., Monteiro, J. B., Tucker, E., Volaufova, J., et al. (2002). Energy intake and energy expenditure: A controlled study comparing dietitians and non-dietitians. *Journal of the American Diet Association, 102,* 1428.

Colditz, G. A., Willet, W. C., Rotnitzky, A., & Manson, J. E. (1995). Weight gain as a risk factor for clinical diabetes mellitus in women. *Annals of Internal Medicine, 122*(7), 481–486.

Cooper, Z., Fairburn, C. G., & Hawker, D. M. (2003). *Cognitive-behavioral treatment of obesity: A clinician's guide.* New York: Guilford.

Epstein, L. H. (1986). Treatment of childhood obesity. In K. D. Brownell & J. P. Foreyt (Eds.), *Handbook of eating disorders* (pp. 159–178). New York: Basic Books.

Epstein, L. H., Valoski, A. M., Kalarchian, M. A., & McCurley, J. (1995). Do children lose and maintain weight easier than adults: A comparison of child and parent weight changes from six months to ten years. *Obesity Research, 3,* 411–417.

Fabricatore, A. N., Crerand, C. E., Wadden, T. A., Sarwer, D. B., & Krasucki, J. L. (2006). How do mental health professionals evaluate candidates for bariatric surgery? Survey results. *Obesity Surgery, 16*(5), 567–573.

Fairburn, C. G. (1995). *Overcoming binge eating.* New York: Guilford.

Finer, N. (2002). Sibutramine: Its mode of action and efficacy. *International Journal of Obesity, 26,* S29–S33.

Flechtner-Mors, M., Ditschuneit, H. H., Johnson, T. D., Suchard, M. A., & Adler, G. (2000). Metabolic and weight loss effects of long-term dietary intervention in obese patients: Four-year results. *Obesity Research, 8,* 399.

Foster, G. D., Wadden, T. A., Vogt, R. A., & Brewer, G. (1997). What is a reasonable weight loss? Patients' expectations and evaluations of obesity treatment outcomes. *Journal of Consulting and Clinical Psychology, 65,* 79–85.

Foster, G. D., Wyatt, H. R., Hill, J. O., McGuckin, B. G., Brill, C., Mohammed, B. S., et. al. (2003). A randomized trial of a low-carbohydrate diet for obesity. *New England Journal of Medicine, 348* (21), 2082–2090.

Freudenheim, M. (2003, August 29). Hospitals pressured by soaring demand for obesity surgery. *New York Times,* sect 1.

Glaeser, E., Shapiro, J., & Cutler, D. (2003, December 13). Make it cheaper, and cheaper. *Economist, 369,* 6–9.

Jakicic, J. M., Winters, C., Lang, W., & Wing, R. R. (1999). Effects of intermittent exercise and use of home exercise equipment on adherence, weight loss, and fitness in overweight women: A randomized trial. *Journal of the American Medical Association, 282,* 1554.

Jeffery R. W., Drewnowski, A., Epstein, L., Stunkard, A. J., Wilson, G. T., Wing, R. R., et al. (2000). Long-term maintenance of weight loss: Current status. *Health Psychology, 19,* 5–16.

Kalarchian, M. A., & Marcus, M. D. (2003). Management of the bariatric surgery patient: Is there a role for the cognitive behavior therapist? *Cognitive and Behavioral Practice, 10,* 112–119.

Knowler, W. C., Barrett-Connor, E., Fowler, S. E., Hamman, R. F., Lachin, J. M., Walker, E. A., et al. (2002). Reduction in the incidence of type 2 diabetes with lifestyle intervention or metformin. *New England Journal of Medicine, 346,* 393–403.

Kushner, R. F. (2003). *Roadmaps for clinical practice: Case studies in disease prevention and health promotion-assessment and management of adult obesity: A primer for physicians.* Chicago: American Medical Association.

Latifi, R., Kellum, J. M., De Maria, E. J., & Sugerman, H. J. (2002). Surgical treatment of obesity. In T. A. Wadden & A. J. Stunkard (Eds.), *Handbook of obesity treatment* (pp. 339–356). New York: Guilford.

Lee, L., Kumar, S., & Leong, L.C. (1994). The impact of five-month basic military training on the body weight and body fat of 197 moderately to severely obese Singaporean males aged 17 to 19 years. *International Journal of Obesity Related Metabolic Disorders 18*(2), 105–109.

Leung, W. Y., Thomas, G. N., Chan, J. C., & Tomlinson, B. (2003). Weight management and current options in pharmacotherapy: Orlistat and Sibutramine. *Clinical Therapeutics, 25*(1), 58–80.

Lucas, K. H., & Kaplan-Machlis, B. (2001). Orlistat—a novel weight loss therapy. *Annals of Pharmacotherapy, 35,* 314–328.

Miller, W. C., Koceja, D. M., & Hamilton, E. J. (1997). A meta-analysis of the past 25 years of weight loss research using diet, exercise or diet plus exercise intervention. *International Journal of Obesity, 21,* 941.

Mitka, M. (2003). Surgery for obesity: Demand soars amid scientific, ethical questions. *Journal of the American Medical Association, 289,* 1761–1762.

Moran, R. (1999). Evaluation and treatment of childhood obesity. *American Family Physician, 59*(4), 861.

National Alliance for Nutrition and Activity. (2002). *From wallet to waistline: The hidden cost of super sizing.* Retrieved January 5, 2007, from http://www.cspinet.org/w2w.pdf

National Center for Health Statistics. (2006). *Health, United States, 2006.* Washington, DC: U.S. Government Printing Office.

National Institutes of Health and National Heart, Lung and Blood Institute. (1998). *Obesity education initiative: Clinical guidelines on the identification, evaluation, and treatment of overweight and obesity in adults.* Bethesda, MD: U.S. Department of Health and Human Services.

Newman, C. (2004, August). Why are we so fat? *National Geographic, 4,* 48–61.

O'Brien, P. E., McPhail, T., Chaston, T. B., & Dixon, J. B. (2006). Systematic review of medium-term weight loss after bariatric operations. *Obesity Surgery, 16*(8), 1032–1040.

Padwal, R., Li, S. K., & Lau, D. C. (2004). Long-term pharmacotherapy for obesity and overweight. *Cochrane Database of Systematic Reviews, 3,* CD004094.

Perri, M. G. (1998). The maintenance of treatment effects in the long-term management of obesity. *Clinical Psychology: Science and Practice, 5,* 526–543.

Perri, M. G. (2002). Improving maintenance in behavioral treatment. In C. G. Fairburn & K. D. Brownell (Eds.), *Eating disorders and obesity: A comprehensive handbook* (2nd ed., 593–598). New York: Guilford.

Pirozzo, S., Summerbell, C., Cameron, C., & Glasziou, P. (2002). *Advice on low-fat diets for obesity.* Cochrane Database System Review, CD003640.

Powlow, L. A., O'Neil, P. M., White, M. A., & Byrne, T. K. (2005). Findings and outcomes of psychological evaluations of gastric bypass applicants. *Surgery for Obesity and Related Diseases,*1(6), 523–527.

Rosen, J. C., Orosan, P., and Reiter, J. (1995). Cognitive behavior therapy for negative body image in obese women. *Behavior Therapy, 26,* 25–42.

Rossner, S. (1992). Factors determining the long-term outcome of obesity treatment. In P. Bjorntorp & B.N. Brodoff (Eds.), *Obesity.* Philadelphia: Lipincott.

Samaha, F. F., Iqbal, N., Seshadri, P., & Chicano, K. L. (2003). A low-carbohydrate as compared with a low-fat diet in severe obesity. *New England Journal of Medicine, 348,* 2074.

Schoeller, D. A., Shay, K., & Kushner, R. F. (1997). How much physical activity is needed to minimize weight gain in previously obese women? *America Journal of Clinical Nutrition, 66*(3), 551–556.

Seidell, J. C., Verschuren, W. M., van Leer, E. M., & Kromhout, D. (1996). Overweight, underweight, and mortality: A prospective study of 48,287 men and women. *Archives of Internal Medicine, 1569,* 958–963.

Serdula, M. K., Khan, L. K., & Dietz, W. H. (2003). Weight loss counseling revisited. *Journal of the American Medical Association, 289*(14), 1747–1750.

Sjostrom, C. D., Lissner, L., Wedel, H., & Sjostrom, L. (1999). Reduction in incidence of diabetes, hypertension and lipid disturbances after intentional weight loss induced by bariatric surgery: The SOS intervention study. *Obesity Research, 7,* 477–484.

Stein, C. J., & Colditz, G. A. (2005). Obesity. In C. N. Dulmus & L. A. Rapp-Paglicci (Eds.), *Handbook of preventive interventions for adults* (pp. 252–279). Hoboken, NJ: Wiley.

Stunkard, A. J., Berkowitz, R., Wadden, T., Tanrikut, C., Reiss, E., & Young, L. (1996). Binge eating disorder and the night eating syndrome. *International Journal of Obesity, 20,* 1–6.

Stunkard, A., Harris, J., Pederson, N., & McClearn, G. E. (1990). The body-mass index of twins who have been reared apart. *New England Journal of Medicine, 322,* 1483–1487.

U.S. Department of Health and Human Services. (2001). *The Surgeon General's call to action to prevent and decrease overweight and obesity.* Rockville, MD: U.S. Department of Health and Human Services, Public Health Service, Office of the Surgeon General.

Wadden, T. A., & Sarwer, D. B. (2006). Behavioral assessment of candidates for bariatric surgery: A patient-oriented approach. *Surgery for Obesity and Related Diseases, 2*(2), 171–179.

Wilson, G. T., & Brownell, K. D. (2002). Behavioral treatment for obesity. In C. G. Fairburn & K. D. Brownell (Eds.), *Eating disorders and obesity: A comprehensive handbook* (2nd ed., 484–489). New York: Guilford.

Wing, R. R., & Jeffrey, R. W. (1999). Benefits of recruiting participants with friends and increasing social support for weight loss and maintenance. *Journal of Consulting and Clinical Psychology, 67*(1), 132–238.

Wing, R. R., Jeffrey, R. W., Burton, L. R., Thorson, C., Sperber-Nissinoff, K., & Baxter, J. E. (1996). Food provision vs. structured meal plans in the behavioral treatment of obesity. *International Journal of Obesity, 20,* 56–62.

Witteman, J. C., Willet, W. C., Stampfer, M. J., Colditz, G. A., Sacks, F. M., Speizer, F. E., et al. (1989). A prospective study of nutritional factors and hypertension among U. S. women. *Circulation, 80*(5), 1320–1327.

Womble, L. G., Wang, S. S., & Wadden, T. A. (2002). Commercial and self-help weight loss programs. In T. A. Wadden & A. J. Stunkard (Eds.), *Handbook of obesity treatment* (pp. 395–415). New York: Guilford.

CHAPTER 5

Tobacco Cessation

M. INDIRA PAHARIA

INTRODUCTION

Tobacco use takes various forms, including smoking (cigarette, cigar, and pipe) and smokeless (snuff and chewing tobacco). Cigarette smoking is the most common form of tobacco use, and is therefore the focus of this chapter. However, the treatment described may be appropriate for other types of tobacco use, as nicotine in all types of tobacco causes addiction (U.S. Department of Health and Human Services [USDHHS], 1988).

The words of U.S. Surgeon General Koop, spoken over 2 decades ago, hold true today: "Cigarette smoking is the chief, single avoidable cause of death in our society and the most important public health issue of our time" (USDHHS, 1982, p. 9). Smoking causes more deaths than AIDS, cocaine, heroin, alcohol, auto accidents, fires, homicides, and suicides combined (Dodgen, 2005). Although smoking has sharply declined in the United States since 1965, when nearly 42% of Americans over the age of 18 smoked, nearly 21% of this population continues to smoke today (National Center for Health Statistics [NCHS], 2006). In general, men smoke more than women (23% vs. 19%), and among minority groups, smoking rates are highest for American Indian or Alaska Native men (34%) and women (29%). Smoking is three times more likely among adults with less than a high school education, as compared to those with an education at the bachelor's level or higher. Nearly one-quarter of high school students are also current smokers (NCHS, 2006; see Figure 5.1).

More than 430,000 Americans die each year as a result of cigarette smoking (Centers for Disease Control and Prevention [CDC], 1997b). Over 90% of smokers know that smoking is harmful to their health, yet they continue to smoke (Rigotti, 1997). Cigarette smoking causes several types of cancer (lung, oral, bladder, larynx, esophagus, and pharynx), heart disease, and chronic obstructive pulmonary disease (COPD), and significantly contributes to stroke and other cancers (cervical, pancreatic, and kidney; USDHHS, 2000b, 2004). Smokeless tobacco also causes oral cancer (USDHHS, 2000b). Seventy-five percent of deaths from oral and pharyngeal cancer are caused by tobacco use (CDC, 2000). Smoking is responsible for 80 to 90% of COPD deaths and approximately 90% of lung cancer deaths (CDC, 2004). Women who use oral contraceptives and smoke are at increased risk of myocardial infarction and stroke (Rigotti, 1997). For most, tobacco use eventually takes its toll in deteriorating quality of life

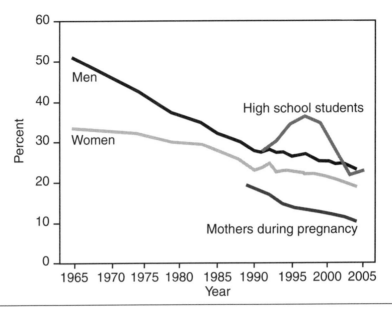

Figure 5.1 Cigarette smoking

and related emotional suffering. Our society as a whole also pays a high price for this addiction.

The economic impact of tobacco use is staggering. In developed countries, up to 15% of total health care expenditures is attributed to smoking (Parrott & Godfrey, 2005). Even so, the majority of the world's tobacco consumption is found in developing countries, with China and India as the largest consumers, respectively. Second-hand smoke is estimated to account for 19% of American health care expenditures on childhood respiratory conditions (Parrott & Godfrey). The total annual cost of smoking in the United States is over $167 billion, including $92 billion in productivity losses (indirect costs) and $75.5 billion in medical expenditures (direct costs; CDC, 2005).

TREATMENT

The demand for smoking cessation has never been higher, and is driven by policies that ban public and workplace smoking, by the smokers themselves, and by health care providers. Smoking ban policies have resulted in large part from rising smoking-related health care costs. Smokers on average cost employers 25% more in health care than nonsmokers (Cornwell, 2006). Seventy percent of smokers want to quit smoking completely (CDC, 1997a), but each year, only 7% of the 46% of smokers who attempt to quit are abstinent a year later (USDHHS, 2000c). Given the health consequences of tobacco use, health care providers see the value of incorporating smoking cessation into medical treatment plans. For instance, quitting smoking, even after a diagnosis of COPD, can substantially slow the progression of this disease (for more information on COPD, the interested reader is referred to Chapter 12).

Smoking is strongly reinforced for a variety of reasons. First, it is highly physiologically addictive. Second, because cigarettes are readily available and legal, the habit of smoking pervades the smoker's life and becomes associated with most daily activities. Addressing this physiological addiction and continuous behavioral reinforcement is the cornerstone of treatment.

Assessment

The assessment phase of treatment may take several sessions. In addition to a standard psychological intake, the following five areas should be addressed: (1) nicotine addiction; (2) smoking and quit history; (3) medical history; (4) comorbid psychological conditions; and (5) motivation, self-efficacy, and readiness to change.

Nicotine Addiction   Cigarette smoke consists of over 4,800 chemicals, 69 of which are known carcinogens (CDC, 2004). Patients are often surprised to learn of certain cigarette contents, such as tar, ammonia, formaldehyde, carbon monoxide, and pesticide and fungicide residues. The addictive substance in tobacco is nicotine, and has been found to be as physically addictive as cocaine or heroin (USDHHS, 1988). In fact, smoking relapse rates are almost identical to that of heroin. Use of nicotine releases neurotransmitters such as norepinephrine, serotonin, and dopamine, and dopamine has been suggested as a mechanism for addiction (Benowitz, 1998). Nicotine affects the central nervous system such that it can cause increased heart rate and blood pressure (Dodgen, 2005).

According to the *Diagnostic and Statistical Manual of Mental Disorders,* fourth edition (*DSM-IV;* American Psychiatric Association [APA], 1994), nicotine-related disorders include nicotine dependence and nicotine withdrawal (nicotine withdrawal is discussed in the *Intervention Strategies* section in this chapter). A diagnostic category of nicotine abuse does not currently exist, because it is unlikely for abuse to exist without dependence (Colby, Tiffany, Shiffman, & Niaura, 2000b). Nicotine Dependence Disorder (NDD) is diagnosed by endorsing three of the seven criteria listed in Exhibit 5.1 within the last 12 months.

In addition to the *DSM-IV* (APA, 1994) diagnosis, there are other screening measures available to assess nicotine dependence. The most commonly used self-report measure is the Fagerstrom Tolerance Questionnaire (FTQ). The FTQ consists of eight items with a maximum score of 11; 0 indicates minimum physical dependence and 11 indicates maximum physical dependence (Fagerstrom, 1978). Through extensive research, the FTQ has been found to effectively determine dependence; however, it may not be as applicable with adolescent smokers (Dodgen, 2005). Because criteria for NDD and items on the FTQ assess different aspects of dependence, it is useful to use

---

Exhibit 5.1
Nicotine Dependence Disorder

1. Tolerance: need for greater amount of nicotine or diminished effect with the same amount.
2. Withdrawal: distressful symptoms in the absence of nicotine or relief of these symptoms upon use.
3. Substance is used in larger amounts or over a longer period than was intended.
4. Persistent desire or unsuccessful efforts to cut down or control nicotine use.
5. A great deal of time is used to obtain or use nicotine or to recover from its effects.
6. Important activities are given up or reduced due to nicotine use.
7. Continued use despite awareness of nicotine related physical or psychological problems.

Note: If item 1 or 2 is endorsed, physiological dependence is specified.
Source: Adapted from the *DSM-IV* (American Psychiatric Association, 1994).

both. Smoking more than 25 cigarettes per day and having the first cigarette within 30 minutes of awakening is indicative of dependence and later withdrawal (Rigotti, 1997). Typically, the more NDD criteria endorsed, and the higher the FTQ score, the more likely it is that the patient may require adjunctive pharmacotherapy.

Smoking History   This includes the age of smoking initiation, daily average for number of cigarettes smoked and progression to this amount, and cigarette brand(s). Knowing the cigarette brand allows the clinician to investigate nicotine and tar levels, information that will prove useful if fading is a chosen intervention. A detailed quit history includes all significant quit attempts. For each attempt, ask when the attempt took place, how long the patient was able to abstain from smoking, what methods were used ("cold turkey," fading, pharmacotherapy, hypnosis, formal cessation program, etc.), and reasons for relapse. Reasons for relapse shed light on triggers to smoking, barriers to success, and factors impacting self-efficacy. Additionally, inquire about other smokers in the patient's home, friends and coworkers who smoke, and any close friends or family who do not smoke. If the patient's spouse and most others in his or her life are smokers, this may necessitate a couples approach to cessation and the patient may need to acquire assertiveness skills to create a nonsmoking environment.

Medical History   Conditions frequently observed in long-term smokers include COPD, lung, throat, and oral cancers, and heart disease. A detailed medical history should be obtained, including current medications. It is not uncommon for patients seeking smoking cessation to have recently been diagnosed with a life-threatening medical condition, as this is often the impetus for quitting. Depending on the patient's perspective of his or her medical condition, this can be leveraged by the clinician and the patient's loved ones to enhance motivation for quitting. If the patient does not seem concerned about the condition, this is an opportunity to further educate the patient about the seriousness of the condition and the benefits of smoking cessation. Other conditions to be aware of include hypertension and history of seizures, as these are contraindicated in the use of certain types of smoking cessation pharmacotherapy (transdermal patch, Bupropion).

Comorbid Psychological Conditions   This includes screening for depression, anxiety, and substance abuse. If the patient is clinically depressed, treatment of depression will likely take precedence over smoking cessation. However, if psychiatric medication is elected, the antidepressant Bupropion (Wellbutrin), also marketed as the smoking cessation drug Zyban, may prove an effective choice. Depression is also more likely when the patient has been diagnosed with a smoking-related disease, such as lung cancer.

Although smokers commonly report that smoking helps to reduce anxiety and stress, current research suggests that smoking may in fact be anxiogenic (i.e., anxiety-inducing) rather than anxiolytic (i.e., anxiety-reducing; Dodgen, 2005). Patients suffering with a diagnosable anxiety disorder or subclinical levels of anxiety may benefit from this information. If the patient is actively abusing other substances (illicit drugs, alcohol), it is recommended that all addictions be treated simultaneously, given common underlying addiction processes (USDHHS, 2000c).

Among the seriously mentally ill (SMI) population (schizophrenia, bipolar disorder), smoking is alarmingly overrepresented. In the United States, 88% of adults with schizophrenia and 70% of adults with bipolar disorder are smokers (Dodgen, 2005). This may be attributed to hospital policies that allowed psychiatric inpatients to leave their units for smoking breaks, thereby reinforcing smoking behavior in this population. Smoking also increases the metabolism of psychotropic medications, meaning that SMI patients who smoke require higher doses of medications to achieve a therapeutic level (Dodgen, 2005). Therefore, cessation in the SMI population is critical, and there is a current trend toward banning all hospital employee and patient smoking.

Coping is another important area of assessment. Given that many use smoking as a coping mechanism, alternative forms of coping may be lacking. This being the case, patients can benefit from stress management as a treatment component to adopt, for example, problem-solving and relaxation skills (e.g., diaphragmatic breathing, progressive muscle relaxation, guided imagery). Such skills are best taught early in the treatment, as it is unwise for smokers to give up cigarettes without alternative modes of coping in place. The level of current stress should also be assessed to determine the feasibility of undertaking cessation at that time.

Motivation, Self-Efficacy, and Readiness to Change   Most smokers have attempted to quit several times and failed for various reasons, leaving them with a lack of confidence about quitting. However, patients often benefit from learning that, on average, it takes multiple quit attempts to achieve lasting abstinence (Schachter, 1982). Self-efficacy and motivation are constructs that are inextricably linked and therefore impact one another. For instance, as confidence improves, motivation is likely to be enhanced. To assess motivation and self-efficacy, a 10-point rating scale can be employed, followed by a discussion of reasons for the assigned number. This rating scale can be used throughout treatment. Barriers to change and pros and cons of treatment should also be explored in detail (e.g., fear of weight gain, irritability, and other withdrawal symptoms). Self-efficacy may be enhanced by asking the patient to consider other times when he or she was able to successfully make changes in his or her life and how these skills are transferable to quitting smoking as well. In addition, motivation can be strengthened by asking the patient to list the reasons why he or she wants to quit (e.g., smoker's cough, medical condition, loved ones).

In smoking cessation, as with most addiction treatments, assessing readiness to change is crucial. It is recommended that formal cessation efforts not be attempted until the patient has at least reached the preparation stage of change (for details on stages of change assessment, see Chapter 3). At this stage, the patient is able to use more active change processes. However, this is not to imply that precontemplators and contemplators should be abandoned. Rather, useful techniques such as consciousness raising (i.e., learning about the negative consequences of smoking and the benefits of smoking cessation) and addressing ambivalence to change (i.e., having patients consider what they enjoy about smoking and alternatives to achieving these things), can help move patients along the continuum of change (Prochaska & DiClemente, 1983; Rollnick, Butler, & Stott, 1997). These strategies may also be used to enhance motivation after relapse. For a detailed discussion on theories of behavior change (e.g., motivational interviewing, stages of change, social cognitive theory), the interested reader is referred to Chapter 3.

INTERVENTION STRATEGIES

The benefits of smoking cessation are almost immediate, and the body continues to repair itself as the person continues to abstain. Remarkably, after only 20 minutes of cessation, blood pressure and heart rate drop to normal; after 3 months lung function improves by up to 30%, after 9 months respiratory symptoms decrease, after 1 year risk of coronary heart disease decreases by 50%, after 10 years precancerous cells are replaced by normal cells, thereby decreasing cancer risk, and after 15 years death rates are nearly the same for ex-smokers as they are for those who never smoked (USDHHS, 1990). Given the hopelessness with which many patients approach quitting smoking, they are often stunned and relieved to learn these facts, which help to enhance motivation.

Research has demonstrated that increased abstinence rates are related to greater intensity of treatment. In terms of efficacy by type of treatment, individual counseling produced the highest abstinence rate when compared to group and phone counseling (USDHHS, 2000c). Increased patient contact also produced better outcomes. Increased length of sessions and more follow-up visits have superior outcomes over brief interventions for smoking cessation (Lichtenstein & Glasgow, 1992; Wilson et al., 1988; USDHHS, 2000c). Greater contact also leads to better long-term cessation rates. Thirty to 90 minutes of counseling for four sessions or more was three times more effective in producing long-term cessation than the no-contact control group (USDHHS). Additionally, treatment success increases with the number of intervention modalities used, generally achieving long-term abstinence rates of 25 to 30% (USDHHS).

The intervention strategies detailed in the following assume a preparation or action stage of change and an individual versus a group therapy approach to treatment; however, these interventions can be modified to fit a group format.

Self-Monitoring   Instructing the patient to begin self-monitoring is one of the earliest interventions. Monitoring sheets may be provided to the patient that allow for daily recording of each cigarette smoked, with related emotions and behaviors. Patients are instructed to smoke in their typical fashion for the first week or two to establish a baseline. It is not unusual for patients to notice an automatic reduction in their smoking as an initial response to this self-observation and heightened awareness of smoking behavior. This data provides information about emotional and behavioral triggers to smoking, and useful patterns related to people, places, and situations associated with smoking. In line with social cognitive theory, the triggers are the antecedents to the behavior of smoking, followed by reinforcing consequences (relaxation, heightened alertness; Bandura, 1997). By identifying this chain of events, the clinician can help the patient unlearn this behavior. Adherence with this stage of treatment is essential, and any nonadherence should be addressed early in the treatment. For instance, in addition to the intrusion of self-monitoring, patients may experience embarrassment or surprise by the amount of their daily smoking. These daily assessments should be used until the quit day.

Set Quit Date   Setting the quit date early in treatment is important for several reasons. First, it establishes a clear goal that the patient is working toward. Second, it provides a timeframe for the therapist to assist the patient in developing coping strategies before quitting. The quit date should be set for a time of lowered stress for the patient and not around significant events (anniversary of loved one's death, Thanksgiving, etc.). The patient should be seen on the quit day and again within 72 hours, as this is the time period of most intense withdrawal symptoms (Brown, 2003). To prepare for the quit day, patients will need to remove all cigarettes and paraphernalia (matches, lighters, ashtrays) out of their home, car, and work environment, and should clean to remove the smell of smoke (vacuum, wash clothes, bed linens, etc.). Generally, the quit date is set within 3 weeks of beginning treatment (Brown, 2003). However, this can be extended, depending on additional strategies employed. For instance, the full effect of Bupropion can take several weeks to reach. In addition, if fading is used, this will also extend the time before the quit date.

Fading   Fading is a process whereby the nicotine level is gradually reduced. This is accomplished through altering the brand smoked (brand fading) and/or the number of cigarettes smoked per day (rate fading). Fading can be especially useful with long-term smokers who experience significant addiction to nicotine. Reduced intensity of withdrawal symptoms on the quit day is the rationale for the fading technique. However, patients will experience milder forms of withdrawal during the fading process.

When possible, lower-nicotine cigarettes should be chosen from patients' preferred brand, given the strong brand loyalty that many smokers exhibit. For instance, the Camel brand sells nonfilter regular (nicotine = 1.7 mg/cigarette; tar = 23 mg/cigarette), filter light (nicotine = 0.9 mg/cigarette; tar =11 mg/cigarette), and filter ultra-light (nicotine = 0.4 mg/cigarette; tar = 5 mg/cigarette) cigarette varieties (U. S. Federal Trade Commission, 1997). Thus, with each switch, nicotine levels are cut in half. Information on nicotine and tar yields for most domestic cigarette brands can by obtained from the U. S. Federal Trade Commission's 1997 report. While brand fading reduces nicotine intake per cigarette, rate fading reduces daily nicotine intake and has the added advantage of breaking some behavioral associations. As the number of cigarettes smoked per day is reduced, it is recommended that patients not smoke less than 10 cigarettes per day, as these become overly reinforced (Brown, 2003).

Brand and rate fading can be used simultaneously. During fading, patients should be instructed to avoid compensatory smoking behaviors (inhaling more deeply, covering filter holes, smoking to base of cigarette). In cases where pharmacotherapy is contraindicated, fading can be an effective alternative (Brown, 2003). Success during fading can also bolster self-efficacy for quitting (Dodgen, 2005).

Self-Regulation   Once triggers (people, places, situations, emotions) to smoking have been identified from self-monitoring records, patients can begin to alter their environments and behaviors accordingly. For instance, the patient can replace smoking with chewing gum when talking on the phone, or use relaxation strategies in place of smoking when stressed (i.e., counter-conditioning), or watch television in a non-smoking room of his or her home (i.e., stimulus control). This may initially also require the use of avoidance (local bar, friends who smoke). As mentioned previously, because smoking permeates most of a patient's life, the opportunities for stimulus control are endless. The clinician can brainstorm with the patient to identify creative ways to break associations and change the environment. The clinician should also consistently review throughout the treatment how the identified strategies are working and whether changes need to be made. These self-regulatory techniques are typically introduced before the quit date (Dodgen, 2005). Once the patient has quit, reinforcement strategies can also be employed. For instance, it is easy to calculate the monetary savings from quitting smoking, and patients can put this money aside to reward themselves during treatment at interval milestones (1 week; 1 month; 6 months; 1 year). The patient's support system can also be instrumental in providing positive reinforcement.

Monitoring Withdrawal   Unpleasant withdrawal symptoms often lead to relapse (Dodgen, 2005). Therefore, withdrawal must be frequently monitored and actively managed. *DSM-IV* (APA, 1994) criteria for Nicotine Withdrawal are listed in Exhibit 5.2.

Exhibit 5.2
Nicotine Withdrawal

1. Daily use of nicotine for at least several weeks.
2. Reduction or cessation followed by 4 or more of the following symptoms within 24 hours:
   a. Restlessness
   b. Decreased heart rate
   c. Difficulty concentrating
   d. Increased appetite or weight gain
   e. Dysphoric or depressed mood
   f. Anxiety
   g. Insomnia
   h. Anger, frustration, or irritability
3. The symptoms cause significant distress or impairment in functioning.

Source: Adapted from the *DSM-IV* (American Psychiatric Association, 1994).

Because withdrawal symptoms and their severity can fluctuate, in addition to the *DSM-IV*(APA, 1994) diagnosis, a weekly self-report measure can be administered. A frequently used measure is the Minnesota Nicotine Withdrawal Scale (MNWS; Hughes & Hatsukami, 1986). It includes 15 items that measure withdrawal on a scale from none to severe. However, as a research tool the MNWS has been evaluated to have only face validity and is lacking in reliability and validity (Patten & Martin, 1996). Even so, as a clinical tool, it can be a helpful guage of the patient's level of withdrawal and related distress.

Withdrawal symptoms are most severe during the first week after quitting and typically subside after 2 to 3 weeks (Brown, 2003). If the fading technique was used, this will lessen the severity of withdrawal symptoms after the quit date. Depending on the patient's experience of withdrawal, an active or passive strategy may be employed. Management of withdrawal can include exercise, use of nicotine replacement therapy (NRT; gum, patch), use of active distraction techniques (knitting, crossword puzzles), and time spent with supportive others. Patients should be reminded that these symptoms will gradually lessen and fade within 3 weeks. Interestingly, some researchers have noted a difference in response to withdrawal between men and women. These differences may be mediated by the menstrual cycle (Perkins et al., 2000) and certain treatments (NRT) may be less effective in women (USDHHS, 2000c).

Managing High-Risk Situations   Frequent triggers identified during the early phase of self-monitoring are likely to become situations that put the patient at risk for relapse (e.g., negative emotions, celebrations involving alcohol, being around other smokers). For instance, if the patient tended to smoke more when dealing with a difficult family member, the quality of this relationship may undermine the patient's progress. Therefore, once these high-risk situations are identified, patients should strategize ahead of time with the clinician on how best to handle these situations without turning to cigarettes. In this example, he or she could use assertiveness skills, or even avoidance if necessary, to manage the relationship. As the patient remains abstinent and becomes more confident, he or she can slowly reintroduce those things that were triggers to smoking with the help of the clinician (e.g., having a beer, being around other smokers, drinking coffee).

Bolstering Social Support   As mentioned earlier, a spouse, other family members, friends, and coworkers who smoke can present obstacles to creating a smoke-free environment. The patient's goal to quit smoking may be perceived as threatening or abandoning to those who choose to continue. While some people in the patient's life can be avoided until he or she feels confident enough to be around smokers while abstaining, a spouse, children, or parents living with the patient who smoke will make the quit attempt very difficult. In this case, it may be useful to conduct couples or family sessions to empower the patient to ask for the support that he or she needs (e.g., no smoking in home or car, no smoking near the patient). The patient can be encouraged to consider behaviors from others in his or her life that he or she finds supportive, and behaviors found to be unsupportive before asserting needs. Supportive people in the patient's life can be a source of motivation and positive reinforcement, and also provide a buffer against stress (Brown, 2003). If the patient lacks a support network, group programs such as Nicotine Anonymous (NA) can provide ongoing adjunctive support during treatment.

Addressing Weight Gain   Precessation concerns about weight gain can impede quitting (French, Jeffery, Pirie, & McBride, 1992), and post-cessation weight gain often leads to relapse (Hall, Ginsberg, & Jones, 1986). Therefore, clinicians should openly address post-cessation weight gain concerns and acknowledge that weight gain is likely but typically limited. Almost 80% of smokers will gain weight after quitting (USDHHS, 1990), with average weight gain between 5 and 10 lbs (Williamson, Madans, Anda, Kleinman, Giovino, & Byers, 1991). As compared to men, women typically gain more weight, express greater concern about gaining weight pre-cessation, and more commonly report weight gain as a reason for relapse (Williamson et al., 1991). Addressing weight concerns with cognitive-behavioral therapy was found to improve smoking cessation outcomes in women concerned with weight gain (Perkins et al., 2001).

Nicotine increases metabolic rate and acts as an appetite suppressant, thereby suppressing weight (Dodgen, 2005). Patients can be encouraged to make changes in their diet and begin or increase exercise regimens to prevent weight gain. Exercise has the added benefit of reducing stress and improving mood, and vigorous exercise is incompatible with smoking (Brown, 2003). Pharmacotherapy, particularly bupropion and nicotine gum, can delay (but not prevent) weight gain (Dodgen, 2005).

Maintenance and Relapse Prevention   Once the patient has been able to abstain from smoking, a focus on maintenance and preventing relapse begins. A barrier to maintenance is the experience of cravings, or urges, to resume smoking. These urges are usually brought about by old triggers to smoking. Researchers have found that the majority of lapses were attributable to urges (Catley, O'Connell, & Shiffman, 2000; Killen & Fortmann, 1997). This provides a window of opportunity to actively manage urges before leading to relapse (Dodgen, 2005). Urges can be triggered by emotions, environmental cues, or physiology (fatigue). It should be explained to patients that urges are time limited, lasting approximately 20 minutes (Dodgen, 2005). Therefore, if the patient can initiate active coping strategies (exercise, NRT, distraction, relaxation) for this time period, the urge will subside. Brown (2003) recommends the use of imagery during these periods and suggests that patients view the urges as waves in the ocean that rise and fall, while the patient is like a surfer riding the wave until it washes up against the shore. To enhance motivation that can wax and wane during the maintenance phase of treatment, patients can be asked about any benefits to quitting they have noticed, encouraged to remind themselves of their reasons for quitting, and instructed to review strategies for managing high-risk situations.

The difference between a lapse and a relapse and the management of these should be discussed. A lapse, or a slip, is a discrete episode of smoking, whereas a relapse is the return to a baseline level of smoking (Brown, 2003). Experiencing a lapse during treatment is likely and should be normalized; however, future lapses should be prevented (Brown). A lapse may be viewed by the exsmoker as a total failure instead of a normal part of recovery from addiction. Therefore, lapses must be dealt with before they lead to relapse. The abstinence violation effect (AVE; Marlatt & Gordon, 1985) is a useful framework to present to patients. The AVE consists of negative self-attributions that the patient makes after a slip or relapse (e.g., "I'm a failure, I can't do it") that will most likely lead to relapse. Patients should also be informed that they are likely to experience negative emotions (guilt, frustration, anger, sadness) after a slip that can then lead to self-defeating attributions. The AVE leads a patient to believe that a slip means that he or she is again a smoker, which then becomes a rationale for relapse. Therefore, if the patient can cognitively reframe the experience of a slip with the help of the clinician, it is much less likely to undermine the patient's progress. This can be accomplished by examining the reasons for the slip, learning from these mistakes, and resuming abstinence. Enlisting support from others and use of positive reinforcing can bolster self-efficacy that may be diminished by slips.

Emotions such as grief, regret, and anger may arise during the maintenance phase. Patients can report experiencing loss over quitting smoking, similar to losing a friend. For some, smoking has been a long-time companion of sorts, which the patient now misses. Further, for those who have serious medical conditions as a result of smoking (lung cancer, COPD), this may also be a time of regret and anger toward oneself, and the patient's loved ones may share these sentiments. As patients move further along in maintenance, they can become nostalgic ("I really miss smoking when driving") or overconfident ("I'm doing so well, I could handle just one cigarette") regarding smoking (Brown, 2003). If these thoughts arise in treatment, clinicians should challenge these directly, as thoughts such as these can lead to relapse. As termination to treatment approaches, sessions can move to every other week and then to once per month before termination, to establish the patient's ability to abstain without treatment. Further, even after termination, the patient may require future booster sessions should he or she face a slip or relapse, such as during a time of crisis.

Other Techniques   Cognitive dissonance can be created by asking patients to consider their most important personal values and whether smoking is complementary or contradictory to these values (Dodgen, 2005). Aversion techniques such as rapid smoking and covert sensitization have not demonstrated better outcomes than intensive counseling (USDHHS, 2000c). Furthermore, rapid smoking poses potential medical risks, such as increased heart rate and elevated blood pressure (Dodgen). Brief physician advice, such as the 5 As (see Table 5.1), has demonstrated lower efficacy results as compared to intensive counseling (USDHHS). This may be attributed to the brevity of the intervention. However, given that physicians are often the first to address a patient's smoking, this brief advice can provide a window of opportunity and influence the patient to comply with more intensive treatment, especially for pregnant and adolescent smokers. Physicians see an estimated 70% of smokers per year (Rigotti, 1997). Given this and many other reasons (physician support, pharmacotherapy, medical management), it is beneficial for the health psychologist to work collaboratively with the patient's physician(s) during the course of treatment.

Table 5.1

The 5 As: Brief Physician Advice for Smoking Cessation

1. Ask	Systematically identify all tobacco users at every visit. Implement an office-wide system that ensures that, for every patient at every clinic visit, tobacco-use status is queried and documented.
2. Advise	Strongly urge all tobacco users to quit. In a clear, strong, and personalized manner urge every tobacco user to quit.
3. Asess	Determine willingness to make a quit attempt. Ask every tobacco user if he or she is willing to make a quit attempt at this time.
4. Assist	Aid the patient in quitting. Help the patient with a quit plan; provide practical counseling; provide intratreatment social support; help the patient obtain extratreatment social support; recommend use of approved pharmacotherapy except in special circumstances; provide supplementary materials.
5. Arrange	Schedule follow-up contact in person or over telephone.

Source: Adapted from the Tobacco Use and Dependence Clinical Practice Guideline Panel, Staff, and Consortium Representatives (2000). *A clinical practice guideline for treating tobacco use and dependence: A US public health service report.*

Numerous other smoking cessation programs exist that are beyond the scope of this chapter, such as NA, Smokenders, SmokeStoppers, programs sponsored by hospitals, insurance companies, and nonprofit organizations (American Cancer Society, American Lung Association), and so forth. Most of these use aspects of the aforementioned strategies.

PHARMACOTHERAPY

The FDA has approved the use of over-the-counter (OTC) and prescription medications for nicotine dependence. Nicotine replacement therapy (NRT) is available both OTC (gum, lozenge, and patch) and by prescription (nasal spray and inhaler). Prescription medications include bupropion (Zyban) and varenicline (Chantix). These are considered first-line medications for nicotine dependence.

Nicotine replacement therapy is used to reduce withdrawal symptoms through low doses of nicotine that are free from other chemicals and toxins found in cigarettes. Although some patients worry that they may become addicted to NRT, long-term dependence on NRT is not common (USDHHS, 2000c). The OTC NRTs are more commonly used, most likely because they are easy to use and do not require a prescription. However, the nicotine inhaler and nasal spray have been proven to have a higher abstinence rate than placebo (22.8 vs. 10.5, 30.5 vs. 13.9, respectively; USDHHS). The gum and the lozenge can be especially helpful for those patients who wish to occupy their mouth, but not with smoking. As compared to a placebo, nicotine polacrilex (nicotine gum) was found to have a higher abstinence rate (23.7% vs. 17.1%; USDHHS). The gum is available in 2 mg and 4 mg doses. The patient is instructed to chew the gum for a few seconds to release the nicotine into the buccal mucosa and then "park it" against the cheek. Patients should not use more than 20 pieces per day of the 4 mg dose or more than 30 pieces per day of the 2 mg dose (USDHHS, 2000a). The transdermal nicotine patch provides a continuous dose of nicotine (0.9 mg per hour), and one patch is worn per 24-hour period (USDHHS, 2000a).

The patch was found to have a higher abstinence rate than placebo (17.7% vs. 10%; USDHHS, 2000c). There is limited efficacy data available on the nicotine lozenge;

however, the lozenge is easy to use and delivers nicotine more effectively than the nicotine gum (Dodgen, 2005).

Bupropion was found to have a higher abstinence rate than placebo (30.5% vs. 17.3%; USDHHS, 2000c). The medication is started 1 to 2 weeks before the quit date, with dosage beginning at 150 mg once daily for 3 days, followed by 150 mg twice daily for up to 6 months postcessation for maintenance (USDHHS, 2000a). Because bupropion is an antidepressant (i.e., Wellbutrin, Zyban), it can be a good choice for the smoker who is suffering with depression. It works by blocking dopamine and norepinephrine reuptake in the central nervous system, which decreases withdrawal symptoms, including nicotine cravings (Dodgen, 2005). Varenicline (Chantix) is the newest prescription medication available for smoking cessation. Patients who use insulin, asthma medications, or blood thinners, or who receive dialysis, are not advised to take this medication. Varenicline is started at least 1 week before the quit date and is typically used for up to 12 weeks. Dosage begins at 0.5 mg once per day for 3 days, then 0.5 mg twice per day for the next 4 days, and moves to 1 mg twice per day from day 8 on. It works by preventing nicotine from binding to nicotinic receptors (Pfizer Inc., 2006). This medication was released to the public at the end of 2006; therefore, efficacy data from independent studies are not yet available.

Multiple pharmacotherapy is also an option for those with severe nicotine dependence. Bupropion may be safely combined with any of the NRTs (USDHHS, 2000a), and NRTs may be used in combinations. For instance, the patch is used to provide a baseline level of nicotine with a second form of NRT (gum), used as needed (Dodgen, 2005). Combination NRT is considered a second-line medication treatment because of insufficient safety data and concerns about nicotine overdose (Dodgen, 2005). Additionally, combining pharmacotherapy and counseling enhances treatment outcomes over either approach alone (Hajek, 1996; Stitzer & Walsh, 1997). With patients who have medical contraindications (e.g., heart disease, hypertension, seizures), pharmacotherapy should only be used with careful physician monitoring. In any event, the patient should not begin any type of pharmacotherapy, including OTC, before consulting his or her physician.

SPECIAL POPULATIONS

This section covers additional considerations for helping pregnant women and teens to quit smoking.

PREGNANT WOMEN

Smoking during pregnancy has significantly declined, from 20% in 1989 to 10% in 2004 (NCHS, 2006). Smoking during pregnancy causes spontaneous abortion, low birth weight (20 to 30%), and sudden infant death syndrome, and contributes to premature delivery (14%), low IQ, and birth defects (DiFranza & Lew, 1995; USDHHS, 2005). Both smoking during pregnancy and exposure to secondhand smoke in the home environment place children at greater risk for developing asthma (DiFranza, Aligne, & Weitzman, 2004). It is estimated that 22% of U.S. children and adolescents are exposed to secondhand smoke at home (CDC, 1997c). Annual medical costs in the United States related to smoking during pregnancy are approximately $366 million (CDC, 2002). However, when smokers quit in the first trimester, their infants have similar body weights and measurements to those of nonsmokers' infants (CDC, 2002).

Therefore, intervening early in a woman's pregnancy can benefit the health of the fetus, and obstetricians and gynecologists are uniquely situated to screen and advise women smokers before and during pregnancy. Because pharmacotherapy is typically contraindicated during pregnancy and has not been approved by the FDA for use during pregnancy, behavioral interventions should be initiated first (USDHHS, 2000a; Prokhorov, Hudmon, & Stancic, 2003). However, for pregnant women who are heavy smokers or are otherwise unable to quit, pharmacotherapy can be used at the physician's discretion, provided that the benefits of such use outweigh the risks of continued smoking (USDHHS, 2000c).

ADOLESCENTS

Although smoking rates have steadily declined in the adult population over the last few decades, some surveys show that teen smoking increased through 1997 and has since remained unchanged (NCHS, 1999). Currently, nearly one-quarter of high school students smoke (NCHS, 2006). Approximately 90% of smokers begin before the age of 18, and two-thirds of adolescents have tried smoking by age 18 (USDHHS, 1994). Each day about 3,000 teenagers become daily smokers (CDC, 1996). Sadly, most adolescent smokers believe they will not be smoking in adulthood, yet approximately 75% of them do (Colby, Tiffany, Shiffman, & Niaura, 2000a). Despite these grim statistics, from the time of initiation, it takes up to 3 years to become a regular smoker (USDHHS, 1994), meaning that there is a large window of opportunity to intervene. In fact, the majority of adolescent smokers report wanting to quit (USDHHS, 1994). Risk factors include low self-efficacy, lack of knowledge regarding health consequences and nicotine addiction, and peer pressure to smoke (Elder, Iniguez, & Larios, 2004). Also, because nicotine is an appetite suppressant, many teenage girls start smoking to lose weight.

Adolescents do experience nicotine dependence and withdrawal; however, pharmacotherapy for use with this population of smokers has not been FDA approved (McDonald, Colwell, Backinger, Husten, & Maule, 2003; Prokhorov et al., 2003). Because adolescent smoking tends to be more erratic (only smoking on weekends; only smoking when parents are not around, etc.) than that of adults, they tend to be lighter smokers who have lower levels of dependency than adults; therefore the use of NRT may actually provide more nicotine than the teenager is getting from smoking (Dodgen, 2005; McDonald et al.). Pharmacotherapy can be considered with adolescents if the level of dependence is severe (Dodgen, 2005; USDHHS, 2000c; Milton, Maule, Backinger, & Gregory, 2003).

The assessment areas and intervention strategies detailed previously can be age adjusted and safely used with adolescents with some added considerations. McDonald and colleagues (2003) found that the majority of effective tobacco cessation programs for adolescents were based on cognitive-behavioral principles. The peer group has a powerful influence over teenagers, and if most of the patient's friends are smokers, he or she may need to learn assertiveness and social skills in order to abstain from smoking. Similar to adults, teen smokers benefit from learning coping skills such as relaxation, problem solving, and management of negative emotions (Milton et al., 2003). Further, given that teenagers are actively marketed to by cigarette companies (Cummings, Morley, Horan, Steger, & Leavell, 2002), they are mistakenly led to believe that smoking is safe and "cool." Therefore, the clinician may need to spend significant time educating the patient about the later health consequences of smoking and the addiction of nicotine. Because teenagers seldom believe that bad things can happen to them (i.e., belief in invulnerability), it may be beneficial for teen patients to speak with older smokers suffering health consequences. Weight gain may be a more significant impediment to quitting for teenage girls and should be addressed openly. Clinicians can also involve parents in the smoking cessation effort; however, this can interfere with the level of teen disclosure, and the parents may be smokers themselves. If parents or siblings are also smokers, the clinician can work with the entire family on cessation efforts. Otherwise, it will be challenging for the teen to quit while others are smoking in the home. This can be an opportunity for parents and teens to work as a team to support one another's quit efforts.

Adolescents are difficult to get into treatment. Given this, the window before regular smoking occurs, and the percentage of smokers that start in adolescence, prevention during adolescence is crucial. This is an ideal time for community- and school-sponsored prevention programs. These types of programs can help to combat the barrage of tobacco marketing directed toward teens. The tobacco companies (e.g., Philip Morris [now known as the Altria Group], RJ Reynolds) are well aware that if 90% of their clients start in their teens, they must continue to target adolescents to survive. Landers (2002) reports that even after the FDA banned marketing in magazines with more than two million readers under the age of 18 (or >15%) in 1998, RJ Reynolds placed ads in magazines with just under 2 million teen readers and Philip Morris advertised in magazines with just under 15% teen readers in 1999. Companies such as these claim that they have begun online smoking prevention campaigns to help prevent teen smoking. However, these types of industry-sponsored prevention programs focus on smoking as an adult choice, lack of parental guidance as a problem, and the law as a reason not to smoke, and there is little mention of the devastating health effects of smoking (Landman, Ling, & Glantz, 2002). By focusing on smoking as an adult choice, this makes smoking appear as forbidden fruit, or a way to prematurely assert independence, which may make smoking even more enticing. Moreover, their prevention efforts do not target the at-risk teenage age group of 15–18, but rather the 10- to 14-year-olds (Landman et al.). The industry uses so-called prevention efforts to influence politicians, undermine tobacco regulation initiatives, and to enhance public relations (Landman et al.). In addition, the industry is also able to maintain its access to this teenage group in order to glean needed psychographic marketing data (these programs require teens to log onto industry web sites and fill out various surveys). In order to protect adolescents from this aggressive marketing, our educational (in-school prevention and cessation classes), governmental (raise and enforce the legal age to purchase cigarettes, increase cigarette excise tax; ban Internet cigarette vendors), and health care (screening and intervention and reimbursement for such services) systems must consistently provide strong antitobacco messages to this vulnerable population.

CASE ILLUSTRATION

Jane, a 58-year-old African American female, was referred for tobacco cessation by her pulmonologist, who had diagnosed her with COPD 1 year prior. She had been smoking regularly for 43 years since the age of 15. She smoked unfiltered regular Camel cigarettes (nicotine = 1.7 mg/cigarette; tar = 23 mg/cigarette) up until 10 years ago, at which time she switched to filtered Camel lights (nicotine = 0.9 mg/cigarette; tar = 11 mg/cigarette), thereby cutting her nicotine intake in half. Jane reported doing so because her husband of 35 years had expressed concern about her smoking. At the time of intake, the patient reported smoking approximately 30 cigarettes (1.5 packs) per day. In the last 5 years, the patient had attempted quitting on four separate occasions, each time "cold turkey" with assistance, including hypnosis and the transdermal patch. With each attempt, she was able to abstain from smoking for no more than 1 week, and she reported that the patch had elevated her blood pressure. The patient was living with her husband, who she felt was very supportive. She stated that he smoked an occasional cigar in their home. Although she reported having many friends who smoked, she had a handful of nonsmoking friends and coworkers as well. In addition to her recent diagnosis of COPD, the patient had a history of hypertension and was currently taking blood pressure medication. She denied any history of or current alcohol or drug abuse and reported an "occasional beer" with friends. Although she denied any history of or current suicidal ideation, the patient did endorse enough depressive symptoms to warrant an evaluation for depression. She did not meet full criteria for a *DSM-IV* (APA, 1994) diagnosis of major depressive disorder and scored in the mild range on the Beck Depression Inventory. However, the patient's subclinical depression was causing her some distress and interfering somewhat with her work and daily functioning. Upon further questioning, it became clearer that her symptoms were closely related to the diagnosis of COPD, which was her major motivation for seeking treatment for tobacco cessation. Throughout treatment, time was spent helping her deal with feelings of regret, guilt, and anger related to the COPD. As she came to terms with the diagnosis, her depressive symptoms lessened.

On a 10-point scale, the patient's reported motivation was a 5 and her self-efficacy was a 2 at the time of intake. She stated that while she knew she had to quit, her past "failures" left her doubtful of her ability to do so, and because she really enjoyed smoking, she was less motivated. The patient met *DSM-IV* (APA, 1994) criteria for NDD, and scored 9 on the FTQ, indicating a substantial level of nicotine dependence, which was not surprising given her long-term use. Her current stress level was low, but given the pervasiveness of smoking in her life, she had few other coping mechanisms. The most significant barrier to change was the amount of pleasure the patient derived from smoking. Despite her low motivation and confidence levels, she was quite determined to quit. The patient described herself as consistent with the preparation stage of change (Prochaska & DiClemente, 1983), as she was greatly concerned about her COPD and was well aware of the impact that smoking cessation could have in slowing its progression. She was presently diagnosed with a mild classification (Forced Expiratory Volume in 1 Second [FEV1] $\geq 80\%$ predicted) of COPD, with chronic symptoms (cough, sputum production) and was using a short-acting bronchodilator.

With permission from the patient, this psychologist consulted with her primary care physician regarding her level of addiction and her subclinical depression. The physician and patient decided it would be best to use Zyban as an adjunct to treatment. The patient was started on Zyban. Due to her hypertension, however, her blood pressure elevated to 169/99 (stage 2 hypertension) within 1 week, at which point her physician immediately discontinued the medication. He then started her on a newer medication, Chantix, which the patient responded well to without side effects. The patient was simultaneously monitoring her daily smoking and associated emotions, thoughts, and behaviors. Given the length of her smoking history and her physiological and psychological dependence, fading was used. Her quit date was set for 4 weeks after she began Chantix, to allow the medication to become fully effective and to provide the opportunity to use the fading technique. Her baseline smoking was 25 cigarettes per day (slight decrease from 30 due to monitoring). Initially, rate fading was used and the avoidance of compensatory smoking was discussed. Each subsequent week, her daily smoking allowance was reduced by 5 cigarettes (wk 1 = 20; wk 2 = 15; wk 3 = 10). The patient was very successful at reducing her weekly rate of smoking and reported using cognitive techniques to restrict her daily use (e.g., thinking "No, I cannot have one yet; I have to wait"). During week four, she was instructed to switch to Camel ultra light filter cigarettes (nicotine = 0.4 mg/cigarette; tar = 5 mg/cigarette), thereby again cutting her nicotine intake in half. Switching brands was not attempted, given that she had been smoking Camels for 43 years. She was very resistant to switching to ultra lights, claiming that they "had no taste," which was somewhat surprising, given her quick compliance with rate fading. The patient felt that she would not be able to enjoy these cigarettes. It was explained to her that this was in fact the goal. She received great pleasure from smoking, and this association needed to be broken. The patient unhappily agreed and smoked Camel ultra lights during her last week of smoking 10 cigarettes per day. On the session before her quit date, her motivation and self-efficacy were reassessed and were found to be significantly higher. In addition, the patient described being in an action stage of change (Prochaska & DiClemente, 1983). Her withdrawal symptoms were monitored weekly using the MNWS, and she did endorse several symptoms on a mild to moderate level, which she successfully managed with distraction techniques (walking, knitting, crossword puzzles).

During the 4 weeks leading up to her quit date, many interventions were employed. First, numerous consistent triggers were identified from her self-monitoring sheets. After these were compiled, the patient was asked to rate the intensity of each trigger on a 10-point scale. Strategies were then developed to manage each of these, paying close attention to the most intense triggers. For example, she rated her morning coffee as 10. To manage this trigger, the patient agreed to have her coffee first and then wait as long as possible before having her first cigarette of the day. Initially she could only wait about 5 minutes, but by the time of her quit date, the patient was able to wait a full hour between coffee and smoking. She actively used these strategies to manage her triggers to smoking. The intensity of these triggers was reassessed several weeks later, and all had dramatically reduced in intensity by the patient's ratings. This was a particularly helpful activity, as the patient had stated still feeling controlled by her smoking. After comparing initial and later ratings, she was surprised and pleased to learn that she was in fact mastering her triggers and increasing her control. Because the patient was so emotionally attached to smoking, time was spent identifying what she liked most about smoking and the things she could do to achieve the same effects in alternate ways. For example, she reported that she liked how smoking relaxed her by taking her mind off her troubles. In place of smoking, she identified using the relaxation strategies she was taught as a way to achieve this same effect. Deep breathing was especially useful for her, given that this was also a technique used during her pulmonary rehabilitation. She also began taking walks regularly, as she was somewhat concerned about postcessation weight gain.

On the session before her quit date, the patient was asked to prepare by removing all cigarettes and paraphernalia out of her home, car, and office desk, and to clean to remove the smell of smoke. She also asked her husband not to smoke cigars in the house, to which he agreed. The patient had chosen a weekday for her quit date because she felt work would be a good distraction and provide some structure. She was seen on a Tuesday (quit day) and again that Friday to monitor her progress and withdrawal symptoms. The patient did very well the first week and reported only a few mild withdrawal symptoms. This decreased intensity of withdrawal symptoms resulted from the combined use of Chantix and fading. Given this and her hypertension, it was decided not to use NRT. The patient also began putting money aside (the cost of one pack per day) to later reward herself. Strategies were developed to manage high-risk situations such as being around her friends who smoke and their reactions to her quitting.

The patient was taught the AVE and the difference between a slip and a relapse. She reported experiencing urges that were often triggered by environmental cues. She was able to ride these out but found them to be extremely frustrating, stating "Will there ever be a time when I don't want a cigarette?" The patient had successfully abstained for 3 months, when her husband was diagnosed with a serious medical illness. Jane slipped and smoked about 10 cigarettes over the course of 2 days. Significant time was spent on the negative emotions she was experiencing, including sadness and anger. Jane was seen for another 3 months, during which time treatment focused on coping with her husband's health and remaining abstinent from smoking, which she was able to do until the end of treatment.

CONCLUSION

Our society pays dearly for nicotine addiction, in lives lost, diminished quality of life, and skyrocketing health care expenditures. Health psychologists and physicians of various specialties (internal medicine, family medicine, pulmonology, cardiology, gynecology, obstetrics, pediatrics) are uniquely positioned to intervene not only with chronic smokers, but also with teens as part of an early intervention or prevention program, as most smokers begin in adolescence. Tobacco cessation requires a multidisciplinary approach to treatment, including pharmacotherapy and cognitive-behavioral techniques. Screening to identify smokers is the first step, and intervening with more than one approach from more than one discipline is more effective than any one intervention strategy alone. Psychologists possess the knowledge and skills to not only provide these interventions on an individual and group level, but to also assist in designing, implementing, and evaluating community-, hospital-, and school-based smoking cessation programming. As a society, we must continue to work with our health care, educational, and governmental systems to protect our environment, our health, and our youth from the dangers of nicotine addiction and the proliferation of the tobacco industry. Although we have made great strides, there is still much work to be done.

REFERENCES

American Psychiatric Association. (1994). *Diagnostic and statistical manual of mental disorders* (4th ed.). Washington, DC: Author.

Bandura, A. (1997). *Self-efficacy: The exercise of control.* New York: W. H. Freeman.

Benowitz, N. L. (1998). Pharmacology of nicotine. In R. E. Tarter & R. T. Ammerman (Eds.), *Handbook of substance abuse: Neurobehavioral pharmacology* (pp. 283–297). New York: Plenum.

Brown, R. A. (2003). Intensive behavioral treatment. In D. B. Abrams et al. (Eds.), *The tobacco dependence treatment handbook: A guide to best practices* (pp. 118–117). New York: Guilford.

Catley, D., O'Connell, K. A., & Shiffman, S. (2000). Absentminded lapses during smoking cessation. *Psychology of Addictive Behaviors, 14*(1), 73–76.

Centers for Disease Control and Prevention. (1996). The great American smokeout. *Morbidity and Mortality Weekly Report, 45*(44), 961.

Centers for Disease Control and Prevention. (1997a). Cigarette smoking among adults. *Morbidity and Mortality Weekly Report, 46*, 1217–1220.

Centers for Disease Control and Prevention. (1997b). Cigarette smoking-attributable mortality and years of potential life lost. *Morbidity and Mortality Weekly Report, 46*(20), 444–451.

Centers for Disease Control and Prevention. (1997c). State-specific prevalence of cigarette smoking among adults, and children's and adolescents' exposure to environmental tobacco smoke. *Morbidity and Mortality Weekly Report, 46*, 1038–1043.

Centers for Disease Control and Prevention. (2000). Oral health in America: A report of the Surgeon General. *Morbidity and Mortality Weekly Report, 41*, 325–327.

Centers for Disease Control and Prevention. (2002). Annual smoking-attributable mortality, years of potential life lost, and economic costs–U.S., 1995–1999. *Morbidity and Mortality Weekly Report, 51*(14), 300–303.

Centers for Disease Control and Prevention. (2004). *Tobacco use in the United States.* Washington, DC: National Center for Chronic Disease Prevention and Health Promotion. Tobacco Information and Prevention Source.

Centers for Disease Control and Prevention. (2005). Annual smoking-attributable mortality, years of potential life lost, and productivity losses–U.S., 1997–2001. *Morbidity and Mortality Weekly Report, 54*(25).

Colby, S. M., Tiffany, S. T., Shiffman, S., & Niaura, R. S. (2000a). Are adolescent smokers dependent on nicotine? A review of the evidence. *Drug and Alcohol Dependence, 59*(Suppl. 1), S83–S95.

Colby, S. M., Tiffany, S. T., Shiffman, S., & Niaura, R. S. (2000b). Measuring nicotine dependence among youth: A review of available approaches and instruments. *Drug and Alcohol Dependence, 59*(Suppl. 1), S23–S39.

Cornwell, L. (2006, February 16). Employers charging smoker extra for health insurance. The Associated Press, pp. 1–3.

Cummings, K. M., Morley, C. P., Horan, J. K, Steger, C., & Leavell, N. R. (2002). Marketing to America's youth: Evidence from corporate documents. *Tobacco Control, 11*(S1), 5–17.

DiFranza, J. R., Aligne, C. A., & Weitzman, M. (2004). Prenatal and postnatal environmental tobacco smoke exposure and children's health. *Pediatrics, 113*(4), 1007–1015.

DiFranza, J. R., & Lew, R. A. (1995). Effect of maternal cigarette smoking on pregnancy complications and sudden infant death syndrome. *Journal of Family Practice, 40*(4), 385–394.

Dodgen, C. E. (2005). *Nicotine dependence: Understanding and applying the most effective treatment interventions.* Washington, DC: American Psychological Association.

Elder, J. P., Iniguez, E. M., & Larios, S. (2004). Tobacco use. In L. A. Rapp-Paglicci, C. N. Dulmus, & J. S. Wodarski (Eds.), *Handbook of preventive interventions for children and adolescents,* (pp. 255–274). Hoboken, NJ: Wiley.

Fagerstrom, K. O. (1978). Measuring degree of physical dependence to tobacco smoking with reference to individualization of treatment. *Addictive Behaviors, 3*, 235–241.

French, S. A., Jeffery, R. W., Pirie, P. L., & McBride, C. M. (1992). Do weight concerns hinder smoking cessation efforts? *Addictive Behaviors, 17*(3), 219–226.

Hajek, P. (1996). Current issues in behavioral and pharmacological approaches to smoking cessation. *Addictive Behaviors, 21*, 699–707.

Hall, S. M., Ginsberg, D., & Jones, R. T. (1986). Smoking cessation and weight gain. *Journal of Consulting and Clinical Psychology, 54*(3), 342–346.

Hughes, J. R., & Hatsukami, D. K. (1986). Signs and symptoms of tobacco withdrawal. *Archives of General Psychiatry, 43*, 289–294.

Killen, J. D., & Fortmann, S. P. (1997). Craving is associated with smoking relapse: Findings from three prospective studies. *Experimental and Clinical Psychopharmacology, 5*(2), 137–142.

Landers, S. J. (2002). Antitobacco activists lift smokescreen behind teen smoking. *American Medical News, 45*(13), 46–47.

Landman, A., Ling, P. M., & Glantz, S. A. (2002). Tobacco industry youth smoking prevention programs: Protecting the industry. *American Journal of Public Health, 92*(6), 917–930.

Lichtenstein, E., & Glasgow, R. E. (1992). Smoking cessation: What have we learned over the past decade? *Journal of Consulting and Clinical Psychology, 60*(4), 518–527.

Marlatt, G. A., & Gordon, J. R. (Eds.). (1985). *Relapse prevention: Maintenance strategies in the treatment of addictive behaviors.* New York: Guilford.

McDonald, P., Colwell, B., Backinger, C. L., Husten, C., & Maule, C. O. (2003). Better practices for youth tobacco cessation: Evidence of review panel. *American Journal of Health Behavior, 27*(Suppl. 2), S144–S158.

Milton, M. H., Maule, C. O., Backinger, C. L., & Gregory, D. M. (2003). Recommendations and guidance for practice in youth tobacco cessation. *American Journal of Health Behavior, 27*(Suppl. 2), S159–S169.

National Center for Health Statistics (1999). *Healthy people 2000 review, 1998-1997.* Hyattsville, MD: Public Health Service.

National Center for Health Statistics (2006). *Health, United States, 2006.* Washington, DC: U.S. Government Printing Office.

Parrott, S. & Godfrey, C. (2005). Economics of smoking cessation. *British Medical Journal, 328*, 947–949.

Patten, C. A., & Martin, J. E. (1996). Measuring tobacco withdrawal: A review of self-report questionnaires. *Journal of Substance Abuse, 8*(1), 93–113.

Perkins, K. A., Levine, M., Marcus, M., Shiffman, S., D'Amico, D., Miller, A., et al. (2000). Tobacco withdrawal in women and menstrual cycle phase. *Journal of Consulting and Clinical Psychology, 68*(1), 176–180.

Perkins, K. A., Marcus, M., Shiffman, S., Levine, M., D'Amico, D., Miller, A., et al. (2001). Cognitive-behavioral therapy to reduce weight concerns improves smoking cessation outcome in weight-concerned women. *Journal of Consulting and Clinical Psychology, 69*(4), 604–613.

Pfizer, Inc. (2006, May). Chantix prescribing information. Retrieved December 24, 2006, from http://www.pfizer.com/pfizer/download/uspi_chantix.pdf

Prochaska, J. O., & DiClemente, C. C. (1983). Stages and processes of self-change of smoking: Toward an integrative model of change. *Journal of Consulting and Clinical Psychology, 51*(3), 390–395.

Prokhorov, A. V., Hudmon, K. S., & Stancic, N. (2003). Adolescent smoking: Epidemiology and approaches for achieving cessation. *Pediatric Drugs, 5*(1), 1-10.

Rigotti, N. A. (1997). Smoking. In M. D. Feldman & J. F. Christensen (Eds.), *Behavioral medicine in primary care: A practical guide* (pp. 141–149). Stamford, CT: Appleton & Lange.

Rollnick, S., Butler, C. C., & Stott, N. (1997). Helping smokers make decisions: The enhancement of brief intervention for general medical practice. *Patient Education and Counseling, 31*, 191–203.

Schachter, S. (1982). Recidivism and self-cure of smoking and obesity. *American Psychologist, 37*, 436–444.

Stitzer, M. L., & Walsh, S. L. (1997). Psychostimulant abuse: The case for combined behavioral and pharmacological treatments. *Pharmacology, Biochemistry and Behavior, 57*, 457–470.

Tobacco Use and Dependence Clinical Practice Guideline Panel, Staff, and Consortium Representatives. (2000). A clinical practice guideline for treating tobacco use and dependence: A US public health service report. *Journal of the American Medical Association, 283*(24), 3244–3254.

U.S. Department of Health and Human Services. (1982). *The health consequences of smoking: Cancer: A report of the Surgeon General* (DHHS Publication no. PHS 82-50179). Washington, DC: U.S. Government Printing Office.

U.S. Department of Health and Human Services. (1988). *The health consequences of smoking: Nicotine addiction: A report of the Surgeon General* (DHHS Publication no. CDC 88-8406). Washington, DC: U.S. Government Printing Office.

U.S. Department of Health and Human Services. (1990). *The health benefits of smoking cessation: A report of the Surgeon General* (DHHS Publication No. CDC 90-8416). Washington, DC: U.S. Government Printing Office.

U.S. Department of Health and Human Services. (1994). *Preventing tobacco use among young people: A report of the Surgeon General.* Atlanta, GA: Author.

U.S. Department of Health and Human Services. (2000a). *Reducing tobacco use: A report of the Surgeon General.* Atlanta, GA: Author.

U.S. Department of Health and Human Services. (2000b). *Tobacco use. In Healthy People 2010: Vol. 2. Understanding and improving health and objectives for improving health* (2nd ed., pp. 27-3–27-40). Washington, DC: U.S. Government Printing Office.

U.S. Department of Health and Human Services. (2000c). *Treating tobacco use and dependence: Clinical practice guideline.* Rockville, MD: Author.

U. S. Department of Health and Human Services (2004). *The health consequences of smoking: A report of the Surgeon General.* Atlanta, GA: Centers for Disease Control and Prevention.

U.S. Department of Health and Human Services (2005). *Women and Smoking: A report of the Surgeon General, 2001. National vital statistic reports. Births: Final data for 2003.* Washington, DC: U.S. Government Printing Office.

U. S. Federal Trade Commission (1997). *Report of tar, nicotine, and carbon monoxide of the smoke of 1206 varieties of domestic cigarettes.* Washington, DC: Author.

Williamson, D. F., Madans, J., Anda, R. F., Kleinman, J. C., Giovino, G. A., & Byers, T. (1991). Smoking cessation and severity of weight gain in a national cohort. *New England Journal of Medicine, 324*(11), 739–745.

Wilson, D. M., Taylor, D. W., Gilbert, J. R., Best, J. A., Lindsay, E. A., Willms, D. G., & Singer, J. (1988). A randomized trial of a family physician intervention for smoking cessation. *Journal of the American Medical Association, 260*(11), 1570–1574.

PART III

Common Disease States

CHAPTER 6

Cardiovascular Disease

ALBERT J. BELLG

INTRODUCTION

In cardiovascular disease (CVD), psychological factors are essential to understanding the onset and progress of the disease, its treatment, and how patients make lifestyle changes and cope with the issues associated with cardiac conditions. However, CVD is more complex than many of the diseases covered in this handbook, and there are many tests and treatments to identify and control it. This chapter will cover three broad areas of CVD that are commonly addressed in the practice of health psychology with heart patients. Each has its own psychological issues and challenges.

BRIEF DESCRIPTION OF DISEASE STATES

The first area of CVD that cardiac psychology focuses on is coronary artery disease (CAD), or the accumulation of hardened atherosclerotic plaques or deposits along the inner lining of the arteries (Heger, Niemann, & Criley, 2003; except where indicated, this text is the source for the information on cardiovascular disease, tests, and treatment in this chapter). People with CAD may have a heart attack (myocardial infarction) or chest pain (angina). Psychological factors (e.g., stress, depression, and social isolation) and behavioral factors (e.g., diet, exercise, weight control, and adherence to prescribed medications) affect the development of atherosclerotic plaques throughout the course of the disease, and are therefore addressed as both primary risk factors influencing the onset of the disease and secondary risk factors affecting disease progression. Cardiac rehabilitation programs typically combine a variety of psychological and behavioral approaches to aid the recovery of heart patients and reduce their risk factors.

The second area is heart failure (cardiomyopathy), in which a weakened and often enlarged heart is no longer able to pump blood effectively to the rest of the body. For heart failure, although there are some behavioral factors associated with the onset of cardiomyopathy (e.g., drug and alcohol abuse), the key focus in controlling the disease is secondary prevention to minimize the impact of the disease on the patient's life and slow down its progress. Psychological and behavioral interventions to control secondary risk factors, such as dietary sodium and fluid consumption, are important to reduce the incidence of congestive heart failure (CHF), which is essentially fluid retention resulting from poor kidney function associated with the weakened heart.

The third area of CVD is the broad collection of heart rhythm disorders (arrhythmias) and valvular disease. For both arrhythmias and valvular disease, prevention is less important than an overall behavioral focus on medical disease management (e.g., medication adherence) and coping with potentially severe treatment consequences such as shocks from an implanted cardiac pacemaker/defibrillator.

In all three areas of CVD, the psychological issues associated with illness coping and treatment adherence are a focus of patient concern and psychological intervention. In addition, the onset and progress of cardiovascular disease has a significant body of research indicating that it is directly affected by psychological factors such as stress, depression, and social isolation. Consequently, there are three main areas of focus for the psychological issues associated with cardiovascular disease.

1. The facilitation of health-promoting behavioral changes and adherence to recommended medical treatment.
2. Helping patients address illness-related psychopathology and coping issues.
3. Intervention with psychological risk factors that directly influence the onset and progress of disease.

PREVALENCE

Almost one in four Americans has some form of cardiovascular disease. It has been the main cause of death in the United States for every year since 1900 except for 1918, the year of the Spanish flu pandemic. Approximately 910,600 people died in 2003 with CVD as the primary cause (American Heart Association [AHA], 2006; except where indicated, this is the source for the incidence, prevalence, and mortality statistics on heart disease in this chapter).

Coronary artery disease has often been erroneously identified as a man's disease, in part because there are many more unexpected deaths (deaths at an earlier age than the average life expectancy) from CAD in men than in women. A protective effect associated with women's reproductive hormones results in women having only one-fourth as many heart attacks as men under the age of 65 (and a lower proportion at younger ages; above age 65, however, men and women are equally likely to have a heart attack). On average, acute events such as heart attacks and sudden death occur about 10 years earlier in men than in women. Women start to catch up as they get older, however, and by the end of life, slightly fewer men than women have died from all forms of CVD (AHA, 2006).

The type of CVD that men and women develop tends to be different, however. Under age 75, American men have more coronary artery disease (CAD) than women, and women have more congestive heart failure (CHF) than men (AHA, 2006). The number of people with CVD also differs by race. At any given time, 34.3% of Caucasian males and 32.4% of Caucasian females have CVD. By comparison, the prevalence of CVD in African American males is 20% higher than in Caucasian males, and 38% higher in African American females than in Caucasian females. The prevalence in Mexican American males is 14.8 % less than in Caucasian males, and 10.6% less in Mexican American females than in Caucasian females (AHA).

Heart failure is the only area of CVD that has been significantly increasing, and the incidence is growing at over 3% per year for reasons that are not well understood. Congestive heart failure (CHF), its most common manifestation, occurs in five million Americans and results in 57,200 deaths per year (AHA, 2006).

DISEASE FACTORS

There are many manifestations of cardiovascular disease and many patient responses as a consequence. The following sections review the various forms of CVD with a focus on some of the key factors affecting patient coping and behavior.

CORONARY ARTERY DISEASE

Coronary artery disease has three major clinical syndromes: angina pectoris, myocardial infarction, and sudden cardiac death. A 70% or greater stenosis (narrowing) in one or more of the three main coronary arteries or their branches is usually necessary for symptoms of these syndromes to be evident (Heger, Niemann, & Criley, 2003). CAD can also present as silent ischemia, which is a blockage of blood flow to the heart without pain or discomfort, and ischemic cardiomyopathy, in which a portion of the heart muscle no longer functions due to its not having sufficient blood (Heger, Niemann, & Criley).

Angina Pectoris   Inadequate blood flow to the heart muscle often results in anginal pain or a sensation of pressure or fullness, but no permanent damage to the heart. Stress or physical activity may cause angina, because partially blocked arteries may not supply the heart with the needed increase in blood during those experiences. An arterial spasm can also cause angina. Symptoms of angina can either remain unchanging for years, or unstable angina may occur without warning with symptoms that can be as severe as those in a heart attack (Heger, Niemann & Criley, 2003).

A key coping issue is how patients respond to this early symptom of CAD. Some patients will take angina as a wakeup call to get checked out by their physician, make healthy lifestyle changes, take medications to reduce risks from high cholesterol or high blood pressure, and make sure they have regular visits with their physician. Others may continue with old habits, coping with the prospect of more severe and life-threatening disease with denial or avoidance strategies. Unfortunately, those strategies often result in more severe disease that is far more difficult to deny or avoid.

Myocardial Infarction   A blood clot (coronary thrombosis or occlusion) or the rupture of an atherosclerotic plaque can result in complete blockage of the coronary arteries, producing a heart attack (myocardial infarction). A heart attack can also result from a severe arterial spasm. Heart attacks often occur without warning, with 80% occurring in patients who have never had long-standing angina. About 20% of heart attacks occur either without being noticed by the patient or without being identified by the patient from the symptoms that are experienced (Kannel & Feinleib, 1972).

Common symptoms of a heart attack (American Heart Association [AHA], 2006) include:

- Uncomfortable pressure, fullness, squeezing or pain in the center of the chest that lasts more than a few minutes, or goes away and comes back.
- Pain that spreads to the shoulders, neck, or arms.

- Chest discomfort with lightheadedness, fainting, sweating, nausea, or shortness of breath.

A key coping issue is whether to take immediate action when symptoms of a heart attack occur. Even with textbook symptoms of a heart attack, patients often delay action and hope the symptoms will go away. Some wait hours before going to the emergency room for treatment, in part to avoid feeling foolish if there is "nothing wrong." During that time, the heart muscle may become more severely damaged or death may occur. Heart attacks with less-than-typical symptoms also can cause additional delays in response, particularly for women who are both more likely to have atypical symptoms and who also may not consider themselves to be at risk for a heart problem.

Sudden Cardiac Death (SCD)   About 50% of all sudden death from heart disease in men and 64% in women occurs without warning in people who have had no previous symptoms of CVD. Although atherosclerotic plaques in two or more major coronary arteries are present in the great majority of patients who have SCD, most sudden deaths are caused by a rapid heartbeat (ventricular tachycardia) or an irregular heartbeat (ventricular fibrillation; AHA, 2006).

Perhaps surprisingly, there is a key coping factor associated with sudden cardiac death. People with SCD often have subtle, preclinical symptoms of possible heart disease prior to their sudden death, and survivors of the person who died frequently feel guilt and remorse for not doing more to urge their loved one to seek help that might have saved his or her life. Such guilt generally has a negative effect on the grieving process. In addition, possible accusations that some people should have done more than they did for their loved one may result in the breakdown of family members' support for each other.

CORONARY ARTERY DISEASE RISK FACTORS

There are a wide variety of medical risk factors for coronary artery disease (see Table 6.1). These risk factors may result in any of the manifestations of CAD already discussed.

Dyslipidemias   Total cholesterol above 200 mg/dl is generally a concern, and about half of all Americans are above that level (AHA, 2006). Lipid-lowering medications decrease the number of deaths in men with mildly to moderately elevated total cholesterol (Shepherd, Cobbe, & Ford, 1995) and also reduce the number of further coronary events in post-heart attack patients with normal cholesterol (Sacks et al., 1996). HMG CoA reductase inhibitors (the "statins"; e.g., atorvastatin, simvastatin) are commonly used to reduce total cholesterol or low density lipoprotein (LDL; "bad" cholesterol). Some patients, however, may experience muscle aches severe enough to lead to discontinuation of the medication (Heger, Niemann, & Criley, 2003). Other medications for lipid management can also have significant side effects that reduce patient tolerance and adherence (Bellg, Rivkin, & Rosenson, 2002). Smoking cessation, exercise, and reduction in body weight and dietary fat are also recommended to control lipid disorders (AHA).

A key coping issue is whether patients will commit to long-term use of lipid-lowering medication that does not directly treat a disease and that reduces a risk factor with no physical symptoms. Research has found that, in a general clinic setting, cholesterol-lowering medications were most likely to be discontinued by women, pa-

Table 6.1

Risk Factors for Coronary Artery Disease

Unmodifiable risks
- Increasing age
- Male gender
- Heredity

Modifiable risks
- Smoking
- High overall or "bad" cholesterol (low density lipoprotein; LDL)
- Low "good" cholesterol (high density lipoprotein; HDL)
- Hypertension
- Diabetes mellitus
- Sedentary lifestyle
- Obesity 35% or more above ideal body weight
- Individual response to stress
- Presymptomatic atherosclerosis (per coronary CT scan)
- Type A behavior, notably hostility
- Clinical depression
- Social isolation
- High triglycerides
- High blood viscosity

Source: Adapted from American Heart Association (2006) and Scheidt (1996).

tients younger than 50 years old, and patients who had previously been treated for high cholesterol (Caspard, Chan, & Walker, 2005). Further adherence difficulties can also occur when low-level but ongoing side effects become harder to tolerate as time goes on.

Hypertension (HTN)   High blood pressure or hypertension is found in 32.3% of adult Americans (AHA, 2006). Certain groups are at greater risk, however. *Hypertension* is two to three times more common in women taking oral contraceptives than in women not taking them (AHA). Also, African Americans develop HTN earlier and have more severe HTN than Caucasian Americans, with a death rate associated with HTN about three times higher (AHA). Even mild HTN (blood pressure greater than or equal to 140/90 mmHg) is associated with increased risk of CVD (Joint National Committee on Detection, Evaluation, and Treatment of High Blood Pressure, Fifth Report [JNC V], 1993). Lifestyle modifications such as sodium restriction, weight reduction, and increased physical activity can help most patients with HTN (Blanchard, 1994), but medications are often needed to reliably lower more severe cases. The drugs used include diuretics, beta blockers, calcium channel blockers, and angiotensin-converting enzyme (ACE) inhibitors. Unfortunately, side effects (particularly those from beta blockers and, usually to a lesser extent, ACE inhibitors) may negatively influence quality of life and result in depression, fatigue, insomnia, and sexual dysfunction.

A key coping factor for antihypertensive medication, as with cholesterol-lowering medications, is medication adherence. However, subtle erosion of quality of life may be an even more significant coping issue for many patients. Side effects of medication to reduce blood pressure may be hard to identify and may be attributed to other physical problems. For instance, fatigue and mild depression may be a side effect overlooked in the context of other illness symptoms. Even sexual dysfunction, a common side effect of beta blockers, may be attributed to advancing age or stress associated with illness. Fortunately, when side effects occur, alternative medications are often available. Patients should be encouraged to approach their physicians to explore alternative treatments, if needed, to maintain their quality of life.

Metabolic Syndrome (MetS)   Metabolic syndrome increases the risk of plaque forming on the walls of coronary arteries, primarily due to obesity and a metabolic process called insulin resistance. It consists of three or more of five main elements: (1) abdominal obesity; (2) elevated triglycerides; (3) reduced HDL; (4) elevated blood pressure; and (5) elevated fasting glucose (AHA, 2006). Lifestyle modifications such as increasing physical activity, lowering dietary fat, and reducing weight are the recommended treatments for MetS, in part because medical treatment of elevated blood pressure can increase insulin resistance (Flack & Sowers, 1991).

HEART FAILURE AND TRANSPLANT

When the heart muscle is damaged and unable to function normally, heart failure (usually presenting as congestive heart failure) is the result. The heart is a pump, and when it is unable to pump effectively, blood does not circulate adequately. As it moves sluggishly, it can cause shortness of breath and edema, or swelling of the extremities. It can also interfere with sleep by making it difficult for the patient to lie flat in bed. The kidneys also have a more difficult time removing water, waste products, and sodium from the body, making the symptoms more severe.

A number of other diseases of the heart muscle that affect its ability to pump are called cardiomyopathies. Cardiomyopathy (CM) may result from a heart attack, hypertension, valve disease, alcoholism, and other causes. The varieties of cardiomyopathy include dilated CM (an enlarged and therefore weakened heart) and hypertrophic CM (a thickening of the left ventricle that impairs the ability of the heart to pump; Heger, Niemann, & Criley, 2003).

One important way to evaluate the severity of heart failure is to assess the heart's ejection fraction (EF), or the percentage of blood that is released when the heart contracts. The average EF in a healthy person is approximately 55 to 65%. An EF of 25% or less, along with other clinical factors, will often result in a patient being considered for heart transplantation.

A key coping factor in heart failure is associated with the apparent health of most heart failure patients and the absence of symptoms when they are resting or inactive. Other people in the patient's life may wonder why the patient can no longer work, cut the grass, or do housework. They may accuse the patient of laziness or lack of motivation. These statements are hurtful to heart failure patients, who may find their fatigue or shortness of breath so severe that they may be able to participate in normal activities for no more than a few minutes before having to rest. Patients also commonly experience days when their energy and abilities feel almost normal again, but if they push themselves (or are pushed by others) to engage in what used to be a normal day's activities, they may pay a high price the next day by having severe fatigue.

ARRHYTHMIAS

Irregular heartbeats are associated with erratic electrical impulses caused by abnormal electrolytes (e.g., potassium, magnesium, or calcium), addictive substances (alcohol, nicotine, or other recreational drugs), medications such as digoxin and theophylline, and other causes. Most cases of sudden cardiac death are associated with an arrhythmia called ventricular fibrillation. Other arrhythmias include sinus arrhythmia, premature atrial contractions (PACs), premature ventricular contractions (PVCs), and atrial fibrillation. Arrhythmias may be kept under control with medication or with implanted electrical cardiac pacemakers, which often include a defibrillator to restore normal heart rhythm with an electrical shock.

A key coping issue is associated with implanted defibrillators. Although a life-threatening arrhythmia may be controlled with an implanted cardiac pacemaker and defibrillator, if the defibrillator gives a patient a repeated electric shock to reestablish a normal cardiac rhythm, that patient may develop acute anxiety, phobic avoidance behaviors in situations where he or she anticipates receiving such shocks, and posttraumatic stress disorder symptoms (Mello & Batista, 2001). Particularly problematic are shocks that occur in places far from medical help or in public places where a patient feels conspicuous and embarrassed. Support groups consisting of patients who are also coping with this problem and individual counseling for anxiety and phobias are often effective at restoring a patient's confidence and enabling him or her to resume normal life activities.

Valvular Disease

Problems with heart valves make it more difficult for the heart to pump effectively. The symptoms can be shortness of breath, fatigue, or chest pain. The stethoscope can usually reveal heart sounds such as clicks or snaps, changes in the intensity or timing of the heart sounds, or heart murmurs that result from irregularly formed valves creating turbulence in the bloodstream. Valve problems can be congenital or caused by infections. Treatments include use of medication or surgery to replace or reconstruct the valve.

A key coping issue is awareness of heart sounds. Some patients become aware of irregular heart sounds and may become anxious, wondering whether their heart is functioning normally. After surgery to replace a valve, the new valve may also produce a different sound that the patient becomes aware of. As with most physical symptoms causing anxiety, improving coping strategies is usually effective.

Other Cardiac Issues

Cardiac Infections   Infections of the heart usually occur around the pericardium (a fibrous membrane and a dense sack surrounding the heart) or on the heart valves, due to an infection in the bloodstream. Symptoms of pericardial disease can be similar to a heart attack or congestive heart failure. Endocarditis results when bacteria enter the blood from dental or other procedures (Heger, Niemann, & Criley, 2003). Both types of infection are hard to treat due to the difficulty of effectively delivering an antibiotic to the infected areas, and surgery may be required.

A key coping issue has to do with the uncertainty of treatment. Long courses of antibiotics may be administered, but patients may worry about whether therapy will be effective and anxious regarding the prospect of surgery at some point in the future if it is not. Even if treatment is successful, they may also worry about a recurrence of the disease.

Aortic Aneurysms   An aneurysm is a widening or ballooning of the wall of a vein or artery. It is of considerable concern when it occurs in the aorta, the artery that carries blood from the heart to the body. One quarter of the hospitalizations associated with aortic aneurysms result in death (Heger, Niemann, & Criley, 2003). Lowering blood pressure and placing a surgical patch on the aneurysm is the usual treatment.

A key coping issue is fear of sudden death. Many people with aneurysms; even those who are being effectively treated feel that they could die at any time. This sense of fear can result in excessively constrained activity and anxiety symptoms. Typically this fear subsides over time, but psychotherapy is often helpful.

REGIMEN FACTORS

The regimen for patients with heart disease nearly always involves a complex combination of diagnostic procedures, symptom monitoring, treatment, and monitoring of treatment effects.

DIAGNOSTIC PROCEDURES

Ischemic heart disease constricts the flow of blood to the heart, and when a person exercises, the heart's increased demand for blood flow may not be capable of being met and symptoms may result. An exercise stress test uses carefully administered amounts of exercise, based on the person's age, to increase demand on the heart. If a person has arterial blockages or partial blockages, symptoms such as fatigue, shortness of breath, rapid heartbeat, chest pain due to angina, blood pressure changes, or electrocardiogram changes, coronary artery disease may be revealed. However, an exercise stress test can only detect blockages greater than 50% to 75%, which means that there are often false negative results for the presence of disease that could be clinically significant. False positive results are more likely in groups that are unlikely to have actual CAD, such as people with few or no risk factors or women prior to menopause (Heger, Niemann, & Criley, 2003).

A more recent and accurate screening test is the 64–slice coronary computed tomography (CT) scan. This relatively new type of CT scan creates a three-dimensional image of the heart that is detailed enough to detect nearly all coronary artery disease and identify its degree of severity, with the exception of blockages found in highly calcified areas (Heger, Niemann, & Criley, 2003). This promising technology can be used as a highly accurate screening test, although it is too expensive to be covered by most insurers for that purpose. However, when disease is suspected due to the presence of possible symptoms, it can be one of the most accurate ways of discovering whether disease is present, approaching the diagnostic accuracy of coronary catheterization. The 64–slice CT is rapidly replacing the ultra-fast electron beam computed tomography (EBCT) scans that are used to produce an image of calcium deposits in the coronary arteries that are associated with increased risk of CAD (Heger, Niemann, & Criley).

A key coping issue occurs when a person with many CAD risk factors has a negative exercise stress test. The result is often his or her minimization of the need to address his or her risk factors. The apparent absence of disease provides them with false reassurance that they do not have heart disease. Because a stress test is unlikely to detect blockages less than 50%, it is more accurate to believe that nearly everyone with several coronary risk factors has some degree of CAD, and whether it can be detected by a stress test is irrelevant to the need to reduce those risk factors to keep the CAD from progressing. It is not uncommon for people to know or have heard of someone who had a negative stress test who developed symptoms of heart disease or had a heart attack within the following year.

Tests for a Heart Attack   The death of muscle tissue associated with a heart attack is signaled by elevated cardiac enzymes, particularly creatine kinase (CK or CPK) and the proteins troponin T and troponin I. These chemicals are among the first things examined when a patient is brought to the emergency room with a suspected heart attack. However, enzyme levels often take 6 hours or more to become elevated after a heart attack (Heger, Niemann, & Criley, 2003), so lab tests do not provide useful information during that time.

An electrocardiogram (ECG) shows the electrical activity of the heart. The presence of abnormal activity may be indicative of a heart attack, although an initial ECG may be nondiagnostic in 20 to 50% of cases of acute heart attack (McGuinnes, Begg, & Semple, 1976). If elevated cardiac enzymes or an abnormal ECG are present along with other symptoms congruent with a diagnosis of heart attack, patients are typically referred for cardiac catheterization to obtain a definitive diagnosis.

Cardiac catheterization involves running a catheter through a vein or artery in the leg up into the heart. With the use of imaging technology to monitor contrast dye injected into the coronary arteries, blockages can be definitively identified. Simultaneously with the diagnosis of a blockage, balloon angioplasty with a stent can often be used to open the artery. In addition, depending on the diagnostic need, other information on ventricular ejection fraction, wall motion of the heart, and valve function can be obtained (Heger, Niemann, & Criley, 2003). Catheterization is relatively safe, with fewer than 1% of cases involving complications (Fighali et al., 1985; Hansing, 1979). Cardiac catheterization can also be used to biopsy transplanted hearts to test for rejection (Heger, Niemann, & Criley, 2003).

A key coping factor is associated with the increased chance that a heart attack may be misdiagnosed when it presents with atypical symptoms or when it occurs in low-risk groups. Women frequently confront both issues, being more likely to experience atypical symptoms of a heart attack (for example, neck or back pain) as well as being in a group assumed to be at lower risk of a heart problem. This potentially deadly combination may result in a delay of weeks or months in obtaining the correct diagnosis and treatment for their heart problem (Hayes, 2006). Many women heart patients are understandably frustrated and angry that their heart problem took so long to diagnose, and some become advocates for greater awareness in the medical community regarding women's heart problems. This issue is getting considerably more attention from primary care physicians and emergency room staff, as well as cardiologists (Tsang, Barnes, Gersh, & Hayes, 2000).

Other Cardiac Tests   Echocardiography is a noninvasive procedure that uses ultrasound to provide moving images of cardiac structures. An "echo" can show cardiac valves, wall motion, flow-velocity patterns, and chamber dimensions and function. They are typically used in patients suspected of ischemic heart disease, heart failure, and valvular disease (Heger, Niemann, & Criley, 2003).

There are also several noninvasive imaging techniques that use radioisotopes. Myocardial perfusion imaging uses thallium-201 or other radioisotopes to identify areas of the heart that are not adequately perfused with blood after exercise. Infarct avid imaging identifies damaged heart tissue following a heart attack by using an interaction between calcium and technetium pyrophosphate. Radionuclide angiography can create images of various parts of the heart, calculate the ventricular ejection fraction, and identify valvular disease and heart wall motion abnormalities. Positron emission tomography (PET scans) is helpful in evaluating healthy heart tissue and can also test for CAD and myocardium function.

Magnetic resonance imaging (MRI) or nuclear magnetic resonance (NMR) images can be used to evaluate damage to the heart from a heart attack, identify some congenital heart defects, and examine disease in larger blood vessels. Magnetic resonance imaging tests have traditionally been a source of stress and even phobic responses in some patients, since they require patients to enter a narrow, confining tube and remain motionless while the equipment operates, producing a loud sound. Cognitive behavioral therapy for phobias is often successful. Newer, open-MRI equipment is open at the sides and is usually better tolerated.

Medical and Surgical Treatments for Coronary Artery Disease

Angina, the least severe form of symptomatic coronary artery disease, is usually treated with three types of drugs: nitrates, beta blockers, and calcium channel blockers. Nitrates (e.g., nitroglycerin) increase blood to the heart tissue by dilating the coronary arteries to improve collateral blood flow. Beta-adrenergic blocking agents reduce heart rate and blood pressure, thereby lowering the amount of oxygen the heart requires. Calcium channel blockers lower the effort put out by the heart and reduce constriction of the coronary arteries (Heger, Niemann, & Criley, 2003). The physical interventions to open blood vessels are percutaneous transluminal coronary angioplasty (PTCA) and coronary artery bypass graft surgery (CABG). Percutaneous transluminal coronary angioplasty is considered to be a medical procedure and is performed by interventional cardiologists. Coronary artery bypass graft surgery is a surgical procedure and is performed by cardiac surgeons.

When CAD becomes more severe and results in a heart attack, urgent medical and often surgical intervention is required. Fast response is critical, since the longer a coronary artery is blocked by a plaque or a blood clot, the greater the damage to the heart muscle. Once a patient is diagnosed with a heart attack, a clot-dissolving (thrombolytic) agent is often administered to start the process of reopening the artery. Emergency PTCA or CABG surgery may follow, sometimes in less than an hour, to physically open the arteries and improve blood flow (Heger, Niemann, & Criley, 2003). Various blood thinners can be used in the short term to prevent further blockages and clots, while the long-term use of aspirin can not only reduce the chance of clots but can stabilize plaques. Recovery of partially damaged heart muscle can be aided by drugs that promote vasodilation, such as nitrates, beta blockers and angiotensin-converting enzyme (ACE) inhibitors (Heger, Niemann, & Criley).

Percutaneous transluminal coronary angioplasty (balloon angioplasty) is often used to open up partially blocked arteries in patients with CAD. A small incision is usually made in the inner thigh near the groin, and a guide wire is passed through the arteries up into the narrowed area of the coronary artery. The procedure is monitored with fluoroscopic imaging. Then a narrow balloon on the end of a catheter is threaded through the guide wire, and the balloon is then inflated to compress the plaque. Without the use of stents (a wire mesh tube used to hold the artery open), the blockage is likely to recur within 6 months in about 25% of patients (Heger, Niemann, & Criley, 2003). Stents can reduce this to about 10%, and medically coated stents reduce the chance of recurrent blockage to about 3%. Other catheterization procedures may involve removing the plaque itself (atherectomy). Anticoagulant medications and sometimes radiation are also used to reduce the likelihood of blockage recurring (Heger, Niemann, & Criley).

Coronary artery bypass graft surgery (CABG) involves surgically implanting a vein from the patient to convey blood around the blockage. The main reason this procedure is possible is because atherosclerotic plaques almost always occur in specific locations and can be bypassed (Heger, Niemann, & Criley, 2003). Although traditional CABG procedures involve cutting through the sternum and opening up the chest, for some patients a variation on the procedure, called minimally invasive coronary artery bypass (Mid CAB) can be used. This involves entering between the ribs and is less physically stressful (Heger, Niemann, & Criley). Some CABG procedures are associated with increased risk of stroke, and reduced cognitive functioning (usually temporary) is found in up to 25% of CABG patients (Selnes, McKhann, Borowicz, & Grega, 2006).

A new angina-reducing procedure called transmyocardial laser revascularization (TMLR) uses a laser to burn holes to increase blood flow in areas of the heart muscle that are impaired but not entirely dead. The heart muscle then receives blood directly from the interior of the heart. A percutaneous version of this procedure (percutaneous myocardial revascularization, or PTMR) can be conducted similarly to cardiac catheterization. Percutaneous myocardial revascularization or TMLR is sometimes used as an alternative treatment for patients with angina who cannot be treated medically (Heger, Niemann, & Criley, 2003).

Enhanced external counterpulsation (EECP) treatment for angina involves the use of leg cuffs rapidly inflated precisely at the time during the heartbeat when pressure on the legs can reduce strain on the heart and increase the return of blood through the coronary arteries, thereby increasing flow to the heart muscle. Patients usually have 35 sessions of EECP over 5 to 7 weeks. About two-thirds of patients with severe angina have reduced symptoms as a result of this procedure (Arora et al., 1999), and about half have improvements that last a year or more (Arora et al., 2002).

A key coping factor for any medical or surgical intervention for a heart attack has to do with the patient's concern regarding how much of his or her previous ability to function will be regainable. Although a wait and see attitude is appropriate and common, many patients with financial stress are worried about being able to resume their jobs or their role as breadwinners. Others may worry that they can no longer be involved in personal or family activities the way they used to. Some may be impatient at the slow rate of rehabilitation recommended by cardiac rehabilitation staff to promote complete healing and recovery. Others may be concerned about restrictions on the amount of weight they should lift or activity they should engage in the months following CABG surgery. Such concerns often exacerbate difficulties with self-worth, particularly for patients who define themselves primarily by what they are capable of doing. For patients with supportive families, encouraging them to listen to what their loved ones are saying regarding how much they are valued and cared for may be helpful. The basic cognitive reframing strategy of focusing patients on what they can do rather than what they can't do may also be useful.

Medical and Surgical Treatments for Heart Failure

Treatment can improve CHF as long as specific causes can be identified (e.g., hypertension, abnormal valves). Even lifestyle changes such as sodium and fluid restriction, and changes in physical activity level, may help patients with relatively mild non-symptomatic heart failure. For symptomatic CHF, medical therapy usually includes ACE inhibitors, diuretics to reduce the body's sodium and fluid load, and inotropic agents to improve the ability of the heart to pump. ACE inhibitors reduce the load on the heart by dilating blood vessels and decreasing blood pressure. Beta blockers may also be helpful. For more severe heart failure requiring medications that cannot be administered at home, patients may come to a hospital infusion clinic several times a week for up to 8 hours to receive their medicines intravenously (Heger, Niemann, & Criley, 2003). This regimen is often quite disruptive to the patient's life.

A heart transplant is considered when the patient is at risk of dying because his or her severely damaged heart is not responding to medical treatment and cannot benefit from CABG surgery. Although 2,198 heart transplants were performed in the United States in 2000, as many as 40,000 patients each year could benefit from a transplant each year, so most patients eligible for transplant die while they are waiting for a heart. About 70% of heart transplant patients survive for 5 years, and the 1-year survival rate is approximately 85% (AHA, 2006). Survival requires transplant patients to take 8 to 12 medications per day to reduce the chance of rejecting the transplanted heart, fight infection, and control blood pressure (Heger, Niemann, & Criley, 2003). This is often a difficult treatment regimen to follow, particularly since some of these medications (such as immunosuppressive steroids) can affect mood and mental status (Brown, Beard, Frol, & Rush, 2006).

Some heart failure patients appear to benefit from ventricular reduction surgery, which increases the heart's ability to pump efficiently. A left ventricular assist device (LVAD) can also be used to temporarily assist the heart while a patient waits for transplantation, and in some cases may be available for patients not eligible for transplantation. This mechanical pump may allow patients to resume many of their normal activities, although it requires careful monitoring and frequent battery changes. The audible sound of the pump may also make some patients self-conscious.

A key coping factor for heart failure patients and patients following cardiac transplantation is adherence to treatment. Heart failure patients with even mild cardiomyopathy may have a difficult time maintaining the lifestyle changes that will slow the progress of their disease and minimize its effect on their lives. Following transplantation, however, even a few days of nonadherence to antirejection medications may put a patient's life at risk. Prior to being considered for transplantation, patients often undergo a psychological screening and evaluation to determine their likely adherence to posttransplant medication. Factors considered may include past medication adherence, issues with authority, willingness to cooperate with the medical team, cognitive function that may affect the patient's ability to remember directions, and emotional issues potentially affecting the patient's adherence behavior. Transplantation programs vary considerably in what psychosocial factors they consider relevant to heart transplantation.

INDIVIDUAL FACTORS

A variety of individual factors influence how well patients handle heart disease and cope with their treatment regimen.

KNOWLEDGE AND INFORMATION

Heart patients are frequently surprised by the onset of a heart attack or the diagnosis of heart disease. Lack of knowledge frequently exacerbates their sense of being threatened by their heart problem, and information from their medical or surgical care-givers is crucial to helping them manage heart disease and cope more successfully with it. Medical literacy is a key factor as well, since older patients in particular (and therefore most heart patients) may not know the language of medical care (Baker, 1999). Assessing and improving patient understanding of any new aspect of their disease or intervention is essential to good patient care.

RELATIONSHIPS WITH MEDICAL PROVIDERS

Patients who develop heart disease typically meet many new medical providers in a short period of time. Patients who are somewhat insecure about their care or their illness may become anxious when their providers do not all characterize the patient's problems or the severity of those problems in the same way. Unless there is a clear policy governing how patients and their families obtain information, providers may also offer different recommendations for treatment. This natural variation may lead to misunderstandings, anxiety, and mistrust of the caregiving team. Under better circumstances, however, positive relationships with providers can improve coping and reduce stress that can impair the process of healing (Broadbent, Petrie, Alley, and Booth, 2003).

AGE

Because of the age of onset of heart disease, cardiac patients and preventive cardiology patients are usually middle-aged and older men and women. Older medical patients deal about as well with health behavior change issues as younger patients, but younger patients may have more illness adjustment problems since their heart problem may interfere more with their family and work life. Older heart patients may be less likely to deal well with distress and follow through with psychological treatment for illness adjustment problems since they may be less interested in and experienced with psychological perspectives, less articulate about feelings and internal experiences, and less inclined to look to others for support (Rybarczyk, 1994). Alexithymia, or the inability to understand or talk about feelings due to a lack of emotional awareness, is also somewhat more common in older than younger heart patients and can result in reduced social skills and greater difficulty with illness coping (Lumley, Ovies, Stettner, Wehmer, & Lakey, 1996). However, age in itself is no barrier to effective psychological treatment, and treatment expectations for cooperative older heart patients should remain high.

Age can also be an issue with younger cardiac patients or preventive cardiology patients. Risk factors such as elevated cholesterol can run in families, and when younger family members show signs of familial hypercholesterolemia, changing their eating and exercise behavior may require the entire family to make lifestyle changes. Parents have more effect on the eating behavior of heart patients under 10 years old, especially when the parents eat in the way they are recommending to their children (Brown & Ogden, 2004). Teenagers may be dealing with other kinds of lifestyle change issues such as peer pressure, self-confidence, psychological developmental issues, and less ability to control the stimulus effect of their environment.

GENDER

Gender affects the psychological consequences of heart disease and also plays a role in identifying and treating cardiac risk factors. Men tend to develop heart disease earlier in their lives, which means that their coping issues more frequently involve the effects of their illness on their ability to work, their income, their physical capabilities, and their ability to fulfill family roles. Men are also less likely to identify the need for help and seek professional assistance in order to make health behavior changes and deal with illness-related psychopathology (Warren, 1983). The difference in the age of onset of heart disease in men and women has also resulted in women's awareness and concerns in the prevention and treatment of heart disease being underemphasized until recently. For instance, women are more concerned about dying of breast cancer than heart disease, even though they are 12 times more likely to die of a cardiac condition; one in 2.6 women die of heart disease (AHA, 2006). Because of this lack of awareness, women are also less likely to participate in screening for cardiovascular disease and to be aware of the need to address cardiac risk factors. Lower illness rates for women in study populations is also a factor in women being underrepresented in treatment research and studies of psychosocial factors affecting CVD outcomes (Frasure-Smith, Lesperance, & Talajic, 1995a).

The medical issues associated with heart disease are also different for men and women. Women have a poorer prognosis after a heart attack than men (AHA, 2006). Smoking is also a more significant risk factor for women than men, since a first heart attack occurs approximately 7 years earlier in smoking men than nonsmoking men, but 19 years earlier in smoking women than nonsmoking women (Hansen, Anderson, & Von Eyben, 1993). Smoking thus effectively eliminates the gender advantage women have in avoiding heart disease at younger ages. Men and women also differ in risk factors such as cardiovascular reactivity, triggering events for a heart attack, and types of stressors associated with increases in cardiovascular disease (Jacobs & Sherwood, 1996). There are currently significant efforts to include more women in prevention and treatment research in order to better understand all aspects of heart disease and cardiac risks among women (Tsang, Barnes, Gersh, & Hayes, 2000).

COMORBID PSYCHOPATHOLOGY

DEPRESSION

Clinical depression may be found in 18 to 44% of cardiac patients over the course of their disease (Fernandez, 1993). Psychological or physical processes often lead to clinical depression or anxiety in heart patients after they have received a diagnosis of coronary artery disease or have suffered a heart attack. Psychological issues such as awareness of one's mortality, loss of income or work, or changes in family roles can lead to anxiety or depression. Treatment goals for depression in heart patients may include reduction of anger, irritability, social withdrawal, anhedonia, and loss of interest. Diagnoses also need to distinguish depressed and anxious thoughts from reasonable concern, worry, and sadness about having a heart problem.

Depression also appears to be implicated in the onset of heart disease (Nemeroff, Musselman, & Evans, 1998). People with depression have high sympathetic tone, hypercortisolemia, elevated catecholamine levels, abnormal platelet activation, increased inflammatory markers, and endothelial dysfunction—and so do people with a diagnosis of heart disease (Rumsfeld & Ho, 2005). Depression not only makes it more likely for heart disease to develop initially, but also increases the likelihood of death in the months following a heart attack (Frasure-Smith, Lesperance, & Talajic, 1995b). Depression can increase blood pressure, alter blood clotting, affect heart rhythms, and raise cholesterol and insulin levels, but the physiological mechanisms by which it does this are not well understood at present (Rumsfeld & Ho).

ANXIETY

Similar to clinical depression, anxiety is an independent risk factor for heart disease and has a complex association with other cardiac risk factors. Generalized anxiety disorder, in particular, has been associated with high blood pressure, diabetes, high cholesterol, body mass index, and increased smoking, all risks for heart disease (Barger & Sydeman, 2005). Phobic anxiety is also a concern, with both men and women with phobic anxiety being more likely to die suddenly of a heart-related problem (Albert, Chae, Rexrode, Manson, & Kawachi, 2005). Posttraumatic stress disorder (PTSD) is also linked with heart disease. Vietnam war veterans with PTSD have been found to have six times the risk of a heart attack as veterans without it (Boscarino, 2004). Posttraumatic stress disorder, persistent depression, and persistent anger also predict lower survival rates following heart transplantation (Dew, Kormos, & Roth, 1999)

Anxiety is also frequently implicated in patients who report chest pain that has noncardiac origins. As many as 30% of patients who experience apparent symptoms of angina have normal angiograms (Cannon et al., 1994; Kemp, Vokonas, Cohn, & Gorlin, 1973). Chest pain resembling a heart attack or angina is common in patients with panic disorders, clinical anxiety, or gastroesophageal reflux disease (GERD). Behavioral and psychopharmacological treatments for anxiety and panic disorders appear to be effective with many of these patients (Cannon et al., 1994; Klimes, Mayhou, Pearce, Coles, & Fagg, 1990).

OTHER PSYCHOLOGICAL DIFFICULTIES

Illness symptoms and treatment side effects also can produce subclinical coping difficulties. Chest pain, pressure, and other physical symptoms of a heart attack may result in fear and anxiety. These experiences may sensitize some patients, who may then develop anxiety at minor pain and avoid or constrain activities more than they need to. Even reasonable limitations on activities may be associated with frustration, loss, and resentment. The side effects of heart medications can also be disruptive, and surgical interventions such as bypass surgery can change quality of life, mood, and cognitive status as well (Gold, 1996).

The experience of being an inpatient can also be stressful. Patients in a coronary care unit (CCU) receive excellent care, but at the cost of being surrounded by and connected to life support machines that may be intimidating or frightening. Hospitalized patients also often feel depersonalized by hospital personnel and procedures. As anonymous patients defined by their medical problems, they find that ordinary hospital procedures (wearing an anonymous hospital gown, for instance) can disconnect them from important parts of their lives and personal identities (Rybarczyk & Bellg, 1997).

ASSESSMENT AND INTERVENTIONS

PSYCHOLOGICAL ASSESSMENT ISSUES

Heart patients often experience clinical depression and anxiety, but these may be a challenge to identify because they may present with atypical symptoms. Major depression, for instance, may reveal itself first as increased irritability or anger. Illness concerns may mask the appearance of anxiety disorders. The physical symptoms of depression (sleep disruption, weight gain or loss) can easily be confounded with disease symptoms and side effects of medication. Assessment of psychopathology in heart patients usually means having to focus on cognitive and emotional symptoms and not rely as much on somatic symptoms (Davidson, Kupfer, Bigger et al., 2006).

Areas of interest to the clinician can be identified with screening questionnaires. Checklists or brief rating scales may be used to identify life stressors, psychopathology symptoms, physical symptoms and functional ability, motivational style, perceived social support, or other areas. Sensitive issues such as substance abuse may be better discussed in a clinical interview after rapport and a level of trust has been established. Lengthy questionnaires, or those that are too overtly "psychological," may create resistance in the patient and should be avoided.

Clinical interviews usually go most easily if the initial topics focus on adjustment to illness and treatment and the patient's perceptions of caregivers. Other topics that may be covered include treatment side effects and adherence, health beliefs (e.g., benefits, barriers) regarding medication and lifestyle recommendations, motivation for risk factor modification, health-related behavior change and maintenance, coping style and resources, accuracy of patient understanding of his or her illness and treatment, psychopathology, substance use and dependence, and mental status and cognitive functioning.

Assessment of potential heart transplant patients generally focuses on how well the patient is likely to take care of a new heart. The transplantation team needs to know the patient's past adherence to medical treatment and recommendations for health behavior change, the patient's attitudes toward medical caregivers (including trust and authority issues), and if appropriate, the patient's willingness to change behaviors associated with substance abuse and dependence. Transplantation programs usually require patients to be abstinent from abused substances, including cigarettes, for at least 6 months. The evaluation also needs to determine whether the patient's spouse or family is able to make a commitment to provide long-term emotional and tangible support (e.g., provide clinic transportation, support medication adherence) for the patient.

Interventions for Psychopathology and Coping

Rapid development of rapport and a treatment alliance is one of the keys to success, since heart patients need to quickly understand the benefits of treatment and develop trust in their therapist in order to continue therapy. Heart patients generally respond well to psychological treatment using a cognitive-behavioral approach (e.g., Beck, Rush, Shaw, & Emery, 1979; Beck & Emery, 1979) or brief interpersonal approach (e.g., Walter & Peller, 1992). Cognitive restructuring (Beck & Emery) may help reduce helplessness and negative ideation, while assertiveness training and support for patient self-efficacy may help the patient deal better with disease symptoms or treatment side effects. When side effects to medications are uncomfortable and alternatives are not available, the patient's tolerance of side effects may be increased by improving coping strategies (e.g., plan activities when drowsiness is not a problem) or helping the patient use cognitive-behavioral techniques (e.g., mindfulness-based stress reduction). Coping after surgery may be aided by promoting patience and realistic expectations for postoperative ability to function, recovery time, and support from family and friends. Group therapy to improve coping may provide support, promote emotional expression, and help patients reprioritize their goals and activities (Spira, 1997).

For hospitalized patients, it is often helpful to encourage the patient to engage in active coping and educate the staff on how to promote patient choice around his or her activities. For instance, giving patients the opportunity to choose to wear their own pajamas or choose the time that vital signs are assessed during the night may help the patient feel more control over what is happening to him or her. Information is also important, and hospitalized heart attack patients have shorter stays when they have good information about their condition and are allowed to participate in their care (Cromwell & Levenkron, 1984). Negative hospital experiences may also be moderated by encouraging social support for the patient, identifying and addressing reasons for "bad" patient behavior (e.g., nonadherence to medications or recommended exercise, or behavior that appears needy), and using CBT to address negative feelings and thoughts associated with hospitalization (Gold, 1996).

Heart patients often benefit from psychotropic medications. Hostility is frequently amenable to medical treatment (with buspirone or a selective serotonin reuptake inhibitor [SSRI], for instance) even if all the criteria for a diagnosis of clinical depression or anxiety are not met (Littman, 1993; Tollefson, 1995). Cardiologists frequently defer to the patient's primary care physician in prescribing and monitoring the effect of antidepressants, since the primary care doctor can see the patient more frequently over a longer period of time. However, psychological treatment for medical patients often includes monitoring the side effects and treatment effects of medications for depression and anxiety. SSRIs are generally safe to use with cardiac patients, although some may elevate levels of beta blockers and other cardiac medications. Tricyclic antidepressants are generally contraindicated since they can result in tachycardia, orthostatic hypotension (sudden fall in blood pressure upon standing up that can result in fainting), and changes in the patient's electrocardiogram. Benzodiazepines are often used with heart patients for anxiety, panic attacks, or insomnia, but long-term use should be avoided because of the risk of physiological dependence (Tabrizi, Littman, Williams, & Scheidt, 1996).

INTERVENTIONS FOR PSYCHOSOCIAL RISK FACTOR REDUCTION

The association of psychosocial factors with CVD risk becomes more persuasive as biological pathways for the effect of psychological factors such as depression, stress, hostility, and social isolation on the development of cardiovascular disease receive better research support (Blumenthal, 2002). Biological pathways linking psychological risk factors and heart disease include platelet activation increasing the chance of blood clots, neuroendocrine activation, elevated cholesterol, onset of arrhythmias, inflammation and injury to the lining of the coronary arteries, and activation of the sympathetic nervous system (Rozanski, Blumenthal, & Kaplan, 1999; Allan & Scheidt, 1996). Many studies show a connection between individual and combined psychosocial factors and CAD (e.g., Boyle, Michalek, & Suarez, 2006), the onset of heart attacks (e.g., Mittleman et al., 1995), post-heart attack hospitalization time (e.g., Allison et al., 1995) and post-heart attack survival (e.g., Thomas, Friedmann, Wimbush & Schron, 1997). Interventions to reduce psychosocial risk factors also have an independent effect in reducing morbidity and mortality (Nunes, Frank, & Kornfield, 1987), even beyond that of standard cardiac rehabilitation (Linden, Stossel, & Maurice, 1996). The effects of psychosocial intervention for these risks are comparable to those of medical treatment in reducing nonfatal heart attacks and cardiac death after a person has been identified with heart disease (Ketterer, 1993).

LONG-TERM MAINTENANCE OF HEALTH BEHAVIOR

The main difficulty in promoting treatment adherence and healthy lifestyle change to reduce cardiovascular risk is that of long-term maintenance. Positive health behavior change remains susceptible to deterioration over time (Behavior Change Consortium, 2002; Burke & Ockene, 2001). Patient adherence to cardiac rehabilitation activities 6 months after Phase 2 cardiac rehabilitation is completed (including exercise, dietary change, smoking cessation, and taking prescribed medications) is only 25 to 40% (U.S. Department of Health and Human Services, 1995).

Readiness to change often is the first thing that needs to change before patients can alter their behavior, since even discussing the health benefits of making a change can be perceived as largely unsought and unpleasant advice. Assessment and intervention using the stages of change model (SOC; Prochaska, Redding, & Evers, 1997; Prochaska et al., 1994) has helped many patients initiate health behavior changes. The SOC model is helpful in assessing both general readiness to engage in psychological intervention for behavior change and readiness to engage in specific behaviors, but it is less useful in promoting long-term behavior maintenance (see Chapter 3 for a full review of the SOC model).

A potentially more effective way to promote long-term maintenance is to help patients develop positive motivation for change with the goal of internalizing and integrating lifestyle changes with their daily routine. Such positive motivation encourages patients to choose healthy behaviors that they enjoy out of a range of options. These self-determined behaviors are more likely to be sustained than extrinsically motivated behaviors that patients experience as being coerced by circumstances or other people (Bellg, Williams, Deci, & Suchman, 1991; Botelho & Skinner, 1995), perhaps because they may be involved in assisting the process of integrated internalization and self-regulation (Bellg, 2003). Studies of self-determination in health behavior change have shown that it has a positive effect on smoking cessation (Williams et al., 2006), adolescent health risk behaviors (Williams, Cox, Hedberg, & Deci, 2001), long-term medication adherence (Williams, Rodin, Ryan, Grolnick, & Deci, 1998), glucose control in patients with diabetes (Williams, Freedman, & Deci, 1998), long-term adherence to exercise (Ryan, Frederick, Lepes, Rubio, & Sheldon, 1997), and long-term weight loss (Williams, Grow, Freedman, Ryan, & Deci, 1996).

Motivational interviewing is a highly effective way to implement a motivational approach. Developed by Rollnick and Miller (1995) as a directive yet client-centered counseling style for eliciting behavior change, it has been effectively adopted by therapists dealing with substance abuse and other behavioral problems, including risky sexual practices, compliance with medical recommendations, and eating disorders. Within this approach, there are five clinical strategies: (1) express empathy, (2) develop discrepancy between the patient's values and his or her behavior, (3) avoid argumentation, (4) roll with resistance, and (5) support self-efficacy to make and sustain change (Miller & Rollnick, 2002). All of these steps encourage patients to identify and act upon their own reasons to change their behavior (see Chapter 3 for a full review of motivational interviewing).

Traditional cognitive-behavioral therapy has not been as successful in producing sustained health behavior change—although it may help patients initiate change—and some cognitive and behavioral techniques can be used to support long-term change. For instance, behavioral self-management strategies with extensive personal contact with medical caregivers and active long-term follow-up can be very effective at enabling heart patients to sustain long-term change (Debusk et al., 1994). These strategies, however, require multiple patient contacts and the personnel and financial resources to make such contact possible. Telephone interventions that more efficiently use clinical time have been successful at reducing rehospitalization rates and patient care costs in heart failure patients (Riegel et al., 2002).

Cognitive strategies, particularly those based on the Health Belief Model, are helpful in understanding how heart patients think about their illness and how they engage or disengage with the health care available to them (Becker & Maiman, 1975; Strecher & Rosenstock, 1997). For instance, many patients minimize the perceived threat of cardiovascular disease in order to control their anxiety, and as a result, they may also underestimate the benefits they would obtain from engaging in cardiac risk reduction. Misinformation and inaccurate appraisal of the benefits of healthy lifestyle change are also common. For instance, heart patients often do not know that even a modest weight loss (less than 10 pounds) or a small increase in exercise (10 minutes of walking a day) can be medically beneficial, or that even infrequent smoking increases their risk of sudden cardiac death (AHA, 2006).

CARDIAC REHABILITATION

The principles for modifying risk factors also apply to the cardiac rehabilitation experience. In addition to facilitating cardiac healing and reducing short-term risk, promoting patient involvement in long-term risk reduction is necessary to maintain control over a variety of coronary risk factors (Lavie & Milani, 1996). Phase 1 rehabilitation involves patients while they are still hospitalized, and resistance to participation often is associated with fear of further damage to the heart or debilitation from illness and treatment symptoms. Phase 1 intervention from a psychological perspective focuses on improving coping and self-efficacy, making it possible for patients to see their activity level improve. Phase 2 cardiac rehabilitation consists of a structured outpatient rehabilitation program intended to aid recovery following an acute event and begin the risk reduction process. Psychological issues in Phase 2 often involve addressing barriers to treatment. These can include the inconvenience of attending the three sessions per week for 6 to 10 weeks (the most common schedule), feeling different than other cardiac rehabilitation patients (e.g., younger patients often feel out of place), being uncomfortable with the experience of exercise, and having fatalistic beliefs. Phase 3 cardiac rehabilitation involves ongoing maintenance of cardiac fitness and a healthy lifestyle. It usually involves only occasional visits to the rehabilitation center, perhaps as few as one per month, but patients have the benefit of receiving regular monitoring and feedback on their cardiovascular status. The psychological difficulties of promoting adherence to long-term risk reduction are somewhat more easily addressed with patients in Phase 3 cardiac rehabilitation than for nonrehabilitation patients, due to the structure of the rehabilitation program and regular contact with cardiac rehabilitation staff.

CASE EXAMPLES

One of the reasons that cardiac psychology is a credible subspecialty of health psychology is that there are so many psychological and behavioral theories, interventions, and issues relevant to the care of heart patients. The following two case examples offer only a small taste of the broad range of issues confronting heart patients and the interventions they can benefit from.

Case Example 1

A 53–year-old female cardiac rehabilitation patient was referred for nonadherence to recommended lifestyle changes, particularly diet and exercise to help her lose weight, reduce high LDL cholesterol, and increase HDL. She had a family history of heart disease, with her father and sister dying of heart attacks in their late 40s.

She had a stressful job selling automobiles to upscale clients. Due to personal financial pressures, she felt that she was unable to cut back on her work as much as she wanted to. Several of her cardiac rehabilitation sessions were interrupted when she answered calls on her cell phone from potential customers or her sales manager. When working, she found that her eating habits were irregular and that she frequently skipped meals or ate fast food. Prior to her heart attack she had exercised intermittently, largely to keep her weight down, but was frustrated at not accomplishing that goal. She was married with adult children out of the home, and described herself as having few close friends.

Her risk reduction goals consisted of obtaining better control over her diet, increasing her exercise level, and reducing stress. Establishing a strategy to achieve these goals was a challenge, since she felt that food was a reward and compensation for her stress at work and she did not want to feel that she was depriving herself. She agreed that fast food was a poor reward for all the stress she endured, so it was relatively easy for her to have lunch at a restaurant near her work where she could order healthier meals she enjoyed. Her encounters with fast food dropped from nearly daily to about twice a month.

It was more difficult to establish regular exercise and stress management routines. After trying several health clubs that catered to people who were potential clients and finding it too stressful to combine exercise with selling cars, she decided to develop a regular walking routine outdoors or inside department stores or malls in bad weather. Her schedule permitted her to fit a 30–minute walk into her daily routine before going to work. She did not feel that she had time for a regular stress management routine, but she was willing to do a walking version of Mindfulness-Based Stress Reduction while she was exercising. She also adopted a brief stress management routine (relaxing with three breaths) to break her normal pattern of stress multiple times during the day.

After 6 months, she was still engaged in her rehabilitation activities. Between changes in her diet, exercise, and regularly taking cholesterol-lowering medication, her LDL had dropped to 103 mg/dl and her HDL had risen to 65 mg/dl. Her weight was down 14 pounds and had stabilized. She ended her initial treatment after eight sessions, and had an additional three sessions about a year later when she needed further help maintaining her new health behaviors.

CASE EXAMPLE 2

A 59–year-old man was referred by the electrophysiologist in our cardiology practice to treat the phobic fear and avoidance behavior that had resulted from his implanted cardiac defibrillator shocking him repeatedly while he was out on Lake Michigan in his 40–foot sailboat. The pacemaker/defibrillator had been implanted to control fairly severe atrial fibrillation, which in this patient was considered to be life threatening. The patient had retired 2 years earlier with the intention of spending the rest of his days sailing the Great Lakes, and his fear and avoidance of sailing as a result of the traumatic experience with his defibrillator was a severe setback for his quality of life and future plans.

The patient felt anxious and panicky when he first tried to go sailing again after his defibrillation incident, and after that first attempt he felt uncomfortable even thinking about going out on his boat. He also had intrusive traumatic thoughts associated with being repeatedly shocked, and he particularly remembered the embarrassment of being shocked in the presence of the friends he was sailing with. Along with refusing to go sailing, the avoidance behavior associated with his fear of being shocked again included his refusal to travel more than 10 miles from the cardiology clinic where he received his care and his avoidance of vigorous activity, which he believed might trigger another incident.

The patient had a history of depression associated with a business failure about 15 years previously, but it had been of short duration and successfully treated with an SSRI and several counseling sessions. He had been widowed 5 years earlier, but had reestablished his social life and felt that he had successfully dealt with his grief, having participated in professional counseling and a support group for several months. He had no other history of psychopathology.

Therapy first focused on relaxation training with a somatic focus (progressive relaxation training and abdominal breathing). The patient then created a hierarchy of situations that he felt fear in (e.g., being too far away from the cardiology clinic, standing on the dock looking at his boat, getting on board, preparing the boat to sail, starting to move away from the dock) and exposed himself to increasingly fearful situations over several weeks while using his relaxation skills to reciprocally inhibit his anxiety. At the end of that time, he was able to go sailing comfortably for several hours on his sailboat. A few months after that, he was planning a trip that would take him away from his home for several weeks, and he currently feels that he has put his anxiety behind him and is emotionally prepared to deal with it if his defibrillator goes off again.

REFERENCES

Albert, C. M., Chae, C. U., Rexrode, K. M., Manson, J. E., & Kawachi, I. (2005). Phobic anxiety and risk of coronary heart disease and sudden cardiac death among women. *Circulation, 111,* 480–487.

Allan, R., & Scheidt, S. (1996). Empirical basis for cardiac psychology. In R. Allen & S. Scheidt (Eds.), *Heart and mind: The practice of cardiac psychology.* Washington, DC: American Psychological Association.

Allison, T. G., Williams, D. E., Miller, T. D., Patten, C. A., Bailey, K. R., Squires, R. W., et al. (1995). Medical and economic costs of psychologic distress in patients with coronary artery disease. *Mayo Clinic Procedures, 70,* 734–742.

American Heart Association. (2006). Heart and stroke statistics–2006 update. *Circulation, 113,* e85–e151.

Arora, R. R., Chou, T. M., Jain, D., Fleishman, B., Crawford, L., McKiernan, T., et al. (1999). The Multicenter Study of Enhanced External Counterpulsation (MUST-EECP): Effect of EECP on exercise-induced myocardial ischemia and anginal episodes. *Journal of the American College of Cardiology, 33,* 1833–1840.

Arora, R. R., Chou, T. M., Jain, D., Fleishman, B., Crawford, L., McKiernan, et al. (2002). Effects of enhanced external counterpulsation on health-related quality of life continue 12 months after treatment: A substudy of the Multicenter Study of Enhanced External Counterpulsation. *Journal of Investigative Medicine, 50,* 25–32.

Baker, D. W. (1999). Reading between the lines: Deciphering the connections between literacy and health. *Journal of General Internal Medicine, 14*(5), 315–317.

Barger, S. D., & Sydeman, S. J. (2005). Does generalized anxiety disorder predict coronary heart disease risk factors independently of major depressive disorder? *Journal of Affective Disorders, 88,* 87–91.

Beck, A., & Emery, G. (1979). *Cognitive therapy of anxiety and phobic disorders.* Philadelphia: Center for Cognitive Therapy.

Beck, A., Rush, A. J., Shaw, B. F., & Emery, G. (1979). *Cognitive therapy of depression.* New York: Guilford.

Becker, M. H., & Maimen, L. A. (1975). Sociobehavioral determinants of compliance with health and medical care recommendations. *Medical Care, 13,* 10–25.

Behavior Change Consortium. (2002). Conceptualizing health behavior change research: Theory comparison and multiple behavior intervention research from the NIH Behavior Change Consortium. In C. R. Nigg, J. P. Allegrante, & M. Ory (Eds.), *Health Education Research, 17*(5), 670–679.

Bellg, A. J. (2003). Maintenance of health behavior change in preventive cardiology: Internalization and self-regulation of new behaviors. *Behavior Modification, 27,* 103–131.

Bellg, A. J., Rivkin, S., & Rosenson, R. S. (2002). Adherence to lipid-altering medications and lifestyle recommendations. In Rose, B. (Ed.), *Up to date in cardiovascular medicine,* 10(1). Wellesley MA: BDR.

Bellg, A. J., Williams, G., Deci, E. L., & Suchman, A. L. (1991, March). *The influence of affects and perceptions on likelihood of compliance.* Paper presented at the Mid-Year Health Communication Conference, Monterey, CA.

Blanchard, E. B. (1994). Behavioral medicine and health psychology. In A. E. Bergin & S. L. Garfield (Eds.), *Handbook of psychotherapy and behavior change.* New York: Wiley.

Blumenthal, J. A. (2002, April). *ENRICHD and beyond: The role of psychosocial interventions in cardiac rehabilitation.* Paper presented at the Society of Behavioral Medicine Conference, Washington, DC.

Boscarino, J. (2004). Posttraumatic stress disorder and physical illness: Results from clinical and epidemiologic studies. *Annals of the New York Academy of Sciences, 1032,* 141–153.

Botelho, R. J., & Skinner, H. (1995). Motivating change in health behavior: Implications for health promotion and disease prevention. *Primary Care, 22,* 565–589.

Boyle, S. H., Michalek, J. E., & Suarez, E. C. (2006). Covariation of psychological attributes and incident coronary heart disease in U.S. Air Force veterans of the Vietnam war. *Psychosomatic Medicine, 68,* 844–850.

Broadbent, E., Petrie, K. J., Alley, P. G., & Booth, R, J. (2003). Psychological stress impairs early wound repair following surgery. *Psychosomatic Medicine, 65*(5), 865–869.

Brown, E. S., Beard, L., Frol, A. B., & Rush, A. J. (2006). Effect of two prednisone exposures on mood and declarative memory. *Neurobiology of Learning and Memory, 86*(1), 28–34.

Brown, R., & Ogden, J. (2004). Children's eating attitudes and behaviour: A study of the modeling and control theories of parental influence. *Health Education Research, 19*(3), 261–271.

Burke, L. E., & Ockene, I. S. (2001). *Compliance in healthcare and research.* American Heart Association Monograph Series. Armonk, NY: Futura.

Cannon, R. O. III, Quyyumi, A. A., Mincemoyer, R., Stine, A. M., Gracely, R. H., Smith, W. B., et al. (1994). Imipramine in patients with chest pain despite normal coronary angiograms. *New England Journal of Medicine, 330,* 1411–1417.

Caspard, H., Chan, A. K., & Walker, A. M. (2005). Compliance with a statin treatment in a usual-care setting: Retrospective database analysis over 3 years after treatment initiation in health maintenance organization enrollees with dyslipidemia. *Clinical Therapeutics: The International Peer-Reviewed Journal of Drug Therapy. 27*(10), 1639–1646.

Cromwell, R. L., & Levenkron, J. C. (1984). Psychological care of acute coronary patients. In A. Steptoe & A. Mathews (Eds.), *Health care and human behaviour.* San Diego: Academic Press.

Davidson, K. W., Kupfer, D. J., Bigger, J. T., Califf, R. M., Carney, R. M., Coyne, J. C., et al. (2006). Assessment and treatment of depression in patients with cardiovascular disease: National Heart, Lung and Blood Institute working group report. *Annals of Behavioral Medicine, 32*(2), 121–126.

Debusk, R. F., Miller, N. H., Superko, H. R., Dennis, C. A., Thomas, R. J., Berger, W. E., et al. (1994). A case-management system for coronary risk factor modification after acute myocardial infarction. *Annals of Internal Medicine, 120,* 721–729.

Dew, M. A., Kormos, R. L., & Roth, L. H. (1999). Early post-transplant medical compliance and mental health predict physical morbidity and mortality one to three years after heart transplantation. *Journal of Heart and Lung Transplantation, 18,* 549–562.

Fernandez, F. (1993). Depression and its treatment in cardiac patients. *Texas Heart Institute Journal, 20,* 188–193.

Fighali, S., Krajcer, Z., Gonzales-Camid, F., Warda, M., Edelman, S., & Leachman, R. (1985). Safety of outpatient cardiac catheterization. *Chest, 88,* 349–351.

Flack, J. M., & Sowers, J. R. (1991). Epidemiologic and clinical aspects of insulin resistance and hyperinsulinemia. *American Journal of Medicine, 91,* 11S–21S.

Frasure-Smith, N., Lesperance, F., & Talajic, M. (1995a). Depression and 18-month prognosis after myocardial infarction. *Circulation, 91*(4), 999–1005.

Frasure-Smith, N., Lesperance, F., & Talajic, M. (1995b). The impact of negative emotions on prognosis following myocardial infarction: Is it more than depression? *Health Psychology, 14,* 388–398.

Gold, J. P. (1996). Psychological issues and coronary artery bypass surgery. In Allen, R., & Scheidt, S. (Eds.), *Heart and mind: The practice of cardiac psychology* (pp. 219–232). Washington, DC: American Psychological Association.

Hansen, E. F., Anderson, L. T., & Von Eyben, F. E. (1993). Cigarette smoking and age at first acute myocardial infarction, and influence of gender and extent of smoking. *American Journal of Cardiology, 71,* 1439–1443.

Hansing, C. E. (1979). The risk and cost of coronary angiography. *JAMA, 242,* 735–740.

Hayes, S. N. (2006). Identification of women with heart disease: A missed opportunity. *Nature Clinical Practice Cardiovascular Medicine, 3,* 522–523.

Heger, J. W., Niemann, J. T., & Criley, J. M. (2003). *Cardiology* (5th ed.). Baltimore: Lippincott Williams & Wilkins.

Jacobs, S. C., & Sherwood, J. B. (1996). The cardiac psychology of women and coronary heart disease. In R. Allen & S. Scheidt (Eds.), *Heart and mind: The practice of cardiac psychology* (pp. 219–232). Washington, DC: American Psychological Association.

Joint National Committee on Detection, Evaluation, and Treatment of High Blood Pressure— Fifth Report (JNC V). (1993). The fifth report of the Joint National Committee on Detection, Evaluation, and Treatment of High Blood Pressure. *Archives of Internal Medicine, 153,* 154–183.

Kannel, W. B., & Feinleib, M. (1972). Natural history of angina pectoris in the Framingham study. *American Journal of Cardiology, 29,* 154–162.

Kemp, H. G., Vokonas, P. S., Cohn, P. F., & Gorlin, R. (1973). The anginal syndrome associated with normal coronary arteriograms: Report of a six year experience. *American Journal of Medicine, 54,* 735–742.

Ketterer, M. W. (1993). Secondary prevention of ischemic heart disease. *Psychosomatics, 34,* 478–484.

Klimes, I., Mayhou, R. A., Pearce, M. J., Coles, L., & Fagg, J. R. (1990). Psychological treatment for atypical non-cardiac chest pain: A controlled evaluation. *Psychological Medicine, 20,* 605–611.

Lavie, C. J., & Milani, R. V. (1996). Effects of nonpharmacologic therapy with cardiac rehabilitation and exercise training in patients with low levels of high-density lipoprotein cholesterol. *American Journal of Cardiology, 78,* 1286–1289.

Linden, W., Stossel C., & Maurice, J. (1996). Psychosocial interventions for patients with coronary artery disease: A meta-analysis. *Archives of Internal Medicine, 156,* 2302–2308.

Littman, A. B. (1993). Review of psychosomatic aspects of cardiovascular disease. *Psychotherapy and Psychosomatics, 60,* 148–167.

Lumley, M. A., Ovies, T., Stettner, L., Wehmer F., & Lakey, B. (1996). Alexithymia, social support and health problems. *Journal of Psychosomatic Research, 41,* 519–530.

McGuinnes, J. B., Begg, T. B., & Semple, T. (1976). First electrocardiogram in recent myocardial infarction. *British Medical Journal, 2,* 449–456.

Mello, M. F., & Batista, F. (2001). Post-traumatic stress disorder in a patient with an implant cardioverter-defibrillator. *International Journal of Psychiatry in Clinical Practice, 5*(4), 291–292.

Miller, W. R., & Rollnick, S. (2002). *Motivational Interviewing: Preparing people for change* (2nd ed.). New York: Guilford.

Mittleman, M. A., Maclure, M., Sherwood, J. B., Mulry, R. P., Tofler, G. H., Jacobs, S. C., Friedman, R., Benson, H., & Muller, J. E., for the Determinants of Myocardial Infarction Onset Study Investigators. (1995). Triggering of acute myocardial infarction onset by episodes of anger. *Circulation, 92,* 1720–1725.

Nemeroff, C. B., Musselman, D. L., & Evans, D. L. (1998). Depression and cardiac disease. *Depression and Anxiety, 8*(Suppl. 1), 71–79.

Nunes, E. V., Frank, K. A., & Kornfield, D. S. (1987). Psychologic treatment for the type A behavior pattern and for coronary heart disease: A meta-analysis of the literature. *Psychosomatic Medicine, 48,* 159–173.

Prochaska, J. O., Redding, C. A., & Evers, K. E. (1997). The transtheoretical model and stages of change. In K. Glanz, F. M. Lewis, & B. K. Rimer, (Eds.) *Health behavior and health education: Theory, research and practice* (pp. 60–84). San Francisco: Jossey-Bass.

Prochaska, J. O., Velicer, W. F., Rossi, J. S., Goldstein, M. G., Marcus, B. H., Rakowski, W., et al. (1994). Stages of change and decisional balance for 12 problem behaviors. *Health Psychology, 13,* 39–50.

Riegel, B., Carlson, B., Kopp, Z., LePetri, B., Glazer, D., & Unger, A. (2002). Effect of a standardized nurse case-management telephone intervention on resource use in patients with chronic heart failure. *Archives of Internal Medicine, 162,* 705–712.

Rollnick, S., & Miller, W. R. (1995). What is motivational interviewing? *Behavioural and Cognitive Psychotherapy, 23,* 325–334.

Rozanski, A., Blumenthal, J. A., & Kaplan, J. (1999). Impact of psychological factors on the pathogenesis of cardiovascular disease and implications for therapy. *Circulation, 99,* 2192–2217.

Rumsfeld, J. S., & Ho, M. (2005). Depression and cardiovascular disease: A call for recognition. *Circulation, 111,* 250–253.

Rybarczyk, B. D. (1994). Diversity among American men: The impact of aging, ethnicity, and race. In C. Kilmartin (Ed.), *The masculine self.* New York: MacMillan.

Rybarczyk, B. D., & Bellg, A. J. (1997). *Listening to life stories: A new approach to stress management in the medical setting.* New York: Springer.

Ryan, R. M., Frederick, C. M., Lepes, D., Rubio, N., & Sheldon, K. M. (1997). Intrinsic motivation and exercise adherence. *International Journal of Sport Psychology, 28,* 335–354.

Sacks, F. M., Pfeffer, M. A., Moye, L. A., Rouleau, J. L., Rutherford, J. D., Cole, T. G., et al. (1996). The effect of pravastatin on coronary events after myocardial infarction in patients with average cholesterol levels. *New England Journal of Medicine, 335,* 1001–1009.

Selnes, O. A., McKhann, G. M., Borowicz, L. M. Jr., & Grega, M. A. (2006). Cognitive and neurobehavioral dysfunction after cardiac bypass procedures. *Neurologic Clinics. 24*(1), 133–145.

Shepherd, J., Cobbe, M., Ford, I. for the West of Scotland Coronary Prevention Study Group. (1995). Prevention of coronary heart disease with pravastatin in men with hypercholesterolemia. *New England Journal of Medicine, 333,* 1301–1307.

Spira, J. L. (1997). Understanding and developing psychotherapy groups for medically ill patients. In J. L. Spira, (Ed.) *Group therapy for medically ill patients* (pp. 3–11). New York: Guilford.

Strecher, V. I., & Rosenstock, I. M. (1997). The health belief model. In K. Glanz, F. M. Lewis, & B. K. Rimer (Eds.), *Health behavior and health education* (2nd ed.; pp. 41–59). San Francisco: Jossey-Bass.

Tabrizi, K., Littman, A., Williams, R. B. Jr., & Scheidt, S. (1996). Psychopharmacology and cardiac disease. In R. Allen & S. Scheidt (Eds.), *Heart and mind: The practice of cardiac psychology.* Washington, DC: American Psychological Association.

Thomas, S. A., Friedmann, E., Wimbush, F., & Schron, E. (1997). Psychosocial factors and survivial in the cardiac arrhythmia suppression trial (CAST): A reexamination. *American Journal of Critical Care, 6,* 116–126.

Tollefson, G. D. (1995). Anger, aggression, and depression. *Journal of Clinical Psychiatry, 56,* 404–418.

Tsang, T. S. M., Barnes, M. E., Gersh, B. J., & Hayes, S. N. (2000). Risks of coronary heart disease in women: Current understanding and evolving concepts. *Mayo Clinic Proceedings, 75,* 1289–1303.

U.S. Department of Health and Human Services. (1995). *Cardiac Rehabilitation Clinical Practice Guideline no. 17.* Rockville, MD: Author.

Walter, J. L., & Peller, J. E. (1992). *Becoming solution-focused in brief therapy.* New York: Brunner/Mazel.

Warren, L. W. (1983). Male intolerance of depression: A review with implications for psychotherapy. *Clinical Psychology Review, 3,* 147–156.

Williams, G. C., Cox, E. M., Hedberg, V. A., & Deci, E. L. (2001). Extrinsic life goals and health risk behaviors in adolescents. *Journal of Applied Social Psychology, 30,* 1756–1771.

Williams, G. C., Freedman, Z. R., & Deci, E. L. (1998). Supporting autonomy to motivate glucose control in patients with diabetes. *Diabetes Care, 21,* 1644–1651.

Williams, G. C., Grow, V. M., Freedman, Z. M., Ryan, R. R., & Deci, E. L. (1996). Motivational predictors of weight loss and weight-loss maintenance. *Journal of Personality and Social Psychology, 70,* 115–126.

Williams, G. C., McGregor, H. A., Sharp, D., Levesque, C., Kouides, R. W., Ryan, R. M., & Deci, E. L. (2006). Testing a self-determination theory intervention for motivating tobacco cessation: Supporting autonomy and competence in a clinical trial. *Health Psychology, 25*(1), 91–101.

Williams, G. C., Rodin, G. C., Ryan, R. M., Grolnick, W. S., & Deci, E. L. (1998) Autonomous regulation and long-term medication adherence in adult outpatients. *Health Psychology, 17,* 269–276.

CHAPTER 7

Cancer

ALYSON B. MOADEl and MELANIE S. HARRIS

INTRODUCTION

Oncology is the study and treatment of cancer, which is represented by a group of diseases whereby uncontrolled growth and spread of abnormal cells occurs (American Cancer Society [ACS], 2006b). Advances in molecular biology, genetics, and epidemiology have brought us closer to understanding the etiology and pathophysiology of cancer, although there are still many questions to be answered. The current model of cancer development suggests that cells undergo a series of genetic mutations or alterations, due to genetic or environmental causes, which results in their inability to respond normally to signals that control cell growth, differentiation, and death (Tannock, Hill, Bristow, & Harrington, 2004). Two gene processes that contribute to tumorigenesis include activation of *oncogenes,* which promote cell proliferation, and inhibition of *tumor suppressor genes,* which promote cancer cell death. To survive and grow, tumors thrive on oxygen and other nutrients easily found in blood supplies and are therefore able to induce blood vessel growth (i.e., angiogenesis) in and around the tumor, potentially through the secretion of various growth factors. Angiogenesis is also one route by which cancer spreads, as single cells break off from the primary tumor and travel through the blood vessels to distal sites in the body where they implant and grow secondary tumors (i.e., metastases). Cancer can also spread through the lymphatic system, a secondary circulatory system involved in the production and transport of fluids throughout the body. If the spread of cancer is uncontrolled, it can interfere with vital organ function and eventually lead to death.

The causes of cancer include environmental factors (i.e., tobacco use, radiation, chemicals), immunoendocrine factors (i.e., infectious organisms, viruses, hormones), and genetic factors (i.e., inherited mutations, metabolism-related mutations; ACS, 2006b). It often takes years after exposure to a carcinogen for cancer to become detectable. While it is sometimes possible to identify a clear cause of cancer (e.g., heavy alcohol and tobacco use history in a head and neck cancer patient, human papillomavirus in a cervical cancer patient), in many cases the exact cause is unknown. There are, however, several risk factors for cancer, including poor nutrition (high intake of fat and red or processed meats, low intake of fruits and vegetables), obesity/overweight, physical inactivity, family history of cancer, increasing age, alcohol and tobacco use, sun exposure, and, in women, extended exposure to estrogen through hormone replacement therapy, early menarche, late menopause, and nulli-parity (i.e., no children).

PREVALENCE

There are approximately 10 million people alive today with a history of cancer in the United States (ACS, 2006b). It is estimated that nearly 1.4 million people will be diagnosed with the disease in 2006. The most prevalent cancers include breast, prostate, lung, and colorectal cancer. Cancer is the second leading cause of death after heart disease, with one of four deaths in the United States attributable to cancer.

Cancer incidence and mortality varies across different sociocultural groups (Center for Disease Control and Prevention [CDC], 2005). Cancer in children is very rare, whereas cancer prevalence increases to nearly one in three in late adulthood. Overall, cancer mortality is 46% higher among men than women. This is in part due to the higher proportion of lung cancer in men, a cancer with a poor survival rate, and the high prevalence of breast and gynecologic cancers in women, which are often readily detectable and treatable (CDC). Gender differences in health–care-seeking behaviors may also play a part, with men less likely to seek care early compared to women (Lantz, Fullerton, Harshburger, & Sadler, 2001). Ethnic disparities in cancer also exist, with African Americans more likely to develop and die of cancer than any other ethnic or racial group in the United States (ACS, 2006b). Among other ethnic minority groups, Hispanic women have the highest rate of cervical cancer, Asians have the highest rate of stomach and liver cancers, and American Indian/Alaska Native women have the lowest cancer incidence rates yet the third highest cancer death rates (Ward et al., 2004). Ashkenazi Jewish women have a greater risk of genetic mutations in specific genes (i.e., BRCA1, BRCA2) that predispose them to breast and ovarian cancer (ACS). Overall, poor and underserved populations are at greatest risk for reduced survival and increased mortality from cancer, indicating that socioeconomic-related factors such as limited knowledge, poor access, inadequate screening, late detection, and nutritional factors may be contributing to cancer disparities.

DISEASE FACTORS

In addition to the site of the disease (e.g., breast, lung, and so on), there are other disease factors that characterize the cancer experience. Two such factors include the onset and progression of disease, as described in the following

ONSET

A diagnosis of cancer can occur through a variety of mechanisms, including a routine screening in an asymptomatic person (e.g., yearly mammography or blood tests); through a gradual process of symptom reporting, testing, and confirmation; or detection during testing/treatment for another medical condition. There are seven common warning signs and symptoms of cancer including: (1) a change in bowel habits or bladder function, (2) sores that do not heal, (3) unusual bleeding or discharge, (4) a lump or thickening in any part of the body (e.g., breast), (5) indigestion or trouble swallowing, (6) a change in a mole or wart, and (7) a cough or hoarseness that does not go away (ACS, 2006e). In addition, some general signs include fever, fatigue, pain, or skin changes. It should be noted that these symptoms can be related to many other health conditions and require examination to determine a differential diagnosis. The location, size, and type of cancer often determine the nature and severity of symptoms.

In the last century, increased national interest around cancer as an enigmatic, nondiscriminatory invader for which known causes and cures are often lacking, and stories of suffering, disability, and death are ubiquitous, have contributed to its reputation as the *dread disease* (Patterson, 1987). Not surprisingly, a diagnosis of cancer is often received with great distress. This is compounded by the fact that there can be minimal, vague, or lack of symptoms leading up to diagnosis, rendering the news of a cancer diagnosis an unexpected shock. In fact, the potentially life-threatening nature of an illness such as cancer is now recognized in the Diagnostic and Statistical Manual of Mental Disorders (4th ed.; *DSM-IV*) as a trauma that can engender reactions such as fear, helplessness, or horror as well as additional symptoms, such as reexperiencing trauma (i.e., intrusive thoughts, nightmares), avoidance of cues associated with the trauma, and increased arousal or irritability (American Psychiatric Association, 1994). As such, one can experience posttraumatic stress disorder from being diagnosed and treated for cancer (as described more fully in the following). It should be noted, however, that the experience of cancer can be as variable as the disease itself, with the stage of disease and treatment course important factors in the psychosocial adjustment trajectory.

DISEASE PROGRESSION

It is estimated that 65% of those diagnosed with cancer will survive at least 5 years (ACS, 2006b). This statistic includes patients who are cured or in remission (i.e., with no evidence of disease), those who have relapsed, and those on treatment. The course of cancer depends on several factors, of which the primary one is the stage of disease at diagnosis. A cancer's stage is determined by the size of the tumor, the location in the body, and the extent of spread (i.e., metastasis). When cancers are detected early, that is, with little to no spread of cells, the prognosis is often favorable. On the other hand, when cancer is at an advanced stage where distal metastases are evident, the chances for long-term survival greatly decrease. Other important factors that can influence the disease trajectory include the type of cancer, treatment options, other illnesses and biological factors, behavioral characteristics, and adherence to the treatment regimen.

Overall, cancer is now considered more of a chronic than acute disease, given advances in treatments to regress and inhibit cancer growth (Beyer, 1995). As a result, it is becoming more and more common for patients with advanced disease to survive several years versus months, and for recurrent disease to remit with treatment rather than lead to inevitable death. In fact, similar to other chronic diseases like multiple sclerosis, some cancer patients may live many years with periods of recurrences and remissions.

Cancer staging is used to determine how extensive the cancer is, which, in turn, is a measure of prognosis (ACS, 2004b). The determination of disease stage is generally based on the American Joint Committee on Cancer's TNM system, whereby *T* stands for tumor size and spread to local tissue, *N* represents lymph node involvement, and *M* describes the presence and extent of distal metastasis (Greene et al., 2002). Once the TNM estimates are gathered, this information is then translated into an overall stage grouping from stage I (the least advanced) to stage IV (the most advanced). Prognosis is better for cancers found at earlier stages, where there is little to no spread and lymph

Table 7.1

TNM Cancer Staging System

Primary Tumor (T)	Lymph Nodes (N)	Metastatis (M)
TX = Tumor can't be measured or found.	NX = Nearby lymph nodes can't be measured or found.	MX = Metastasis can't be measured or found.
T0 = There is no evidence of primary tumor.	N0 = No cancer in nearby lymph nodes.	M0 = There are no known distant metastases.
Tis = The cancer is in situ (the tumor has not started growing into the surrounding structures).	N1–N3 = The size, location, and/or the number of lymph nodes involved. The higher the N number, the greater the lymph node involvement.	M1 = Distant metastases are present.
T1–T4 = The size and/or level of invasion into nearby structures. The higher the T number, the larger the size of the tumor and/or the greater invasion into nearby structures.		

Stage Grouping

I	T1	N0	M0
II	T0–T3	N0–N1	M0
III	T0–T4	N0–N3	M0
IV	Any T	Any N	M1

Source: Based on sources from the American Cancer Society (ACS, 2004b) and American Joint Committee on Cancer (Greene et al., 2002).

node involvement compared to those found at advanced stages. While this is a basic overview of the most common staging system, it is noted that staging subcategories using letters (i.e., A, B) are sometimes used, and that completely distinct staging systems exist for certain cancers such as lymphomas and childhood cancers. The TNM cancer staging system is depicted in Table 7.1.

CANCER TREATMENT

Cancer treatment most commonly involves one or more of the following: surgery, chemotherapy, radiation therapy, and/or hormonal therapy. Surgery and radiation therapy are typically localized treatments that aim to remove or destroy an identifiable tumor(s). Traditional chemotherapies (e.g., alkylating agents) operate systemically in the body by interfering with DNA activity among rapidly dividing cells, thereby inhibiting cell growth and promoting cell death (ACS, 2006h). Hormonal therapy in cancer refers to treatments that block the effects or levels of certain hormones (e.g., estrogen or androgen) that can contribute to the growth and spread of hormone-sensitive cancers (ACS, 2006f, 2006d). Common examples include *Tamoxifen*, an anti-estrogen agent for breast cancer, and *Lupron*, an anti-androgen drug, for prostate cancer.

Other cancer treatments include biological therapy (also known as immunotherapy or biological response modifiers), which functions to enhance the ability of the immune system to fight cancer and infections (ACS, 2006i). More recently, a number of targeted therapies have received FDA approval for use in antineoplastic (i.e., anti-cancer) treatment. For example, *monoclonal antibodies* are laboratory-derived antibodies that are used to carry cancer-toxic substances to targeted cancer cells to which they bind (ACS, 2006g). *Herceptin* is one example of a monoclonal antibody that has been effective with certain forms of breast cancer in preventing cancer cell growth and enhancing immune function.

Bone marrow transplant (BMT) is a procedure whereby stem cells, found in the bone and from which blood cells derive, are purposely destroyed by chemotherapy and/or radiation and then replaced by a donor's or one's own purged stem cells (ACS, 2004a). This procedure is used for patients with hematologic (i.e., blood-born) malignancies such as leukemia or lymphoma, and for those who are no longer able to make the blood cells needed to carry oxygen, fight infection, and prevent bleeding due to previous chemotherapy- and/or radiation-induced stem cell damage.

Given that cancer is not a single disease but rather one with many different presentations, complications, and courses, treatment is often similarly complex. It often includes multiple modes of treatment (e.g., surgery, chemotherapy, and radiation therapy), may involve multiple lines of treatment (i.e., lack of response to one type of chemotherapy leads to treatment with another), and is often supplemented with toxicity control treatments to manage side effects (e.g., pain medications, anti-emetics). Further, the field of therapeutic oncology is replete with experimental treatments to identify more effective means to manage and potentially cure cancer.

Among patients with advanced disease, where treatment options are often limited, many opt to undergo experimental treatment by participating in a *Phase I or II Clinical Trial* (ACS, 2006c). These trials seek to identify the safety and effectiveness of a drug that has only been tested in lab and animal studies (Phase I) or minimally in humans (Phase II). Examples of clinical trials currently underway include anti-angiogenesis agents aimed at blocking the formation of new blood vessels around tumors (ACS, 2006a), and gene therapy approaches whereby genetic material (e.g., "suicide genes") is introduced into cancer cells to induce cell death, replace altered/missing genes with healthy ones, or make cancer cells more sensitive to chemotherapy or radiation therapy (ACS, 2005).

SIDE EFFECTS

Given the aggressive, multimodal, and systemic nature of many cancer protocols, patients can experience a range of short-term, long-term, and late effects of treatment (Souhami & Tobias, 2005). The nontargeted systemic treatments, like chemotherapy, that attack healthy as well as cancer cells often cause the most pervasive side effects through damage to rapidly dividing cells. These include cells in the digestive track, hair follicles, and skin. As a result, nausea, vomiting, diarrhea, appetite changes, hair loss, and dry skin are common short-term effects. A serious complication of chemotherapy is suppression of the immune system, which occurs as a result of toxicity to the rapidly dividing white and red blood cells. Such immunosuppression can lead to infection, anemia, inability to receive further toxic treatment, and in rare cases, death. Cardiotoxicity and peripheral neuropathies (nerve damage) can also infrequently occur.

Fatigue (Cella, Lai, Chang, Peterman, & Slavin, 2002) and pain (Goudas, Bloch, Gialeli-Goudas, Lau, & Carr, 2005) are two commonly reported effects of cancer treatment. Weight changes, insomnia, and psychological distress are also relatively widespread. Both men and women can experience sexual impairment as a result of treatments that directly or indirectly affect the sexual organs and/or hormones (Schover, 1998). For example, a majority of women who experience premature menopause from surgical removal of their ovaries or radiation/chemotherapy-induced ovarian failure, report sexual changes including vaginal dryness, loss of sexual desire, and pain during intercourse (i.e., dyspareunia; Muscari Lin, Aikin, & Good, 1999). Recently, a phenomenon described as *chemobrain* has been identified, suggesting that chemotherapy may produce cognitive impairment, including short-term memory loss and concentration difficulties (Jansen, Miaskowski, Dodd, Dowling, & Kramer, 2005). The targeted therapies, including surgery and radiation therapy, are more localized in effect. For example, wound infections or skin burns may present as a typical outcome. It should be noted that, in rare cases, radiation as well as chemotherapy can contribute to secondary cancers, often years after treatment. To significantly reduce this risk, there are limitations on the lifetime dose of treatment a patient can receive. Bone marrow transplant patients who receive bone marrow from a donor can experience graft-versus-host disease, a condition in which the donor's tissue attacks that of the patient's, resulting in mild to severe inflammation of the internal organs or skin. While depression and menopausal symptoms are potential effects of hormonal treatments, flulike symptoms are more typical among those receiving biological therapy or monoclonal antibodies.

Though this list appears daunting, progress in supportive care has helped to mitigate many of these side effects and substantially improve and preserve quality of life (QOL). In particular, pharmacologic and behavioral interventions have resulted in greater management of nausea, pain, infection, anemia, insomnia, anxiety, and depression. As a reflection of these improvements, surveys of patients in 1983 and 2000 regarding the severity of chemotherapy side effects indicate that physical side effects—at the forefront of patients' concerns years ago—have been surpassed by psychosocial concerns related to family, work, and social life (Carelle et al., 2002). On the other hand, certain issues, particularly hair loss and fatigue, have remained a consistent concern over time.

CANCER CARE COSTS, ACCESSIBILITY, AND BARRIERS

On the national level, the socioeconomic burden of cancer is substantial; the total cost of cancer in the United States in 2005 was $209.9 billion, of which $74 billion went to direct medical expenditures (Mackay, Jemal, Lee, & Parkin, 2006). On the individual level, the direct costs have been found to range from $1,844 to $7,282 per month, dependent upon the type of cancer (Chang et al., 2004). Among the majority of Americans who have health insurance, out-of-pocket expenses, including co-payments, deductibles, and uncovered medical procedures/treatment can exact a heavy financial toll (e.g., $360—$1,455 per month for breast cancer treatment; Siminoff & Ross, 2005). Among the approximately 45 million (15%) Americans who are uninsured (Siminoff & Ross), access to adequate medical care may be exceedingly limited.

In addition to insurance inequities, other patient barriers to quality care include old age, minority race, and low socioeconomic class, which appear to be mediated through cultural attitudes, knowledge, and behavior on the part of both the patient and physician (Mandelblatt, Yabroff, & Kerner, 1999). For example, a newly immigrated patient from South America who has previously received her health care from an indigenous healer may be reticent to accept the approach used in westernized medicine. Specific provider barriers, including lack of cultural competency, poor physician-patient communication, and personal biases, can further impede access to care. Such barriers can take the form of the physician who fails to assess the patient's beliefs about the illness and its treatment, decides upon a treatment without the patient's input, and provides a limited or inaccessible explanation about the choice of treatment.

INDIVIDUAL FACTORS

The experience of cancer, from diagnosis to posttreatment survivorship or end of life, is different for every patient, based on a number of individual factors encompassed by the patient's education, knowledge, attitudes, behaviors, cultural background, beliefs, coping resources, and social support. These patient factors influence cancer prevention behavior (e.g., cancer screening), acceptance and adherence to medical treatment, self-management strategies, and psychosocial adjustment to cancer. A brief review of key individual factors follows.

SOCIOECONOMIC STATUS

Socioeconomic status (SES), encompassing income, education, employment, and living environment, is integrally connected to the cancer experience. Patients with higher SES often report higher health literacy, or the ability to obtain and understand basic health information and services necessary for making informed health decisions, which can impact patients' communication with their health care providers and their medical outcomes (Davis, Williams, Marin, Parker, & Glass, 2002). Patients with lower SES report poorer QOL (Baker, Denniston, Smith, & West, 2005; Eversley et al., 2005), which may in part be due to barriers in receiving appropriate services. In a psychosocial needs assessment survey provided to 248 cancer outpatients in an urban cancer center serving a primarily underserved population, the majority of patients expressed the need for more accessible and understandable medical information, emotional support, and practical assistance in their cancer care (Moadel, Morgan, & Dutcher, 2007).

PERSONAL BELIEFS

People hold a variety of personal beliefs about cancer, its treatment, and their own abilities to manage the disease, many of which can have a direct effect on behavior. For example, women who perceive their risk for breast cancer to be high are more likely to adhere to mammography screening (Katapodi, Lee, Facione, & Dodd, 2004). Internal locus of control, or believing one has an influence over one's cause and/or course of cancer, has been shown to be related to greater use of complementary medicine among breast cancer patients (Henderson & Donatelle, 2003). Similarly, patients' perceptions of self-efficacy, or personal ability to manage cancer-related situations, symptoms, and procedures, may contribute to better psychological adjustment (Manne et al., 2006).

CULTURE

Like personal beliefs, cultural beliefs, values, and behaviors (i.e., those shared and transmitted among members from the same culture) can play a significant role in how someone responds to cancer-related signs and/or a diagnosis of cancer (Meyerowitz, Richardson, Hudson, & Leedham, 1998). For example, cancer fatalism, or the belief that cancer inevitably leads to death, is a commonly held belief among African Americans, women, and those of lower socioeconomic status, which has been associated with delay or avoidance of cancer screening (Powe & Finnie, 2003). Among cultures in which modesty, privacy, and traditional gender roles are strongly valued, patients may have difficulty with invasive examinations and procedures, particularly when a health care provider is of the opposite sex. Accordingly, measures of modesty, shame, or embarrassment among Filipino, Korean, and Mexican women have been found to be inversely associated with mammography utilization (Maxwell, Bastani, & Warda, 1998). In contrast, high levels of acculturation (i.e., assimilation of immigrants to western values, beliefs, and behaviors) have been associated with increased screening practices in the United States.

There are a variety of highly respected systems of healing within different cultures, such as allopathic, homeopathic, naturopathic, Chinese, and Ayurvedic medicine approaches (National Center for Complementary and Alternative Medicine [NCCAM], October 2004). Depending upon the medical system in which they believe, patients may look to medical doctors as well as faith healers, shamans, *curanderos*, or other traditional healers as trusted health care providers. A clash between cultural approaches to health can occur when immigrants who are not highly acculturated face a health crisis. Whereas westernized medicine assumes that each patient should have full autonomy to know, understand, and decide upon cancer/treatment-related matters, in non-Western cultures, such medical disclosure to patients can be considered not only undesirable and inappropriate, but even potentially harmful (Mitchell, 1998). In particular, developing countries and those with patriarchal social values (e.g., Asians, Hispanics, and Eastern Europeans) are less likely to practice or encourage truth telling when it comes to a cancer diagnosis, due to the belief that it might lead a patient to despair and loss of hope, which, in turn, will hasten death. As an alternative, medical decision making is left to the family or doctor rather than the patient.

Medical mistrust appears to be a cultural phenomenon, most frequently evidenced among patients from ethnic minority populations (Doescher, Saver, Franks, & Fiscella, 2000). Perhaps due to historical racial discrimination in medical research or current inequities in the health care system, African Americans are less likely to trust their doctors, and more likely to be concerned with issues of privacy and harmful experimentation. Among Spanish-speaking Hispanics living in the United States, a high level of suspiciousness and mistrust of physicians' motives regarding recommendation of clinical trials has also been documented (Ellington, Wahab, Martin, Field, & Mooney, 2006).

COPING

Coping strategies/styles encompass a range of reactions and behaviors to stressful situations that can result in either increased or decreased psychological adjustment (Folkman & Lazarus, 1988). Numerous coping strategies have been enumerated in cancer patients, including information seeking, seeking social support, positive reframing, distancing, denial, cognitive-behavioral avoidance, fighting spirit, problem-focused, emotion-focused, and the like (Dunkel-Schetter, Feinstein, Taylor, & Falke, 1992; Nelson, Friedman, Baer, Lane, & Smith, 1989; Nordin, Berglund, Terje, & Glimelius, 1999). Cultural differences in coping have also been noted among cancer survivors. For example, African Americans have been found to use more avoidant coping (Rodrigue, 1997), Hispanics use more self-distraction, and both of these ethnic minority groups use humor-based coping less and religion-based coping more than Caucasians. Others have found that African Americans are more likely to use wishful thinking, positive reappraisal, and emotion suppression, while Caucasians tend to rely on problem solving, escapism, and emotional expression (Reynolds et al., 2000).

Coping style has been found to be associated with both self-management behavior and adjustment after cancer. For example, active coping has been associated with greater use of complementary medicine (Sollner et al., 2000), and specific strategies such as acceptance, emotional expression, fighting spirit, and humor have all been linked to better psychological adjustment, while denial and disengagement have been linked to greater distress (Carver et al., 1993). Optimism, resiliency, and social integration are personality constructs considered to be important coping resources for promoting greater engagement in life and one's medical care during and after cancer diagnosis (Carver, 2005).

Fueled by the lack of clear understanding about the causes and treatments for cancer, a burgeoning self-help movement has focused a great deal of attention on the role of stress and coping in cancer. This public interest has led many researchers to empirically examine the relationship between coping styles and cancer diagnosis, survival, and/or recurrence. Several small studies suggest that having a fighting spirit is associated with better medical outcomes, whereas emotional repression, denial, avoidance, and/or helplessness/hopelessness may be associated with poorer outcomes; however, methodological weaknesses and lack of significant findings in the majority of studies suggests that these relationships are weak (Gerits, 2000; Petticrew, Bell, & Hunter, 2002). Nonetheless, psychological factors, particularly depression, have been found to contribute to medical outcomes among cancer patients (see the subsequent section on Depression).

A relatively new psychological concept akin to the area of coping and adjustment has been described under several different terms, including *posttraumatic growth, stress-related growth,* and *benefit finding.* These terms refer to the positive psychological gains experienced as a result of struggling with a highly challenging life situation (Tedeschi, & Calhoun, 2004). Research indicates that many cancer survivors report such psychological gains as greater appreciation/enjoyment of life, improved relationships, and enhanced view of self as a result of living with and facing cancer (Thornton, 2002). Preliminary research has not found a strong association between posttraumatic growth and psychological outcomes (Tomich & Helgeson, 2002). One potential reason for this is that posttraumatic growth may be better conceptualized as a coping *process* that occurs over time rather than a coping strategy and therefore may be less amenable to interpretation when assessed at a static point in time (Brennan, 2001).

SPIRITUALITY

A number of studies highlight the central role that spiritual beliefs play in coping with cancer (Ashing-Giwa et al., 2004; Musick, Koenig, Larson, and Matthews, 1998; Potts, 1996). One finding that emerges consistently is that underserved minority cancer patients, namely African Americans and Hispanics, report a greater level of spirituality/religiosity (Bourjolly, 1998; Mickley & Soeken, 1993) and use of spiritual coping (Culver, Arena, Antoni, & Carver, 2002) than their Caucasian counterparts. In addition, ethnic minority cancer survivors report the greatest level of unmet spiritual and existential needs (Moadel et al., 1999). Based on the limited research in this area, spirituality and spiritual well-being appear to be related to better psychosocial outcomes (Mytko & Knight, 1999) but not medical outcomes in cancer, although more rigorous research is needed to more fully explore this association (Stefanek, McDonald, & Hess, 2005).

SOCIAL SUPPORT

One area of psychosocial functioning that is often affected by cancer, and can be a major coping resource or deficit, is social support. That is, both the quantity and quality of social support can diminish or be enhanced following a diagnosis of cancer (Pardue, Fenton, & Rounds, 1989), and are positively associated with psychosocial well-being (Helgeson & Cohen, 1996). There is some indication that ethnic differences in social support may exist, with specific vulnerabilities among African American and Hispanic cancer survivors noted (Aziz & Rowland, 2002; Bourjolly, Kerson, & Nuamah, 1999; Rodrigue, 1997). While people with strong social support tend to have better health outcomes (Uchino, Cacioppo, & Kiecolt-Glaser, 1996), research specific to cancer survival is lacking.

COMORBID PSYCHOPATHOLOGY

As described earlier, the physical sequelae of symptoms, treatments, and side effects associated with cancer can potentially pervade all aspects of functioning—including emotional, social, occupational, and general daily activities—and ultimately impact the quality of life of patients and their loved ones. Patients must learn to cope with a host of physical changes, loss of social roles, and a new role as "patient"—with its associated treatment schedule and medical visits—all within the context of a looming potential threat to one's life. From a clinical perspective, therefore, emotional distress in response to the diagnosis and treatment of cancer is to some degree expected. Zabora and colleagues (2001) found an overall prevalence rate of clinically significant emotional distress (i.e., using a "caseness" definition) of 35%, in a sample of 2,296 patients (over 50% of whom were newly diagnosed) with 14 types of cancer diagnoses (Zabora, BrintzenhofeSzoc, Curbow, Hooker, & Piantadosi, 2001). It is important to not simply dismiss emotional reactions as normal, however, because in fact, many cancer patients do meet diagnostic criteria for clinical disorders. Therefore, it is crucial to accurately assess and diagnose mood and anxiety disorders.

DEPRESSION

Comorbid depression can potentially complicate treatment of both conditions (Massie, 2004). For example, the multiple stressors associated with cancer can lead to the development or exacerbation of existing depression, and depression in turn can lead to poorer treatment adherence and outcomes (Massie; Spiegel & Giese-Davis, 2003). Newport and Nemeroff (1998) describe a number of factors that may contribute to increased risk for depressive disorders in cancer patients: Physical contributions may include direct effects of treatments such as chemotherapy, radiation, and specific medications (e.g., steroids); increased pain (often indicating more severe illness status); declining physical status; and need for ongoing treatment (Newport & Nemeroff). Psychosocial contributions may include prior history of depression, poor coping skills, and social isolation. Qualitatively, the themes underlying depression in cancer patients may revolve around issues of sadness, loss, and decreased self-esteem related to changes in/loss of control over health, physical appearance (i.e., disfigurement), physical functioning, and role functioning (i.e., work and relationships). Hopelessness about the future can be significant for patients undergoing repeated treatment cycles over the long term, as well as for patients with terminal disease, who face additional grief associated with anticipation of and preparation for the end of life. Although occasional thoughts of death are not uncommon in cancer patients, it is important to assess suicide risk in cancer patients (Chochinov, 2001), as suicidal ideation may emerge around desires to end physical and emotional suffering and control one's time of death.

Prevalence rates of depression spectrum syndromes vary widely, with estimates ranging from 0 to 58% among adults and from 10 to 22% among children and adolescents (Massie, 2004). Among terminally ill patients (advanced cancer), prevalence of depression ranges from 12 to 26% and is not significantly higher than those with non-advanced cancer. Although depression can co-occur with any type of cancer, higher comorbidity rates have been reported for oropharyngeal (22 to 57%), pancreatic (33 to 50%), lung (11 to 44%) and breast (2 to 46%) cancers (Massie). Multiple authors concur that the prevalence of depression is higher among cancer patients than the general population (Massie; Newport & Nemeroff, 1998; van't Spijker, Trijsburg, & Duivenvoorden, 1997). When interpreting prevalence rates, it is imperative to keep in mind the multiple factors that can contribute to the wide variance in depression prevalence data. In addition to typical challenges regarding comparison of data across studies, such as differences in definitions of depression (i.e., depression symptoms versus major depressive disorder), and assessment methods used (i.e., structured interviews versus self-report instruments) (Newport & Nemeroff; Sellick & Crooks, 1999), a central issue is the lack of a depression assessment measure designed specifically for cancer patients (Ronson, 2004). There is often significant overlap between symptoms of depression and of cancer/treatment side effects (Massie; Trask, 2004). It is therefore difficult to determine whether physical symptoms of depression such as changes in appetite/weight, sleep, energy, or concentration are due to depression, cancer, or both. For more information on approaches used to address this overlap in assessment of adults and children, see Trask (2004). A more abstract consideration is the challenge of assessing the normative versus clinical degree of depression within the context of a life-threatening illness (Massie, 2004), in which depressed and variable mood within the course of cancer treatment is somewhat expected.

As alluded to earlier, research on causal relations between psychological factors and cancer has generally *not* supported a strong association between psychosocial variables such as stress, major life events, a "cancer-prone personality," and emotional distress with increased cancer risk or impact on cancer course and survival (Butow et al., 2000; Dalton, Beosen, Ross, Schapiro, & Johansen, 2002; Sampson, 2002; Vigano et al., 2004). One exception, however, is some preliminary research evidence that points to the impact of depression on cancer course and prognosis. One purported physiological mechanism for this association is dysregulation of the hypothalamic-pituitary-adrenal (HPA) axis, which may result in overproduction of glucocorticoids (i.e., cortisol) as part of the stress response in depression and ultimately lead to impairment in immune functioning, thus affecting cancer progression (Spiegel & Giese-Davis, 2003). Future research is needed to clarify these biopsychological connections.

ANXIETY

Anxiety, like depression, can fall on a continuum from normal to clinical levels. The experience of cancer can trigger multiple anxieties, encompassing practical (e.g., maintaining work and household responsibilities while feeling ill and juggling medical appointments), medical (e.g., fears of needles and painful treatments), and existential (e.g., uncertainties about health status and survival) concerns. For some patients, these anxieties might develop into new diagnoses of anxiety disorders, whereas for others, preexisting anxiety disorders might be exacerbated by the specific threats of cancer and its treatments. In either case, clinically significant anxiety can put patients at risk for poor adherence or even termination of treatment (Bottomley, 1998), and has been associated with decreased functional well-being (Stark et al., 2002). Anxiety disorders related to cancer-specific content and which can interfere with treatment may include blood-injection-injury type phobia (interfering with routine medical tests), claustrophobia (interfering with receiving treatments such as MRI or radiation in small rooms), and generalized anxiety disorder, related to the entire illness experience (Bottomley). In addition, patients with obsessive-compulsive disorder may experience an intensification of symptoms related to contamination fears and washing and checking rituals, given extensive contact with perceived germ-laden medical settings.

Prevalence rates for anxiety disorders have ranged anywhere from 1% to 77%, depending on the assessment method and criteria used (Bottomley, 1998; Stark et al., 2002).

In one study, use of a semistructured diagnostic interview for anxiety disorders yielded a prevalence rate of 18%, compared with a 48% rate when self-report measures were used; results also indicated that 28% of patients also had comorbid depression (Stark et al., 2002). As with depression, a key issue in assessment of anxiety disorders is the lack of assessment measures designed specifically for cancer patients (Bottomley, 1998), making it challenging to distinguish between overlapping physical symptoms of anxiety and illness/treatment side effects, such as increased muscle tension, fatigue, sleep disturbance, and difficulty concentrating. Moreover, it is important to recognize that in addition to the psychosocial factors that may contribute to anxiety disorders (i.e., coping styles and preexisting individual factors), *organic anxiety syndromes* can occur as a result of illness or treatment variables such as infection, pain, abnormal hormonal states, and medical treatments such as steroid and antiemetic medications (Bottomley). Moreover, another essential issue is the difficulty of classifying anxiety as abnormal given the very real threat to health and life that cancer patients confront (Stark et al.).

POSTTRAUMATIC STRESS DISORDER

Recently, some authors (e.g., Ronson, 2004) have begun to conceptualize the psychological responses to cancer within the diagnostic framework of posttraumatic stress disorder (PTSD). According to this perspective, symptoms of depression and anxiety can be viewed within the spectrum of traumatic stress responses, from both a biological and psychological perspective. Ronson (2004) argues that PTSD is a more clinically useful diagnosis than adjustment disorder because it is more sensitive to the actual threat of cancer.

Empirical support for PTSD conceptualization in cancer patients is growing (Gurevich, Devins, & Rodin, 2002). Prevalence rates for the PTSD diagnosis have reportedly ranged from 1% to 58%, depending on the assessment approach used and illness variables (Kangas, Henry, & Bryant, 2002). On average, about 8% of adult cancer survivors experience PTSD-like responses after diagnosis (Smith et al., 1999). Risk for PTSD is highest among those with poorer physical, emotional, social, and financial resources, past and current stressors, and younger age (Smith et al.). Use of the diagnosis, however, is controversial. A number of authors (e.g., Kangas, Henry, & Bryant) point out some of the differences between an illness such as cancer and a distinct traumatic event. These include the following: cancer is an ongoing trauma that may include multiple related stressors, thus making it difficult to determine when a person is "post-trauma"; cognitive intrusions related to cancer are often future-oriented, versus past-oriented as in single traumatic events; and arousal symptoms in cancer patients, such as insomnia, irritability, and difficulty concentrating might be confounded with treatment side effects. In addition, the avoidance criteria of PTSD are difficult to apply because the internal nature of cancer and its treatment requirements make cancer-related issues hard to avoid; memory symptoms might be impaired due to treatment side effects, and it is natural for patients to be worried about a foreshortened future due to the very real threat of death.

PERSONALITY DISORDERS

Research literature is scant in the area of personality disorders and cancer care. Virtually any personality disorder can manifest in a problematic way for patients and practitioners during cancer treatment. The health crisis and associated medical stressors (e.g., loss of control, need to follow authority) of cancer can trigger and/or exacerbate the preexisting poor coping styles and interpersonal challenges that are common to those with personality disorders. Patients who present as "difficult patients" to their health care team may in fact have preexisting personality disorders. For example, patients with dependent personality disorder might present as overly needy and intrusive to their health care providers, and call repeatedly for reassurance. Patients with borderline personality disorder, in particular, might be the most challenging for the health care team, as the stress of cancer might trigger the mood lability, anxiety, and problematic interpersonal styles typical of these patients (Hay & Passik, 2000). It is imperative to assess for Axis II disorders because their presence can potentially intensify comorbid mood or anxiety disorders, as well.

NEUROPSYCHOLOGICAL CONDITIONS

There is a growing interest in understanding cognitive impairment associated with cancer treatment, particularly the phenomenon of *chemobrain* (Matsuda et al., 2005). However, patients can experience neuropsychological side effects not only from chemotherapy but from many types of cancer treatment, including surgery, radiation, and hormonal therapy. Patients with cancer have reported problems with attention and concentration, verbal and visual memory, and organization of information, as well as word-finding difficulty and motor skills deficits (Anderson-Hanley, Sherman, Riggs, Agocha, & Compas, 2003; Matsuda et al.). Research indicates that mild cognitive impairment can affect quality of life (Matsuda et al.). This is consistent with anecdotal patient reports regarding the impact of cognitive deficits on their occupational, social, and general daily functioning.

In their literature review, Matsuda and colleagues report prevalence rates of mild cognitive impairment ranging from 17 to 34% across studies of breast cancer patients who have been treated with adjuvant chemotherapy (2005). They note that there is some contention that mild cognitive impairment due to chemotherapy may be reversible; however, some people report continued symptoms as long as 10 years after completing treatment. Results of several recent meta-analyses (Anderson-Hanley et al., 2003; Jansen et al., 2005; Matsuda et al.) converge in their conclusions that there does appear to be an overall general trend of decreased cognitive functioning after cancer treatment, albeit to a mild to moderate degree. Results were generally significant when scores were compared to normative or control group data but not to patients' own baseline scores. The phenomenon of treatment-related cognitive impairment is challenging to study because of the multiple possible confounds. Central questions remain regarding the source of reported cognitive impairment—for example, is it due to the direct neurotoxic effects of the treatments themselves, or to other proposed factors such as reproductive hormone levels, depression, age, infection, impaired sleep/fatigue, stress, medications, or the cancer itself? (Anderson-Hanley et al.; Matsuda et al.). Randomized longitudinal studies are needed to clarify the underlying causes and the specific nature of the differential effects of treatments on cognitive impairment.

A more acute and serious neuropsychological condition that can occur during cancer treatment is delirium. According to *DSM-IV* criteria (APA, 1994), core clinical symptoms of delirium include decreased clarity of awareness of the environment and reduced attention and changes in cognition, including impaired memory, orientation, language, or perception. Unlike dementia, delirium is considered to be reversible. Prevalence estimates range from 15 to 30% among cancer inpatients, 51% among postoperative patients, and as high as 85% in terminal cancer patients, with elderly patients appearing to be particularly vulnerable (Breitbart & Cohen, 1998). There are multiple potential etiologies, such as the direct effects of tumor(s), or indirect effects of cancer or treatment on the central nervous system, including infection, electrolyte imbalances, or side effects of medication (e.g., opioids), chemotherapy, or radiation. Emotional lability associated with delirium can increase pain and decrease accuracy of pain reports. In addition, delirium might increase the risk of suicide, potentially through behavioral disinhibition (Chochinov, 2001).

PSYCHOLOGICAL INTERVENTIONS

An abundance of research in the field of psycho-oncology has been devoted to developing and evaluating psychosocial/behavioral interventions for improving quality of life outcomes in cancer patients. Two meta-analyses of the literature indicate that taken as a whole, psychosocial interventions for cancer patients result in modest to moderate improvements in emotional adjustment (reflected in improved mood and quality of life) and physical symptoms due to side effects of cancer or its treatment (Meyer & Mark, 1995; Rehse & Pukrop, 2003). There is some indication that a psychosocial intervention duration of 12 or more weeks may be more efficacious than shorter interventions (Rehse & Pukrop). There is some limited research indicating a potential impact of psychological interventions on enhanced immune function and prolonged survival (Andersen et al., 2004; Ironson, Antoni, & Lutgendorf, 1995). More research is needed on the effects of psychosocial interventions for ethnic minorities.

A wide array of therapeutic interventions has been applied to address the emotional and physical needs of patients with cancer. These can be delivered in individual or group modalities. In practice, there is some degree of overlap or combinations within intervention categories. The major intervention approaches are herein described.

Educational Interventions

Educational interventions generally fall into two categories. The first focuses on provision of medical information about cancer and its treatments. Throughout treatment, but particularly after receiving an initial diagnosis of cancer, patients often desire and seek out detailed information about their illness. Unfortunately, however, questions may go unanswered, given the time constraints of office visits. Information can serve as a means to provide social support and to enhance coping (van der Molen, 1999) as well as to promote increased participation and decision making regarding treatment in a cost-effective manner (Mossman, Boudioni, & Slevin, 1999).

The second category, psycho-education, is a frequently used approach that focuses on providing participants with educational information about psychological aspects of cancer and offering an array of tools they can use to cope effectively with the stressors and emotional responses to their cancer diagnosis. Fawzy & Fawzy (1994) have pioneered the use of a psychoeducational model tailored specifically to the needs of cancer patients. Their structured intervention consists of four components: health education, stress management awareness and training, coping skills training, and psychological support. Results of their randomized-controlled study delivering this intervention to patients newly diagnosed with malignant melanoma revealed significantly decreased emotional distress and increased use of active coping among intervention participants (Fawzy & Fawzy). In addition, early results indicated increased immune functioning and survival among intervention patients up to 6 years post-treatment; however, these results did not entirely remain at 10–year follow-up (Fawzy, Canada, & Fawzy, 2003). In research studies comparing psychoeducational to supportive group interventions, the majority favored the efficacy of psychoeducational approaches for psychological outcomes (Edelman, Craig, & Kidman, 2000). The advantages of educational interventions are their brevity, ease of modification for a variety of patients and settings by a range of health care professionals, and cost-effectiveness.

Cognitive-Behavioral Therapy Interventions

Cognitive-behavioral therapy (CBT) interventions for cancer patients focus on skills training to modify problematic thinking styles and behavioral responses that can lead to or exacerbate emotional distress associated with cancer. Cognitive-behavioral therapy techniques have also been implemented to address cancer symptoms and treatment side effects. Included in the broad category of CBT are pure cognitive, pure behavioral, and a combination of these techniques, as well as psychoeducation. Cognitive interventions might include teaching cognitive restructuring to modify beliefs related to body image (e.g., loss of hair or body parts), depression (e.g., feelings of worthlessness or hopelessness), and anxiety (e.g., worries about the future), or teaching effective cognitive coping strategies to deal with fears related to medical procedures. Behavioral interventions might include teaching stress management and problem-solving skills to deal with illness-related stressors, communication skills to improve relationships with family, friends, and health care providers, behavioral activation techniques for goal-setting to address activity level, particularly during depressive episodes, and relaxation techniques (e.g., progressive muscle relaxation, deep breathing, and guided imagery) to promote coping with physical symptoms such as nausea and fatigue.

Outcome data indicate that CBT has been found to improve quality of life and mood, particularly depressed mood, when compared to patients who receive supportive therapy or no therapy (Compas, Haaga, Keefe, Leitenberg, & Williams, 1998), and for patients with advanced cancer (Uitterhoeve et al., 2004). Specific data on relaxation training, in particular, suggest it is effective for decreasing distressing emotional states such as depression, anxiety, and hostility (Luebbert, Dahme, & Hasenbring, 2001; Redd, Montgomery, & DuHamel, 2001). Data on the use of CBT to address health conditions are promising. A number of studies support the use of CBT techniques, particularly relaxation training, for management of treatment-related side effects such as nausea, vomiting, and pain (Compas et al.; Devine, 2003; Luebbert et al.; Redd et al.; Tatrow & Montgomery, 2006). In addition, limited but positive data exist to support the use of CBT techniques (e.g., sleep restriction, stimulus control, progressive muscle relaxation, sleep hygiene, cognitive interventions to decrease worry before sleep) to improve sleep difficulties and fatigue (Smith, Huang, & Manber, 2005).

SUPPORTIVE-EXPRESSIVE THERAPY

Supportive-expressive therapy interventions for cancer patients focus on providing emotional and social support to participants and encouraging emotional expression. Within this category are approaches that focus on existential and spiritual themes such as the search for meaning in cancer, confronting suffering, and exploring religion and faith; these interventions are often directed to patients with advanced cancer (see Breitbart, 2002 for a description). Perhaps the most well-known research studies on supportive-expressive group therapy are by Spiegel and colleagues (Spiegel, Bloom, Kraemer, & Gottheil, 1989; Spiegel, Bloom, & Yalom, 1981). In their prospective randomized-controlled studies of women with metastatic breast cancer, they found that those who participated in support groups over the course of 1 year exhibited significantly less depression, phobias, tension, fatigue, confusion, and maladaptive coping compared to women in the control group. Moreover, at 10–year follow-up, results indicated that support group participants exhibited significantly longer survival times (average = 18 months longer). Although these results have raised great excitement and have been followed by a few small studies with similarly positive findings, there have also been several studies that failed to find a benefit to medical outcome, and large prospective randomized trials have not yet confirmed positive findings (Sagar & Cassileth, 2005).

PHYSICAL EXERCISE

Exercise has been used as an intervention to address both physical and psychological symptoms associated with cancer. There is a growing body of evidence to support the beneficial effects of exercise in cancer patients for improving physical well-being in areas such as nausea, functional capacity, and muscle strength, as well as emotional well-being, in areas such as personality functioning, self-esteem, and mood, particularly for psychological symptoms such as anxiety and depression (Courneya &

Friedenreich, 1999; Galvao & Newton, 2005). In addition, there is strong empirical support for use of aerobic exercise interventions to reduce fatigue, particularly among women with breast cancer. However, results need to be viewed with caution because many studies are limited by lack of randomized-control designs and small samples (Courneya & Friedenreich; Galvao & Newton).

COMPLEMENTARY AND ALTERNATIVE MEDICINE

Complementary and Alternative Medicine (CAM) is of interest to a growing number of patients and researchers. According to a branch of the National Institutes of Health entitled the National Center for Complementary and Alternative Medicine (NCCAM), the broad rubric of CAM "is a group of diverse medical and health care systems, practices, and products that are not presently considered to be part of conventional medicine" (NCCAM, 2002). A distinction is made between complementary and alternative medicine approaches. Whereas *complementary medicine* serves as an adjunct or *complement* to mainstream medicine with practices such as yoga and acupuncture, *alternative medicine* is used to *replace* mainstream medicine, with practices such as using herbal supplements in place of standard cancer treatment. Although appealing to many patients, with estimates ranging from 10 to 80% of cancer patients using CAM, the lack of both controlled studies of CAM and governmental regulation over CAM modalities leads to the risk that CAM modalities will be at best, ineffective, and at worst, physically harmful (Cassileth, 1999; Cassileth & Deng, 2004).

Mind-body medicine is one area of complementary medicine that focuses on the potential for mental, emotional, social, behavioral, and spiritual processes to affect health and personal growth (NCCAM, 2005). While psychotherapy, support groups, and physical exercise are all conventional forms of mind-body medicine, newer mind-body therapies borrowing from cultural or creative practices are becoming a highly popular and intriguing option for both patients and behavioral researchers alike (Richardson, Sanders, Palmer, Greisinger, & Singletary, 2000; White, 2002). Examples include yoga, meditation, prayer, and expressive arts such as dance, art, and music. Although mind-body techniques can enhance patients' symptom management, coping, and quality of life, evidence does not support the idea that patients can control the course or outcome of their cancer with mental or emotional work, as is sometimes promoted by the popular media; in fact, this idea can promote guilt among patients who do not see a change in disease outcome (Sagar & Cassileth, 2005). There is currently a dearth of randomized-controlled studies to evaluate the newer mind-body therapies. There is preliminary evidence, however, to indicate that mindfulness meditation (Ott, Norris, & Bauer-Wu, 2006) and yoga (Bower, Woolery, Sternlieb, & Garet, 2005) may be associated with improvements in various measures of quality of life, and that such interventions (i.e., yoga) are well-received and effective among underserved and ethnic minority populations (Moadel et al., in press).

SPECIAL POPULATIONS

For comprehensiveness, a word must be added about two special populations who are faced with cancer and its challenges from their own unique perspectives. These include children and adolescents with cancer, as well as family members.

PEDIATRIC ONCOLOGY

Although cancer incidence is rare in children, when it does occur, it engenders many of the medical, physical, psychological, and social issues described throughout this chapter as experienced within a developmental and familial context (Kreitler& Weyl-Ben-Arush, 2004). Issues around medical procedures, pain, disfigurement, and displacement from normal life, including school, are central themes facing the child with cancer; adolescents often grapple with body image, independence/dependence conflicts, and social relationship distress; long-term survivors of childhood cancer are prone to experiencing a range of potential medical and psychosocial sequelae (Bottomley & Kassner, 2003). Overall, however, survivors of pediatric cancer often fare as well as their healthy peers in emotional and social adaptation (Stam & Last, 2001). A variety of behavioral interventions, often applied in combination, have been used to reduce distress and increase cooperation in children undergoing cancer treatment; these include contingency management, cognitive/attentional distraction, hypnosis, systematic desensitization, modeling, and behavioral rehearsal (DuHamel, Redd, & Vickberg, 1999).

FAMILIES AND CANCER

When cancer is diagnosed, it typically affects the entire family system. For siblings of children with cancer, feelings of loss, loneliness, anger, jealousy, and guilt are frequently experienced, although gains in personal growth, maturity, and independence are also seen (Wilkins & Woodgate, 2005). Parents of children with cancer often experience intense emotional reactions, feelings of helplessness, loss of control, psychiatric disorders, and marital distress (Grootenhuis & Last, 1997), and may even experience PTSD (Kazak et al., 1997; Stuber, Christakis, Houskamp, & Kazak, 1996). Caregiver stress and burnout is another phenomenon that affects many families in which a member has cancer. As a result of chronic psychological, social, and physical demands of caring for a loved one with cancer, family members of cancer patients may experience anxiety, depression, interpersonal and work-related disruption, physical symptoms, and financial stress (Grov, Dahl, Moum, & Fossa, 2005; Kitrungrote & Cohen, 2006; Northouse et al., 2002; Weitzner, Haley, & Chen, 2000). On the other hand, caregiving may also provide positive rewards such as enriched purpose or meaning in life and improved self-esteem (Hunt, 2003). While there is some research indicating that cognitive-behavioral family therapy interventions for adolescent cancer survivors and their families may help reduce PTSD and anxiety symptoms (Kazak et al., 1999), more research is clearly needed to help identify and evaluate effective interventions for promoting adjustment and reducing stress among family caregivers (Harding & Higginson, 2003).

CASE EXAMPLE

Mrs. R. is a 64–year-old married woman who was born and raised in Jamaica but has lived in an urban area of the United States throughout most of her adult life. Mrs. R. was referred for psychosocial oncology services following a major depressive episode that was triggered by a recent diagnosis of breast cancer. Initially withdrawn and reserved in her meeting with the psychologist, Mrs. R. slowly revealed a well of despair and guilt related to her cancer and the underlying meanings it had for her.

Mrs. R. was convinced that her cancer was a punishment from God. Having strayed away from her Christian upbringing, she felt her "lack of faith" was a sin for which she had silently carried great shame. Further complicating her depression was her grief around losing her breast and the fear that her husband would not be attracted to her anymore. In order to preempt his potential rejection, she avoided any intimate contact with him, and made sure not to expose her unclothed chest to him in any way. The therapeutic approach was oriented toward acknowledging and validating Mrs. R.'s feelings of loss and despair and eliciting her beliefs and experiences about religion/spirituality and the marital relationship. Two important aspects of her life were revealed: First, Mrs. R. had never been baptized, which symbolized for her a barrier to building a relationship with God. Second, her perceptions of marital life were degraded by several extramarital affairs undertaken by her husband in the early years of their marriage. Given that Mrs. R.'s most acute distress revolved around her spiritual conflict, therapeutic energies were first focused on this issue. Through the use of cognitive-behavioral and existential therapeutic strategies, the therapist guided the patient to identify and assess the validity of the beliefs that were causing her emotional distress (e.g., "I am being punished by God for my lack of faith"), and to explore personally meaningful and proactive strategies in which she may be able to respond to her beliefs. Through an open-ended discussion about how she could "regain or build her faith," Mrs. R. came upon a resolution that held great meaning to her. Arranged with the help of a relative who was a minister, Mrs. R. was baptized in a traditional ceremony. This symbolic act provided a tremendous sense of relief and freedom, and served to redirect her attentions to the underlying feelings of loss and shame related to her body disfigurement and her relationship with a man from whom she had felt rejected in the past. Once again, CBT was used to help her separate her fears from reality, expand her definitions of beauty and femininity, and model communication skills whereby she could share her thoughts, feelings, and needs with her husband. Over time, Mrs. R. began to accept her new body and more openly discuss her fears of rejection with her husband, whose expressions of commitment to her helped her to begin to explore intimacy with him again. Feeling significantly more optimistic and less distressed, Mrs. R. discontinued therapy after just a couple of months. While it is not known the extent to which she was able to further and/or reinforce her progress, as is true in most cases, it is probably the case with Mrs. R. that she experienced steps forward and steps backward in her journey living with and beyond cancer.

REFERENCES

American Cancer Society. (2004a). *Bone marrow and peripheral blood stem cell transplants*. Retrieved September, 2004, from http://www.cancer.org/docroot/ETO/eto_1_3_Bone_Marrow.asp

American Cancer Society. (2004b). *Staging*. Retrieved September, 2004, from http://www.cancer.org/docroot/ETO/content/ETO_1_2X_Staging.asp

American Cancer Society. (2005). *What is gene therapy?* Retrieved February, 2005, from http://www.cancer.org/docroot/ETO/content/ETO_1_4X_What_Is_Gene_Therapy.asp

American Cancer Society. (2006a). *Antiangiogenesis treatment*.Retrieved November, 2006, from http://www.cancer.org/docroot/ETO/ eto_1_3_Antiangiogenesis_Therapy.asp?sitearea= &level=

American Cancer Society. (2006b). *Cancer Facts and Figures 2006*. Atlanta: American Cancer Society.

American Cancer Society. (2006c). *Clinical trials: What you need to know*. Retrieved August, 2006, from http://www.cancer.org/docroot/ETO/content/ETO_6_3_Clinical_Trials_Patient _Participation.asp

American Cancer Society. (2006d). *Detailed guide: Breast cancer hormone therapy*. Retrieved September, 2006, from http://www.cancer.org/docroot/CRI/content/CRI_2_4_4X_Hormone _Therapy_5.asp?sitearea=

American Cancer Society. (2006e). *Detailed guide: Cancer (general information): Signs and symptoms of cancer*. Retrieved February 28, 2006, from http://www.cancer.org/docroot/CRI/content/ CRI_2_4_3X_What_are_the_signs_and_symptoms_of_cancer.asp?sitearea=CRI&viewmode =print&

American Cancer Society. (2006f). *Detailed guide: Prostate cancer hormone (androgen deprivation) therapy*. Retrieved July, 2006, from http://www.cancer.org/docroot/CRI/content/CRI_2 _4_4X_Androgen_Suppression_Hormone_Therapy_36.asp?sitearea=

American Cancer Society. (2006g). *Monoclonal antibodies*. Retrieved December, 2006, from http://www.cancer.org/docroot/ETO/content/ETO_1_4X_Monoclonal_Antibody_Therapy _Passive_Immunotherapy.asp?sitearea=ETO

American Cancer Society. (2006h). *What are the different types of chemotherapy drugs?* Retrieved November, 2006, from http://www.cancer.org/docroot/ETO/content/ETO_1_4X_What_Are _The_Different_Types_Of_Chemotherapy_Drugs.asp?sitearea=ETO

American Cancer Society. (2006i). *What is immunotherapy?* Retrieved December, 2006, from http://www.cancer.org/docroot/ETO/content/ETO_1_4X_What_Is_Immunotherapy.asp ?sitearea=ETO

American Psychiatric Association. (1994). *Diagnostic and statistical manual of mental disorders* (4th ed.). Washington, DC: Author.

Andersen, B. L., Farrar, W. B., Golden-Kreutz, D. M., Glaser, R., Emery, C. F., Crespin, T. R., et al. (2004). Psychological, behavioral, and immune changes after a psychological intervention: A clinical trial. *Journal of Clinical Oncology, 22*(17), 3570–3580.

Anderson-Hanley, C., Sherman, M. L., Riggs, R., Agocha, V. B., & Compas, B. E. (2003). Neuropsychological effects of treatments for adults with cancer: A meta-analysis and review of the literature. *J Int Neuropsychol Soc, 9*(7), 967–982.

Ashing-Giwa, K T., Padilla, G. Tejero, J., Kraemer, J., Wright, K., Coscarelli, A., et al. (2004). Understanding the Breast Cancer Experience of Women: A Qualitative Study of African American, Asian American, Latina and Caucasian Cancer Survivors. *Psycho-Oncology, 13*, 408-428.

Aziz, N. M., & Rowland, J. H. (2002). Cancer survivorship research among ethnic minority and medically underserved groups. *Oncology Nursing Forum, 29*(5), 789–801.

Baker, F., Denniston, M., Smith, T., & West, M. M. (2005). Adult cancer survivors: How are they faring? *Cancer, 104*(S11), 2565–2576.

Beyer, D. A. (1995). Cancer is a chronic disease. *Nurse Practitioner Forum, 6*(4), 201–206.

Bottomley, A. (1998). Anxiety and the adult cancer patient. *European Journal of Cancer Care, 7*, 217–224.

Bottomley, S. J., & Kassner, E. (2003). Late effects of childhood cancer therapy. *Journal of Pediatric Nursing, 18*(2), 126–133.

Bourjolly, J. N. (1998). Differences in religiousness among black and white women with breast cancer. *Social Work in Health Care, 28*(1), 21–39.

Bourjolly, J. N., Kerson, T. S., & Nuamah, I. F. (1999). A comparison of social functioning among Black women with breast cancer. *Social Work in Health Care, 28*(3), 1–20.

Bower, J.E., Woolery, A., Sternlieb, B., & Garet, D. (2005). Yoga for Cancer Patients and Survivors. *Cancer Control, 12*(3), 165–171.

Breitbart, W. (2002). Spirituality and meaning in supportive care: Spirituallity- and meaning-centered group psychotherapy interventions in advanced cancer. *Supportive Care in Cancer, 10*(4), 272–280.

Breitbart, W., & Cohen, K. R. (1998). Delirium. In J. C. Holland (Ed.), *Psycho-Oncology* (pp. 564–575). New York: Oxford University Press.

Brennan, J. (2001). Adjustment to cancer—coping or personal transition? *Psycho-Oncology, 10,* 1–18.

Butow, P. N., Hiller, J. E., Price, M. A., Thackway, S. V., Kricker, A., & Tennant, C. C. (2000). Epidemiological evidence for a relationship between life events, coping style, and personality factors in the development of breast cancer. *Journal of Psychosomatic Research, 49,* 169–181.

Carelle, N., Piotto, E., Bellanger, A., Germanaud, J., Thuillier, A., & Khayat, D. (2002). Changing patient perceptions of the side effects of cancer chemotherapy. *Cancer, 95*(1), 155–163.

Carver, C. S. (2005). Enhancing adaptation during treatment and the role of individual differences. *Cancer, 104*(S11), 2602–2607.

Carver, C. S., Pozo, C., Harris, S. D., Noriega, V., Scheier, M. F., Robinson, D. S., et al. (1993). How coping mediates the effect of optimism on distress: A study of women with early stage breast cancer. *J Pers Soc Psychol, 65*(2), 375–390.

Cassileth, B. R. (1999). Evaluating complementary and alternative therapies for cancer patients. *CA-A Cancer Journal for Clinicians, 49*(6), 363–375.

Cassileth, B. R., & Deng, G. (2004). Complementary and alternative therapies for cancer. *Oncologist, 9*(1), 80–89.

Cella, D., Lai, J. S., Chang, C. H., Peterman, A., & Slavin, M. (2002). Fatigue in cancer patients compared with fatigue in the general United States population. *Cancer, 94*(2), 528–538.

Center for Disease Control and Prevention (CDC). (2005). *United States Cancer Statistics: 1999–2002 Incidence and Mortality Web–based Report Version.* Atlanta: Department of Health and Human Services, Centers for Disease Control and Prevention, and National Cancer Institute. U.S. Cancer Statistics Working Group. Available at: www.cdc.gov/cancer/npcr/uscs/

Chang, S., Long, S. R., Kutikova, L., Bowman, L., Finley, D., Crown, W. H., et al. (2004). Estimating the cost of cancer: Results on the basis of claims data analyses for cancer patients diagnosed with seven types of cancer during 1999 to 2000. *J Clin Oncol, 22*(17), 3524–3530.

Chochinov, H. M. (2001). Depression in cancer patients. *The Lancet, 2,* 499–505.

Compas, B. E., Haaga, D. A. F., Keefe, F. J., Leitenberg, H., & Williams, D. A. (1998). Sampling of empirically supported psychological treatments from health psychology: Smoking, chronic pain, cancer and bulimia nervosa. *Journal of Consulting and Clinical Psychology, 66*(1), 89–112.

Courneya, K. S., & Friedenreich, C. M. (1999). Physical exercise and quality of life following cancer diagnosis: A literature review. *Annals of Behavioral Medicine, 21*(2), 171–179.

Culver, J. L., Arena, P. L., Antoni, M. H., & Carver, C. S. (2002). Coping and distress among women under treatment for early stage breast cancer: Comparing African Americans, Hispanics and non-Hispanic Whites. *Psycho-Oncology, 11,* 495–504.

Dalton, S. O., Beosen, E. H., Ross, L., Schapiro, I. R., & Johansen, C. (2002). Mind and cancer: Do psychological factors cause cancer? *European Journal of Cancer, 38,* 1313–1323.

Davis, T. C., Williams, M. V., Marin, E., Parker, R. M., & Glass, J. (2002). Health literacy and cancer communication. *CA Cancer J Clin, 52*(3), 134–149.

Devine, E. C. (2003). Meta-analysis of the effect of psychoeducational interventions on pain in adults with cancer. *Oncology Nursing Forum, 30*(1), 75–89.

Doescher, M. P., Saver, B. G., Franks, P., & Fiscella, K. (2000). Racial and ethnic disparities in perceptions of physician style and trust. *Arch Fam Med, 9*(10), 1156–1163.

DuHamel, K. N., Redd, W. H., & Vickberg, S. M. (1999). Behavioral interventions in the diagnosis, treatment and rehabilitation of children with cancer. *Acta Oncol, 38*(6), 719–734.

Dunkel-Schetter, C., Feinstein, L. G., Taylor, S. E., & Falke, R. L. (1992). Patterns of coping with cancer. *Health Psychol, 11*(2), 79–87.

Edelman, S., Craig, A., & Kidman, A. (2000). Group interventions with cancer patients: Efficacy of psychoeducational versus supportive groups. *Journal of Psychosocial Oncology, 18*(3), 67–85.

Ellington, L., Wahab, S., Martin, S. S., Field, R., & Mooney, K. H. (2006). Factors that influence Spanish- and English-speaking participants' decision to enroll in cancer randomized clinical trials. *Psycho-Oncology, 15*(4), 273–284.

Eversley, R., Estrin, D., Dibble, S., Wardlaw, L., Pedrosa, M., & Favila-Penney, W. (2005). Post-treatment symptoms among ethnic minority breast cancer survivors. *Oncology Nursing Forum, 32*(2), 250–256.

Fawzy, F. I., Canada, A. L., & Fawzy, N. W. (2003). Malignant melanoma: Effects of a brief, structured psychiatric intervention on survival and recurrence at 10–year follow-up. *Archives of General Psychiatry, 60,* 100–103.

Fawzy, F. I., & Fawzy, N. W. (1994). A structured psychoeducational intervention for cancer patients. *General Hospital Psychiatry, 16*(3), 149–192.

Folkman, S., & Lazarus, R. S. (1988). Coping as a mediator of emotion. *J Pers Soc Psychol, 54*(3), 466–475.

Galvao, D. A., & Newton, R. U. (2005). Review of exercise intervention studies in cancer patients. *Journal of Clinical Oncology, 23*(4), 899–909.

Gerits, P. (2000). Life events, coping and breast cancer: State of the art. *Biomedecine & Pharmacotherapy, 54*(5), 229–233.

Goudas, L. C., Bloch, R., Gialeli-Goudas, M., Lau, J., & Carr, D. B. (2005). The epidemiology of cancer pain. *Cancer Invest, 23*(2), 182–190.

Greene, F., Page, D., Fleming, I., Fritz, A., Balch, C., Haller, D., et al. (2002). *American Joint Committee on Cancer Staging Manual* (6th ed.). New York: Springer.

Grootenhuis, M. A., & Last, B.F. (1997). Adjustment and coping by parents of children with cancer: A review of the literature. *Support Care Cancer, 5*(6), 466–484.

Grov, E. K., Dahl, A. A., Moum, T., & Fossa, S. D. (2005). Anxiety, depression, and quality of life in caregivers of patients with cancer in late palliative phase. *Annals of Oncology, 16,* 1185–1191.

Gurevich, M., Devins, G. M., & Rodin, G. M. (2002). Stress response syndromes and cancer: Conceptual and assessment issues. *Psychosomatics, 43*(4), 259–281.

Harding, R., & Higginson, I.J. (2003). What is the best way to help caregivers in cancer and palliative care? A systematic literature review of interventions and their effectiveness. *Palliative Medicine, 17*(1), 63–74.

Hay, J. L., & Passik, S. D. (2000). The cancer patient with borderline personality disorder: Suggestions for symptom-focused management in the medical setting. *Psycho-Oncology, 9,* 91–100.

Helgeson, V. S., & Cohen, S. (1996). Social support and adjustment to cancer: Reconciling descriptive, correlational, and intervention research. *Health Psychology, 15*(2), 135–148.

Henderson, J. W., & Donatelle, R. J. (2003). The relationship between cancer locus of control and complementary and alternative medicine use by women diagnosed with breast cancer. *Psycho-Oncology, 12*(1), 59–67.

Hunt, C. K. (2003). Concepts in caregiver research. *Journal of Nursing Scholarshop, 35*(1), 27–32.

Ironson, G., Antoni, M., & Lutgendorf, S. (1995). Can psychological interventions affect immunity and survival? Present findings and suggested targets with a focus on cancer and human immunodeficiency virus. *Mind/Body Medicine, 1*(2), 85–110.

Jansen, C. E., Miaskowski, C., Dodd, M., Dowling, G., & Kramer, J. (2005). A meta-analysis of studies of the effects of cancer chemotherapy on various domains of cognitive function. *Cancer, 104*(10), 2222–2233.

Kangas, M., Henry, J. L., & Bryant, R. A. (2002). Posttraumatic stress disorder following cancer: A conceptual and empirical review. *Clinical Psychology Review, 22*, 499–524.

Katapodi, M. C., Lee, K. A., Facione, N. C., & Dodd, M. J. (2004). Predictors of perceived breast cancer risk and the relation between perceived risk and breast cancer screening: A meta-analytic review. *Preventive Medicine, 38*(4), 388–402.

Kazak, A. E., Barakat, L. P., Meeske, K., Christakis, D., Meadows, A. T., Casey, R., et al. (1997). Posttraumatic stress, family functioning, and social support in survivors of childhood leukemia and their mothers and fathers. *J Consult Clin Psychol, 65*(1), 120–129.

Kazak, A. E., Simms, S., Barakat, L., Hobbie, W., Foley, B., Golomb, V., et al. (1999). Surviving cancer competently intervention program (SCCIP): A cognitive-behavioral and family therapy intervention for adolescent survivors of childhood cancer and their families. *Family Process, 38*(2), 175–191.

Kitrungrote, L., & Cohen, M. Z. (2006). Quality of life of family caregivers of patients with cancer: A literature review. *Oncology Nursing Forum, 33*(3), 625–632.

Kreitler, S., & Weyl-Ben-Arush, M. (Eds). (2004). *Psychosocial Aspects of Pediatric Oncology.* Hoboken, NJ: Wiley.

Lantz, J. M., Fullerton, J. T., Harshburger, R. J., & Sadler, R. (2001). Promoting screening and early detection of cancer in men. *Nursing & Health Sciences, 3*(4), 189–196.

Luebbert, K., Dahme, B., & Hasenbring, M. (2001). The effectiveness of relaxation training in reducing treatment-related symptoms and improving emotional adjustment in acute nonsurgical cancer treatment: A meta-analytical review. *Psycho-Oncology, 10*, 490–502.

Mackay, J., Jemal, A., Lee, N. C.,& Parkin, D. M. (2006). *The Cancer Atlas.* Atlanta: American Cancer Society.

Mandelblatt, J. S., Yabroff, K. R., & Kerner, J. F. (1999). Equitable access to cancer services. *Cancer, 86*(11), 2378–2390.

Manne, S. L., Ostroff, J. S., Norton, T. R., Fox, K., Grana, G., & Goldstein, L. (2006). Cancer-specific self-efficacy and psychosocial and functional adaptation to early stage breast cancer. *Annals of Behavioral Medicine, 31*(2), 145–154.

Massie, M. J. (2004). Prevalence of depression in patients with cancer. *Journal of the National Cancer Institute Monographs, 32*, 57–71.

Matsuda, T., Takayama, T., Tashiro, M., Nakamura, Y., Ohashi, Y., & Shimozuma, K. (2005). Mild cognitive impairment after adjuvant chemotherapy in breast cancer patients: Evaluation of appropriate research design and methodology to measure symptoms. *Breast Cancer, 12*(4), 279–287.

Maxwell, A. E., Bastani, R., & Warda, U. S. (1998). Misconceptions and mammography use among Filipino- and Korean-American women. *Ethnicity & Disease, 8*(3), 377–384.

Meyer, T. J., & Mark, M. M. (1995). Effects of psychosocial interventions with adult cancer patients: A meta-analysis of randomized experiments. *Health Psychology, 14*(2), 101–108.

Meyerowitz, B. E., Richardson, J., Hudson, S., & Leedham, B. (1998). Ethnicity and cancer outcomes: Behavioral and psychosocial considerations. *Psychological Bulletin, 123*(1), 47–70.

Mickley, J., & Soeken, K. (1993). Religiousness and hope in Hispanic- and Anglo-American women with breast cancer. *Oncology Nursing Forum, 20*(8), 1171–1177.

Mitchell, J. L. (1998). Cross-cultural issues in the disclosure of cancer. *Cancer Pract, 6*(3), 153–160.

Moadel, A., Morgan, C., & Dutcher, J. (2007). Psychosocial needs assessment among an underserved, ethnically diverse cancer patient population. *Cancer* 109(2 Suppl.)P: 446–454.

Moadel, A., Morgan, C., Fatone, A., Grennan, J., Carter, J., Laruffa, G., et al. (1999). Seeking meaning and hope: Self-reported spiritual and existential needs among an ethnically diverse cancer patient population. *Psycho-Oncology, 8*, 378–385.

Moadel, A. B., Shah, C., Wylie-Rosett, J., Patel, S., Harris, M., & Sparano, J. (in press). Randomized-controlled trial of yoga among a multi-ethnic breast cancer sample: Effects on quality of life. *Journal of Clinical Oncology.*

Mossman, J., Boudioni, M., & Slevin, M. L. (1999). Cancer information: A cost-effective intervention. *European Journal of Cancer, 35*(11), 1587–1591.

Muscari Lin, E., Aikin, J. L., & Good, B. C. (1999). Premature menopause after cancer treatment. *Cancer Practice, 7*(3), 114–121.

Musick, M., Koenig, H. G., Larson, D., & Matthews, D. (1998). Religion and spiritual beliefs. In J. Holland (Ed.), *Psycho-Oncology* (pp. 780–789). New York: Oxford University Press.

Mytko, J. J., & Knight, S. J. (1999). Body, mind and spirit: Towards the integration of religiosity and spirituality in cancer quality of life research. *Psycho-Oncology, 8*(5), 439–450.

National Center for Complementary and Alternative Medicine (NCCAM). (2002). *What is complementary and alternative medicine (CAM)?* Retrieved April, 2005, from http://nccam.nih.gov/health/whatiscam/

National Center for Complementary and Alternative Medicine (NCCAM). (2004). *Whole medical systems: An overview:* National Center for Complementary and Alternative Medicine, National Institutes of Health, U.S. Department of Health and Human Services. Retrieved October, 2004, from http://nccam.nih.gov/health/backgrounds/wholemed.pdf

National Center for Complementary and Alternative Medicine (NCCAM). (2005). *Mind-body medicine: An overview.* Retrieved August, 2006, from http://nccam.nih.gov/health/backgrounds/mindbody.htm

Nelson, D. V., Friedman, L. C., Baer, P. E., Lane, M., & Smith, F. E. (1989). Attitudes of cancer: Psychometric properties of fighting spirit and denial. *J Behav Med, 12*(4), 341–355.

Newport, D. J., & Nemeroff, C. B. (1998). Assessment and treatment of depression in the cancer patient. *Journal of Psychosomatic Research, 45*, 215–237.

Nordin, K., Berglund, G., Terje, I., & Glimelius, B. (1999). The Mental Adjustment to Cancer Scale: A psychometric analysis and the concept of coping. *Psycho-Oncology, 8*(3), 250–259.

Northouse, L. L., Mood, D., Kershaw, T., Schafenacker, A., Mellon, S., Walker, J., et al. (2002). Quality of life of women with recurrent breast cancer and their family members. *Journal of Clinical Oncology, 20*(19), 4050–4064.

Ott, M. J., Norris, R. L., & Bauer-Wu, S. M. (2006). Mindfulness meditation for oncology patients: A discussion and critical review. *Integr Cancer Ther, 5*(2), 98–108.

Pardue, S. F., Fenton, M. V., & Rounds, L. R. (1989). The social impact of cancer. *Dimens Oncol Nurs, 3*(1), 5–13.

Patterson, J. T. (1987). *The dread disease: Cancer and modern American culture.* Cambridge: Harvard University Press.

Petticrew, M., Bell, R., & Hunter, D. (2002). Influence of psychological coping on survival and recurrence in people with cancer: Systematic review. *BMJ, 325*(7372), 1066.

Potts, R. G. (1996). Spirituality and the experience of cancer in an African-American community: Implications for psychosocial oncology. *Journal of Psychosocial Oncology, 14*(1), 1–19.

Powe, B. D., & Finnie, R. (2003). Cancer fatalism: The state of the science. *Cancer Nurs, 26*(6), 454–464.

Redd, W. H., Montgomery, G. H., & DuHamel, K. N. (2001). Behavioral intervention for cancer treatment side effects. *Journal of the National Cancer Institute, 93*(11), 810–823.

Rehse, B., & Pukrop, R. (2003). Effects of psychosocial interventions on quality of life in adult cancer patients: Meta analysis of 37 published controlled outcome studies. *Patient Education & Counseling, 50*(2), 179–186.

Reynolds, P., Hurley, S., Torres, M., Jackson, J., Boyd, P., & Chen, V. W. (2000). Use of coping strategies and breast cancer survival: Results from the Black/White Cancer Survival Study. *Am J Epidemiology, 152*(10), 940–949.

Richardson, M. A., Sanders, T., Palmer, J. L., Greisinger, A., & Singletary, S. E. (2000). Complementary/Alternative medicine use in a comprehensive cancer center and the implications for oncology. *Journal of Clinical Oncology, 18*(13), 2505–2514.

Rodrigue, J. R. (1997). An examination of race differences in patients' psychological adjustment to cancer. *Journal of Clinical Psychology in Medical Settings, 4*(3), 271–280.

Ronson, A. (2004). Psychiatric disorders in oncology: Recent therapeutic advances and new conceptual frameworks. *Current Opinion in Oncology, 16*, 318–323.

Sagar, S. M., & Cassileth, B. R. (2005). Integrative oncology for comprehensive cancer centres: Definitions, scope, and policy. *Current Oncology, 12*(3), 103–117.

Sampson, W. (2002). Controversies in cancer and the mind: Effects of psychosocial support. *Seminars in Oncology, 29*(6), 595–600.

Schover, L. R. (1998). Sexual dysfunction. In J. C. Holland (Ed.), *Psycho-oncology* (pp. 494–499). New York: Oxford University Press.

Sellick, S. M., & Crooks, D. L. (1999). Depression and cancer: An appraisal of the literature for prevalence, detection, and practice guideline development for psychological interventions. *Psycho-Oncology, 8*, 315–333.

Siminoff, L. A., & Ross, L. (2005). Access and equity to cancer care in the USA: A review and assessment. *Postgrad Med J, 81*(961), 674–679.

Smith, M. T., Huang, M. I., & Manber, R. (2005). Cognitive behavior therapy for chronic insomnia occurring within the context of medical and psychiatric disorders. *Clinical Psychology Review, 25*, 559–592.

Smith, M.Y., Redd, W.H., Peyser, C., & Vogl, D. (1999). Post-traumatic stress disorder in cancer: A review. *Psycho-Oncology, 8*(6), 521–537.

Sollner, W., Maislinger, S., DeVries, A., Steixner, E., Rumpold, G., & Lukas, P. (2000). Use of complementary and alternative medicine by cancer patients is not associated with perceived distress or poor compliance with standard treatment but with active coping behavior. *Cancer, 89*, 873–880.

Souhami, R. L., & Tobias, J. S. (2005). *Cancer and its management*. Malden, UK: Blackwell.

Spiegel, D., Bloom, J. R., Kraemer, H. C., & Gottheil, E. (1989). Effect of psychosocial treatment on survival of patients with metastatic breast cancer. *The Lancet, 2*, 888–891.

Spiegel, D., Bloom, J. R., & Yalom, I. (1981). Group support for patients with metastatic cancer. *Arch Gen Psychiatry, 38*, 527–531.

Spiegel, D., & Giese-Davis, J. (2003). Depression and cancer: Mechanisms and disease progression. *Biological Psychiatry, 54*, 269–282.

Stam, H., Grootenhuis, M. A., & Last, B. F. (2001). Social and emotional adjustment in young survivors of childhood cancer. *Support Care Cancer, 9*(7), 489–513.

Stark, D., Kiely, M., Smith, A., Velikova, G., House, A., & Selby, P. (2002). Anxiety disorders in cancer patients: Their nature, associations, and relation to quality of life. *Journal of Clinical Oncology, 20*(14), 3137–3148.

Stefanek, M., McDonald, P. G., & Hess, S. A. (2005). Religion, spirituality and cancer: Current status and methodological challenges. *Psycho-Oncology, 14*(6), 450–463.

Stuber, M. L., Christakis, D. A., Houskamp, B., & Kazak, A. E. (1996). Posttrauma symptoms in childhood leukemia survivors and their parents. *Psychosomatics, 37*(3), 254–261.

Tannock, I. F., Hill, R. P., Bristow, R. G., & Harrington, L. (2004). *The basic science of oncology*. New York: McGraw-Hill.

Tatrow, K., & Montgomery, G. H. (2006). Cognitive behavioral therapy techniques for distress and pain in breast cancer patients: A meta-analysis. *Journal of Behavioral Medicine, 29*(1), 17–27.

Tedeschi, R. G., & Calhoun, L.G. (2004). Posttraumatic growth: Conceptual foundations and empirical evidence. *Psychological Inquiry, 15*(1), 1–18.

Thornton, A. A. (2002). Perceiving benefits in the cancer experience. *Journal of Clinical Psychology in Medical Settings, 9*(2), 153–165.

Tomich, P. L., & Helgeson, V. S. (2002). Five years later: A cross-sectional comparison of breast cancer survivors with healthy women. *Psycho-Oncology, 11,* 154–169.

Trask, P. C. (2004). Assessment of depression in cancer patients. *Journal of the National Cancer Institute Monographs, 32,* 80–92.

Uchino, B. N., Cacioppo, J. T., & Kiecolt-Glaser, J. K. (1996). The relationship between social support and physiological processes: A review with emphasis on underlying mechanisms and implications for health. *Psychol Bull, 119*(3), 488–531.

Uitterhoeve, R. J., Vernooy, M., Litjens, M., Potting, K., Bensing, J., De Mulder, P., et al. (2004). Psychosocial interventions for patients with advance cancer: A systematic review of the literature. *British Journal of Cancer, 91,* 1050–1062.

van der Molen, B. (1999). Relating information needs to the cancer experience: 1. Information as a key coping strategy. *European Journal of Cancer Care, 8*(4), 238–244.

van't Spijker, A., Trijsburg, R. W., & Duivenvoorden, H. J. (1997). Psychological sequelae of cancer diagnosis: A meta-analytical review of 58 studies after 1980. *Psychosomatic Medicine, 59*(3), 280–293.

Vigano, A., Donaldson, N., Higginson, I. J., Bruera, E., Mahmud, S., & Suarez-Almazor, M. (2004). Quality of life and survival prediction in terminal cancer patients: A multicenter study. *Cancer, 101*(5), 1090–1098.

Ward, E., Jemal, A., Cokkinides, V., Singh, G. K., Cardinez, C., Ghafoor, A., et al. (2004). Cancer disparities by race/ethnicity and socioeconomic status. *CA Cancer J Clin, 54*(2), 78–93.

Weitzner, M. A., Haley, W. E., & Chen, H. (2000). The family caregiver of the older cancer patient. *Hematol Oncol Clin North Am., 14*(1), 269–281.

White, J. D. (2002). Complementary and alternative medicine research: A National Cancer Institute perspective. *Seminars in Oncology, 29*(6), 546–551.

Wilkins, K. L., & Woodgate, R. L. (2005). A review of qualitative research on the childhood cancer experience from the perspective of siblings: A need to give them a voice. *Journal of Pediatric Oncology Nursing, 22*(6), 305–319.

Zabora, J., BrintzenhofeSzoc, K., Curbow, B., Hooker, C., & Piantadosi, S. (2001). The prevalence of psychological distress by cancer site. *Psycho-Oncology, 10*(1), 19–28.

CHAPTER 8

Diabetes

BRET A. BOYER

DEFINITION OF DIABETES

Diabetes occurs when an individual develops a dysfunction in insulin production and/or insulin action, which induces an inability to metabolize blood glucose. Insulin is a hormone produced by beta cells within the pancreas; it is necessary for the body's cells to metabolize glucose carried within the blood stream (American Diabetes Association [ADA], 2006c; http://www.diabetes.org/type-2-diabetes/insulin.jsp). As discussed in the Disease Factors section, persistently high blood glucose (BG) increases the risk of many serious complications. Although islet cell transplantation shows great promise as a cure for diabetes (Bertuzzi, Marzorati, & Secchi, 2006), these treatments have not become available to the public, and the primary goal of treatment remains the management of BG within, or as close as possible to, normal levels (~90–130 mg/dl; ADA).

Diabetes is identified as one of several types. Type I diabetes was formerly referred to as Juvenile diabetes or insulin-dependent diabetes. These names have fallen from favor, since Type I diabetes can develop at almost any age (even though it more commonly begins during childhood, adolescence, or young adulthood). With Type I diabetes, the body destroys the insulin-producing beta cells of the pancreas in what appears to be an autoimmune reaction. Without insulin production, an individual will die, necessitating the use of exogenous insulin. Since insulin is destroyed by the digestive process, it cannot be taken orally, and must be delivered by some form of injection (see the following Regimen Factors section). The term Type I has become preferred over insulin dependent, since individuals with Type II diabetes may progress to need insulin, thereby becoming truly insulin-dependent.

Type II diabetes, previously called adult-onset diabetes, begins with the development of insulin resistance. As the cells do not properly utilize the available insulin, the demand for insulin production increases and the pancreas eventually fails to produce sufficient insulin. Risk factors for Type II diabetes include obesity, older age, family history of diabetes, and physical inactivity (Centers for Disease Control and Prevention [CDC], 2005). Individuals of some racial ethnicities, particularly African Americans, Hispanic/Latino Americans, Native American Indians, Asian Americans, and Native Hawaiians show higher rates of Type II diabetes than Caucasians (CDC). In recent years, there has been a dramatic increase in the number of adolescents developing Type II diabetes, and it is hypothesized that increases in pediatric obesity are primary factors in this phenomena (Porter & Barrett, 2004).

Gestational diabetes occurs during pregnancy and usually remits after delivery. Women who are African American, Hispanic/Latino, or Native American, are obese, or with a family history of diabetes are more likely to develop gestational diabetes. Five to ten percent of women with gestational diabetes develop Type II diabetes after the pregnancy (CDC, 2005).

As part of the interdisciplinary medical team, psychologists, dietitians, and other therapists must appreciate issues of diabetes medical assessment that may be well known to physicians and nurses reading this book. There are three primary measurements of physical function relevant to diabetes: measurement of immediate blood glucose (BG), measurement of long-term glycemic control (i.e., the ongoing consistency and level of BG), and measurement related to development of long-term diabetic complications. With current technology, BG can be easily measured with a "fingerstick," using devices the size of a computer mouse or smaller that report the BG value in 5 to 30 seconds of the blood application. These glucometers are widely used by patients to monitor their own BG and are considered a crucial aspect of diabetes mellitus (DM) self-management (as described in the following in the Regimen Factors section. Blood glucose, however, is extremely unstable. One could measure his or her blood glucose at one point in time and have a drastically different value within 2 to 4 hours, depending upon what he or she ate and whether/which medications were taken. For this reason, long-term glycemic control is usually measured by a glycosulated hemoglobin assay, usually an Hb A1c, which is performed upon whole blood drawn intravenously. The glycosulated hemoglobin, or Hb A1c, indicates the average BG over the past 6 weeks to 3 months. Glycosulated hemoglobin is generally used to assess overall glycemic control. The American Diabetes Association (ADA, 2006c) guidelines refer to Hb A1c of 7.0 or lower to represent tight control, and utilize this as a goal for treatment. In addition, tests such as microalbumin in urine to assess for changes in kidney function and microscopic inspection of the retinas by an ophthalmologist to detect early signs of retinopathy (a breakdown of the light-sensitive lining in the eyes) are important on a yearly basis (ADA).

Because glycosulated hemoglobin and current BG, as well as subtle changes in kidney and retina function, are not readily detected by subjective self-observation of patients, individuals with DM often look to these tests as indicators of their treatment success, and for reassurance that their health is not deteriorating. Current goals for treatment include BG of 70–130mg/dl and an HB A1c of < 7.0 (ADA, 2006c).

PREVALENCE

It is estimated that 20.8 million individuals in the United States, or approximately 7% of the population, have diabetes. Among individuals aged 20 or younger, approximately 176,500 people have diabetes, representing one in every 400 to 600 persons in that age bracket (CDC, 2005). About 90 to 95% of all individuals with diabetes have Type II diabetes, with 5 to 10% having a Type I onset (CDC).

DISEASE FACTORS

Since the disease factors for Type I diabetes and Type II diabetes are somewhat different, issues regarding disease onset, disease progression, and symptoms will be discussed specific to each type of onset.

DISEASE ONSET

The onset of diabetes is notably different for Type I and Type II diabetes. In Type I diabetes, symptoms usually develop over several weeks. The symptoms are fairly vague and, at the outset, not so disturbing. Individuals usually experience increased thirst, increased urination, increased hunger, fatigue, and weight loss. As symptoms progress, and as the person seeks medical attention, the diagnosis is easily made by simple finger-stick or blood tests. In such cases, the news of the diagnosis is often perceived as more stressful than the symptoms themselves. That is, the news and the need for life adjustment and management are often more daunting than the symptoms are frightening or intolerable. In contrast, however, some individuals do not seek medical attention, progress to dangerously elevated BG levels, and develop diabetic ketoacidosis, which can induce coma and can be fatal. In this case, the patient may experience the onset as frightening or possibly traumatic. Due to these potential differences in the onset and diagnosis, it is important to consider how each person's Type I onset occurred.

Type II onset is slow and insidious, and can often go on for considerable time without subjective symptoms. For this reason, many individuals do not get the disease diagnosed until it has been present for some time or has progressed significantly. Since Type II diabetes is often diagnosed during a routine medical examination, the patient may experience the news of the diagnosis as being far more disturbing than the rather unnoticeable symptoms. As discussed in the Regimen Factors section, the treatment of Type II diabetes may change over time, as the diabetes progresses. This, in turn, creates the experience that each progression and treatment change represents an onset of new stresses and demands.

DISEASE PROGRESSION

The course of diabetes over time is chronic and constant. The need for self-management of BG persists every day, and carries the expectation that it will be a lifelong endeavor. Type I diabetes is really not progressive. Many individuals may experience what is called a "honeymoon" period, in which some residual insulin production continues (Abdul-Rasoul, Habib, & Al-Khouly, 2006). Once this brief period is over, however, the disease itself is rather stable over time. In contrast, persistent high BG places the patient at increased risk for many other health complications. If these complications begin to develop, diabetes may seem progressive, because the progressive addition of each new complication adds further stress and demands for coping.

Type II diabetes may have a progressive course, with the impaired insulin metabolism worsening over time. Individuals whose Type II diabetes progresses, necessitating a series of changes to more and more intensive treatment regimens may experience these changes as signs of their own failure, even if they had successfully engaged in the self-management behaviors of the previous regimen. Individuals who were consistent and active in their self-management, only to experience the progression of the disease, may be at risk of becoming frustrated and/or hopeless about their ability to prevent the worsening of their condition.

Diabetes of either type places individuals at increased risk for diabetic retinopathy and blindness; peripheral neuropathy, generating numbness and pain in the feet and legs; stroke; myocardial infarction (heart attack); peripheral vascular problems; end-stage renal disease; impaired healing, particularly at the periphery, and amputation of lower extremities (WebMD, 2006). Although the threat of these complications may be daunting, research has indicated that, when BG is maintained at levels near normal range (~70 to 130 mg/dl), the development and progression of diabetic complications is significantly reduced (Diabetes Control and Complications Trial Research Group [DCCT], 1993).

SYMPTOMS

It is important to remember that the symptoms of diabetes result from elevated or insufficient blood glucose (BG), not directly from having the condition. That is, if the individual maintains BG within or as close as possible to normal range, there are likely to be no symptoms other than the demands of the regimen needed to maintain BG (i.e., the regimen factors may still be bothersome, as discussed in the Regimen Factors section).

When BG becomes elevated (hyperglycemia), individuals may experience thirst, frequent need to urinate, fatigue, headache, mood changes, nausea and vomiting, and/or any combination of these symptoms (ADA, 2006a). Many individuals, however, do not begin to experience symptoms from high BG until BG becomes very high, or remains high for an extended period of time. For this reason, self-observation of symptoms is not a reliable means to detect high BG, and monitoring of BG by blood testing becomes essential for maintaining BG.

Conversely, when insulin or particular oral medications[1] drive BG too low, symptoms may begin more immediately than they do with hyperglycemia. These symptoms include two types of reactions: adrenergic symptoms and neuroglycopenia. Adrenergic symptoms include tremor, sweating, restlessness, nausea, headache, nervousness, intense hunger, palpitations, increased respiration rate, weakness, or tingling sensations around the mouth. As hypoglycemia worsens, or at more significantly low BG, neuroglycopenia may ensue, referring to acute transient neuropsychological symptoms induced by low BG. These may include confusion, word-finding problems (dysnomia), emotional lability, impaired thinking and judgment, dizziness, amnesia, stupor, difficulty walking or coordinating motor movement (ataxia, dyspraxia, respectively), and at extreme levels, delirious or psychotic-like functioning, unconsciousness, or seizure (ADA, 2006b; Cox et al., 1999). Although the individual only needs to eat carbohydrates or glucose tablets to remedy his or her low BG, hypoglycemia can be extremely uncomfortable and/or frightening for affected individuals (as discussed later in the section on anxiety in the Comorbid Psychopathology section). If individuals become too impaired secondary to hypoglycemia, they may need help from others, either to get something for them to eat, or administer other BG-elevating interventions (e.g., intramuscular injection of glucagon, intravenous administration of dextrose serums). In addition, patients who become fearful during hypoglycemic episodes may overreact and overeat, thereby elevating their BG more than they intend to, then needing to administer insulin to bring their BG back down and creating a dysregulated too low→too high→too low→too high cycle.

REGIMEN FACTORS

Although there are multiple regimens for Type I and Type II diabetes (see Table 8.1), regardless of which regimen an individual needs or chooses, he or she all pose the risk of the following barriers: High *complexity* of the regimen, *intrusiveness* regarding

---

1. Typically, sulfonylurea or meglitinide will induce hypoglycemia, while other oral medications will not.

lifestyle, significant *cost* of the regimen, and most involve activities with some *discomfort* or *pain*.

Regardless of which regimen a patient is using, the diabetes self-management regimens usually include some or all of the following: monitoring BG levels with finger sticks, taking medication (oral antihyperglycemic medicine for Type II, insulin by injection or insulin pump for Type I) in proper dosage at proper times, needle insertion (if using insulin, by self-administering injections or placement of insulin pump infusion sets), eating appropriate amounts of particular foodstuffs (either restricting carbohydrates or counting carbohydrates to match insulin dosage), exercise, checking one's feet to prevent infection, regular blood assays to monitor glycemic control, yearly or semi-yearly visits to an ophthalmologist to prevent/treat retinal breakdown, prevention and/or treatment of hypoglycemia (i.e., low BG), and carrying supplies needed to accomplish all of the above activities. As such, the self-management regimens are *complex*. The required activities are multifactorial. Additionally, they involve the achievement of balance rather than being linear in their goals. That is, BG needs to be maintained at a level that is not *too high* or *too low*. This is difficult for individuals who are more cognitively limited. For example, patients with DM2 may have difficulty understanding that they should avoid concentrated carbohydrates in their daily food intake, but may need to quickly eat concentrated carbohydrates if their BG becomes low. These regimens also demand ongoing consistency. Since DM is not episodic, maintaining BG requires consistent daily activity.

In addition, the required accomplishment of these activities is, for many individuals, intrusive relative to their previous lifestyle. Many individuals experience distress regarding their loss of convenience, freedom, or flexibility. Depending upon the individual's insurance and prescription plan, these activities may be costly. For example, the retail cost of glucometer strips for home testing of BG are often about $1.00 per strip, and may not be fully covered by all prescription plans. In operant behavioral terms, the increased cost for more active testing serves to financially punish self-monitoring behavior. Finally, the activities of injection or finger sticks for BG monitoring may induce at least mild pain or discomfort, further serving as a barrier for some individuals.

Schilling, Grey, and Knafl (2002) have made a clear distinction between self-management and adherence. *Adherence* describes the accuracy and consistency with which a patient executes the prescriptions of the regimen and treatment team recommendations. *Self-management* refers to an active, patient-directed process, with components identifiable as *process* to execute the *activities* to reach self-management *goals*. This distinction between adherence and self-management emphasizes that, although self-management requires collaboration with the medical team, it also requires that patients and their families understand the behaviors that affect BG (e.g., food intake [carbohydrates, fats], insulin dosage, timing of food intake and insulin dosage, BG monitoring, exercise, stress management), behaviors that prevent diabetic complications (foot care, ophthalmologic screening), and strategically execute these behaviors actively over time. For medical professionals providing assistance to individuals with DM, the availability of various regimens in the twenty-first century adds further clinical complexity. The variety of regimens available to individuals with DM is accompanied by a corresponding variety in the particular self-management activities that are relevant to each regimen (Boyer, Ikunga, Cantor, & Scheiner, 2006).

One example is the initiation of a basal/bolus insulin regimen, using either a multiple daily injection (MDI) schedule (with the 24-hour insulin preparation, Glargine [basal], and analog insulin injections for each meal/snack [bolus]), or continuous sub-cutaneous insulin infusion (CSII) pumps. These regimens deliver either one injection (with Glargine) or a continuous subcutaneous delivery of analog insulin on a unit-per-hour basis as a *basal* dose, to manage the normal metabolic release of glucose into the bloodstream. The regimen then requires either a *bolus* injection for each meal/snack (with MDI) or the delivery of a *"bolus"* for each meal/snack (with the CSII pump) to manage BG from food intake. These basal/bolus regimens allow the individual to independently dose for the two functional elements that increase BG (i.e., the ongoing metabolic process and food intake), rather than targeting the overall level of BG-lowering medication, as in traditional insulin regimens (with intermediate and short-acting insulin combinations) or oral medications regimens.

Given the multiple regimens available for those with DM1 and DM2, clinicians must focus on the demands of each regimen. Although this is somewhat oversimpli-fied, it is conceivable to categorize regimens into four types: no medication (using only diet and exercise, for DM2), oral medication regimen (for DM2), traditional insulin regimen (using intermediate insulin [MPH, Lente] and short-acting insulin), or basal/bolus insulin regimen. For individuals using no medication, successfully limit-ing food intake and intake of concentrated carbohydrates and consistently exercising are crucial where there is no medication, no injections, and a lower frequency of BG monitoring. If individuals with DM2 are using oral medications, consistency of exer-cise and success in limiting overall food intake and concentrated carbohydrate intake remain crucial, with the added demand to take oral medications consistently. For in-dividuals with DM1 or advanced DM2 who use a traditional insulin regimen (with combined intermediate and short-acting insulin), the individual faces the need for two to three injections per day, the need to eat consistent amounts at consistent times across the day, and the need to test BG about four times daily—but he or she may not need as consistent and strenuous an exercise regimen. Risk of hypoglycemia becomes high, and the knowledge and skills to prevent and treat hypoglycemia become im-perative. With the MDI basal/bolus insulin regimen, the individual needs to take more injections (about four or more daily), pay more attention to carbohydrate count-ing, and tailor the units of insulin to each episode of eating, but is afforded a greater flexibility regarding the frequency of eating, timing of eating, how much to eat at any given time, and the basal/bolus regimens do not require the avoidance of concen-trated carbohydrates (so long as the patient accurately doses for grams of carbohy-drates eaten).

To date, insulin pumps permit the greatest flexibility and functions to maximize control of BG. Pumps benefit from all the advantages cited earlier for the MDI regimen but involve no injections other than replacing the infusion, set once every third day, and allow basal rates to be highly individualized, with hour-by-hour dosage settings, to exactly match the varied insulin basal needs of individuals across the day. When in-sulin needs were empirically tested among 322 individuals with DM1, no two indi-viduals had exactly the same profile of basal doses over the 24-hour day (Scheiner & Boyer, 2005). Unlike basal doses delivered by the dosing of a single injection in MDI regimens, CSII pumps allow the basal profile to be set with almost unlimited flexibil-ity. In addition, pumps allow insulin to be delivered in .1 unit or .05 unit increments, doses in far finer increments than possible with syringes or insulin pens for injecting insulin. With pumps, temporary basal rates can be set to reduce basal insulin while ex-ercising (thereby preventing hypoglycemia) or increase basal rates (to prevent fats in foods from increasing BG 4 to 8 hours after eating).

Attention to each of these regimen-specific demands is imperative for clinicians to guide individuals in the appropriate skills essential for their successful BG management and not misguide them regarding the skills that may be relevant to others' regimens but irrelevant to theirs. Since the initiation of the basal/bolus insulin regimen (e.g., MDI and CSII pumps), for example, individuals with DM1 may not need to eat at scheduled times, and may not need to avoid concentrated carbohydrates (since accurate dosing of boli for carbohydrates with analog insulin may prevent elevated BG, even with sweeter foods, although individuals may need to avoid concentrated carbohydrates for the same reasons as those without DM [to avoid weight gain]). These patients may face frustrations, since the actual demands of their regimen are different from the nonmedical social understanding of DM management. Significant others in their family and social lives may chastise them for eating certain foods that, given their regimen, they need not avoid. Patients using basal/bolus regimens may need to educate others, who urge them to eat at certain times to prevent hypoglycemia when it is not necessary. This variety of regimen and regimen-specific self-management activities also affects assessment of self-management and adherence (since certain activities are or are not relevant to particular regimens), as well as intervention to assist patients' self-management (since self-management is specific to each patient's particular regimen; Boyer et al., 2006). For this reason, health psychologists, certified diabetes educators, nurses, physicians, and dietitians need to understand the exact demands relevant to each diabetes regimen. Table 8.1 overviews the relevance and implications regarding DM-management behaviors specific to each category of regimen.

As described in the previous Disease Factors section, individuals with DM2 may need to employ progressively more rigorous regimens if their BG impairment progresses. This requires the patient to learn new and different skills at certain junctures in treatment. For example, an individual may learn the information and skills to manage BG using diet and exercise, then transition to medication taking if oral hypoglycemic medication is added to the regimen. Depending on the type of oral medication, this may necessitate the patient to learn about preventing and managing hypoglycemia. If oral medications do not adequately maintain his or her BG, insulin may be added to the regimen, requiring individuals to learn and apply skills for filling syringes and giving themselves shots or using an insulin pen. If a combination of oral antihyperglycemic medication and insulin does not adequately control BG, the patient may need to initiate an insulin regimen that parallels an insulin regimen for DM1. Patients may be at risk of feeling overwhelmed at these times of transition, and may feel helpless or hopeless, as if the need to increase the intensity of intervention or need for different regimen signals a failure on their part.

INDIVIDUAL FACTORS

Due to the need for self-management of DM, *information* and *knowledge* are of crucial importance. Research has demonstrated that knowledge about DM and its self-management is crucial to regimen adherence (Hanson, Henggeler, & Burghen, 1987), to metabolic control (Gray, Marrero, Godfrey, Orr, & Golden, 1988), tends to increase with age for individuals diagnosed when children or adolescents (Johnson, 1995; Wysocki et al., 1996), but is vulnerable to worsen over time and require ongoing reassessment and support (Johnson). Even when a patient is well informed and maintains accurate diabetes-specific knowledge, this knowledge appears necessary but in-

Table 8.1

Specific Self-Management Activities and Lifestyle Factors Relevant to Current Insulin Regimen

Type of Regimen	Exercise and Diet only, No Medication	Oral Medications only, No Insulin	Combination of Oral Medications and Insulin	Long-acting Basal Insulin only (for Type II DM)	Traditional injection therapy with intermediate insulin and rapid insulin (but not at every meal) (e.g., Twice daily NPH [morning and dinnertime possibly bedtime] with Regular, Aspart, or Lispro injections prior to breakfast and dinner)	Multiple Daily Injection (MDI)Regimen; basal/bolustherapy by injections, with bolus taken at every meal (e.g., Glargine with Aspart or Lispro injections each time you eat)	CSII; Pump Therapy
Regular exercise	Essential	Essential	Essential	Essential	Helpful but not essential for BG management, helpful for overall health and reduction of DM complications	Helpful but not essential for BG management, helpful for overall health and reduction of DM complications	Helpful but not essential for BG management, helpful for overall health and reduction of DM complications
Need to restrict amounts of food, amounts of carbohydrates	High	Moderate to high	Moderate to high	Moderate to high	Low to moderate	Low to none	Low to none
Threat of hypoglycemia, need to manage hypoglycemia	Usually not relevant	Low, unless using sulfonylurea or meglitinide. If these oral medications are used, risk of hypoglycemia is moderate	Low to moderate	Low to moderate	High	Moderate to high	Moderate to High
Frequency of BG monitoring	Low to moderate	Low to moderate	Low to moderate	Low to moderate	High, ~4 times daily	High, ~4 times daily	High, ~4 times daily

Factor	No injections	No injections	Varied, dependent upon format. If long-acting insulin is used, ~ 1 injection/day. If per-meal analogue insulin is used, injections equal number of meals.	Multiple daily injection/day	Fewer, 2 to 3/day	More injections, (number of meals + number of snacks + 1 administration of Glargine), usually > 4 (depending of frequency of eating)	No daily injections. Only infusion set changes, 1/every third day
Frequency of injection (or needle Insertion)	No injections	No injections	Varied, dependent upon format. If long-acting insulin is used, ~ 1 injection/day. If per-meal analogue insulin is used, injections equal number of meals.	Multiple daily injection/day	Fewer, 2 to 3/day	More injections, (number of meals + number of snacks + 1 administration of Glargine), usually > 4 (depending of frequency of eating)	No daily injections. Only infusion set changes, 1/every third day
Need for consistency in mealtimes	Low	Low to moderate (depending on type of med)	Moderate	Moderate	High	Moderate	Low
Flexibility in mealtimes	Moderate	Moderate	Moderate	Moderate	Low	Moderate	High
Flexibility regarding amounts of food eaten/meal	Low to moderate	Low to moderate	Low to moderate	Low to moderate	Low (for meals covered by intermediate insulin) or high (for meals covered by rapid insulin)	High	High
Need for carbohydrate counting	Varied, but can accomplish control without carbohydrate counting	Varied, but can accomplish control without carbohydrate counting	Varied, but can accomplish control without carbohydrate counting	Varied, but can accomplish control without carbohydrate counting	Moderate. Varied, but can accomplish control without carbohydrate counting	High	High
Demand to execute arithmetic for meal insulin-to-carbohydrate ratios	Not relevant	Not relevant	Not relevant	Not relevant	Varied, but low if patient is not carbohydrate counting	High	High, but low with newer pump models, in which ratios can be entered into pump
Ability to dose with insulin for effects of dietary fats upon BG	Not relevant	Not relevant	Low, very difficult	Low, very difficult	Low, very difficult	Low, very difficult	High, ease with use of temporary basal rates
Ability to achieve optimal BG with exercise/sports activity	High	Moderate	Moderate	Moderate	Low	Moderate	High

sufficient for many individuals (Wysocki, Greco, & Buckloh, 2003). Indeed, many factors other than knowledge impact self-management and glycemic control, including the complexity, cost, and inconvenience of the regimen, discussed previously. With increased cost–cutting, due to financial concerns in medical service provision, many informational services have been reduced in hospital settings. The increased pressure for diabetes teaching to occur in the context of primary care physicians' office visits, or in endocrinologists' office visits, often without the resources of certified diabetes educators and/or dietitians, has strained the consistency of diabetes education. Even if patients and families are well educated, many other factors may serve as barriers to consistent application of this knowledge (Wysocki, Greco, & Buckloh).

Culture may pose particular difficulties for some individuals' self-management. Some cultural diets are high in carbohydrates, fats, sweet food preparations, or fried foods, and may require more significant changes for the person with Type II diabetes than cultural diets high in fresh vegetables, or with spice patterns that utilize less sugars or fats. Cultural factors may also affect beliefs about the cause, course, and treatment of DM. For example, ethnographic research indicates that individuals within the Navajo culture may process diabetes diagnosis and treatment demands through a postcolonial perspective, affected by multigenerational trauma and oppression by Anglo groups (Huttlinger, 1995). Research has identified beliefs that "sustos" (a scare or emotionally traumatic experience) may induce the onset of Type II DM, that God may control the onset or course of DM, or that the course of the disease is unalterable (i.e., a *fatalistic* belief about disease progression) to be common among some but not all Hispanic cultures (Caban & Walker, 2006). The relationship of these beliefs to DM management and glycemic control among Hispanic cultures requires further investigation (Caban & Walker). Other cultural phenomena, like some older African Americans' belief that "everyone has sugar," may more accurately represent differences in *health beliefs* and *coping* rather then behavior patterns inherent in a particular culture.

HEALTH BELIEFS AND COPING

Some research has indicated that active, approach-oriented coping strategies are associated with better quality of life among adults with diabetes (Coelho, Amorim, & Prata, 2003), and better glycemic control among adolescents with DM (Seiffe-Krenke & Stemmler, 2003). Karlsen and Bru (2002) found that those with Type II DM showed greater use of avoidant coping than those with Type I DM, but note that this may be more related to older age and lower education among the sample with Type II DM. Avoidant coping and self-blame were also found to be more prevalent among women with Type I DM who developed eating disorders than those without eating disorders (Grylli, Wagner, Hafferl-Gattermayer, Schober, & Karwautz, 2005). Coping and perceived social support have been associated with psychological well-being among adults with both Type I and II DM (Karlsen, Idsoe, Hanes, Murberg, & Bru, 2004). Perceived support from family members appeared to be more important than support from the medical treatment team, and coping appeared to mediate the relationship between social support and psychological outcomes. Other studies have found that patient identity and perceptions of the impact of diabetes predicted emotional well-being among adolescents, and this relationship was not mediated by differences in coping (Edgar & Skinner, 2003).

COMORBID PSYCHOPATHOLOGY

A considerable literature has investigated the rates of psychological difficulties for individuals with diabetes. In the following section the differences between individuals with and without diabetes will be discussed, as well as the ways in which psychological difficulties pose risks for difficulties with self-management, glycemic control, and medical outcomes.

Depression

The comorbidity of diabetes and depression has received enough empirical investigation to generate several meta-analytic studies to summarize the findings. First, a meta-analysis of nine studies published prior to January, 2005 that assessed the relationship of depression to the subsequent development of Type II DM suggests that depressed adults are 37% more likely than those without depression to develop Type II DM (Knol et al., 2006). In addition, depression appears more common among individuals who have diabetes than those without diabetes. Although some studies have found depression to be six times higher among those with diabetes (Lustman, Griffith, Clouse, & Cryer, 1986), a meta-analysis of 42 studies indicates an odds ratio of 2:1, indicating depression to be twice the prevalence among those with diabetes compared to those without diabetes (Anderson, Freedland, Clouse, & Lustman, 2001). Among those with diabetes, rates were 28% among women and 18% among men, with rates as high as 32% in samples seeking clinical services (Anderson et al.). Although women showed higher absolute rates of depression than men, the odds ratio was consistent for sexes, as well as for Type I and Type II DM, with twice the rate of depression among both women and men with either type of DM. A review of depression prevalence among individuals with Type I DM that included five studies since the Anderson and colleagues' meta-analysis (2001) indicated 12% of persons with diabetes had comorbid depression, compared to a 3.2% rate of depression for those without diabetes (Barnard, Skinner, & Peveler, 2006). A recent study of 2,672 individuals aged 10 to 21 years found that 14% reported mild depression symptoms, 8.6% reported moderate or severe depression symptoms, and that greater depression was associated with hyperglycemia and frequency of emergency medical visits. At particularly high risk for depression within this study were males with juvenile Type II DM and women with Type I DM who had comorbidities (compared to women without comorbidities; Lawrence et al., 2006). Twenty-seven percent of individuals diagnosed with DM in childhood or adolescence experienced a major depressive episode within 10 years after the DM diagnosis (Kovacs, Goldston, Obrosky, & Bonar, 1997). In addition, meta-analytic studies have shown significant and consistent relationships between depression and poor glycemic control (Lustman et al., 2000; Lustman & Clouse, 2005) and increased diabetic complications (de Groot, Anderson, Freedland, Clouse, & Lustman, 2001). Depression has also been shown to relate to greater perceived symptom burden, perceived lack of control, and expectations for worse outcomes among individuals with Type II DM, as well as poorer quality of life (Paschalides et al., 2004). In a series of studies of more than 4,000 individuals with diabetes, comorbid depression corresponded to a tenfold increase in disability and a fourfold increase in peoples' experience of 20 or more days of reduced household work, compared to those without depression (Von Korff et al., 2005), and to a 70% increase in health care cost (Simon et al., 2005). Furthermore, individuals with Type II DM who reported either comorbid major depression or minor depression (i.e., clinically significant depression that was subdiagnostic for a major depressive episode) were significantly more likely to die than those without depression over the subsequent 3 years (Katon et al., 2005).

Taken together, depression appears to be a significant risk factor for developing Type II DM, DM appears to place people at twice the risk for depression, and depression is associated with poorer glycemic control and greater development of diabetic complications, such as nephropathy, neuropathy, retinopathy, macrovascular changes, and sexual dysfunction (de Groot et al., 2001). Despite the increased prevalence of depression among those with DM, and the deleterious impact upon medical outcomes, depression continues to be underdiagnosed and undertreated, despite evidence that effective treatments exist (Steed, Cooke, & Newman, 2003). Among patients with diabetes from nine primary care practices who reported clinically significant depression in a systematic screening, 49% were not diagnosed or treated. Of the 51% whose depression was detected, 43% received antidepressant pharmacotherapy, and only 6.7% received four or more psychotherapy sessions during the previous 12 months (Katon et al., 2004), indicating that many of those diagnosed were not adequately treated.

ANXIETY

Thirteen percent of youth diagnosed with Type I DM developed an anxiety disorder within ten years after the DM diagnosis (Kovacs et al., 1997). A meta-analysis of anxiety prevalence among individuals with diabetes, with a combined sample of 2,584 participants with DM and 1,492 nondiabetic control participants, indicated that 14% of those with DM experienced Generalized Anxiety Disorder, and that 40% experienced elevated anxiety symptoms (Grigsby, Anderson, Freedland, Clouse, & Lustman, 2002). Although anxiety symptoms were higher among women than men, there were similar rates for those with Type I and Type II DM. In a meta-analysis of 11 studies assessing the relationship between anxiety and glycemic control, the overall sample indicated no significant relationship of anxiety to control of BG. However, when only studies that utilized diagnostic interviews to assess anxiety were included, anxiety was significantly related to glycemic control, with a significant effect size (Anderson et al., 2002). The authors conclude that the lack of relationship in the larger sample may be due to methodological factors and, when more rigorously evaluated, anxiety appears related to hyperglycemia.

Some individuals have exhibited diabetes-specific anxiety, such as fear of hypoglycemia (FH). Studies have found relationships between FH and poorer glycemic control (Cox, Irvine, Gonder-Frederick, Nowacek, & Butterfield, 1987), higher trait anxiety and past hypoglycemic experiences, difficulty distinguishing between anxiety and hypoglycemia, (Polonsky, Davis, Jacobson, & Anderson, 1992), as well as higher perceived stress, frequency of past hypoglycemic episodes, and greater daily variations in BG (Irvine, Cox, & Gonder-Frederick, 1992). Some individuals attempt to avoid this FH, compromising their glycemic control by administering lower insulin dosage/maintaining higher BG levels (Surwit, Scovern, & Feinglos, 1982), or overeating in response to early signs of hypoglycemia (Cox et al., 1987). If individuals engage in these avoidance behaviors, they may increase risk for the long-term medical complications associated with hyperglycemia.

One study has investigated whether this pattern of hypoglycemia-specific anxiety may constitute a subset of posttraumatic stress (PTS) symptomatology. Since some individuals 1) report ongoing intrusive worry about hypoglycemia; 2) become anxious in response to this intrusive ideation, even when BG is not low; and 3) react with avoidance behaviors that compromise their diabetes regimen and pose serious long-term health risks, the authors evaluated the full PTS symptomatology among individuals using tight control insulin regimens (CSII insulin pumps and basal/bolus injection regimen). Twenty-five percent of the patients reported symptoms consistent with current posttraumatic stress disorder (PTSD) about hypoglycemia (Myers, Boyer, Herbert, Barakat & Scheiner, in press).

Studies assessing parental adjustment to a DM diagnosis have found PTSD in 24% of mothers and 22% of fathers of children newly diagnosed with Type I DM (Landolt et al., 2002). A longitudinal follow-up at 6 weeks, 6 months, and 12 months after their child's diagnosis reported the following PTSD rates (Landolt, Vollrath, Laimbacher, Gnehm, & Sennhauser, 2005). For mothers: 22.4% at 6 weeks, 16.3% at 6 months, and 20.4% at 12 months reported PTSD. For fathers: 14.6% at 6 weeks, 10.4% at 6 months, and 8.3% at 12 months reported PTSD. Studies comparing parental PTS among parents of children with diabetes compared to cancer, however, have found lower rates of PTS/PTSD among parents of diabetes patients than among families facing cancer (Fuemmeler, Mullins, Van Pelt, Carpentier, & Parkhurst, 2005; Landolt, Vollrath, Ribi, Gnehm, & Sennhauser, 2003).

While an important literature has begun to investigate FH, indicating that it may interfere with self-management, more thorough investigation of these phenomena appears warranted, and may serve to guide clinical intervention that reduces anxiety, improves quality of life, and optimizes metabolic outcomes.

DYSREGULATED EATING

It has been estimated that approximately 16% of people with DM1 experience a concurrent eating disorder (Kelly, Howe, Hendler, Lipman, 2005), and many more will suffer from subclinical levels of dysregulated eating. Research also suggests that DM may trigger disordered eating, and may exacerbate body dissatisfaction, in part to their higher-than-average-base weight (Colton, 1999). A meta-analysis investigating rates of anorexia among women with DM1 found no higher rates of anorexia among those with DM than among the general public (Nielsen, 2002). Anorexia appears much more dangerous, however, among those with diabetes, with a death rate of 34.6 per 1000 person years, compared to 2.2 per 1000 person years among those with anorexia but without diabetes (Nielsen, Emborg, & Molback, 2002).

A meta-analysis investigating bulimia among those with DM1 found that patients with DM1 are significantly more likely to develop bulimia than those without diabetes (Mannucci et al., 2005). In addition, it is appears that 60-80% of people with DM1 engage in episodes of binging that are subclinical to a diagnosis of bulimia (La Greca, Schwarz, & Satin, 1987).

Of particular importance among women with diabetes is the behavior of intentionally omitting or underdosing insulin relative to the amount of food eaten. As many as 30% of adolescents with DM1 intentionally omit their insulin doses, or take insufficient insulin doses in order to control their weight (Kelly, Howe, Hendler, & Lipman, 2005). In the clinical context, the current author has observed the following behaviors: (1) episodically taking insufficient insulin for food, or omitting insulin when eating, only when acutely distressed about weight; (2) intentionally taking insufficient doses of insulin for each episode of food intake, in a steady, ongoing fashion; or (3) taking basal insulin (i.e., via glargine injection or CSII pump basal rates), but omitting insulin boli for each snack or meal eaten (Boyer, Myers, & Lehman, in press). While these strategies do indeed serve to reduce weight or weight gain, they accomplish it at the expense of glycemic control and expose patients to an increased risk for the complications of persistent hyperglycemia. Indeed, research has found greater levels of diabetes complications among those with diabetes and eating disorders (Rydall, Rodin, Olmstead, Devenyi, & Daneman, 1997). The study of therapy outcomes for eating disorders has suffered from several logistical impediments. Conducting treatment efficacy or effectiveness studies with large samples, comparison to control groups, and random assignment of participants to treatment groups have been difficult, due to low overall prevalence of certain eating disorders (e.g., anorexia), need for long treatment and long follow-up to discern maintenance of treatment gains, low participation rates among many populations with disordered eating, and the high acuity of clients with extremely low weight status precludes assignment to control conditions (Wilson & Fairburn, 2002). The literature addressing treatment of dysregulated eating among those with DM is even more limited. One study, however, compared outcomes for two groups of women with diabetes and bulimia: one received inpatient treatment ($N = 9$) and the other received no inpatient treatment ($N = 10$). Three years after treatment, the women who received inpatient treatment showed better glycemic control (measured by Hb A1c) as well as less depression, anxiety, and binge eating and purging behaviors. Although this study utilized a relatively small sample, it may suggest that initiating therapy for women with bulimia and DM with an inpatient treatment component may generate better long-term outcomes. Outcome studies assessing the effectiveness of treatment for dysregulated eating, specific to individuals with DM, are greatly needed.

PSYCHOSIS

There is growing evidence that many antipsychosis medications may induce diabetes (Ananth & Kolli, 2005). The impact of atypical antipsychotic medications on diabetes risk, however, appears related to research design and possibly to dosage factors (Gianfrancesco, Wang, & Nasrallah, 2006). Needless to say, individuals with a psychotic disorder may have particular difficulties managing diabetes, and may require additional training and intervention for adequate diabetes management (El-Mallakh, 2006).

HEALTH PSYCHOLOGY TREATMENTS

Several meta-analyses and reviews have been recently published regarding the utility of various psychotherapies for improving diabetes outcomes (Drotar, 2006; Snoek & Skinner, 2002; Lustman & Clouse, 2002; Ismail, Winkley, & Rabe-Hesketh, 2004; Christie & Wilson, 2005; Wysocki, Greco, & Buckloh, 2003). Taken together with studies published since these reviews, evidence indicates that several interventions have been proven to increase glycemic control. That is, cognitive-behavior therapy (CBT) has been effective in reducing depression and improving glycemic control among those with DM2 (Snoek & Skinner; Ismail, Winkley, & Rabe-Hesketh). A problem-solving training with a diabetes self-management focus (Delameter et al., 1990) and coping skills training (Grey, Boland, Davidson, Li, & Tamborlane, 2000; Grey & Berry, 2004) have been shown to improve glycemic control among youths with pediatric

DM1. A family teamwork intervention, provided in the context of adolescents' outpatient office visits, targeting appropriate parental involvement in DM management, produced improved glycemic control as well as reduced family conflict (Anderson, Brackett, Ho, & Laffel, 1999). A group therapy addressing diabetes-related stress, coping, well-being, and metabolic control showed a positive impact on glycemic control among adults with DM1 and DM2 (Karlsen et al., 2004).

In contrast, some interventions have been effective in ameliorating important psychological and behavioral difficulties associated with DM but did not produce actual changes in glycemic control. For example, behavioral family systems therapy was effective in reducing familial conflict but did not improve regimen adherence or metabolic control (Wysocki, Greco, Harris, & White, 2000; Wysocki et al., 2000). Similarly, stress-management training for adolescents with DM1 yielded improvements in diabetes-related stress, but not in treatment adherence or glycemic control (Boardway, Delamater, Tomakowsky, & Gutai, 1993).

Whereas depression has been shown to worsen medical outcomes for those with diabetes, enhanced depression treatment for those with comorbid depression and diabetes have not consistently shown improvement in patients' self-management (Lin et al., 2006) or glycemic control (Katon et al., 2004).

Research is needed to further test the effectiveness of psychological interventions for improvements in multiple classes of important outcomes, including psychological adjustment factors, family adjustment, ease and success with DM self-management, glycemic control, and prevention of diabetic complications. The existing research, however, indicates that there is symptom specificity in the treatment outcomes, with interventions producing positive change in the functional features that are directly addressed by the therapy, but there is often failure to produce positive change in elements not directly addressed. For example, some therapies have facilitated effective treatment of depression or family conflict without successfully improving glycosulated hemoglobin, when the DM-management issues were not more directly addressed in the therapy.

CASE EXAMPLE

This case was chosen as an example because it differs from many examples and from well-investigated clinical issues, such as clinical depression reducing an individual's consistency of self-management, and represents an adult case rather than a family and child case of pediatric DM, as highlighted in Chapter 15.

A 36-year-old woman, Ginger, had been diagnosed with Type 1 diabetes at age 12. Ginger was referred to the health psychologist because her glycosulated hemoglobin (Hb A1c) was 10.6. Her endocrinologist was perplexed because Ginger was employed, high functioning socially, and appeared very educated about her diabetes management. Regarding her DM regimen, Ginger had required insulin since her diagnosis, for many years using NPH (an intermediate action insulin) and Regular (the traditional fast-acting insulin) in three injections per day, and eating three meals with three snacks between meals. Within the last 5 years, however, with the availability of Glargine and Analog insulins, as well as CSII pumps, she decided to change to a regimen that allowed more flexibility in her eating schedule. She actively researched the relative costs and benefits of MDI basal/bolus injection regimens and the CSII pump, and decided to initiate pump therapy. She quickly learned the activities relevant to the pump regimen, such as carbohydrate counting, dosing her insulin using a *units of insulin-to-grams of carbohydrate* ratios for meal boli, and refilling her pump and placing her infusion set. Her endocrinologist had assessed Ginger's knowledge to determine whether she was misunderstanding some of the information and tasks, but found that her understanding and retention of the relevant skills and knowledge were astoundingly good. When Ginger informed her physician that she had become extremely fearful of her BG getting low, the endocrinologist referred her to the health psychologist.

In the first session with the psychologist, it became apparent that she was not depressed, was socially and professionally active, and was engaged to a man with whom she lived and planned to marry within the next 2 years. Although she did not describe any general or social anxiety, she reported that she had become extremely anxious about her blood sugar "crashing." Although she had not had frequent episodes of hypoglycemia, she described the following event. Eight months prior, she had experienced a hypoglycemic episode at a work party. She had calculated her dosage of insulin for a grain salad, which someone told her was oats and vegetables, but was really pearl barley, which has a much lower glycemic index and does not elevate BG as quickly as oats. In retrospect, she probably slightly misdosed for several mixed food items that evening, and collectively took in slightly too much insulin boli for the food.

She began to feel dizzy, sweating, and was unable to effectively communicate to her coworkers. They called 911, and paramedics came, administering intravenous D50, a glucose serum that quickly elevates BG. She recovered immediately, with all hypoglycemic symptoms remitting within 15 minutes of the D50 administration, and a mild headache remitting over the next half hour to an hour. She was extremely frightened, felt embarrassed in front of her coworkers, and feared constantly that this would happen again. She also reported feeling that she couldn't quite trust her calculations regarding carbohydrate contents, and that all this "carb-counting" was more tricky, with hidden inaccuracies that felt uncertain.

Since that time, she reported that she was testing her BG approximately 15 times per day. When she was driving on long highway trips she would stop about every third to fourth exit, pull from the highway, and check her BG. She found that the information that her BG was not low, or even high (e.g., 200–275) did not reassure her that it would not crash, and she felt safer with BGs in the 200s, accompanied by the following reasoning: "If my BG is 250, and it quickly drops 100 or 150, it will still be in a safe range. If it's 120, and it drops only 50 or so, I'll be in big trouble." The life contexts in which she felt she needed to keep her BG over 200 or 250 were: (1) at work, (2) when out in the evening at social events, (3) when driving, or (4) when sleeping alone. As such, this included most of her typical days. She had begun to carry candies in her purse, and when she became fearful that her BG might be getting low, but was somewhere in which she felt self-conscious to check her BG (e.g., in a public restaurant or in a professional meeting), she would begin eating them. She had also begun to mistake the increased sympathetic nervous system arousal associated with this anxiety for signs of hypoglycemia, and would often eat something despite having a BG reading in the 200s.

The psychologist began by empathizing with the frightening experience, and reassuring Ginger that this type of anxious reaction made perfect sense, given her experience, but was now interfering with her BG management. This symptomatology clearly indicated a fear of hypoglycemia (Cox et al., 1987), but displayed aspects that paralleled obsessive-compulsive disorder (i.e., worrying about hypoglycemia, testing as a solution but feeling that this reassurance lasted only a short time before the worry returned), and posttraumatic stress (intrusive worry and events serving as triggers to the intrusive ideation, anxious arousal related to this event-related intrusive ideation, and avoidance behaviors). The therapist utilized the posttraumatic diagnostic scale as an interview, and found that Ginger clearly reported symptoms consistent with current PTSD, characterized by frequent intrusive ideation about hypoglycemia and triggering of this ideation by any stimulus condition perceived to be dangerous or embarrassing if her BG crashed, anxious arousal subsequent to these fears, and multiple avoidance strategies (all of which served to elevate and destabilize Ginger's BG). Therapy began by reframing her efforts to maintain safe BG levels as misplaced, since she was actually attempting to ameliorate her *anxiety* about the unsafe BG levels and was mistakenly focusing on BG itself. The therapy involved three distinct but related aspects: (1) increasing her certainty and self-efficacy regarding methods to address low BG, (2) ensuring that Ginger had effective methods to reduce and/or tolerate her anxiety independent of altering her BG, and (3) plans to reduce her overly frequent BG monitoring, which was serving to trigger avoidance behaviors.

Since ignoring signs of low BG is indeed foolish and could pose danger, the first step involved reviewing Ginger's knowledge and beliefs about strategies to manage low BG. She rationally understood that most of her 15 or more BG tests/day were unnecessary and increased (rather than decreased) her anxiety. She also acknowledged that, when she ate candies to stop her feared hypoglycemia, this was usually when she felt anxious and knew her BG was fine (or even high). After discussing these phenomena, it was collectively decided that taking glucose tablets in a meeting, for example, felt more like a medical intervention than eating candies, and would be harder for her to justify to herself or feel as if she were below the "social radar" about. She also reviewed and understood that the predictable quantity of carbohydrates in glucose tablets would prevent her from the uncertainty that drove her to eat too much when her BG appeared low. After a review of the sensations she felt when she became anxious about hypoglycemia, it became clear that they were distinguishable from when her BG really was low. She agreed that she would carry packets of glucose tablets in her purse and pockets and stock her home, office, car, and friend's homes with glucose tablets, so as to have no reason to fear lack of access to them.

The second step was to limit the over-monitoring of her BG. Ginger described that, when she took insulin to lower her BG, she would begin testing her BG within the next 1.5 to 2 hours, to prevent it from getting too low. Upon review, her correction ratio (a ratio of units of insulin per number of mg/dl above goal BG) worked well and was accurately set. She also knew, from monitoring, that high BG would require at least 2.75 to 3 hours after her correction bolus to reach the goal BG, and would only begin to reduce at about 2 to 1.5 hours after the bolus. She reported that, over the past months, she would test at 2 hours, and if her BG had reduced at all, even if still elevated, she would eat something in fear that it would now precipitously plummet. She knew, however, that this was not what would happen. She agreed that she would never test her BG before 2.5 hours after a correction bolus, or 3 hours after eating (unless eating and bolusing for another food intake). As such, the plan was to monitor her BG in the morning, before each meal, before each time she drove her car (unless within a short time of a previous test and drive, such as if she had just tested and drove to the store, and was driving back home within the half hour), and before bedtime (approximately six times per day). She worked with the therapist to plan what to do when, as she kept to these limits regarding testing, she became anxious and needed to alleviate the elevated anxiety that induced her otherwise to test or to eat.

After assessing the activities Ginger typically used to relax or soothe herself, and discovering that smoking cigarettes was the sole method, she decided to learn and apply new and different means to manage arousal. Since her anxious experience had both physiological and cognitive symptoms for Ginger, an imagery intervention was chosen. Ginger identified a vacation house in the mountains with a lake, where she always felt relaxed and safe. Incorporating diaphragmatic breathing, and a vivid recreation of the mountain spot, Ginger could reduce her anxious arousal within 5 to 15 minutes by imagining wading into the lake at sundown, creating a multisensory covert experience to divert her attention from the fearful cognitions and images regarding hypoglycemia (Boyer, 1998). After practicing this 15-minute imagery for a week or two, the therapist worked with Ginger to select a quick and unitary image that she could present to herself for only a moment when she became acutely fearful regarding hypoglycemia but knew that her BG was fine.

As these plans were laid and applied, the psychologist also inquired about the hypoglycemic event that spawned her persisting fear. The psychologist assessed for changes in the anxious experience, with some concern that more intensive therapy, such as extended exposure (Rothbaum, Meadows, & Foy, 2000) or eye movement desensitization and reprocessing may be necessary (Davidson & Parker, 2001; Shapiro, 1989). Within two months, Ginger was testing her BG about six times per day, continuing to test before driving each time, and had reduced her average BG from 243 to 137. Her next Hb A1c, at 4 months after the initiation of therapy was 7.1, greatly reduced from 10.6. She reported that both the frequency and the intensity of her fears regarding hypoglycemia had reduced and almost remitted.

REFERENCES

Abdul-Rasoul, M., Habib, H., & Al-Khouly, M. (2006). The "honeymoon phase" in children with type 1 diabetes mellitus: Frequency, duration, and influential factors. *Pediatric Diabetes, 7,* 101–107.

American Diabetes Association. (2006a). *Hyperglycemia.* Retrieved November 30, 2006, from http://www.diabetes.org/type-1–diabetes/hyperglycemia.jsp

American Diabetes Association. (2006b). *Hypoglycemia.* Retrieved November 30, 2006, from http://www.diabetes.org/type-1–diabetes/hypoglycemia.jsp

American Diabetes Association. (2006c). Standards of medical care in diabetes. *Diabetes Care.* 29(supplement 1), S4 -S42.

Ananth, J., & Kolli, S. (2005). Atypical antipsychotic agents and increased risk ofdiabetes: Class action or differential action? *Expert Opinion on Drug Safety, 4,* 55–68.

Anderson, B. J., Brackett, J., Ho, J., & Laffel, L. M. B. (1999). An office-based intervention to maintain parent-adolescent teamwork in diabetes management. *Diabetes Care, 22,* 713–731.

Anderson, R. J., Freedland, K. E., Clouse, R. E., & Lustman, P. J. (2001). The prevalence of co-morbid depression in adults with diabetes: A meta-analysis. *Diabetes Care, 24,* 1069–1078.

Anderson, R. J., Grigsby, A. B., Freedland, K. E., de Groot, M., McGill, J. B., Clouse, R. E., & Lustman, P. J. (2002). Anxiety and poor glycemic control: A meta-analytic review of the literature. *International Journal of Psychiatry in Medicine, 32,* 235–247.

Barnard, K. D., Skinner, T. C., & Peveler, R. (2006). The prevalence of co-morbid depression in adults with Type 1 diabetes: Systematic literature review. *Diabetic Medicine, 23,* 445–448.

Bertuzzi, F., Marzorati, S., & Secchi, A. (2006). Islet cell transplantation. *Current Molecular Medicine, 6,* 369–374.

Boardway, R. H., Delamater, A. M., Tomakowsky, J., & Gutai, J. P. (1993). Stress management training for adolescents with diabetes. *Journal of Pediatric Psychology, 18,* 29–45.

Boyer, B. A., Myers, V. H., & Lehman, D. (in press). Psychological aspects of Type 1 Diabetes in adults. In S. Jabbour, E. A. Stephens, I. Hirsch, B. J. Goldstein, S. Garg, & M. Riddle (Eds.). *Type 1 Diabetes in Adults: Principles and Practices.* New York: Informa Healthcare.

Boyer, B. A., Ikunga, A., Cantor, R. K., & Scheiner, G. (March, 2006). *Diabetes self-management in the 21st century: Self-care behaviors relevant to current treatment regimens.* Poster presented at the 27th Annual Meeting of the Society of Behavioral Medicine, San Francisco, CA.

Caban, A., & Walker, E. A. (2006). A systematic review of research on culturally relevant issues for Hispanics with diabetes. *The Diabetes Educator, 32,* 584–595.

Centers for Disease Control and Prevention. National diabetes fact sheet: General information and national estimates on diabetes in the United States, 2005. Atlanta: U.S. Department of Health and Human Services, Centers for Disease Control and Prevention, 2005.

Christie, D., & Wilson, C. (2005). CBT in paediatric and adolescent health settings: A review of practice-based evidence. *Pediatric Rehabilitation, 8,* 241–247.

Ciechanowski, P. S., Katon, W. J., & Russo, J. E. (2005). The association of depression and perceptions of interpersonal relationships in patients with diabetes. *Journal of Psychosomatic Research, 58,* 139–144.

Coelho, R., Amorim, I., & Prata, J. (2003). Coping styles and quality of life in patients with non-insulin-dependent diabetes mellitus. *Psychosomatics, 44,* 312–318.

Colton, P.A. (1999). Eating disturbances in young women with diabetes mellitus: Mechanics and consequences. *Psychiatric Annals, 29,* 213–218.

Cox, D. J., Gonder-Frederick, L. A., Kovatchev, B. P., Young-Hyman, D. L., Donner, T. W., Julian, D. M., & Clarke, W. L. (1999). Biopsychobehavioral model of severe hypoglycemia. II. Understanding the risk of severe hypoglycemia. *Diabetes Care, 22,* 2018–2025.

Cox, D. J., Irvine, A., Gonder-Frederick, L. A., Nowacek, G., & Butterfield, J. (1987). Fear of hypoglycemia: Quantification, validation, and utilization. *Diabetes Care, 10*(5), 617–621.

Davidson, P. R., & Parker, K. C. H. (2001). Eye movement desensitization and reprocessing (EMDR): A meta-analysis. *Journal of Consulting and Clinical Psychology, 69,* 305-316.

de Groot, M., Anderson, R. J., Freedland, K. E., Clouse, R. E., & Lustman, P. J. (2001). Association of depression and diabetes complications: A meta-analysis. *Psychosomatic Medicine, 63,* 619–630.

Delamater, A. M., Bubb, J., Davis, S., Smith J. A., Schmidt, L., White, N. H., & Santiago, J. V., (1990). Randomized prospective study of self-management training with newly diagnosed diabetic children. *Diabetes Care, 13,* 492–498.

Diabetes Control and Complications Trial Research Group. (1993). The effect of intensive treatment of diabetes on the development and progression of long-term complications in insulin-dependent diabetes mellitus. *New England Journal of Medicine, 329,* 977–986.

Drotar, D. (2006). Psychological interventions: Diabetes. In D. Drotar (Ed.) *Psychological interventions in childhood chronic illness,* 139-155. Washington, DC: American Psychological Association.

Edgar, K. A., & Skinner, T. C. (2003). Illness representations and coping as predictors of emotional well-being in adolescents with Type 1 Diabetes. *Journal of Pediatric Psychology, 28,* 485–493.

El-Mallakh, P. (2006). Evolving self-care in individuals with schizophrenia and diabetes mellitus. *Archives of Psychiatric Nursing, 20,* 55–64.

Fuemmeler, B. F., Mullins, L. L., Van Pelt, J., Carpentier, M. Y., & Parkhurst, J. (2005). Posttraumatic stress symptoms and distress among parents of children with cancer. *Children's Health Care, 34,* 289–303.

Gianfrancesco, F., Wang, R. H., & Nasrallah, H. A. (2006). The influence of study design on the results of pharmacoepidemiologic studies of diabetes risk with antipsychotic therapy. *Annals of Clinical Psychiatry, 18*, 9–17.

Gray, D. L., Marrero, D. G., Godfrey, C., Orr, D. P., & Golden, M. P. (1988). Chronic poor metabolic control in the pediatric population: A stepwise intervention program. *Diabetes Educator, 14*, 516–520.

Grey, M., & Berry, D. (2004). Coping skills training and problem solving in diabetes. *Current Diabetes Reports, 4*, 126–131.

Grey, M., Boland, E. A., Davidson, M., Li, J., & Tamborlane, W. V. (2000). Coping skills training for youths with diabetes mellitus has long-lasting effects on metabolic control and quality of life. *Journal of Pediatrics, 137*, 107–113.

Grigsby, A. B., Anderson, R. J., Freedland, K. E., Clouse, R. E., & Lustman, P. J. (2002). Prevalence of anxiety in adults with diabetes: A systematic review. *Journal of Psychosomatic Research, 53*, 1053–1060.

Grylli, V., Wagner, G., Hafferl-Gattermayer, A., Schober, E., & Karwautz, A. (2005). Disturbed eating attitudes, coping styles, and subjective quality of life in adolescents with Type 1 diabetes. *Journal of Psychosomatic Research, 59*, 265–272.

Hanson, C. L., Henggeler, S. W., & Burghen, G. (1987). Social competence and parental support as mediators of the link between stress and metabolic control in adolescents with insulin-dependent diabetes mellitus. *Journal of Consulting and Clinical Psychology, 55*, 529–533.

Huttlinger, K. W. (1995). A Navajo perspective of diabetes. *Family & Community Health, 18*, 9–16.

Irvine, A. A., Cox, D., & Gonder-Frederick, L. (1992). Fear of hypoglycemia: Relationship to physical and psychological symptoms in patients with insulin-dependent diabetes mellitus. *Health Psychology, 11*(2), 135–138.

Ismail, K., Winkley, K., & Rabe-Hesketh, S. (2004). Systematic review and meta-analysis of randomized controlled trials of psychological interventions to improve glycemic control in patients with type 2 diabetes. *Lancet, 363*, 1589–1597.

Johnson, S. B. (1995). Insulin–dependent diabetes mellitus in childhood. In M. C. Roberts (Ed.), *Handbook of pediatric psychology* (2nd ed., pp. 263–285). New York: Guilford.

Karlsen, B., Idsoe, T., Dirdal, I., Rokne Hanestad, B., & Bru, E. (2004). Effects of a group-based counseling programme on diabetes-related stress, coping, psychological well-being and metabolic control in adults with type 1 or type 2 diabetes. *Patient Education and Counseling, 53*, 299–308.

Katon, W. J., Rutter, C., Simon, G., Lin, E. H., Ludman, E., Ciechanowski, P., et al., (2005). The association of comorbid depression with mortality in patients with type 2 diabetes. *Diabetes Care, 28*, 2668–2672.

Katon, W. J., Simon, G., Russo, J., Von Korff, M., Lin, E. H., Ludman, E., et al., (2004). Quality of depression care in a population-based sample of patients with diabetes and major depression. *Medical Care, 42*, 1222–1229.

Katon, W. J., Von Korff, M., Lin, E. H., Simon, G., Ludman, E., Russo, J., et al., (2004). The Pathways Study: A randomized trial of collaborative care in patients with diabetes and depression. *Archives of General Psychiatry, 61*, 1042–1049.

Karlsen, B., & Bru, E. (2002). Coping styles among adults with Type 1 and Type 2 diabetes. *Psychology, Health & Medicine, 7*, 245–259.

Kelly, S. D., Howe, S. J., Hendler, J. P., & Lipman, T. H. (2005). Disordered eating behaviors in youth with type 1 diabetes. *Diabetes Educator, 34*, 572–583.

Knol, M. J., Twisk, J. W., Beekman, A. T., Heine, R. J., Snoek, F. J., & Pouwer, F. (2006). Depression as a risk factor for the onset of type 2 diabetes mellitus: A meta-analysis. *Diabetologia, 49*, 837–845.

Kovacs, M., Goldston, D., Obrosky, D. S., & Bonar, L. K. (1997). Psychiatric disorders in youths with IDDM: Rates and risk factors. *Diabetes Care, 20,* 36–44.

La Greca, A. M., Schwarz, L. T., & Satin, W. (1987). Eating patterns in young women with IDDM: Another look. *Diabetes Care 1987, 10,* 659–660.

Landolt, M. A., Ribi, K., Laimbacher, J., Vollrath, M., Gnehm, H. E., & Sennhauser, F. H. (2002) Posttraumatic stress disorder in parents of children with newly diagnosed Type 1 daibetes. *Journal of Pediatric Psychology, 27,* 647–652.

Landolt, M. A., Vollrath, M., Laimbacher, J., Gnehm, H. E., & Sennhauser, F. H. (2005). Prospective study of posttraumatic stress disorder in parents of children with newly diagnosed type 1 diabetes. *Journal of the American Academy of Child & Adolescent Psychiatry, 44,* 682–689.

Landolt, M. A., Vollrath, M., Ribi, K., Gnehm, H. E., & Sennhauser, F. H. (2003). Incidence and associations of parental and child posttraumatic stress symptoms in pediatric patients. *Journal of Child Psychology and Psychiatry, 44,* 1199–1207.

Lawence, J. M., Standiford, D. A., Loots, B., Klingensmith, G. J., Williams, D. E., Ruggiero, A., et al., (2006). Prevalence and correlates of depressed mood among youth with diabetes: The SEARCH for Diabetes in Youth study. *Pediatrics, 117,* 1348–1358.

Lin, E. H., Katon, W., Rutter, C., Simon, G. E., Ludman, E. J., Von Korff, M., et al., (2006). Effects of enhanced depression treatment on diabetes self-care. *Annals of Family Medicine, 4,* 46–53.

Lustman, P. J., Anderson, R. J., Freedland, K. E., de Groot, M., Carney, R. M., & Clouse, R. E. (2000). Depression and poor glycemic control: A meta-analytic review of the literature. *Diabetes Care, 23,* 934–942.

Lustman, P. J., & Clouse, R. E. (2002). Treatment of depression in diabetes: Impact on mood and medical outcomes. *Journal of Psychosomatic Research, 53,* 917–924.

Lustman, P. J., & Clouse, R. E. (2005). Depression in diabetic patients: The relationship between mood and glycemic control. *Journal of Diabetes and Its Complications, 19,* 113–122.

Lustman P. J., Griffith L. S., Clouse, R. E., & Cryer, P. E. (1986). Psychiatric illness in diabetes mellitus: Relationship to symptoms and glucose control. *The Journal of Nervous and Mental Disease, 174,* 736–742.

Mannucci, E., Rotella, F., Ricca, V., Moretti, S., Placidi, G. F., & Rotella, C. M. (2005). Eating disorders in patients with type 1 diabetes: A meta-analysis. *Journal of endocrinological investigation, 28,* 417–419.

Myers, V. H., Boyer, B. A., Herbert, J. D., Barakat, L. P., & Scheiner, G. (2007). Fear of hypoglycemia and self reported posttraumatic stress in adults with type I diabetes treated by intensive regimens. *Journal of Clinical Psychology in Medical Settings, 14,* 11-21.

Nielsen, S. (2002). Eating disorders in females with type 1 diabetes: An update of a meta-analysis. *European Eating Disorders Review, 10,* 241–254.

Nielsen, S., Emborg, C., & Molback, A. G. (2002). Mortality in concurrent type 1 diabetes and anorexia nervosa. *Diabetes Care, 25,* 309–312.

Paschalides, C., Wearden, A. J., Dunkerley, R., Bundy, C., Davies, R., & Dickens, C. M. (2004). The associations of anxiety, depression and personal illness representations with glycaemic control and health-related quality of life in patients with type 2 diabetes mellitus. *Journal of Psychosomatic Research, 57,* 557–564.

Polonsky, W. H., Davis, C. L., Jacobson, A. M., & Anderson, B. J. (1992). Correlates of hypoglycemic fear in Type I and Type II diabetes mellitus. *Health Psychology, 11*(3), 199–202.

Porter, J. R., & Barret, T. G. (2004). Acquired non-type 1 diabetes in childhood: Subtypes, diagnosis, and management. *Archives of Disease In Childhood, 89,* 1138–1144.

Rothbaum, B. O., Meadows, E. A., Resick, P., & Foy, D. W. (2000). Cognitive-Behavior Therapies. In E. B. Foa, T. M. Keane, & M. J. Friedman (Eds.), *Effective Treatments for PTSD,* 320–325. New York: Guilford Press.

Rydall, A. C., Rodin, G. M., Olmsted, M. P., Devenyi, R. G., & Daneman, D. (1997). Disordered eating behavior and microvascular complications in young women with insulin-dependent diabetes mellitus. *New England Journal of Medicine, 336,* 1849–1854.

Scheiner, G., & Boyer, B. A. (2005). Characteristics of basal insulin requirements by age and gender in patients with Type-I diabetes. *Diabetes Research and Clinical Practice, 69,* 14–21.

Schilling, L. S., Grey, M., & Knafl, K. A. (2002). The concept of self-management of type I diabetes in children and adolescents: An evolutionary concept analysis. *Journal of Advanced Nursing, 37,* 87–99.

Seiffge-Krenke, & Stemmler, M. I. (2003). Coping with everyday stress and links to medical and psychosocial adaptation in diabetic adolescents. *Journal of Adolescent Health, 33,* 180–188.

Shapiro, F. (1989a). Efficacy of the eye movement desensitization procedure in the treatment of traumatic memories. *Journal of Traumatic Stress, 2,* 199–223.

Simon, G. E., Katon, W. J., Lin, E. H., Ludman, E., VonKorff, M., Ciechanowski, P., & Young, B. A. (2005). Diabetes complications and depression as predictors of health service costs. *General Hospital Psychiatry, 27,* 344–351.

Snoek, F. J., & Skinner, T. C. (2002). Psychological counseling in problematic diabetes: Does it help? *Diabetic Medicine, 19,* 265–273.

Steed, L., Cooke, D., & Newman, S., (2003). A systematic review of psychosocial outcomes following education, self-management and psychological interventions in diabetes mellitus. *Patient Education and Counseling, 51,* 5–15.

Surwit, R. S., Scovern, A. W., & Feinglos, M. N. (1982). The role of behavior in diabetes care. *Diabetes Care, 5,* 337–342.

Takii, M., Uchigata, Y., Komaki, G., Nozaki, T., Kawai, H., Iwamoto, Y., et al. (2003). An integrated inpatient therapy for type 1 diabetic females with bulimia nervosa: A 3–year follow-up study. *Journal of Psychosomatic Research, 55,* 349–356.

Von Korff, M., Katon, W., Lin, E. H., Simon, G., Ludman, E., Oliver, M., et al., (2005). Potentially modifiable factors associated with disability among people with diabetes. *Psychosomatic Medicine, 67,* 233–240.

WebMD. (2006). *Diabetes.* Retrieved October 24, 2006, from http://www.webmd.com/content/article/59/

Wilson, G. T., & Fairburn, C. G. (2002). Treatments for eating disorders. In P. E. Nathan & J. M. Gorman (Eds.), *A guide to treatments that work* (2nd ed.; pp. 559–592). New York: Oxford University Press.

Wysocki, T., Greco, P., & Buckloh, L. M. (2003). Childhood diabetes in psychological context. In M. C. Roberts (Ed.), *Handbook of pediatric psychology* (3rd ed.; pp. 304–320). New York: Guilford.

Wysocki, T., Greco, P., Harris, M. A., White, N. H. (2000). Behavioral family systems therapy for adolescents with diabetes. In D. Drotar (Ed.), *Promoting adherence to medical treatment in chronic childhood illness: Concepts, methods, and interventions.* (pp. 367–381). Mahwah, NJ: Lawrence Erlbaum.

Wysocki, T., Harris, M. A., Greco, P., Bubb, J., Danda, C. E., Harvey, I. M., et al. (2000). Randomized, controlled trial behavior therapy for families of adolescents with insulin-dependent diabetes mellitus. *Journal of Pediatric Psychology, 25,* 23–33.

Wysocki, T., Meinhold, P. Taylor, A., Hough, B. S., Barnard, M. U., Clarke, W. L., et al. (1996). Psychometric properties and normative data for the parent version of the Diabetes Independence Survey. *Diabetes Educator, 22,* 587–591.

CHAPTER 9

HIV/AIDS

LYNDA M. SAGRESTANO, AMY ROGERS, and ARRON SERVICE

PREVALENCE

Worldwide, more than 40 million people were living with human immunodeficiency virus (HIV) in 2005, including 38 million adults and 2.3 million children. Close to 5 million new people were infected with HIV and over 3 million people died from acquired immunodeficiency syndrome (AIDS) in 2005. AIDS has killed more than 25 million people since if was first identified (Joint United Nations Programme on HIV/AIDS [UNAIDS], 2005). The first cases of what would later be known as AIDS were reported in the United States in June of 1981 (Centers for Disease Control and Prevention [CDC], 1981). Since that time, more than 1.5 million people in the United States have been infected with HIV, including more than 500,000 who have already died (CDC, 2005). At the end of 2003, an estimated 1,039,000 to 1,185,000 persons in the United States were living with HIV/AIDS (CDC, 2006a; Glynn & Rhodes, 2005). The CDC estimates that approximately 40,000 Americans become infected with HIV each year (CDC, 1999b). From 2001 through 2004, the total number of new cases of HIV/AIDS decreased slightly in 35 areas (33 of the states within the United States, Guam, and the U.S. Virgin Islands); however, with long-term, confidential, name-based HIV reporting, HIV/AIDS prevalence (i.e., the number of persons living with HIV/AIDS) increased during this time (CDC, 2006a). Because the disease is spread through modifiable behaviors, understanding both transmission rates and patterns and the course of the illness progression is imperative for primary, secondary, and tertiary prevention.

HIV/AIDS continues to affect certain groups in the population that characteristically engage in high-risk sexual behaviors, such as high-risk heterosexuals (HRH; i.e., heterosexual individuals who engage in high-risk sexual activities such as having sex without condoms or having sex with partners who use injected drugs), men who have sex with men (MSM), injected drug users (IDU), and sex workers (i.e., individuals who earn their living by exchanging sex for money, drugs, or shelter). From 2001 through 2004, the estimated number of HIV/AIDS cases increased among MSM and decreased among IDU, MSM who were also IDU, HRH, adolescents, and children. Eighty percent of all HIV/AIDS cases diagnosed in 2004 were accounted for by MSM (47%) and persons exposed through heterosexual contact (33%; CDC, 2006a).

In addition to specific risk groups, racial and ethnic minorities have been disproportionately affected by HIV/AIDS since the beginning of the epidemic. Minority Americans now represent the majority of new AIDS cases (71%), and the majority of those estimated to be living with AIDS (64%) in 2003 (CDC, 2006b). African Americans have the highest HIV case rates of any racial/ethnic group, followed by Latinos, American Indian/Alaska Natives, whites and Asian/Pacific Islanders. The AIDS case rate per 100,000 population for African Americans was 9.5 times that of whites in 2003. HIV was the third leading cause of death among African Americans between the ages of 25 and 34 in 2001, and the sixth leading cause of death for Latinos and whites in this age group (CDC, 2006b).

In the United States, women are the fastest-growing population group with HIV, and half of these infections are attributed to heterosexual sex. Women in racial and ethnic minority communities have been particularly affected by HIV. For example, although Latinas comprise only about 10% of the female population, they constitute 20% of women with AIDS (CDC, 2005). Despite these increases in transmission rates for women, males still accounted for 73% of all HIV/AIDS cases among adults and adolescents in 2004 (CDC, 2006a).

DISEASE STATES

HIV is a retrovirus that binds to cells that carry the CD4 molecule, including T helper lymphocytes (T-cells), monocytes, and macrophages, which are primary components of the immune system. The function of the T-cell is to respond to attacks from foreign agents by mounting an immune response, which should neutralize the foreign agent. HIV takes over the T-cells and multiplies, which destroys more T-cells and ultimately damages the body's defenses against infection. As the number of T-cells drops, people with HIV become more susceptible to other infections and certain types of cancer, which their bodies are no longer able to fight. As their immune system becomes increasingly deficient, they are diagnosed with AIDS (Kalichman, 1998; Klatt, 2005).

Transmission   HIV is transmitted via three primary routes: sexual, blood-borne (parenteral), and perinatal. The rate of transmission varies by both the route of transmission and the specific circumstances surrounding transmission (Greenblatt & Hessol, 2001; Kalichman, 1998). Sexual transmission is the worldwide leading mode of transmission (Quinn, 1996). Three body fluids carry sufficient concentrations of HIV to spread the virus (blood, semen, vaginal fluids), whereas saliva, urine, and feces, in the absence of blood, do not (Kalichman). Saliva, in particular, does not carry sufficient concentrations of HIV to transmit the virus via kissing or oral-genital contact, and in addition, enzymes in the saliva inactivate the virus (Bergey et al., 1993).

Anal intercourse carries the highest risk, as the high concentration of HIV in semen and blood are exposed to the anal cavity, which is highly vascularized, leading to rapid absorption into the bloodstream. Anal intercourse poses risk for both receptive and insertive partners, although insertive partners experience a relatively lower risk level than receptive partners. Nonetheless, the risk for insertive partners is still high, as the outer surface of the penis experiences microlacerations during insertive anal sex (Caceres & van Griensven, 1994; Kalichman, 1998; Ostrow, DiFranceisco, Chmeil, Wagstaff, & Wesch, 1995).

Vaginal intercourse accounts for the largest proportion of HIV infections worldwide (World Health Organization, 2002). The mode of transmission is similar to anal intercourse, as insertive vaginal intercourse can lead to microlacerations of the vaginal walls and the penis, exposing both partners to high concentrations of the virus (Kalichman, 1998). The female partner in vaginal intercourse is at relatively higher risk than her male partner, although the male partner is still at significant risk for infection from vaginal intercourse with an infected partner (Downs & De Vincenzi, 1996; Haverkos & Battjes, 1992; Padian, Shiboski, & Jewell, 1991).

The risks associated with oral-penile intercourse are less clear, with conflicting research findings (Kalichman, 1998). In addition, it has been very difficult to assess the findings related to this question. Although evidence from several studies suggests that the risk is very low (De Vincenzi, 1994; Ostrow et al., 1995), several case studies have documented HIV infection where receptive oral intercourse was the only risk factor. Such case examples are hard to interpret, as there is evidence that some individuals may deny engaging in risky anal or vaginal intercourse and provide inaccurate information (Brody, 1995). The equivocal findings have led to inconsistent education in preventive intervention, leading to mixed messages about the level of risk associated with oral sex (Kalichman, 1998).

Parenteral transmission can take place when blood recipients receive infected blood products, through sharing of needles by injection drug users, and through needle sticks among health care workers (Greenblatt & Hessol, 2001). Perinatal transmission can result from exposure in utero, during labor and delivery, and through breastfeeding (Anderson, 2001; Greenblatt & Hessol, 2001). Perinatal transmission occurs at a rate of 25% without antiretroviral therapy, although 60 to 75% of transmissions occur at the time of delivery (Mofenson, 1997). Evidence suggests that use of antiretroviral agents reduces the transmission rate to as low as 2% (CDC, 2001).

DISEASE FACTORS

The onset and progression of HIV varies substantially, making early testing and diagnosis critical for effective treatment.

Onset

One of the first signs of HIV infection is acute seroconversion syndrome, which typically occurs 6 to 9 months after infection (Feinberg & Maenza, 2001). These symptoms are classically those of seronegative mononucleosis or flu, such as fever, aches, pharyngitis, lymphadenopathy, and frequently rash, although the range of possible clinical manifestations of acute HIV infection is very broad. In fact, an individual newly infected with HIV may not experience any symptoms: the onset of HIV can be acutely asymptomatic. Of the estimated 1,039,000 to 1,185,000 persons living with HIV (not AIDS), approximately 25% are unaware they are infected (Greenwald, Burstein, Pincus, & Branson, 2006) and approximately 8 to 15% have no symptoms (Munoz et al., 1995). Therefore, people living with HIV (PLWHIV) are often indistinguishable from most people seen in primary care today.

Disease Progression

Because of the long incubation period (8 to 10 yr on average) and the success of treatment regimens, HIV has become a chronic disease that foreshortens life expectancy. Although an individual with HIV may feel healthy, he or she is still infectious and can transmit the virus to others. T-cells (CD4 cells) are a major target of the virus, and

Table 9.1
CDC (1986; 1992) Classification System of HIV Progression

Stage	CD4 Cell Count	Clinical Manifestations
A (relatively normal)	500 cells/mm^3	Minimal immune injury
B	200–499 cells/mm^3	Conditions worsened by HIV infection
C (severely depleted)	< 200 cells/mm^3	Conditions that are AIDS defining

therefore circulating levels of CD4 cells in the blood have been used as a way of measuring the amount of damage HIV has done to the immune system. Most people experience a gradual decline in CD4 and T-cell counts, and when untreated, the body progresses through characteristic clinical stages, ending in AIDS (Greenblatt & Hessol, 2001; Klatt, 2005).

In 1986, the CDC developed a classification system of the stages of HIV progression, which was later revised in 1992 (CDC, 1986, 1992). The classification system acknowledges that certain symptoms and clinical conditions tend to occur at differing levels of immunological damage associated with CD4 cell counts. Use of a staging system allows for more consistent clinical evaluation and treatment planning (Greenblatt & Hessol, 2001). Although there are several staging systems, the CDC's system is the most widely used in industrialized nations.

The stages are defined by two types of information: CD4 cell counts in the blood and clinical manifestations of the disease (see Table 9.1). The CD4 cell categories include >500 cells/mm^3 (relatively normal), 200–499 cells/mm^3, and <200 cells/mm^3 (severely depleted; CDC's clinical definition of AIDS). The clinical manifestations are also separated into three categories: Category A (minimal immune injury), Category B (conditions worsened by the HIV infection), and Category C (conditions that are AIDS defining, even when CD4 cell counts are above 200 cells/mm^3). Therefore, a person can be diagnosed with AIDS either based on CD4 cell counts below 200 cells/mm^3, or based on Category C clinical manifestations of HIV (CDC, 1992; Greenblatt & Hessol, 2001). Studies of the time course of HIV before the development of highly active antiretroviral therapy (HAART) indicate that approximately half of adults infected with the virus will develop an AIDS-defining condition (Category C) within 10 years of infection, and most of those patients will die (Greenblatt & Hessol). A small group of people (8 to 15%) infected with the virus remain symptom free for long periods of time, either because their CD4 cell counts stay stable or because they do not develop any AIDS-defining conditions, even with a low cell count (Munoz et al. 1995; Schrager, Young, Fowler, Mathieson, & Vermund, 1994). Of all HIV infections diagnosed in 2003, 39% progressed to AIDS within 12 months after HIV infection was diagnosed (Klein, Hurley, Merrill, & Quesenberry, 2003). Morbidity and mortality related to HIV has decreased significantly as a result of HAART (Bartlett, 2002; Michaels, Clark, & Kissinger, 1998; Palella et al., 1998), although recipients of the therapy do continue to experience declines in their health status (Ledergerber et al., 1999), in part due to viral resistance to components of HAART (Richman, 1996).

REGIMEN FACTORS

When AIDS was first discovered in the early 1980s, there were no effective treatments for either the underlying immune deficiency or the opportunistic diseases that resulted from the virus, and patients only lived a few years. Although there is not yet a cure for HIV, developments in treatment have resulted in drugs to fight both HIV infection and the associated opportunistic diseases, and patients now live longer and healthier lives (United States Department of Health and Human Services [USDHHS], 2006; National Institutes of Health [NIH], 2005, 2006).

TREATMENT REGIMENS

There are three classes of antiretroviral medications (26 drugs) approved by the Food and Drug Administration. The first class, reverse transcriptase (RT) inhibitors, interrupt the process of the HIV life cycle (reverse transcription) so that the virus cannot make copies of itself, thus slowing the spread of HIV in the body. The two main types of RTs are nucleoside/nucleotide RT inhibitors (NRTI) and non-nucleoside RT inhibitors (NNRTI). The second class of drugs, protease inhibitors (PI), also interrupts the process of the HIV life cycle, but at a later step in the cycle. The third class is fusion inhibitors, which block the virus' ability to merge with the membranes of other cells, which blocks entry into immune cells. Given that as HIV reproduces itself different strains of the virus emerge that are resistant to antiretroviral drugs, these drugs are used in combination. Highly active antiretroviral therapy typically combines drugs from at least two classes, and has been shown to effectively suppress the virus and lower the rate of opportunistic infections, thus lowering the number of deaths from AIDS in the United States. (USDHHS, 2006; NIH, 2005, 2006).

BARRIERS TO SELF-MANAGEMENT

Barriers to successful self-management of the treatment regimen are substantial and multifaceted, including the complexity of the regimen, pill burden, the long-term nature of the treatment, side effects, and costs (Starace, Massa, Amico, & Fisher, 2006). Specifically, the regimen is highly complex, with some patients taking up to 20 pills per day on a precise schedule (i.e., pill burden), yet if patients deviate from following the regimen exactly as prescribed, they can develop resistance and weaken the effects of the drugs. If these drug-resistant strains are then passed on to others, some antiretroviral therapies will fail in new patients (Bangsburg, Moss, & Deeks, 2004; Catz, Kelly, Bogart, Bentsch, & McAuliffe, 2000; Chesney, Morin, & Sherr, 2000; Little et al., 2002). Therefore, strict adherence to treatment regimens is critical. Nonetheless, evidence suggests that adherence is inconsistent, with reports ranging from 33% to 88% adherence (Altice & Friedland, 1998; Bartlett, 2002).

Side effects associated with HAART can be severe (Fellay et al., 2001). The USDHHS (2006) notes that some of the side effects may be life threatening, and therefore careful monitoring of treatment regimens and side effects are necessary. Among the most common side effects are liver problems, diabetes, abnormal fat distribution, high cholesterol, increased bleeding in patients with hemophilia, decreased bone density, skin rash, pancreatitis, and nerve problems. More minor side effects such as fever, nausea, and fatigue may also indicate other underlying problems and must therefore also be monitored. Comorbid conditions and the use of combinations of different medications may increase the likelihood of certain side effects (e.g., drug-drug interactions).

The cost of treatment can be a significant barrier to successful self-management of HIV. Several studies have shown that HAART is a cost-effective use of resources (Freedberg et al., 2001), and over the past decade the total cost of care has decreased (Bozzette et al., 2001). In the mid to late 1990s, data indicated that, although the cost of pharmaceuticals had increased, these increases were offset by decreased hospital costs, resulting in a shift in monthly costs per person from $20,300 in 1996 to $18,300 in 1998. In addition, people living with HIV without insurance had the lowest pharmaceutical costs, but the highest hospital costs (Bozzette et al.). HIV disproportionately affects people who have fewer resources, and in addition, HIV may lead to job loss from inability to work, thus resulting in loss of employer-provided insurance and income. The Ryan White Comprehensive AIDS Resource Emergency (CARE) Act was passed by Congress in 1990 to provide funding for health care and support services to people living with HIV. Programs funded by the CARE Act are meant to fill gaps not covered by other sources, such as private insurance or Medicaid. Services provided through the CARE Act are focused on reducing inpatient care by increasing access to primary care for underserved populations (Health Resources and Services Administration, n.d.).

INDIVIDUAL FACTORS

With the advent of HAART treatments and the resultant decreases in morbidity and mortality, self-management of HIV/AIDS has largely been conceptualized as adherence to HAART regimens. Because stringent adherence is critical to effective treatment for the individual and the prevention of drug-resistant strains of the virus, much study has been devoted to the individual factors related to this aspect of treatment. Despite some inconsistencies across studies and between subpopulations, several factors are reliably associated with medication adherence.

PROVIDER/CLIENT RELATIONSHIP

The quality of communication and trust between the patient and provider is associated with adherence (Murphy, Marelich, Hoffman, & Steers, 2004), especially for minority populations (e.g., van Servellen, Brown, Lombardi, & Herrera, 2003; Whetten et al. 2006) and adolescents (Murphy, Wilson, Durako, Muenz, & Belzer, 2001). Particularly important is communication that effectively improves health literacy by conveying the way the medications work and the importance and precision of dosing schedules. Indeed, knowledge about the way HAART medications work predicts adherence (Bing, Kilbourne, Brooks, Lazarus, & Senak, 1999; Stone, Hogan, & Schuman, 2001).

Open dialogue between patient and provider, which leads to consensus concerning the seriousness of both the diagnosis and treatment, is also key (Altice, Mostashari, & Friedland, 2001; Chesney, 2003; Murphy, Roberts, Martin, Marelich, & Hoffman, 2000; Murri et al., 2002; van Servellen, Chang, Garcia, & Lombardi, 2002). Furthermore, because medication adherence is a lifelong concern for persons living with HIV (PLWHIV), and adherence rates decline over time (Gross, Bilker, Friedman, & Strom, 2001; Mannheimer, Friedland, Matts, Child, & Chesney, 2002; Tuldra & Wu, 2002), communication about medications needs to be ongoing (Uldall, Palmer, Whetten, & Mellins, 2004).

Patient Characteristics

Although poor communication is often targeted as the cause of poor patient understanding of illness and/or treatment dynamics, other individual factors could account for these deficits. For example, PLWHIV who show general cognitive deficits or memory problems have worse medication adherence. Indeed, AIDS itself can lead to cognitive deficits (Lawrence & Major, 2002; Llorente et al., 1998), of which impaired mental flexibility is most strongly associated with poor medication adherence (Avants, Margolin, & Warburton, 2001; Hinkin et al., 2002).

Most demographic variables, other than age, are only sporadically associated with adherence to drug regimens. The relation of gender, education level, race, unemployment, economic status, and HIV exposure category to adherence are inconsistent and sometimes counterintuitive; only increasing age is consistently associated with better adherence. The inconsistency of the importance of demographic variables can often be attributed to the inclusion or exclusion of variables that covary with demographics. For example, many of the aforementioned demographic variables covary with stress. When stress is included in studies, the effects of these demographics may be negligible; however, if stress is not included, the demographic variables may become a proxy measure for stress and become important to medication adherence.

It is not surprising that stressful life conditions lower adherence. For example, relationship instability, housing instability, history of incarceration, and unemployment all increase the likelihood of nonadherence (Bouhnik et al., 2002). People who report high care-giving responsibilities for children or sick partners, or just generally high life stress have poorer adherence (Chesney, 2003; Mellins, Kang, Leu, Havens, & Chesney, 2003). Interestingly, studies show that perceived stress is enough to reduce adherence (Bottonari, Roberts, Ciesla, & Hewett, 2005; Murphy, Greenwell, & Hoffman, 2002), especially when comorbid with depression (Bottonari et al., 2005).

Psychiatric comorbidity is also associated with adherence to medication regimens such that depression (Gordillo, del Amo, Soriano, & Gonzalez-Lahoz, 1999; Kleeberger, Phair, & Strathdee, 2001; Perry et al., 2002; Schuman et al., 2001; Simoni, Frick, Lockhart, & Liebovitz, 2002; Starace et al., 2002), generalized anxiety disorder and panic disorder (Tucker, Burnam, Sherbourne, Kung, & Gifford, 2003), posttraumatic stress disorder (Delahanty, Bogart, & Figler, 2004), social phobia (Ingersoll, 2004), and stress (Mellins et al., 2003) all reduce adherence. The relation between psychiatric diagnosis and poor adherence seems to be especially pronounced among women (Mellins et al., 2002, 2003; Morrison et al., 2002; Turner, Laine, Cosler, & Hauck, 2003), and people with past or present substance use (Wagner, Kanouse, Koegel, & Sullivan, 2004).

Health Beliefs

A number of health-related beliefs have proven to be notable in understanding variable adherence rates. Self-efficacy in the area of medication adherence is a key factor across a variety of populations (Chesney et al., 2000; Gifford & Groessl, 2000; Tuldra & Wu, 2002; van Servellen et al., 2003; Weidle et al., 1999). People living with HIV who believe they are capable of managing medications actually do achieve better adherence. Furthermore, people who adhere less report feeling less in control of their behavior than those effectively managing their medications (Murphy et al., 2004). Other health beliefs are also related to adherence; beliefs that "the disease is not progressing" or that "medicines have stopped working" are associated with nonadherence (Aversa & Kimberlin, 1996; Muma, Ross, Parcel, & Pollard, 1995; Smith, Rapkin, Morrison, & Kammerman, 1997). Finally, higher belief in HIV/AIDS stigma is also associated with poor adherence to medications, such that some PLWHIV decide to not take medications because others might see or otherwise know of their HIV/AIDS status due to telltale side effects (e.g., lipodystrophy, wasting). They fear resulting negative social consequences such as social rejection, loss of employment, or violence (van Servellen et al., 2002).

Social Support and Coping

Social support has been shown to provide general benefits for medication adherence (Bamberger et al., 2000; Catz et al., 2000; Simoni et al., 2002). Some of the positive effects of social support are through its effect on depression, such that high social support decreases depression, which increases adherence (Jia et al., 2004). The construct of social support, however, has been divided into subcategories that reveal differing patterns of facilitation. Relationships specifically supportive of medication adherence (Broadhead et al., 2002; Catz et al., 2000), living with others (Mellins et al., 2002), greater emotional ties, reassurance of worth, and reliable alliances (Murphy et al., 2004) predicted greater medication adherence. Conversely, Murphy and colleagues also found that greater social attachment and overall higher scores on the Social Provisions Scale (Cutrona & Russell, 1987) actually hurt adherence.

In addition to the physical aspects of effective self-management of HIV/AIDS reflected in medication adherence, self-management also involves the psychological aspect of coping. Coping is relevant to self-management from the early aspects of deciding to test for HIV, through every stage of the disease, to coping with death-related issues. Two basic functions of coping have been identified by Lazarus and Folkman (1984). *Problem-focused coping* is behavior designed to change or improve stressful situations (e.g., problem solving, information seeking, conflict resolution); conversely, *emotion-focused coping* addresses emotional reactions to stressful situation (e.g., reappraisal, reframing, distraction). In general, problem-focused is a more adaptive response to controllable/changeable stressors and emotion-focused to uncontrollable/unchangeable stressors (Chesney, Folkman, & Chambers, 1996).

The importance of coping arises early in the etiology of HIV. It is estimated that 40% of people with elevated risk for HIV have never been tested (Berrios et al., 1993). Research suggests that worries about inability to cope with test results (Zapka, Stoddard, Zorn, McCusker, & Mayer, 1991) and fear of dealing with discrimination and stigma (Myers, Orr, Locker, & Jackson, 1993) are significant contributors to the lack of testing. For PLWHIV, coping is critical in managing aspects of their physical quality of life (e.g., functioning, pain, viral levels) and their psychological quality of life (e.g., bereavement, stigma, mortality).

Passive and avoidant forms of coping have been found to be detrimental to health-related quality-of-life indices, including nonadherence to medication, skipped medical appointments, lower immune function, and generally worse physical health outcomes, although not specifically examined among PLWHIV (Goodkin, Fuchs, Feaster, Leeka, & Rishel, 1992; Herbert & Cohen, 1993; Ironson et al., 2005; Leserman et al., 2002; Pereira et al., 2004; van Servellen et al., 2002).

Psychological quality of life for PLWHIV is also influenced by coping patterns. Adaptive coping, that which is appropriately matched to controllability/changeability of stressor, lowers AIDS-related burnout and perceptions of stress and increases feelings of wellbeing (Chesney et al., 1996). Adaptive coping has also been shown to reduce depression (Heckman et al., 2004), grief, and psychological distress (Sikkema, Kalichman, Kelly, & Koob, 1995). Avoidant coping, however, is tied to emotional distress (Heckman et al. 2004), less optimism, and more hopelessness (Rogers, Hansen, Levy, Tate, & Sikkema, 2005). Various interventions have been shown effective at improving coping skills for PLWHIV in general (Chesney et al., 1996), for bereavement (Sikkema et al., 1995), among the elderly (Heckman et al., 2001), and for the acutely ill (Côté & Pepler, 2005).

STIGMA

One prominent stressor that must be negotiated by PLWHIV is stigma. Because HIV transmission is linked to behaviors that often are regarded as breaches of society's moral codes (e.g., homosexuality, injected drug use, promiscuity) there is significant stigma attached to PLWHIV. Furthermore, the presence of incurability, youthful death, contagiousness, and homophobia make the HIV/AIDS stigma stronger (Green, 1995; Leiker, Taub, & Gast, 1995). Stigma influences efforts to prevent the spread of HIV as well as the coping and effective treatment of PLWHIV. One such manifestation of stigma involves gay men's reluctance to openly express their homosexuality. This stigma-based reluctance is, in turn, tied to quicker progression of HIV infection (Cole, Kemeny, Taylor, Visscher, & Fahey, 1996).

COMORBID PSYCHOPATHOLOGY

In addition to the association of psychological disorders with medication adherence, HIV/AIDS is found to be comorbid with a number of psychiatric/psychological disorders, and these influence many aspects of the disease. As is true with most people suffering from a chronic health condition, PLWHIV suffer a range of emotional and psychiatric disorders. The mechanisms of psychiatric comorbidity seem to be both psychological (e.g., death anxiety, bereavement, changed life expectations) and physical. Evidence suggests that many forms of comorbidity are associated with viral infection of the central nervous system or other attacks of the disease. Mania, for example, accompanies the onset of AIDS, is associated with AIDS-dementia, and is associated with higher counts of helper/inducer lymphocyte (CD3+/CD4+). Furthermore, AIDS-related mania manifests differently than mania associated with bipolar disorder, suggesting it is physically linked to the disorder (Lyketsos et al., 1993; Mijch, Judd, Lyketsos, & Cockram, 1999).

DEPRESSION

The most striking psychiatric comorbidity is the prevalence of PLWHIV with clinical levels of depression. Compared to the general population rates of 15% (Yun, Maravi, Koayashi, Barton, & Davidson, 2005), PLWHIV have a lifetime prevalence rate of clinical depression ranging between 22 to 45% (Rosenberger et al., 1993; Maj et al., 1994). Indeed, meta-analysis (Ciesla & Roberts, 2001) suggests the prevalence rate to be double that of the non-HIV infected. Furthermore, the likelihood of suffering from depression increases with years living with HIV/AIDS (Zinkernagel et al., 2001).

The prevalence of depression across populations with HIV/AIDS or disease stage is not constant. Gay and bisexual men (Berg, Mimiaga, & Safren, 2004; Rosenberger et al., 1993), people with less social support (Kalichman, DiMarco, Austin, Luke, & DiFonzo, 2003; Mizuno, Purcell, Dawson-Rose, & Parsons, 2003), people outside of relationships, people under stress, and people with a history of illegal drug use (Komiti et al., 2003) have higher rates of depression. Depression is more likely at the time of initial diagnosis and again at the onset of HIV-related symptoms (Hoffman, 1991). The onset of symptoms tends to produce depression and anxiety surrounding employment and autonomy issues (Hoffman), concern over the unknown elements of disease progression (Tross & Hirsch, 1988), and concern about stigma from social support networks, including friends and family (Walkey, Taylor, & Green, 1990).

The consequences of comorbid HIV/AIDS and depression extend well beyond additive symptomatologies. People with depression are less likely to receive prescriptions for antiretroviral therapy (Gordillo et al., 1999) and are harder to diagnose because of symptom overlap (e.g., pain, anorexia, fatigue). Treatment adherence is worse among depressed PLWHIV (Kleeberger et al., 2004; Starace et al., 2002) and negative physical HIV-related outcomes are increased (Ickovics et al., 2001; Leserman et al., 2002). Depressed PLWHIV engage in higher levels of risk-taking behaviors (Rahav, Nuttbrock, Rivera, & Link, 1998) and report lower quality of life (Tate et al. 2003; Trepanier et al., 2005). Finally, mortality rates are higher in depressed seropositive women (Cook et al., 2004; Ickovics et al., 2001) than in their nondepressed peers.

Clearly, depression accompanies a host of negative consequences for PLWHIV. To compound the problem, when a diagnosis of major depression or dysthymia is made, only approximately 43% of PLWHIV receive antidepressants (Vitiello, Burnam, Bing, Beckman, & Shapiro, 2003). This finding is in juxtaposition to the fact that depression among PLWHIV is responsive to medication (Himelhoch & Medoff, 2005) and therapy (Antoni et al., 1991; Kelly et al., 1993; Lutgendorf et al., 1997). Furthermore, when treated, negative consequences related to immune function (Antoni et al.), and speed of disease progression (Ironson et al., 1994) tend to abate. Thus, both pharmacotherapies and psychotherapies have been shown to be effective in treating depression among those with HIV/AIDS and may help optimize medical outcomes, but remain underutilized.

ANXIETY

Although not as common as depression, anxiety is still a common issue for PLWHIV. Prevalence rates suggest that generalized anxiety disorders affect between 16% (Bing et al., 2001) and 32% (Kilbourne, Justice, & Rabeneck, 2001) of PLWHIV. As in depression, the likelihood of suffering from an anxiety disorder increases with length of time living with HIV/AIDS (Zinkernagel et al., 2001). The prevalence of anxiety across populations with HIV/AIDS is not constant. Gay and bisexual men experience higher levels of anxiety than other groups (Berg et al., 2004). In addition to general anxiety disorder, PLWHIV are disproportionately affected by posttraumatic stress disorder (PTSD), with some studies finding rates at 50% (Safren, Gershuny, & Hendriksen, 2003). Anxiety has been found amenable to treatment, such that there is a drop in anxiety with group therapy and relaxation techniques (Lutgendorf et al., 1997) and cognitive behavioral stress management therapy (Antoni et al., 2000).

COGNITIVE IMPAIRMENT

The evidence suggesting cognitive impairment resulting from HIV/AIDS is compelling. Many, but not all PLWHIV have shown patterns of reduced executive functioning early in the disease progression (Basso & Bornstein, 2000; Sahakian et al., 1995) and more diffuse cognitive deficit in later stages of the illness (Heaton et al., 1995). The fact of inconsistent impairment has generated research to identify factors leading to greater or lesser risk. Three factors seem to be particularly important in understanding the association between HIV/AIDS and cognitive decline. Strong evidence suggests that much of the decline in functioning is linked to immunological health (Basso & Bornstein; Heaton et al.). Indeed, cognitive decline often is reversed with successful response to HAART, such that deficits are transitory rather than permanent. The role of alcohol and other substance abuse is also important. Among those drinking or using drugs, cognitive impairment is consistently more severe (Green, Saveanu, & Bornstein, 2004). Finally, a particularly interesting finding has been dubbed "cognitive reserve" (Satz, 1993). Individuals with higher premorbid levels of intelligence seem to experience substantially less cognitive decline (Basso & Bornstein, 2000; Maj et al., 1994; Satz et al., 1993; Stern, Silva, Chaisson, & Evans, 1996). The interpretation is that they possess a cognitive reserve that buffers them from impairment.

PERSONALITY DISORDERS

Personality disorders, especially antisocial and borderline disorders, are more common among people involved in HIV-related risk behaviors and among PLWHIV than in the general population (Jacobsberg, Frances, & Perry, 1995; Johnson, Williams, Rabkin, Goetz, & Remien, 1995; Perkins, Davidson, Leserman, Liao, & Evans, 1993). Furthermore, within groups at high risk for HIV, people with personality disorders are more likely to engage in the riskiest behaviors (Kelley & Petry, 2000; Verheul, Ball, & van der Brink, 1998). When compared to others with HIV/AIDS, people with personality disorders express more maladaptive ways of coping, more depression, and more anxiety (Johnson et al.; Perkins et al.). Clearly, the aspects of personality disorders that make people more susceptible to HIV also increase the likelihood of poorer adherence to medication (e.g., poor impulse control) and further spread of HIV through continued high-risk behaviors. Interesting preliminary research suggests that comorbidity of HIV/AIDS and personality disorders produces a resistance to the improvements in cognitive functioning that are typically found among PLWHIV once they begin HAART (Bauer & Shanley, 2006). This resistance is not caused by a lack of medication adherence and has yet to be fully explained.

PSYCHOSIS

Psychosis is expressed at higher rates among PLWHIV. Comorbidity seems to take two distinct paths. First, people with preexisting psychosis are more likely to become infected with HIV, with prevalence rates between 5 and 7% (Sewell, 1996). Second, HIV is associated with "new-onset" psychosis such that between 0.2 and 15% of PLWHIV will express such a psychosis (Sewell). The prevalence of psychosis among PLWHIV is increasing (Carey, Weinhardt, & Carey, 1995) and appears to be related to advanced progression of the disease. This particular combination of disorders is also associated with higher levels of HIV-related morbidity and mortality than AIDS alone.

These elevated rates may be due to low medication adherence associated with elements of the psychotic illness (Cuffel, Alford, Fischer, & Owen, 1996).

PREVENTION AND INTERVENTION

The prevention of HIV/AIDS begins with the recognition that individuals can make poor sex- and drug-related health decisions that consequently place them at risk for contracting HIV/AIDS. Risk reduction behavior describes various methods (e.g., safe sex) that can reduce the probability of sexually transmitted infection (STI) and HIV transmission. The general goal of prevention efforts is to either eliminate high-risk behaviors (e.g., abstinence) or encourage individuals to engage in risk reduction (e.g., condom use, use of sterilized needles). HIV/AIDS risk reduction involves three components; (1) preventing HIV-negative (–) individuals from becoming infected in the first place (primary prevention), (2) preventing HIV-positive (+) individuals from spreading the disease to uninfected individuals (secondary prevention), and (3) preventing HIV+ individuals from acquiring a more virulent strain of the disease (tertiary prevention). Specifically, secondary prevention of HIV aims to limit the spread of HIV to an infected woman's fetus (if she is pregnant), partners, and in turn, partners' partners (Simoni, Walters, & Nero, 2000). Tertiary prevention efforts among HIV+ individuals may involve prevention from becoming reinfected with HIV (i.e., "superloading"), contracting different strains of HIV, and acquiring other STIs that may complicate diagnoses (Simoni, Mason, Marks, Ruiz, & Richardson, 1995).

It is a challenge to recommend a single approach for risk-reduction interventions, considering the wide array of possible demographic and psychosocial correlates of high-risk behavior. Perhaps as a result, much of the research contributed by health psychology attempts to provide an understanding of the processes that underlie individual health behaviors. This research attempts to uncover the underlying decision-making processes that are occurring and often suggests intervention strategies that aim to change unhealthy behaviors.

Individuals are an essential unit of health education and health behavior theory, research, and practice (Rimer, 1997). In terms of the prevention of a disease like AIDS, behavior change is at the root of any prevention solution. If, in addition to understanding *who* may be engaging in high-risk behaviors (i.e., demographic factors), we can understand *what* influences people to engage in high-risk behaviors (e.g., psychosocial factors), health scientists may be able to develop appropriate interventions to help individuals enact positive behavioral change. Theoretical models such as the Health Belief Model (HBM) with self-efficacy, the Theory of Reasoned Action (TRA), the Transtheoretical Model (TTM) and Stages of Change (SOC), and the AIDS Risk Reduction Model (ARRM) are examples of models that have been heavily relied on by researchers in their attempts to understand what factors influence an individual's health behavior.

The health belief model (HBM) was developed with the view that there is a direct association between demographic characteristics and risk reduction behavior (Bandura, 1986; Becker et al., 1977; Rosenstock, 1974). The model suggests that appraisals of how threatening a disease is, how effective a recommended behavioral response will be, and how many barriers there are to adopting the response are the determinants of health behavior. In the model, health behavior can be explained using four constructs: perceived susceptibility, perceived severity, perceived benefits, and perceived barriers. According to the HBM, individuals will be more likely to practice a particular health behavior if they perceive themselves as being susceptible to a disease that has negative consequences and if they believe that the benefits of practicing the behavior outweigh the barriers. Self-efficacy was later added to the HBM, and has increased the model's predictive utility (Strecher & Rosenstock, 1997).

Belief in one's personal efficacy to exercise control over one's sexual behavior often emerges as a reliable predictor of sexual risk-taking behavior (e.g., Sterk, Theall, & Elifson, 2003). The lower the perceived self-efficacy, the higher the likelihood of high-risk behavior. Even when individuals acknowledge that safe sex and drug practices reduce their risk of infection, they will not adopt them if they believe that they cannot exercise control over their sexual relations (Siegel, Mesagno, Chen, & Christ, 1989).

One aspect that is lacking in the HBM is that there is no mechanism from which appraisal of the threat of AIDS can develop into action. An action mechanism was introduced by the theory of reasoned action (TRA), which suggests that the formation of a behavioral intention (e.g., "I plan on using a condom every time I have sex") is the catalyst of action and mediates the influence of other variables (Ajzen & Fishbein, 1980). According to the TRA, attitudes and subjective norms are the psychological prerequisites of intention formation. Attitudes are thought to be based on beliefs about, and evaluations of, the consequences of action, including beliefs about action effectiveness and barriers specified by the HBM. Subjective norms are derived from beliefs about what other people think one should do and from motivation to comply with these people's views (Ajzen & Fishbein).

A number of empirical studies have tested the ability of the TRA to account for condom use and other sexual behaviors that influence a person's risk of contracting HIV. With rare exceptions (e.g., Valdiserri, Arena, Proctor, & Bonati, 1989), intentions to use condoms consistently have been found to positively correlate with condom use in heterosexual and homosexual populations, among adolescents and adults, and among persons of color and Whites in the United States. (Fisher, Fisher, & Rye, 1995; Reinicke, Schmit, & Ajzen, 1996; Sheeran & Orbell, 1998; St. Lawrence et al., 1998; Wulfert, Wan, & Backus, 1996).

The TTM (Prochaska, DiClemente, & Norcross, 1992; Prochaska, Redding, & Evers, 2002) was developed to address the stages through which people pass when attempting to make long-term behavior modifications. The model includes five stages. In the precontemplation stage, the individual is not considering change in the near future. In the contemplation stage, the individual is considering change sometime in the next several months. In the preparation stage, the individual makes a commitment to attempt to change behavior and develops a behavior change plan. In the action stage, the individual implements the behavior change plan. After several months of successful action, the individual enters the maintenance stage and focuses on avoiding relapse (DiClemente, 1993; Prochaska et al.). One implication of the TTM is that community-based interventions will be more effective and cost effective when they correspond to the appropriate SOC (Prochaska, 1991).

Lauby and colleagues (1998) found that self-efficacy acted as a mediating variable for the stages of change such that self-efficacy for condom use increased with stage of change (i.e., as participants moved closer to action, their self-efficacy increased). Further support for the TTM was provided by Gielen and colleagues (2001) when the SOC was used to implement and evaluate a condom promotion intervention for HIV+ and at-risk women who were recruited from clinic and community settings in two U.S. cities. Participants were assigned to receive standard reproductive health services or enhanced services (standard plus SOC peer-advocate intervention). Results indicated that, compared with the standard intervention group, HIV+ women in the enhanced group were significantly more likely to have progressed in the SOC model or to have maintained consistent condom use and were less likely to have relapsed or stayed in the precontemplation stage. Among the women at high risk, exposure to the enhanced intervention was associated with being at a higher SOC and being less likely to relapse relative to the standard intervention group. Generally, these results suggest that stage-based interventions with high-risk and HIV+ women can promote movement along the SOC toward consistent condom use with main male sex partners.

Catania, Kegeles, and Coates (1990) have proposed a three-stage model to examine the psychosocial processes involved with behavioral changes necessary to prevent transmission of HIV. The AIDS risk reduction model (ARRM) is a combination of perceptual and attitudinal factors in the theory of reasoned action (Ajzen & Fishbein, 1980), social-cognitive theory (Bandura, 1986), and the health belief model (Rosenstock, 1990). In the ARRM, risk behavior change is viewed as a three-stage process: (1) recognition and labeling of one's sexual behaviors as high risk for contracting HIV, (2) making a commitment to reduce high-risk behaviors, and (3) seeking and engaging in strategies to obtain these goals. Generally, people engaging in high-risk behaviors may or may not perceive that their behavior presents a possible source of HIV infection. If they do, they may decide to change their behavior and act on this decision.

In addition to modeling change behaviors over time, the ARRM helps identify where in the change process particular types of public health messages may have their greatest impact on those at risk (Catana et al., 1990). Messages focusing on behaviors that lead to HIV transmission are hypothesized to influence labeling of high-risk behaviors as problematic (Stage 1). The reluctance of many mass media health efforts to move beyond this type of message suggests that the major influence of these efforts will be on Stage 1 outcomes. Influencing Stage 2 outcomes (commitment to change) was hypothesized to occur through education in the form of specific instructions focusing on the health utility and enjoyment of various risk-reducing behaviors (i.e., using condoms). Programs that are hypothesized to affect Stage 3 outcomes include those that focus specifically on how to achieve beneficial change and that inform people as to where they could get help to accomplish this task (Kowalewski, Longshore, & Anglin, 1994).

To successfully move from behavior change theory to the implementation of a psychosocial intervention demands careful consideration of the context in which individuals conduct their everyday lives. Therefore, understanding the mechanisms through which individuals change their behaviors and the social contexts where they may engage in risky behaviors is central to successful HIV intervention efforts. For example, the influence of peer leaders and outreach has been identified as an important leverage point for community-based interventions seeking to reduce the amount of risky sexual behavior taking place in the gay male community (Kegeles, & Hart, 1998; Kegeles, Hays, Pollack, & Coates, 1999). Successful injected drug use interventions have recognized that the provision of clean needles through syringe exchange programs can prevent HIV transmission without encouraging illegal drug use (National Research Council and Institute of Medicine, 1994; Office of Technology Assessment, 1995). Prevention among those 25 yr of age and younger often involves sex education that can take two forms. Abstinence-only programs typically promote abstinence from sex before marriage or a committed relationship and generally avoid specific discussions of contraception. Comprehensive sexuality education often encourages abstinence but also includes discussion of contraceptives, condom use, abortion, and homosexuality. Two recent reviews examined the evidence supporting abstinence-only and comprehensive sexuality programs in the United States and Canada (Kirby, 2001; Manlove, Romano-Papillo, and Ikramullah, 2004). Both reviews demonstrated that comprehensive sexuality education effectively promoted abstinence as well as other protective behaviors. In contrast, Kirby found no scientific evidence that abstinence-only programs demonstrate efficacy in delaying initiation of sexual intercourse. Although federal support for abstinence-only programs has grown rapidly since 1996 in the United States, existing evaluations of such programs either do not meet standards for scientific evaluation or lack evidence of efficacy in delaying initiation of intercourse (Santelli et al., 2006).

A common thread that ties successful prevention interventions together is that they are often tailored to reach specific audiences. The one size fits all approach to prevention often fails to reach those groups at greatest risk, including young people of color and gay men. In 1999, the CDC released a compendium of tested, proven-effective HIV prevention interventions, most of them targeted at specific groups (CDC, 1999a). Further, HIV prevention interventions are most effective when they reach people on multiple levels (Coates & Collins, 1999). For example, the impact of a safe sex initiative may be greatly reduced if participants leave the program and reenter communities where there is no social support for maintaining risk reduction behaviors.

Psychotherapeutic intervention approaches have been successful in reducing depression, denial coping (Carrico et al., 2006), and stress, and increasing protective factors such as social support, positive states of mind, and medication adherence (Carrico et al., 2005). Specifically, cognitive-behavioral stress management interventions have been shown to be particularly effective in improving medication adherence by affecting critical factors such as social support, mood, and coping in PLWHIV (e.g., Carrico, 2005). Further, stress-management techniques such as relaxation training and imagery, cognitive restructuring, coping skills training, and interpersonal skills training may reduce anxiety, depression, and social isolation in PLWHIV by lowering physical tension and increasing a sense of control and self-efficacy (Antoni, 2003).

CASE EXAMPLE

For Steve, a recent college graduate who had grown up in the Midwest, moving to San Francisco to live the "gay boy life" seemed like the thing to do in 1978. Working at a trendy restaurant staffed primarily by gay men, he formed some of the deepest friendships of his life. Little prepared him for the loss he would experience in the coming years, as AIDS took its toll on the gay community. It began with an article in the *San Francisco Chronicle* in 1981: Six gay men in Los Angeles had contracted a strange disease. Over the next weeks and months, more and more articles and cases surfaced, and the news media began calling the disease the "gay cancer." As the news became more prominent, Steve became more scared, and as it moved to the front page, Steve stopped reading the newspaper altogether. There was no cure, and everyone with the disease had a short time to live. Many theories surfaced, from government plots, to bioweapons tested on gay men, to contaminated products that gay men used. It took 5 years for researchers to figure out that the disease was a sexually transmitted virus. By then, Steve had watched this disease go from people in the newspaper to people he knew: people he worked with, people in his neighborhood, friends.

While addressing the health of others, he was in denial about his own situation. He knew he had done everything that gay men did, but he tried to talk himself out of believing he could be infected. He tried to convince himself that gay behavior was the cause, and so he tried to give it up. He liked women, too, so he switched to straight sex because he thought it would protect him. He became involved with a woman, and after 4 years he wanted to marry her. Before marrying they decided to get tested for HIV. They went to an anonymous clinic and waited in a huge room packed with over 100 people. The pretest counseling consisted of a video with the message that you should hope you don't have AIDS because there is no cure. They waited for 2 weeks before returning for the results. His girlfriend was negative. Steve was nearly the last to get his results that day. The counselor asked him if he wanted to know his results, taunting him and telling him that once he knows, he can never "not know." Then, with a big grin on his face, he told Steve he was positive. As prepared as Steve was (he went in thinking he was positive), he was unprepared for the impact—it hit him like a ton of bricks.

Steve had seen and observed many friends get ill. He had taken care of friends. He had lost friends. He knew what was ahead. He went home and spent a month in bed crying and waiting to die. His first CD4-count test (October 1987) indicated he had been positive for about 6–7 years (since 1981), and they estimated he had 18 months to live. He was devastated, but began getting his affairs in order. When he did not die he ended his relationship to protect his girlfriend and went to law school as a diversion. He knew he was living on borrowed time.

His closest friends and roommates continued falling ill and failing. As he lost roommates, he moved new roommates into his five-bedroom flat. Most poignantly, he cared for his good friend, Johnny. Together they were able to find humor in the situation, doing a Lucy and Ethel routine to keep their spirits up. Steve lost Johnny in January of 1991; he died in Steve's car on the way to the emergency room. This had a profound impact on Steve—he could not keep moving people in just to watch them die. Although San Francisco was one of the few places you could get treatment, Steve knew that treatment was not enough. One of the most horrible aspects he had witnessed was the secrecy surrounding AIDS. Many can't tell anyone who matters. Because of the stigma, people deprive themselves of support. There is guilt in telling and in not telling. He consulted with a health psychologist, who helped Steve problem-solve means to cope with the level of stress he was currently experiencing. With the therapist, he surveyed the scope of social support available to him and the degree of stress he was experiencing, given the loss and ongoing losses of friends. He decided to return home to his family. Steve was lucky to have family that knew his HIV status and were supportive.

When he returned to the rural community he put his energy into redoing his house and the farm, planting flowers that were already fully grown because he could not wait for them to grow. He was not going to assume he would see anything. The process was wonderful therapy for him.

However, he began to get sicker, and by 1996 he was showing symptoms and wasting—he knew he was failing.

His normal weight had been 190, and in January of 1996 he was down to 117. There were no doctors in the rural area where he lived; he traveled to a doctor referred by a friend. The nurses would close the glass between Steve and themselves and talk to him through closed glass out of fear. Steve heard about a doctor about 185 miles away. He went there for treatment for 5 years until there was a doctor in his area who could treat him. This new doctor assessed him and signed him up for some studies in Evanston. Participating in the studies was Steve's way of giving his life meaning, or giving something back. He spent months in research hospitals in medication studies and met lots of people. He saw that he was not alone, took comfort from others, and made lasting friendships. In 1996 work started with triple combination therapy, and Steve's doctor put him on it immediately. After 5 weeks on the new therapy, his t-cell count, which had dipped to 12, was up to 325. His weight came back. Now he had to exercise and eat modestly to avoid gaining too much.

Steve remembers both dates—the date they told him he was going to die, and then, after 5 years of preparing to die, the date he was told he was not going to die. It still has an impact on him. Each time a regimen fails (he has been through several and become resistant) he thinks he is going to die. It is a roller coaster of living and dying. At these points Steve utilizes the health psychologist in order to discuss the fear and uncertainty, to refocus his coping efforts, to utilize both guided imagery and diaphragmatic breathing to reduce the stress-related arousal, and to continue focusing on the good he has gotten out of his experience. He "would not trade it." AIDS has led him to think about the beautiful things in life and brought him to realize what is important. He has been lucky and blessed in friendship, the people he has known and lost, those who stuck with him, his family. It has not been all dark and gloomy. Steve, here, evidences what Lazarus (1999) and others have referred to as positive reinterpretation, as a coping strategy.

Steve decided, once again, to consult with a therapist that was experienced with HIV/AIDS. This therapy gave him the context to discuss existential issues related to his life-and-death experiences and to reflect on his choices of plans for his life and relationships. Together, they discussed Steve's delight at the response he encountered when he returned to the community of his origin. Steve's decision to come back home to a small community proved to be a good one for him. In San Francisco he was surrounded by the disease but felt he had no way to fight it. But in his hometown there was no strong voice for HIV. He discussed with the therapist the options for taking an active coping stance, not just for himself, but for a larger social impact. After surveying the risks and benefits with the therapist regarding disclosure of his HIV status on a larger scale, and the satisfaction that the politically active strategy would bear, he decided to become a public voice for understanding HIV/AIDS. Becoming that voice gave him a cause and a reason to keep going. He also found out that he misjudged how people would react to him. He thought he would not be accepted, but he can truly say there is no one who knows who has not been supportive. He has received kindness, love, and support from people he would not have expected it from. In his job, working as an AIDS activist, he feels good about connecting with people going through the same thing because he can talk them through it in a way that others cannot. As his voice became stronger, his passion for helping others with HIV led him to become active at the state level, serving as his county's coordinator of HIV prevention and outreach.

Steve has a strong, loving relationship and an ever-increasing circle of friends that he is not sure he would have had if he had stayed in San Francisco. He keeps hoping his medications will not fail again, and he has faith that there will always be something new. Steve is now 50, has been living with AIDS for 25 years, and sees every birthday as a blessing.

CONCLUSION

Twenty-five years have passed since the first cases of what was to become known as AIDS were diagnosed. Although no cure has been found, great strides have been made in understanding the causes, consequences, and treatment of this virus. Although the search for the cure continues, through prevention and treatment break-throughs, the toll of AIDS has been reduced in the United States. Challenges still remain in the search for a cure, development of nonresistant pharmaceuticals, prevention of new cases, and most notably, in stemming the tide of AIDS in the developing world.

REFERENCES

Ajzen, I., & Fishbein, M. (1980). *Understanding attitudes and predicting social behavior.* Englewood-Cliffs, NJ: Prentice Hall.

Altice, F. L., & Friedland, G. H. (1998). The era of adherence to HIV therapy. *Annals of Internal Medicine, 129,* 503–504.

Altice, F. L., Mostashari, F., & Friedland, G. H. (2001). Trust and acceptance of and adherence to antiretroviral therapy. *Journal of Acquired Immune Deficiency Syndromes, 28,* 47–58.

Anderson, J. R. (2001). HIV and reproduction. In J. R. Anderson (Ed.), *A guide to the clinical care of women with HIV* (pp. 213–273). Washington, DC: U.S. Department of Health and Human Services, Health Resources and Services Administration.

Antoni, M. H. (2003). Stress management and psychoneuroimmunology in HIV infection. *CNS Spectrums, 8,* 40–51.

Antoni, M. H., Baggett, L., Ironson, G., LaPerriere, A., August, S., Klimas, N., et al. (1991). Cognitive behavioral stress management intervention buffers distress responses and immunologic changes following notification of HIV-1 seropositivity. *Journal of Consulting and Clinical Psychology, 59,* 906–915.

Antoni, M. H., Cruess, S., Lutgendorf, S., Kumar, M., Ironson, G., Klimas, N., et al. (2000). Cognitive-behavioral stress management intervention effects on anxiety, 24-hr urinary norepinephrine output, and T-cytoxic/suppressor cells over time among symptomatic HIV-infected gay men. *Journal of Consulting and Clinical Psychology, 68,* 31–45.

Avants, S. K., Margolin, A., & Warburton, L. A. (2001). Predictors of non-adherence to HIV-related medication regimens during methadone stabilization. *American Journal of Addictions, 10,* 69–78.

Aversa, S. L., & Kimberlin, C. (1996). Psychosocial aspects of antiretroviral medication use among HIV patients. *Patient Education and Counseling, 29,* 207–219.

Bamberger, J. D., Unick, J., Klein, P., Fraser, M., Chesney, M., & Katz, M. H. (2000). Helping the urban poor stay with antiretroviral HIV drug therapy. *American Journal of Public Health, 90,* 699–701.

Bandura, A. (1986). *Social foundations of thought and action: A social cognitive theory.* Englewood Cliffs, NJ: Prentice Hall.

Bangsberg, D. R., Moss, A. R., Deeks, S. G. (2004). Paradoxes of adherence and drug resistance to HIV antiretroviral therapy. *Journal of Antimicrobial Chemotherapy, 53,* 696–699.

Bartlett, J. A. (2002). Addressing the challenges of adherence. *Journal of AIDS, 29,* S2–S10.

Basso, M. R., & Bornstein, R. A. (2000). Estimated premorbid intelligence mediates neurobehavioral change in individuals infected with HIV across 12 months. *Journal of Clinical & Experimental Neuropsychology, 22*(2), 208–219.

Bauer, L. O., & Shanley, J. D. (2006). ASPD blunts the effects of HIV and antiretroviral treatment on event-related brain potentials. *Neuropsychobiology, 53,* 17–25.

Becker, M. H., Heafner, D. P., Kasl, S. V., Kirscht, J. P., Maiman, L. A., & Rosenstock, I. M. (1977).

Selected psychosocial models and correlates of individual health-related behaviors. *Medical Care, 15*(Suppl. 5), 27–46.

Berg, M. B., Mimiaga, M. J., & Safren, S. A. (2004). Mental health concerns of HIV-infected gay and bisexual men seeking mental health services: An observational study. *AIDS Patient Care and STDs, 18*, 635–643.

Bergey, E. J., Cho, M. I., Hammarskjold, M. L., Rekosh, D., Levine, M. J., Blumberg, B. M., et al., (1993). Aggregation of human immunodeficiency virus type 1 by human salivary secretions. *Critical Review of Oral Biological Medicine, 4*, 467–474.

Berrios, D., Hearst, N., Coates, T., Stall, R., Hudes, E., Turner, H., Eversley, R., & Catania, J. (1993). HIV antibody testing among those at risk for HIV infection: The National AIDS Behavior Survey (NABS). *Journal of the American Medical Association, 270*, 1576–1580.

Bing, E. G., Burnam, M. A., Longshore, D., Fleishman, J. A., Sherbourne, C. D., London, A. S., et al. (2001). Psychiatric disorders and drug use among human immunodeficiency virus-infected adults in the United States. *Archives of General Psychiatry, 58*, 721–728.

Bing, E. G., Kilbourne, A. M., Brooks, R. A., Lazarus, E. F., & Senak, M. (1999). Protease inhibitor use among a community sample of people with HIV disease. *Journal of Acquired Immune Deficiency Syndromes, 20*, 474–480.

Bottonari, K. A., Roberts, J. E., Ciesla, J. A., & Hewett, R. G. (2005). Life stress and adherence to antiretroviral therapy among HIV-positive individuals: A preliminary investigation. *AIDS Patient Care and STDs, 19*, 719–727.

Bouhnik, A. D., Chesney, M., Carrieri, P., Gallais, H., Moreau, J., Moatti, J. P., et al. (2002). Nonadherence among HIV-infected injecting drug users: The impact of social instability. *Journal of Acquired Immune Deficiency Syndromes, 31*, S149–S153.

Bozzette, S. A., Joyce, G., McCaffrey, D. F., Leibowitz, A. A., Morton, S. C., Berry, S. H., et al. (2001). Expenditures for care of HIV-infected patients in the era of highly active antiretroviral therapy. *New England Journal of Medicine, 344*, 817–823.

Broadhead, R. S., Heckathorn, D. D., Altice, F. L., Hulst, Y., van Carbone, M., Friedland, G. H., et al. (2002). Increasing drug users' adherence to HIV treatment: Results of a peer-driven intervention feasibility study. *Social Science and Medicine, 55*, 235–246.

Brody, S. (1995). Patients misrepresenting their risk factors of AIDS. *International Journal of STD & AIDS, 6*, 392–398.

Caceres, C. F., & van Griensven, G. (1994). Male homosexual transmission of HIV-1. *AIDS, 8*, 1051–1061.

Carey, M. P., Weinhardt, L. S., & Carey, K. B. (1995). Prevalence of infection with HIV among the seriously mentally ill: Review of research and implications for practice. *Professional Psychology: Research and Practice, 26*, 262–268.

Carrico, A. W., Antoni, M. H., Duran, R. E., Ironson, G., Penedo, F., Fletcher, M. A., et al. (2006). Reductions in depressed mood and denial coping during cognitive behavioral stress management with HIV-positive gay men treated with HAART. *Annals of Behavioral Medicine, 31*, 1155–1164.

Carrico, A. W., Antoni, M. H., Pereira, D. B., Fletcher, M. A., Klimas, N., Lechner, S. C., et al. (2005). Cognitive behavioral stress management effects on mood, social support, and a marker of antiviral immunity are maintained up to 1 year in HIV-infected gay men. *International Journal of Behavioral Medicine, 12*, 218–226.

Catania, J. C., Kegeles, S. M., & Coates, T. J. (1990). Towards an understanding of risk behavior: An AIDS risk reduction model (ARRM). *Health Education Quarterly, 17*, 53–72.

Catz, S. L., Kelly, J. A., Bogart, L. M., Bentsch, E. G., & McAuliffe, T. L. (2000). Patterns, correlates, and barriers to medication adherence among persons prescribed new treatments for HIV disease. *Health Psychology, 19*, 124–133.

Centers for Disease Control and Prevention (1981). Pneumocystis pneumonia—Los Angeles. *MMWR, 30,* 250–252.

Centers for Disease Control and Prevention (1986). Classification system for human T-lymphotropic virus type III/lymphadenopathy-associated virus infections. *MMWR, 35,* 334.

Centers for Disease Control and Prevention (1992). 1993 revised classification system for HIV infection and expanded surveillance case definition for AIDS among adolescents and adults. *MMWR, 41,* 961–962.

Centers for Disease Control and Prevention (1999a). *Compendium of HIV prevention interventions with evidence of effectiveness.* Retrieved November, 1999, at http://www.cdc.gov/hiv/pubs/hivcompendium/hivcompendium.pdf

Centers for Disease Control and Prevention (1999b). Guidelines for national human immunodeficiency virus case surveillance, including monitoring for human immunodeficiency virus infection and acquired immunodeficiency syndrome. *MMWR, 48,* 1–28.

Centers for Disease Control and Prevention. (2001). Revised recommendations for HIV screening of pregnant women. *MMWR, 1,* 59–85.

Centers for Disease Control and Prevention (2005). HIV/AIDS surveillance report: HIV infection and AIDS in the United States, 2004. *CDC, 16,* 1–46.

Centers for Disease Control and Prevention (2006a). Cases of HIV infection and AIDS in the United States, by race/ethnicity, 2000–2004. *HIV/AIDS Surveillance Supplemental Report, 12,* 1–36.

Centers for Disease Control and Prevention (2006b). Racial/ethnic disparities in diagnoses of HIV/AIDS. *MMWR, 55,* 121–125.

Chesney, M. (2003). Adherence to HAART regimens. *AIDS Patient Care and STDs, 17,* 169–177.

Chesney, M. A., Folkman, S., & Chambers, D. (1996). Coping effectiveness training for men living with HIV: Preliminary findings. *International Journal of STD and AIDS, 7* (Suppl. 2), 75–83.

Chesney, M. A., Morin, M., & Sherr, L. (2000). Adherence to HIV combination therapy. *Social Science Medicine, 50,* 1599–1605.

Ciesla, J. A., & Roberts, J. E. (2001). Meta-analysis of the relationship between HIV infection and risk for depressive disorders. *American Journal of Psychiatry, 158,* 725–730.

Coates, T., & Collins, C. (1999). HIV prevention: We don't need to wait for a vaccine. In M. D. Glantz and C. R. Hartel (Eds.), *Drug abuse: Origins and interventions* (pp. 309–330). Washington, DC: American Psychological Association.

Cole, S. W., Kemeny, M. E., Taylor, S. E., Visscher, B. R., & Fahey, J. L. (1996). Accelerated course of human immunodeficiency virus infection in gay men who conceal their homosexual identity. *Psychosomatic Medicine, 58,* 219–231.

Cook, J. A., Grey, D., Burke, J., Cohen, M. H., Gurtman, A. C., Richardson, J. L., et al. (2004). Depressive symptoms and AIDS-related mortality among a multisite cohort of HIV-positive women. *American Journal of Public Health, 94,* 1133–1140.

Côté, J. K., & Pepler, C. (2005). Cognitive coping intervention for acutely ill HIV-positive men. *Journal of Clinical Nursing, 14,* 321–326.

Cuffel, B. J., Alford, J., Fischer, E., & Owen, R. R. (1996). Awareness of illness in schizophrenia and outpatient treatment adherence. *Journal of Nervous and Mental Disease, 184,* 653–659.

Cutrona, C. E., & Russell, D. W. (1987). The provisions of social relationships and adaptation to stress. In W. H. Jones & D. Perlman (Eds.), *Advances in personal relationships* (pp. 37–67). Greenwich, CT: JAI.

Delahanty, D. L., Bogart, L. M., & Figler, J. L. (2004). Posttraumatic stress disorder symptoms, salivary cortisol, medication adherence, and CD4 levels in HIV-positive individuals. *AIDS Care, 16,* 247–260.

De Vincenzi, I. (1994). A longitudinal study of human immunodeficiency virus transmission by heterosexual partners. *New England Journal of Medicine, 331,* 341–346.

DiClemente, C. C. (1993). Changing addictive behaviors: A process perspective. *Current Directions in Psychological Science, 2,* 101–105.

Downs, A. M., & De Vincenzi, I. (1996). Probabiltiy of heterosexual HIV transmission of HIV: Relationships to the number of unprotected sexual contacts. *Journal of AIDS and Human Retrovirology, 11,* 388–395.

Feinberg, J., & Maenza, J. (2001). Primary medical care. In J. R. Anderson (Ed.), *A guide to the clinical care of women with HIV* (pp. 77–137). Washington, DC: U.S. Department of Health and Human Services, Health Resources and Services Administration.

Fellay, J., Boubaker, K., Ledergeber, B., et al. (2001). Prevalence of adverse events associated with potent antiretroviral treatment: Swiss HIV Cohort Study. *Lancet, 358,* 1322–1327.

Fisher, W. A., Fisher, J. D., & Rye, B. J. (1995). Understanding and promoting AIDS-preventative behavior. *Health Psychology, 14,* 255–264.

Freedberg, K. A., Losina, E., Weinstein, M. C., Paltiel, A. D., Cohen, C. J., Seage, G. R., et al. (2001). The cost effectiveness of combination antiretroviral therapy for HIV disease. *New England Journal of Medicine, 344,* 824–831.

Gielen, A. C., Fogarty, L. A., Armstrong, K., Green, B. M., Cabral, R., Milstein, B., et al. (2001). Promoting condom use with main partners: A behavioral intervention trial for women. *AIDS and Behavior, 5,* 193–204.

Gifford, A. L., & Groessl, E. J. (2002). Chronic disease self-management and adherence to HIV medications. *Journal of Acquired Immune Deficiency Syndromes, 31,* S163–S166.

Glynn, M. K., & Rhodes, P. (2005, June). Estimated HIV prevalence in the United States at the end of 2003. Paper presented at the 2005 National HIV Prevention Conference, Atlanta.

Goodkin, K., Fuchs, I., Feaster, D., Leeka, J., & Rishel, D. D. (1992). Life stressors and coping style are associated with immune measures in HIV-1 infection: A preliminary report. *International Journal of Psychiatry in Medicine, 22*(2), 155–172.

Gordillo, V., del Amo, J., Soriano, V., & Gonzalez-Lahoz, J. (1999). Sociodemographic and psychological variables influencing adherence to antiretroviral therapy. *AIDS, 13,* 1763–1769.

Green, G. (1995). Attitudes towards people with HIV: Are they as stigmatizing as people with HIV perceive them to be? *Social Science & Medicine, 41,* 557–568.

Green, J., Saveanu, R., & Bornstein, R. (2004). The effect of previous alcohol abuse on cognitive function in HIV infection. *American Journal of Psychiatry, 161,* 249–254.

Greenblatt, R. M., & Hessol, N. A. (2001). Epidemiology and natural history of HIV infection in women. In J. R. Anderson (Ed.), *A guide to the clinical care of women with HIV* (pp. 1–32). Washington, DC: U.S. Department of Health and Human Services, Health Resources and Services Administration.

Greenwald, J. L., Burstein, G. R., Pincus, J., & Branson, B. (2006). A rapid review of rapid antibody tests. *Current Infections Disease Reports, 8,* 125–131.

Gross, R., Bilker, W. B., Friedman, H. M., & Strom, B. L. (2001). Effects of adherence to newly initiated antiretroviral therapy on plasma viral load. *AIDS, 15,* 2109–2117.

Haverkos, H. W., & Battjes, R. J. (1992). Female to male transmission of HIV. *JAMA, 268,* 1855–1856.

Health Resources and Services Administration. (HRSA; n.d.). Ryan White CARE ACT: Purpose of the CARE Act. Retrieved June 1, 2006, from http://hab.hrsa.gov/history/purpose.htm

Heaton, R. K., Grant, I., Butters, N., White, D. A., Kirson, D., Atkinson, J. H., et al. (1995). The HNRC 500—neuropsychology of HIV infection at different disease stages. HIV Neurobehavioral Research Center. *Journal of the International Neuropsychological Society, 1,* 231–251.

Heckman, T. G., Anderson, E. S., Sikkema, K. J., Kochman, A., Kalichman, S. C., & Anderson, T. (2004). Persons living with HIV disease enrolled in a telephone-delivered, coping improvement group intervention. *Health Psychology, 23,* 94–100.

Heckman, T. G., Kochman, A., Sikkema, K. J., Kalichman, S. C., Masten, J., Bergholte, J., et al. (2001). A pilot coping improvement intervention for late middle-aged and older adults living with HIV/AIDS in the USA. *AIDS Care, 13,* 129–139.

Herbert, T. B., & Cohen, S. (1993). Stress and immunity in humans: a meta-analytic review. *Psychosomatic Medicine, 55,* 364–379.

Himelhoch, S., & Medoff, D. R. (2005). Efficacy of antidepressant medication among HIV positive individuals with depression: A systematic review and meta-analysis. *AIDS Patient Care and STDs, 19,* 813–822.

Hinkin, C. H., Castellon, S. A., Durvasula, R. S., Hardy, D. J., Lam, M. N., Mason, K. I., et al. (2002). Medication adherence among HIV+ adults. *Neurology, 59,* 1944–1950.

Hoffman, M. A. (1991). Counseling the HIV-infected client: A psychosocial model for assessment and intervention. *The Counseling Psychologist, 19,* 467–542.

Ickovics, J. R., Hamburger, M. E., Vlahov, D., Schoenbaum, E. E., Schuman, P., Boland, R. J., et al. (2001). Mortality, CD4 cell count decline, and depressive symptoms among HIV-seropositive women: Longitudinal analysis from the HIV Epidemiology Research Study. *Journal of the American Medical Association, 285,* 1466–1474.

Ingersoll, K. (2004). The impact of psychiatric symptoms, drug use, and medication regimen on non-adherence to HIV treatment. *AIDS Care, 16,* 199–211.

Ironson, G., Balbin, E., Stuetzle, R., Fletcher, M. A., O'Cleirigh, C., Laurenceau, J. P., et al. (2005). Dispositional optimism and the mechanisms by which it predicts slower disease progression in HIV: Proactive behavior, avoidant coping, and depression. *International Journal of Behavioral Medicine, 12,* 86–97.

Ironson, G., Friedman, A., Klimas, N., Antoni, M., Fletcher, M. A., LaPerriere, A., et al. (1994). Distress, denial, and low adherence to behavioral interventions predict faster disease progression in gay men infected with human immunodeficiency virus. *International Journal of Behavioral Medicine, 1,* 90–105.

Jacobsberg, L., Frances, A., & Perry, S. (1995). Axis II diagnoses among volunteers for HIV testing and counseling. *American Journal of Psychiatry, 152,* 1222–1224.

Jia, H., Uphold, C. R., Wu, S., Reid, K., Findley, K., & Duncan, P. R. (2004). Health-related quality of life among men with HIV infection: Effects of social support, coping, and depression. *AIDS Patient Care and STDs, 18,* 594–603.

Johnson, J. G., Williams, J. B., Rabkin, J. G., Goetz, R. R., & Remien, R. H. (1995). Axis I psychiatric symptoms associated with HIV infection and personality disorder. *American Journal of Psychiatry, 152,* 551–554.

Joint United Nations Programme on HIV/AIDS (UNIAIDS). (2005, December). *AIDS epidemic update: December 2005.* Geneva: UNAIDS/World Health Organization.

Kalichman, S. C. (1998). *Preventing AIDS: A sourcebook for behavioral interventions.* Mahwah, NJ: Lawrence Erlbaum.

Kalichman, S. C., DiMarco, M., Austin, J., Luke, W., & DiFonzo, K. (2003). Stress, social support, and HIV-status disclosure to family and friends among HIV-positive men and women. *Journal of Behavioral Medicine, 26,* 315–332.

Kegeles, S. M., & Hart, G. J. (1998). Recent HIV prevention interventions for gay men: Individual, small-group and community-level interventions. *AIDS, 12,* 209–215.

Kegeles, S. M., Hays, R. B., Pollack, L., & Coates, T. J. (1999). Mobilizing young gay men for HIV prevention: A two community study. *AIDS, 13,* 1753–1762.

Kelley, J. L., & Petry, N. M. (2000). HIV risk behaviors in male substance abusers with and without antisocial personality disorder. *Journal of Substance Abuse Treatment, 19,* 59–66.

Kelly, J. A., Murphy, D. A., Bahr, G. R., Kalichman, S. C., Morgan, M. G., Stevenson, L. Y., et al. (1993). Outcomes of cognitive-behavioral and support group brief therapies for depressed persons diagnosed with HIV infection. *American Journal of Psychiatry, 150,* 1679–1686.

Kilbourne, A. M., Justice, A. C., & Rabeneck, L. (2001). General medical and psychiatric comorbidity. *Journal of Clinical Epidemiology, 54*(Suppl.), S22–S28.

Kirby, D. (2001). *Emerging answers: Research findings on programs to reduce teen pregnancy.* Washington, DC: National Campaign to Prevent Teen Pregnancy, 2001.

Klatt, E. C. (2005). *Pathology of AIDS, Version 16.* Retrieved May 23, 2006, from http://medstat.med.utah.edu/WebPath/TUTORIAL/AIDS/AIDS.html

Kleeberger, C. A., Buechner, J., Palella, F., Detels, R., Riddler, S., Godfrey R., et al. (2004). Changes in adherence to highly active antiretroviral therapy medications in the Multicenter AIDS Cohort Study. *AIDS, 18,* 683–688.

Kleeberger, C. A., Phair, J. P., & Strathdee, S. A. (2001). Determinants of heterogeneous adherence to HIV antiretroviral therapies in the Multicenter AIDS Cohort Study. *Journal of Acquired Immune Deficiency Syndromes, 26,* 82–92.

Klein, D., Hurley, L. B., Merrill, D., & Quesenberry, C. P. (2003). Review of medical encounters in the 5 years before a diagnosis of HIV-1 infection: Implications for early detection. *Journal of Acquired Immune Deficiency Syndromes, 32,* 143–153.

Komiti, A., Judd, F., Grech, P., Mijch, A., Hoy, J., Williams, B., et al. (2003). Depression in people living with HIV/AIDS attending primary care and outpatient clinics. *Australian and New Zealand Journal of Psychiatry, 37,* 70–77.

Kowalewski, M. R., Longshore, D., & Anglin, M. D. (1994). The AIDS risk reduction model: Examining intentions to use condoms among injection drug users. *Journal of Applied Psychology, 24,* 2002–2027.

Lauby, J. L., Semaan, S., Cohen, A., Leviton, L., Gielen, A., Pulley, L., et al. (1998). Self-efficacy, decisional balance and stages of change for condom use among women at risk for HIV infection. *Health Education Research, 13,* 343–356.

Lawrence, D. M., & Major, E. O. (2002). HIV-1 and the brain: Connections between HIV-1–associated dementia, neuropathology and neuroimmunology. *Microbes Infect, 4,* 301–308.

Lazarus, R. S. (1999). *Stress and emotion: A new synthesis.* New York: Springer Publishing Company.

Lazarus, R. S., & Folkman, S. (1984). *Stress, appraisal, and coping.* New York: Springer.

Ledergerber, B., Egger, M., Oprovil, M., et al. (1999). Clinical progression and virologic failure on highly active antiretroviral therapy in HIV-1 patients: A prospective cohort study. *Lancet, 353,* 863–868.

Leiker, J., Taub, D., & Gast, J. (1995). The stigma of AIDS: Persons with AIDS and social distance. *Deviant Behavior, 16,* 333–351.

Leserman, J., Petitto, J. M., Gu, H., Gaynes, B. N., Barroso, J., Golden, R., et al. (2002). Progression to AIDS, a clinical AIDS condition and mortality: Psychosocial and physiological predictors. *Psychological Medicine, 32,* 1059–1073.

Little, S. J., Holte, S., Routy, J., Daar, E. S., Markowitz, M., Collier, A. C., et al. (2002). Antiretroviral drug resistance among patients recently infected with HIV. *New England Journal of Medicine, 347,* 385–394.

Llorente, A. M., Miller, E. N., D'Elia, L. F., Selnes, O. A., Wesch, J., Becker, J. T., et al. (1998). Slowed information processing in HIV-1 disease. *Journal of Clinical Experimental Neuropsychology, 20,* 60–72.

Lutgendorf, S. K., Starr, K., McCabe, P., Antoni, M. H., Ironson, G., Klimas, N., et al. (1997). Cognitive behavioral stress management decreases dysphoric mood and herpes simplex virus type 2 antibody titers in symptomatic HIV-seropositive gay men. *Journal of Consulting and Clinical Psychology, 65*, 31–43.

Lyketsos, C. G., Hanson, A. L., Fishman, M., Rosenblatt, A., McHugh, P. R., & Treisman, G. J. (1993). Manic syndrome early and late in the course of HIV. *American Journal of Psychiatry, 150*, 326–327.

Maj, M., Satz, P., Janssen, R., Zaudig, M., Starace, F., D'Elia, L., et al. (1994). WHO neuropsychiatric AIDS study, cross-sectional phase II. Neuropsychological and neurological findings. *Archives of General Psychiatry, 51*, 51–61.

Manlove, J., Romano-Papillo, A., & Ikramullah, E. (2004). *Not yet: Programs to delay first sex among teens.* Washington, DC: National Campaign to Prevent Teen Pregnancy, 2004.

Mannheimer, S., Friedland, G., Matts, J., Child, C., & Chesney, M. A. (2002). The consistency of adherence to antiretroviral therapy predicts biologic outcomes for HIV persons in clinical trials. *Clinical Infectious Diseases, 34*, 1115–1121.

Mellins, C. A., Havens, J. F., McCaskill, E., Leu, C. S., Brudney, K., & Chesney, M. (2002). Mental health, substance use and disclosure are significantly associated with the medical treatment adherence of HIV-infected mothers. *Psychology, Health and Medicine, 7*, 451–460.

Mellins, C. A., Kang, E., Leu, C. S., Havens, J. F. & Chesney, M. A. (2003). Longitudinal study of mental health and psychosocial predictors of medical treatment adherence in mothers living with HIV disease. *AIDS Patient Care and STDs, 17*, 407–416.

Michaels, S. H., Clark, R., & Kissinger, P. (1998). Declining morbidity and mortality among patients with advanced human immunodeficiency virus infection. *New England Journal of Medicine, 339*, 405–406.

Mijch, A. M., Judd, F. K., Lyketsos, C. G., Ellen, S., & Cockram, A. (1999). Secondary mania in patients with HIV infection: Are antiretrovirals protective? *Journal of Neuropsychiatry and Clinical Neuroscience, 11*, 475–480.

Mizuno, Y., Purcell, D. W., Dawson-Rose, C., & Parsons, J. T. (2003). Correlates of depressive symptoms among HIV-positive injection drug users: The role of social support. *AIDS Care, 15*, 689–698.

Mofenson, L. M. (1997). Interaction between timing of perinatal human immunodeficiency virus infection and the design of preventive and therapeutic interventions. *Acta Pediatr Suppl, 491*: 1–9.

Morrison, M. F., Petito, J. M., Have, T. T., Gettes, D. R., Chiapini, M. S., Weber, A. L., et al. (2002). Depressive and anxiety disorders in women with HIV Infection. *American Journal of Psychiatry, 159*, 789–796.

Muma, R. D., Ross, M. W., Parcel, G. S., & Pollard, R. B. (1995). Zidovudine adherence among individuals with HIV infection. *AIDS Care, 7*, 439–447.

Munoz, A., Kirby, A. J., He, Y. D., Margolick, J., Visscher, B., Rinaldo, C., et al. (1995). Long-term survivors with HIV-1 infection: Incubation period and longitudinal patterns of CD4+ lymphocytes. *Journal of Acquired Immune Deficiency Syndromes & Human Retrovirology, 8*, 496–506.

Murphy, D. A., Greenwell, L., & Hoffman, D. (2002). Factors associated with antiretroviral adherence among HIV-infected women with children. *Women & Health, 36*, 97–111.

Murphy, D. A., Marelich, W. D., Hoffman, D., & Steers, W. N. (2004). Predictors of antiretroviral adherence. *AIDS Care, 16*, 471–484.

Murphy, D. A., Roberts, K. J., Martin, D. J., Marelich, W., & Hoffman, D. (2000). Barriers to antiretroviral adherence among HIV-infected adults. *AIDS Patient Care and STDs, 14*, 47–58.

Murphy, D. A., Wilson, C. M., Durako, S. J., Muenz, L. R., & Belzer, M. (2001). Antiretroviral medication adherence among the REACH HIV-infected adolescent cohort. *AIDS Care, 13*, 27–40.

Murri, R., Antinori, A., Ammassari, A., Nappa, S., Orofino, G., Abrescia, N., et al. (2002). Physician estimates of adherence and the patient-physician relationship as a setting to improve adherence to antiretroviral therapy. *Journal of Acquired Immune Deficiency Syndromes, 31,* S158–S162.

Myers, T., Orr, P., Locker, D., & Jackson, E. (1993). Factors affecting gay and bisexual men's decisions and intentions to seek HIV testing decision. *Inquiry, 28,* 226–235.

National Institutes of Health (2005, March). *HIV infection and AIDS: An overview.* Retrieved May 25, 2006, from http://www.niaid.nih.gov/factsheets/hivinf.htm

National Institutes of Health (2006, April). *Treatment of HIV infection.* Retrieved April 25, 2006, from http://www.niaid.nih.gov/factsheets/treat-hiv.htm

National Research Council and Institute of Medicine (1994). *Proceedings, Workshop on Needle Exchange and Bleach Distribution Programs.* Washington, DC: National Academy.

Office of Technology Assessment (1995). *The effectiveness of AIDS prevention efforts.* Washington, DC: Office of Technology Assessment.

Ostrow, D. G., DiFranceisco, W., Chmeil, J., Wagstaff, D. & Wesch, J. (1995). A case control study of human immunodeficiency virus type-1 seroconversion and risk-related behaviors in the Chicago MACS/CCS cohort, 1984–1992. *American Journal of Epidemiology, 142,* 1–10.

Padian, N. S., Shiboski, C. S., & Jewell, N. P. (1991). Female to male transmission of human immunodeficiency virus. *JAMA, 266,* 1664–1667.

Palella, F. J., Delaney, K. M., Moorman, A. C., Loveless, M. O., Fuhrer, J., Satten, G. A., et al. (1998). Declining morbidity and mortality among patients with advanced human immunodeficiency virus infection: HIV outpatient study investigators. *New England Journal of Medicine, 338,* 853–860.

Pereira, D. B., Antoni, M. H., Danielson, A., Simon, T., Efantis-Potter, J., & O'Sullivan, M. (2004). Inhibited interpersonal coping style predicts poorer adherence to scheduled clinic visits in human immunodeficiency virus infected women at risk for cervical cancer. *Annals of Behavioral Medicine, 28,* 195–202.

Perkins, D. O., Davidson, E. J., Leserman, J., Liao, D., & Evans, D. L. (1993). Personality disorder in patients infected with HIV: A controlled study with implications for clinical care. *American Journal of Psychiatry, 150*(2), 309–315.

Perry, S., Bangsberg, D. B., Charlebois, E. D., Clark, R., Karasic, D., Dilley, J., et al. (2002). Depressive symptoms predict adherence, treatment duration and survival in an urban poor cohort. XIV International AIDS Conference, abstract TuPeC4724, Barcelona, Spain.

Prochaska, J. O. (1991). Prescribing to the stages and levels of change. *Psychotherapy, 28,* 463–468.

Prochaska, J. O., DiClemente, C. C., & Norcross, J. C. (1992). In search of how people change: Applications to addictive behaviors. *American Psychologist, 47,* 1102–1114.

Prochaska, J. O., Redding, C. A., & Evers, K. E. (2002). The transtheoretical model and stages of change. In K. Glantz, B. K. Rimer, & F. M. Lewis (Eds.), *Health behavior and health education: Theory, research, and practice* (pp. 99–120). San Francisco: Jossey-Bass.

Quinn, T. C. (1996). Global burden of the HIV pandemic. *Lancet, 348,* 99–106.

Rahav, M., Nuttbrock, L., Rivera, J. J., & Link, B. (1998). HIV infection risks among homeless, mentally ill, chemical misusing men. *Substance Use & Misuse, 33,* 1407–1426.

Reinecke, J., Schmidt, P., & Ajzen, I. (1996). Application of the theory of planned behavior to adolescents' condom use: A panel study. *Journal of Applied Social Psychology, 26,* 749–772.

Richmond, D. D. (1996). Antiretroviral drug resistance: Mechanisms, pathogenesis, clinical significance. *Antiretroviral Chemotherapy, 4,* 383–395.

Rimer, B. K. (1997). Toward an improved behavioral medicine. *Annals of Behavioral Medicine, 19,* 6–10.

Rogers, M. E., Hansen, N. B., Levy, B. R., Tate, D. C., & Sikkema, K. J. (2005). Optimism and coping with loss in bereaved HIV-infected men and women. *Journal of Social & Clinical Psychology, 24*, 341–360.

Rosenberger, P. H., Bornstein, R. A., Nasrallah, H. A., Para, M. F., Whitaker, C. C., Fass, R. J., et al. (1993). Psychopathology in human immunodeficiency virus infection: Lifetime and current assessment. *Comprehensive Psychiatry, 34*, 150–158.

Rosenstock, I. M. (1974). Historical origins of the health beliefs model. *Health Education Monographs, 2*, 328–335.

Rosenstock, I. M. (1990). The health belief model: Explaining health behavior through expectancies. In K. Glanz, F. Lewis, and B. Rimer (Eds.), *Health behavior and education* (pp. 39–62). San Francisco: Jossey-Bass.

Safren, S. A., Gershuny, B. S., & Hendriksen, E. (2003). Symptoms of posttraumatic stress and death anxiety in persons with HIV and medication adherence difficulties. *AIDS Patient Care and STDs, 17*, 657–664.

Sahakian, B. J., Elliott, R., Low, N., Mehta, M., Clark, R. T., Pozniak, A. L. (1995). Neuropsychological deficits in tests of executive function in asymptomatic and symptomatic HIV-1 seropositive men. *Psychological Medicine, 25*, 1233–1246.

Santelli, J., Ott, M. A., Lyon, M., Rogers, J., Summers, D., & Schleifer, R. (2006). Abstinence and abstinence-only education: A review of U.S. policies and programs. *Journal of Adolescent Health, 38*, 72–81.

Satz, P. (1993). Brain reserve capacity on symptom onset after brain injury: A formulation and review of evidence for threshold theory. *Neuropsychology, 7*, 273–295.

Satz, P., Morgenstern, H., Miller, E. N., Selnes, O. A., McArthur, J. C., Cohen, B. A., et al. (1993). Low education as a possible risk factor for early cognitive abnormalities in HIV-1: Findings from the Multicenter AIDS Cohort Study (MACS). *Journal of Acquired Immune Deficiency Syndromes, 6*, 503–511.

Schrager, L. K., Young, J. M., Fowler, M. G., Mathieson, B. J., & Vermund, S. H. (1994). Long-term survivors of HIV-1 infection: Definitions and research challenges. *AIDS, 8*, S95–S108.

Schuman, P., Ohmit, S. E., Moore, J., Schoenbaum, E., Boland, R., Rompalo, A., et al. (2001). Perceived need for and use of mental health services by women living with or at risk of human immunodeficiency virus infection. *Journal of the American Medical Women's Association, 56*, 4–8.

Sewell, D. D. (1996). Schizophrenia and HIV. *Schizophrenia Bulletin, 22*, 465–473.

Sheeran, P., & Orbell, S. (1998). Do intentions predict condom use? Meta-analysis and examination of six moderator variables. *British Journal of Social Psychology, 37*, 231–250.

Siegel, K., Mesagno, F. P., Chen, J., & Christ, G. (1989). Factors distinguishing homosexual males practicing risky and safer sex. *Social Science Medicine, 28*, 561–569.

Sikkema, K. J., Kalichman, S. C., Kelly, J. A., & Koob, J. J. (1995). Group intervention to improve coping with AIDS-related bereavement: Model development and an illustrative clinical example. *AIDS Care, 7*, 463–475.

Simoni, J. M., Frick, P. A., Lockhart, D., & Liebovitz, D. (2002). Mediators of social support and antiretroviral adherence among an indigent population in New York City. *AIDS Patient Care and STDs, 16*, 431–440.

Simoni, J. M., Mason, H. R. C., Marks, G., Ruiz, M. S., & Richardson, J. L. (1995). Women living with HIV: Sexual behaviors and counseling experiences. *Women and Health, 23*, 17–26.

Simoni, J. M., Walters, K. L., & Nero, D. K. (2000). Safer sex relationships among HIV+ women: The role of relationships. *Sex Roles, 42*, 691–708.

Smith, M. Y., Rapkin, B. D., Morrison, A., & Kammerman, S. (1997). Zidovudine adherence in persons with AIDS: The relation of patient beliefs about medication to self-termination of therapy. *Journal of General Internal Medicine, 12*, 216–223.

Starace, F., Ammassari, A., Trotta, M. P., Murri, R., De Longis, P., Izzo, C., et al. (2002). Depression is a risk factor for suboptimal adherence to highly active antiretroviral therapy. *Journal of Acquired Immune Deficiency Syndromes, 31*(Suppl. 3), S136–S139.

Starace, F., Massa, A., Amico, K. R., & Fisher, J. D. (2006). Adherence to antiretroviral therapy: An empirical test of the information-motivation-behavioral skills model. *Health Psychology, 25*, 153–162.

Sterk, C., Theall, K., & Elifson, K. (2003). Effectiveness of an HIV risk reduction intervention among African American women who use crack cocaine. *AIDS Education and Prevention, 15*, 15–32.

Stern, R. A., Silva, S. G., Chaisson, N., & Evans, D. L. (1996). Influence of cognitive reserve on neuropsychological functioning in asymptomatic human immunodeficiency virus-1 infection. *Archives of Neurology, 53*, 148–153.

St. Lawrence, J. S., Eldridge, G. D., Reitman, D., Little, C. E., Shelby, M. C., & Brasfield, T. L. (1998). Factors influencing condom use among African American women: Implications for risk reduction intervention. *American Journal of Community Psychology, 26*, 728.

Stone, V. E., Hogan, J. W., & Schuman, P. (2001). Antiretroviral regimen complexity, self-reported adherence, and HIV patients' understanding of their regimens: Survey of women in the HER study. *Journal of Acquired Immune Deficiency Syndromes, 28*, 124–131.

Strecher, V. J., & Rosenstock, I. M. (1997). The health belief model. In K. Glanz, B. K. Rimer, & F. M. Lewis (Eds.), *Health behavior and health education: Research, theory and practice*. San Francisco: Jossey-Bass.

Tate, D., Paul, R. H., Flanigan, T. P., Tashima, K., Nash, J., Adair, C., et al. (2003). The impact of apathy and depression on quality of life in patients infected with HIV. *AIDS Patient Care and STDs, 17*, 115–120.

Trepanier, L. L., Rourke, S. B, Bayoumi, A. M., Halman, M. H., Krzyzanowski, S., & Power, C. (2005). The impact of neuropsychological impairment and depression on health-related quality of life in HIV-infection. *Journal of Clinical and Experimental Neuropsychology, 27*, 1–15.

Tross, S., & Hirsch, D. A. (1988). Psychological distress and neuropsychological complications of HIV infection and AIDS. *American Psychologist, 43*, 929–934.

Tucker, J. S., Burnam, M. A., Sherbourne, C. D., Kung, F. Y., & Gifford, A. L. (2003). Substance use and mental health correlates of nonadherence to antiretroviral medications in a sample of patients with human immunodeficiency virus infection. *American Journal of Medicine, 114*, 573–580.

Tuldra, A., & Wu, A. W. (2002). Interventions to improve adherence to antiretroviral therapy. *Journal of Acquired Immune Deficiency Syndromes, 31*, S154–S157.

Turner, B. J., Laine, C., Cosler, L., & Hauck, W. W. (2003). Relationship of gender, depression, and health care delivery with antiretroviral adherence in HIV-infected drug users. *Journal of General Internal Medicine, 18*, 248–257.

Uldall, K. K., Palmer, N. B., Whetten, K., & Mellins, C. (2004). Adherence in people living with HIV/AIDS, mental illness, and chemical dependency: A review of the literature. *AIDS Care, 16*, s71–s96.

U.S. Department of Health and Human Services (2006, May). Guidelines for the use of antiretroviral agents in HIV-1–infected adults and adolescent. Retrieved May 30, 2006, from http://AIDSinfo.nih.gov

Valdiserri, R. O., Arena, V. C., Proctor, D., & Bonati, F. (1989). The relationship between women's attitudes about condoms and their use: Implications for condom promotion programs. *American Journal of Public Health, 79*, 499–501.

van Servellen, G., Brown, J. S., Lombardi, E., & Herrera, G. (2003). Health literacy in low-income Latino men and women receiving antiretroviral therapy in community-based treatment centers. *AIDS Patient Care and STDs, 17*, 283–298.

van Servellen, G., Chang, B., Garcia, L., & Lombardi, E. (2002). Individual and system level factors associated with treatment nonadherence in human immunodeficiency virus-infected men and women. *AIDS Patient Care STDS, 16*, 269–281.

Verheul, R., Ball, S. A., & van der Brink, W. (1998). Substance abuse and personality disorders. In H. R. Kranzler & B. J. Rounsavill (Eds.), *Dual diagnosis and treatment: Substance abuse and comorbid medical and psychiatric disorders.* New York: Marcel Dekker.

Vitiello, B., Burnam, M. A., Bing, E. G., Beckman, R., & Shapiro, M. F. (2003). Use of psychotropic medications among HIV-infected patients in the United States. *American Journal of Psychiatry, 160*, 547–554.

Wagner, G. J., Kanouse, D. E., Koegel, P., & Sullivan, G. (2004). Correlates of HIV antiretroviral adherence in persons with serious mental illness. *AIDS Care, 16*, 501–506.

Walkey, F. H., Taylor, A. J., & Green, D. E. (1990). Attitudes to AIDS: A comparative analysis of a new and negative stereotype. *Social Science Medicine, 30*, 549–552.

Weidle, P. J., Ganera, C. E., Irwin, K. L., McGowan, J. P., Ernst, J. A., Olivo, N., et al. (1999). Adherence to antiretroviral medications in an inner-city population. *Journal of Acquired Immune Deficiency Syndromes, 22*, 498–502.

Whetten, K., Leserman, J., Whetten, R., Ostermann, J., Thielman, N., Swartz, M., et al. (2006). Exploring lack of trust in care providers and the government as a barrier to health service use. *American Journal of Public Health, 96*, 716–721.

World Health Organization, Joint United Nations Programme on HIV/AIDS. (2002). *Report on the global HIV/AIDS epidemic.* Geneva, Switzerland: World Health Organization.

Wulfert, E., Wan, C. K., & Backus, C. (1996). Gay men's safer sex behavior. *Journal of Behavioral Medicine, 19*, 345–366.

Yun, L. W. H., Maravi, M., Koayashi, J. S., Barton, P. L., & Davidson, A. J. (2005). Antidepressant treatment improves adherence to antiretroviral therapy among depressed HIV-infected patients. *Journal of Acquired Immune Deficiency Syndromes, 38*, 432–438.

Zapka, J., Stoddard, A., Zorn, M., McCusker, J., & Mayer, K. (1991) HIV antibody test result knowledge, risk perceptions and behavior among homosexually active men. *Patient Education and Counseling, 18*, 9–17.

Zinkernagel, C., Taffe, P., Rickenbach, M., Amiet, R., Ledergerber, B., Volkart, A. C., et al. (2001). Importance of mental health assessment in HIV-infected outpatients. *Journal of Acquired Immune Deficiency Syndromes, 28*, 240–249.

CHAPTER 10

Spinal Cord Injury

ELIZABETH J. RICHARDSON, J. SCOTT RICHARDS, and BRET A. BOYER

SPINAL CORD INJURY

The spinal cord is a vital communication pathway between the brain and body. It houses the major fibers innervating our muscles, sensory afferents enabling us to perceive the environment, and reflex arcs involved in autonomic and homeostatic mechanisms. Thus, damage to the spinal cord, as occurs in spinal cord injury (SCI), can drastically affect day-to-day living. Although SCI can occur as a result of disease (e.g., tumor) or birth complication (e.g., spina bifida), most SCIs are caused by blunt trauma.

How a SCI will affect an individual functionally depends on both the level and extent of the injury. The neurological level of injury (Figure 10.1) is determined by locating the areas of the body with diminished or absent sensory or motor function. *Tetraplegia* denotes an injury to the spinal cord located in the cervical vertebrae, which results in sensory or motor loss—or both—throughout the body, including the upper limbs. *Paraplegia* denotes injury to the cord at the level of the first thoracic vertebra or below and is typically characterized by preserved arm/hand function but sensory and/or motor loss in the lower limbs and/or lower portions of the trunk. The extent of spared sensory and motor function below the level of spinal cord damage determines whether the injury is complete or incomplete. In complete injuries, no feeling or movement will be present on either side of the body below the level of injury. Persons with incomplete injuries may have widely varied residual sensory and motor function below the level of injury, ranging from sensory sparing only, with no motor function, to minimal deficits.

PREVALENCE, ETIOLOGY, AND DEMOGRAPHICS

Based on state registry, census, and survey information, it is estimated that 250,000 persons in the United States are currently living with SCI and 11,000 persons sustain an SCI each year (National Spinal Cord Injury Statistical Center [NSCISC], 2005a). A more comprehensive look at demographic and etiological characteristics associated with SCI has, in large part, been made possible by the existence of the Model SCI Systems of Care Program funded by the National Institute on Disability and Rehabilitation Research. Data from this source (NSCISC, 2005b) indicate that 81% of SCI cases

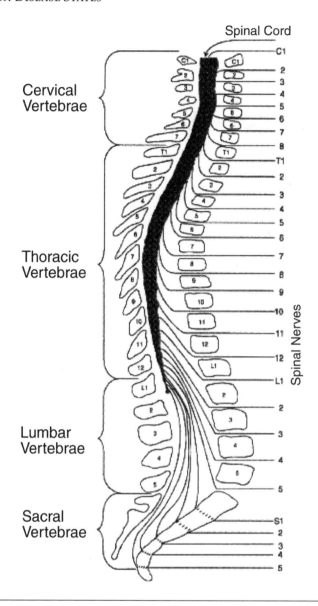

Figure 10.1 Human spinal cord in vertebral column. Vertebrae are numbered with respect to location in spine. Cord segments and spinal nerves are also numbered to indicate corresponding vertebrae

are male and that injuries are most likely to occur between 16 and 30 years of age. Of those injured since 2000, 62.9% are Caucasian, 22% African American, and 12.6% Hispanic; figures that reflect a higher proportion of African Americans concurrent with a lower proportion of Caucasians when compared to the general population (Grieco & Cassidy, 2001).

In the United States, automobile crashes account for nearly 35% of SCIs and are the leading cause of injury. The second and third leading causes of SCI are falls (19.7%) and gunshot wounds (16.2%), respectively (NSCISC, 2005b). However, leading causes of SCI may vary with age. While vehicle crashes remain the leading cause for individuals injured as children or adolescents, sports accidents (24.1%) and violence (23.5%) represent the second and third most common causes of SCI, respectively. For individuals injured over the age of sixty, automobile crashes and violence decline while falls emerge as the leading cause of SCI (NSCISC, 2005b).

Nearly half of those who sustain a SCI have graduated from high school, approximately 25% have some high school education, 10% an 8th grade education or less, and 9% completed college- or graduate-level education. Almost two-thirds of persons who sustain a SCI are employed at the time of injury. The employment rate decreases considerably during the initial years postinjury; only 22.8% are employed by their fifth year after injury (NSCISC, 2005b). The jobs held by individuals with chronic SCI typically tend to be professional or administrative jobs—those usually requiring higher education levels and involving fewer physical demands (NSCISC, 2005b). Over half of individuals who sustain a SCI are single at the time of injury. This is most likely attributable to the young age at which the injuries occur. Individuals who are single at the time of injury have a reduced likelihood of getting married in the post-injury years compared to the able-bodied population (NSCISC, 2005a).

DISEASE FACTORS

Although considerable advances have been made in the basic sciences in terms of understanding the neurophysiological cascade of events that occur at the cord level following injury (Hulbert, 2006; Keirstead & Steward, 2003), clinically, at least, we are not yet able to reverse spinal cord injury and the devastating consequences it can produce. The reality for most who have sustained a SCI is the formidable challenge of adapting, both physically and emotionally, to some degree of permanent disability. Aside from the immediate and obvious physical impairments resulting from a SCI, many individuals with SCI will also face a number of secondary complications affecting a variety of organ systems and physiological processes throughout their lives.

RESPIRATORY COMPLICATIONS

Respiratory complications rank as the leading cause of death among persons with SCI (NSCISC, 2005b). The level of injury sustained will determine the risk and degree of respiratory complications that may arise. Mid- to high-level cervical injuries pose the greatest risk of respiratory dysfunction due to paralysis of the respiratory muscles, thereby reducing vital lung capacity (Sassoon & Baydur, 2003). However, those with paraplegia or injuries at the thoracic level may have impairment in abdominal muscles that provide diaphragmatic support (Lanig and Peterson, 2000). In the days immediately following the onset of SCI, potential pulmonary complications include total or partial collapse of the lung (atelectasis) and respiratory failure. Thus, intubation or ventilatory support may be required. For individuals with a cord injury above C3, such aggressive respiratory management may unfortunately be a necessity for the remainder of their lives (Lanig & Peterson). For others with lower-level injuries, this need may diminish once medically stable and the focus of medical management may shift to long-term preventive care. Due to disruptions in airflow mechanics and therefore a reduced ability to cough and clear the respiratory tract, there is an increase in risk for pneumonia and other respiratory infections (Sassoon & Baydur). Thus, many persons with SCI will require incorporating techniques such as manually or mechanically assisted cough techniques into their daily routine (Sassoon & Baydur).

CARDIOVASCULAR COMPLICATIONS

In addition to pulmonary dysfunction, persons with SCI are susceptible to adverse cardiovascular consequences. Reductions in sympathetic nervous system activity can lead to reduced blood pressure, orthostatic hypotension, bradycardia, and possible cardiac arrest, particularly in the acute phases of SCI (Campagnolo & Merli, 2002; Sabharwal, 2003). As the duration of injury progresses, however, individuals with high-level SCIs may paradoxically experience bouts of abrupt and potentially life-threatening increases in blood pressure. This condition, known as *autonomic dysreflexia*, primarily affects those with injuries at thoracic levels T6 and above and is caused by a dysregulation of the ascending and descending autonomic pathways (Sabharwal). Specifically, noxious stimuli experienced below the level of injury may trigger a sympathetic response, causing hypertension, headache, anxiety, sweating, and flushing of the face (Campagnolo & Merli). Because descending spinal regulatory systems that maintain homeostasis cannot descend past the level of the injury, the sympathetic mechanism is left unchecked and the physiological responses that ensue can become extreme (Mallory, 2003). Common stimuli that may trigger an episode of autonomic dysreflexia include overfilling of the bladder, urinary tract infections, bowel problems, and wounds or pressure sores. Thus, adherence to medical management regimens is important, such as adherence to bowel programs and proper catheterization procedures.

Over time, diminished mobility results in decreases in muscle mass coupled with increases in adiposity. Consequently, negative metabolic changes may occur, resulting in unfavorable blood lipid profiles, impaired glucose tolerance, and increased blood platelet aggregation due to stasis (Baumen & Spungen, 2000). As such, pharmacological therapy may be required in conjunction with dietary and lifestyle changes.

URINARY AND GASTROINTESTINAL COMPLICATIONS

Bladder and bowel dysfunction are common secondary complications to SCI that can have a tremendous impact on not only physical health, but psychosocial functioning as well. Nearly 63% of individuals with SCI experience gastrointestinal difficulties (Han, Kim, & Kwon, 1998). Depending on the areas that are denervated, possible bowel complications include incontinence, inability to sense the need for elimination, reduced motility, and constipation (Stiens, Fajardo, & Korsten, 2003). Individualized bowel programs are often required in order to effectively maintain gastrointestinal health. This process can be quite time consuming for many and may require the assistance of others. Glickman and Kamm (1996) found that nearly half of individuals with SCI reported that it required more than 30 minutes to complete their daily bowel regimen. Furthermore, these researchers found that the amount of time required to complete the process was positively associated with the level of reported depression.

Bladder functioning can also be significantly altered after sustaining an SCI. Depending on the extent and level of injury, persons may experience spontaneous bladder muscle contractions resulting in incontinence. For others, cord damage may lead to a lack of coordination between the bladder and sphincter muscle, rendering the individual unable to completely void and at increased risk for urinary reflux to the kidneys, causing renal damage (Bodner & Perkash, 2003). The physiological changes and urinary management techniques (e.g., catheterization) employed may often lead to the development of a urinary tract infection (UTI). The onset of a UTI in persons with SCI may trigger episodes of autonomic dysreflexia, spasticity in the lower limbs, and if left untreated, may result in renal dysfunction or failure (Cardenas, Farrell-Roberts, Sipski, & Rubner, 1995). Thus, adherence to proper urine drainage techniques and schedules is essential for maintaining health post-SCI.

Pressure Sores

Data from the Model Systems SCI database indicate that approximately one third of persons will develop a pressure sore in the acute rehabilitation phase, and 15 to 27% will develop a pressure sore in later postinjury years (NSCISC, 2005b). Pressure sores result from deficient or complete lack of blood flow due to compression of soft tissue (Priebe, Martin, Wuermser, Castillo, & McFarlin, 2003); a condition most likely to occur on areas of the skin that overlie bony areas and are in contact with the bed or seat of a wheelchair. If left unrelieved, the compressed tissue will eventually become necrotic and an ulcer will develop (Priebe et al.). The recovery process from a pressure sore can substantially interfere with the inpatient rehabilitation progress and, for individuals in the community, can bring daily activities to a near halt. In severe cases, skin flap surgery may be required to close the wound and promote healing (Montroy & Eltorai, 2003). Thus, in addition to the use of special wheelchair cushions or mattresses, education in preventive measures is an integral component of the rehabilitative process. Good prevention entails proactive behavior on the part of the individual, including frequent skin checks to identify early signs of ulcers and routine pressure releases or weight shifts to reduce the compression time for a given surface area (Priebe et al.).

Spasticity

Spinal cord injuries can disrupt the coordination of sensory afferent and motor efferent activity required for normal voluntary movement (Nance, 2003). As a result, increased tone and spasticity can occur in muscles below the level of injury, resulting in uncontrolled limb movements. Consequently, bone fractures, dislocations, and pain can often occur. Spasticity in the trunk muscles may increase the risk for falling out of a wheelchair or create difficulty when transferring[1] (LeViseur & Sonka-Maarek, 2003). Spasticity may also have adverse psychosocial effects, as having spasms in public has been found to be a source of considerable social discomfort among persons with SCI (Dunn, 1977). Pharmacologic treatment of spasticity often includes the use of drugs that help to increase neural inhibition, such as GABA agonists or benzodiazepines (Nance). Other methods include passive range of motion exercises, massage, acupuncture, and programmable implanted intrathecal pumps (Nance).

Sexual Functioning

Significant changes in the physiological mechanisms underlying sexual functioning can occur. Men with injuries above the T6 level may still be capable of having an erec-

---

1. Among rehabilitation specialists, the term "transferring" denotes the act of transitioning from one sitting/lying posture or place to another, such as from bed to wheelchair, wheelchair into a car, and so on.

tion via a reflex arc located in the sacral regions (Elliot, 2003). This type of erection can be induced by contact that can occur in the absence of psychological arousal. Lower-level injuries may preclude reflexogenic erections; however, the ability to have a psychogenic (i.e., mental imagery, introduction of erotic stimuli) erection may be preserved. Various methods, such as external vacuum devices, injections, and oral medications have been found to improve sexual functioning and experience (Richards, Lloyd, James, & Brown, 1992). Difficulties with ejaculation coupled with reduced sperm quality and motility may prove problematic for men with SCI who would like to father a child. Nevertheless, fatherhood remains a viable option with various techniques available to obtain semen and assisted reproductive methods such as in vitro fertilization (Linsenmeyer, 2000).

In women with higher-level SCIs, reflex vaginal lubrication can still occur, whereas those with incomplete injuries may still maintain both reflexive and psychogenic lubrication (Sipski, Alexander, & Rosen, 1995). Although some reports suggest a decrease in the ability to achieve orgasm (Jackson, Wadley, Richards, & DeVivo, 1995), other studies indicate that many of the physiological experiences including orgasm can still occur (Sipski, Alexander & Rosen; Jackson, 2003).

It is common for women to experience disruptions in menstrual cycles, especially during the more acute phases of SCI. Most will resume regular menstruation and hormonal cycles within the first year after injury. Pregnancy and the ability to carry a fetus to full term are probable; however, potential complications resulting from SCI-related conditions such as urinary dysfunction, autonomic dysreflexia, and spasticity warrant careful follow-up during pregnancy, labor, and delivery (Jackson, 2003).

Spinal Cord Injury-Related Pain

One of the most frequently occurring physical sequelae following SCI is persistent pain, with almost 80% of individuals reporting some form of chronic pain post-SCI (Bryce & Ragnarsson, 2003). Pain can be localized with respect to the neurological level of the injury, described as occurring above-level, at-level, or below-level (Bryce & Ragnarsson, 2000; Bryce & Ragnarsson, 2003). In addition to location, the type of pain may be characterized as musculoskeletal, visceral, or neuropathic pain (Siddall, Yezierski, & Loeser, 2000). *Musculoskeletal pain* is most evident in regions of preserved innervation above the level of injury, and commonly results from the wear and tear on muscles, joints, and tendons. Thus, this form of nociceptive pain is often experienced in shoulders, elbows, and wrists secondary to prolonged use of manual wheelchairs and use of the upper limbs when transferring. Musculoskeletal pain can also be experienced below the level of injury in individuals with sensory incomplete injuries. *Visceral pain* originates from abdominal or pelvic organs, may be difficult to localize, and often results from physiological disturbances such as urinary tract infections, bowel impaction, and kidney or bladder stones. *Neuropathic pain* occurs in a region of sensory disturbance and can be experienced around the zone of injury (resulting from damage within the spinal cord itself or proximal nerve roots) or below the level of injury (resulting from an imbalance in the central nervous system). Neuropathic pain descriptively differs from nociceptive pain, being reported as sharp, burning, and/or electric, or feelings of "pins and needles" (Bryce & Ragnarsson, 2000). The functional impairments arising from pain are pervasive, disrupting mood and psychosocial functioning (Richards, Meredith, Nepomuceno, Fine, & Bennett; Elliott & Harkins,

1991), occupational activities (Rose, Robinson, Ellis, & Cole, 1988), and basic needs such as sleep (Budh, Hultling, & Lundeberg, 2005; Widerström-Noga, Felipe-Cuervo, & Turk, 2001). Thus, it is not surprising that pain, among other complications of SCI, has been consistently associated with lower quality of life post injury (Richards, 2005; Putzke, Richards, Hicken, & DeVivo, 2002; Lundqvist, Siösteen, Blomstrand, Lind, & Sullivan, 1991).

REGIMEN FACTORS

An optimal treatment regimen for individuals who have sustained a SCI is one that is tailored to meet their various needs across all phases of care. Such a comprehensive service delivery system is the underlying concept of the SCI Model Systems, a network of rehabilitation centers located throughout the United States. Each Model System provides a multidisciplinary continuum of care, from the time of injury through maintenance and long-term follow-up. Specifically, there are five clinical service components of a Model system, including (1) emergency services and stabilization immediately following injury, (2) acute care from a specialized team of personnel, (3) physical rehabilitation, (4) psychosocial and vocational rehabilitation, and (5) life-long follow-up and health maintenance (Thomas, 1995). A system's ultimate goal is to improve quality of life, community integration, and to help the individual reach maximum potential in both physical and psychological functioning. Once a patient is medically stable after an injury, acute inpatient rehabilitation can begin. Physical and occupational therapists can provide a coordinated effort to assist the individual in gaining optimal mobility and functioning in day-to-day activities. Functional goals are established for each patient, regularly scheduled physical and occupational therapy sessions are conducted to achieve these goals, and any assistive equipment that will be needed is introduced. This phase of care also involves a great deal of education for both patients and family members. Patient and caregivers learn proper bladder, bowel, and skin care procedures that will need to be incorporated into their day-to-day living.

In addition to increasing functional independence in basic daily living skills, it is also important to address any potential barriers to social role fulfillment that may impede successful community reintegration after discharge. Vocational rehabilitation services can assist the individual in returning to previous work or in obtaining training to prepare for a job post injury. In addition, transportation or adaptive equipment may also be introduced in order to achieve social and economic independence. Psychosocial services in the form of individual and family counseling may help persons with SCI anticipate potential challenges post discharge and provide them with resources to provide for a successful transition. Individuals with SCI who reside in the community may continue to receive outpatient physical, occupational, vocational, physical, and psychological services. Periodic medical care will also be needed for general health maintenance and treatment of secondary complications that may arise.

When a person is fully invested in rehabilitation, extraordinary gains can occur. However, the rehabilitative process can prove taxing to even the most motivated of individuals. Pain associated with therapy can be severe enough to discourage full participation in routine sessions. In addition, many of the self-care regimens can be intrusive. Many individuals with SCI will need to devote a substantial amount of time to daily urinary and bowel programs. Proper skin care will require constant mindfulness of when to conduct routine pressure releases and skin checks. Lack of transportation can significantly impede post-rehabilitative care, vocational, and social interactions that are beneficial in health and successful community integration. Finally, post-SCI care can be quite costly. The estimated cost of care within the first year of injury for someone with a high cervical lesion can be as high as $710,275, with an expense of $127,227 each subsequent year (NSCISC, 2005a).

INDIVIDUAL FACTORS

Spinal cord injury per se does not present as a singular, isolated stressor; its occurrence induces a number of challenging sequelae that permeate a variety of life domains. Physical and psychological outcomes are, in large part, mediated by various personal, social, and environmental factors. Certain characteristics, such as gender or ethnicity, warrant mindfulness of the clinician when developing rehabilitation goals. However, factors such as the way in which one copes, attributional styles, and the quality and amount of social support available are potentially malleable and may be the direct focus of therapeutic intervention within the rehabilitation setting.

RACE AND GENDER

Studies examining effects of race and ethnicity on post-SCI physical and mental health outcomes are sparse; however, the data that exist suggest minority groups to be at a heightened risk for mood disturbance and restricted access to the community. Increased rates of depression have been found among Hispanic (Kemp, Krause, & Adkins 1999) and African American (Krause, Kemp & Coker, 2000) persons with SCI when compared to their Caucasian counterparts. Employment after injury, one marker for successful community reintegration, has also been shown to be lower among African Americans and lower still among Hispanics (Krause et al., 1999). However, race, in and of itself, may serve as a proxy variable mediating the relationship of SCI outcomes. When other demographic, medical, and geographic factors were taken into consideration, no significant differences were seen with respect to functional independence, degree of handicap, satisfaction with life, and perceived physical and mental health between African Americans and Caucasians with SCI (Putzke, Hicken, & Richards, 2002). Rather than targeting specific ethnic groups per se, interventions geared toward improving the mediating factors such as level of education and restricted access to occupational and social activities could be more effective.

Women comprise a small proportion of those with SCI. As such, less is known about how their unique concerns may impact adjustment post-SCI. There is evidence to suggest that among persons with SCI, women tend to report more depressive symptomatology than men (Fuhrer, Rintala, Hart, Clearman, & Young, 1993; Krause & Broderick, 2004). Women with SCI also tend to have lower mobility (Fuhrer et al.), are less likely to have a favorable score on an environmental access measure (Richards et al., 1999), and have lower odds of employment post injury than men (Krause et al., 1999). These barriers to social integration may mediate the relationship between gender and psychological functioning post SCI. Gender, like race, may serve as a marker variable to denote when specific intervention approaches are warranted, such as those aimed at improving social and environmental access.

COPING AND ATTRIBUTIONAL STYLES

Prior conceptualizations of psychological adjustment post SCI were similar to a grief stage process (Bracken & Shepard, 1980). This stage theory posited that once an SCI was incurred, a series of psychological reactions was automatically set in motion. The role of the clinician was a passive one, providing support while the individual works through the process with the goal of reaching a final endpoint of accepting the injury and consequent life changes. We now, however, appreciate the dynamic interplay of various psychosocial, biological, and environmental factors contributing to successful adjustment. Viewing adjustment to SCI as a continual, transactional process rather than a fixed linear sequence of predetermined stages places the clinician in a more active role, with the opportunity to intervene on one or more contributing factors.

One of the mediating factors of successful adaptation to SCI is the way in which one copes with the injury and its effects. Frank and colleagues (1987) conducted a study that was one of the first attempts to explore in detail various coping styles and their relationship to psychological adjustment post SCI. These researchers found that individuals who utilized wishful thinking, self-blame, and relied on more coping attempts in general showed increased psychological distress. In addition, these persons attributed their overall health outcome to be in the control of powerful others or merely a matter of chance. Conversely, persons with SCI who relied less on these coping strategies and had more internal orientation with respect to their outcome evidenced less distress.

Later researchers investigating attribution of responsibility (i.e., self-blame) found that individuals in the acute phase of rehabilitation who held themselves responsible for sustaining the SCI showed greater psychological distress and lower life satisfaction during rehabilitation (Hanson, Buckelew, Hewett, & O'Neal, 1993; Richards, Elliott, Shewchuk, & Fine, 1997). However, whether one blamed him- or herself for the injury did not have much of an effect on adjustment after the first year of injury (Richards et al.). Rather, individuals in the chronic phases of SCI utilizing coping strategies centered on cognitive restructuring showed more acceptance of their disability, whereas wishful thinking was associated with poorer emotional adjustment (Hanson et al.). These findings suggest that interventions targeting self-blame and possible distortions in self-views may be more effective during the acute phases of SCI; however, long-term adjustment may be improved by facilitating cognitive restructuring of the various life implications resulting from the injury that evolve with time.

FAMILY/SOCIAL SUPPORT

Support from others is unquestionably a vital element facilitating successful outcome in a variety of life areas for a person with long-term disability. Individuals with SCI who report low levels of social and family support have poorer community reintegration (Song, 2005), an increased incidence of health complications (Rintala, Young, Hart, Clearman, & Fuhrer, 1992; Anson, Stanwyck, & Krause, 1993), increased feelings of helplessness and lack of control (Elfström, Kreuter, Rydén, Persson, & Sullivan, 2002), and thus not surprisingly, more depressive symptoms (Schulz & Decker, 1985). More perceived social support has also been shown to reduce the development of PTSD among injured veterans (Danner & Radnitz, 2000), but not to improve the recovery from PTSD (Radnitz & Danner, 2002).

However, the mere presence of social support does not necessarily mean that it is beneficial. The value of social support as a resource is, in great part, defined by the quality of relationships and nature of social interactions within one's immediate and extended social network. Persons with SCI whose family environment was characterized by open communication and appropriate emotional responses in various situations fared better in overall functional independence (McGowan & Roth, 1987). Family or social relationships that foster personal worth and reinforce one's confidence in his or her ability have been associated with lower levels of depression among persons with SCI (Elliot, Herrick, Witty, Godshall, & Spruell, 1992). Yet, the dynamic nature of family and social interactions necessitates consideration of the individual's own personality and disposition. Elliott and colleagues (1991) examined possible interactive effects and found that persons with SCI who were more assertive in disposition reported more depressive symptomatology when in relationships that were characterized by advice giving and more direct guidance. Conversely, persons with SCI who were low in assertiveness showed less depression in the presence of guidance support in addition to having relationships that reassured their sense of self-worth and self-competency. Perhaps persons with SCI involved in relationships that are guidance driven and more unidirectional in communication may feel their voice to be overshadowed, and thus their own thoughts, opinions, and judgments to be somewhat devalued. In contrast, persons with SCI who are less assertive may feel less self-confident in directing their rehabilitative process and thus feel reassured by those providing more structured guidance that promotes self-worth, skill, and competence.

COMORBID PSYCHOPATHOLOGY

Each individual who sustains an SCI must face considerable life changes occurring in nearly every facet of living—challenges that can prove quite formidable to those with limited personal and environmental resources. As for anyone in the general population, psychological and emotional adaptation after a life-altering event depends on a multitude of factors, such as history of psychopathology, coping styles, and availability of social support. Rather than rendering subsequent psychological distress as inevitable, it is more likely that SCI may increase the risk for the development of or exacerbate a pre-existing psychological disorder.

DEPRESSION

Prevalence rates of major depression among persons with SCI have been found to range from 11% to over 30% (Frank et al., 1992; Bombardier, Richards, Krause, Tulsky, & Tate, 2004; Krause et al., 2000; Fuhrer et al., 1993), exceeding the 6.7% found in the general population (Kessler, Chiu, Demler, & Walters, 2005). A common misconception is that the injury itself is the underlying factor to any depressive symptomatology that may emerge, and that nearly all individuals who sustain an SCI will experience similar emotional, psychological, and behavioral reactions. This assumption may unfortunately bias the subjective attitudes and perceptions of rehabilitation personnel (Cushman & Dijkers, 1990, Siösteen, Kreuter, Lampic, & Persson, 2005). However, depression following SCI is neither an inevitable emotional reaction nor a stage that is necessary for an individual to go through in order to successfully adjust (Frank, Elliott, Corcoran, & Wonderlich, 1987).

Although depression post SCI is not a universal occurrence, it is important to assess each person post SCI for the presence of depressive symptoms. This is underscored by findings that depression has been associated with longer hospital stays (Kennedy & Rogers, 2000), increased risk for secondary health complications (Herrick, Elliott, & Crow, 1994), and decreased mobility and social integration within the community (Fuhrer et al., 1993). Moreover, depression may lead to suicidal thoughts and behaviors. Prior studies have noted that 6.3 to 9% of deaths among persons with SCI are attributable to suicide (DeVivo, Black, Richards, & Stover, 1991; Charlifue, Kenneth, & Gerhart, 1991; Soden et al., 2000). Suicide risk appears greatest during the first few years post injury and gradually tapers with each subsequent year (Dijkers, Abela, Gans, & Gordon, 1995). Thus, there is a heightened need to both detect and address suicidality in the initial phases of injury. Suicide is most often associated with an overt act of self-harm; however, suicide among persons with SCI may also take the form of self-neglect or refusal of care (Dijkers et al.). If suicidal ideation is suspected, an individual's intent, possible plan, history of prior attempts, drug/alcohol use, and access to lethal means should be assessed as these are risk factors associated with suicide (Fichtenbaum & Kirshblum (2002).

ANXIETY

Similar to the depression literature, reports have varied regarding prevalence rates of anxiety among those with SCI. Nevertheless, data indicate a relatively greater prevalence of anxiety compared to the general population. Kennedy & Rogers (2000) followed SCI patients from rehabilitation to reintegration within the community, and found anxiety rates to range from 10 to 60%, with the highest rates occurring right before initial discharge. Given the traumatic nature in which most injuries are acquired, more focus has been given to the prevalence of posttraumatic stress disorder (PTSD). Compared to a lifetime prevalence rate of 8% for PTSD in the general population (APA, 2000), estimates of the prevalence of PTSD in the SCI population are typically higher, ranging from approximately 10 to 44% (Kennedy & Duff, 2001). Among children and adolescents who sustain SCI, 25 to 33% experience current PTSD symptoms (Boyer, Knolls, Kafkalas, Tollen, & Swartz, 2000; Boyer, Ware, Knolls, & Kafkalas, 2003, Boyer, Tollen, & Kafkalas, 1998). Radnitz and colleagues (1998) investigated the rate of PTSD relative to the level and type of injury and found the incidence of lifetime PTSD in those with paraplegia to be 44%, whereas the lifetime prevalence among those with tetraplegia was found to be only 13%. These authors suggest that higher-level injuries may impair the physiological mechanisms that allow for sympathetic arousal—a hallmark symptom of PTSD. Nevertheless, consideration of possible PTSD is important regardless of injury type, as symptoms may directly interfere with rehabilitative progress. Indeed, PTSD symptoms have been found to negatively impact functional independence post-inpatient rehabilitation (Boyer, Knolls, Kafkalas, & Tollen, 2000), and mediate the relationship between family functioning and post-rehabilitation functional outcomes (Boyer, Hitelman, Knolls, & Kafkalas, 2003). Individuals with SCI may have frequent and distressing recollections of the event that caused the injury (motor vehicle accident, violence) and may subsequently begin to avoid situations or individuals that remind them of the incident. For example, intense fears of riding in the automobile may lead to the avoidance of required follow-up visits or engaging in other social activities that require transportation. The interference may be further compounded by any concurrent PTSD experienced by family and caregivers, as Boyer and colleagues (2000, 2003) have noted that 30 to 41% of mothers and 11 to 36% of fathers of children with SCI report PTSD symptomatology.

The social implications of disability may also increase the risk for developing social anxiety. Individuals with SCI may become self-conscious about requiring accommodations in their environment and may fear others' reactions to their physical limitations. Social fears specific to secondary complications may also be present, such as fears of having catheter malfunctions, accidental bowel movements, or spasms in public (Dunn, 1977). These fears may in turn lead to the tendency to socially withdraw and isolate, thus decreasing the likelihood of successful community reintegration and increasing the risk for depression or other mood disturbances. In addition, concerns regarding disclosure to others of bowel and bladder needs may affect individuals' comfort when developing intimate relationships. Components of the rehabilitative process that target these potential issues, in conjunction with general gastrointestinal health education, are essential for psychosocial equilibrium in the subsequent years post injury (Trieschmann, 1988).

Substance Abuse

The prevalence of alcohol abuse among community-residing individuals with SCI has been estimated to be 21% (Young, Rintala, Rossi, Hart, & Fuhrer, 1995), which exceeds rates found in the general population (Kessler et al., 2005; APA, 2000). The increased rate among persons with SCI does not necessarily imply that the injury per se increases one's risk for alcohol abuse; rather, it may reflect a continuation of premorbid substance abuse behaviors (Heinemann, Doll, & Schnoll, 1989). Studies indicate that 35 to 57% reported heavy drinking before injury, (Kolakowsky-Hayner et al., 1999; Bombardier & Rimmele, 1998; Bombardier, Stroud, Esselman, & Rimmele, 2004), and intoxication at the time of injury is a probable contributory factor in sustaining an SCI for many persons (McKinley, Kolakowsky, & Kreutzer, 1999; Heinemann, Mamott, & Schnoll, 1990). Unfortunately, problem drinking behaviors persisting in both the acute and chronic phases of post-SCI care can have profound consequences, including negative pain outcomes (Tate, Forchheimer, Krause, Meade, & Bombardier, 2004), increased likelihood of developing pressure sores (Elliott, Kurylo, Chen, & Hicken, 2002), and lower rates of functional improvement during inpatient rehabilitation (Bombardier, Stroud, et al., 2004). The acute rehabilitation phase may represent a pivotal moment for many individuals with SCI who also have a premorbid substance abuse disorder. The realization of the grave consequences of substance misuse, concern from loved ones regarding their well-being, and intensive, continual interaction with the rehabilitation team may present the initial rehabilitation process as an opportune time to incorporate substance abuse treatment (Bombardier and Rimmele, 1998). Indeed, individuals with recently sustained SCIs who experienced greater alcohol-related life problems showed a greater readiness to change in the days following their injury (Bombardier and Rimmele). Although formal treatment approaches may be difficult to incorporate into the already time-constrained context of acute medical, physical, and occupational rehabilitation, a brief intervention technique such as Motivational Interviewing may prove both effective and feasible (Bombardier, 1995).

Less is known about illicit drug use among persons with SCI. Although some studies indicate an increased prevalence (Heinemann et al., 1990, Kolakowsky-Hayner et al., 2002), others found that the prevalence of use was actually lower than the rate found in the general population (Young et al., 1995). It is likely that self-report or questionnaire data regarding illicit substance use has questionable reliability due to response bias and thus may be a cause for underreporting (Richards, Kewman, & Pierce 2000). Also, many individuals with SCI-related pain may be prescribed narcotic analgesics, anxiolytics, or other medications to treat secondary conditions. These medications have the potential for abuse and certain individuals may become dependent or develop a pattern of overuse under the premise that there is not a problem as long as the drug itself was prescribed by their physician. Education regarding the differences between proper use and abuse may reduce the risk for abuse and dependency among persons with SCI who require these medications.

COGNITIVE IMPAIRMENT

Given the nature in which most SCIs are sustained, there is an increased likelihood of concomitant cerebral insult. Accompanying head injury in persons with recent-onset SCI may be obvious if there is blunt trauma to the skull; however, in some circumstances brain injury may be occult, as in cases of intracranial brain-skull contact from rapid deceleration. It is estimated that approximately 40 to 50% of persons sustaining SCI experience posttraumatic amnesia or loss of consciousness at the time of injury (Davidoff, Morris, Roth, & Bleiberg, 1985; Davidoff et al., 1988; Roth et al., 1989), Symptoms suggestive of traumatic brain injury (TBr). Concomitant TBI, depending on the location and extent of cerebral damage, can be associated with cognitive deficits in attention, memory, learning, reasoning, and problem solving (Davidoff, Roth, & Richards, 1992). Rehabilitation post SCI is intensive, involving the new learning of many skills and incorporating them into virtually every aspect of living. Consequently, persons lacking adequate cognitive functioning are at a disadvantage in terms of gaining the full benefit of the rehabilitation process. Indeed, persons dually diagnosed with both SCI and TBI show less functional gain in a similar duration of acute rehabilitation compared to those with SCI only (Macciocchi, Bowman, Coker, Apple, & Leslie, 2004). A further complication is the possibility of premorbid learning disorders or conditions that may interfere with the learning of new information such as attention-deficit/hyperactivity disorder (ADHD). Such cognitive profiles may make it difficult to tease apart deficits observed post-injury in terms of their etiological basis (Alford, Boyer, & Goldberg, 2004; Marchese, Boyer, & Goldberg, 2005). For these reasons, neuropsychological assessment, for those in whom impairment is suspected, can help the rehabilitation team tailor treatment protocols according to each individual's level of cognitive functioning. Furthermore, because cognitive status may change in those with concomitant TBI (Richards, Brown, Hagglund, Bua, & Reeder, 1988), follow-up assessments may aid in determining possible adjustments needed in long-term care.

PSYCHOLOGICAL INTERVENTIONS

Clinical practice in the SCI rehabilitation setting has, for the most part, focused on importing various existing psychotherapeutic approaches and not techniques or modalities specifically modified or developed for individuals with SCI (Consortium for Spinal Cord Medicine, 1998). The lack of SCI-specific guidelines likely reflects the limited number of existing empirical studies regarding the efficacy of these general approaches or any new or modified versions, for that matter, within the SCI population

(Richards, Kogos, & Richardson, 2006; Sipski & Richards, 2006). This is an area that needs to be addressed, as evidence suggests that the personality and dispositional make-up of many who incur a SCI render traditional approaches that are more insight-oriented less suitable (Rohe & Krause, 1993). Kemp and colleagues (2004) did find a cognitive-behavioral approach that emphasized coping with SCI to be beneficial. These researchers provided 6 months of individual cognitive-behavioral therapy (CBT) in conjunction with antidepressant treatment to community-residing persons with chronic SCI. Psychotherapy sessions centered on education regarding the nature and effects of depression, increasing positive problem-solving skills, and addressing problematic life areas that were a source of dissatisfaction for each individual. A 40% increase in community activities was noted at 8 weeks and an overall 57% decrease in depressive symptoms at the end of the 6 months (Kemp, Kahan, Krause, Adkins, & Nava, 2004).

Group psychological interventions conducted within the acute rehabilitation setting have also shown promise. Craig, Hancock, Dickson, & Chang (1997) and Craig, Hancock, Chang, & Dickson investigated the effects of a 10–week group CBT aimed at promoting cognitive and behavioral skills for smoother transition and integration into community living. At 1-year follow-up, only those with initial high levels of self-reported depression showed significant improvement (Craig et al., 1997). Two years later, however, overall reductions in depressive symptomatology were found across subjects receiving group CBT during their inpatient rehabilitation compared to those receiving only physical and occupational therapy (Craig et al., 1998).

Consideration of SCI as a chronic health condition has prompted other researchers to utilize approaches that operate within a theoretical framework that considers the effects of stress and coping on health. Coping Effectiveness Training (CET) is a group-based variant of CBT that is based on the stress and coping model of health developed by Lazarus and Folkman (1984). Using this approach, Kennedy, Duff, Evans, & Beedie (2003) conducted twice-weekly group sessions for newly injured persons in the acute rehabilitation setting. The therapy focused on increasing one's ability to appraise stressful situations and develop positive problem-solving and coping skills with which to better deal with those situations. Group sessions involved learning strategies for choosing appropriate coping skills and practicing these skills with scenarios or situations that may be commonly experienced in day-to-day living with SCI. Results indicated that those who underwent CET showed an overall decrease in depressive symptomatology regardless of baseline levels. Furthermore, anxiety symptoms and negative perceptions associated with the injury were also significantly reduced (Kennedy et al.).

INTERVENTIONS TO REDUCE RISK OF SECONDARY COMPLICATIONS

Negative health behaviors such as poor diet, smoking, and noncompliance with self-care regimens can increase the risk for secondary complications among persons with SCI. As such, there are multiple areas in which behavioral change strategies could be employed in order to reduce the risk of adverse health consequences among persons with SCI. As noted previously, pressure sores are one of the most commonly occurring yet paradoxically, highly preventable secondary complications following SCI. There exist several studies examining the effectiveness of behavioral modification techniques aimed at increasing the frequency with which one engages in pressure releases or wheelchair "push-ups." Although the use of negative reinforcement (e.g., performing a pressure release in order to avoid an alarm) and contingency management (positive reinforcement for clear skin checks) show short-term benefit, long-term changes in behavior remain questionable (Merbitz, King, Bleiberg, & Grip, 1985; White, Mathews, & Fawcett, 1989; Jones, Mathewson, Adkins, & Ayllon, 2003). Perhaps these techniques would serve well as an initial break in the cycle, until an individual is aided in the development of effective problem-solving skills and social supports necessary for long-term change (Jones et al.).

CASE EXAMPLE

R. G. was 25 years old when he left home for the first time and worked on a construction crew. While on the job, he fell into an excavated pit onto an iron rebar and was instantly rendered paraplegic at the T6 level. Once medically stable and transferred to the rehabilitation unit, he was referred for psychological evaluation and treatment.

Assessing R. G.'s psychosocial background revealed him to be the youngest of seven children of a divorced mother. School records indicated his IQ to be in the low 70s. He received special education throughout his school years. Participation in activities outside of the home was hindered by his inability to master driving and obtain a license. After his high school years, he continued to live at home with his mother, had minimal dating experience, and worked occasional odd jobs. Consequently, R. G. was quite dependent as a young adult; thus, signing on to work for a construction crew was a major first attempt on his part to increase his independence.

R. G. was reported not to have lost consciousness at the scene of the accident. Upon interview, however, he was unable to recall some aspects of the events immediately surrounding the occurrence of his injury. During his acute rehabilitation, R. G. was initially agitated and fearful of the rehabilitation personnel and therapeutic regimens, yet was comforted, to some extent, by the presence of his family. To ease his distress, members of the rehabilitation team were encouraged to adhere to an established routine as much as possible by maintaining consistency in protocol, providing continuity of staff-patient contact, and discussing events/activities prior to their occurrence so as to increase predictability for R. G. Anxiolytics were prescribed as well. In addition, his cognitive limitations warranted tailoring certain aspects of his regimen, such as the use of very simple terms when providing instructions on various tasks in his therapies. His family was also asked to participate as much as possible in the rehabilitation process, including educational sessions of self-care and day-to-day health maintenance.

After a number of visits from the rehabilitation psychologist, when R. G. developed trust and began to share his thoughts and concerns, it became apparent that he had several symptoms of PTSD. By discharge, he achieved only a moderate level of physical independence, an outcome likely hindered by several factors, including the severity of his injuries, his limited cognitive skills, and emotional disturbance. R. G. continued outpatient weekly psychotherapy sessions, and within a few months post discharge, began experiencing frequent nightmares that would often involve "falling," as had happened at injury. As a corollary to his increased anxiety, R. G. became more dependent and demanding on his sister, exhibiting extreme distress if she were not immediately available. A graded exposure program for PTSD was implemented in his psychotherapy sessions. Shortly after this was initiated, his recollection of the accident occurred spontaneously and his PTSD symptoms diminished.

R. G. received a large settlement because of his injuries, and because of his cognitive limitations, a guardianship arrangement was made with his sister to assist in managing his finances. R. G.'s sister was a strong advocate for his health throughout his initial rehabilitation and was proactive in arranging medical or psychological follow-up appointments during the first several years post discharge. Over time, however, the follow-up visits became less frequent, and those that were made were oftentimes cancelled. When he was finally brought back for an annual evaluation, he was so debilitated physically that he was immediately admitted. He presented with flat and guarded affect, a marked change from his usual presentation. When interviewed by the psychologist alone, R. G. revealed a pattern of physical and emotional abuse by his sister and a suspicion that she had been misappropriating his funds. Legal authorities were contacted and it was deemed necessary to change R. G.'s guardianship to another family member. He regained his health once guardianship was changed and he began receiving better attendant care. His emotional status improved substantially via ongoing psychological follow-up in combination with antidepressant medication. Over the subsequent years, behavioral plans were initiated to address noncompliance with various regimens. R. G. eventually died at the age of 47, due to severe secondary complications, primarily renal failure and respiratory complications.

This case illustrates the complexity of some of the persons who present with spinal cord injury. This was a young man who, with his cognitive limitations and emotional reactions, was unable to achieve an optimal level of independence. This was compounded by his extreme psychological dependence upon family and lack of self-confidence in his capabilities. Behavioral techniques were implemented to alleviate his anxiety and PTSD symptoms along with family guidance on how to incorporate such techniques in his home life in order to maintain psychotherapeutic progress. In addition, a competency assessment was required to aid in establishing an appropriate level of guardianship. In later years, family dynamics and physical/emotional abuse and neglect had to be addressed. Such issues are often complex, and may require working with various professionals from law enforcement to the court systems. R. G. eventually was able to attain a reasonable emotional and behavioral equilibrium with substantial support and vigilance from a number of different sources. However, this is the kind of case that requires virtually every skill in the psychologist's armamentarium, from assessment to therapy and consultation. It further illustrates the importance of a thorough understanding of the strengths, limitations, and background experiences someone brings to a spinal cord injury, as they play a critical role in the level of adjustment that is possible post injury.

REFERENCES

Alford, H. L., Boyer, B. A., & Goldberg, K.B. (2004). Pediatric traumatic brain injury and spinal cord injury: Considering the psychological impact of combination injury. *SCI Psychosocial Process, 17*, 316–321.

American Psychiatric Association. (2000). *Diagnostic and statistical manual of mental disorders* (4th ed., text revision). Washington, DC: Author.

Anson, C. A., Stanwyck, D. J., & Krause, J. S. (1993). Social support and health status in spinal cord injury. *Paraplegia, 31*, 632–638.

Bauman, W. A., & Spungen, A. M. (2000). Metabolic changes in persons after spinal cord injury. *Physical Medicine and Rehabilitation Clinics of North America, 11*(1), 109–140.

Bodner, D. R., & Perkash, I. (2003). Urologic management in spinal cord injury. In V. W. Lin et al. (Eds.), *Spinal cord medicine: Principles and practice* (pp. 299–305). New York: Demos.

Bombardier, C. (1995). Alcohol use and traumatic brain injury. *Western Journal of Medicine, 162,* 150–151.

Bombardier, C. H., Richards, J. S., Krause, J. S., Tulsky, D., & Tate, D. G. (2004). Symptoms of major depression in people with spinal cord injury: Implications for screening. *Archives of Physical Medicine & Rehabilitation, 85,* 1749–1755.

Bombardier, C. H., & Rimmele, C. T. (1998). Alcohol use and readiness to change after spinal cord injury. *Archives of Physical Medicine & Rehabilitation, 79,* 1110–1115.

Bombardier, C. H., Stroud, M. W., Esselman, P. C., & Rimmele, C. T. (2004). Do preinjury alcohol problems predict poorer rehabilitation progress in persons with spinal cord injury? *Archives of Physical Medicine and Rehabilitation, 85,* 1488–1492.

Boyer, B. A., Hitelman, J. S., Knolls, M. L., & Kafkalas, C. (2003). Posttraumatic stress and family functioning in pediatric spinal cord injuries: Moderation or mediation? *American Journal of Family Therapy, 31,* 23–37.

Boyer, B. A., Knolls, M. L., Kafkalas, C. M., & Tollen, L. G. (2000). Prevalence of Posttraumatic Stress Disorder in Patients with Pediatric Spinal Cord Injury: Relationship to Functional Independence *Topics in Spinal Cord Injury Rehabilitation, 6*(Suppl), 125–133.

Boyer, B. A., Knolls, M. L., Kafkalas, C. M., Tollen, L. G., & Swartz, M. (2000). Prevalence and relationships of posttraumatic stress in families experiencing pediatric spinal cord injury. *Rehabilitation Psychology, 45,* 339–355.

Boyer, B. A., Tollen, L., & Kafkalas, C. M. (1998). A pilot study of posttraumatic stress disorder in children and adolescents with spinal cord injury. *SCI Psychosocial Process, 11,* 75–81.

Boyer, B. A., Ware, C. J., Knolls, M. L., & Kafkalas, C. M. (2003). Posttraumatic stress in families with pediatric spinal cord injury: A replication. *SCI Psychosocial Process, 16,* 85–94.

Bracken, M. B., & Shepard, M. J. (1980). Coping and adaptation following acute spinal cord injury: A theoretical analysis. *Paraplegia, 18,* 74–85.

Bryce, T. N., & Ragnarsson, K. T. (2000). Pain after spinal cord injury. *Physical Medicine and Rehabilitation Clinics of North America, 11*(1), 157–168.

Bryce, T. N., & Ragnarsson, K. T. (2003). Pain management in persons with spinal cord disorders. In V. W. Lin et al. (Eds.), *Spinal cord medicine: Principles and practice* (pp. 441–460). New York: Demos.

Budh, C. N., Hultling, C., & Lundeberg, T. (2005). Quality of sleep in individuals with spinal cord injury: A comparison between patients with and without pain. *Spinal Cord, 43,* 85–95.

Campagnolo, D. I., & Merli, G. J. (2002). Autonomic and cardiovascular complications of spinal cord injury. In S. Kirshblum, D. Campagnolo, & J. A. DeLisa (Eds.), *Spinal cord injury medicine* (pp. 123–134). Philadelphia: Lippincott Williams & Wilkins.

Cardenas, D. D., Farrell-Roberts, L., Sipski, M. L., & Rubner, D. (1995). Management of gastrointestinal genitourinary, and sexual function. In S. L. Stover, J. A. DeLisa, & G. G. Whiteneck (Eds.), *Spinal cord injury: Clinical outcomes from the model systems* (pp. 120–144). Gaithersburg, MD: Aspen.

Charlifue, S. W., Kenneth, M. A., & Gerhart, M. S. (1991). Behavioral and demographic predictors of suicide after traumatic spinal cord injury. *Archives of Physical Medicine & Rehabilitation, 72,* 488–492.

Consortium for Spinal Cord Medicine. (1998). *Depression following spinal cord injury: A clinical practice guideline for primary care physicians.* Washington, DC: Paralyzed Veterans of America.

Craig, A., Hancock, K., Chang, E., & Dickson, H. (1998). Immunizing against depression and anxiety after spinal cord injury. *Archives of Physical Medicine & Rehabilitation, 79,* 375–377.

Craig, A., Hancock, K., Dickson, H., & Chang, E. (1997). Long-term psychological outcomes in spinal cord injured persons: Results of a controlled trial using cognitive behavior therapy. *Archives of Physical Medicine & Rehabilitation, 78,* 33–38.

Cushman, L. A., & Dijkers, M. P. (1990). Depressed mood in spinal cord injured patients: Staff perceptions and patient realities. *Archives of Physical Medicine & Rehabilitation, 71,* 191–196.

Danner, G., & Radnitz, C.L. (2000). Protective factors and posttraumatic stress disorder in veterans with spinal cord injury. *International Journal of Rehabilitation & Health, 5,* 195–203.

Davidoff, G., Morris, J., Roth, E., & Bleiberg, J. (1985). Cognitive dysfunction in mild closed head injury in traumatic spinal cord injury. *Archives of Physical Medicine & Rehabilitation, 66,* 489–491.

Davidoff, G. N., Roth, E. J., & Richards, J. S. (1992). Cognitive deficits in spinal cord injury: Epidemiology and outcome. *Archives of Physical Medicine & Rehabilitation, 73,* 275–284.

Davidoff, G., Thomas, P., Johnson, M., Berent, S., Dijkers, M., & Doljanac, R. (1988). Closed head injury in acute traumatic spinal cord injury: Incidence and risk factors. *Archives of Physical Medicine & Rehabilitation, 69,* 869–872.

DeVivo, M. J., Black, K. J., Richards, J. S., & Stover, S. L. (1991). Suicide following spinal cord injury. *Paraplegia, 29,* 620–627.

Dijkers, M. P., Abela, M. B., Gans, B., & Gordon, W.A. (1995). The aftermath of spinal cord injury. In S. L. Stover, J. A. DeLisa, & G. G. Whiteneck (Eds.), *Spinal cord injury: Clinical outcomes from the model systems* (pp. 185–212). Gaithersburg, MD: Aspen.

Dunn, M. (1977). Social discomfort in the patient with spinal cord injury. *Archives of Physical Medicine & Rehabilitation, 58,* 257–260.

Elfström, M. L., Kreuter, M., Rydén, A., Persson, L.-O., & Sullivan, M. (2002). Effects of coping on psychological outcome when controlling for background variables: A study of traumatically spinal cord lesioned persons. *Spinal Cord, 40,* 408–415.

Elliot, S. (2003). Sexual dysfunction and infertility in men with spinal cord disorders. In V. W. Lin et al. (Eds.), *Spinal cord medicine: Principles and practice* (pp. 349–365). New York: Demos.

Elliott, T. R., & Harkins, S. W. (1991). Psychosocial concomitants of persistent pain among persons with spinal cord injuries. *NeuroRehabilitation, 1*(4), 7–16.

Elliott, T. R., Herrick, S. M., Patti, A. M., Witty, T. E., Godshall, F. J., & Spruell, M. (1991). Assertiveness, social support, and psychological adjustment following spinal cord injury. *Behavior Research and Therapy, 29*(5), 485–493.

Elliott, T. R., Herrick, S. M., Witty, T. E., Godshall, F., & Spruell, M. (1992). Social support and depression following spinal cord injury. *Rehabilitation Psychology, 37,* 37–48.

Elliott, T. R., Kurylo, M., Chen, Y., & Hicken, B. (2002). Alcohol abuse history and adjustment following spinal cord injury. *Rehabilitation Psychology, 47,* 278–290.

Fichtenbaum, J., & Kirshblum, S. (2002). Psychological adaptation to spinal cord injury. In S. Kirshblum, D. Campagnolo, & J. A. DeLisa (Eds.), *Spinal cord medicine* (pp. 300–311). Philadelphia: Lippincott Williams & Wilkins.

Frank, R. G., Chaney, J. M., Clay, D. L., Shutty, M. S., Beck, N. C., Kay, D. R., et al. (1992). Dysphoria: A major symptom factor in persons with disability or chronic illness. *Psychiatry Research, 43,* 231–241.

Frank, R. G., Elliott, T. R., Corcoran, J. R., & Wonderlich, S. A. (1987). Depression after spinal cord injury: Is it necessary? *Clinical Psychology Review, 7,* 611–630.

Frank, R. G., Umlauf, R. L., Wonderlich, S. A., Askanazi, G. S., Buckelew, S. P., & Elliott, T.R. (1987). Differences in coping styles among persons with spinal cord injury: A cluster-analytic approach. *Journal of Consulting and Clinical Psychology, 55*(5), 727–731.

Fuhrer, M. J., Rintala, D. H., Hart, K. A., Clearman, R., & Young, M. E. (1993). Depressive symptomatology in persons with spinal cord injury who reside in the community. *Archives of Physical Medicine & Rehabilitation, 74,* 255–260.

Glickman, S., & Kamm, M. A. (1996). Bowel dysfunction in spinal cord injury patients. *Lancet, 347,* 1651–1653.

Grieco, E. M., & Cassidy, R. C. (2001, March). *Overview of race and Hispanic origin: Census 2000 Brief.* Retrieved July 15, 2006, from U.S. Census Bureau web site, at http://www.census.gov/prod/2001pubs/c2kbr01-1.pdf

Han, T. R., Kim, J. H., & Kwon, B. S. (1998). Chronic gastrointestinal problems and bowel dysfunction in patients with spinal cord injury. *Spinal Cord, 36,* 485–490.

Hanson, S., Buckelew, S. P., Hewett, J., & O'Neal, G. (1993). The relationship between coping and adjustment after spinal cord injury: A 5–year follow-up study. *Rehabilitation Psychology, 38,* 41–52.

Heinemann, A. W., Doll, M., & Schnoll, S. (1989). Treatment of alcohol abuse in persons with recent spinal cord injuries. *Alcohol Health & Research World, 13,* 110–117.

Heinemann, A. W., Mamott, B. D., & Schnoll, S. (1990). Substance use by persons with recent spinal cord injuries. *Rehabilitation Psychology, 35,* 217–228.

Herrick, S., Elliott, T. R., & Crow, F. (1994) Social support and the prediction of health complications among persons with spinal cord injuries. *Rehabilitation Psychology, 39,* 231–250.

Hulbert, R. J. (2006). Strategies of medical intervention in the management of acute spinal cord injury. *Spine, 31*(11 Suppl.), S16–S21.

Jackson, A. (2003). Women's health challenges after spinal cord injury. In V. W. Lin et al. (Eds.), *Spinal cord medicine: Principles and practice* (pp. 839–849). New York: Demos.

Jackson, A. J., Wadley, V. G., Richards, J. S., & DeVivo, M. J. (1995). Sexual behavior and function among spinal cord injured women [Abstract]. *Journal of Spinal Cord Medicine, 18,* 141.

Jones, M. L., Mathewson, C. S., Adkins, V. K., & Ayllon, T. (2003). Use of behavioral contingencies to promote prevention of recurrent pressure ulcers. *Archives of Physical Medicine & Rehabilitation, 84,* 796–802.

Keirstead, H. S., & Steward, O. (2003). Recent advances in neural regeneration. In V. W. Lin et al. (Eds.), *Spinal cord medicine: Principles and practice* (pp. 785–800). New York: Demos.

Kemp, B. J., Kahan, J., Krause, J., Adkins, R. H., & Nava, G. (2004). Treatment of major depression in individuals with spinal cord injury. *Journal of Spinal Cord Medicine, 27,* 22–28.

Kemp, B. J., Krause, J. S., & Adkins, R. A. (1999). Depressive symptomatology among African-American, Latino, and Caucasian participants with spinal cord injury. *Rehabilitation Psychology, 44,* 235–247.

Kennedy, P., & Duff, J. (2001). Post traumatic stress disorder and spinal cord injuries. *Spinal Cord, 39,* 1–10.

Kennedy, P., Duff, J., Evans, M., & Beedie, A. (2003). Coping effectiveness training reduces depression and anxiety following traumatic spinal cord injuries. *British Journal of Clinical Psychology, 42,* 41–52.

Kennedy, P., & Rogers, B. A. (2000). Anxiety and depression after spinal cord injury: A longitudinal analysis. *Archives of Physical Medicine & Rehabilitation, 81,* 932–937.

Kessler, R. C., Chiu, W. T., Demler, O., & Walters, E. E. (2005). Prevalence, severity, and comorbidity of twelve-month *DSM-IV* disorders in the National Comorbidity Survey Replication (NCS-R). *Archives of General Psychiatry, 62,* 617–627.

Kolakowsky-Hayner, S. A., Gourley, E. V., Kreutzer, J. S., Marwitz, J. H., Cifu, D. X., & McKinley, W. O. (1999). Pre-injury substance abuse among persons with brain injury and persons with spinal cord injury. *Brain Injury, 13,* 571–581.

Kolakowsky-Hayner, S. A., Gourley, E. V., Kreutzer, J. S., Marwitz, J. H., Meade, M. A., & Cifu, D. X. (2002). Post-injury substance abuse among persons with brain injury and persons with spinal cord injury. *Brain Injury, 16,* 583–592.

Krause, J. S., & Broderick, L. E. (2004). Outcomes after spinal cord injury: Comparisons as a function of gender and race and ethnicity. *Archives of Physical Medicine & Rehabilitation, 85,* 355–362.

Krause, J. S., Kemp, B., & Coker, J. (2000). Depression after spinal cord injury: Relation to gender, ethnicity, aging, and socioeconomic indicators. *Archives of Physical Medicine & Rehabilitation, 81,* 1099–1109.

Krause, J. S., Kewman, D., DeVivo, M. J., Maynard, F., Coker, J., Roach, M. J., & Ducharme, S. (1999). Employment after spinal cord injury: An analysis of cases from the model spinal cord injury systems. *Archives of Physical Medicine & Rehabilitation, 80,* 1492–1500.

Lanig, I. S., & Peterson, W. P. (2000). The respiratory system in spinal cord injury. *Physical Medicine and Rehabilitation Clinics of North America, 11*(1), 29–43.

Lazarus, R. S., & Folkman, S. (1984). *Stress, appraisal and coping.* New York: Springer.

LeViseur, C., & Sonka-Maarek, S. (2003). Activities of daily living. In V. W. Lin et al. (Eds.), *Spinal cord medicine: Principles and practice* (pp. 691–704). New York: Demos.

Linsenmeyer, T. A. (2000). Sexual function and infertility following spinal cord injury. *Physical Medicine and Rehabilitation Clinics of North America, 11*(1), 141–156.

Lundqvist, C., Siösteen, A., Blomstrand, C., Lind, B., & Sullivan, M. (1991). Spinal cord injuries: Clinical, functional and emotional status. *Spine, 16,* 78–83.

Macciocchi, S. N., Bowman, B., Coker, J., Apple, D., & Leslie, D. (2004). Effect of co-morbid traumatic brain injury on functional outcome of persons with spinal cord injuries. *American Journal of Physical Medicine & Rehabilitation, 83,* 22–26.

Mallory, B. (2003). Autonomic dysfunction in spinal cord disease. In V. W. Lin et al. (Eds.), *Spinal cord medicine: Principles and practice* (pp. 477–500). New York: Demos.

Marchese, K., Boyer, B. A., & Goldberg, K. B. (2005). Pediatric spinal cord injury and mild traumatic brain injury: A brief guide to differential diagnosis and treatment recommendations in combination injury. *SCI Psychosocial Process, 18,* 40–45.

McGowan, M. B., & Roth, S. (1987). Family functioning and functional independence in spinal cord injury adjustment. *Paraplegia, 25,* 357–365.

McKinley, W. O., Kolakowsky, S. A., & Kreutzer, J. S. (1999). Substance abuse, violence, and outcome after traumatic spinal cord injury. *American Journal of Physical Medicine & Rehabilitation, 78,* 306–312.

Merbitz, C. T., King, R. B., Bleiberg, J., & Grip, J. C. (1985). Wheelchair push-ups: Measuring pressure relief frequency. *Archives of Physical Medicine & Rehabilitation, 66,* 433–438.

Montroy, R. E., & Eltorai, I. (2003). The surgical management of pressure ulcers. In V. W. Lin et al. (Eds.), *Spinal cord medicine: Principles and practice* (pp. 591–612). New York: Demos.

Nance, P. W. (2003). Management of spasticity. In V. W. Lin et al. (Eds.), *Spinal cord medicine: Principles and practice* (pp. 461–476). New York: Demos.

National Spinal Cord Injury Statistical Center. (2005a). Spinal cord injury: Facts and figures at a glance. *Journal of Spinal Cord Medicine, 28,* 379–380.

National Spinal Cord Injury Statistical Center. (2005b). The 2005 annual statistical report for the model spinal cord injury systems. Retrieved June 2, 2006, from the University of Alabama at Birmingham Spinal Cord Injury Information Network web site at http://images.main.uab .edu/spinalcord/pdffiles/facts05.pdf

Priebe, M. M., Martin, M., Wuermser, L. A., Castillo, T., & McFarlin, J. (2003). The medical management of pressure ulcers. In V. W. Lin et al. (Eds.), *Spinal cord medicine: Principles and practice* (pp. 567–589). New York: Demos.

Putzke, J. D., Hicken, B. L., & Richards, J. S. (2002). Race: Predictor versus proxy variable? Outcomes after spinal cord injury. *Archives of Physical Medicine & Rehabilitation, 83,* 1603–1611.

Putzke, J. D., Richards, J. S., Hicken, B. L., & DeVivo, M. J. (2002). Interference due to pain following spinal cord injury: Important predictors and impact on quality of life. *Pain, 100,* 231–242.

Radnitz, C., & Danner, G. (2002). Recovery from posttraumatic stress disorder in veterans with spinal cord injury. *SCI Psychosocial Process, 15,* [185], 190, 192–7.

Radnitz, C. L., Hsu, L., Tirch, D. D., Willard, J., Lillian, L. B., Walczak, S., et al. (1998). A comparison of posttraumatic stress disorder in veterans with and without spinal cord injury. *Journal of Abnormal Psychology, 107,* 676–680.

Richards, J. S. (2005). Spinal cord injury pain: Impact, classification, treatment trends, and implications from translational research. *Rehabilitation Psychology, 50,* 99–102.

Richards, J. S., Bombardier, C. H., Tate, D., Dijkers, M., Gordon, W., Shewchuk, R., & DeVivo, M. J. (1999). Access to the environment and life satisfaction after spinal cord injury. *Archives of Physical Medicine & Rehabilitation, 80,* 1501–1506.

Richards, J. S., Brown, L., Hagglund K., Bua, G., & Reeder, K. (1988). Spinal cord injury and concomitant traumatic brain injury: Results of a longitudinal investigation. *American Journal of Physical Medicine & Rehabilitation, 67,* 211–216.

Richards, J. S., Elliott, T. R., Shewchuk, R. M., & Fine, P. R. (1997). Attribution of responsibility for onset of spinal cord injury and psychosocial outcomes in the first year post injury. *Rehabilitation Psychology, 42,* 115–124.

Richards, J. S., Kewman, D. G., & Pierce, C. A. (2000). Spinal cord injury. In R. G. Frank & T. R. Elliott (Eds.), *Handbook of Rehabilitation Psychology* (pp. 11–27.) Washington, DC: American Psychological Association.

Richards, J. S., Kogos, S. C., & Richardson, E. J. (2006). Psychosocial measures for clinical trials in spinal cord injury: Quality of life, depression, and anxiety. *Topics in Spinal Cord Injury Rehabilitation, 11*(3), 24–35.

Richards, J. S., Lloyd, L. K., James, J. W., & Brown, J. (1992). Treatment of erectile dysfunction secondary to spinal cord injury: Sexual and psychosocial impact on couples. *Rehabilitation Psychology, 37,* 205–213.

Richards, J. S., Meredith, R. L., Nepomuceno, C., Fine, P. R., & Bennett, G. (1980). Psychosocial aspects of chronic pain in spinal cord injury. *Pain, 8,* 355–366.

Rintala, D. H., Young, M. E., Hart, K. A., Clearman, R. R., & Fuhrer, M. J. (1992). Social support and the well-being of persons with spinal cord injury living in the community. *Rehabilitation Psychology, 37,* 155–163.

Rohe, D. E., & Krause, J. S. (1993, August). *The five factor model of personality: Findings among males with spinal cord injury.* Paper presented at the 101st Annual Convention of the American Psychological Association, Toronto.

Rose, M., Robinson, J., Ells, P., & Cole, J. (1988). Pain following spinal cord injury: Results from a postal survey. *Pain, 34,* 101–102.

Roth, E., Davidoff, G., Thomas, P., Doljanac, R., Dijkers, M., Berent, S., et al. (1989). A controlled study of neuropsychological deficits in acute spinal cord injury patients. *Paraplegia, 27,* 480–489.

Sabharwal, S. (2003). Cardiovascular dysfunction in spinal cord disorders. In V. W. Lin et al. (Eds.), *Spinal cord medicine: Principles and practice* (pp. 179–192). New York: Demos.

Sassoon, C. S. H., & Baydur, A. (2003). Respiratory dysfunction in spinal cord disorders. In V. W. Lin et al. (Eds.), *Spinal cord medicine: Principles and practice* (pp. 155–168). New York: Demos.

Schulz, R., & Decker, S. (1985). Long-term adjustment to physical disability: The role of social support, perceived control, and self-blame. *Journal of Personality and Social Psychology, 48,* 1162–1172.

Siddall, P. J., Yezierski, R. P., & Loeser, J. D. (2000). Pain following spinal cord injury: Clinical features, prevalence, and taxonomy. *International Association for the Study of Pain Newsletter, 3,* 3–7.

Siösteen, A., Kreuter, M., Lampic, C., & Persson, L. O. (2005). Patient-staff agreement in the perception of spinal cord lesioned patients' problems, emotional well-being, and coping pattern. *Spinal Cord, 43,* 179–186.

Sipski, M. L., Alexander, C. J., & Rosen, R. C. (1995). Physiologic responses associated with orgasm in SCI women [Abstract]. *Journal of Spinal Cord Medicine, 18,* 140.

Sipski, M. L., & Richards, J. S. (2006). Spinal cord injury rehabilitation: State of the science. *American Journal of Physical Medicine & Rehabilitation, 85,* 310–342.

Soden, R. J., Walsh, J., Middleton, J. W., Craven, M. L., Rutkowski, S. B., & Yeo, J.D. (2000). Causes of death after spinal cord injury. *Spinal Cord, 38,* 604–610.

Song, H.-Y. (2005). Modeling social reintegration in persons with spinal cord injury. *Disability & Rehabilitation, 27*(3), 131–141.

Stiens, S., Fajardo, N. R., & Korsten, M. A. (2003). The gastrointestinal system after spinal cord injury. In V. W. Lin et al. (Eds.), *Spinal cord medicine: Principles and practice* (pp. 321–348). New York: Demos.

Tate, D. G., Forchheimer, M. B., Krause, J. S., Meade, M. A., & Bombardier, C. H. (2004). Patterns of alcohol and substance use and abuse in persons with spinal cord injury: Risk factors and correlates. *Archives of Physical Medicine & Rehabilitation, 85,* 1837–1847.

Thomas, J. P. (1995). The model spinal cord injury concept: Development and implementation. In S. L. Stover, J. A. DeLisa, & G. G. Whiteneck (Eds.), *Spinal cord injury: Clinical outcomes from the model systems* (pp. 1–9). Gaithersburg, MD: Aspen.

Trieschmann, R. B. (1988). *Spinal cord injuries: Psychological, social, and vocational rehabilitation* (2nd ed.). New York: Demos.

White, G. W., Mathews, M., & Fawcett, S. B. (1989). Reducing risk of pressure sores: Effects of watch prompts and alarm avoidance on wheelchair push-ups. *Journal of Applied Behavior Analysis, 22,* 287–295

Widerström-Noga, E. G., Felipe-Cuervo, E., & Yezierski, R. P. (2001). Chronic pain after spinal injury: Interference with sleep and daily activities. *Archives of Physical Medicine & Rehabilitation, 82,* 1571–1577.

Widerstöm-Noga, E. G., & Turk, D. C. (2004). Exacerbation of chronic pain following spinal cord injury. *Journal of Neurotrauma, 21,* 1384–1395.

Young, M. E., Rintala, D. H., Rossi, C. D., Hart, K. A., & Fuhrer, M. J. (1995). Alcohol and marijuana use in a community-based sample of persons with spinal cord injury. *Archives of Physical Medicine & Rehabilitation, 76,* 525–532.

CHAPTER 11

Asthma

DAPHNE KOINIS MITCHELL and ELIZABETH MCQUAID

INTRODUCTION: PATHOPHYSIOLOGY

Asthma is a complex disease of the airways, characterized by both episodic and chronic features. The Guidelines for the Diagnosis and Management of Asthma, developed by the National Heart, Lung and Blood Institute, define asthma as a chronic inflammatory airway disorder, in which many cells and cellular elements play a role (National Institutes of Health [NIH], 1997). Asthma involves bronchial hyperresponsiveness (i.e., an exaggerated bronchoconstrictor response to stimuli) and bronchospasm, leading to airflow limitation and intermittent and variable periods of airway obstruction. Chronic inflammation of the airways, even in milder forms of the disease, is also recognized as a core feature (NIH). Current treatment approaches highlight the need for ongoing management for all forms of the disease.

Specifically, the pathophysiology of asthma involves multiple overlapping processes, including smooth muscle dysfunction, airway inflammation, airway hyperresponsiveness to various triggers, swelling of the airways, and mucus production (NIH, 1997). Smooth muscle contraction causes bronchial constriction. If the inflammation is chronic, smooth muscle hypertrophy (an increase in cell size), hyperplasia (an increase in the number of cells), and bronchial hyperresponsiveness develop. An influx of inflammatory cells (i.e., mast cells, eosinophils, and Type 2 helper T lymphocytes) is associated with airway inflammation. Airway inflammation and bronchoconstriction can result in a range of symptoms, including coughing, wheezing, breathlessness, and chest tightness, particularly at night or early in the morning. Episodes involving one or many of these symptoms are associated with widespread but variable airflow obstruction that is often reversible, either spontaneously or with treatment.

If not properly treated, symptoms can persist and can impose limitations on physical functioning, including a restriction of activities, missed sleep, and overall quality of life. Other outcomes of asthma morbidity that can be affected by frequent asthma symptoms include an increase in school absences for children, missed work for adults, and an increase in emergency department (ED) visits and hospitalizations. For children and adults, the presence of symptoms can also impair concentration and the ability to attend. Nocturnal allergic symptoms can compromise children's quality of sleep and ability to focus while in school (Diette, Markson, Skinner, Nguen, & Algatt-Bergstrom, 2000). If untreated and/or severe, asthma can result in death.

RISK FOR ASTHMA

Although there is not a clear understanding of the cause of asthma, several factors are thought to contribute to its development (Arruda, Sole, Baena-Cagnani, & Naspitz, 2005). Genetic factors, such as a family history, are now thought to play a central role (Samet, Wiesch, & Ahmed, 2001). The presence of familial aggregation in asthma among related individuals may indicate either shared genes or a common household environment, as a study of monozygotic twins showed higher concordance rates than in dizygotic twins (Samet et al.). A maternal history of asthma has also been associated with a larger increase in asthma risk (Liu et al., 2003; Martinez, 2001a). This research has evidenced maternal effects on a developing fetus' immune system that may extend from the fetal period to the postnatal period through breast milk and environmental conditions. Further, exclusive breastfeeding for at least 4 months has been associated with protection for the development of asthma (Oddy, 2004); however, other studies have failed to demonstrate this protective effect (Sears et al., 2002).

In general, asthma is thought to be a complex genetic disorder with variable phenotypes, largely attributed to the interactions of the environment and multiple genes (Halapi & Hakonarson, 2004). Specific alleles have been identified for immunoglobulin E (IgE; Cookson & Young, 1992) and bronchoreactivity (Postma et al. 1995). A genomic-wide search for genes associated with asthma, asthma-associated phenotypes, elevated IgE levels, and bronchial hyperresponsiveness is underway, and numerous loci and a variety of candidate genes have been identified (Anon, 1997). Recently two allergy and asthma susceptibility genes, ADAM33 and PHFII, have been reported (Zang et al. 2003). However, only a few genes conferring significant risk have been mapped (Halapi & Hakonarson), and the clinical implications of the genetic variations within these genes remain largely undetermined (Halapi & Hakonarson). Efforts to examine ethnic group differences in genetic predispositions and risk for development of asthma have also been suggested, and some variations in genetic profile by ethnic group have been found (e.g., Burchard et al., 2004). Further work is needed to determine the importance of the genes identified.

The propensity to have an allergy (known as *atopy*), as defined by IgE or allergen skin testing, is highly related to asthma (Gergen, Mullally, & Evans, 1988). Increasing levels of atopy, as defined by the number of positive allergen skin tests, has been related to the severity of asthma in children (Zimmerman et al. 1988), but not in adults (Inouye et al. 1985). Allergic rhinitis (Bousquet, Van Cauwenberge, Khaltaev, & World Health Organization, 2001) and atopic dermatitis (Fernandez-Mayoralas, Caballero, & Garcia-Marcos, 2004) have been shown to be risk factors for asthma. Not all allergens appear to be related to asthma occurrence, as cross-sectional and longitudinal research have documented a link between allergen skin reactivity to dust mites, cats, and asthma in children from birth to age 13 (Marks et al., 2006; Sears et al. 1989), yet grass pollen was not associated with asthma. The amount of allergen to which an individual is exposed also appears to play a role in the development and severity of asthma, as increasing levels of exposure to house dust mites or cockroaches has been associated with asthma in some children (Rosenstreich et al., 1997). Other forms of atopy, such as infantile eczema and hay fever, have also been associated with asthma (Jenkins, Hopper, Flander, Carlin, & Giles, 1993).

Male sex also appears to be a risk factor for asthma onset, but only up to the age of puberty. This may be linked with boys' lower maximal expiratory flow at a given lung volume, possible immune factor differences, and hormonal changes. Airway size is also smaller in boys than girls during early development, and subsequently increases more rapidly in boys than in girls (Martinez, 2001b). Boys also have greater airway hyperresponsiveness (PausJenssen & Cockcroft, 2003).

Other factors can precipitate the onset of asthma, including environmental factors such as exposure to viruses, allergens, and irritants (Busse & Lemanske, 2001). Environmental stimuli might affect gene expression and phenotypic outcome, and the interactions may be subject to change over time, depending on the developmental state and the immulogic milieu (Vercelli, 2004). Viral infections have been implicated in at least three ways to the pathogenesis of asthma: inception, prevention, and exacerbations (Lemanske, 2004). Asthma inception after early childhood respiratory tract infection may be influenced by genetic, environmental (type of virus and concomittant allergen exposure), and developmental factors (age at which infection occurs). Studies have pointed to an association between respiratory syncytial virus (RSV), bronchiolitis, and other early respiratory tract infections, with recurrent wheezing during the first 4 to 7 years of life (Lemanske). Early sensitization has been associated with an increased risk for persistent asthma, bronchial hyperresponsiveness, and with a greater loss of lung function (Platts-Mills, Blumenthal, Perzanowski, & Woodfolk, 2000). Paradoxically, repetitive viral infections may actually exert a protective effect on the development of asthma, due to certain effects on the immune system (Lemanske).

The risk of having asthma appears to be compounded by certain modern lifestyle factors, including indoor environment, diet, air pollution, and psychological stress (Colilla et al., 2003). The length, timing, and type of exposure to infectious agents have been shown either to promote or to suppress an inflammatory process and to influence a subsequent history of asthma (de Marco, Pattaro, Locatelli, Svanes, & ECRHS Study Group, 2004). Maternal smoking during pregnancy and children's exposure to environmental tobacco smoke (ETS) have been associated with the risk for the development of asthma (DiFranza, Aligne, & Weitzman, 2004). Environmental tobacco smoke increases the prevalence and severity of asthma exacerbations, as indicated by increases in the frequency of attacks and the number of ED visits (DiFranza et al.). Exposure to air pollutants, including nitrogen oxides, carbon monoxide, sulfur dioxide, and parental atopy were significantly associated with physician-diagnosed asthma among children 6 to 15 years of age in Taiwan (Lee, Lin, Hsiue, Hwang, & Guo, 2003). Few studies have evaluated exposure to air pollutants prospectively and its relation to the development of asthma. Links between obesity and asthma have also been shown, with associations between inflammatory markers and body mass index (e.g., Barros et al., 2006).

Widespread research has shown an association between psychological factors such as stress and the development of asthma (Kattan et al., 2005; Mrazek & Klinnert, 1991). Some evidence also suggests that psychological stress may influence the development and pathophysiology of asthma through increased risk of respiratory infections (Wright & Taussig, 1998). Recent research has indicated that maternal factors, such as difficulties in parenting, may have an impact on asthma risk (Klinnert, Mrazek, & Mrazek, 1994; Klinnert et al., 2001). Klinnert and colleagues (2001) conducted an investigation of physiological and psychological influences on asthma onset, using a prospective design. Results showed that two early indicators, an index of allergy, and an index of global parenting difficulty at 3 weeks of age, were independent predictors of asthma status between ages 6 and 8. These findings suggest that stressful events and/or the quality of the caregiving may affect the emotional and physiologic regulation of the infant in the direction of increased allergic response.

Some theories have been proposed that attempt to further understanding about the development of asthma. It has been theorized that the development of asthma may be due to increased exposure to indoor allergens related to overall lifestyle changes (i.e., reduction in time spent outside by both children and adults). Additionally, the "hygiene hypothesis" involves the argument that the frequent use of antibiotics and decreased exposure to infections early in life might alter the immune response, which could lead to an increased likelihood of developing asthma (Mattes & Karmaus, 1999). Taken together, what is known about the proclivity to have asthma and the risk to develop asthma over time point to the complex interaction between genes and environment, with potential contributions from additional contextual and social factors exacerbating onset and expression of symptoms.

PREVALENCE

The overall prevalence of asthma in the United States increased approximately 58.6% between 1982 and 1996 (Centers for Disease Control [CDC], 1996). Recent data suggest that rising asthma prevalence rates may have demonstrated a plateau in the late 1990s, but the general trend over the past several decades has been toward an increase (Annual Report 2005: The Future of Lung Health, 2005).

Statistics regarding asthma prevalence typically differentiate between current asthma (people who have been diagnosed with asthma by a health professional and who still have asthma), and lifetime asthma (people who have ever been diagnosed with asthma). According to statistics from the CDC, in 2002, estimates of current asthma prevalence included 72 people per 1,000, or 20 million people in the United States. In terms of lifetime prevalence rates, in 2002, 30.8 million people (111 people per 1,000) had ever been diagnosed with asthma during their lifetime.

Asthma prevalence rates appear to decrease with age. In 2002, 83 per 1,000 children under 17 years of age have a current diagnosis of asthma, compared to 68 per 1,000 adults 18 years and over. Females had a 30% higher prevalence compared to males. This pattern, however, was reversed among children. The current asthma prevalence rate for boys aged 0–17 years (94 per 1,000) was 30% higher than the rate among girls (71 per 1,000; CDC, 2002).

ASTHMA BURDEN

The burden from asthma in the United States has increased over the past 2 decades, despite advances in asthma treatment. Increases in asthma morbidity and mortality are overrepresented in the pediatric population (CDC, 2002). Uncontrolled asthma can also impose serious limitations on daily life. Asthma is the leading cause of school absenteeism due to chronic illness, with approximately 14.7 million school days missed per year due to asthma symptoms by children 5–17 years of age (NIH, 2002). This problem is compounded by an estimated $1 billion in lost productivity for their working parents (NIH). For adults, asthma is the second most important respiratory condition to cause home confinement. In 2002, adults 18 years of age and over who were currently employed missed 11.8 million work days due to asthma (NIH). Each year, asthma causes more than 18 million days of restricted activity (NIH).

Asthma accounts for millions of visits to physicians' offices and to the ED. In 2002, there were an estimated 13.9 million outpatient asthma visits to private physician offices and hospital outpatient departments (CDC, 2002). Children aged 0–17 years accounted for approximately 5 million visits, and adults accounted for close to nine million visits. There were approximately 1.9 million visits to EDs for asthma in 2002, with the highest rates among children aged 0–4 years (CDC). In addition, asthma accounted for approximately 484,000 hospitalizations in 2002. Hospitalizations were also highest among children 0–4 years. Females had a hospitalization rate about 35% higher than males (CDC).

Asthma-related health care costs for the United States were approximately $10.7 billion in 1994, including a direct health care cost of $6.1 billion (CDC, 2002). A large proportion of asthma health care costs are allocated for serious consequences of the disease, such as hospitalizations and ED visits, which could potentially be avoided through the implementation of optimal pharmacologic intervention and self-management techniques (Smith & Strunk, 1999). The rising rates and associated burdens that asthma can impose have made the condition a public health concern of significant social magnitude and a priority for health care providers working with individuals with asthma.

ASTHMA MORTALITY

Compared to other chronic illnesses, asthma-related fatalities are relatively rare; however, death rates from pediatric asthma have risen considerably in the past 2 decades (Weiss & Wagener, 1990). From 1975 to 1979, the death rate was 8.2 per 100,000 people. That rate jumped from 1993–1995 to 17.9 per 100,000. The death rate from asthma for children ages 5 to 14 doubled from 1980 to 1993. In total, asthma claims approximately 5,000 lives annually in the United States. Deaths from asthma have been linked to a number of risk factors, including medication nonadherence and inaccuracies in perceiving the severity of symptoms (NIH, 1995).

DISPROPORTIONATE IMPACT OF ASTHMA

Asthma's prevalence, morbidity, and mortality is disproportionately present among ethnic minority youth and adults, urban communities, and low-income populations (CDC, 2002). In terms of prevalence rates, when race and ethnicity is considered, Puerto Ricans had a current asthma prevalence that was 80% higher than non-Hispanic Whites. Non-Hispanic blacks and American Indians had a current asthma prevalence that was 30% higher than non-Hispanic Whites (CDC). Overall estimates for Hispanics are somewhat misleading, as they mask striking subgroup variations. Among all racial and ethnic groups, in 2002, Puerto Ricans had the highest rate of lifetime asthma (196 per 1,000) and Mexicans the lowest (61 per 1,000). Puerto Ricans were almost 80% more likely, and non-Hispanic blacks and American Indians were about 25% more likely to have ever been diagnosed with asthma than non-Hispanic Whites.

Ethnic minorities demonstrate higher rates of asthma, more health care utilization related to asthma, and more fatalities from asthma than Caucasians (CDC, 2002; Lozano, Sullivan, Smith, & Weiss, 1999; Weiss, Gergen, & Crain, 1992). In 2002, non-Hispanic blacks were the most likely to die from asthma, and had an asthma death rate over 200% higher than non-Hispanic whites and 160% higher than Hispanics. National estimates for Hispanic subgroups, such as Puerto Ricans and Mexicans, are not available. However, studies have shown that overall, asthma mortality in the U.S. has been decreasing since 1999 among Hispanics and non-Hispanics (e.g., Sly, 2006). For example, deaths from asthma among Hispanics decreased from 320 in 1999 to 274 in 2001 (from 1.0 per 100,000 to .7 in 2001), whereas deaths among non-Hispanics decreased from 4,324 to 3,976 (1.84 to 1.6).

Confounding factors related to ethnic group status and urban living may explain the disparities in asthma outcomes (Miller, 2000). For example, low-income status (Miller), urban residence (Grant, Lyttle, & Weiss, 2000), ethnic minority status/race (Lieu et al., 2002), beliefs about medications (Bearison, Minian, & Granowetter, 2002), language barriers, environmental triggers (e.g., pollution; Brugge et al., 2003), and access to consistent asthma care (Crain, Kercsmar, Weiss, Mitchell, & Lynn, 1998) are among the factors shown to independently account for poor health management behaviors and health care utilization among urban groups (Wallace et al., 2003). The increasing prevalence of asthma in urban populations underscores the need for new therapies to prevent asthma and reduce its prevalence in these groups.

DISEASE FACTORS

When asthma symptoms typically first present in a given individual they are intricately linked with a host of factors involving genetic predisposition, such as maternal contributions, environmental conditions related to prenatal development early in life (e.g., allergens and irritants, respiratory infections), perceptions of stress, and psychological processes. One typically is born with a susceptibility to develop sensitive airways; however, environmental and/or psychological reactions to specific conditions can precipitate or worsen symptoms. More research is still needed to clarify this complex puzzle regarding asthma onset; however, due to such differences, several profiles of asthma onset and response to symptoms over the life course among individuals are common. For example, some children exhibit symptoms early on in infancy, only as the result of respiratory infections, yet do not experience symptoms in response to other triggers. It is possible that these children's symptom presentation will wax and wane throughout their life. Other children may be symptomatic in the presence of many triggers over time or during specific seasons and may remain with a diagnosis of severe asthma throughout their development. There are developmental variations, individual characteristics, changes in season, and differences in exposure to environmental elements that may impact when one will first develop symptoms, and one's overall asthma response trajectory over time. It is more common for most individuals with asthma to present with symptoms in the first 2 years of life; however, adult onset asthma (e.g., during pregnancy) is not uncommon (NIH, 2002).

Disease Progression

Asthma's course is intermittent and variable. The chronic underlying inflammation does not typically produce noticeable symptoms. Symptoms commonly occur as a result of airway hyperresponsiveness to a variety of triggers. Asthma exacerbations can vary from mild to life threatening, and episodes can range in duration. Early warning signs that may show the onset of asthma symptoms can include watery eyes, behavioral quieting, runny nose, or circles under the eyes. Symptoms can then become more severe if not treated with quick-relief medication. When severe, symptoms include changes in accessory muscle groups, such as retractions (the skin on the neck and by the ribcage sink in during breathing), cyanosis (evidence of poor oxygen saturation, such as a blue tinge to the fingertips or lips), and difficulty walking and speaking comfortably. An individual's response to specific triggers and symptom expression can also change over development and contexts, depending on the individual, seasonality, response to medications, and exposure to triggers. Many factors can trigger an asthma attack, including allergens (e.g., dust), respiratory infections, exercise, seasonal factors such as abrupt changes in the weather, or exposure to airway irritants, such as tobacco smoke. Triggers vary by individual, and sensitivity can change over the course of illness, underscoring the need for individualized treatment plans that specify asthma triggers, symptoms, and medication needs for a particular patient.

While the airway obstruction associated with asthma is typically reversible without resulting in lung damage, more permanent remodeling of the airways has been recognized as a potential consequence of the disease (Academy of Allergy, Asthma and Immunology [AAAAI], 2000). Recent research in the pediatric asthma population suggests that early recognition and treatment of the disease during the first 5 years of life may play a role in preventing the progressive loss of lung function that can occur later in childhood (Martinez et al., 1995).

REGIMEN FACTORS

Effective asthma management requires acceptance of the chronic, episodic nature of the illness, and belief in the efficacy of medications used for treatment. A physician skilled in asthma diagnosis, treatment, and symptom monitoring is needed to coordinate care. Depending on the severity and course of the condition, asthma may be medically managed by a primary care pediatrician or may necessitate the involvement of a specialty provider, such as a pulmonologist or an allergist.

An array of treatment recommendations is typically made for control of persistent symptoms. Recommendations regarding matching the level of care to disease severity have been broadly adopted (NIH, 1997). Typical recommendations include separate medications for symptom control and for management of exacerbations, and identification of triggers and measures to avoid or minimize exposure to them (NIH). Patients are instructed that adherence to these treatment recommendations can lead to greater symptom control, decreased need for urgent health care visits, and enhanced quality of life. The more complex a treatment regimen becomes, however, the more challenging it becomes for patients and families to follow it effectively.

Quick-relief medications are used to provide prompt relief of symptoms associated with bronchoconstriction, a core feature of asthma episodes. These include short-acting beta$_2$–agonists, and systemic corticosteroids for more severe asthma episodes. Short-acting beta$_2$–agonists (e.g., albuterol) are inexpensive and are typically prescribed to be used by metered-dose inhaler. For patients with intermittent asthma that involves infrequent exacerbations, a quick-relief medication may be the only form of treatment prescribed. Oral steroids (e.g., prednisone) are also recommended for prompt reversal of asthma symptoms when repeated administration of beta$_2$–agonists is not effective. It is important to note that quick-relief medications are only recommended for short-term use. Excessive use of quick-relief medications may be an important indicator that asthma is insufficiently managed and that more aggressive treatment, such as addition of a long-term-control medication, should be considered.

Long-term-control medications are intended for daily use for extended periods of time to control persistent asthma symptoms. Patients with persistent asthma symptoms are typically prescribed both quick-relief medication and some form of long-term-control medication. Several forms of these preventive medications are available. Inhaled corticosteroids are the most commonly prescribed, as they are regarded as the most effective anti-inflammatory technique currently available for daily control of symptoms (NIH, 1997, 2002). These are typically available in inhaled form, such as through a metered dose inhaler or a dry powder inhaler. Leukotriene modifiers (e.g., Singulair®), which are available in oral tablet form, can be considered alternative treatment or additional treatment for significant symptoms (NIH). Some forms of medication offer a dual delivery of inhaled corticosteriod along with a long-acting $beta_2$–agonist in a single therapeutic dose for patients who require both forms of preventive medication (e.g., Advair®).

Clinical recommendations for asthma management also include measures for trigger reduction in the home setting. This often includes strategies such as counseling patients and/or family members to quit smoking, to remove pets from the home, and to employ measures to reduce dust mites, such as frequent cleaning and washing of bedclothes in hot water.

One of the most significant challenges in following treatment recommendations for asthma appears to be adhering to recommendations for consistent use of controller medications. Nonadherence to controller medications is a pervasive problem for both children (Bender et al., 2000) and adults (Apter, Reisine, Affleck, Barrows, & ZuWallack, 1998) with asthma, with objective measures indicating that, on average, patients take approximately half of prescribed doses (McQuaid, Kopel, Klein, & Fritz, 2003). Although there is more limited research regarding adherence to environmental control recommendations, adherence in this area also appears to be low. Studies consistently show that adults with asthma do not have lower smoking rates that those without asthma (Lemiere & Boulet, 2005), a large proportion of parents of children with asthma continue to smoke (Kattan et al., 1997), and approximately two-thirds of households of children with asthma have household pets (Wamboldt et al., 2002).

Some key features of asthma and the recommendations for care may impede appropriate adherence. Asthma's variable symptom presentation makes it difficult to link specific triggers to exacerbations on a consistent basis (e.g., "the cat hasn't been bothering my asthma lately"), which may decrease motivation to follow through on certain strategies. Additionally, medications for long-term control must be taken consistently for proper effect, yet they provide no immediate feedback on symptoms. As a result, patients may forget to take medications regularly, particularly during asymptomatic periods (Penza-Clyve, Mansell, & McQuaid, 2004). For children with asthma, effective communication between children, parents, and other caregivers is necessary for ongoing symptom management and disease control. Differing perspectives regarding responsibility for asthma management from various players in the system may result in poor adherence (Walders, Drotar, & Kercsmar, 2000).

Family stressors can also serve as barriers to successful illness management. Family processes that impact family functioning and the emotional climate of the family, such as parental distress, conflict, stressful life events, or lack of spousal or caretaker support can compromise illness management and contribute to poor asthma management.

For children, developmental issues can also present as challenges to effective asthma control. The implementation of skills for optimal pediatric asthma management results from a complex set of interactions between parent and child. Children's active participation may vary widely by age, developmental maturity, and attitude toward illness (McQuaid et al., 2001). Preadolescent children tend to assume responsi-

bility for tasks of identifying and managing symptoms when asthma symptoms occur. They are less likely to assume responsibility for tasks of preventive management,
such as avoiding triggers or taking regular medications (McQuaid, Kopel, & Nassau,
2001). Adolescence is a time in which difficulties in adherence to medications can be
more pronounced for children with asthma (Bender et al., 2000; McQuaid et al., 2000).
Consideration of appropriate developmental expectations for an individual's self-
management of illness is important for the successful control of asthma.

INDIVIDUAL FACTORS

Several individual factors have been found to be associated with variations in asthma
management behaviors and morbidity in children and adults. A review of some of the
key factors is presented here. Achieving developmental milestones associated with
specific age ranges may affect how these processes impact asthma management behaviors.

INTELLIGENCE

The link between intelligence and asthma management behaviors and morbidity has
not been closely looked at in representative samples with different age groups; however, consistent differences in intelligence between children with and without asthma
have not been found (Annett, Aylward, Lapidus, Bender, & DuHamel, 2000). In a
group of over 1,000 children aged 5 to 12, lower IQ was found to be a risk factor for hospitalizations due to asthma in the previous year (Bacharier et al., 2003). Some research
has shown differences in how individuals perceive their asthma symptoms. Higher
levels of IQ were found to be associated with more accurate perception of asthma
symptoms in children (Fritz, McQuaid, Spirito, & Klein, 1996). The academic functioning of children with asthma has been a focus of some studies. Higher levels of
asthma severity have been associated with problems in academic achievement
(Austin, Huberty, Huster, & Dunn, 1998) and lower standardized examination scores
(Silverstein et al., 2001). Results suggest that several factors may explain the relation
between asthma and academic problems, such as predisposing individual differences,
illness severity, or treatment-related factors such as medication side effects. It seems
plausible to assume that higher levels of intelligence may be related to optimal management behaviors in individuals across different age groups; however, more work
that includes adults and that examines the relation between IQ and specific asthma
management behaviors is needed.

KNOWLEDGE AND INFORMATION

Understanding accurate information on the nature of asthma and its specific treatment components are integral for effective asthma control (NIH, 2002). Examples of
inadequate knowledge of asthma include inaccuracies regarding the type and use of
medications, lack of understanding concerning the etiology and course of asthma, and
incorrect beliefs concerning asthma management techniques (Celano, Geller, Phillips,
& Ziman, 1998; Zimmerman, Bonner, Evans, & Mellins, 1999). Higher levels of asthma
knowledge are consistently shown to be related to lower levels of asthma morbidity in
families from Anglo (Bender, Milgrom, Rand, & Ackerson, 1998) and ethnic minority
backgrounds (e.g., Koinis Mitchell & Murdock, 2005).

It is important to educate people with asthma about different facets of asthma management, including mechanisms of asthma medications (daily medications and as needed) and the distinction between common but harmless side effects and uncommon but dangerous side effects. Further, some research suggests that children with asthma of school age have many misperceptions about the illness and fail to understand the preventive use of medications (Kieckhefer & Spitzer, 1995). Educational efforts need to be developmentally appropriate and reinforced regularly by physicians and other health care providers to ensure adequate understanding of disease and management strategies (McQuaid et al., 2007).

Literacy   Some research has examined the impact of health literacy on asthma outcomes over time in adults. Lower levels of health literacy were associated with poorer quality of life and more ED visits related to asthma over 2 years (Mancuso & Rincon, 2006a). Patients with lower literacy may likely not to want to participate in decisions about their care (Mancuso & Rincon, 2006b). Respondents with inadequate health literacy know significantly less about their disease than those with adequate literacy. Efforts to improve asthma outcomes should focus on improving literacy skills that are required to learn, understand, and implement effective self-management. There are many opportunities to improve patients' knowledge of their chronic disease(s), and efforts need to consider their health literacy skills (Gazmararian, Williams, Peel, & Baker, 2003). These results provide additional incentives for physicians to find better ways to explain asthma treatments to low-literacy patients. Further, increasing the availability and use of written asthma management plans that meet recognized readability standards may help to improve asthma outcomes, especially in poor populations in which there is both low literacy and the greatest prevalence and severity of asthma (Forbis & Aligene, 2002).

Culture and Health Beliefs

The role of cultural factors in asthma management is not an area that has received much attention but certainly warrants further exploration, given the prevalence of asthma morbidity in ethnic minority populations. Most of the pediatric asthma research tends to look at the association of ethnic minority status or racial background and asthma morbidity. Some studies have found an independent relationship between ethnic minority status and asthma morbidity, even after controlling for socioeconomic status (Lieu et al., 2002). Other research has shown that socioeconomic status explains a large proportion of the disparities in specific indices of morbidity outcomes between Latino and African American individuals and their White counterparts (Miller, 2000). One study examines the association between multiple risks related to urban poverty and ethnic minority status, which may have a bearing on asthma morbidity in children, such as acculturative stress and discrimination (Koinis Mitchell et al., forthcoming). Results show that cumulative risks, including those associated with asthma, culture, and context account for more morbidity in children than one single risk factor, such as poverty or asthma severity. Since more ethnic minority families tend to live in urban environments, more work is needed to examine interactive affects of experiences related to context and culture that may have an impact on management behaviors and morbidity for children and adults from specific ethnic minority groups.

Language barriers have been frequently used as a proxy for acculturation, and are associated with lower rates of medication adherence (Apter et al., 1998). In one study,

Latino children and adolescents from Spanish-speaking homes had lower rates of peak flow monitoring and poorer asthma knowledge than Latino children and adolescents from English-speaking homes (Chan, Keeler, Schonlau, Rosen, & Mangione-Smith, 2005). Results suggested that language barriers seem to contribute to poorer asthma management practices and knowledge. Efforts to increase knowledge in this group, such as through use of an interpreter, may enhance asthma self-care and limit the morbidity associated with asthma.

There also appears to be some use of alternative practices (e.g., prayers, rubs, herbal remedies) in African American (Braganza, Ozuah, & Sharif, 2003) and Latino (Bearison et al., 2002) families with children who have asthma. An individual's health beliefs should be considered when attempting to understand potential variations in asthma management behaviors among ethnic minority groups (Flores, 2004). Some research has focused on families' and parents' belief systems regarding medication that may contribute to low medication adherence rates in ethnic minorities. For example, for African American and Latino inner city families, parents' beliefs or concerns about their child's medications (e.g., the dangers of dependence or long-term effects) can affect the underuse of daily, preventive asthma medications (Conn et al., 2005; Riekert et al., 2003). These findings are consistent with those of qualitative research including African American adult patients with asthma (George & Apter, 2004; George, Freedman, Norfleet, Feldman, & Apter, 2003). In these studies, health beliefs and attitudes have been proposed as partial explanations for low adherence to medical therapy and the consequent high burden of morbidity. Health beliefs that influenced adherence included patients' reliance on their assessment of asthma control over that of the health provider and concern over the adverse effects of inhaled corticosteroid (ICS) therapy. Results also indicated mistrust of the medical establishment. More research is needed to identify specific values by ethnic groups and subgroups who may be associated with a balance between use of traditional and alternative medications in various ethnic groups.

There are many common misperceptions about the nature of asthma and specific components of asthma management that are often believed by patients with asthma, regardless of their ethnic or racial background. For example, many individuals fail to recognize that asthma is a chronic illness with a symptom course that may not be directly associated with medication use. Thus, in the absence of symptoms, patients with persistent levels of this disease may not continue to take their daily controller medications. This "acute disease belief" has been associated with lower adherence to inhaled daily corticosteroids in adults with asthma (Halm, Mora, & Leventhal, 2006). Concerns about the affects of long-term daily controller use on children's growth may also cause parents to resist using these medications. Fear about having children involved in physical activity that may bring about an asthma exacerbation can also lead a parent to recommend that his or her child refrain from exercise. All of these concerns can have a bearing on the individual's effective asthma control and participation in developmentally appropriate social activities.

Coping

The relationship between adaptive coping and optimal psychosocial adjustment is well documented in the wider chronic illness literature (e.g., Compas, Connor-Smith, Saltzman, Thomsen, & Wadsworth, 2001). However, few studies have clarified how variations in coping styles/strategies can impact specific asthma management behaviors, and most of this research has focused on children. One theme that has emerged across studies is that children with asthma use a range of coping strategies when faced with the stresses imposed by asthma management. For example, findings by Noeker and Petermann (1998) indicate that children tended to employ cognitive coping resources when faced with asthma-related stresses. Other research has shown that repressive defense styles (operationalized as the management of distress and self-restraint in children's socioemotional functioning) were associated with greater perceptual accuracy of children's symptom management (Fritz et al., 1996). The researchers in this study explained that, for a portion of children with asthma in this sample, some degree of repression or lack of worrying regarding possible symptoms was associated with more accurate symptom perception. Brook and Tepper (1997) found that children with asthma tended to use avoidant coping as their primary mode of coping with stressful situations when compared to healthy children. In a study including low-income, urban children, a significant relationship emerged between children's employment of higher levels of active and avoidance coping strategies when faced with asthma-related stress, and their increased participation in activities and optimal asthma management. These results suggest that coping strategies that have been traditionally viewed as less optimal (e.g., avoidance coping strategies) have been shown to be associated with healthier asthma outcomes in the short term. Whether avoidant coping strategies will serve long-term healthy asthma outcomes is still questionable.

COMORBID PSYCHOPATHOLOGY

Psychological symptoms have been recognized as having a role in initiating asthma episodes for individuals. A large body of evidence has documented an association between psychiatric symptoms and asthma exacerbations in children (Ortega et al., 2003) and adults (Feldman et al., 2005; Solis, Khan, & Brown, 2006). In general, research has not identified direct causal pathways between asthma and psychological problems. Still, results suggest that a wide range of psychiatric problems is more commonly presented in individuals with asthma (e.g., Bender et al., 2000; Wamboldt, Fritz, Mansell, McQuaid, & Klein, 1998). Internalizing the stress associated with having asthma can influence the development of psychological problems (Bender et al.; Mrazek, 1992). Psychiatric symptoms (e.g., panic/fear symptoms) may also be associated with asthma exacerbations through hyperventilation (e.g., Carr, 1998). Other results indicate that psychiatric problems in children may challenge effective asthma management abilities (e.g., Weil et al., 1999) and asthma control in adults (Lavoie et al., 2005). Studies have emphasized a specific relation between asthma, anxiety, and depressive symptoms across samples of different age groups (e.g., Solis et al., 2006; M. Wamboldt et al., 1998; Waxmonsky et al., 2006).

DEPRESSIVE SYMPTOMS AND ASTHMA

Clinic-based studies have indicated a link between higher levels of internalizing symptoms and childhood asthma (e.g., Ortega, Huertas, Canino, & Rubio-Stipec, 2002). A meta-analysis including 26 studies demonstrated a modest but consistent association between asthma and global internalizing problems in children (McQuaid et al., 2001). A relation between depressed mood, poor asthma management, and morbidity has also been documented in children (Galil, 2000; Waxmonsky et al., 2006) and adults (Heaney, Conway, Kelly, & Gamble, 2005). In a population-based epidemiological sample, the parental report of asthma diagnosis in children and attacks was associated with depressive symptoms (Ortega, McQuaid, Canino, Goodwin, & Fritz, 2004). In addition, one study found depressive symptoms to be above the clinical cutoff on the Children's Depression Rating Scale, Revised (CDRS-R) in 30% of a sample of inner-city children with asthma (Morrison, Goli, Van Wagoner, Brown, & Khan, 2002). Higher levels of perceived neighborhood problems were also found to be associated with increased depressive symptoms among adults with asthma, even when asthma severity was taken into account (Yen, Yelin, Katz, Eisner, & Blanc, 2006). It is possible that the stress associated with asthma increases the likelihood of the development of depressive symptoms in children (Morrison et al., 2002) and adults (Bender, 2006; Solis et al., 2006).

ANXIETY AND ASTHMA

Investigators have theorized that both anxiety and asthma symptoms frequently lead to fearful cognitions (i.e., catastrophizing), a sense of being out of control, the need for help and support (Carr, Lehrer, Rausch, & Hochron, 1994), and feelings of panic (Butz & Alexander, 1993). Interest in this association stems from symptoms these illnesses share, such as sensations of being smothered, choking, and hyperventilation-induced dyspnea (Katon, Richardson, Lozano, & McCauley, 2004).

An increased likelihood and higher prevalence of anxiety disorders (e.g., separation anxiety, overanxious disorder, specific phobia, panic attacks) among children with asthma versus healthy controls and children with other chronic illnesses has been demonstrated (e.g., Ortega et al., 2002). A recent review showed that in child/adolescent populations with asthma, up to one third met criteria for comorbid anxiety disorders (Katon et al., 2004). Recent research, including a community-sample, published since the Katon review, has also shown an association between asthma symptoms and anxiety (Halterman et al., 2006). It also appears that children with severe asthma may be particularly likely to have an anxiety disorder (Ortega et al., 2002).

In general, individuals with asthma who have comorbid psychiatric problems may have more difficulties with asthma management and, consequently, greater morbidity (Deshmukh, Toelle, Usherwood, O'grady, & Jenkins, in press; Weil et al., 1999). A constellation of factors, such as severe asthma, psychiatric comorbidity, and increased functional limitations from asthma, can have a significant impact on functioning. Identification of comorbid psychological problems in individuals with asthma, and appropriate referral for treatment, if indicated, should be clear priorities for health care providers.

NEUROPSYCHOLOGICAL AND COGNITIVE IMPAIRMENT

There has been little research in the area of neuropsychological and cognitive functioning in children and adults with asthma. Asthma symptoms and stresses associated with management may affect attention and focus; however, the presence of asthma symptoms typically does not bring about extreme cognitive impairment. In children with asthma exposed to chronic and intermittent hypoxia (low levels of oxygen desaturation), however, a review of data across several studies showed an adverse impact on their development, behavior, and academic achievement (Bass et al., 2004). Few studies in this area have either focused on neuropsychological correlates that may be associated with asthma or the affects of asthma medications on functioning. Differences in neurocognitive functioning between children with and without asthma have not been found (Annett & DuHamel, 2000).

Although studies have shown that children with asthma are at an increased risk for exhibiting behavioral problems (e.g., McQuaid, Kopel et al., 2001), results have also failed to support a substantial relation between Attention Deficit Hyperactive Disorder (ADHD) and asthma status in children (e.g., Biederman, 1994). One large, multicenter pediatric study, however, assessed the association between asthma severity, asthma status, and attention (Annett et al.. 2000). Children with asthma scored between two-thirds and one standard deviation below the normative value on a measure of attention-assessing impulse control when compared to children without asthma. Despite their level of severity, children with asthma had difficulties with the modulation and the control of impulsive behaviors. It may be that lack of attention and impulse control problems can have a bearing on specific asthma management strategies.

A small body of research has focused on the affects of asthma medications on an individual's cognitive functioning. Specifically, the potential side effects of asthma medications (both as needed medications and daily controllers) on learning and activity level have been studied, and the results from this research are inconsistent. Common quick-relief medicines for asthma, such as albuterol, do not appear to significantly increase the activity level of children with asthma (Hadjikoumi, Loader, Bracken, & Milner, 2002). Oral corticosteroids used in severe asthma may impair school performance (Suess, Stump, Chai, & Kalisker, 1986) and can result in hyperactive symptoms (Hederos, 2004); however, this has not been demonstrated consistently (Bender, Lerner, & Poland, 1991). It is noteworthy that many children who use as-needed or preventive long-term medicines to treat asthma have minimal side effects (Bender et al.) and the benefits of using medication consistently to control symptoms likely outweigh the costs. Consideration of the use of asthma medications, the extent of individuals' adherence to them, and their potential side effects is clearly warranted in research with specific populations who have asthma.

INTERVENTIONS

Interventions that incorporate medical, behavioral, and educational approaches to assist in enhancing asthma control have been shown to be the most beneficial to patients across different age groups (Clark, 1998). Interdisciplinary approaches to asthma management that integrate the expertise of a variety of providers, such as physicians, psychologists, nurses, and health educators, have also proven to be the most effective (e.g., Bratton et al., 2001; Evans et al., 1999). Although the NIH has established criteria for the medical management of asthma, it has also highlighted the benefits of an interdisciplinary approach to asthma management. A four-tiered strategy is typically recommended for asthma symptom management. This includes (1) avoiding or minimizing exposures to known allergens and irritants in the environment, (2) using medication as prescribed by the patient's physician, (3) evaluating the patient for the effectiveness of medication, assessing potential symptom presentation, and whether allergy testing is necessary, and (4) patient and family education regarding the disease and its management (AAAAI, 2000).

In addition to the pharmacological treatment of asthma management, a variety of supplemental educational, environmental, and psychosocial interventions have been suggested to optimize asthma control. These include recommendations and problem-solving strategies aimed at the control of environmental triggers and educational and psychosocial interventions to provide basic knowledge of the illness and support for the individual's asthma-related behaviors (AAAAI, 2000). As pharmacologic management has been reviewed in the previous sections, we outline commonly used interventions that have been employed as adjuncts to pharmacological care as well as treatment approaches that combine various elements of these approaches.

EDUCATIONAL INTERVENTIONS

Education on appropriate asthma self-management behaviors has been shown to assist in enhancing symptom-free days and decreasing ED visits due to asthma in children (Portnoy & Jennings, 2006; Wood, Tumiel-Berhalter, Owen, Taylor, & Kattan, 2006) and adults (Urek et al., 2005). Such interventions have included inner-city populations and have been implemented in community-based settings. Education typically consists of information regarding the basics of asthma etiology, symptom management, and trigger control as foundations for effective care (AAAAI, 2000; National Institutes of Health, 1997, 2002). Educational programs also address inaccuracies of asthma information and treatment.

Some educational efforts have resulted in reduced asthma morbidity and improved adherence (e.g., Fritzpatrick, Coughlin, & Chamberlin, 1992), while other programs have not been successful at decreasing asthma morbidity (Bernard-Bonnin, Stachenko, Bonin, Charette, & Rousseau, 1995). Educational programs that fail to address barriers to optimal asthma management (e.g., consistent medication use and a review of the proper technique to use the medication) and that do not incorporate strategies for translating knowledge into healthy behavioral patterns may not be effective in reducing asthma morbidity (Clark & Gong, 2000). Establishing the efficacy of educational programs is challenging. However, the medical field of asthma continues to advance with the development of new medications, new delivery systems for medicine, new guidelines for assessing severity level, and new methods of disease management. In order to provide consistency in the educational strategies provided to patients and ensure that state-of-the-art asthma education is being implemented by qualified providers, the National Asthma Educator Certification Board (NAECB) has been established to regulate the certification of health care professionals as Asthma Educators (AE-C).

ENVIRONMENTAL CONTROL STRATEGIES

An essential component of effective asthma control includes a focus on trigger reduction in the home setting. Strategies include emphasis on removing pets from the home and employing measures to reduce dust mites, such as washing bedclothes in hot water. Although allergen avoidance is widely recommended as part of a secondary and tertiary prevention strategy for asthma and allergic diseases, a clear-cut demonstration of its effectiveness is lacking (Marinho, Simpson, & Custovic, 2006). One randomized control study focusing on reducing early life exposure to house dust mites during infancy found no differences in the prevention of the onset of asthma or atopy in high-risk children (Marks et al., 2006). However, some specific measures to reduce individual triggers in the home, such as mattress covers to minimize dust mite exposure, have been shown to reduce allergen levels (e.g., Marks et al., 1994).

Low-income households are more likely to be reservoirs for certain triggers (e.g., cockroaches, rodents; see Kattan et al., 2005), and some families may lack the resources to implement more expensive strategies for trigger control, such as carpet removal. In addition, focusing efforts related to trigger control on the individual's bedroom is a more feasible goal for patients. Although few randomized smoking prevention and cessation trials including individuals with asthma have been conducted, tobacco counseling strategies have been suggested for clinicians who treat these patients (see Tye & Throckmorton-Belzer for a review [2006]). In addition, the danger of exposure to environmental tobacco smoke is essential to review. Taking into consideration an individual's economic circumstances and his or her specific allergic profile when offering environmental control suggestions can increase acceptance of the recommendations. Data has shown that an individualized approach, such as trigger reduction strategies based on the patient's skin testing profile, can be useful in reducing allergen exposure and asthma symptoms (Morgan et al., 2004).

PSYCHOSOCIAL INTERVENTIONS

Several psychosocial interventions for asthma are implemented in clinical practice, including self-management training, problem-solving techniques, family-based interventions, and psychophysiologic modalities to reduce symptoms (i.e., relaxation training and biofeedback). A review of studies on the effectiveness of psychological interventions for reducing morbidity in adults with asthma showed some promising results. Relaxation therapy was found to be helpful for reducing the use of as-needed medications, and cognitive-behavioral therapy was shown effective for enhancing quality of life (Yorke, Fleming, & Shuldham, in press).

Some recent interventions have explicitly focused on increasing child adherence to medication use. For example, promising results from one study showed that targeting enhancing adherence to medication use during home visits helped increase appropriate use of daily medications in inner-city children (Bartlett, Lukk, Butz, Lampros-Klein, & Rand, 2002). Efforts to pilot test such an intervention included employing social cognitive strategies (e.g., goal-setting, monitoring, and feedback) and targeting known barriers to medication use. Psychosocial interventions can play an important role in identifying difficulties in asthma management, addressing poor treatment adherence, and facilitating cooperation between families and physicians (Lemanek, Kamps, & Chung, 2001).

Psychophysiologic approaches such as relaxation training and biofeedback have also been implemented as adjunctive treatments for asthma symptoms. A review of different forms of biofeedback and relaxation techniques in pediatric asthma (McQuaid & Nassau, 1999) showed that some forms of biofeedback to modify asthma symptoms have empirical support, yet more research is needed to determine if these strategies effect clinically significant changes in asthma symptoms. Heart rate variability biofeedback as an adjunct to asthma treatment has also been shown to effectively improve pulmonary function and decrease asthma symptoms in some adult patients, although further evaluation of this method is warranted (e.g., Lehrer et al., 2004).

MULTICOMPONENT APPROACHES

Given that asthma is a multifaceted chronic illness with a complicated etiology, asthma intervention approaches that integrate several components of treatment in a coordinated fashion are likely to have the most significant and sustained results. For example, one recent study evaluated the effectiveness of a comprehensive school-based asthma program on indices of asthma morbidity and school functioning (Clark et al., 2004). This program included asthma education for the general school population through classroom sessions for children, asthma education for school personnel, and school fairs regarding asthma ("Open Airways for Schools"; Evans et al., 1987). The program also involved school "walk-throughs" to identify problems in indoor air quality in order to reduce environmental asthma triggers. Written communication regarding the child's participation in this school program was shared with the health care providers of children with asthma to encourage coordination of care. Results indicated significant reductions in asthma symptoms, particularly for children with persistent asthma. Few differences in academic functioning were shown, with the exception of higher grades in science and fewer school absences related to asthma for the treatment group (Clark et al.). These results suggest that although combined interventions can be costly and labor intensive, they are successful at reducing morbidity and sustaining these effects on asthma control. Further development and evaluation of multicomponent interventions that include representative populations are clearly needed.

CASE EXAMPLE

Jose is an 8-year-old Latino boy who was born in the United States and currently resides in an urban neighborhood in the United States. Both of his parents were born in Puerto Rico and moved to the mainland when they were 20 years of age. Jose's parents' medical history is not significant, except for his mother's having asthma. She was diagnosed with asthma when she came to the United States.

Jose's infancy and toddlerhood were characterized with bouts of breathing difficulty and asthma symptoms, particularly during the winter season. As an infant, he wheezed as the result of a respiratory infection, but his symptoms responded to quick-relief medication. When he was 4 years old, his mother realized that his asthma symptoms became more frequent and occurred in the absence of illness and in response to cold weather and exercise. Based on the frequency and nature of his symptoms, Jose was prescribed a daily controller medication to take two times a day, in addition to his quick-relief medication. Initially, Jose's mother had many concerns about her son taking this medication, and often preferred to try natural remedies or over-the-counter treatments as a first line of intervention. Over time, she was able to share her concerns with her son's physician. Jose's mother also shared her son's difficulty taking medication. She indicated that he often forgets to take his medications, and she is not sure about what to do when he has symptoms. Additionally, Jose's grandmother, who cares for him certain weekday afternoons, is hesitant to administer medications herself.

In response to Jose's mother's concerns, the physician developed an asthma action plan with the family that consisted of a detailed review of what Jose and the family should do when he is having breathing difficulty. She referred the family to a community-based asthma education program and suggested that Jose's grandmother attend educational sessions as well, given her central role in caretaking. The program additionally offered individual consultation with psychologists, if needed, to address barriers to medication use, to enhance family support around asthma management, to increase self-confidence in what to do when faced with symptoms, and to offer strategies for effective asthma management. For instance, the psychologist asked Jose to pair his medications with other routine behaviors (e.g., brushing his teeth, eating a meal) and then assisted the grandmother in implementing positive reinforcement (e.g., use of praise, placing a sticker on a calendar for each good day). This strategy was successful in increasing his adherence to consistent medication use.

CONCLUSION

Asthma is a chronic illness with a complex pathophysiology and disease course. Multiple risk factors have been implicated in the development of asthma, including genetic, environmental, social, and psychological processes. Asthma disproportionately affects ethnic minority individuals and is increasing in prevalence in school-aged children. Much research is devoted to understanding the mechanisms that underlie asthma health disparities among individuals from specific ethnic groups. This research is quickly evolving, with different dimensions of risk factors being considered.

Treatments for asthma comprise two basic strategies: (1) trigger control for symptom prevention and (2) medication use for symptom prevention and relief. The role of patient and family education in trigger avoidance, symptom monitoring, and appropriate use of medication has been increasingly emphasized in guidelines for effective medical care (AAAAI, 2000; NIH, 2002). A variety of psychosocial and behavioral interventions are available to supplement medical treatments for asthma. An individual's cultural background and experiences will likely impact his or her beliefs about and behaviors related to specific asthma treatment components. More research that examines interactions between individual, family, and social risk and protective factors and their impact on asthma management among specific groups is needed (Koinis Mitchell, Murdock, & Bender Berz, 2004). A coordinated treatment plan that involves ongoing communication between the family, professional caregivers, and the individual with asthma is necessary for optimal disease management.

REFERENCES

Academy of Allergy, Asthma and Immunology (AAAAI). (2000). *The allergy report: Science-based findings on the diagnosis and treatment of allergic disorders.* Milwaukee: American Academy of Allergy Asthma and Immunology.

American Lung Association. (2005). *Annual report 2005: The future of lung health.* New York: Author.

Annett, R., Aylward, E. H., Lapidus, J, Bender, B. G., & DuHamel, T. (2000). Neurocognitive functioning in children with milk and moderate asthma in the childhood asthma management program. The Childhood Asthma Management Program (CAMP) Group. *Journal of Allergy and Clinical Immunology, 105,* 717–724.

Anon. (1997). A genome-wide search for asthma susceptibility loci in ethnically diverse populations: The collaborative study on the genetics of asthma (CSGA). *Nature Genetics, 15,* 389–392.

Apter, A. J., Reisine, S. T., Affleck, G., Barrows, E., & ZuWallack, R. L. (1998). Adherence with twice-daily dosing of inhaled steroids. Socioeconomic and health-belief differences. *American Journal of Respiratory and Critical Care Medicine, 157*(6, Pt. 1), 1810–1817.

Arruda, L. K., Sole, D., Baena-Cagnani, C. E., & Naspitz, C. K. (2005). Risk factors for asthma and atopy. *Current Opinions in Allergy and Clinical Immunology, 5*(2), 153–159.

Austin, J. K., Huberty, T. J., Huster, G. A., & Dunn, D. W. (1998). Academic achievement in children with epilepsy or asthma. *Developmental Medicine and Child Neurology, 40*(4), 248–255.

Bacharier, L. B., Dawson, C., Bloomberg, G. R., Bender, B., Wilson, L., Strunk, R. C., et al. (2003). Hospitalization for asthma: Atopic, pulmonary function, and psychological correlates among participants in the Childhood Asthma Management Program. *Pediatrics, 112*(2), e85–92.

Barros, R., Moreira, A., Fonseca, J., Moreira, P., Fernandes, L., de Oliveira, J. F., et al. (2006). Obesity and airway inflammation in asthma. *Journal of Allergy and Clinical Immunology, 117*(6), 1501–1502.

Bartlett, S. J., Lukk, P., Butz, A., Lampros-Klein, F., & Rand, C. S. (2002). Enhancing medication adherence among inner-city children with asthma: Results from pilot studies. *Journal of Asthma, 39,* 47–54.

Bass, J. L., Corwin, M., Gozal, D., Moore, C., Nishida, H., Parker, S., et al. (2004). The effect of chronic or intermittent hypoxia on cognition in childhood: A review of the evidence. *Pediatrics, 114*(3), 805–816.

Bearison, D. J., Minian, N., & Granowetter, L. (2002). Medical management of asthma and folk medicine in a Hispanic community. *Journal of Pediatric Psychology, 27,* 385–392.

Bender, B. G. (2006). Risk taking, depression, adherence, and symptom control in adolescents and young adults with asthma. *American Journal of Respiratory and Critical Care Medicine, 173*(9), 953–957.

Bender, B. G., Annett, R. D., Ikle, D., DuHamel, T. R., Rand, C., & Strunk, R. C. (2000). Relationship between disease and psychological adaptation in children in the Childhood Asthma Management Program and their families. CAMP Research Group. *Arch Pediatr Adolesc Med, 154*(7), 706–713.

Bender, B. G., Lerner, J. A., & Poland, J. E. (1991). Association between corticosteroids and psychologic change in hospitalized asthmatic children. *Annals of Allergy, 66,* 414–419.

Bender, B. G., Milgrom, H., Rand, C., & Ackerson, L. (1998). Psychological factors associated with medication nonadherence in asthmatic children. *Journal of Asthma, 35,* 347–353.

Bernard-Bonnin, A., Stachenko, S., Bonin, D., Charette, C., & Rousseau, E. (1995). Self management teaching programs and morbidity of pediatric asthma: A meta-analysis. *Journal of Allergy and Clinical Immunology, 90,* 135–138.

Biederman, J., Milberger, S, Faraone, S. V., Guite, J, & Warburton, R. (1994). Associations between childhood asthma and ADHD: Issues of psychiatric comorbidity and familiality. *Journal of the American Academy of Child and Adolescent Psychiatry, 33*(6), 842–848.

Bousquet, J., Van Cauwenberge, P., Khaltaev, N., & World Health Organization. (2001). Allergic rhinitis and its impact on asthma: Aria workshop report. *Journal of Allergy and Clinical Immunology, 108*(5), S147–S334.

Braganza, S., Ozuah, P. O., & Sharif, I. (2003). The use of complementary therapies in inner-city asthmatic children. *Journal of Asthma, 40*(7), 823–827.

Bratton, D. L., Price, M., Gavin, L., Glenn, K., Brenner, M., Gelfand, E. W., et al. (2001). Impact of a multidisciplinary day program on disease and healthcare costs in children and adolescents with severe asthma: A two-year follow-up study. *Pediatric Pulmonology, 31,* 177–189.

Brook, U., & Tepper, I. (1997). Self-image, coping and familial interaction among asthmatic children in Israel. *Patient Education and Counseling, 30,* 187–192.

Brugge, D. V., Vallarino, J., Ascolillo, L., Osgood, N. D., Steinback, S., & Spengler, J. (2003). Comparison of multiple environmental factors for asthmatic children in public housing. *Indoor Air, 13*(1), 18–27.

Burchard, E. G., Avila, P. C., Nazarlo, S., Casal, J., Torres, A., Rodriguez-Santana, J. R., et al. (2004). Lower bronchodilator responsiveness in Puerto Rican than in Mexican subjects with asthma. *American Journal of Respiratory and Critical Care Medicine, 169,* 386–392.

Busse, W. W., & Lemanske, R. F. J. (2001). Advances in immunology: Asthma. *The New England Journal of Medicine, 344*(5), 350–362.

Butz, A., & Alexander, C. (1993). Anxiety in children with asthma. *Journal of Asthma, 30*(3), 199–209.

Carr, R. (1998). Panic disorder and asthma: Causes, effects and research implications. *Journal of Psychosomatic Research, 44*(1), 43–52.

Carr, R., Lehrer, P., Rausch, L., & Hochron, S. (1994). Anxiety sensitivity and panic attacks in an asthmatic population. *Behaviour Research and Therapy, 32*(4), 411–418.

Celano, M., Geller, R. J., Phillips, K. M., & Ziman, R. (1998). Treatment adherence among low-income children with asthma. *Journal of Pediatric Psychology, 23,* 345–349.

Centers for Disease Control. (1996). Asthma morbidity and hospitalization among children and young adults—US 1980–1993. *Morbidity and Mortality Weekly Report, 45,* 350–353.

Centers for Disease Control. (2002). Surveillance for asthma—United States, 1980–1999. *Morbidity and Mortality Weekly Report, 51* (SSOI), 1–13.

Chan, S. C., Keeler, E., Schonlau, M., Rosen, M., & Mangione-Smith, R. (2005). How do ethnicity and primary language spoken at home affect management practices and outcome in children and adolescents with asthma? *Archives of Pediatric and Adolescent Medicine, 159*(3), 283–289.

Clark, N. M. (1998). Management of asthma by parents and children. In A. H. Harry Kotses (Ed.), *Self-management of asthma* (vol. 113, pp. 271–292). New York: Marcel Dekker.

Clark, N. M., Brown, R., Joseph, C. L. M., Anderson, E. W., & Liu, M., & Valerio, M.A. (2004). Effects of a comprehensive school-based asthma mangement program on symptoms, parent management, grades and absenteeism. *Chest, 1125,* 1674–1679.

Clark, N. M., & Gong, M. (2000). Management of chronic disease by practitioners and patients: Are we teaching the wrong things? *British Medical Journal, 320,* 572–575.

Colilla, S., Nicolea, D., Pluzhnikov, A., Blumenthal, M. N., Beaty, T. H., Bleekcker, E. R., et al. (2003). Evidence for gene-environment interactions in a linage study of asthma and smoking exposure. *Journal of Allergy and Clinical Immunology, 111,* 840–846.

Compas, B. E., Connor-Smith, J. K., Saltzman, H., Thomsen, A. H., & Wadsworth, M. E. (2001). Coping with stress during childhood and adolescence: problems, progress, and potential in theory and research. *Psychological Bulletin, 127*(1), 87–127.

Conn, K. M., Halterman, J. S., Fisher, S. G., Yoos, H. L., Chin, N. P., & Szilagyi, P. G. (2005). Parental beliefs about medications and medication adherence among urban children with ashtma. *Ambulatory Pediatrics, 5*(5), 306–310.

Cookson, W. O. C. M., & Young, R. P. (1992). Maternal inheritance of atopic IgE responsiveness on Chromosome 11Q. *Lancet, 340*(8816), 381–384.

Crain, E. F., Kercsmar, C., Weiss, K. B., Mitchell, H., & Lynn, H. (1998). Reported difficulties in access to quality care for children with asthma in the inner city. *Archives of Pediatric and Adolescent Medicine, 151,* 333–339.

de Marco, R., Pattaro, C., Locatelli, F., Svanes, C., & ECRHS Study Group. (2004). Influence of early life exposures on indidence and remission of asthma throughout life. *Journal of Allergy and Clinical Immunology, 113,* 845–852.

Deshmukh, V. M., Toelle, B. G., Usherwood, T., O'grady, B., & Jenkins, C. R. (in press). Anxiety, panic and adult asthma: A cognitive-behavioral perspective. *Respiratory Medicine.*

Diette, G. B., Markson, L., Skinner, E. A., Nguen, T. T., & Algatt-Bergstrom, P. (2000). Nocturnal asthma in children affects school attendance, school performance and parents' work attendance. *Archives of Pediatric Adolescent Medicine, 154,* 923–928.

DiFranza, J. R., Aligne, C. A., & Weitzman, M. (2004). Prenatal and postnatal environmental tobacco smoke exposure and children's health. *Pediatrics, 113*(Suppl. 4), 1007–1015.

Evans, D., Clark, N. M., Feldman, C. H., Rips, J., Kaplan, D., Levinson, J. J., et al. (1987). A school health education program for children with asthma aged 8–11 years. *Health Education Quarterly, 14,* 267–279.

Evans, R., Gergen, P. J., Mitchell, H., Kattan, M., Kercsmar, C., Crain, E., et al. (1999). A randomized clinical trial to reduce asthma morbidity among inner-city children: Results of the National Cooperative Inner-City Asthma Study. *Journal of Pediatrics, 135,* 332–338.

Feldman, J. M., Siddique, M. I., Morales, E., Kaminski, B., Ju, S. E., & Lehrer, P. M. (2005). Psychiatric disorders and asthma outcomes among high-risk inner-city patients. *Psychosomatic Medicine, 67*(6), 989–996.

Fernandez-Mayoralas, M., Caballero, J. M. M., & Garcia-Marcos, A. L. (2004). Association between atopic dermatitis, allergic rhinitis and asthma in schoolchildren ages 13–14 years old. *Anales de Pediatría, 60,* 236–242.

Flores, G. (2004). Culture, ethnicity, and linguistic issues in pediatric care: Urgent priorities and unanswered questions. *Ambulatory Pediatrics, 4,* 276–282.

Forbis, S. G., & Aligene, A. A. (2002). Poor readability of written asthma management plans found in national guidelines. *Pediarics, 109*(4), e52.

Fritz, G. K., McQuaid, E. L., Spirito, A., & Klein, R. B. (1996). Symptom perception in pediatric asthma: Relationship to functional morbidity and psychological factors. *Journal of the American Academy of Child and Adolescent Psychiatry, 35,* 1033–1041.

Fritzpatrick, S. B., Coughlin, S. S., & Chamberlin, J. (1992). A novel asthma camp intervention for childhood asthma among urban blacks. *Journal of the National Medical Association, 84,* 233–237.

Galil, N. (2000). Depression and asthma in children. *Current Opinion in Pediatrics, 12*(4), 331–335.

Gazmararian, J. A., Williams, M. V., Peel, J., & Baker, D. W. (2003). Health literacy and knowledge of chronic disease. *Patient Education and Counseling, 51*(3), 267–275.

George, M., & Apter, A. J. (2004). Gaining insight into patients' beliefs using qualitative research methodologies. *Current Opinion in Allergy and Clinical Immunology, 4*(3), 185–189.

George, M., Freedman, T. G., Norfleet, A. L., Feldman, H. I., & Apter, A. J. (2003). Qualitative research-enhanced understanding of patients' low-income, urban, African American adults with asthma. *Journal of Allergy and Clinical Immunology, 111*(5), 967–973.

Gergen, P. J., Mullally, D. I., & Evans, R. (1988). National survey of prevalence of asthma among children in the United States, 1976 to 1980. *Pediatrics, 81*(1), 1–7.

Grant, E. N., Lyttle, C. S., & Weiss, K. B. (2000). The relation of socioeconomic factors in racial/ethnic differences in US asthma mortality. *American Journal of Public Health, 90*(12), 1923–1925.

Hadjikoumi, I., Loader, P., Bracken, M., & Milner, A. D. (2002). Bronchodilator therapy and hyperactivity in preschool children. *Archives of Disease in Childhood, 86,* 202–203.

Halapi, E., & Hakonarson, H. (2004). Recent development in genomic and proteomic research for asthma. *Current Opinion in Pulmonary Medicine, 10,* 22–30.

Halm, E. A., Mora, P., & Leventhal, H. (2006). No symptoms, no asthma: The acute episodic disease belief is associated with poor self-management among inner-city adults with persistent asthma. *Chest, 129*(3), 573–580.

Halterman, J., Conn, K., Forbes-Jones, E., Fagnano, M., Hightower, A., & Szilagyi, P. (2006). Behavior problems among inner-city children with asthma: Findings from a community-based sample. *Pediatrics, 117*(2), 192–199.

Heaney, L. G., Conway, E., Kelly, C., & Gamble, J. (2005). Prevalence of psychiatric morbidity in a difficult asthma population: Relationship to asthma outcome. *Respiratory Medicine, 99*(9), 1152–1159.

Hederos, C. (2004). Neuropsychologic changes and inhaled corticosteroids. *Journal of Allergy and Clinical Immunology, 114,* 451–452.

Inouye, T., Tarlo, S., Broder, I., Corey, P., Davies, G., Lenznoff, A., et al. (1985). Severity of asthma in skin test-negative and skin test-positive patients. *Journal of Allergy and Clinical Immunology, 75*(2), 313–319.

Jenkins, M. A., Hopper, J. L., Flander, L. B., Carlin, J. B., & Giles, G. G. (1993). The associations between childhood asthma and atopy, and parental asthma, hay fever and smoking. *Pediatric and Perinatal Epidemiology, 7*(1), 67–76.

Katon, W., Richardson, L., Lozano, P., & McCauley, E. (2004). The relationship of asthma and anxiety disorders. *Psychosomatic Medicine, 66,* 349–355.

Kattan, M., Mitchell, H., Eggleston, P., Gergen, P., Crain, E., Redline, S., et al. (1997). Characteristics of inner-city children with asthma: The National Cooperative Inner-City Asthma Study. *Pediatric Pulmonology, 24*(4), 253–262.

Kattan, M., Stearns, S., Crain, E., Stout, J., Gergen, P., Evans, R., et al. (2005). Cost-effectiveness of a home-based environmental intervention for inner-city children with asthma. *Journal of Allergy and Clinical Immunology, 116*(5) 1058–1063.

Kieckhefer, G. M., & Spitzer, A. (1995). School-age children's understanding of the relations between their behavior and their asthma management. *Clinical Nursing Research, 4,* 149–167.

Klinnert, M. D., Mrazek, P. J., & Mrazek, D. A. (1994). Early asthma onset: The interaction between family stressors and adaptive parenting. *Psychiatry, 57*(1), 51–61.

Klinnert, M. D., Nelson, H. S., Price, M. R., Adinoff, A. D., Leung, D. Y. M., & Marzek, D. A. (2001). Onset and persistence of childhood asthma: Predictors from infancy. *Pediatrics, 108*(4), e69–77.

Koinis Mitchell, D., & Murdock, K. K. (2005). Identifying risk and resource factors in children with asthma from urban settings: The context-health-development model. *Journal of Asthma, 42*(6), 425–436.

Koinis Mitchell, D., McQuaid, E. L., Seifer, R., Kopel, S. J., Esteban, C., Garcia Coll, C., et al. (2007). Multiple urban and asthma-related risks and their association with asthma morbidity in children. *Journal of Pediatric Psychology, 44,* 449–453.

Koinis Mitchell, D., Murdock, K. M., & Bender Berz, J. (2004). Developmental, gender, and health-related variations in self-competence and depressed mood among school-aged urban children with asthma: A pilot study. *Journal of Clinical Psychology in Medical Settings, 11*(4), 434–355.

Lavoie, K. L., Cartier, A., Labrecque, M., Bacon, S. L., Semiere, C., Malo, J. L., et al. (2005). Are psychiatric disorders associated with worse asthma control and quality of life in asthma patients? *Respiratory Medicine, 99*(10), 1249–1257.

Lee, Y. L., Lin, Y. C., Hsiue, T. R., Hwang, B. F., & Guo, Y. L. (2003). Indoor and outdoor environmental exposures, parental atopy, and physician-diagnosed asthma in Taiwanese school children. *Pediatrics, 112*(e389–e395).

Lehrer, P. M., Vaschillo, E., Vaschillo, B., Lu, S. E., Scardella, A., Siddique, M., et al. (2004). Biofeedback treatment for asthma. *Chest, 126*(2), 352–361.

Lemanek, K. L., Kamps, J., & Chung, N. B. (2001). Empirically supported treatments in pediatric psychology: Regimen adherence. *Journal of Pediatric Psychology, 26,* 279–282.

Lemanske, R. F., Jr. (2004). Viral infections and asthma inception. *Journal of Allergy and Clinical Immunology, 114,* 1023–1026.

Lemiere, C., & Boulet, L. P. (2005). Cigarete smoking and asthma: A dangerous mix. *Canadian Respiratory Journal : Journal of the Canadian Thoracic Society, 12*(2), 79–80.

Lieu, T. A., Lozano, P., Finkelstein, J. A., Chi, F. W., Jensvold, N. G., Capra, A. M., et al. (2002). Racial/ethnic variation in asthma status and management practices among children in managed medicaid. *Pediatrics, 109*(5), 857–865.

Liu, C. A., Wang, C. L., Chauang, H., Ou, C. Y., Hsu, T. Y., & Yang, K. D. (2003). Prenatal prediction of infant atopy by maternal but not paternal total IgE levels. *Journal of Allergy and Clinical Immunology, 112*(5), 899–904.

Lozano, P., Sullivan, S. D., Smith, D. H., & Weiss, K. B. (1999). The economic burden of asthma in US children: Estimates from the National Medical Expenditure Survey. *Journal of Allergy and Clinical Immunology, 104*(5), 957–963.

Mancuso, C. A., & Rincon, M. (2006a). Asthma patients' assessments of health care and medical decision making: The role of health literacy. *Journal of Asthma, 43*(1), 41–44.

Mancuso, C. A., & Rincon, M. (2006b). Impact of health literacy on longitudinal asthma outcomes. *Journal of Internal Medicine, 21*(8), 813–817.

Marinho, S., Simpson, A., & Custovic, A. (2006). Allergen avoidance in the secondary and tertiary prevention of allergic diseases: Does it work? *Primary Care Repository Journal, 15*(3), 152–158.

Marks, G., Mihrshahi, S., Kemp, A. S., Tovey, E. R., Webb, K., Almgvist, C., et al. (2006). Prevention of asthma during the first 5 years of life: A randomized controlled trial. *Journal of Allergy and Clinical Immunology, 118*(1), 53–61.

Marks, G., Tovey, E. R., Green, W., Shearer, M., Salome, C. M., & Wooldock, A. J. (1994). House dust mite allergen avoidance: A randomized controlled trial of surface chemical treatment and encasement of bedding. *Clinical and Experimental Allergy, 24*, 1078–1083.

Martinez, F. D. (2001a). Links between pediatric and adult asthma. *J Allergy Clin Immunol, 107*(Suppl. 5), S449–455.

Martinez, F. D. (2001b). Risk factors for the development of asthma. In C. K. Naspitz, S. J. Szefler, J. O. Warner, & D. G. Tinkelman (Eds.), *Textbook of pediatric asthma* (pp. 67–82). London: Martin.

Martinez, F. D., Wright, A. L., Taussig, L. M., Holberg, C. J., Halonen, M., Morgan, W. J., et al. (1995). Asthma and wheezing in the first six years of life. *New England Journal of Medicine, 332*, 133–138.

Mattes, J., & Karmaus, W. (1999). The use of antibiotics in the first year of life and the development of asthma: Which comes first? *Clinical and Experimental Allergy, 29*, 729–732.

McQuaid, E. L., Fritz, G. K., Nassau, J. H., Mansell, A., Lilly, M. K., & Klein, R. (2000). Stress and airway resistance in children with asthma. *Journal of Psychosomatic Research, 49*, 239–245.

McQuaid, E. L., Koinis Mitchell, D., Walders, N., Nassau, J., Kopel, S., Klein, R., et al. (2007). Pediatric asthma morbidity: The importance of symptom perception and family response to symptoms. *Journal of Pediatric Psychology, 32*(2), 167–177.

McQuaid, E. L., Kopel, S. J., Klein, R. B., & Fritz, G. K. (2003). Medication adherence in pediatric asthma: Reasoning, responsibility, and behavior. *Journal of Pediatric Psychology, 28*, 323–333.

McQuaid, E. L., Kopel, S. J., & Nassau, J. H. (2001). Behavioral adjustment in children with asthma: A meta-analysis. *Journal of Developmental and Behavioral Pediatrics, 22*, 430–439.

McQuaid, E. L., & Nassau, J. H. (1999). Empirically supported treatments of disease-related symptoms in pediatric psychology: Asthma, diabetes, and cancer. *Journal of Pediatric Psychology, 24*, 306–328.

McQuaid, E. L., Penza-Clyve, S., Nassau, J. H., Fritz, G. K., Klein, R., O'Connor, S., et al. (2001). Sharing family responsibility for asthma management tasks. *Children's Health Care, 30*(3), 183–199.

Miller, J. E. (2000). The effects of race/ethnicity and income on early childhood asthma prevalence and health care issues. *American Journal of Public Health, 90*, 428–430.

Morgan, W. J., Crain, E. F., Gruchalla, R. S., O'Connor, G. T., Kattan, M., Evans, R., et al. (2004).

Results of a home-based environmental intervention among urban children with asthma. *New England Journal of Medicine, 351,* 1068–1080.

Morrison, K. M., Goli, A., Van Wagoner, J., Brown, E. S., & Khan, D. A. (2002). Depressive symptoms in inner-city children with asthma. *Primary Care Companion to the Journal of Clinical Psychiatry, 4*(5), 174–177.

Mrazek, D. (1992). Psychiatric complications of pediatric asthma. *Annals of Allergy, 69*(4), 285–290.

Mrazek, D. A., & Klinnert, M. (1991). *Asthma: Psychoneuroimmunologic considerations* (2nd ed.): Academic Press.

National Institutes of Health. (1995). *Asthma management in minority children: Practical insights for clinicians, researchers and public health planners* (DHHS Publication no. 95–3675). Washington, DC: Author.

National Institutes of Health. (1997). *National Asthma Education and Prevention Program (National Heart, Lung, and Blood Institute) Second Expert Panel on the Management of Asthma. Expert panel report 2: Guidelines for the diagnosis and management of asthma.* Bethesda, MD: Author.

National Institutes of Health. (2002). *National Asthma Education and Prevention Program, Expert Panel, Report. Guidelines for the Diagnosis and Management of Asthma—Update on Selected Topics 2002.* Bethesda, MD: Author.

Noeker, M., & Petermann, F. (1998). Children's and adolescent's perceptions of their asthma bronchiale. *Child Care Health and Development, 24,* 21–30.

Oddy, W. H. (2004). A review of the effects of brestfeeding on respiratory infection, atopy and childhood asthma. *Journal of Asthma, 41,* 605–621.

Ortega, A. N., Gergen, P. J., Paltiel, A. D., Bauchner, H., Belanger, K. D., & Leaderer, B. P. (2002). Impact of site care, race, and Hispanic ethnicity on medication use for childhood asthma. *Pediatrics, 109*(1), E1.

Ortega, A. N., Huertas, S. E., Canino, G., R., R., & Rubio-Stipec, M. (2002). Childhood asthma, chronic illness, and psychiatric disorders. *Journal of Nervous and Mental Disorders, 190*(5), 275–281.

Ortega, A. N., McQuaid, E. L., Canino, G., Goodwin, R. D., & Fritz, G. K. (2004). Comorbidity of asthma and anxiety and depression in Puerto Rican children. *Psychosomatics, 45*(2), 93–99.

Ortega, A. N., McQuaid, E. L., Canino, G., Ramirez, R., Fritz, G. K., & Klein, R. B. (2003). Association of psychiatric disorders and different measures of asthma in island Puerto Rican children. *Soc Psychiatry Psychiatr Epidemiol, 38*(4), 220–226.

PausJenssen, E. S., & Cockcroft, D. W. (2003). Sex differences in asthma, atopy, and airway hyperresponsiveness in a university population. *Annals of Allergy and Asthma Immunology, 91,* 34–37.

Penza-Clyve, S. M., Mansell, C., & McQuaid, E. L. (2004). Why don't children take their asthma medications? A qualitative analysis of children's perspectives on adherence. *Journal of Asthma, 41,* 189–197.

Platts-Mills, T. A., Blumenthal, K., Perzanowski, M., & Woodfolk, T. A. (2000). Determinants of clinical allergic disease: The relevance of indoor allergens to the increase in asthma. *American Journal of Respiratory and Critical Care Medicine, 162,* S128–S133.

Portnoy, J. M., & Jennings, D. (2006). Utilization patterns in an asthma intervention. *Annals of Allergy and Asthma Immunology, 97*(Suppl. 1), S25–30.

Postma, D. S., Bleeker, E. R., Amelung, P. J., Holroyd, K. J., Xu, J., Panhuysen, C. I., et al. (1995). Genetic susceptibility to asthma-broncheal hyperresponsiveness coinherited with a major gene for atopy. *New England Journal of Medicine, 333*(14), 894–900.

Riekert, K. A., Butz, A. M., Eggleston, P. A., Huss, K., Winkelstein, M., & Rand, C. S. (2003). Caregive-physician medication concordance and undertreatment in asthma among inner-city children. *Pediatrics, 111,* 214–220.

Rosenstreich, D. L., Eggleston, P., Kattan, M., Baker, D., Slavin, R. G., Gergen. P., et al. (1997). The role of cockroach allergy and exposure to cockroach allergen in causing morbidity among inner-city children with asthma. *New England Journal of Medicine, 336,* 1356–1363.

Samet, J. M., Wiesch, D. G., & Ahmed, I. H. (2001). Pediatric asthma: Epidemiology and natural history. In C. K. Naspitz, S. J. Szefler, J. O. Warner, & D. G. Tinkelman (Eds.), *Textbook of pediatric asthma* (pp. 35–66). London: Martin.

Sears, M. R., Greene, J. M., Willan, A. R., Taylor, D. R., Flannery, E. M., Cowan, J. O., et al. (2002). Long-term relations between breastfeeding and development of atopy and asthma in children and young adults: A longitudinal study. *Lancet, 360,* 901–907.

Sears, M. R., Herbison, G. P., Holdaway, M. D., Hewitt, C. J., Flannery, E. M., & Silva, P. A. (1989). The relative risks of sensitivity to grass pollen, house dust mite and cat dander in the development of childhood asthma. *Clinical and Experimental Allergy: Journal of the British Society for Allergy and Clinical Immunology, 19*(4), 419–424.

Silverstein, M., Mair, J., Katusic, S., Wollan, P., O'Connell, E., & Yungin, J. (2001). School attendance and school performance: A population-based study of children with asthma. *Journal of Pediatrics, 139,* 278–283.

Smith, S. R., & Strunk, R. C. (1999). Acute asthma in the pediatric emergency department. *Pediatric Clinics of North America, 46*(6), 1145–1165.

Solis, O. L., Khan, D. A., & Brown, E. S. (2006). Age at onset of major depression in inner-city adults with asthma. *Psychosomatics, 47*(4), 330–332.

Suess, W. M., Stump, N., Chai, H., & Kalisker, A. (1986). Mnemonic effects of asthma medication in children. *Journal of Asthma, 23*(6), 291–296.

Tye, V. L., & Throckmorton-Belzer, L. (2006). Smoking rates and the state of smoking interventions for children and adolescents with chronic illness. *Pediatrics, 118*(2), e174–187.

Urek, M. C., Tudoric, N., Plavee, D., Urek, R., Koprivc-Milenovic, T., & Stojic, M. (2005). Effect of educational programs on asthma control and quality of life in adult asthma patients. *Patient Education and Counseling, 58*(1), 47–54.

Vercelli, D. (2004). Genetics, epigenetics, and the environment: Switching, buffering, releasing. *Journal of Allergy and Clinical Immunology, 113,* 373–379.

Walders, N., Drotar, D., & Kercsmar, C. (2000). The allocation of family responsibility for asthma management tasks in African-American adolescents. *Journal of Asthma, 37,* 89–99.

Wallace, L. A., Mitchell, H., O'Connor, G. T., Neas, L., Lippman, M., & Kattan, M., et al. (2003). Particle concentrations in inner-city homes of children with asthma: The effect of smoking, cooking, and outdoor pollution. *Environ Health Perspect, 111*(9), 1265–1272.

Wamboldt, F. S., Ho, J., Milgrom, H., Wamboldt, M. Z., Sanders, B., Szefler, S. J., et al. (2002). Prevalence and correlates of household exposures to tobacco smokers and pets in children with asthma. *The Journal of Pediatrics, 141*(1), 109–115.

Wamboldt, M., Fritz, G. K., Mansell, A., McQuaid, L., & Klein, R. B. (1998). Relationship of asthma severity and psychological problems in children. *Journal of the American Academy of Child and Adolescent Psychiatry, 37,* 943–950.

Waxmonsky, J., Wood, B. L., Stern, T., Ballow, M., Lillis, K., Cramer-Benjamin, D., et al. (2006). Association of depressive symptoms and disease activity in children with asthma: Methodological and clinical implications. *Journal of the American Academy of Child and Adolescent Psychiatry, 45*(8), 945–954.

Weil, C., Wade, S., Bauman, L., Lynn, H., Mitchell, H., & Lavigne, J. (1999). The relationship between psychosocial factors and asthma morbidity in inner-city children with asthma. *Pediatrics, 104,* 1274–1280.

Weiss, K. B., Gergen, P. J., & Crain, E. F. (1992). Inner-city asthma: The epidemiology of an emerging US public health concern. *Chest, 101*(Suppl. 6), 362S–367S.

Weiss, K. B., & Wagener, D. K. (1990). Changing patterns of asthma mortality: Identifying target populations at high risk. *Journal of the American Medical Association, 264,* 1683–1687.

Wood, P., Tumiel-Berhalter, L., Owen, S., Taylor, K., & Kattan, M. (2006). Implementation of an asthma intervention in the inner city. *Annals of Allergy and Asthma Immunology, 97*(Suppl. 1), S20–24.

Wright, A. L., & Taussig, L. M. (1998). Lessons from long-term cohort studies: Childhood asthma. *Eur Respir J Suppl, 27,* 17s–22s.

Yen, I. H., Yelin, E. H., Katz, P., Eisner, M. D., & Blanc, P. D. (2006). Perceived neighborhood problems and quality of life, physical functioning, and depressive symptoms among adults with asthma. *American Journal of Public Health, 96*(5), 973–979.

Yorke, J., Fleming, S. L., & Shuldham, C. (in press). Psychological interventions of adults with asthma: A systematic review. *Respiratory Medicine.*

Zang, Y., Leaves, N. I., Anderson, G. G., Ponting, C. P., Broxholme, J., Holt, R., et al. (2003). Positional cloning of a quantitative trait locus on chromosome 13q14 that influences immunoglobulin E levels and asthma. *Nature Genetics, 34*(2), 181–188.

Zimmerman, B. J., Bonner, S., Evans, D., & Mellins, R. B. (1999). Self-regulating childhood asthma: A developmental model of family change. *Health Education and Behavior, 26,* 55–71.

Zimmerman, B. J., Feanny, S., Reisman, J., Hak, H., Rashed, N., McLaughlin, F. J., et al. (1988). Allergy in asthma I: The dose relationship of allergy to severity of childhood asthma. *Journal of Allergy and Clinical Immunology, 81,* 63–70.

CHAPTER 12

Chronic Obstructive Pulmonary Disease

KIRK STUCKY and JEFF GREENBLATT

DESCRIPTION OF DISEASE STATE

Chronic Obstructive Pulmonary Disease (COPD) is defined as a "disease state characterized by *airflow limitation that is not fully reversible*. The airflow limitation is usually both *progressive* and associated with an abnormal inflammatory response of the lungs to noxious articles or gases" (italics added; Global Initiative for Chronic Obstructive Lung Disease [GOLD], 2005, p. 2). Airflow limitation leads to symptoms of breathlessness and fatigue. Because these airflow limitations are not fully reversible, the chronic baseline deficit may increase but will not return to normal physiologically, even if the patient becomes asymptomatic. Progressive means that the baseline will change negatively over time. These chronic and progressive aspects of COPD play a role in the psychological and social aspects of the disease and the management of patient expectations. Common symptoms that patients with COPD experience and present with include cough, sputum production, dyspnea (a feeling of breathlessness or shortness of breath), and a history of exposure to risk factors for the disease, which very commonly includes smoking. Except where noted, the information on classification, epidemiology, disease factors, and regimen factors is contained within the summary of the Global Initiative for Chronic Obstructive Lung Disease (GOLD, 2005) web site.

Spirometry, a tool used to quantify lung function, confirms the diagnosis. Several parameters are key in this test, and they include:

- *Forced vital capacity* (FVC), which measures the total amount of air that a patient can breath out
- *Forced expiratory volume in 1 second* (FEV1), which measures the maximum amount of air a patient can breath out in the first second of expiration, and
- *The ratio of FEV1 to FVC* (FEV1/FVC)

Combining the symptoms with spirometric parameters allows a classification of COPD into at risk, mild, moderate, severe, and very severe.

Table 12.1
Classification of COPD

0: At risk	Normal spirometry Chronic symptoms (cough, sputum production)
I: Mild COPD	FEV1/FVC < 70% FEV1 ≥ 80% predicted With or without chronic symptoms (cough, sputum production)
II: Moderate COPD	FEV1/FVC < 70% 50% ≤ FEV1 < 80% predicted With or without chronic symptoms (cough, sputum production)
III: Severe COPD	FEV1/FVC < 70% 30% ≤ FEV1 < 50% predicted With or without chronic symptoms (cough, sputum production)
IV: Very Severe COPD	FEV1/FVC < 70% FEV1 < 30% PREDICTED OR FEV1 < 50% predicted plus chronic respiratory failure

It is important to note that there is an imperfect relationship between symptoms and the degree of airflow limitation. Therefore, each patient must be individually assessed to define his or her status in the disease process. Furthermore, a lack of symptoms does not mean that a patient may not have considerable lung function impairment. In developing countries, COPD and tuberculosis (TB) are common and share a similar symptom profile. Therefore, TB needs to be considered in patients who are visiting or have immigrated from developing countries.

Pathogenesis

The hallmark of COPD is chronic airway inflammation. Chronic inflammation of the airways leads to the release of mediators that are capable of damaging the lungs. Other precursors include the imbalance of proteases (enzymes that destroy proteins) and antiproteases, and oxidative stress. Both cigarette smoking and other noxious stimuli cause airway inflammation and directly damage the lungs.

Pathology

Inflammation of the airways leads to mucus hypersecretion and remodeling of airways, causing airway narrowing and fixed airway obstruction. In addition, the imbalance of proteases and antiproteases, and perhaps oxidative stress, destroys lung tissue and leads to the development of emphysema. These pathologic changes are linked to the symptoms characteristic of COPD:

1. Mucus hypersecretion and ciliary dysfunction that leads to chronic cough and sputum production (cilia are small, hairlike projections from mucous cells lining the airways that in normal lungs work to move mucus out of the airways).
2. Lung tissue destruction and narrowing, leading to dyspnea

3. Vascular changes that contribute to the development of pulmonary hypertension and cor pulmonale[1]. *Pulmonary hypertension* is increased pressure in the vessels that carry deoxygenated blood from the right side of the heart to the lungs for oxygenation. Prolonged increases can lead to enlargement and failure of the right side of the heart. These changes are associated with a poor prognosis.

There are several risk factors that account for the heterogeneity in the patient population and that can be broken down into host and environmental factors. Host factors include straightforward genetic and more complex multifactorial conditions. Alpha-1 antitrypsin is a well-recognized entity that occurs in one of every 2,000 to 5,000 individuals. It is associated with early-onset emphysema, especially in those who smoke. Effective but expensive replacement therapy of Alpha-1 antitrypsin is available (Stoller & Aboussouan, 2005). Other host factors that contribute to the onset of COPD include a history of airway hyperresponsiveness (e.g., asthma) and in utero or childhood exposures that retard lung growth. In addition, a recent study by Coxson, Chan, Mayo, and Hlynsky (2004) found that patients who suffer from anorexia nervosa were more likely to have early-onset COPD, which is posited to be caused by the malnutrition seen in this disease. Apart from the obvious tobacco exposure, including second-hand smoke, other environmental exposures also increase the risk of developing COPD. These include outdoor and indoor pollution, a history of severe childhood lung infections, and lower socioeconomic status, which may be mediated by the interplay of factors such as poor nutrition, pollution exposure, overcrowding, and others.

PREVALENCE

The prevalence of the disease is substantial and increasing, particularly in developing countries, likely due to the increasing prevalence of smoking in these regions. Worldwide, it is estimated that by the year 2020 COPD will be the fifth leading cause of death. Differences in prevalence from country to country exist and may be multifactorial in origin, affected by types and amounts of indoor and outdoor pollution, smoking behaviors, type of tobacco, processing differences of cigarettes, genetic factors, and climate (Hurd, 2000). In the United States there are approximately 24 million adults with impaired lung function, although the actual number of physician-reported cases is less than half that figure, indicating a great deal of underdiagnosis. It is currently the fourth leading cause of death behind myocardial infarction, cancer, and stroke. The burden of disease on the health care system is substantial, with 8 million annual office visits, 1.5 million emergency room visits, 726,000 hospitalizations, and 119,000 deaths. The incidence has more than doubled between 1980 and 2000, and for the first time the number of women dying from COPD has exceeded that of men. In addition to the upward trend in females, there has also been an increase in the incidence in African Americans, although this trend has recently demonstrated a reversal. One trend in the opposite direction is a decline in the prevalence of COPD for those ages 25 to 54, probably as a result of a decrease in smoking behavior. This suggests that the upward trend in hospitalizations and mortality may not persist (Mannino, Homa,

---

1. *Cor pulmonale* is an increase in the size (hypertrophy) of the right side of the heart, usually brought on by disease of the lung. This can eventually lead to right-sided heart failure, characterized by swelling of the legs, increases in liver size, and fluid in the abdomen (ascites).

Akinbami, Ford, & Redd, 2002). The economic burden is also substantial, with an annual cost that exceeds $14 billion. Cigarette smoking accounts for the majority of cases, and only 15% of COPD is work related (Boschetto, Quintavalle, Miotto, Cascio, Zeni, & Mapp, 2006).

DISEASE FACTORS

The onset of the chronic obstructive pulmonary disease is often insidious and may be preceded by years of chronic cough and mucus production. There are a number of environmental, social, and individual risk factors, which interact in a complex fashion. A more detailed discussion regarding disease factors is provided below.

Onset

As mentioned earlier, there is a poor correlation between symptoms and severity of disease, and symptoms such as chronic cough and mucus production may precede the diagnosis of COPD by years. A "smoker's cough" may give the patient a false sense of security, since a cough does not necessarily herald the onset of COPD. Thus, patients may opt to self-medicate. The cough can actually be a self-protective mechanism to overcome ciliary dysfunction induced by smoking, and thus self-medication may predispose patients to developing acute bronchitis and worsening lung function. In addition, self-medication of symptoms may delay patients seeking diagnosis and treatment. Since the disease is progressive, early detection can be helpful in slowing the progression by the removal of causative factors (e.g., cigarette smoking). The first hospitalization may in fact be the initiation of a diagnostic evaluation for COPD. Once the diagnosis is made, communicating the seriousness of this condition is essential to promoting optimal patient and family coping.

Disease Progression

COPD is characterized by a chronic progressive course, punctuated by acute exacerbations that may be life threatening. Furthermore, exacerbations account for approximately 70% of the medical care costs in patients with COPD (Niewoehner, 2006). Not infrequently, treatment for severe exacerbations requires a period of mechanical ventilation accompanied with intubation. Patients who have suffered an exacerbation of their underlying disease may not return to their baseline status due to further lung damage. As will be discussed in the Regimen Factors section, treatment, once initiated, is also progressive. Therefore, exacerbations may herald the need for additional therapy. In its late stages, patients with COPD are extremely limited in their ability to carry on activities of daily living and may be placed on continuous oxygen therapy, which restricts mobility. The most severely affected patients are sometimes placed on long-term mechanical ventilation. According to the MIMAP description, in Chapter 1, COPD would be considered a chronic episodic condition, usually with worsening of the between-episode baseline after episodes of exacerbation.

REGIMEN FACTORS

Although most therapeutic interventions are well tolerated except in the most severe cases or during acute exacerbations, the lack of effective cures and the progressive nature of the disease are challenging for both the patient and clinician. The goals of COPD management are not mutually exclusive, and include:

- Prevent progression
- Relieve symptoms
- Increase exercise tolerance
- Increase health status
- Prevent and treat complications
- Prevent and treat exacerbations
- Decrease mortality (GOLD, 2005)

Once initiated, reduction of baseline therapy is not possible. As the disease progresses, additional therapies are required. Because exacerbations impair a patient's quality of life and decrease his or her health status, aggressive efforts are necessary to prevent exacerbations. Comorbidities that must be considered include bronchial cancer, tuberculosis, sleep apnea, and left heart failure (GOLD, 2005).

SMOKING CESSATION

Cigarette smoking is a major risk factor in the development of COPD and accounts for the vast majority of patients with the illness. Therefore, smoking cessation is an essential component of treatment. The executive summary for the Global Initiative for Chronic Obstructive Lung Disease (GOLD, 2005) states, "Smoking cessation is the single most effective and cost effective intervention to reduce the risk of developing COPD and stop its progression." (GOLD, p. 9) Thus, treatment of tobacco addiction is recommended for every patient. Brief tobacco-dependence treatment has an impact on usage rates and, even though there is a high rate of recidivism, every opportunity should be taken to offer this at each clinical contact. Optimally, counseling sessions lasting longer than 10 minutes appear to offer the best abstinence rate, but brief interventions lasting less than 3 minutes may increase abstinence rates by 30%. Three types of counseling are primarily recommended—practical counseling, social support as part of treatment, and social support outside of treatment (Creer, Bender, & Lucas, 2006). Practical counseling can relatively easily be incorporated into routine care, and focuses on the clinician providing problem solving and skills training to the smoker. These counseling topics include recognizing danger situations that may promote smoking, developing appropriate coping skills, and providing basic information about smoking and successful quitting (Fiore, Bailey, Cohen, Dorfman, Goldstein, & Gritz, 2000). One brief recommended interventional tool for primary care clinicians is the 5 As system, which utilizes in part Prochaska's transtheoretical model of the stages of change (Prochaska & DiClemente, 1983). The GOLD summary (p. 10) provides the following table (see Table 12.2), which outlines the system.

It should be emphasized that the effectiveness of interventions such as pulmonary rehabilitation, medications, and psychotherapy are dependent on the patient abstaining from tobacco. Additionally, the maintenance of abstinence from smoking is complicated and mediated by a number of factors, including physician and social support. Although 70% of smokers report wanting to quit, 88% of smokers who do stop eventually resume smoking (Ockene et al. 2000). It should also be noted that, in those patients with a history of depression who do successfully quit smoking, there is a sevenfold increase in the risk for reoccurrence of major depression relative to those who

Table 12.2

5 As Brief Physician Advice for Smoking Cessation

1. **Ask:** Systematically identify all tobacco users at every visit. Implement an office-wide system that ensures that, for every patient at every clinic visit, tobacco-use status is queried and documented.

2. **Advise:** Strongly urge all tobacco users to quit. In a clear, strong, and personalized manner urge every tobacco user to quit.

3. **Assess:** Determine willingness to make a quit attempt. Ask every tobacco user if he or she is willing to make a quit attempt at this time (e.g., within the next 30 days).

4. **Assist:** Aid the patient in quitting. Help the patient with a quit plan, provide practical counseling, provide intratreatment social support, help the patient obtain extra-treatment social support, recommend use of approved pharmacotherapy except in special circumstances, and provide supplementary materials.

5. **Arrange:** Schedule follow-up contact. Schedule follow-up contact either in person or via telephone.

---

continue to smoke (Covey, 1999). These findings have raised questions regarding the biochemical and biophysiologic mechanisms between smoking, COPD, and depression (Clary, Palmer, & Doraiswamy, 2002). For a comprehensive review of smoking cessation treatment, the interested reader is referred to Chapter 5 and to Wagena and colleagues (2004) for a review of smoking-cessation efficacy specific to COPD.

Pharmacotherapy and counseling are additive. Pharmacotherapy must be used with caution in light smokers and with patients with medical contraindications or pregnancy. Occupational exposures can be reduced through interventions to decrease inhalation of particulate matter. For indoor and outdoor pollution, high-risk individuals should be advised to avoid vigorous outdoor exercise during times of increased pollution. Unfortunately, air cleaners have not been shown to be beneficial.

For those with stable disease there should be a stepwise approach to therapeutic interventions. Education can play a role in improving the patient's response to exacerbations, decreasing smoking, as well as improving adaptive skills, coping ability, and health status. Educational interventions also include discussing advanced directives and end-of-life care.

Pharmacologic therapeutic intervention for COPD proceeds in an additive fashion. The goals for therapy include reductions in the number of exacerbations, improvements in functional status, and increasing exercise tolerance. The first step is prescription of a bronchodilator delivered in a multidose inhaler. Inhalers can be effective and are usually well-tolerated, since they are delivered to the lungs locally rather than systematically. Care must be taken to ensure that the patient uses proper techniques or the medicine will not reach small enough airways to be effective. Mechanical spacers can be added to the inhaler to more effectively deliver the medicine. All inhalers have been shown to improve exercise tolerance. Initially using a short-acting inhaler in mild forms of the disease is an appropriate approach. However, when the patient passes into the moderate stage, one or more longer-acting bronchodilators are indicated, usually given two to four times per day, depending on the drug. Oral bronchodilators are available, but systemic side effects are more common. As more bronchodilators are added to the regimen the complexity of the treatment regimen increases. However, there are formulations that combine medications that can decrease the complexity. Patients with severe or very severe COPD benefit from the addition of an inhaled glucocorticosteroid, which has been shown to decrease exacerbations. Oral glucocorticosteroids, although not supported by clinical trials, are still utilized by practitioners in those patients with severe and very severe COPD. Side effects from these systemic steroids can be substantial, including osteoporosis, problems with glucose metabolism, susceptibility to infections, psychiatric complications, and muscle weakness that can worsen lung function (GOLD, 2005). For patients who become chronically hypoxic in the later stages of the disease, supplemental oxygen more than 15 hours per day can be provided, and will decrease the cardiovascular effects of prolonged hypoxia, as well as increase survival, exercise capacity, lung mechanics, and possibly prevent the development of cognitive problems (GOLD). However, even though oxygen therapy can have many beneficial effects, patient acceptability may be an issue that needs to be addressed with the patient and his or her family.

Patients with COPD often steadily decrease their physical and social activity levels in order to reduce the intensity of their dyspnea or distress. This results in further deconditioning and subsequent increases in fatigue and/or breathlessness (Reardon, Lareau, & ZuWallack, 2006). Pulmonary rehabilitation at all stages will increase exercise tolerance and decrease dyspnea and fatigue (GOLD, 2005). However, even though it is proven to be effective in the short term, long-term gains have not been shown to be maintained. Rehabilitation interventions are discussed in more detail at the end of this chapter. Recently, lung reduction surgery for those with very severe disease was studied. Although initial reports were promising, recent data indicates that the procedure carries significant morbidity, has high overall costs, and currently must be reserved for only selected groups of patients (GOLD). However, in the right patient population, done in a high-performing center, there are long-term benefits.

INDIVIDUAL FACTORS

Sir William Osler, MD, wrote, "It is more important to understand what patient has a disease, than what disease the patient has." (Osler, 1919). In this statement he summarized what researchers have demonstrated over the past 30 years—that a patient's perception of illness, personal belief system, and coping style can significantly influence disease outcome independent of physiological factors (Everly, 1989; Boll, Johnson, Perry, & Rozensky, 2006; Gatchel and Oordt., 2003).

The experiences patients have with chronic illness can vary widely due to the influence of various individual factors, such as education and culture. For example, typical pulmonary function measures, such as FEV1, are not very well correlated with patients' reports regarding quality of life or overall perception of symptoms (Ries, 2006). Physician and psychologist researchers have begun to explore variables that influence the course of chronic illness in an attempt to develop comprehensive, cost-effective interventions with greater overall efficacy. Essentially, patients with COPD often have similar physical symptoms and disease parameters, but a complex interplay of intrapersonal and interpersonal factors influence the way in which they express these symptoms and how these symptoms impact their lives. Research in health psychology has revealed social and psychological factors that impact not only the experience of chronic illness and quality of life, but in some cases morbidity and mortality as well. In this section we summarize findings from studies addressing this topic in patients with COPD. There is not a broad depth of literature regarding individual factors specific to patients with COPD, and some of the findings are in conflict, indicating that additional research is required to better understand the interplay between the disease and psychosocial variables. Thus, the review provided here is by no means exhaustive, and the perceptive reader will recognize that a great deal more study needs to be done with pulmonary patients before more definitive statements can be made.

KNOWLEDGE AND INFORMATION

Educational level appears to have an impact on disease outcomes, with higher levels of education generally associated with increased interest in obtaining information and better long-term outcomes (Koster, Bosma, Kempen, van Lenthe, van Eijk, & Mackenbach, 2004). In a study on health disparities, those with less education had lower life expectancy, and individuals with less than a ninth-grade education had the lowest (Wong, Shapiro, Boscardin, & Ettner, 2002). These findings were consistent across multiple chronic illness groups, including lung disease. Additionally, a number of studies have found that patients with lung disease are often uninformed regarding their diagnosis and may not know which practical behavioral strategies would be most effective in managing their illness (Boot, van der Gulden, Vercoulen, van den Borne, Orbin, & Rooijackers, 2005). Interestingly, the same study found that 30% of the COPD patients did not know their correct diagnosis. This lack of understanding could have been related to multiple factors, such as low educational attainment, lack of exposure to or ineffective educational materials, cognitive deficits, and/or the patients' lack of interest in becoming informed regarding their illness.

Socioeconomic status has been associated with morbidity and mortality in a variety of chronic diseases, including COPD. In fact, some authors have found that higher chronic disease severity was less predictive of mobility and functional decline than socioeconomic status (Koster et al. 2004). In a study based on 14,223 individuals in Copenhagen, both income and education were associated with lung function, independent of smoking behavior (Prescott, Lange, & Vestbo, 1999). This association was true for both males and females. Additionally, individuals in the lowest socioeconomic group were three times more likely to be hospitalized for the illness relative to patients in the highest socioeconomic group. These findings were similar to those from another Norwegian study, in which education level acted as an independent risk factor for COPD even after occupational exposure was controlled (Bakke, Hanoa, and Gulsvik, 1995).

HEALTH BELIEFS

Not surprisingly, a patient's understanding of illness and treatment can affect health outcome as well as overall adherence. In part, obtaining this knowledge and information is dependent upon the individual patient's interest and assertiveness in educating themselves. Some patients can be aggressive information seekers while others are passive and willingly allow clinicians to manage their treatment without a need to understand it (Miller, Shoda, & Hurley, 1996). Unfortunately, clinicians may not necessarily recognize or respond to this asymmetry strategically. Psychologists have discussed these phenomena in the context of an individual's locus of control and self-efficacy. *Health locus of control* refers to a patient's personal beliefs regarding the degree to which he or she is able to change or influence his or her own health status. The importance of personal perception in determining the functional impact of COPD cannot be overstated. Several studies have pointed out that work-related disability and sick leave are more associated with the patient's perceived symptoms and health complaints than they are with actual pulmonary function measures, such as FEV 1 (Boot et al., 2005; Kubzansky, Wright, Cohen, Weiss, Rosner, & Sparrow, 2002). Overall, research suggests that individuals who expect poor function often fulfill those expectations while individuals who are more optimistic, even when it is somewhat unrealistic, tend to function better in a variety of life roles.

Researchers often refer to a person's perceived level of control over health and treatment outcome as self-efficacy. Essentially, self-efficacy refers to an individual's belief regarding his or her ability to perform a particular behavior or set of behaviors (Bandura, 1977). In other words, self-efficacy involves the individual's perceived level of control over his or her symptoms and illness. Individuals with an internal locus of control believe that they are primarily in control of their health status. These patients are often confident that by doing certain things they can prevent or control the expression of symptoms. Conversely, individuals with an external locus of control view their health as primarily influenced by outside factors such as chance, powerful others, or the environment. These individuals may minimize the importance of behavioral change, such as smoking cessation. They may also be unaware of behaviors that exacerbate their symptoms or may believe that symptoms will occur regardless of their efforts. Not surprisingly, personality researchers have identified internal and external locus of control as important predictors of a patient's interest in learning more about his or her illness (Everly, 1989; Boll et al. 2006, Gatchel & Oordt, 2003).

Social Support

As in other patient groups, positive social support has consistently been associated with lower levels of depression and anxiety. Not surprisingly, patients who are dissatisfied with their relationships tend to report more problems with loneliness and depression. Furthermore, patients who report more frequent negative interactions with individuals in their social group tend to experience higher levels of depression (McCathie, Spence, & Tate, 2002). It is important to emphasize that these studies addressed the patient's perception of social support, not the actual level of support. While some clinicians might view a patient's social support as suboptimal, if the patient does not share this perception he or she typically receives a certain level of benefit. These findings also suggest that patients may be at greater risk for depression, even when they have considerable resources and support, but do not appreciate or utilize them.

Coping

Hans Selye, a physiologist who was a pioneer in studying the human stress response, stated, "It's not the stress that kills us, it is our reaction to it" (Selye, 1974). The concept of coping in chronic illness is complex, but generally refers to the thoughts, beliefs, behaviors, compensatory strategies, and adaptive techniques an individual uses or applies in an effort to adjust to his or her health condition. Thus, coping has to do with an individual's cognitive and behavioral efforts to reduce, adapt, or tolerate the internal and external impact of an event, situation, injury, or illness (Lazarus, 1999). Coping strategies can be productive or unproductive, active or passive. *Passive coping styles* are characterized by ignoring or avoiding a situation in hopes that it will go away, or that something external will solve the problem. *Active coping* typically refers to proactive efforts directed at resolving or controlling a health-related condition. Although active coping is often believed to result in healthier outcomes, there are exceptions, which are influenced in part by the natural disease course and the availability of effective disease interventions. For example, an individual with COPD who develops a belief that he or she can eventually breathe normally without the use of medication, and actively pursues this goal, may expend valuable physical and psychological energy on an unobtainable goal. In other words, an active coping style directed at attempting to change something that is not subject to change can be unproductive or can potentially set an individual up for disappointment and further decline. Multiple studies have demonstrated the influence that desirable or undesirable coping styles can have on disease progression and outcome (McCathie, Spence, & Tate, 2002). Avoidant coping styles often lead to poor follow-through on positive disease management behaviors. Examples of avoidant coping styles in COPD would include procrastinating with regard to habit change, such as smoking cessation, and/or avoiding exercise. Generally, lower levels of self-efficacy and a tendency to use withdrawal as a coping strategy have been associated with higher levels of depression and reduced quality of life. Consequently, authors have suggested that interventions that successfully increase a patient's belief in personal control and challenge misperceptions regarding the consequences and course of illness can lead to improvements in physical, role, and social functioning (Scharloo, Kaptein, Weinman, Hazes, Willems, & Bergman, 1998).

There is also evidence that desirable psychological characteristics, such as optimism, have a positive impact on disease progression and outcome. Kubzansky and colleagues (2002) found that optimism was associated with a slower rate of decline in FEV 1 over time. These findings were found to be independent of cigarette smoking behavior. The authors concluded, "The results of this study suggest that modifying cognitive or emotional styles, such as optimistic or pessimistic explanatory style, may help to delay or attenuate potential decline in individuals at risk of poor pulmonary health" (Kubzansky et al. 2002, p. 351). Similar to this finding, Scharloo and colleagues (1998) conducted a cross-sectional study in patients with rheumatoid arthritis, COPD, and psoriasis. They wrote, "strong illness identity, passive coping style, belief in long illness duration, belief in more severe consequences, and an unfavorable score on medical variables were associated with worse outcome on disease-specific measures of functioning and on general role and social functioning. Coping by seeking social support and beliefs in controllability/curability of the disease were significantly related to better functioning" (Scharloo et al. 1998, p. 573).

Chronic obstructive pulmonary disease and asthma, although both diseases of the lung, were found to differ in how coping styles interacted with quality of life (Hesselink, Penninx, Schlosser, Wijnhoven, van der Windt, & Kriegsman, 2004). It was hypothesized that these differences could be explained because asthma patients might feel a greater sense of control and tended to have a more benign course than those with COPD. Another study from the Netherlands (Scharloo et al. 1998) that focused on patients with chronic illnesses, including COPD, found that disease-specific functioning, role, and social functioning were influenced by the illness identity and coping strategy. In particular, passive coping and a strong illness identity were found to be negatively associated with functional status. Those patients who believed they had more control over their illness and sought social support as a coping strategy had better overall functional status.

COMORBID PSYCHOPATHOLOGY

The occurance of anxiety, depression, and other psychiatric disorders is quite common in chronic illness populations. COPD is certainly no exception. However, the identification and treatment of co-morbid psychopathology in patients with COPD has been described as inadequate. A more detailed discussion regarding common, complicating psychological issues and their impact on disease outcome has been provided below.

DEPRESSION AND ANXIETY

There is a moderate body of literature indicating that, as a group, patients with COPD have a higher incidence of depression and anxiety. Figures vary, but generally studies indicate a prevalence of emotional disorders between 25 to 50% in patients with COPD. In a recent study, Roundy and colleagues (2005) found that 49% of 102 patients had an anxiety or depressive disorder. They commented that while recognition of emotional issues had improved in this population, there were still inefficiencies in providing patient education within the primary care setting. Craven (1990) found that approximately 50% of 116 lung transplant candidates had a diagnosable psychiatric disorder. On personality assessment inventories such as the Minnesota Multiphasic Personality Inventory (MMPI-2; Graham, 1990) studies have reported a high incidence of depression and preoccupation with somatic concerns (Prigatano, Parsons, Wright, Levin, & Hawryluk, 1987; Grant, Heaton, McSweeny, Adams, & Timms,1982). Furthermore, not surprisingly, the profiles of COPD patients on inventories like this were similar to other patient groups with chronic medical illness or disability.

Overall levels of stress, debility, and degree of hypoxemia most likely also contribute to the development of depression. Studies have shown that patients' risk for affective disturbances generally escalate as the severity of illness increases. In a sample of 92 males with COPD, higher levels of depression were found in those patients with coping strategies that focused on catastrophic withdrawal and had lower levels of self-efficacy. Less anxiety and depression were found in patients with higher levels of perceived social support (McCathie, Spence, & Tate, 2002).

Quality of life (QOL) studies have consistently demonstrated that, relative to controls, patients with COPD score lower on all dimensions. Fan and colleagues (2002) found that, in a sample of 601 patients with lung disease, lower quality of life was a strong predictor of all-cause mortality and hospitalization. Additionally, patients who experience the most frequent exacerbations often experience a more rapid decline in QOL (Niewoehner, 2006). Several studies have suggested that anxiety and depression have a more important influence on determining a patient's quality of life than COPD severity (Roundy et al. 2005; Burgess, Kunik, & Stanley, 2005). Thus, the identification of emotional disturbance in this and other chronic illness populations is critical as depression alone, independent of other factors, has been found to be a significant predictor for increased morbidity and mortality (Fan et al.).

NEUROPSYCHOLOGICAL IMPAIRMENT

There is a growing body of literature documenting changes in neuropsychological functioning for patients with COPD. Grant and colleagues (1982) studied the effects of advanced hypoxemia in 203 patients. The authors applied a liberal cutoff score of 1 standard deviation below the mean as being indicative of cognitive impairment. They found that, compared to a sample of matched controls, COPD patients displayed inefficiencies on tasks requiring flexible thought, abstraction abilities, perceptual-motor integration, and simple motor skills. In the sample, 77% were found to have some form of cognitive impairment, and 42% exhibited moderate to severe neuropsychological impairment. Generally, studies have found a dose-response type relationship between severity of hypoxemia and degree of neuropsychological impairment. In other words, there appears to be rather consistent evidence that those patients with more severe and progressive hypoxemia perform worse on neuropsychological measures than those patients with less severe COPD. Grant and colleagues (1987) conducted a factor analysis and found that as the degree of hypoxemia increased, patients scored progressively worse in the domains of perceptual learning, problem solving, alertness-psychomotor speed, and simple motor function. They summarized the results, indicating that the rate of cognitive impairment increased from 27% in patients with mild hypoxemia to 61% in patients with severe hypoxemia.

Crews and colleagues (2001) studied the neuropsychological data for 47 patients with end-stage COPD who were being evaluated as candidates for lung transplantation. As in other studies, these authors used scores that were 1 standard deviation below the mean as the criterion for impairment. The highest frequency of impairment was found on a test of verbal learning and memory. Specifically, 50% of patients earned scores suggesting impaired immediate free recall. Approximately 44% of these patients displayed deficient long-term retrieval while 32% had an elevated number of intrusion errors. Intrusion errors are often observed in individuals with memory disorders and typically indicate the presence of difficulty discriminating newly learned information from other information. These findings were consistent with other studies that identified verbal memory impairments in patients with COPD (Incalz, Gemma, Marra, Capparella, Fuso, & Carbonin, 1997; Incalzi, Gemma, Marra, Muzzolon, Capparella, & Carbonin, 1993). On tests assessing mental flexibility, over 20% of patients exhibited scores 1 standard deviation below the normative mean. Thus, although the criterion for impairment was somewhat liberal in these studies, there appears to be scientific evidence of a trend toward cognitive decline or inefficiency, especially as disease severity increases.

Additionally, clinicians and researchers have speculated that patients with mild hypoxemia, or even those with relatively stable COPD, may be experiencing subtle cognitive changes, which negatively impacts their capacity to benefit from educational materials or to learn coping strategies. In a study, Liesker and colleagues (2004) indicated that 30 patients with stable COPD demonstrated impaired speed-of-information processing, but relatively intact verbal memory relative to a control group. They hypothesized that deficient cognitive function in nonhypoxemic patients could be related to chronic nocturnal desaturation, or perhaps the effects of certain medications commonly used in this population. Encouragingly, several studies have also documented a positive effect of oxygen therapy on cognitive performance (Hjalmarsen, Waterloo, & Dahl, 1999; Krop, Block, & Cohen, 1973; Heaton, Grant, & McSweeny, 1983).

Overall, the findings regarding neuropsychological functioning in patients with COPD raise important concerns with regard to how to approach assessment and treatment in this population. It should be stressed that this particular area requires a great deal more study before definitive statements can be made. The studies reviewed had rather low subject numbers and the criterion for impairment was liberal in most. How-

Table 12.3
Guidelines to Consider Referral for Neuropsychological Assessment

Disease parameters	Symptoms	Functional Issues
Moderate-to-severe COPD	Memory or concentration complaints. Reports being disorganized, forgetful, or unmotivated	Forgets medications more than twice a week
Frequent exacerbations or hospitalizations due to hypoxemia	High level of dependency on others to remember medications or treatment program	Forgets appointments periodically
Any episode of delirium or hypoxic encephalopathy	Exhibits symptoms of depression or anxiety with concurrent treatment adherence issues	Family or friends report cognitive issues affecting social or day to day function

ever, determining a patient's capacity to learn and remember new information is understandably important for physicians who may be prescribing rather complicated treatment or medication regimens. By determining the patient's cognitive strengths and weakness, specific compensatory strategies could be taught to increase the chance of better compliance. Additionally, if patients were identified as having cognitive impairments early on, clinicians would most likely be able make adjustments to increase the probability of education retention and adherence. For example, in those patients with significant cognitive limitations, clinicians would be wise to include or even primarily rely on caregivers and/or family members to ensure the correct implementation and follow-through on treatment protocols. Certain compensatory memory strategies or devices, such as planners, alarms/pager systems, and/or consistent routines or schedules might be the most effective way to help these patients. Furthermore, patients with memory or concentration deficits typically benefit when medical information is written down, reviewed slowly, and repeated several times to help ensure understanding and retention. Additionally, the simplification of information may be critical in patients with lower levels of educational attainment or identified cognitive impairments.

Personality Disorders

There is no evidence to indicate a greater prevalence of personality disorders in individuals with COPD or lung disease. However, there is a body of literature, primarily using the MMPI-2 as an instrument, which suggests that many patients with COPD tend to become overly focused on somatic symptoms, which in turn leads to increasing levels of anxiety and depression (Crews, Jefferson, Bolduc, Elliott, Ferro, & Broshek, 2001). This personality style is not unique to COPD and has been observed in a number of patient groups with chronic medical conditions (e.g., chronic pain). However, understanding this characterological dynamic is important for the treating clinician, as it has strong implications as to how the individual approaches his or her illness and to what degree he or she perceives some level of personal control. Typically, individuals with the type of profile identified by research expend a large amount of cognitive and emotional energy focusing on things that are not within their personal control, which in turn promotes the development and maintenance of emotional disorders. These emotional problems in turn lead to further exacerbation of real physical symptoms, which inevitably discourages the patient from participating in desirable behaviors. Thus, a vicious cycle of increasing anxiety, hopelessness, decreased productive activity, and subsequent declines in physical functioning occurs over time. These findings once again stress the importance of understanding the way in which a patient self-perceives and talks about his or her illness. As will be seen in the case study presented later in this chapter, patients often adopt a defeatist or hopeless attitude with regard to their illness, which in turn acts as a barrier to establishing more healthy behaviors.

Psychosis

There is no evidence that psychiatric conditions, such as schizophrenia or bipolar disorder, occur with greater frequency in patients with COPD. However, some patients with COPD go on to develop delirium secondary to hypoxic injury or iatrogenic effects of medication. In an extensive literature search, the prevalence rates for these particular complications in patients with COPD could not be found. We are unaware of studies identifying the incidence of delirium in this population. Furthermore, the most common contributing variable to delirium in this population is not known. The authors' personal experience with patients diagnosed with COPD suggests that moderate to severe hypoxic events or the iatrogenic effects of medication would be the most common precursors to delirium.

INTERVENTIONS

The three primary approaches to treatment of COPD are medication, smoking cessation, and rehabilitation. Although pulmonary rehabilitation programs sometimes include psychotherapeutic interventions and smoking cessation, many focus primarily on exercise. Unfortunately, a global standard of care recommending an interdisciplinary, multitiered approach has not been established, although this would most likely be the ideal standard of care (Creer, Bender, and Lucas, 2006). These three primary interventions are discussed briefly and separately.

Pulmonary Rehabilitation

Chronic obstructive pulmonary disease, by definition, is a chronic illness that will become progressively worse over time. Treatment is not curative but is aimed at slowing down illness progression, improving function, and enhancing overall quality of life. Thus, an effective treatment program establishes goals and targets symptoms that can be modified, as opposed to focusing on uncontrollable aspects of the condition. Lox and Freehill (1999) pointed out that pulmonary physical rehabilitation did not become recognized as an effective strategy for COPD management until the mid 1970s. They wrote, "Pulmonary rehabilitation has been defined as 'an art of medical practice wherein an individually tailored, multidisciplinary program is formulated which, through accurate diagnosis, therapy, emotional support, and education, stabilizes or reverses both the physio- and psychopathology of pulmonary disease and attempts to return the patient to the highest possible functional capacity allowed by his pulmonary handicap and overall life situation' (American Thoracic Society, 1981, p. 209)." A more recent definition characterizes it as a "multidisciplinary program of care for patients with chronic respiratory impairment that is individually tailored and designed to optimize physical and social performance and autonomy" (quoted in American Association of Respiratory Care, 2002, p. 617).

Thus, pulmonary rehabilitation provides a structured approach to optimizing functional capacity, reducing the impact of symptoms on quality of life, and establishing proactive habits to prevent or slow down disease progression. These programs typically provide exercise training, psychosocial support, education, and instruction on respiratory techniques. Ries and colleagues (1995) found that comprehensive pulmonary rehabilitation produced a significantly greater increase in endurance and maximal oxygen uptake. However, relative to an education-alone group, there was no difference in measures of lung function, overall quality of life, or depression. In a meta-analysis of pulmonary rehabilitation for patients with COPD that primarily focused on exercise, Lacasse and colleagues (1996) found positive benefits. Furthermore, recent reviews of the literature on pulmonary rehabilitation indicate that overall research has consistently demonstrated improved exercise tolerance, perception of dyspnea, and quality of life (Creer, Bender, and Lucas, 2006). Additionally, there is evidence indicating that rehabilitation reduces the likelihood and/or frequency of hospitalization (Prescott, Lange, & Vestbo,1999).

Although a unified consensus on the definition or measurement of quality of life (QOL) has not been developed, there has been a great deal of interest in the concept. Generally, QOL refers to an individual's overall satisfaction with areas in his or her life, such as health, relationships, and treatment (Fan et al. 2002). In other words, it is possible for an individual to be unhappy with his or her health but satisfied with the level of support he or she receives from family and friends. The Chronic Respiratory Disease Questionnaire (CRQ) is a commonly used instrument in studying QOL in patients with COPD. Researchers using this instrument have reported mixed findings regarding an overall improvement in QOL for patients who participate in pulmonary rehabilitation (Lox & Freehill, 1999).

While the benefits of formal pulmonary rehabilitation programs on endurance and physical function are well known, the maintenance of desirable health-promoting habits learned in these programs has been poor, ranging between 25 and 50% of participants. Emery, Schein, Hauck, & MacIntyre (2003) evaluated the 1-year outcome of a self-directed exercise activity on cognitive functioning and psychological well-being in 28 patients with COPD. After a 10-week program, participants were given exercise and behavioral prescriptions to follow. Of the 28 patients, 11 remained adherent and subsequently maintained their initial gains. Nonadherent individuals experienced declines in functional capacity, cognitive performance, and psychological well-being. This and other studies emphasize the importance of developing interventions that increase the chances of maintaining patient adherence over time. Additionally, several studies have found no significant differences in the rate of depression or survival in patients who participate in these programs (Clary, Palmer, & Doraiswamy, 2002). Effective treatment of emotional issues in patients with COPD is considered by most as critical to overall program success, because studies have identified psychological factors such as mood, personal beliefs, and certain coping styles as predictive of better outcome maintenance. Consequently, Wempe and Wijkstra, (2004) suggested a program duration of at least 3 months with behavioral modification and regular physical/social activities within the post-rehabilitation period. Recently, the executive summary for the Global Initiative for Chronic Obstructive Lung Disease (GOLD, 2005) indicated that the minimum length of an effective pulmonary rehabilitation program was 2 months, and that longer programs were associated with better results. To date, a structured, cost-effective approach that maintains treatment effects after formal rehabilitation ends has not been established (GOLD).

PSYCHOTHERAPY

As noted throughout this chapter, high self-efficacy, optimism, and an internal locus of control have all been identified as predictive of better disease outcome and treatment adherence. Furthermore, maladaptive coping strategies and maintenance of unhealthy behavior can quickly undermine the efforts of physicians who are attempting to manage COPD. Psychotherapy has been shown to be an effective way to help patients modify counterproductive coping strategies and beliefs (Wampold, 2001; Taylor and Asmundson, 2004). Unfortunately, studies have indicated that fewer than 30% of health care providers appropriately assess for and recognize anxiety and depression, and fewer still follow recommended practice guidelines (Burgess, Kunik, & Stanley, 2005). These findings raise major concerns regarding the overall quality of care in patients with COPD.

Early recognition of emotional adjustment issues is important, as literature suggests that the longer these conditions go untreated the more resistant to intervention they become (Keller et al. 1992; Roundy et al. 2004; Taylor & Asmundson, 2004). Significant reduction in depression and anxiety most likely would lead patients to more consistency in their follow-through on wellness behaviors. Additionally, a great deal has been published regarding the use of motivational interviewing (MI) techniques in patients with addictive disorders. This treatment approach first attempts to determine an individual's interest in changing his or her behavior. Patients who recognize a need to change but have limited interest are referred to as *precontemplative*, while patients who are beginning to make active attempts to change are described as *contemplative*. Once an individual's motivation for change has been established, efforts are made by the therapist to move the patient toward consideration and ultimately enactment of positive behavioral change (Miller and Rollnick, 2002).

While cognitive-behavioral psychotherapy (CBT) generally has the most research support in treating anxiety and depression, it is important to remember that effective psychotherapeutic intervention requires the establishment of a trusting treatment alliance (Taylor & Asmundson, 2004). Thus, the individual skill of the psychotherapist is a critical variable in influencing treatment effectiveness (Wampold, 2001). It should also be stressed that MI techniques are tailored to increase an individual's motivation for change. Thus, MI is often used within the framework of CBT. In Table 12.4 some general guidelines are provided for clinicians who are considering a referral for psychotherapeutic intervention.

CASE EXAMPLE

Mr. Kellogg was a 46-year-old married man referred for psychotherapy by his internal medicine physician. He had been diagnosed with COPD 5 years prior to the appointment. His disease was related to a 30-year history of smoking and exposure to asbestos when he worked as an electrician. He was on 2 liters per minute oxygen via nasal can-

Table 12.4
When to Consider Referral for Cognitive Behavioral Psychotherapy
and/or Motivational Interviewing

Patient meets DSM-IV criterion for depression	CBT
Patient meets DSM-IV criterion for anxiety disorder	CBT
Patient indicates a desire to quit smoking or other problematic behavior but feels powerless to stop	MI
Patient has difficulty managing or following through on exercise or other activities he or she recognizes as potentially helpful	MI / CBT
Patient is socially isolated or does not perceive his or her social support group as helpful	CBT
	CBT

ula[2]. He was able to independently ambulate with a cane and perform self care as long as he paced himself. The patient had been on long-term disability for 5 years.

Mr. Kellogg's medical condition was negatively affected by morbid obesity, an ongoing one-pack-a-day smoking habit, and sedentary lifestyle. His physician had recommended psychotherapy and smoking cessation on several occasions, but the patient had refused. The patient finally agreed to see a psychologist after he had experienced a mild burn while smoking with his oxygen tank on. This burn injury was witnessed by the patient's wife and children, which promoted a significant amount of familial concern. Furthermore, the physician had noted significant declines in the patient's overall respiratory function, and had informed the family that if Mr. Kellogg continued to maintain the same daily routine and unhealthy lifestyle that he would most likely decline rapidly. A combination of these factors brought the patient into psychotherapy.

INTAKE EVALUATION

In the first session, Mr. Kellogg verbally stated ambivalence with regard to seeing a psychologist. He felt that he knew what he was doing and was not "crazy." Time was spent explaining that he was not being seen because of this, but because he was engaged in a number of counterproductive behaviors that were affecting his health. He seemed somewhat relieved to learn that health psychologists were involved in the care of many patients with various medical conditions.

Mr. Kellogg was ambivalent with regard to his smoking and desire to abstain. He tended to focus on his exposure to asbestos at the age of 30, and felt that this had caused his COPD. He was able to agree that his continued smoking was affecting his health, but he pointed out that he had a number of friends who smoked as much as him and were fine. Furthermore, he expressed a sense of hopelessness with regard to being able to change his condition and maintained a desire to continue smoking because it was one of the few things he still enjoyed. Finally, he complained of some cognitive changes and admitted that the quality of his life was lower than what he wanted. At the same time, he did not feel there was anything he could do about this. Motiva-

---

2. *Nasal canula* is delivery of oxygen via tubing that ends with two prongs placed in the patient's nostrils with the tubing draped over the patient's ears. It is a very well-tolerated delivery system and is the least invasive method.

tional interviewing techniques were utilized to gauge the patient's interest in change. Overall, it seemed that Mr. Kellogg was primarily in a precontemplative stage. He was ambivalent about quitting smoking and becoming more physically active. Psychologically he meet criterion for dysthymia with interspersed bouts of major depression over the past 5 years. With regard to strengths, it was clear that Mr. Kellogg was very connected with his wife and three children (ages 15, 18, and 20). He enjoyed going to his children's school and social events, but his shortness of breath (SOB) and general lack of exercise was affecting his ability to do this. Furthermore, Mr. Kellogg was intelligent and capable of listing the pros and cons of change. It was clear that he had already done a fair amount of thinking with regard to his options. Unfortunately, he had come to the conclusion that quitting smoking or changing his eating habits would not make a significant enough impact on his quality of life. He felt that his family was overreacting to the "tiny explosion" and indicated on several occasions that he was only in my office because his kids and wife would not stop "bugging him about it."

Time was also spent asking the patient to describe his medical condition, physician's treatment plan, and prognosis. He was fairly well informed regarding the nature of his condition. However, he was unaware that his mild concentration and memory complaints might have been related to COPD and oxygen deprivation.

INITIAL IMPRESSION

Mr. Kellogg was not invested in changing his behavior and thus not a very good candidate for individual psychotherapy. He maintained a number of fixed beliefs with regard to his lifestyle and medical condition that were both inaccurate and counterproductive. The chances of instigating sustained cognitive and behavioral change for Mr. Kellogg would hinge on several factors:

1. Establishing a therapeutic alliance.
2. Family support and willingness to change their own behavior.
3. Modifying the patient's belief system.
4. Moving him toward or into a contemplative stage for behavioral change.

After the first session, I asked the patient if I could meet with his family in the next session. He willingly agreed. Additionally, I recommended a brief neuropsychological evaluation to investigate his complaints of memory and concentration problems.

FIRST FAMILY SESSION

Mr. Kellogg's family enjoyed one another's company and had close relationships. There was a trend toward being overweight, with the exception of Mr. Kellogg's 15-year-old son, who was in wrestling and was quite fit. His 18-year-old daughter sang in the school and church choir. His 20-year-old son was still living at home and working in construction. Mr. Kellogg had been married to his wife for 22 years, and she had primarily been a "stay at home" mother while he worked. For the past 6 years she had worked part time as a cashier to help the family make ends meet.

Unlike Mr. Kellogg, the family was very concerned about his continued smoking and the physician's statement that his behaviors would shorten his life. Mr. Kellogg maintained that the physician was using scare tactics and that he was okay. Furthermore, the family spent time discussing the "explosion," and this had clearly been frightening, especially for the wife and daughter.

Family interviews revealed that, despite their concern, all family members were engaged in counterproductive, supportive behavior. They would get Mr. Kellogg things to eat, cigarettes, and other items, despite his ability to walk and get them himself. The wife bought his cigarettes for him. Also, Mr. Kellogg smoked in the house, and the family often watched movies together while he did so. Most family members were ambivalent with regard to their support behavior, but listed "feeling sorry for" or "you do what Dad tells you" as primary reasons for continuing. Also, Mr. Kellogg had resorted to relentless complaining and making statements such as "you don't understand how hard it is for me" when family members had refused to bring or buy him cigarettes in the past.

By the end of the session the family agreed to do several things. First, the wife would no longer buy Mr. Kellogg's cigarettes. If he wanted them he would have to drive to the store and get them himself. Second, the children agreed not to fetch things for their father any longer and instead would encourage him to walk more about the house. Third, family members agreed that they would not watch television with Mr. Kellogg when he was smoking. Fourth, the wife agreed to begin changing the family meals and managing a healthier diet for the family. Understandably, Mr. Kellogg was not happy with the discussion, but reluctantly was able to verbalize that he recognized that his family would be doing these things in an effort to help him.

FOLLOWING SESSIONS

Over the course of 10 additional sessions, I met with the patient and his family. Three of these sessions were individual sessions. Initially Mr. Kellogg became more tearful, tended to lay "guilt trips" with family members, and was angry with the therapist. He attempted to refuse to continue psychotherapy, but as his family remained steadfast in their resolve this melted. Initially the patient continued to smoke, but he shared that it was more difficult to continue when family members actively avoided him when he did. Furthermore, he missed family time watching television, as initially he refused to quit smoking in front of the TV. To the family's credit, they maintained this boycott despite the patient's complaints and not being able to watch much TV for the first 3 weeks.

Neuropsychological evaluation had revealed average intellectual skills. Mr. Kellogg's functioning within multiple cognitive domains was average, but low average performances on tasks requiring speed of information processing and verbal memory were noted. Interestingly this assessment heightened Mr. Kellogg's concern about his memory, as he felt he should have done much better. Despite reassurances, he spent several sessions complaining that his cognitive problems were part of the reason he could not change his habits.

OUTCOME

Within 2 months, the patient was smoking approximately five cigarettes a day. He had reluctantly agreed to participate in a pulmonary rehabilitation program at the urging of his family, physician, and psychologist. He was no longer smoking in the house. Furthermore the wife had changed the family meals and, combined with the family members requiring Mr. Kellogg to get things himself, he had lost 10 pounds.

After 5 months the patient had lost 45 pounds. The physician reported improvements in his overall activity level and Mr. Kellogg had not suffered any exacerbations that required hospitalization. Psychologically, Mr. Kellogg was able to recognize that his endurance had significantly improved. He was more comfortable at school-related events. He started making statements such as "When I finally quit smoking . . ." His conversation shifted from blaming and making excuses to talking about how he could accomplish certain things. The family planned a camping trip for the summer, which was something Mr. Kellogg had enjoyed but stopped doing years ago.

After 7 months he had lost 50 pounds and was no longer smoking. He was maintaining a home exercise program that had been initiated by pulmonary rehabilitation. His youngest son took time out to exercise with his father, which encouraged him to continue.

CONCLUSION

In this case the patient was not a good candidate for individual psychotherapy alone because of his unwillingness to change. Additionally, patients in a precontemplative stage are often prone to procrastinating with regard to physician recommendations, as was the case here. The change agent and leverage in this case was the family, who were inadvertently facilitating Mr. Kellogg's inactivity and smoking habit. Fortunately, the family was ready to make significant changes in their behavior due to fear and concern for the patient's health. If this motivation and tenacity had not been present in the family it is doubtful that any significant behavioral change would have occurred. Fortunately, in this case the patient experienced positive changes in his health and activity, which contradicted fixed negative beliefs. This experience led to healthy changes in his beliefs and self-talk as well. This positive cognitive change fueled his motivation to maintain healthy behaviors and shift into a contemplative stage of change, and eventually resulted in actual behavior change.

REFERENCES

American Association for Respiratory Care (AARC). (2002). AARC clinical practice guideline: Pulmonary rehabilitation. *Respiratory Care, 47,* 617–625.

American Thoracic Society. (1995). Standards for the diagnosis and care of patients with chronic obstructive pulmonary disease. *American Journal of Respiratory Critical Care Medicine, 152,* S77–S121.

Andenaes, R., & Kalfoss, M. H. (2004). Psychological distress in hospitalized patients with chronic obstructive pulmonary disease. *European Journal of Epidemiology, 19,* 851–859.

Bakke, P. S., Hanoa, R., & Gulsvik, A. (1995). Educational level and obstructive lung disease given smoking habits and occupational airborne exposure: A Norwegian community study. *American Journal of Epidemiology, 141,* 1080–1088.

Bandura, A. (1977). Self-efficacy: Toward a unifying theory of behavioral change. *Psychological Review, 84,* 191–215.

Boll, T. J., Johnson, S. B., Perry, N. W., & Rozensky, R. (Eds.). (2006). *Handbook of clinical health psychology.* Washington, DC: American Psychological Association.

Boot, C. R. L., van der Gulden, J. W. J., Vercoulen, J. H. M. M., van den Borne, B. H. W., Orbin, K. H., & Rooijackers, J. (2005). Knowledge about asthma and COPD: Associations with sick leave, health complaints, functional limitations, adaptation, and perceived control. *Patient Education and Counseling, 59,* 103–109.

Boschetto, P., Quintavalle, S., Miotto, D., Cascio, N., Zeni, E., & Mapp, C. E. (2006).Chronic obstructive pulmonary disease and occupational exposures. *Journal of Occupational Medicine and Toxicology, (1)*11, 1745–1766.

Bourbeau, J., Nault, D., & Dang-Tan, T. (2004). Self-management and behaviour modification in COPD . *Patient Education and Counseling, 52,* 271–277.

Burgess, A., Kunik, M. E., & Stanley, M. (2005). Chronic obstructive pulmonary disease: Assessing and treating psychological issues in patients with COPD. ProQuest Medical Library. *Geriatrics, 60,* 18.

Clary, G. L., Palmer, S. M., & Doraiswamy, P. M. (2002). Mood disorders and chronic obstructive pulmonary disease: Current research and future needs. *Curr Psychiatry Rep, 4,* 213–221.

Covey, L. S. (1999). Tobacco cessation among patients with depression: Primary care. *Clinical Office Practice North America, 26,* 691–706.

Coxson, H. O., Chan, I. H., Mayo, J. R., & Hlynsky, J. (2004). Early emphysema in patients with anorexia nervosa. *American Journal of Respiratory and Critical Care Medicine, 170,* 748–752.

Craven, J. (1990). Psychiatric aspects of lung transplantation: The Toronto Lung Transplant Group. *Canadian Journal of Psychiatry, 35,* 759–764.

Creer, T. L., Bender, B. G., and Lucas, D. O. (2006). Diseases of the respiratory system. In T. J. Boll, S. B. Johnson, N. W. Perry, & R. Rozensky (Eds.), *Handbook of clinical health psychology.* Washington, DC: American Psychological Association.

Crews, D. W., Jefferson, A. L., Bolduc, T., Elliott, J. B., Ferro, N. M., & Broshek, D. K. (2001). Neuropsychological dysfunction in patients suffering from end-stage chronic obstructive pulmonary disease. *Archives of Clinical Neuropsychology, 16,* 643–652.

Emery, C. F., Schein, R. L., Hauck, E. R., & MacIntyre, N. R. (1998). Psychological and cognitive outcomes of a randomized trial of exercise among patients with chronic obstructive pulmonary disease. *Health Psychology, 17,* 232–240.

Emery, C. F., Shermer, R. L., Hauck, E. R., Hsiao, E. T., & MacIntyre, N. R. (2003). Cognitive and psychological outcomes of exercise in a 1-year follow-up study of patients with chronic obstructive pulmonary disease. *Health Psychology, 22,* 598–604.

Everly, George (1989). *A clinical guide to the treatment of the human stress response.* New York: Plenum.

Fan, V. S., Curtis, J. R., Shin-Ping, T., McDonell, M. B., & Fihn, S.D., Ambulatory care quality improvement project investigators. (2002). Using quality of life to predict hospitalization and mortality in patients with obstructive lung disease. *Chest, 122,* 429–436.

Fiore, M. C., Bailey, W. C., Cohen, S. J., Dorfman, S. F., Goldstein, M. G., Gritz, E. R., et al. (2000). *Treating tobacco use and dependence: Quick reference guide for clinicians.* Rockville, MD: US Department of Health and Human Services.

Garuti, G., Cilione, C., Dell'Orso, D., Gorini, P., Lorenzi, M. C., Totaro, L, et al. (2003). Impact of comprehensive pulmonary rehabilitation on anxiety and depression in hospitalized COPD patients. *Monaldi Archives or Chest Disease, 59,* 56–61.

Gatchel, R. J., & Oordt, M. S. (2003). *Clinical health psychology and primary care: Practical advice and clinical guidance for successful collaboration.* Washington, DC: American Psychological Association.

Global Initiative for Chronic Obstructive Lung Disease (GOLD). (2005). *Global strategy for the diagnosis, management, and prevention of chronic obstructive pulmonary disease—Updated July 2004.* National Institutes of Health. Retrieved October 15, 2006, from http://www.goldcopd.org

Graham, J. R. (1990). *MMPI-2: Assessing personality and psychopathology.* New York: Oxford University Press.

Grant, I., Heaton, R. K., McSweeny, A. J., Adams, K. M., & Timms, T. M. (1982). Neuropsychologic findings in hypoxemic chronic obstructive pulmonary disease. *Archives of Internal Medicine, 142,* 1470–1476.

Grant, I., Prigatano, G. P., Heaton, R. K., McSweeny, A. J., Wright, E. C., & Adams, K. M. (1987). Progressive neuropsychologic impairment and hypoxemia. *Archives of General Psychiatry, 44,* 999–1006.

Heaton, R. K., Grant, I., & McSweeny, A. J. (1983). Psychologic effects of continuous and nocturnal oxygen therapy in hypoxemic chronic obstructive pulmonary disease. *Archives of Internal Medicine, 143,* 1941–1947.

Hesselink, A. E., Penninx, B. W., Schlosser, M. A., Wijnhoven, H. A., van der Windt, D. A., & Kriegsman, D. M. (2004). The role of coping resources and coping style in quality of life of patients with asthma or COPD. *Quality of Life Research, 13,* 509–518.

Hjalmarsen, A., Waterloo, K., & Dahl, A., (1999). Effect of long-term oxygen therapy on cognitive and neurological dysfunction in chronic obstructive pulmonary disease, *European Neurology, 42,* 27–35.

Hurd, S. (2000). The Impact of COPD on lung health worldwide: Epidemiology and incidence. *Chest, 117,* 1S–4S.

Incalzi, R. A., Gemma, A., Marra, C., Capparella, O., Fuso, L, & Carbonin, P. (1997). Verbal memory impairment in COPD: Its mechanisms and clinical relevance. *Chest, 112,* 1506–1513.

Incalzi, R. A., Gemma, A., Marra, C., Muzzolon, R., Capparella, O., & Carbonin, P. (1993). Chronic obstructive pulmonary disease: an original model of cognitive decline. *American Review of Respiratory Disease, 148,* 418–424.

Kales, H. C., DiNardo, A. R., Blow, F. C, McCarthy, J. F., Ignacio, R. V., & Riba, M. B. (2006). International medical graduates and the diagnosis and treatment of late-life depression. *Academic Medicine. 81,* 171–175.

Kanervisto, M., Paavilainen, E., & Astedt-Kurki, P. (2003). Impact of chronic obstructive pulmonary disease on family functioning. *Heart & Lung, 32*(6), 360–367.

Keller, M. B., Lavori, P. W., & Mueller, T. I. (1992). Time to recovery, chronicity, and levels of psychopathology in major depression: A 5–year prospective follow-up of 431 subjects, *Archives of General Psychiatry, 49,* 809–816.

Koster, A., Bosma, H., Kempen, G., van Lenthe, F., van Eijk, J., & Mackenbach, J. (2004). Socioeconomic inequalities in mobility decline in chronic disease groups (asthma/COPD, heart disease, diabetes mellitus, low back pain): Only a minor role for disease severity and comorbidity. *Journal of Epidemiology and Community Health, 58,* 862–869.

Krop, H. D., Block, A. J., & Cohen, E. (1973). Neuropsychologic effects of continuous oxygen therapy in chronic obstructive pulmonary disease. *Chest, 64,* 317–322.

Kubzansky L. D., Wright, R. J., Cohen, S., Weiss, S., Rosner, B., & Sparrow, D. (2002). Breathing easy: A prospective study of optimism and pulmonary function in the normative aging study. *Annals of Behavioral Medicine, 24,* 345–353.

Lacasse, Y., Wong, E., Guyatt, G. H., King, D., Cook, D. J., & Goldstein, R.S. (1996). Meta-analysis of respiratory rehabilitation in chronic obstructive pulmonary disease. *Lancet, 348,* 1115–1119.

Lazarus, R. S. (1999). *Stress and emotion: A new synthesis.* New York: Springer.

Liesker, J. J. W., Postma, D. S., Beukema, R. J., ten Hacken, N. H., Van der Molen, T., & Riemersma, R. A. (2004). Cognitive performance in patients with COPD. *Respiratory Medicine, 98,* 351–356.

Lox, C., & Freehill, A. (1999). Impact of pulmonary rehabilitation on self-efficacy, quality of life, and exercise tolerance. *Rehabilitation Psychology, 44,*(2), 208–221.

Mannino, D. M., Homa, D. M., Akinbami, L. J., Ford, E. S., & Redd, S. C. (2002). *Chronic Obstructive Pulmonary Disease Surveillance—United States,* 1971–2000. MMWR, 51(SS06), 1–16.

McCathie, H. C. F., Spence, S. H., & Tate, R. L. (2002). Adjustment to chronic obstructive pulmonary disease: The importance of psychological factors. *European Respiratory Journal, 19,* 47–53.

Miller, S. M., Shoda, Y., & Hurley, K. (1996). Applying cognitive-social theory to health-protective behavior: Breast self-examination in cancer screening. *Psychological Bulletin, 119,* 70–94.

Miller, W. R., & Rollnick, S. (2002). *Motivational interviewing: Preparing people for change* (2nd ed.). New York: Guilford.

Monninkhof, E., van der Valk, P., van der Palen, P., van Herwaarden, C., Partridge, M. R., & Ziel-huis, G. (2003). Self-management education for patients with chronic obstructive pulmonary disease: A systematic review. *Thorax, 58,* 394–398.

Niewoehner, D. E. (2006). The impact of severe exacerbations on quality of life and the clinical course of chronic obstructive pulmonary disease, *The American Journal of Medicine (suppl.), 119,* S38–S45.

Ockene, J. K., Emmons, K. M., Mermelstein, R. J., Perkins, K. A., Bonollo, D. S., Voorhees, C. C., et al. (2000). Relapse and maintenance issues for smoking cessation. *Health Psychology, 19*(Suppl.), 17–31.

Osler, W. (1919). A way of life. Address delivered to Yale students, April 20th, 1913. Springfield, IL: C. C. Thomas.

Pang, S. M., Chan, K. S., Chung, B. P., Lau, K. S., Leung, E. M., & Leung, A. W. (2005). Assessing quality of life of patients with advanced chronic obstructive pulmonary disease in the end of life. *Journal of Palliative Care, 21,* 180–187.

Prescott, E., Lange, P., & Vestbo, J. (1999). Socioeconomic status, lung function and admission to hospital for COPD: Results from the Copenhagen City Heart Study, *The European Respiratory Journal: Official Journal of the European Society for Clinical Respiratory Physiology, 13,* 1109–1114.

Prigatano, G. P., Parsons, O., Wright, E., Levin, D. C., & Hawryluk, G. (1983). Neuropsychological test performance in mildly hypoxemic COPD patients. *Journal of Consulting and Clinical Psychology, 51,* 108–116.

Prochaska, J. O., & DiClemente, C. C. (1983). Stages and processes of self-change of smoking: Toward an integrative model of change. *Journal of Consulting and Clinical Psychology, 51,* 390–395

Reardon, J. Z., Lareau, S. C., & ZuWallack, R. (2006). Functional status and the quality of life in chronic obstructive pulmonary disease. *The American Journal of Medicine 119*(Suppl.), S32–S37.

Ries, A. L. (1990). Position paper of the American Association of Cardiovascular and Pulmonary Rehabilitation: Scientific basis of pulmonary rehabilitation. *Journal of Cardiopulmonary Rehabilitation, 13,* 51–54.

Ries, A. L. (2006). Impact of chronic obstructive pulmonary disease on quality of life: The role of dyspnea. *The American Journal of Medicine 119*(Suppl.), S12–S20.

Ries, A. L., Kaplan, R. M., Limberg, T. M., & Prewitt, L.M. (1995). Effects of pulmonary rehabilitation on physiologic and psychosocial outcomes in patients with chronic obstructive pulmonary disease. *Annals of Internal Medicine, 122,* 823–832.

Rose, C., Wallace, L., Dickson, R., Ayres, J., Lehman, R., Searle, Y. et al., (2002). The most effective psychologically based treatments to reduce anxiety and panic in patients with chronic obstructive pulmonary disease (COPD): A systematic review. *Patient Education and Counseling, 47,* 311–318.

Roundy, K., Cully, J. A., Stanley, M. A., Veazey, C., Souchek, J., Wray, N. P., et al. (2005). Are anxiety and depression addressed in primary care patients with chronic obstructive pulmonary disease? A chart review prim care companion. *Primary Care Companion to the Journal of Clinical Psychiatry. 7,* 213–218.

Russell, C. K., Geraci, T. Hooper, A., Shull, L., & Gregory, D. M. (1998). Patients' explanatory models for heart failure and COPD exacerbations. *Clinical Nursing Research, 7,* 164–188.

Salman, G. F., Mosier, M. C., Beasley, B. W., & Calkins, D. R. (2003). Rehabilitation for patients with chronic obstructive pulmonary disease: Meta-analysis of randomized controlled trials. *Journal of General Internal Medicine, 18,* 213–221.

Santo-Tomas, L. H., & Varkey, B. (2004). Improving health-related quality of life in chronic obstructive pulmonary disease. *Pulmonary Medicine, 10,* 120–127.

Scharloo, M., Kaptein, A. A., Weinman, J., Hazes, J. M., Willems, L. N., & Bergman, W., et al. (1998). Illness perceptions, coping and functioning in patients with rheumatoid arthritis, chronic obstructive pulmonary disease and psoriasis. *Journal of Psychosomatic Research, 44,* 573–585.

Searight, H. R., & Gafford, J. (2006). Behavioral science education and the international medical graduate. *Academic Medicine, 81,* 164–170.

Selye, H. (1974). *Stress without distress.* Toronto: McClelland Stewart.

Singer, H. K., Ruchinkas, K. C., Riley, K. C., Broshek, D. K., & Barth, J. T. (2001). The psychological impact of end-stage lung disease. *Chest, 120,* 1246–1252.

Stoller, J. K., & Aboussouan, L. S. (2005). Alpha1–antitrypsin deficiency. *Lancet, 365,* 2225–2236.

Taylor, S., & Asmundson, G. (2004). *Treating health anxiety: A cognitive-behavioral approach.* New York: Guilford.

Vermeire, P. (2002). The burden of chronic obstructive pulmonary disease. *Respiratory Medicine, 96*(Suppl. C), S3–S10.

Wagena, E. J., van der Meer, R. M., Ostelo R. J., Jacobs J. E., & van Schayck, C. P. (2004). The efficacy of smoking cessation strategies in people with chronic obstructive pulmonary disease: Results from a systematic review. *Respiratory Medicine, 98,* 805–815.

Wampold, B. (2001). *The great psychotherapy debate: Models, methods, and findings.* Mahwah, NJ: Lawrence Erlbaum.

Wempe, J. B., & Wijkstra, P. J. (2004). The influence of rehabilitation on behaviour modification in COPD. *Patient Education and Counseling, 52,* 237–241.

Wong, M. D., Shapiro, M. F., Boscardin W. J., & Ettner, S. L. (2002). Contribution of major diseases to disparities in mortality. *New England Journal of Medicine, 347,* 1585–1592.

Worth, H., & Dhein, Y. (2004). Does patient education modify behaviour in the management of COPD? *Patient Education and Counseling, 52,* 267–270.

CHAPTER 13

End-Stage Renal Disease

ALLAN GOODY, NICOLE MONSERRATE, and ANU BODETTI

DESCRIPTION OF DISEASE STATES

Chronic kidney disease is highly prevalent in the United States. The National Institute of Diabetes and Digestive and Kidney Diseases (NIDDK) estimates that up to 20 million Americans have chronic kidney disease. Many of these individuals will ultimately progress to End-Stage Renal Disease (ESRD), as defined as the need for renal replacement therapy in the form of dialysis or renal transplantation, with over 104,000 Americans beginning treatment for ESRD in 2004 (United States Renal Data Center [USRDS], 2006).

Chronic kidney disease, previously termed *chronic renal insufficiency* or *chronic renal failure*, by definition implies an inability of the kidneys to function normally. Functions of the kidneys include excretion and filtration of the nitrogenous wastes generated by the body each day and the maintenance of homeostasis in the form of fluid/electrolyte balance. The kidneys also have profound effects on other organs. They act as endocrine organs, releasing hormones such as angiotensin to regulate blood pressure, and erythropoietin, which stimulates the bone marrow to produce red blood cells. The kidneys are also involved in the regulation of calcium and phosphate. Given such diverse roles in the body, the impact of chronic kidney disease can be quite profound (Amir & Winchester, 1999).

One of the earliest markers for renal damage manifests itself as detectable protein in the urine. The most severe form of chronic kidney disease is classified as End-Stage Renal Disease. The NIDDK, in conjunction with the National Kidney Foundation (NKF), have sought to classify chronic kidney disease (The National Kidney Foundation Kidney Disease Outcomes Quality Initiative [NKF, K/DOQI], 2003). In 2002, the NKF implemented a classification scheme for measuring renal function that declines in progressive renal diseases, using the Modification in Diet in Renal Disease (MDRD) formula for estimating glomerular filtration rate (GFR; NKF, K/DOQI). This was put in place to try to simplify diverse previous classifications and terminology (Table 13.1).

The MDRD equation has become the standard for estimation of renal function, replacing other, cruder estimates such as the blood urea nitrogen level or serum creatinine level (Levey, Bosch, Lewis, Greene, Rogers, & Roth, 1999). In many renal diseases, such as diabetic nephropathy or hypertensive nephropathy, there is a predictable decline in the GFR, which precedes patient symptoms. As the GFR declines, the impact

Table 13.1

Classification of Chronic Kidney Disease (NKF, K/DOQI, 2003)

Stage	Description	GFR (ml/min/1.73 m^2)	Action*
	At Increased Risk	> or equal to 90	Screening, CKD risk reduction
1	Kidney Damage with normal or increased GFR	> or equal to 90	Diagnosis and treatment, treatment of comorbid conditions, slowing progression, CVD risk reduction
2	Kidney Damage with mild decreased GFR	60–89	Estimating Progression
3	Moderately decreased GFR	30–59	Evaluating and Treating Complications
4	Severely decreased GFR	15–29	Preparation for kidney replacement therapy
5	Kidney Failure	<15 (or dialysis)	Replacement (if uremia present)

* Includes actions from preceding stages

of chronic kidney disease on the patient becomes more apparent. Unfortunately, patients do not often realize the impact of their disease until progression has become much more pronounced in the later stages of disease, usually at Stage 4 or 5 of chronic kidney disease. The earliest signs of chronic kidney disease are apparent much earlier to the clinician via routine laboratory testing. Renal osteodystophy—weakening of the bones because of impaired calcium and phosphate metabolism—can be detected at GFR levels below 60 (NKF, K/DOQI, 2003). Untreated renal osteodystrophy can eventually lead to fractures and associated morbidity. Anemia can be seen at all levels of renal dysfunction, but becomes highly prevalent in CKD stages 3 and 4, and almost universal in stage 5 (NKF, K/DOQI). Patients with anemia often present with nonspecific symptoms of fatigue. Treatment of anemia with erythropoeitin stimulating factors can improve not only fatigue, but can ameliorate other comorbidities such as cardiac performance, libido, and concentration. Erythropoietin therapy is both expensive and requires patients' adherence. Adherence is improved once renal replacement therapy is instituted, and effective treatment of anemia can improve mortality (Wolfe, Hulbert-Shearon, Ashby, Mahadevan, & Port, 2005).

Diabetes mellitus is the most common cause of ESRD in the United States. Hypertension is also highly prevalent among patients with ESRD. Hypertensive nephropathy is the second leading cause of ESRD in the United States (USRDS, 2006). Other disease states such as diabetes, polycystic kidney disease, and congestive heart failure often have hypertension as an associated morbidity. With chronic long-standing hypertension, the chronic kidney disease/ESRD patient can develop hypertrophic cardiomyopathy and left ventricular hypertrophy (for cardiac conditions, see Chapter 6). The prevalence of cardiovascular disease is higher in ESRD than in age-matched controls (USRDS). Morbidity associated with cardiovascular disease is disproportionately high in patients with ESRD. This cannot be fully explained on the basis of traditional cardiac risk factors alone, such as hyperlipidemia, hypertension, diabetes, smoking, and family history. One report suggested that the use of atorvastatin, a cholesterol-lowering agent efficacious in the general population, did not have the same cardiovascular benefits in patients with ESRD (Wanner et al., 2005). Sudden cardiac death is also more prevalent in ESRD populations than in age-matched controls. Uremia, the end result of untreated ESRD, affects nutritional, hematological, and immune status. End-stage renal disease patients with higher serum albumin levels appear to have a survival advantage compared to those with lower serum albumin levels, in some circumstances reflecting more effective renal replacement therapy, resulting in better nutrition and appetite (USRDS). Infection is a major cause of morbidity in ESRD patients. Catheter-associated infections are a frequent cause of hospitalizations and mortality/morbidity in patients on hemodialysis. The use of ateriovenous fistulas for hemodialysis access has been emphasized by the NKF, Medicare, and in the Healthy People 2010 guidelines, and has increased, although the incidence of patients starting hemodialysis with working ateriovenous fistulas still remains below goals (USRDS).

There are currently three major modes of therapy for the patient who develops ESRD: hemodialysis, peritoneal dialysis, and renal transplantation. A survival advantage for patients who undergo renal transplantation has been documented (USRDS, 2006). Successful renal transplant patients have an improved sense of well-being compared to ESRD patients treated with either hemodialysis or peritoneal dialysis. Unfortunately, there are significant barriers to transplantation. The waiting list for a cadaveric transplant is growing. The ESRD patient must be a suitable surgical candidate, often a problem given associated comorbidities. Waiting times for donor organs differ in different areas of the country, but can be up to years. Many patients die from complications of their disease while awaiting transplantation. Living related renal transplant donation provides the optimal graft and patient survival rates, but requires a healthy, compatible, willing donor, usually a family member or close friend. Renal transplantation is not always successful, and patients must deal with the complications of long-term immunosuppressive medications and the risk of graft rejection. Despite these barriers and complications, ESRD patients should be actively supported to pursue transplantation due to its improved overall survival rate (USRDS).

In the United States, the majority of patients with ESRD are treated with hemodialysis, usually in an in-center setting. Hemodialysis requires a vascular access, either a large in-dwelling catheter or an ateriovenous access. An *ateriovenous access* is a surgically created anastamosis between an artery and vein that with time will develop, allowing the placement of two large needles for blood access. An ateriovenous fistula is a connection between an artery and vein using the patient's native vessels, while a graft is created with a small piece of tubing, such as Gore-Tex, when the native vessels are too small or too far apart for the creation of an ateriovenous fistula (Ross & Yankulin, 1999). Hemodialysis treatments are usually performed three times a week, for 4 hours at a time, at a dialysis center. Home hemodialysis has increased in prevalence in the United States, but is still much less frequently performed compared with in-center hemodialysis. Peritoneal dialysis requires the surgical placement of an intraabdominal catheter. Fluid is then filled and drained by gravity in the peritoneum and dialysis occurs across the peritoneal membrane. Typically exchanges take place at home either four or five times a day or at nighttime.

Risk factors for the development of ESRD can be both primary and secondary. Primary risk factors such as nephrotic syndrome, nephritis, and polycystic kidney disease are less common than secondary risk diseases such as diabetes mellitus and hypertension. Other systemic diseases can result in the development of ESRD, including lupus nephritis, multiple myeloma, and amyloidosis. Given the epidemic of diabetes mellitus in the United States, diabetes mellitus is by far the most prevalent disease state that results in ESRD. Diabetes mellitus and hypertension tend to disproportionately affect certain demographic areas, such as African Americans, and the incidence of ESRD tends to be higher in these populations. Treatment strategies for chronic progressive disease focus on ideal blood pressure control, the reduction of proteinuria (usually with the use of angiotensin converting inhibitors), aggressive management of comorbid conditions including diabetes, dyslipidemia, and cardiovascular disease, and management of the complications of CKD. Treatment regimens for chronic kidney disease invariably focus on the forestalling of ESRD rather than the cure of chronic kidney disease (USRDS, 2006).

PREVALENCE

During the 1990s, the incidence of ESRD exploded dramatically in the United States. This rate has fallen slightly between 2002–2004 according to United States Renal Data System (USRDS, 2006) statistics. With the increasing rise of diabetes mellitus and hypertension, the incidence of ESRD in the elderly population has risen dramatically among individuals over the age of 75. Between 1992 and 2002, there was a 96% increase in the incidence of ESRD in those over 75. However, the overall incidence rate has declined since 2002 (USRDS). The incidence rate in Caucasians has remained stable since 2002, with the majority of improvement found in African American, and Asian patients. Even with this, the overall incidence rate of ESRD remains disproportionately high in African Americans compared to Caucasians, estimated at 3.7 times greater (USRDS).

The incidence of diabetes mellitus in the general population has grown in the 1990s, and thus the incidence of ESRD secondary to diabetes mellitus has also grown (USRDS, 2006). Since 2002, there has been a slight reduction in the overall incidence rate of diabetes mellitus in the general population, and correspondingly a slight decrease in the incidence rate of ESRD. Unfortunately, the incidence rates for ESRD remain drastically higher than the goals laid forth in the national Healthy People 2010 initiative (goal incident rate of 217 cases of ESRD per million population, versus 2004 statistics showing an incident rate of 339 cases of ESRD per million population). It is clear that we still have a long way to go to achieve this goal (USRDS).

Cardiovascular disease remains the leading cause of death among patients with ESRD. Overall mortality due to atherosclerotic disease has fallen 36% since 1991, and the rate of death due to acute myocardial infarction has also dropped in the same time period. Despite some improvement in the outcomes for cardiovascular disease, ESRD patients remain at increased risk for cardiovascular death compared to age-matched controls. Death rates from cardiovascular disease also continue to fall short of the Healthy People 2010 guidelines (USRDS, 2006).

DISEASE FACTORS

The onset of ESRD is predictable in many chronic diseases. Uncontrolled diabetes mellitus and hypertension are the most common presenting factors. Decline in renal function is often detected in the course of routine medical care, when routine laboratory examinations or urinalysis show the presence of elevated creatinine or proteinuria. Patients are often asymptomatic at this point, and referrals to specialists can be delayed, which can result in worsened outcomes. Also, because of the lack of symptoms at this point, many patients are reticent to seek medical care unless they have personal experiences with ESRD. They often lack signs of uremia, which are not usually seen until later in disease progression, and are often nonspecific. When they develop, uremic symptoms can include fatigue, nausea, vomiting, anorexia, pruritis, and decreased cognition (Ouyang & Rakowski, 1999). Patients who do not receive routine medical care may present with signs of uremia or metabolic abnormalities requiring urgent and acute renal replacement therapy. For patients who are routinely followed as their CKD progresses, the early placement of an arteriovenous fistula is recommended for patients who opt for hemodialysis as their method of renal replacement therapy. The Fistula First Program seeks to increase the percentage of patients using ateriovenous fistulae for their hemodialysis access (USRDS, 2006). Ateriovenous fistulae have decreased complications, lower infectious rates, and better flow rates versus ateriovenous grafts or catheters. Ateriovenous fistula result in better overall survival (Astor, Eustace, Powe, Klag, Fink, & Coresh, 2005). While guidelines suggest that placement of arteriovenous fistulae be done prior to the initiation of renal replacement therapy, in 2003 only 36.3% of all hemodialysis patients had an ateriovenous fistula as their primary access when starting hemodialysis (USRDS). Fistula placements are least common in African Americans, and their incidence is less in women compared to men, which is postulated to be due to smaller vessel size in women (USRDS; NKF, K/DOQI, 2003).

In addition to chronic kidney disease, a smaller percentage of ESRD patients present after an episode of acute renal failure, often with underlying chronic kidney disease. Acute onset can be associated with a variety of causes, including obstruction, autoimmune diseases, toxins, crush injuries, and trauma. Patients with acute renal failure are often hospitalized, sometimes in the intensive care unit, and can be more complicated to manage in this setting (Ross & Yankulin, 1999). In many cases of acute renal failure, renal function improves and the patient does not progress to ESRD, even when renal replacement therapy is needed for the acute renal failure. The development of acute renal failure and the need for renal replacement therapy is a poor prognostic indicator for patient overall survival, and patients who develop acute renal failure spend longer in the hospital. Patients who recover renal function may often be left with residual chronic kidney disease and may be at more risk for developing ESRD in the future (USRDS, 2006).

DISEASE PROGRESSION

Both acute and chronic disease can lead to ESRD, as just described. By far, the majority of incident ESRD patients have underlying chronic kidney disease, even when an acute insult leads to the requirement for renal replacement therapy. Despite optimal management, chronic kidney disease can progress to ESRD. Hypertension occurs in 85 to 95% of patients with ESRD, while control of hypertension prior to ESRD slows the progression to ESRD for patients with chronic kidney disease (Amir & Winchester, 1999). Autosomal dominant polycystic kidney disease leads to ESRD in many affected patients and is usually associated with a family history. Glomerulonephritis can remit or in some circumstances (lupus nephritis) be treatable with immunosuppressive medications. Typically, hypertension becomes more difficult to control as renal function declines, further worsening progression. Renal transplantation remains the optimal outcome for patients who require renal replacement therapy. While the supply of donor organs has increased, the number of patients who have ESRD has grown at a faster rate. Patients with comorbidities such as hypertension and diabetes mellitus as the cause of their ESRD are least likely to receive an organ transplant. Comparatively, patients who have cystic kidney disease or glomerulonephritis, and often less cardiovascular comorbidity, are more likely to be wait-listed for an organ. A referral bias exists, with younger patients being most likely to receive a transplant, especially children. Males are more likely to be on the wait list for renal transplantation than females (USRDS, 2006). Asians are most likely to be on the wait list compared to other races (USRDS). Asian renal transplantation recipients have the highest allograft survival rates of all racial groups (Katznelson & Cecka, 1997). However, while Asians and Pacific Islanders experience better survival after transplantation than white individuals, they have substantially lower transplantation rates (Hall, Sugihara, Go, & Chertow, 2005). Kidney organ donation rates are low among ethnic minorities, which is felt to be multifactorial, and not due to specific cultural or religious barriers despite ethnic minorities being aware of the urgent need for donors (Morgan, Hooper, Mayblin, & Jones 2006). The number of all ESRD patients who are on the wait list for a renal transplant or undergo renal transplantation within 1 year of initiating renal replacement therapy remains disappointingly low at 15%, and rates of transplantation after 3 years for all ESRD patients also remain below goals (USRDS).

While many patients perceive renal transplantation as a cure for ESRD, it should be considered another modality of treatment. Renal transplantation entails the risks of surgery and the use of chronic immunosuppressive medications, with complications including infection, rejection, and malignancy. Renal transplantation may not be an alternative for some ESRD patients because of associated comorbidities.

End-stage renal disease portends a shortened life expectancy compared to age-matched controls. Survival rates for patients with diabetes mellitus and ESRD remain especially low, with a 27.2% 5-year survival on hemodialysis for an ESRD patient with diabetes mellitus between 1995–1999 (USRDS, 2006). Controversy exists over whether peritoneal dialysis or hemodialysis provide the longest survivability, as comparisons between the different regimens are fraught with selection and compliance bias. The incidence of peritoneal dialysis as a treatment modality for ESRD has decreased over the last decade. The decision between peritoneal dialysis and hemodialysis often becomes an individual or provider-based decision. Home hemodialysis may soon provide another option (USRDS).

REGIMEN FACTORS

The requirement for renal replacement therapy heralds the diagnosis of ESRD. Once a patient requires renal replacement therapy, there are three different modalities available in the United States. In-center hemodialysis remains the most common modality, with peritoneal dialysis being utilized in a smaller patient population. Renal transplantation remains the optimal therapy. Recently, home hemodialysis has become an alternative in some areas, but utilization of this modality still remains low. Peritoneal dialysis is utilized more outside of the United States (USRDS, 2006).

In-center hemodialysis is a complex process involving the exchange of the patient's blood across a semipermeable membrane (the *dialyzer*) through a vascular access. Many patients consider dialysis an invasive treatment, and its use should be included in end-of-life discussions between medical staff and patients. As such, the decision to initiate hemodialysis, especially in the patient with multiple comorbidities or in the critically ill patient, often is discussed at the same time as resuscitation decisions.

As described previously, the patient must have an access, either an ateriovenous fistula or graft or a large-bore intravenous catheter, placed before beginning hemodialysis. This is an invasive procedure. Once access is established, hypotension and cramping secondary to fluid shifts may be problematic to patients. Treatments are typically performed on a three-times-a-week basis, either Monday-Wednesday-Friday or Tuesday-Thursday-Saturday. Trained dialysis nurses and technicians must be present in order to supervise the procedure. Patients typically sit in a dialysis chair, or reclining chair, which can present difficulties for those with osteoarthritis or back conditions. There is a risk for blood contamination, and patients are vaccinated for hepatitis B; those with hepatitis B are isolated from other patients during their hemodialysis treatment. Transport from the hemodialysis unit to and from home is an ongoing issue for many patients, especially in rural areas where centers are not conveniently close. In some circumstances, peritoneal dialysis would be favored for patients who needed to travel long distances to the nearest dialysis center (USRDS, 2006). Hemodialysis is a costly procedure. The majority of the cost of hemodialysis is borne by the Medicare program. Patients who develop ESRD are usually eligible for Medicare regardless of whether they are 65 years of age (Lockridge 2004). The cost of dialysis for one patient per year was estimated at $66,650 in 2004, a number that can significantly increase depending on vascular access problems and hospitalizations (USRDS). Included in these costs for a stable outpatient are substantial costs for erythropoietin therapy and intravenous iron for treatment of anemia and intravenous medications for the treatment of dialysis-related bone disease. Adherence remains a major barrier to successful hemodialysis. Chronic hemodialysis patients who skip treatments, and thus receive inadequate hemodialysis, are more likely to suffer the complications of untreated uremia and face increased morbidity and mortality (USRDS). Despite this, some patients thrive in the hemodialysis setting, as it provides both a source of new friends and a social outlay. In addition to the demands of renal replacement therapy, the self-management demands for the ESRD patient are great. Dietary restrictions include salt, potassium, phosphorous, and fluid. Despite these restrictions, nutritional status has an important impact on overall survival for patients on dialysis (USRDS).

The intrusiveness of treatment of ESRD has also been evaluated. Intrusiveness is hypothesized to represent a fundamental determinant of the psychosocial impact of chronic conditions (Devins, Edworthy, Seland, Klein, Paul, & Mandin, 1993). Patients who perceived increased intrusiveness in their lives because of their ESRD correlated this intrusiveness with negative and decreased positive mood (Devins, Binik, Hutchinson, Hollomby, Barre, & Guttmann, 1983–1984). Patients' perceptions of intrusiveness from their ESRD correlated with treatment time requirements, uremic symptoms, intercurrent nonrenal illnesses, fatigue, and difficulties in daily activities (Devins et al. 1990). Regular and increased involvement in leisure activities and overall life happiness, defined as an even mixture of unhappiness and happiness, have been found to be independent predictors of increased survival times in ESRD (Devins et al. 1990).

Peritoneal dialysis can be less intrusive compared to hemodialysis. There is no requirement for a machine to perform dialysis for the patient. Instead, exchange of fluid and solute occurs across the peritoneal membrane in the abdomen. Fluid is drained from the peritoneum and instilled by gravity. Prior to beginning peritoneal dialysis, a peritoneal dialysis catheter needs to be inserted into the peritoneum surgically. Post-catheter placement there is usually a 4- to 6-week period before the catheter can be used to begin dialysis, during which the patient undergoes an intensive training period, usually lasting about a week. Given these time constraints, acute peritoneal dialysis has largely been replaced by acute hemodialysis in the United States, with the decision to switch to peritoneal dialysis often being made at a later date. Peritoneal dialysis is felt by some patients to provide greater freedom. Supplies for peritoneal dialysis are delivered to the patient's home. Fluid and electrolyte control can be easier with peritoneal dialysis as dialysis is ongoing each day rather than intermittently. For this reason, congestive heart failure and hyperkalemia are easier to control and patient's diet is more liberal compared with hemodialysis. Peritoneal dialysis patients face the same issues of anemia and renal osteodystrophy as hemodialysis patients and must also be appropriately treated for these. Compliance for peritoneal dialysis patients remains an issue. Unlike in-center hemodialysis, patients do not have someone observing their treatments. Peritoneal dialysis with a cycler, where a small portable machine performs the fluid exchanges while the patient sleeps, may alleviate some of these issues. Peritoneal dialysis has a similar cost per year as hemodialysis (USRDS, 2006).

As stated previously, renal transplant provides the optimal therapy for ESRD. Patients who receive a renal transplant have a better sense of well-being and longer long-term survival versus those on peritoneal dialysis or hemodialysis. Wait times for organs are long, despite efforts to encourage donation, for the patient who does not have a living, related donor. Transplantation is an invasive surgical procedure and patients must be healthy enough to endure the surgery. This is often a concern, given the increased risk of cardiovascular complications in this patient population. Close monitoring for rejection and infection is necessitated during the first year after transplantation, and then less frequently if the patient is doing well. Patients must take immunosuppressive medications to reduce the risk of rejection for lifetime with associated side effects. These side effects can include increased risks of infection, hyperlipidemia, malignancy, hyperglycemia, and in some circumstances, bone marrow suppression (Silkensen, 1999). A renal transplant is estimated to cost $99,000 in the first year, but is cost effective when successful and compared to dialysis (USRDS, 2006).

INDIVIDUAL FACTORS

Intelligence, awareness of the disease process, and the implications of the chosen treatment modality enable the ESRD patient to adjust better to his or her disease in the long term. The well-informed ESRD patient can support the treatment process by understanding the disorder and the treatment, complying with diet and fluid restrictions, meeting scheduled dialysis appointments consistently, and continuing to participate in work, leisure, and social activities. Among chronic hemodialysis patients, those living in rural areas, unemployed men, female patients, and those with diabetes tend to demonstrate increased frequency of psychiatric symptoms, including a high incidence of general distress, anxiety, and sexual problems. (Livesley, 1981; D'Elia et al. 1981).

Patients with chronic diseases need both medical and psychological support and education regarding their disease. The ESRD patient needs adequate knowledge of the disease and the treatment process. Support from medical personnel and family members is important to cope with the long-term changes to their lives. Patients can experience difficulties with medical providers, such as the use of unfamiliar medical terminology, a lack of time for adequate discussion and answering of questions, and uncertainty concerning their future and expectations. The complexity of their medical issues can also cause significant burdens on the quality of life of caregivers and family members (Belasco, Barbosa, Bettencourt, Diccini, & Sesso, 2006).

When adequate education is not provided, patients can become fearful, anxious, and demonstrate adjustment difficulties. This may in turn lead to avoidance of treatment activities. Patients with chronic kidney disease need to be educated and prepared for their treatment modality before beginning renal replacement therapy, in order to adapt and accept the change in their lives. Chronically ill patients who participate in planned educational experiences are able to cope with their illness and comply with their regimens more adequately than patients not offered comparable experiences (Ksch, 1980). Education, despite being an essential tool, does not guarantee that all patients will adapt well to their illness. End-stage renal disease requires patients to make numerous lifestyle and behavioral changes.

Women on dialysis perceive a lower health-related quality of life compared to men. This may reflect gender-related differences in the general population and the higher prevalence of trait anxiety and depressive symptoms in women (Vasquez et al. 2004).

Good rapport with medical service providers improves patients' adaptation and adherence to the treatment regimen. Patients who receive adequate information in advance and receive good medical care are more likely to adapt to their ESRD (Devins, Mendelssohn, Barre, Taub, & Binik, 2005).

Cultural beliefs play a large role in patients' adaptation to ESRD and their treatment. In a study of 102 African American patients on hemodialysis, patients used multiple strategies to cope with their illness and its treatment. Putting trust in God was the most frequently identified strategy (Burns, 2004). Patients' spiritual and religious beliefs correlated with increased perception of social support and quality of life, and less negative perceptions of the effects of their illness and less depression (Patel, Shah, Peterson, & Kimmel, 2002).

Ethnicity plays an important role in the patients' adjustment to ESRD and the treatment. In the Dialysis Outcomes and Practice Patterns Study (DOPPS) study, 6,151 hemodialysis patients treated in 148 U. S. dialysis facilities completed the Kidney Disease Quality of Life Short Form (Lopes, Bragg-Gresham, & Satayathum, 2003). Scores for three components of quality of life were determined: Physical Component Summary (PCS), Mental Component Summary (MCS), and Kidney Disease Component Summary (KDCS). African Americans had higher scores in all three components but had significantly lower scores in patient satisfaction. Lower scores in patient satisfaction also were observed for Asians and Hispanics (Lopes, Bragg-Gresham, & Satayathum). It is important to note that lower levels of patient satisfaction with medical care among African Americans, Asians, and Hispanics than among whites does not seem to be a finding restricted to dialysis treatment (Dosecher, Saver, Franks, & Fiscella, 2000; Cooper-Patrick et al. 1999; Mayberry, Mili, & Ofili, 2000). Data suggest that patients from ethnic minorities, with different health problems, are less likely to be satisfied with their physicians or the care they receive when hospitalized. They are also more likely to believe that their duration of hospitalization is too short, even when income, insurance coverage, disease severity, and co-morbidities are taken into account (Mayberry, Mili, & Ofili, 2000; Blendon, Aiken, Freeman, & Corey, 1989).

A patient's health beliefs can have a major influence on their adaptation to illness. Patients who have slowly progressive renal failure and chronic kidney disease are better adapted to renal replacement therapy compared to patients with acute renal failure or patients who develop ESRD more rapidly. Patients who have been ill and have complications en route to progression to ESRD are less likely to adapt well to dialysis. Traveling to the dialysis center, usually three times a week, impacts both patients and their caregivers. Caregivers of ESRD patients experience significant burdens and an adverse effect on their quality of life (Belasco & Sesso, 2002).

COMORBID PSYCHOPATHOLOGY

There is a wide range of comorbid psychopathology that can be seen in patients with ESRD. Depression, anxiety, sleep disturbances, neuropsychological and cognitive impairment, and personality disorders can be seen in many patients and require attention from clinicians, nurses, and the patients they affect.

Depression

There is a high incidence and prevalence of depression in patients with ESRD on dialysis. It is estimated that depression occurs in 30% of dialysis patients. Depression in patients with ESRD is associated with mortality (Kimmel, Weihs, & Peterson, 1993). A multicenter prospective cohort study of patients within 10 days of initiating dialysis showed a 44% prevalence of depression based on scores above the validated cut-off value in the Beck Depression Inventory. Only 16% of depressed patients were being treated at enrollment (Watnick, Kirwin, Mahnensmith, & Concato, 2003). Pain also played a significant role, with a higher prevalence of depression in patients with moderate or severe chronic pain compared to patients with mild or no pain (Davison & Jhangri, 2005). Patients with depression have also been found to have lower hemoglobin levels and lower albumin levels, (Walters, Hays, Spritzer, Fridman, & Carter, 2002), which also independently predict worse morbidity and mortality in ESRD patients (USRDS, 2006).

Nurses are often better equipped to diagnose depression in the dialysis patient, as they spend more face-to-face time with ESRD patients and can be an important part of the patients' overall care. In one study, the Beck Depression Inventory (BDI) score was used as a gold standard for the detection or screening for depression among chronic hemodialysis patients. Screening with the BDI was then correlated with the patient's primary nurse and the nephrology team's, including physicians', assessment. Depression as measured by the BDI score, nurse, and nephrology team was diagnosed in 38.7%, 41.9%, and 24.2% of patients, respectively. Using the BDI as a gold standard, the nurses' diagnosis of depression had an agreement of 74.2% versus only 24.2% with the nephrology team, highlighting the need for effective nursing in ESRD patients (Wilson et al. 2006). In the dialysis outcomes and practice pattern study (DOPPS), depressive symptoms were assessed in 9,382 patients in multiple countries using the short version of the Center for Epidemiological Studies Depression Screening Index (CES-D). Overall prevalence of physician-diagnosed depression was 13.9%, while the prevalence using the CES-D scale with a cutoff of greater than or equal to 10 was 43%. This suggests that depression is underdiagnosed and undertreated among hemodialysis patients (Lopes et al., 2004).

Physician-diagnosed depression has been associated with increased hospitalization rate and length of stay (Hedayatii et al., 2005). Depression is also associated with larger interdialytic weight gain, suggesting a role in patient adherence with dietary restrictions (Taskapan et al., 2005). Depression is also associated with increased morbidity and mortality (Einwohner, Bernardini, Fried, & Piraino, 2004). Depression has been negatively associated with compliance with medical regimens (DiMatteo, Lepper, & Croghan, 2000). In one study, however, hemodialysis behavorial compliance did not seem to correlate with depressive affect. Instead, a positive relationship was found between patients' satisfaction with their nephrologist and compliance (Kovac, Patel, Peterson, & Kimmel, 2002).

ANXIETY

Anxiety was found in 45% of 128 dialysis patients in one study (Kutner, Fair, & Kutner, 1985). The mean anxiety score of hemodialysis patients has been found to be significantly higher than that of CKD-free subjects (Livesley, 1982). When assessed, women on dialysis had higher anxiety scores and were more frequently personally disturbed and personally ill (Livesley).

SLEEP DISTURBANCES

Sleep-related complaints affect 50 to 80% of patients on hemodialysis, causing significant lifestyle impairments. Insomnia is the most common sleep disorder. There is a higher prevalence of insomnia in patients with moderate or severe chronic pain compared to mild or no pain (Davison & Jhangri, 2005). Consideration of withdrawal from dialysis was significantly associated with moderate or severe pain compared to mild or no pain (Davison & Jhangri). Sleep problems are not as common among transplant patients compared to ESRD patients treated with dialysis, but still higher than non-ESRD patients. These sleep disturbances also correlate with depression (Eryilmaz, Ozdemir, Yurtman, Cilli, & Karaman, 2005).

NEUROPSYCHOLOGICAL AND COGNITIVE IMPAIRMENT

Uremia is associated with cognitive impairment. There is an increased frequency and severity of psychological symptoms in patients with ESRD on hemodialysis (Rocco, Gassman, Wang, & Kaplan, 1997; Weisbord et al., 2005). This correlates directly with impaired quality of life and depression. Cognitive impairment is particularly important in older patients. In one study, a total of 51 older dialysis patients (> 70 yrs) were assessed, of which 30 to 47% of patients had cognitive impairment and 60% percent of patients were depressed, highlighting the need for regular assessment in this population (Tyrell, Paturel, Cadec, Capezzali, & Poussin, 2005). Verbal, performance, and full-scale IQs of patients with ESRD are significantly lower than sibling controls (Bawden et al., 2004).

PERSONALITY

Personality plays an important role in adjustment to end-stage renal disease and dialysis. In one study, patients with chronic kidney disease and high neuroticism had a higher mortality rate, as did patients with low conscientiousness (Christensen et al., 2002). Persons with personality disorders are less likely to comply with treatment for depression, resulting in treatment failure (Wuerth, Finkelstein, & Finkelstein, 2005).

INTERVENTIONS

Patients who have increased confidence in self-care strategies are associated with more positive mood states, health status, and perceived adherence to fluid restriction, and less symptom distress. Interventions designed to increase patients' self-care efficacy may yield positive results (Lev & Owen, 1998; Tsay & Hung, 2004).

Transplantation prior to dialysis results in less psychological and physical impact for patients and their spouses (Starzomski & Hilton, 2000). Patients should be offered transplantation early in the process of discussion about renal replacement therapy.

There is an increased frequency and severity of both physical symptoms and psychological symptoms in patients with ESRD on hemodialysis (Rocco, Gassman, Wang, & Kaplan, 1997; Weisbord et al., 2005). These correlate directly with impaired quality of life and depression. Incorporating a standard assessment of symptoms into the care provided for maintenance dialysis patients may provide a means to improve quality of life in this patient population. National Kidney Foundation K-DOQI guidelines recommend that every dialysis patient be seen by a dialysis social worker at initiation of dialysis, and at least biannually thereafter to assess the patient's psychological status, with specific focus on the presence of depression, anxiety, and hostility (NKF, K/DOQI, 2003). Education, including psychoeducational interventions, of the chronic kidney disease patient prior to the onset of ESRD may delay time to initiation of dialysis (Devins, Mendelssohn, Barre, & Binik, 2003).

Adequate dialysis and anemia are important contributors to overall well-being and quality of life for dialysis patients. These factors, combined with an assessment of patient's physical health and potential medicine side effects, should be evaluated as possible contributors to depression and anxiety states.

Erectile dysfunction is common in ESRD patients and is associated with decreased emotional well-being and poorer social function (Rosas et al., 2003). Recent advances in therapies for erectile dysfunction warrant diagnosis and treatment of erectile dysfunction. Assessment and treatment should be done routinely by nephrologists, as it may improve the quality of life of patients. For a more detailed discussion of erectile dysfunction, see Chapter 17.

A Cochrane Review on depression (identifying only randomized control trials) comparing antidepressants to placebo and a comparison of antidepressants against a combination of ECT and antidepressants, found only one trial, with 12 patients of 8 weeks' duration, which compared fluoxetine against placebo in depressed patients on chronic dialysis and did not show statistical difference (Rabindranath et al., 2005). Further trials are necessary.

A nonrandomized study in peritoneal dialysis patients found an improvement in BDI scores after 12 weeks of pharmacologic treatment (Wuerth, Finkelstein, & Finkelstein, 2005). The levels of depression, anxiety, and functional and occupational impairment do not remit spontaneously in untreated depressed hemodialysis patients. (Soykan et al., 2004).

Treatment of depression with paroxetine has been found to improve nutritional status (Koo et al., 2005). The application of an appropriate exercise program can improve psychological status, quality of life, and work capacity in long-term maintenance dialysis patients (Levendoglu et al., 2004; Kouidi, 2004; Suh, Jung, Kim, Park, & Yang, 2002). Patients should be encouraged to exercise at least three times a week. Psychoeducational intervention studies have been designed to reduce interdialytic weight gain in hemodialysis patients, but further research is needed (Welch & Thomas-Hawkins, 2005). Progressive muscle relaxation training has been utilized in dialysis patients to decrease state- and trait-anxiety levels and to improve quality of life (Yildirim & Fadiloglu, 2006).

CASE EXAMPLE

J. S. is an 84-year-old woman with a history of diabetes mellitus for 25 years and hypertension for 15 years. She has been under the care of a nephrologist for 8 years after a referral for evaluation of an elevated serum creatinine and proteinuria, found on routine examination by her primary care physician. She has diabetic retinopathy and neuropathy, a history of breast cancer and has difficulty ambulating without assistance. Her blood pressure is well controlled on a combination of an angiotensin-converting enzyme inhibitor and a diuretic. She has developed fatigue and anemia and is treated with erythropoietin each week and phosphate-binding medications. Despite these interventions, her renal function has declined over the past year. After discussion with her nephrologist, she was felt not to be a renal transplant candidate because of her age and history of breast cancer. She lives close to a dialysis center in a metropolitan area and currently lives in assisted living close to her family. She had elected to have hemodialysis when renal replacement therapy was needed, and had an arteriovenous fistula placed four months prior to initiation. Despite this, she was reticent to begin dialysis until she developed uremic symptoms of nausea, fatigue, and anorexia. Dialysis was initiated during a 3-day hospitalization, and she now receives renal replacement therapy in her local dialysis center. She has trouble coping with her new dietary and fluid restrictions. She does not like the needle sticks and pain associated with using her fistula for dialysis access. Transport was initially provided by her family, but subsequently she enrolled in a local metro-access program in which a wheelchair van comes to take her to dialysis three times a week. This was set up by the dialysis unit social worker, who is present at the unit three times a week and provides valuable counseling and support. This support included coordinating transport, addressing insurance concerns, and providing emotional support for the patient and her family. She experiences cramping at the end of hemodialysis despite adjustment of her dialysis prescription. She is frequently in the hospital for lower extremity, diabetes-related ulcers. Her dialysis monthly lab measures are adequate but she continues to decline because of her associated comorbidities. After experiencing a cerebrovascular accident, she is hospitalized in an intensive care unit. Her family has many discussions with her physicians regarding end-of-life issues. The patient had always maintained that as long as she had independence she would want to continue with dialysis. With the reality that she would need long-term nursing home placement, without a meaningful quality of life for her, the patient's family decides to discontinue dialysis.

This case illustrates the many battles that hemodialysis patients undergo during treatment of their ESRD. Associated comorbidities and challenges with transport, vascular access, hypotension, and the medical system contribute to the stressors that patients face when dealing with ESRD. Family involvement is often helpful, but cannot always be relied upon. Patients ultimately face shortened survival compared to age-matched controls; continued improvement in the modalities of treatment for ESRD are needed, such as expanding the organ donor pool, shortening the time to renal transplant, and improving access to new modalities.

REFERENCES

Amir, A. R., & Winchester, J. F. (1999). Chronic renal failure. In C. Tisher & C. Wilcox (Ed.), *Nephrology and hypertension* (4th ed., pp. 236–247). Philadelphia: Lippincott, Williams, & Wilkins.

Astor, B. C., Eustace, J. A., Powe, N. R., Klag, M. J., Fink, N. E., & Coresh, J. et al. (2005). Types of vascular access and survival among incident hemodialysis patients: The choices for healthy outcomes in caring for ESRD (CHOICE) study. *Journal American Society of Nephrology, 16*(5): 1449–1455.

Bawden, H. N., Acott, P., Carter, J., Lirenman, D., MacDonald, G. W., McAllister, M., et al. (2004). Neuropsychological functioning in end-stage renal disease. *Archive of Disease in Childhood, 89*(7):644–7.

Belasco, A., Barbosa, D., Bettencourt, A. R., Diccini, S., & Sesso, R. (2006). Quality of life of family caregivers of elderly patients on hemodialysis and peritoneal dialysis. *American Journal of Kidney Disease, 48*(6): 955–963.

Belasco, A. G., & Sesso, R. (2002). Burden and quality of life of caregivers for hemodialysis patients. *American Journal of Kidney Disease, 39*(4): 805–812.

Blendon, R. J., Aiken, L. H., Freeman, H. E., & Corey, C.R. (1989). Access to medical care for black and white Americans: A matter of continuing concern. *JAMA, 261,* 278–281.

Burns, D. (2004) Physical and psychosocial adaptation of blacks on hemodialysis. *Applied Nursing Research, 17*(2), 116–124.

Christensen, A. J., Ehlers, S. L., Wiebe, J. S., Moran, P. J., Raichle, K., Femeyhough, K., et al. (2002). Patient personality and mortality:A 4 year prospective examination of chronic renal insufficiency. *Health Psychology, 21* (4), 315–320.

Cooper-Patrick, L., Gallo, J. J., Gonzales, J. J., Vu, H. T., Powe, N.R., Nelson, C., et al. (1999). Race, gender, and partnership in the patient-physician relationship. *JAMA, 282,* 583–589.

Davison, S. N., & Jhangri, G. S. (2005). The impact of chronic pain on depression, sleep and the desire to withdraw from dialysis in hemodialysis patients. *Journal of Pain Symptom Management, 30*(5), 465–473.

D'Elia, J. A., Piening, S., Kaldany, A., Malarick, C., Unger, K., Ice, S., et al. (1981). Psychosocial crisis in diabetic renal failure. *Diabetes Care, 4,* 99–103.

Devins, G. M., Binik, Y. M., Hutchinson, T. A., Hollomby, D. J., Barre, P. E., & Guttmann, R. D. (1983–1984). The emotional impact of end-stage renal disease: Importance of patients' perception of intrusiveness and control. *Int J Psychiatry Med, 13*(4), 327–343.

Devins, G. M., Edworthy, S. M., Seland, T. P., Klein, G. M., Paul, L. C., & Mandin, H. (1993). Differences in illness intrusiveness across rheumatoid arthritis, end-stage renal disease, and multiple sclerosis. *J Nerv Ment Dis, 18,* 377–381.

Devins, G. M., Mann, J., Mandin, H., Paul, L. C., Hons, R. B., Burgess, E. D., et al. (1990). Psychosocial predictors of survival in end-stage renal disease. *J Nerv Ment Dis,* February, 127–133.

Devins, G. M., Mendelssohn, D. C., Barre, P. E., & Binik, Y.M. (2003). Predialysis psychoeducational intervention and coping styles influence time to dialysis in chronic kidney disease. *Am J Kidney Dis, 42*(4), 693–703.

Devins, G., Mendelssohn, D. C., Barre, P. E., Taub, K., & Binik, Y. (2005). Predialysis psychoeducational intervention extends survival in CKD: A 20–year follow-up. *American Journal of Kidney Diseases,* December, 1088–1098.

DiMatteo, M. R., Lepper, H. S., & Croghan, T. W. (2000). Depression is a risk factor for noncompliance with medical treatment: Meta-analysis of the effects of anxiety and depression on patient adherence. *Archives of Internal Medicine, 160*(14), 2101–2107.

Doescher, M. P., Saver, B. G., Franks, P., & Fiscella, K. (2000). Racial and ethnic disparities in perceptions of physician style and trust. *Arch Fam Med, 9,* 1156–1163.

Einwohner, R., Bernardini, J., Fried, L., & Piraino, B. (2004) The effect of depressive symptoms on survival in peritoneal dialysis patients. *Perit Dial Int, 24*(3), 256–263.

Eryilmaz, M. M., Ozdemir, C., Yurtman, F., Cilli, A., & Karaman, T. (2005). Quality of sleep and quality of life in renal transplantation patients. *Transplant Proc, 37*(5), 2072–2076.

Hall, Y. N., Sugihara, J. G., Go, A. S., & Chertow, G. M. (2005). Differential mortality and transplantation rates among Asians and Pacific Islanders with ESRD. *Journal American Society of Nephrology, 16*(12), 3461–3463.

Hedayati, S. S., Grambow, S. C., Szczech, L. A., Stechuchak, K. M., Allen, A. S., & Bosworth, H. B. (2005). Physician-diagnosed depression as a correlate of hospitalizations in patients receiving long-term hemodialysis. *American Journal of Kidney Diseases, 46*(4), 642–649.

Kalender, B., Ozdemir, A. C., & Koroglu, G. (2006). Association of depression with markers of nutrition and inflammation in chronic kidney disease and end stage renal disease. *Nephron Clin Pract, 102*(3–4), c115–121.

Katznelson, S., & Cecka, J. M. The great success of Asian kidney transplant recipients. *Transplantation, 64*(12), 1850–1852.

Kimmel, P. L., Weihs, K., & Peterson, R. A. (1993). Survival in hemodialysis patients: The role of depression. *Journal of the American Society of Nephrology,* vol. 4, 12–27.

Koo, J. R., Yoon, J. Y., Joo, M. H., Lee, H. S., Oh, J. E., Kim, S. G., et al. (2005). Treatment of depression and effect of antidepression treatment on nutritional status in chronic hemodialysis patients. *Am J Med Sci, 329*(1), 1–5.

Kouidi, E. (2004) Health-related quality of life in end stage renal disease patients: The effects of renal rehabilitation. *Clinical Nephrology, 61* (Suppl. 1), S60–S71.

Kovac, J. A., Patel, S. S., Peterson, R. A., & Kimmel P. L. (2002). Patient satisfaction with care and behavorial compliance in end-stage renal disease patients treated with hemodialysis. *American Journal of Kidney Disease, 39*(6), 1236–1244.

Ksch, C. K. (1980). Some thoughts on patient education. *Dialysis and you,* Spring/Summer, 9.

Kutner, N. G., Fair, P. L., & Kutner, M. H. (1985). Assessing depression and anxiety in chronic dialysis patients. *Psychosom Res, 29,* 23–31.

Lee, S. K., Lee, H. S., Lee, T. B., Kim, D. H., Koo, J. R., Kim, Y. K., et al. (2004). The effects of antidepressant treatment on serum cytokines and nutritional status in hemodialysis patients. *J Korean Med Sci, 19*(3), 384–389.

Lev, E. L., & Owen, S. V. (1998). A prospective study of adjustment to dialysis. *Anna Journal, 25*(5), 495–504.

Levendoglu, F., Altintepe, L., Okudan, N., Ugurlu, H., Gokbel, H., Tonbul, Z., et al. (2004). A twelve week exercise program improves the psychological status, quality of life and work capacity in hemodialysis patients. *J Nephrolo, 17*(6), 826–832.

Levey, A., Bosch, J. P., Lewis, J. B., Greene, T., Rogers, N., & Roth, D. (1999). A more accurate method to estimate glomerular filtration rate from serum creatinine: A new prediction equation. *Ann Intern Med, 130,* 461–470.

Livesley, W. J. (1981). Factors associated with psychiatric symptoms in patients undergoing chronic hemodialysis. *Can. J Psychiatry, 26,* 562–566.

Livesley, W. J. (1982). Symptoms of anxiety and depression in patients undergoing chronic hemodialysis. *Psychosom Res, 29,* 581–584.

Lockridge, R. S. (2004). The direction of end-stage renal disease reimbursement in the United States. *Semin Dial, 17*(2), 125–130.

Lopes, A. A., Albert, J. M., Young, E. W., Satayathum, S., Pisoni, R.L., Andreucci, V. E., et al. (2004). Screening for depression in hemodialysis patients: associations with diagnosis, treatment, and outcomes in the DOPPS. *Kidney Int, 66*(5), 2047–2053.

Lopes, A. A., Bragg- Gresham, J. L., & Satayathum, S. (2003). Health-related quality of life and associated outcomes among hemodialysis patients of different ethnicities in the United States: The Dialysis Outcomes and Practice Patterns Study (DOPPS). *American Journal of Kidney Diseases, 41*(3), 605–615.

Mayberry, R. M., Mili, F., & Ofili, E. (2000). Racial and ethnic differences in access to medical care. *Med Care Res Rev, 57,* 108–145.

Morgan, M., Hooper, R., Mayblin, M., & Jones, R. (2006). Attitudes to kidney donation and registering as a donor among ethnic groups in the UK. *Journal of Public Health,* September, 226–234.

NKF, K/DOQI. (2003). Clinical practice guidelines for chronic kidney disease: Evaluation, classification and stratification. *American Journal of Kidney Diseases, 39* (Suppl. 1), S1–S266.

Ouyang, W., & Rakowski, T. A. (1999). Chronic renal failure. In C. Tisher & C. Wilcox (Ed.), *Nephrology and hypertension* (4th ed., pp. 13–18). Philadelphia: Lippincott, Williams, & Wilkins.

Patel, S. S., Shah, V. S., Peterson, R. A., & Kimmel, P. L. (2002). Psychosocial variables, quality of life, and religious beliefs in ESRD patients treated with hemodialysis. *American Journal of Kidney Diseases, 40*(5), 1013–1022.

Rabindranath, K. S., Butler, J. A., Macleod, A. M., Roderick, P., Wallace, S. A., & Daly, C. (2005). Physical measures for treating depression in dialysis patients. *Cochrane Database Syst Rev, 18*(2):CD004541.

Rocco, M. V., Gassman, J. J., Wang, S. R., & Kaplan, R. (1997). Cross-sectional study of quality of life and symptoms in chronic renal disease patients: The Modification of Diet in Renal Disease Study. *American Journal of Kidney Diseases, 29*(6), 888–896.

Rosas, S. E., Joffe, M., Franklin, E., Strom, B. L., Kotzker, W., Brensinger, C., et al. (2003). Association of decreased quality of life and erectile dysfunction in hemodialysis patients. *Kidney Int, 64*(1), 232–238.

Ross, E., & Yankulin, L. (1999). Hemodialysis and continuous therapies. In C. Tisher & C. Wilcox (Ed.), *Nephrology and hypertension* (4th ed., pp. 250–251). Philadelphia: Lippincott, Williams, & Wilkins.

Silkensen, J. R. (1999). Chronic renal failure. In C. Tisher & C. Wilcox (Ed.) *Nephrology and hypertension* (4th ed., pp. 270–289). Philadelphia: Lippincott, Williams, & Wilkins.

Soykan, A., Boztas, H., Kutlay, S., Ince, E., Aygor, B., Ozden, A., et al. (2004). Depression and its 6–month course in untreated hemodialysis patients: A preliminary follow-up study in Turkey. *Int J Behav Med, 11*(4), 243–246.

Starzomski, R., & Hilton, A. (2000). Patient and family adjustment to kidney transplantation without an interim period of dialysis. *Journal of the American Nephrology Nurses Association, 27*(1), 17–18, 21–32.

Suh, M. R., Jung, H. H., Kim, S. B., Park, J. S., & Yang, W.S. (2002). Effects of regular exercise on anxiety, depression and quality of life in maintenance hemodialysis patients. *Renal Failure, 24*(3), 337–345.

Taskapan, H., Ates, F., Kaya, B., Emul, M., Kaya, M., Taskapan, C., et al. (2005). Psychiatric disorders and large interdialytic weight gain in patients on chronic hemodialysis. *Nephrology, 10*(1), 15.

Tsay, S. L., & Hung, L.O. (2004). Empowerment of patients with end-stage renal disease: A randomized controlled trial. *Int J Nurs Stud, 41*(1), 59–65.

Tyrrell, J., Paturel, L., Cadec, B., Capezzali, E., & Poussin, G. (2005). Patients undergoing dialysis treatment: Cognitive functioning, depressive mood and health related quality of life. *Aging and Mental Health, 9*(4), 374–379.

United States Renal Data System. (2006). *Annual data report: Atlas of end-stage renal disease in the United States.* Bethesda, MD: National Institutes of Health, National Institute of Diabetes and Digestive and Kidney Diseases.

Vasquez, I., Valderrabano, F., Fort, I., Jofre, R., Lopez-Gomez, J. M., Moreno, F., et al. (2004). Differences in health-related quality of life between male and female dialysis patients. *Nefrologia, 24*(2), 167–178.

Walters, B. J., Hays, R. D., Spritzer, K. L., Fridman, M., & Carter, W. B. (2002). Health related quality of life, depressive symptoms, anemia and malnutrition at hemodialysis initiation. *American Journal of Kidney Diseases, 40*(6), 1185–1194.

Wanner, C., Krane, V., Marz, W., Olschewski, M. Sc., Mann, J., Ruf, G., et al. (2005). Atorvastatin in patients with Type 2 diabetes mellitus undergoing hemodialysis. *New England Journal of Medicine, 353,* 238–248.

Watnick, S., Kirwin P., Mahnensmith, R., & Concato, J. (2003). The prevalence and treatment of depression among patients starting dialysis. *American Journal of Kidney Diseases, 41*(1), 105–110.

Weisbord, S. D., Fried, L. F., Arnold, R. M., Fine, M. J., Levenson, D. J., Peterson, R. A., et al. (2005). Prevalence, severity and importance of physical and emotional symptoms in chronic hemodialysis patients. *J Am Soc Nephrol, 16*(8), 2487–2494.

Welch, J. L., & Thomas-Hawkins, C. (2005). Psycho-educational strategies to promote fluid adherence in adult hemodialysis patients: A review of intervention studies. *International Journal of Nursing Studies, 42*(5), 597–608.

Wilson, B., Spittal, J., Heidenheim, P., Herman, M., Leonard, M., Johnston, A., et al. (2006). Screening for depression in chronic hemodialysis patients: Comparison of the Beck Depression Inventory, primary nurse, and nephrology team. *Hemodial Int, 10*(1), 35–41.

Wolfe, R .A., Hulbert-Shearon, T. E., Ashby, V. B., Mahadevan, S., & Port, F. K. (2005). Improvements in dialysis patient mortality are associated with improvements in urea reduction ratio and hematocrit, 1999 to 2002. *American Journal of Kidney Diseases, 45*(1), 127–135.

Wuerth, D., Finkelstein, S. H., & Finkelstein, F. O. (2005). The identification and treatment of depression in patients maintained on dialysis. *Semin Dial, 18*(2), 142–146.

Yildirim, Y. K., & Fadiloglu, C. (2006). The effect of progressive muscle relaxation training on anxiety levels and quality of life in dialysis patients. *Edtna-Erca Journal, 32*(2), 86–88.

CHAPTER 14

Inflammatory Bowel Disease
and Liver Disease

KEVIN A. HOMMEL

INTRODUCTION

Individuals with inflammatory bowel disease (IBD) and/or liver disease account for a considerable proportion of patients with organic disease in pediatric and adult gastroenterology health care. Although the diseases affect different areas of the gastrointestinal system (see Figure 14.1), these patients face similar long-term adjustment challenges with respect to the course of their illness, treatment regimens, changes in functional ability, and psychosocial sequelae. Further, both IBD and liver disease represent populations that have been understudied from a clinical health psychology perspective; yet, these patients are likely to significantly benefit from comprehensive health care that integrates medical and behavioral health factors of their illness and treatment. Thus, inflammatory bowel disease and liver disease are presented together in this chapter in order to compare and contrast the biopsychosocial issues each illness presents.

INFLAMMATORY BOWEL DISEASE

Inflammatory bowel disease (IBD), which is comprised of Crohn's disease and ulcerative colitis, is a chronic inflammatory disease of the gastrointestinal tract resulting in symptoms such as recurrent diarrhea, rectal bleeding, abdominal pain, anemia, decreased appetite, fatigue, arthritis, growth delay, delayed puberty, and perianal (i.e., around the anus) disease (Drossman & Ringel, 2003; Mackner & Crandall, 2006). Crohn's disease can affect any area of the gastrointestinal tract, from the mouth to the anus, but most commonly affects the small intestine. Moreover, inflammation can occur in multiple places along the gastrointestinal tract simultaneously with healthy, unaffected areas in between inflammation sites. This inflammation can cause pain and bleeding and result in frequent emptying of the bowel and diarrhea (National Institutes of Health [NIH], 2006e). In contrast to Crohn's disease, ulcerative colitis is limited to the large intestine (i.e., colon) and rectum. Ulcerative colitis results in inflammation and ulceration of the top layer of the intestinal wall, as opposed to Crohn's disease, in which inflammation can occur deeper within the intestinal wall (NIH, 2006h).

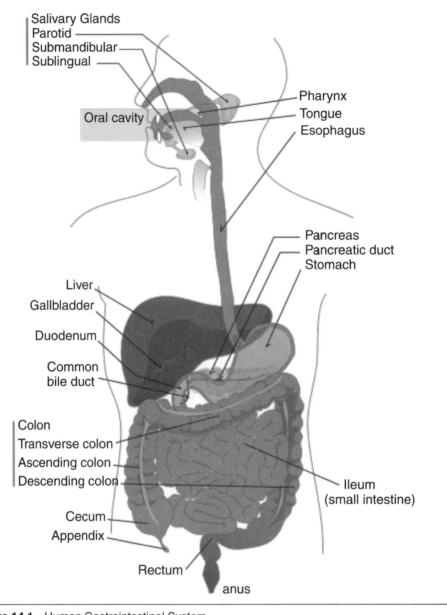

Salivary Glands
Parotid
Submandibular
Sublingual

Oral cavity

Pharynx
Tongue
Esophagus

Pancreas
Pancreatic duct
Stomach

Liver
Gallbladder
Duodenum
Common bile duct

Colon
Transverse colon
Ascending colon
Descending colon

Ileum
(small intestine)

Cecum
Appendix

Rectum
anus

Figure 14.1   Human Gastrointestinal System

LIVER DISEASE

Liver disease represents a number of specific diseases of various etiology, symptoms, and outcome. For the purpose of this chapter, the most common liver diseases, which may affect patients across their lifespan and necessitate involvement of a clinical health psychologist, will be discussed. These diseases include biliary atresia, primary sclerosing cholangitis (PSC), nonalcoholic steatohepatitis (NASH) and nonalcoholic fatty liver disease (NAFLD), autoimmune hepatitis, viral hepatitis, and associated outcomes of liver disease such as cirrhosis and liver transplant.

Biliary atresia is a rare condition that develops during infancy, in which bile is not drained into the intestine properly due to malfunction and loss of the bile ducts. Buildup of this bile in the liver results in scarring and loss of tissue and eventually cirrhosis and liver failure. Transplant is usually required within the first 2 years of life if the condition is not treated properly, as discussed in the following section. Symptoms of biliary atresia include jaundice (i.e., yellow pigmentation in the skin, mucous membranes, and eyes), darkened urine, and pale, gray, or white bowel movements (NIH, 2006b). Primary sclerosing cholangitis is a disease in which the bile ducts both inside and outside the liver exhibit inflammation and scarring, resulting in blockage of the ducts and accumulation of bile. Over time, bile accumulates and causes significant liver damage, requiring liver transplantation. Symptoms of PSC include jaundice, itching caused by bile products deposited in the skin, and fatigue (NIH, 2006g).

The hallmark features of NASH are fat in the liver as well as inflammation and damage. This condition resembles alcoholic liver disease but there is no history of alcohol abuse in patients with this disease. Nonalcoholic fatty liver disease is a similar condition in which fat collects in the liver; however, in NAFLD, the liver is not inflamed or damaged. Both conditions are associated with overweight, and NAFLD can involve insulin resistance. Patients with NASH or NAFLD are generally asymptomatic in the early stages of the disease. When the disease advances, generally over the course of several years, symptoms such as fatigue, weakness, and weight loss may occur, and cirrhosis can develop. Indeed, NASH is one of the leading causes of cirrhosis behind hepatitis C and alcoholic liver disease (NIH, 2006f; Harrison & DiBisceglie, 2003).

Autoimmune hepatitis is a condition in which the immune system attacks cells in the liver, causing inflammation (i.e., hepatitis). The most common symptom of autoimmune hepatitis is fatigue; however, other symptoms include jaundice, itching, abdominal and joint pain, nausea and vomiting, urine darkening, or light-colored stools. This disease is usually serious and progressive, and can result in cirrhosis and liver failure if left untreated or inadequately treated (NIH, 2006a). Viral hepatitis represents a cluster of liver diseases named hepatitis A, B, C, D, and E; each of these involve inflammation of the liver and are caused by different viruses. Each virus causes short-term hepatitis, and hepatitis B, C, and D can cause long-term or chronic hepatitis. Hepatitis C (HCV) develops into chronic hepatitis in approximately 75% of cases. Although some individuals are asymptomatic, common symptoms include jaundice, fatigue, loss of appetite, abdominal pain, nausea and vomiting, diarrhea, and low-grade fever (NIH, 2006i; NIH, 2006c). Cirrhosis is an irreversible liver disease that often presents as a comorbid complication of another condition, such as alcoholic liver disease or HCV. It is characterized by scar tissue development, which eventually hardens the liver and blocks blood flow through the organ. Symptoms can include exhaustion, loss of appetite, nausea, and abdominal pain. Cirrhosis is associated with chronic and progressive liver diseases, such as those discussed in this chapter, and ultimately results in liver transplantation or death (NIH, 2006d). Eventually, any of the aforementioned liver diseases might result in liver transplantation. This process involves being placed on a waiting list kept at the United Network for Organ Sharing (UNOS). Liver transplant can involve whole liver (i.e., cadaveric) transplant from someone recently deceased or a partial or split liver from a living donor.

ETIOLOGY AND EPIDEMIOLOGY

The etiology of IBD and liver diseases presented in this chapter are complex and multifactorial across diseases. Epidemiologic data presented primarily represents estimates for the United States; if available, data for other geographic regions are presented as well.

INFLAMMATORY BOWEL DISEASE

Inflammatory bowel disease affects approximately 9 in 100,000 individuals (Lindberg, Lindquist, Holmquist, & Hildebrand, 2000), and it is equally represented in men and women (NIH, 2006e; NIH, 2006h). It can occur at any age, but is most common in people ages 15 to 30, and is less common in individuals 50 to 70 years of age. Approximately one fourth of IBD patients are diagnosed as children or adolescents (i.e., under 18 years of age). Inflammatory bowel disease tends to run in families, with approximately 20% of individuals having a blood relative with the disease. Caucasians constitute the vast majority of the IBD population, and individuals of Jewish heritage are overrepresented. The cause of IBD remains unknown. Leading theories suggest a multifactorial process involving genetic susceptibility, environmental exposure to antigens (e.g., bacterial or viral infection), and autoimmune response, in which normal bacteria and other substances are mistaken as foreign (NIH, 2006e; NIH 2006h, McClung, 1994). Due to the unknown etiology of IBD, there are no identifiable behavioral or physiological risk factors for development of either Crohn's disease or ulcerative colitis. Nevertheless, Caucasian individuals, and particularly those of Jewish heritage, are at increased risk for IBD, whereas African Americans are at decreased risk (NIH, 2006e; NIH, 2006h).

LIVER DISEASE

Biliary atresia affects approximately 1 in 10,000 children, and is more common in girls and African American and Asian children. It is the most common reason for pediatric liver transplantation in the United States. The cause of the disease is unknown, but two types exist: a fetal form, which arises during fetal development and is present at birth, and the more common perinatal form, which presents in the second to fourth week of life (NIH, 2006b). The etiology of PSC is also unknown, though bacteria, viruses, and immune dysfunction appear to play a role. Primary sclerosing cholangitis generally begins between ages 30 and 60 years, with a mean age at diagnosis of 40 years; however, it can occur in children as well. It has an annual incidence of 0.9–1.31 per 100,000 and point prevalence of 8.5–13.6 per 100,000, and men are affected approximately twice as often as women (Worthington & Chapman, 2006; NIH, 2006g). Nonalcoholic steatohepatitis affects approximately 2 to 5% of individuals in the United States, with NAFLD affecting an additional 10 to 20% or approximately 15 million people in the United States. The causes of NASH and NAFLD are unknown; however, they are associated with overweight, obesity, and diabetes. With the growing prevalence of obesity, these diseases are becoming more common (NIH, 2006f; Wang, 2003).

Autoimmune hepatitis is caused by the immune system attacking liver cells, causing inflammation of the liver. It is unclear why this autoimmune response occurs, but it is speculated that individuals affected by this disease have a genetic predisposition to autoimmune diseases. Approximately 70% of individuals with autoimmune hepatitis are women, and the disease occurs primarily between the ages of 15 and 40 years. Autoimmune hepatitis is classified as type I or type II. Type I is more common in North America and women, and can occur at any age. Type II is less common and primarily affects girls between the ages of 2 and 14 (NIH, 2006a). The incidence of type I auto-immune hepatitis varies depending on geographic region. In North America and Europe, annual incidence ranges from 0.1 to 1.9 per 100,000. Type II autoimmune hepatitis is more common in southern Europe than northern Europe, the United States, or Japan (Boberg, 2002).

Hepatitis A virus (HAV) is generally spread through oral contact with something that has been contaminated with the stool of an infected individual. Approximately one-third of individuals in America have been infected (CDC, 2006a). Hepatitis B virus (HBV) is contracted via blood or unprotected sexual contact with an infected individual. The annual number of new infections is approximately 60,000, and an estimated 1.25 million Americans have chronic infection (CDC, 2006b). Hepatitis C virus (HCV) accounts for 15% of acute viral hepatitis infections, 60 to 70% of chronic hepatitis, and 50% of cirrhosis, end-stage liver disease, and liver cancer (NIH, 2006c). Transmission of HCV occurs through contact with infected blood or maternal-infant transmission. Approximately 55 to 85% of individuals develop chronic infection, 70% of which develop chronic liver disease. Approximately 1.6%, or 4.1 million Americans have been infected with HCV virus, with 3.2 million developing chronic infection. The number of new infections each year is about 26,000. Hepatitis C virus accounts for 10,000 to 12,000 deaths annually in the United States (CDC, 2006c; NIH, 2006c). Hepatitis D virus (HDV) can only occur in individuals already infected with HBV and is transmitted in the same manner. Prevalence data are unavailable for HDV (CDC, 2006d). Hepatitis E virus (HEV) is transmitted in the same manner as HAV, but is uncommon in the United States. Prevalence data are also unavailable for HEV (CDC, 2006e).

Cirrhosis is an irreversible liver disease that can present as a complication of the aforementioned liver diseases. Chronic alcoholism and HCV are the most common causes of cirrhosis in the United States, whereas HBV is likely the most common cause worldwide (NIH, 2006d). Mortality resulting from cirrhosis is highest among the Latino population compared to other ethnic groups in the United States (Stinson, Grant, & Dufour, 2001). Moreover, cirrhosis accounts for approximately 26,000 deaths annually and is the twelfth leading cause of death by disease (NIH, 2006d).

Similar to IBD, behavioral or physiological risk factors for liver disease are largely unclear. Due to the unknown etiology of biliary atresia and PSC, there are no identified risk factors; however, PSC appears to be associated with ulcerative colitis (NIH, 2006b; NIH, 2006g). Although the underlying causes of NASH and NAFLD are not clearly understood, it occurs most often in overweight and middle-aged individuals (NIH, 2006f). Individuals whose weight is greater than 140% of their ideal body weight and those with diabetes mellitus are at increased risk for developing NAFLD (Wang, 2003). There may be a genetic susceptibility to development of autoimmune disorders in individuals who have autoimmune hepatitis, although no specific risk factors exist for this particular disease (NIH, 2006a). Risk factors for hepatitis A include exposure to infected individuals or contaminated food or water. Risk factors for hepatitis B include contact with infected blood, sexual contact with an infected person, or maternal-infant transmission (NIH, 2006i). Hepatitis C risk factors include sharing of needles for intravenous drug use. Blood transfusions were once considered a risk factor; however, routine screening for HCV antibody since 1991 has virtually erased the spread of HCV via transfusions. Other risk factors include suffering needle stick accidents from a person with HCV, maternal-infant transmission, and sexual transmission (NIH, 2006c). Hepatitis D occurs only in individuals with HBV, and risk factors include exposure to infected blood. Risk factors for hepatitis E include international travel and exposure to infected individuals or contaminated food or water (NIH, 2006i).

DISEASE FACTORS

Disease factors, such as disease severity, exacerbation of symptoms (i.e., flares), and overall illness course, associated with IBD and liver diseases vary across diseases and may be biological and/or behavioral in nature. These issues are discussed in the following.

INFLAMMATORY BOWEL DISEASE COURSE

Although stress was once thought to be causal in the onset of IBD, this theory has been discredited. However, this presumption still persists in the general public. This misunderstanding of the origin of IBD likely also accounts for the common misperception that IBD and irritable bowel syndrome (IBS) are synonymous diseases. On the contrary, the two diseases are quite different in terms of physical findings, symptom presentation, and effective treatments. Irritable bowel syndrome symptoms may include abdominal pain and cramping, constipation, increased frequency of stools, and diarrhea. However, patients with IBS do not demonstrate any physical signs of inflammation or disease, and symptoms are more often mediated by stress. In contrast, IBD patients may present with a variety of symptoms such as diarrhea, hematochezia (i.e., blood in stool), abdominal pain, fevers, and growth delay/failure. Unfortunately, some of these symptoms may not be perceived as severe enough by patients to warrant further medical attention at first. For example, occasional fevers with abdominal pain and diarrhea may be perceived as a stomach virus by some patients, whereas others might immediately seek a referral to a gastroenterolgist. However, symptoms are often more severe or concerning enough (e.g., blood in stool) that patients are referred and undergo medical evaluation by a gastroenterololgist relatively quickly. While the diagnosis of IBD is not generally perceived by patients to be traumatic, many patients exhibit a degree of discomfort about discussing bowel disease. This is particularly true for children and adolescents with IBD who may be subject to "bathroom humor" and teasing by other children (Mackner & Crandall, 2006).

Inflammatory bowel disease is a chronic and episodic illness regardless of specific disease (i.e., Crohn's disease or ulcerative colitis). Symptom flares are unpredictable despite disease management efforts, and progression of the illness can vary considerably depending on the individual patient. Moreover, disease symptoms and severity are variable both across and within patients. That is, two patients with IBD may present with very different symptoms and severity, and each patient may experience unique variation in symptoms and symptom severity each time his or her disease flares. As a whole, IBD patients may experience disease complications such as intestinal blockage, fistulas, fissures, and abscesses, which may necessitate surgical intervention to repair damaged tissue. Severity of disease flares does not necessarily progressively worsen over time, and patients generally return to baseline functioning in terms of their functional ability, with the possible exception of temporary or permanent changes due to surgical intervention. Inflammatory bowel disease can also involve malabsorption of nutrients, leading to deficiencies in calories, vitamins, minerals, and proteins (NIH, 2006e; NIH, 2006h). Additionally, stress can play a functional role in exacerbating symptoms such as diarrhea in that anxiety regarding bowel movement urgency in social situations can increase abdominal cramping, thus intensifying anxiety. This circular pattern can exist at a subdiagnostic level as well, but is pronounced in patients with IBD. Extraintestinal manifestations of IBD that may develop over the course of the illness include arthritis, inflammation of the eyes, kidney stones or gallstones, and liver disease (NIH, 2006e; NIH, 2006h). Finally, ulcerative colitis patients in particular are at increased risk for developing colon cancer (NIH, 2006h).

LIVER DISEASE COURSE

The onset and progression of liver diseases vary considerably depending on the specific disease. Biliary atresia develops quite rapidly, with symptoms presenting either at birth or within the first several weeks of life. The course of biliary atresia depends on the success of surgical intervention (i.e., Kasai procedure, described in the Regimen Factors section) and follow-up care. If surgery does not correct the flow of bile, patients will require liver transplantation within the first 2 years of life (NIH, 2006b). Even after initial success and improved bile flow, the majority of patients will ultimately require liver transplantation during their life. Thus, biliary atresia is a chronic yet potentially curable disease, depending on the success of surgical correction or liver transplantation. In contrast to biliary atresia, PSC generally develops more slowly. Scarring and blockage of the bile ducts can begin before patients become symptomatic. Primary sclerosing cholangitis is a chronic and progressive disease, with treatment aimed at improving symptoms. For those patients who develop advanced disease, liver transplant is the only definitive treatment option (Worthington & Chapman, 2006; NIH, 2006g). The onset of NASH and NAFLD is insidious, with patients experiencing few or no symptoms of liver disease for years. Only as NASH becomes more advanced, or as cirrhosis develops, will patients present with symptoms. The progression of NASH and NAFLD can vary considerably across patients. Either condition can remit without future relapse, or can continue as chronic and potentially develop further complications such as insulin resistance (NIH, 2006f; Harrison & DiBisceglie, 2003). The most serious complications of NASH and NAFLD are cirrhosis and liver transplantation. Autoimmune hepatitis is a chronic condition that can usually be controlled with treatment, particularly if treatment is initiated early in the disease course. Patients may present with symptoms similar to other forms of hepatitis, which underscores the importance of accurate diagnosis. Type I autoimmune hepatitis is associated with other autoimmune disorders such as type I diabetes, Grave's disease, and ulcerative colitis. Since treatment is focused on suppressing the immune system, patients have an increased susceptibility to infection. In advanced stages of the disease, patients may develop ascites (i.e., fluid accumulation in the peritoneal cavity) and confusion, and ultimately may require liver transplantation (NIH, 2006a). Patients with viral hepatitis may be symptomatic or asymptomatic. Hepatitis B virus, HCV, and HDV can cause chronic hepatitis, while HAV and HEV usually resolve on their own (NIH, 2006i). While the onset of these diseases may not be traumatic, the patient may have contracted the disease via a traumatic event (e.g., rape by an infected individual). Further, HCV patients may be stigmatized due to the lack of understanding of how the disease is transmitted. Chronic infection of HBV, HCV, or HDV can involve serious morbidity, particularly in HCV, leading to advanced cirrhosis and end-stage liver disease (NIH, 2006c). Cirrhosis can develop quite slowly, and many people are asymptomatic in the early stages of the disease. As it progresses, patients may develop symptoms and complications such as edema and ascites, bruising, portal hypertension, varices (i.e., dilated sub-mucosal veins), diabetes, and liver cancer. Although cirrhosis is a chronic and irreversible condition, treatment can potentially delay or stop further damage to the liver; however, liver transplantation is often necessary (NIH, 2006d). Finally, all liver diseases have the potential to be life-shortening illnesses depending on treatment response; thus, issues pertaining to terminal illness planning, fear of dying, and palliative and hospice care need to be incorporated into treatment if applicable.

REGIMEN FACTORS

Treatment regimens for IBD and liver diseases can be quite complex and demanding, involving medication, nutritional, surgical, and behavioral aspects of care. General treatment regimen considerations and associated challenges are discussed in the following.

Inflammatory Bowel Disease Treatment Regimen Factors

Treatment for IBD can involve various medications, dietary changes, and potentially surgery. The goals of treatment are to induce remission, control inflammation, relieve symptoms, and correct nutritional deficiencies. Treatment depends not only on the specific disease, but also on the location of inflammation, associated symptoms, and patient response to treatment. Medication treatment involves anti-inflammatory agents such as aminosalicylates or corticosteroids, immunomodulators such as azathioprine and 6–mercaptopurine, antidiarrheal medications, and antibiotics for bacterial overgrowth. Infliximab, which is a tumor necrosis factor inhibitor, may be prescribed in severe IBD that is unresponsive to other treatments. Nutritional therapy involves adding high-calorie liquid or powder supplements to patients' diet. Some patients may also require nasogastric tube feeding or intravenous feeding to treat malnutrition and growth failure associated with malabsorption (NIH, 2006e; NIH, 2006h, Rice & Chuang, 1999). Approximately one third to three fourths of Crohn's disease patients and 25 to 40% of ulcerative colitis patients will require surgery at some point during the course of their disease (Langholtz, Munkholm, Krasilnikoff, & Binder, 1997; NIH, 2006e; NIH, 2006h). Surgery can involve removal of sections of diseased bowel and ileostomy or ileoanal anastomosis. Ileostomy involves disconnecting the small intestine and routing it through the abdominal wall through a hole called a stoma. In ileoanal anastomosis, the colon is removed and the small intestine is attached to the rectum and anus to allow typical, albeit more frequent and watery, bowel movements (NIH, 2006e; NIH, 2006h). Overall, treatment regimens for IBD are variable and can be quite complex, making adherence difficult. Further, adverse side effects of some medications (e.g., weight gain from corticosteroids) may be prohibitive for some patients, particularly adolescents who are generally more sensitive about changes in their appearance. Ostomy care might also be neglected by children and adolescents who perceive this process to be gross or embarrassing. Adherence to dietary recommendations is challenging for anyone, particularly individuals with IBD who have dietary restrictions. Procedures such as endoscopy and colonoscopy and surgical intervention are intrusive, but necessary to determine location and severity of inflammation. Fortunately, these procedures are generally available by gastroenterologists in medical centers, and costs are covered by insurance.

LIVER DISEASE TREATMENT REGIMEN FACTORS

Biliary atresia is treated first via surgical intervention called a Kasai procedure, which involves removal and replacement of the bile ducts with a loop of intestine to allow proper flow of bile through the liver into the intestine. Assuming the procedure is successful, a patient's regimen may consist of a low-fat diet and vitamin supplements, depending on how well bile flow is restored. This restrictive diet may not be difficult for parents/caregivers to maintain during infancy; however, a plethora of opportunities arise for school-age children to consume high-fat foods, making dietary adherence challenging. If bile flow is not restored or complications arise following the Kasai procedure, patients may require liver transplantation (NIH, 2006b). While surgery is an intrusive treatment of the disease, it is necessary for survival. Following the Kasai procedure or transplant, the burden of postoperative treatment regimen adherence is placed solely on the parents/caregivers. Treatment of PSC involves medications to relieve symptoms and antibiotics for infections, vitamin supplements to correct deficiencies in vitamin A, D, and K, and surgery to open bile duct blockages. Liver transplant is also likely in advanced stages of the disease (Worthington & Chapman, 2006; NIH, 2006g). Since PSC is associated with ulcerative colitis, patients who develop this comorbidity are faced with the burden of managing two chronic illnesses with variable symptom presentation and severity. Although treatment regimens for these illnesses do not conflict or pose barriers for one another, they are nevertheless more complex and potentially intrusive.

There are no specific medical treatments for NASH or NAFLD. Patients are encouraged to reduce their weight if they are overweight (see Chapter 4 for obesity treatment), increase physical activity, follow a balanced diet, and avoid unnecessary medications and alcohol. Additionally, because patients with NASH/NAFLD can have comorbid diabetes (see Chapter 8 for diabetes treatment), insulin resistance, and high blood pressure or cholesterol (see Chapter 6 for treatment of cardiovascular disease), treatment is also focused on controlling these conditions (Harrison & DiBisceglie, 2003; NIH, 2006f). Treatment regimens for NASH/NAFLD vary across patients depending on risk factors (e.g., overweight, alcohol consumption) and comorbidity (e.g., diabetes). Given that the majority of patients are overweight and treatment recommendations focus on lifestyle changes, behavior modification is critical to outcome.

The primary treatment for both types of autoimmune hepatitis is daily oral corticosteroids, beginning with high doses and tapering down to lower, maintenance dosing as the disease is controlled. Other immunosuppressive agents such as azathioprine can be used as an adjunct to lower the required dose of prednisone. This reduces undesirable side effects of corticosteroids such as weight gain, cushingoid (i.e., facial puffiness) appearance, diabetes, osteoporosis, and mood lability. Patients who do not respond to standard treatment or have significant side effects may be prescribed other medications such as cyclosporine or tacrolimus. Patients are required to take medications long-term, with approximately one third of patients eventually being able to stop treatment (NIH, 2006a). Potential barriers to autoimmune hepatitis treatment include complex dosing schedules (e.g., tapering of doses) and adverse side effects of the prednisone, resulting in reduced adherence and, consequently, reduced treatment effect.

Treatment of viral hepatitis varies depending on type. Fortunately, individuals can prevent infection of HAV and HBV/HDV with HAV and HBV vaccinations, respectively. In patients who contract HAV or HEV, these viruses generally resolve on their own over several weeks. Hepatitis E acute infection also generally resolves on its own;

however, chronic HBV or HDV infection is usually treated with alpha interferon (NIH, 2006i). Treatment of HCV consists of peginterferon or combination peginterferon and ribavirin therapy (NIH, 2006c). Whereas peginterferon monotherapy results in a sustained response rate of 35%, combination peginterferon and ribavirin treatment results in a sustained response rate of 55%. Thus, combination therapy is now recommended for treatment of HCV. While these treatments are not particularly complex, they require a high degree of self-monitoring and consistency as the dosing is staggered. Subcutaneous injections of peginterferon are given weekly, and oral ribavirin is taken daily (NIH, 2006c). Also, the uncertainty of long-term remission may cause significant stress in patients and result in decreased adherence and poorer disease management.

Since damage to the liver caused by cirrhosis cannot be reversed, treatment is aimed at stopping or delaying further progression and any comorbid conditions. Treatment varies depending on the cause of cirrhosis. Thus, cirrhosis caused by hepatitis is treated with corticosteroids or interferon therapy depending on type, whereas cirrhosis caused by chronic alcohol abuse is treated by abstaining from alcohol consumption. Other lifestyle changes such as eating a healthy diet and maintaining light physical activity can help as well. Diuretics can be used to treat complications such as edema or ascites, antibiotics for infections, and blood pressure medication for portal hypertension (NIH, 2006d). Treatment regimens depend on the etiology of cirrhosis in each patient. If chronic alcohol abuse is the cause of a patient's cirrhosis, treatment of the addictive behavior is imperative. Treatment of alcoholism can be quite challenging, and there is a high rate of relapse (see Chapter 17 for substance abuse treatment). However, abstinence has been shown to increase 5-year survival rate in cirrhosis patients (Schenker, 1984; Borowsky, Strome, & Lott, 1982).

When patients undergo liver transplantation, postoperative treatment is aimed at preventing rejection of the new organ. Naturally, the immune system recognizes and attacks any foreign substance, whether it is a bacterial infection or a new organ. Medications, including cyclosporine and tacrolimus, are used to prevent rejection and act by suppressing immune system function, thereby increasing risk of infection. Special dietary recommendations (e.g., foods that are high in protein and low in fat, sodium, and sugar, alcohol abstinence), vitamins, antibiotics, or blood pressure medication may also continue to be part of a patient's regimen. Thus, complexity of the regimen and maintaining consistency of dosing long term are critical factors in determining outcome of liver transplantation.

INDIVIDUAL FACTORS

Individual factors related to patient and family adjustment, coping, social resources, and health management behaviors can significantly impact health outcomes. These psychological adjustment issues must be taken into consideration when developing treatment plans for patients.

PSYCHOLOGICAL ADJUSTMENT

There are a number of individual factors that are important to consider when evaluating the impact of a chronic illness such as IBD or liver disease on the psychological adjustment of patients and their families. Patient and family intelligence and ability to integrate new knowledge are key to managing the challenges of a chronic illness. Further, the developmental age of child and adolescent patients in particular is important to their understanding of the specific condition and their emotional adjustment to having a chronic illness. However, knowledge alone is not sufficient to maintain optimal disease management and emotional adjustment (e.g., Rapoff, 1999). Indeed, other factors play a significant role in adjustment and disease management. The relationship patients and families have with the health care team is critical to fostering trust, communication, and confidence in treatment outcome (e.g., Gillman, 1994; Drossman & Ringel, 2003; Banez & Cunningham, 2003). Inherent in developing an effective therapeutic relationship between patients and health care teams is the need for providers to understand and respect the cultural background of the patient and his or her family. Obviously, a thorough grasp of the racial and ethnic backgrounds of patients is necessary. However, providing culturally sensitive and effective care also involves understanding the patient's religious background, urban versus rural community influences, and unique family beliefs regarding medical treatment and behavioral health care. In addition, socioeconomic status and economic resources available to the patient and family are important to disease management as, unfortunately, some patients and families are faced with having to choose between paying bills and paying for medication. Health beliefs can play a significant role, particularly in IBD, as medications such as azathioprine and 6-mercaptopurine may take 6–8 weeks before therapeutic levels are achieved and symptom improvement is recognized by patients. Moreover, both IBD and liver disease patients who are prescribed corticosteroids may perceive the cost of negative side effects to outweigh the long-term benefit of the treatment. This may be especially salient in adolescents, who are more sensitive to changes in appearance and susceptible to body image distortion. Finally, patient coping behavior (i.e., problem-focused versus emotion-focused; Lazarus & Folkman, 1984; Fawzy et al., 1993; Baum, Herberman, & Cohen, 1995) is important in both IBD and liver disease given that functional ability may fluctuate over the course of the illness due to disease flares, organ failure, and surgery.

PSYCHOLOGICAL COMORBIDITY

Psychological functioning in individuals with IBD and liver disease has been the subject of much research. A summary of the extant data, gaps in the empirical literature, and considerations for future research are described in the following.

INFLAMMATORY BOWEL DISEASE

Inflammatory bowel disease is clearly a demanding disease from both child and adult patient perspectives. The chronic, intermittent, and unpredictable disease course as well as symptoms that may be painful, embarrassing, and require special planning for activities or social events can be quite stressful for patients of all ages. While stress is not a causal factor in IBD, patients often report increased symptom severity in times of increased stress (NIH, 2006e). Further, there is considerable misperception of the cause of IBD in the general population, which might complicate adjustment and access to appropriate social support. Despite erroneous conclusions from poorly designed studies indicating personality characteristics of individuals with IBD (e.g., Murray, 1930; Prugh, 1951; Engel, 1955; McKegney, Gordon, & Levine, 1970), there is no reliable and valid evidence from well-designed and controlled studies that suggests a correlation between personality factors and IBD diagnosis. Nevertheless, individuals with IBD demonstrate increased risk for psychological maladjustment (e.g., Drossman & Ringel, 2003; Mackner, Crandall, & Szigethy, 2006).

Psychological functioning among IBD patients continues to be discussed as a significant issue in disease activity. Research has begun to provide some empirical support for patient anecdotal reports of the stress-disease activity relationship (Casati & Toner, 2000). For example, stressful life events have been associated with increased disease severity (Garrett, Brantley, Jones, & McKnight 1991; Duffy et al., 1991). More recently, in a review article, Searle and Bennett (2001) concluded that multiple low-level stressors, such as daily hassles, appear to be more salient to disease exacerbations than major life stressors, and this increased disease activity in turn increases psychological distress and symptomatology. Although much of the research has examined stress as a primary psychological factor, other research has demonstrated that patients with IBD exhibit an increased rate of psychological disorders compared to healthy controls and consistent with rates in other chronic illness populations (Guthrie et al., 2002; Kurina, Goldacre, Yeates, & Gill, 2001; Drossman et al., 1991). Further, these psychological disorders are generally nonspecific and represent depression and anxiety symptomatology (Drossman & Ringel, 2003). Children and adolescents with IBD have also shown increased rates of psychological maladjustment (60%), particularly internalizing symptoms (e.g., depression, anxiety), compared to healthy controls (15%; Engstrom, 1992; Szajnberg, Krall, Davis, Treem, & Hyams, 1993), increased rates of depression (14%; Burke, Meyer, Kocoshis, Orenstein, Chandra, Nord, et al., 1989) and anxiety disorders (28%; Burke, Neigut, Kocoshis, Chandra, & Sauer, 1994). In a recent study, adolescents with IBD demonstrated clinically significant social problems and increased anxiety and depressive symptomatology compared to healthy controls (Mackner & Crandall, 2006). Similar to adult IBD research, Mackner and colleagues (2004) concluded that, while children with IBD demonstrate greater psychological and behavioral difficulties, this pathology is consistent with that found in other chronic illness populations. Further, the precise relationship between psychological dysfunction and disease activity remains unclear.

Parents of children/adolescents with IBD have also demonstrated higher rates of psychological distress compared to those of healthy controls (Burke, Neigut, Kocoshis, Chandra, & Sauer, 1994; Engstrom, 1999), and this has been associated with functional disability, depression, and bowel movement frequency in children with IBD (Engstrom, 1999). Similarly, family dysfunction, which has been reported at a higher rate in IBD than in families with healthy children (Engstrom, 1999), has also been associated with physical symptoms (Wood et al., 1989; Tojek, Lumley, Corlis, Ondersma, & Tolia, 2002) and depression (Burke et al., 1989).

Quality of life (QOL) is an important health outcome that has received more attention in the past several years among health care professionals, particularly health psychologists. Research on QOL in IBD has demonstrated results similar to those found in other chronic illness populations. Drossman and Ringel (2003) note that QOL impairment has generally been greater in psychological and social dimensions of QOL than in physical dimensions, and that Crohn's disease patients demonstrate poorer psychosocial QOL than ulcerative colitis patients (Drossman et al., 1991; Drossman, Patrick, Mitchell, Zagami, & Appelbaum, 1989; Farmer, Easley, & Farmer, 1992; Love, Irvine, & Fedorak, 1992). Further, Turnbull and Vallis (1995) found that disease activity alone was not predictive of QOL; however, coping and psychosocial distress combined with disease activity were predictive of QOL. Despite the small sample size in this study, the results are consistent with numerous studies in other populations demonstrating that disease activity alone is not predictive of QOL, but rather psychosocial factors must be taken into account. Quality of life has only recently been examined in pediatric IBD. Research has shown that children/adolescents with IBD have lower QOL in areas including emotional functioning, test/treatments concerns, body image, somatic complaints, autonomy, school absenteeism, and fatigue (Loonan et al., 2002; Loonen, Grootenhuis, Last, de Haan et al., 2002; Loonen, Grootenhuis, Last, Koopman, & Derkx, 2002; Griffiths et al., 1999; Richardson, Griffiths, Miller, & Thomas, 2001), and parents have demonstrated similar QOL impairments (Akobeng et al., 1999). In addition, the relationship between disease severity and QOL in IBD is unclear due to conflicting findings (Loonen, Grootenhuis, Last, de Haan et al., 2002; Shepanski, Markowitz, Mamula, Hurd, & Baldassano, 2004; MacPhee, Hoffenberg, & Feranchak, 1998). Overall, the modest amount and descriptive nature of research on QOL in pediatric IBD leaves many questions unanswered, most importantly the impact of patient psychosocial distress and family dysfunction on QOL.

Interestingly, psychoneuroimmunologic processes have received little attention in IBD research despite the correlation between increased cortisol and depression, memory impairment (Goodyer, Park, & Herbert, 2001), and immune dysfunction, resulting in increased vulnerability to infectious disease (Vedhara et al., 1999). Moreover, animal models have demonstrated effects of stress induction on hypothalamopituitary-adrenal (HPA) axis activity and intestinal inflammation, and increased gut mucosal permeability and inflammation (e.g., Drossman & Ringel, 2003). Unfortunately, the absence of psychophysiological parameters in clinical research does not permit a comprehensive understanding of the biopsychosocial processes in IBD, including antecedents of patient and family dysfunction in IBD and the impact of these factors on salient disease outcome, such as disease severity (Ondersma, Lumley, Corlis, Tojek, & Tolia, 1997) or QOL.

Perhaps the most significant shortcoming in the IBD literature, considering the complex medication and nutritional regimens that both patients and family members must follow, is the lack of research on adherence to medical regimens. Research on adults with IBD suggests that over 40% of patients are nonadherent to medication and that psychological distress plays a significant role in nonadherence (Sewitch et al., 2003). Children/adolescents with IBD have demonstrated nonadherence rates of 52 to 62% (Mackner & Crandall, 2005). Studies in other pediatric populations have demonstrated poorer adherence in children, particularly adolescents (Kovacs et al., 1992; La-Greca, Follansbee, & Skyler, 1990; Anderson, Auslander, Jung, Miller, & Santiago, 1990), with psychological dysfunction (Kovacs, Goldston, Obrosky, & Iyengar, 1992; Jacobson et al., 1990) and general behavioral nonadherence (Christophersen, 1994). Poor family functioning and greater family distress and conflict have also been associated with patient nonadherence (Chaney & Peterson, 1989; Hauser et al., 1990). However, research in pediatric IBD has largely neglected examination of adherence rates and, more importantly, factors such as patient and family dysfunction that may contribute to nonadherence to medical regimens. Finally, a salient yet unexamined area of research regarding adherence in IBD concerns the transition of assisted- to self-management of medical regimens for adolescents and young adults. Patients and practitioners would greatly benefit from guidelines on patient and caregiver characteristics that inform optimal timing of transitioning responsibility of disease management such that young adults with IBD can manage their disease effectively.

LIVER DISEASES

Patients with liver disease and their families face a number of medical and psychosocial challenges related to the disease course and treatment, including liver transplantation, uncertainty regarding morbidity/mortality, functional deficits, psychosocial impairment, and decreased QOL. Research on the psychosocial sequelae of pediatric liver disease is limited, with much of the extant research focused on transplant recipients. Nevertheless, evidence suggests that 43–50% of children with liver disease demonstrate significant emotional and behavioral dysfunction, with 36% of mothers exhibiting significant psychological maladjustment (Bradford, 1994; Adeback, Nemeth, & Fischler, 2003) and family functioning contributing to the psychosocial impairment of these children (Hoffman, Rodrigue, Andres, & Novak, 1995). Children with liver disease demonstrate significantly poorer QOL compared to healthy comparison groups, but comparable QOL to other pediatric chronic illness groups (Bucuvalas et al., 2003; Alonso et al., 2003; Midgley, Bradley, Donohue, Kent, & Alonso, 2000). In one study, patients who had undergone a liver transplant demonstrated increased anxiety compared to healthy controls, whereas those who had not yet been transplanted evidenced decreased perceptions of control over their health compared to transplant recipients and healthy controls (Mastroyannopoulou, Sclare, Baker, & Mowat, 1998). Another study reported that approximately one third of liver transplant recipients demonstrated clinically significant posttraumatic stress disorder symptoms, which was associated with nonadherence in half of those patients (Shemesh et al., 2000). However, one of the measures of nonadherence (i.e., provider estimates) employed in this study is highly unreliable, and the sample size was small. Nevertheless, this study highlighted an understudied yet critical psychological variable in this population. Although the course of pediatric liver disease may be unclear in terms of timing of surgery, morbidity, and mortality, research has yet to examine the impact of perceptions of illness uncertainty on psychosocial outcome in this population despite the saliency of this construct in asthma (Mullins, Chaney, Pace, & Hartman, 1997; Hommel et al., 2003), diabetes (Hoff, Mullins, Chaney, & Hartman, 2003), and cancer (Neville, 1998). In addition, there is an absence of research investigating the role of biological indices of long-term distress in liver disease, despite the correlation between increased cortisol and depression, memory impairment (Goodyer, Park, & Herbert, 2001) and immune dysfunction resulting in increased vulnerability to infectious disease (Vedhara et al., 1999).

Psychosocial issues faced by liver disease patients might also be related to the etiology of their disease or its treatment. For example, HCV patients may have contracted the illness via intravenous drug use, indicating the need to treat the underlying drug addiction as well as the HCV. Research has shown that veterans, a subpopulation in which HCV is overrepresented, are at increased risk for comorbid psychiatric diagnoses. Indeed, 31% of a large sample had a current psychiatric diagnosis, while 86% of that sample had a history of psychiatric diagnosis (el-Serag, Kunik, Richardson, & Rabeneck, 2002). These authors also compared the HCV veteran sample to a non-HCV veteran sample and reported increased rates of depression (45% HCV; 39% non-HCV), posttraumatic stress disorder (33% HCV; 24% non-HCV), other anxiety disorders (40% HCV; 32% non-HCV), psychosis (23% HCV; 20% non-HCV), bipolar disorder (16% HCV; 12% non-HCV), alcohol disorders (77% HCV; 45% non-HCV), and other drug-use disorders (69% HCV; 31% non-HCV). Moreover, both HCV and HBV appear to be overrepresented in individuals with chronic and/or severe mental illnesses, including schizophrenia, schizoaffective disorder, bipolar disorder, and major depressive disorder (Osher, Goldberg, Goodman, & Rosenberg, 2003; Rosenberg et al., 2001). Iatrogenic psychological effects of antiviral treatment have also been reported in the literature. Estimates of depression associated with antiviral treatment range from 2 to 41% (Bonaccacorso et al., 2002; Dieperink, Ho, Thuras, & Willenbring, 2003; Hardy, 1996: Horikawa, Yamazaki, Izumi, & Uchichara, 2003; Janssen, Brouwer, van der Mast, & Schalm, 1994; Kraus, Schafer, Wissmann, Reimer, & Scheurlen, 2003; Miyaoka et al., 1999; Trask, Esper, Riba, & Redman, 2000). Additionally, Kraus and colleagues (2003) reported that 15% of HCV patients demonstrated clinically significant depression prior to initiating interferon alpha-2b treatment, whereas 35% demonstrated significant depression at posttreatment. Another study showed a trend of increasing depression incidence from 4% prior to interferon treatment to 22% at week 4 and 38% at week 12; incidence had decreased to 27% at week 24 (Miyaoka et al., 1999), which might indicate a critical time period for development of depressed mood during interferon treatment. Indeed, Horikawa and colleagues (2003) demonstrated that 74% of patients who developed depressive symptoms during antiviral treatment did so within the first 8 weeks. Further, baseline depression scores have been shown to predict depression severity during peginterferon and ribavirin treatment (Raison et al., 2005). Collectively, these studies indicate that antiviral treatment plays a significant role in the onset and/or maintenance of depressive symptomatology during treatment for HCV, and that there might be a critical time during which treatment of depressed mood would be most beneficial. Other psychological issues that may arise during antiviral treatment include exacerbation of posttraumatic stress symptoms (Maunder, Hunter, & Feinman, 1998) and cognitive impairment; however, deficits in cognitive ability may be only temporary, as subjects were shown to return to baseline functioning at posttreatment (Kraus, Schafer, Wissmann Rimer, & Scheurlen, 2005). Overall, research suggests that individuals with HCV are at high risk for depression prior to antiviral treatment and are also at risk for onset or exacerbation of depressive symptomatology secondary to treatment. Thus, patients are in great need for assessment of psychological functioning and treatment of depression throughout the course of their illness and treatment.

As with HCV patients, concomitant psychosocial issues that may contribute to the etiology of NASH/NAFLD patients include comorbid overweight or obesity. While overweight/obesity might be the focus of behavioral treatment, psychosocial factors that antecede or serve to maintain overweight including depression, low self-esteem, and social skills deficits might also warrant clinical attention. Similarly, chronic alcohol abuse may be the etiologic behavioral issue for many cirrhosis patients, and psychosocial factors related to patients' alcoholism such as depression, posttraumatic stress disorder, and anxiety may require behavioral intervention to ultimately treat the cirrhosis effectively.

The significance of adherence to medical and behavioral regimens applies not only to the treatment of chronic liver disease, but also to posttransplant treatment regimens. Prevalence estimates of nonadherence to immunosuppressive agents range from 9 to 75% (Fennell, Tucker, & Pedersen, 2001; Lurie et al., 2000; Serrano-Ikkos, Lask, Whitehead, & Eisler, 1998). This results in additional health consequences, cost, and health care utilization, and may present health care providers with ethical dilemmas regarding candidacy for retransplantation (Rodrigue & Sobel, 2003). Unfortunately, there is a paucity of research examining barriers to adherence in liver disease and behavioral treatments aimed at improving adherence in both pediatric and adult liver disease populations.

PSYCHOLOGICAL INTERVENTIONS

Psychological interventions to improve health behaviors remain an underdeveloped, yet promising, area of research in IBD and liver disease. The following is a summary of the extant research, and guidelines for assessment and treatment in these illness populations.

INFLAMMATORY BOWEL DISEASE

Psychological interventions for IBD are limited; however, there are some guidelines with respect to assessment and interventions with patients and families. Assessment of patient functioning in IBD should focus on (1) individual factors, such as developmental level and cognitive ability of the patient as well as patient understanding of IBD treatment and disease course, (2) physical effects of IBD unique to the patient and treatment outcomes experienced by the patient, (3) adjustments made by the patient and/or family to provide care, and (4) current versus premorbid psychological/behavioral, academic/work, social, and family functioning, and patient self-care versus assisted care (e.g., Gillman,1994; Banez & Cunningham, 2003). Psychological treatment in IBD patients depends on particular symptomatology of each patient; thus interventions are best if individually tailored. However, some common issues for intervention include (1) patient and family education, which might include working with the medical team to structure how information is presented to optimize patient knowledge acquisition, (2) behavioral treatment of nonadherence, (3) cognitive-behavioral treatment for affective comorbidity such as depression, anxiety, or body image distortion, and (4) stress management/reduction training (e.g., Gillman, 1994).

Specific psychological/behavioral treatments for IBD have focused on improving health outcome via psychotherapeutic intervention. Much of the older treatment studies were marked by methodological limitations including small sample sizes, lack of appropriate controls, and poor designs. However, more recent and scientifically rigorous trials have shown promise. For example, Shaw and Ehrlich (1987) demonstrated reduction in chronic pain in IBD patients who received relaxation training compared to IBD patients in an attention control group. A stress management treatment program utilizing autogenics, personal planning skill training, and communication training resulted in reduced IBD-specific stress and improved physical functioning; however, subjects were not matched on symptom severity, thus confounding these results (Milne, Joachim, & Niedhardt, 1986). Nevertheless, these findings are encouraging. Using a cognitive-behavioral group treatment approach and longitudinal (i.e., 9–month follow-up) design, Mussell and colleagues (2003) demonstrated decreases in disease-related psychological distress at posttreatment and follow-up, with significantly better outcome in female versus male patients. Garcia-Vega and Fernandez-Rodriguez (2004) randomized patients to one of three treatment conditions. Patients receiving stress management training demonstrated significant reductions in tiredness, constipation, abdominal pain, and distension. Those receiving self-directed stress management demonstrated reductions in tiredness and abdominal pain. Patients who received medical treatment alone demonstrated no significant changes, and these group differences were maintained at 12-month follow-up. Treatment in pediatric IBD is quite limited; however, Szigethy and colleagues (2004) have demonstrated reduction in depressive symptoms, improved social functioning, and improved perception of physical health in adolescents who received cognitive-behavioral treatment. In addition, Stark and colleagues (2005) demonstrated significant improvement in adherence to dietary calcium intake in children with IBD using a behavioral treatment program emphasizing parent training in behavior modification techniques and positive reinforcement of health-promoting behavior in children.

LIVER DISEASES

Similar to IBD, psychotherapeutic interventions for liver diseases are scant. Recommendations for treatment depend on the specific liver disease and whether behavioral or lifestyle factors contribute to the onset or maintenance of the disease. Assessment and treatment recommendations for IBD as previously mentioned apply to patients with liver disease as well. Additional recommendations for specific liver diseases are as follows. Parents and siblings of children with biliary atresia can benefit from supportive therapy or participation in support groups. Given the low prevalence of biliary atresia, families are unlikely to find support groups exclusively for this disease; however, support groups for families coping with chronic pediatric illnesses in general would suffice. Since the majority of patients with NASH/NAFLD are also overweight or obese, behavioral treatment to improve diet and reduce weight as well as any comorbid psychological disorder (e.g., depression) is imperative. Hepatitis C patients might benefit from various psychological interventions, depending on the etiology of their HCV and iatrogenic effects of treatment. For example, treatment should be provided for patients who contract HCV from intravenous drug use as well as those who develop depression associated with interferon therapy. Similarly, psychological treatment for alcohol addiction and any comorbid psychological disorder (e.g., posttraumatic stress disorder) should be provided for patients who develop cirrhosis as a result of chronic alcoholism. In addition, liver transplant recipients who are nonadherent to antirejection medical regimens would benefit from behavioral treatment (e.g., Gallucci & Smolinski, 2001). Finally, Rodrigue and colleagues (2003) have argued that psychological assessment and treatment should be an ongoing process from diagnosis through transplantation and posttransplant follow-up. They suggest psychological assessment at 6-month intervals prior to transplant and during the first 2 years posttransplant, followed by annual evaluation thereafter. Assessment and treatment issues would focus on quality of life, adherence, cognitive functioning, psychological comorbidity, and family functioning. Such a comprehensive assessment and treatment approach would undoubtedly improve overall treatment outcome in liver disease and transplant patients.

CASE EXAMPLE

BACKGROUND

Jason was a 13-year-old Caucasian Jewish boy diagnosed with Crohn's disease approximately 2 years prior to being referred to a pediatric psychologist for treatment of depressed mood. He lived with his biological mother, father, and his 10-year-old sister. The family was middle class, and both parents worked full time. Jason's father was a sales representative and his mother worked in marketing for a pharmaceutical company. Jason attended public school and earned a 4.0 grade point average, though his parents' expectations for his performance were simply that he did the best he could.

Jason initially presented to the pediatric gastroenterologist with poor growth, abdominal pain, and diarrhea with occasional blood. He was diagnosed with Crohn's disease and responded well to medical treatment, with decreased inflammation, pain, and diarrhea. However, he was unable to maintain optimal growth despite drinking nutritional supplements to maximize his caloric intake. Both the physician and dietician suspected that Jason was depressed as a result of his poor growth, and referred him to the pediatric psychologist for treatment of his mood and to assist in optimizing his caloric intake via behavior modification.

Jason's parents were very supportive and appeared to have adjusted to their child's illness well since his diagnosis. They were well educated, informed about the medical aspects of Crohn's disease, and attentive to the psychological issues that adolescents and adults with IBD sometimes experience. Jason's sister knew that Jason was diagnosed with Crohn's disease, but was not well informed about the symptoms, treatments, and long-term prognosis. She did not typically ask questions and left her brother alone when he was not feeling well. She also appeared anxious at times to her parents, and complained about how much time her parents spent with Jason rather than her.

During the initial evaluation, Jason exhibited restricted range of affect and reported feeling hopeless, having sleep difficulties, lack of interest in activities he usually enjoyed, and fatigue. He reported that he was disappointed about his poor growth and was concerned that he would not grow any taller. He was also being teased about his size in school and at camp. Jason had approximately three close friends in school, but only saw them between classes and after school. So, he felt little social support. A friend would occasionally defend him when he was teased, but most of the time he had to defend himself. He lacked confidence in his ability to handle these situations appropriately, and often responded with anger. Jason also reported that he did not talk about his IBD with anyone in great detail. His friends did not know he had IBD, and he no longer discussed how he felt with his parents because those interactions became argumentative.

CASE CONCEPTUALIZATION

Based on their report and presentation of symptoms, Jason and his family exhibited three specific areas of focus for psychological treatment. First, he demonstrated depressive symptoms related to his disease. However, some of his depressive symptoms were better explained by disease symptoms (e.g., fatigue). Like most IBD patients, Jason's disease course was characterized by unpredictable symptom exacerbations and variability in severity of symptoms. Further, these symptoms occurred in this manner despite Jason's perceived attempts to adhere well to his medical treatment regimen. In order to maximize control over his illness, he consumed additional supplements. Nevertheless, these efforts were met with failure to maintain an optimal growth trajectory and health, as he experienced an uncontrollable decrease in appetite, weight loss, and growth failure. Second, he experienced routine teasing by his peers at school and camp due to his size, which he attributed to his illness as well. This teasing had further decreased his self-efficacy and confidence in coping with difficult situations. Additionally, Jason had developed pervasive attributions about his likeability via distorted perceptions that most of his peers would laugh and contribute to the teasing during these episodes. Finally, although Jason's family was very supportive and everyone related well with each other, they experienced some difficulty with communication about his disease. His parents would often ask how he was feeling (physically), which became an annoyance to him and resulted in increased tension regarding discussions about his illness. Consequently, Jason began to avoid communication not only about his illness, but about other topics as well (e.g., emotions, peer interactions), resulting in reduced social support. Jason's sister often felt uncertain about how her brother was feeling, even before family communication became problematic. She was concerned about his health and prognosis, but was unsure how to ask those questions. From her perspective, her parents were very concerned about Jason and spent a great deal of time trying to get him to eat more and feel better, so their availability to her was limited. Based on this conceptualization, Jason would be best served by cognitive-behavioral treatment for his depressive symptoms and coping with peer teasing. Family therapy was also necessary to improve communication and understanding of Jason's illness among all family members, with the goal of decreasing tension surrounding his physical and emotional functioning as well as his sister's anxiety about Jason's well-being.

TREATMENT

Initially, treatment focused on coping with peer teasing and treatment of Jason's depressive symptomatology. Peer teasing was addressed first in order to ensure that Jason was not being physically bullied by other adolescents and to provide a brief intervention that would likely improve his self-efficacy. His parents were encouraged to speak with the school officials about the teasing, and Jason was encouraged to talk to teachers or the principal when it occurred. Teasing at camp was approached in the same manner with camp counselors. Next, Jason needed to develop skills both to cope with teasing episodes as well as the negative feelings the episodes generated. Jason spent time during sessions problem solving with the pediatric psychologist how he could decrease the frequency and duration of teasing. He would then test these strategies when teasing would occur. Because he was also under the impression that several peers were laughing at him when he was being teased, he was instructed to observe other students/campers during a teasing episode. During subsequent episodes, he observed that, in fact, other peers were not laughing at him. Further, he found success in decreasing the frequency and duration of episodes by ignoring and walking away from the student/camper teasing him and/or reporting it to a teacher or counselor. He was also successful at using his sense of humor about his height, thus denying those peers further opportunities to tease. With continued success in dealing with teasing as it occurred, Jason's negative feelings and distorted perceptions no longer persisted, and he began to feel more confident about his ability to affect positive change in his life.

Jason's depressive symptoms and disease adjustment difficulties were treated via cognitive-behavioral therapy. Medication was not warranted due to the severity of his symptoms. Initially, treatment focused on affective education and appropriately labeling emotions. Jason primarily responded to stressful situations with anger, which only masked underlying emotions such as sadness, frustration, or anxiety. Next, Jason learned to identify the link between thoughts, emotions, and consequent behaviors. For example, he was able to develop an understanding that thinking he would never feel better, because his symptoms persisted despite taking medicine, resulted in feel-ings of sadness and helplessness. This in turn led to decreased attempts to manage his illness and consequently poorer disease functioning. Identifying these automatic thoughts and other cognitive distortions was a critical aspect of his treatment. He re-ceived homework assignments such as thought monitoring and development of al-ternative explanations/attributions for negative events. This provided consistent op-portunities outside of therapy to practice these new cognitive skills and incorporate them in his daily behavior. The next step for Jason was to find appropriate outlets for him to express his emotions. While therapy provided one outlet, he needed to estab-lish those types of relationships with other people in his life. Communication was a fo-cus of family therapy intervention, as discussed in the following section. However, Ja-son also demonstrated poor communication with his friends, resulting in diminished social support. He acknowledged that he had not discussed his disease with any friends out of embarrassment and fear that they would not understand and begin to tease him like other adolescents. After discussing the nature and quality of his friend-ships and problem solving how to approach talking with his friends about his illness in a safe manner (e.g., one-to-one talks at his home), he was able to disclose personal information he had previously kept secret from his friends. This was an important step in his treatment because he began to understand the value of social support in coping with his illness, and gained confidence in his ability to discuss sensitive issues with-out feeling embarrassed.

As previously mentioned, Jason and his family had developed dysfunctional pat-terns of communication. While he and his parents could discuss general topics, they were no longer able to talk about issues related to his disease (e.g., taking medication, drinking supplements) without arguing and Jason becoming upset. This also indi-cated a separate but related issue, that Jason had significant difficulty adhering to his treatment regimen. Additionally, Jason's parents reported that his sister exhibited some anxiety about Jason's illness and prognosis and that she felt ignored by them. During a family session, Jason's sister was encouraged to ask her brother questions that she was hesitant to ask at home and to talk to her parents about her feeling that she was receiving less attention than Jason. With guidance, she was able to ask her questions, which Jason was comfortable answering since he knew she was concerned. She also received reassurance from her parents regarding her perceived differential at-tention. Further, her parents were encouraged to schedule some special time with her weekly to avoid relapse of these feelings. Conflict resolution between Jason and his parents focused initially on identifying and together expressing each person's percep-tion of the cause of their conflict. Jason reported that his parents were annoying him by asking him how he was feeling all the time and nagging him about eating more and drinking more supplements. His parents reported that they felt sometimes he would refuse to take his medication and maintain adequate caloric intake. In response to these concerns, Jason and his parents were instructed to set aside family time each day (e.g., dinner time) during which talking about IBD was not allowed. Further, with the mutual understanding that Jason would let his parents know when he was not feeling well, his parents were encouraged to stop inquiring about his well-being unless they observed signs of his disease symptoms worsening (e.g., abdominal cramping/pain). Since the majority of the conflict centered on Jason's disease management, interven-tions to improve his adherence to his treatment regimen were employed. First, in an effort to maximize his supplement consumption, a schedule of when he would drink supplements was developed such that he would allow time between supplements and avoid becoming frustrated by being full and unable to drink more. Second, he set goals that he perceived to be realistic and regularly modified these goals to be more challenging. Third, palatability was improved by increasing the flavor variety of the supplements as well as keeping them very cold. Finally, Jason's parents were instructed on use of a token economy system to improve the number of supplements consumed each day as well as his adherence to medication. Jason improved his supplement consumption and medication adherence in response to these interventions. Yet, he was unable to maximize his growth potential with supplements alone. Thus, nasogastric tube feeds were recommended by the gastroenterologist as an alternative to supplements. While this was a necessary treatment, it produced significant anxiety in Jason. Exposure therapy and repeated practice of inserting the tube at home significantly reduced this anxiety.

In summary, after approximately 20 sessions, Jason and his family were able to make significant improvements in their psychological functioning. Jason improved his coping with teasing, and he no longer demonstrated clinically significant depressed mood. He felt more confident in coping with the unpredictability of his illness. His social support was enhanced by discussing his illness with his friends. Jason and his family were able to communicate much more effectively and his adherence to his treatment regimen improved considerably. Jason's sister felt comfortable talking to Jason, and their parents communicated information about his illness more appropriately to her. Finally, Jason's health improved, in part by his increased adherence as well as accelerated growth via nasogastric tube feeds.

REFERENCES

Adeback, P., Nemeth, A., & Fischler, B. (2003). Cognitive and emotional outcome after pediatric liver transplantation. *Pediatric Transplantation, 7*, 385–389.

Akobeng, A. K., Miller, V., Firth, D., Suresh-Babu, M. V., Mirajkar, V., Mir, P., et al. (1999). Quality of life of parents and siblings of children with inflammatory bowel disease. *Journal of Pediatric Gastroenterology and Nutrition, 28*(4), S40–S42.

Alonso, E. M., Neighbors, K., Mattson, C., Sweet, E., Ruch-Ross, H., Berry, C., et al. (2003). Functional outcomes of pediatric liver transplantation. *Journal of Pediatric Gastroenterology and Nutrition, 37*, 155–160.

Anderson, B. J., Auslander, W. F., Jung, K. C., Miller, J. P., & Santiago, J. V. (1990). Assessing family sharing of diabetes responsibilities. *Journal of Pediatric Psychology, 15*, 477–492.

Banez, G. A., & Cunningham, C. (2003). Pediatric gastrointestinal disorders: Recurrent abdominal pain, inflammatory bowel disease, and rumination disorder/cyclic vomiting. In M. C. Roberts (Ed.), *Handbook of Pediatric Psychology* (3rd ed., pp. 462–478). New York: Guilford.

Baum, A., Herberman, H., & Cohen, L. (1995). Managing stress and managing illness: Survival and quality of life in chronic disease. *Journal of Clinical Psychology in Medical Settings, 2*(4), 309–333.

Boberg, K. M. (2002). Prevalence and epidemiology of autoimmune hepatitis. *Clinics in Liver Disease, 6*(3), 635–647.

Bonaccorso, S., Marino, V., Biondi, M., Grimaldi, F., Ippoliti, F., & Maes, M. (2002). Depression induced by treatment with interferon-alpha in patients affected by hepatitis C virus. *Journal of Affective Disorders, 72*, 237–241.

Borowsky, S. A., Strome, L., & Lott, E. (1982). Continued heavy drinking and survival in alcoholic cirrhosis, *Gastroenterology, 80,* 1405–1433.

Bradford, R. (1994). Children with liver disease: Maternal reports of their adjustment and the influence of disease severity on outcomes. *Child: Care, Health & Development, 20*(6), 393–407.

Bucuvalas, J. C., Britto, M., Krug, S., Ryckman, F. C., Atherton, H., Alonso, M. P., et al. (2003). Health-related quality of life in pediatric liver transplant recipients: A single-center study. *Liver Transplantation, 9*(1), 62–71.

Burke, P., Meyer, V., Kocoshis, S., Orenstein, D. M., Chandra, R., Nord, D. J., et. al. (1989). Depression and anxiety in pediatric inflammatory bowel disease and cystic fibrosis. *Journal of the American Academy of Child and Adolescent Psychiatry, 28,* 948–951.

Burke, P., Meyer, V., Kocoshis, S., Orenstein, D. M., Chandra, R., & Sauer, J. (1989). Obsessive-compulsive symptoms in childhood inflammatory bowel disease and cystic fibrosis. *Journal of the American Academy of Child and Adolescent Psychiatry, 28,* 525–527.

Burke, P., Neigut, D., Kocoshis, S., Chandra, R., & Sauer, J. (1994). Correlates of depression in new onset pediatric inflammatory bowel disease. *Child Psychiatry and Human Development, 25,* 275–283.

Casati, J. & Toner, B. B. (2000). Psychosocial aspects of inflammatory bowel disease. *Biomedicine and Pharmacotherapy, 54,* 388–393.

Centers for Disease Control and Prevention (CDC). (2006a). *Viral Hepatitis A fact-sheet.* Retrieved March 4, 2007, from http://www.cdc.gov/ncidod/diseases/hepatitis/a/fact.htm

Centers for Disease Control and Prevention (CDC). (2006b). *Viral Hepatitis B fact-sheet.* Retrieved March 4, 2007, from http://www.cdc.gov/ncidod/diseases/hepatitis/b/fact.htm

Centers for Disease Control and Prevention (CDC). (2006c). *Viral Hepatitis C fact-sheet.* Retrieved March 4, 2007, from http://www.cdc.gov/ncidod/diseases/hepatitis/c/fact.htm

Centers for Disease Control and Prevention (CDC). (2006d). *Viral Hepatitis D fact-sheet.* Retrieved March 4, 2007, from http://www.cdc.gov/ncidod/diseases/hepatitis/d/fact.htm

Centers for Disease Control and Prevention (CDC). (2006e). *Viral Hepatitis E fact-sheet.* Retrieved March 4, 2007, from http://www.cdc.gov/ncidod/diseases/hepatitis/e/fact.htm

Chaney, J. M., & Peterson, L. (1989). Family variables and disease management in juvenile rheumatoid arthritis. *Journal of Pediatric Psychology, 14,* 389–404.

Christophersen, E. R. (1994). *Pediatric compliance: A guide for the primary care physician.* New York: Plenum.

Dieperink, E., Ho, S. B., Thuras, P., & Willenbring, M. L. (2003). A prospective study of neuropsychiatric symptoms associated with interferon-alpha-2b and ribavirin therapy for patients with chronic hepatitis C. *Psychosomatics: Journal of Consultation Liaison Psychiatry, 44,* 104–112.

Drossman, D. A., Lesserman, J., Mitchell, C. M., Li, Z., Zagami, E. A., & Patrick, D. L., (1991). Health status and health care use in persons with inflammatory bowel disease: A national sample. *Digestive Diseases and Sciences, 36,* 1746–1755.

Drossman, D. A., Patrick, D. L., Mitchell, C. M., Zagami, E. A., & Appelbaum, M. I. (1989). Health related quality of life in inflammatory bowel disease: Functional status and patient worries and concerns. *Digestive Diseases and Sciences, 34,* 1379–1386.

Drossman, D. A., & Ringel, Y. (2003). Psychosocial factors in ulcerative colitis and Crohn's disease. In R. B. Sartor & W. Sandborn (Eds.), *Kirsner's inflammatory bowel disease* (6th ed., pp. 340–356). Philadelphia: Saunders.

Duffy, L. C., Zielezny, M. A., Marshall, J. R., Byers, T. E., Weiser, M. M., Phillips, et al. (1991). Relevance of major stress events as an indicator of disease activity prevalence in inflammatory bowel disease. *Behavioral Medicine, 17,* 101–110.

el-Serag, H. B., Kunik, M., Richardson, P. & Rabeneck, L. (2002). Psychiatric disorders among veterans with hepatitis C infection. *Gastroenterology, 123,* 476–482.

Engel, G. L. (1955). Studies of ulcerative colitis. III. The nature of the psychologic process. *American Journal of Medicine, 19*, 231–256.

Engstrom, I. (1992). Mental health and psychological functioning in children and adolescents with inflammatory bowel disease: A comparison with children having other chronic illnesses and with healthy children. *Journal of Child Psychology and Psychiatry, 33*, 563–582.

Engstrom, I. (1999). Inflammatory bowel disease in children and adolescents: Mental health and family functioning. *Journal of Pediatric Gastroenterology and Nutrition, 28*, S28–S33.

Farmer, R. G., Easley, K. A., & Farmer, J. M. (1992). Quality of life assessment by patients with inflammatory bowel disease. *Cleveland Clinic Journal of Medicine, 59*, 35–42.

Fawzy, F. I., Fawzy, N. W., Hyun, C. S., Elashoff, R., Guthrie, D., Fahey, J. L., et al. (1993). Malignant melanoma: Effects of an early structured psychiatric intervention, coping, and affective state on recurrence and survival 6 years later. *Archives of General Psychiatry, 50*, 681–689.

Fennell, R. S., Tucker, C., & Pedersen, T. (2001). Demographic and medical predictors of medication compliance among ethnically difference pediatric renal transplant patients. *Pediatric Transplantation, 5*, 343–348.

Gallucci, G., & Smolinski, J. (2001). Treatment contracts for patients with hepatitis C, psychiatric illness, and substance abuse. *Psychosomatics: Journal of Consultation Liaison Psychiatry, 42*, 353–355.

Garcia-Vega, E., & Fernandez-Rodriguez, C. (2004). A stress management programme for Crohn's disease. *Behaviour Research and Therapy, 42*, 367–383.

Garrett, V. D., Brantley, P. J., Jones, G. N., & McKnight, G. T. (1991). The relationship between daily stress and Crohn's disease. *Journal of Behavioral Medicine, 14*, 87–96.

Gillman, J. B. (1994). Inflammatory bowel diseases: Psychological issues. In R. A. Olson, L. L Mullins, J. B. Gillman, & J. M. Chaney (Eds.), *The sourcebook of pediatric psychology* (pp. 135–144). Needham Heights, MA: Allyn and Bacon.

Goodyer, I. M., Park, R. J., & Herbert, J. (2001). Psychosocial and endocrine features of chronic first-episode major depression in 8–16 year olds. *Biological Psychiatry, 50*, 351–357.

Griffiths, A. M., Nicholas, D., Smith, C., Munk, M., Stephens, D., Durno, C., et al. (1999). Development of a quality of life index for pediatric inflammatory bowel disease: Dealing with differences related to age and IBD type. *Journal of Pediatric Gastroenterology and Nutrition, 28*, S46–S52.

Guthrie, E., Jackson, J., Shjaffer, J., Thompson, D., Tomenson, B., & Creed, F. (2002). Psychological disorder and severity of inflammatory bowel disease predict health-related quality of life in ulcerative colitis and Crohn's disease. *American Journal of Gastroenterology, 97*, 1994–1999.

Hardy, P. (1996). Depressive disorders and interferon alpha. *Gastroenterologie clinique et biologique, 20*, 255–257.

Harrison, S. A., & DiBisceglie, A. M. (2003). Advances in the understanding and treatment of nonalcoholic fatty liver disease. *Drugs, 63*, 2379–2394.

Hauser, S., Jacobson, A., Lavori, P., Wolfsdorf, J., Herskowitz, R., Milley, J., et al. (1990). Adherence among children and adolescents with insulin-dependent diabetes mellitus over a four-year longitudinal follow-up: II. Immediate and long-term linkages with the family milieu. *Journal of Pediatric Psychology, 15*, 511–526.

Hoff, A. L., Mullins, L. L., Chaney, J. M., & Hartman, V. L. (2003). Illness uncertainty, perceived control, and psychological distress among adolescents with Type I diabetes. *Research and Theory in Nursing Practice, 16*, 223–236.

Hoffman, R. G., Rodrigue, J. R., Andres, J. M., & Novak, D. A. (1995). Moderating effects of family functioning on the social adjustment of children with liver disease. *Children's Health Care, 24*(2), 107–117.

Hommel, K. A., Chaney, J. M., Wagner, J. L., White, M. W., Hoff, A. L., & Mullins, L. L. (2003). Anxiety and depression in older adolescents with long-standing asthma: The role of illness uncertainty. *Children's Health Care, 32*(1), 51–63.

Horikawa, N., Yamazaki, T., Izumi, N., & Uchihara, M. (2003). Incidence and clinical course of major depression in patients with chronic hepatitis C undergoing interferon-alpha therapy: A prospective study. *General Hospital Psychiatry, 25*(1), 34–38.

Jacobson, A. M., Hauser, S. T., Lavori, P., Wolfsdorf, J. I., Herskowitz, R. D., Milley, J. E., et al. (1990). Adherence among children and adolescents with insulin-dependent diabetes mellitus over a four-year longitudinal follow-up: I. The influence of patient coping and adjustment. *Journal of Pediatric Psychology, 15*, 511–526.

Janssen, H. L., Brouwer, J. T., van der Mast, R. C., & Schalm, S. W. (1994). Suicide associated with alfa-interferon therapy for chronic viral hepatitis. *Journal of Hepatology, 21*, 241–243.

Kovacs, M., Goldston, D., Obrosky, D. S., & Iyengar, S. (1992). Prevalence and predictors of pervasive noncompliance with medical treatment among youths with insulin- dependent diabetes mellitus. *Journal of the American Academy of Child and Adolescent Psychiatry, 31*, 1112–1119.

Kraus, M. R., Schafer, A., Faler, H., Csef, H., & Scheurlen, M. (2003). Psychiatric symptoms in patients with chronic hepatitis C receiving interferon alfa-2b therapy. *Journal of Clinical Psychiatry, 64*, 708–715.

Kraus, M. R., Schafer, A., Wissmann, S., Reimer, P., & Scheurlen, M. (2005). Neurocognitive changes in patients with hepatitis C receiving interferon alfa-2b and ribavirin. *Clinical Pharmacology and Therapeutics, 77*, 90–100.

Kurina, L. M., Goldacre, M. J., Yeates, D., & Gill, L. E. (2001). Depression and anxiety in people with inflammatory bowel disease. *Journal of Epidemiology and Community Health, 55*, 716–720.

LaGreca, A. M., Follansbee, D., & Skyler, J. S. (1990). Developmental and behavioral aspects of diabetes management in youngsters. *Children's Health Care, 19*, 132–137.

Langholtz, E., Munkholm, P., Krasilnikoff, P. A., & Binder, V. (1997). Inflammatory bowel diseases with onset in childhood: Clinical features, morbidity, and mortality in a regional cohort. *Scandinavian Journal of Gastroenterology, 32*, 139–147.

Lazarus, R. S., & Folkman, S. (1984). Coping and adaptation. In W. D. Gentry (Ed.), *Handbook of behavioral medicine* (pp. 282–325). New York: Guilford.

Lindberg, E., Lindquist, B., Holmquist, L., & Hildebrand, H. (2000). Inflammatory bowel disease in children and adolescents in Sweden, 1984–1995. *Journal of Pediatric Gastroenterology and Nutrition, 30*, 259–264.

Loonen, H. J., Derkx, B. H. F., Koopman, H. M., & Heymans, H. S. (2002). Are parents able to rate the symptoms and quality of life of their offspring with IBD? *Inflammatory Bowel Diseases, 8*, 270–276.

Loonen, H. J., Grootenhuis, M. A., Last, B. F., de Haan, R. J., Bouquet, J., & Derkx, B. H. F. (2002). Measuring quality of life in children with inflammatory bowel disease: The Impact-II (NL). *Quality of Life Research, 11*, 47–56.

Loonen, H. J., Grootenhuis, M. A., Last, B. F., Koopman, H. M., & Derkx, B. H. F. (2002). Quality of life in paediatric inflammatory bowel disease measured by a generic and disease-specific questionnaire. *Acta Paediatrica, 91*, 348–354.

Love, J. R., Irvine, E. J., & Fedorak, R. N. (1992). Quality of life in inflammatory bowel disease. *Journal of Clinical Gastroenterology, 14*, 15–19.

Lurie, S., Shemesh, E., Sheiner, P. A., Emre, S., Tindle, H. L., Melchionna, L., & Shneider, B. L. (2000). Non-adherence in pediatric liver transplant recipients—an assessment of risk factors and natural history. *Pediatric Transplantation, 4*, 200–206.

Mackner, L. M., & Crandall, W. V. (2005). Oral medication adherence in pediatric inflammatory bowel disease. *Inflammatory Bowel Diseases, 11*(11), 1006–1012.

Mackner, L. M., & Crandall, W. V. (2006). Brief report: Psychosocial adjustment in adolescents with inflammatory bowel disease. *Journal of Pediatric Psychology, 31*(3), 281–285.

Mackner, L. M., Crandall, W. V., & Szigethy, E. M. (2006). Psychosocial functioning in pediatric inflammatory bowel disease. *Inflammatory Bowel Diseases, 12*(3), 239–244.

Mackner, L. M., Sisson, D. P., & Crandall, W. V. (2004). Review: Psychosocial issues in pediatric inflammatory bowel disease. *Journal of Pediatric Psychology, 29*(4), 243–257.

MacPhee, M., Hoffenberg, E. J., & Feranchak, A. (1998). Quality of life factors in adolescent inflammatory bowel disease. *Inflammatory Bowel Diseases, 4*, 6–11.

Mastroyannopoulou, K., Sclare, I., Baker, A., & Mowat, A. P. (1998). Psychological effects of liver disease and transplantation. *European Journal of Pediatrics, 157*, 856–860.

Maunder, R. G., Hunter, J. J., & Feinman, S. V. (1998). Interferon treatment of hepatitis C associated with symptoms of PTSD. *Psychosomatics, 39*, 461–464.

McClung, H. J. (1994). Inflammatory bowel diseases. In R. A. Olson, L. L. Mullins, J. B. Gillman, & J. M. Chaney (Eds.), *The sourcebook of pediatric psychology* (pp. 130–149). Needham Heights, MA: Allyn and Bacon.

McKegney, F. P., Gordon, R. O., & Levine, S. M. (1970). A psychosomatic comparison of patients with ulcerative colitis and Crohn's disease. *Psychosomatic Medicine, 32*(2), 153–166.

Midgley, D. E., Bradlee, T. A., Donohoe, C., Kent, K. P., & Alonso, E. M. (2000). Health related quality of life in long-term survivors of pediatric liver transplantation. *Liver Transplantation, 6*(3), 333–339.

Milne, B., Joachim, G., & Niedhardt, J. (1986). A stress management programme for inflammatory bowel disease patients. *Journal of Advanced Nursing, 11*(5), 561–567.

Miyaoka, H., Otsubo, T., Kamijima, K., Ishii, M., Onuki, M., & Mitamura, K. (1999). Depression from interferon therapy in patients with hepatitis C. *The American Journal of Psychiatry, 156*, 1120.

Mullins, L. L., Chaney, J. M., Pace, T. M., & Hartman, V. L. (1997). Illness uncertainty, attributional style, and psychological adjustment in older adolescents and young adults with asthma. *Journal of Pediatric Psychology, 22*, 871–880.

Murray, C. (1930). Psychogenic factors in the etiology of ulcerative colitis and bloody diarrhea. *American Journal of Medical Science, 180*, 239.

Mussell, M., Bocker, U., Nagel, N., Olbrich, R., & Singer, M. V. (2003). Reducing psychological distress in patients with inflammatory bowel disease by cognitive-behavioral treatment: Exploratory study of effectiveness. *Scandinavian Journal of Gastroenterology, 38*(7), 755–762.

National Institutes of Health (NIH): National Digestive Diseases Information Clearinghouse. (2006a). *Autoimmune hepatitis.* Retrieved February 24, 2007, from http://digestive.niddk.nih.gov/ddiseases/pubs/autoimmunehep/index.htm

National Institutes of Health (NIH): National Digestive Diseases Information Clearinghouse. (2006b). *Biliary atresia.* Retrieved February 24, 2007, from http://www.digestive.niddk.nih.gov/ddiseases/pubs/atresia/

National Institutes of Health (NIH): National Digestive Diseases Information Clearinghouse. (2006c). *Chronic hepatitis C: Current disease management.* Retrieved February 24, 2007, from http://digestive.niddk.nih.gov/ddiseases/pubs/chronichepc/index.htm

National Institutes of Health (NIH): National Digestive Diseases Information Clearinghouse. (2006d). *Cirrhosis of the liver.* Retrieved February 24, 2007, from http://digestive.niddk.nih.gov/ddiseases/pubs/cirrhosis/index.htm

National Institutes of Health (NIH): National Digestive Diseases Information Clearinghouse.

(2006e). *Crohn's disease.* Retrieved February 24, 2007, from http://digestive.niddk.nih.gov/ddiseases/pubs/crohns/

National Institutes of Health (NIH): National Digestive Diseases Information Clearinghouse. (2006f). *Nonalcoholic steatohepatitis.* Retrieved February 24, 2007, from http://digestive.niddk.nih.gov/ddiseases/pubs/nash/

National Institutes of Health (NIH): National Digestive Diseases Information Clearinghouse. (2006g). *Primary sclerosing cholangitis.* Retrieved February 24, 2007, from http://digestive.niddk.nih.gov/ddiseases/pubs/primarysclerosingcholangitis/

National Institutes of Health (NIH): National Digestive Diseases Information Clearinghouse. (2006h). *Ulcerative colitis.* Retrieved February 24, 2007, from http://digestive.niddk.nih.gov/ddiseases/pubs/colitis/

National Institutes of Health (NIH): National Digestive Diseases Information Clearinghouse. (2006i). *Viral hepatitis: A through E and beyond.* Retrieved February 24, 2007, from http://digestive.niddk.nih.gov/ddiseases/pubs/viralhepatitis/index.htm

Neville, K. (1998). The relationship among uncertainty, social support, and psychological distress in adolescents recently diagnosed with cancer. *Journal of Pediatric Oncology Nursing, 15,* 37–46.

Ondersma, S. J., Lumley, M. A., Corlis, M. E., Tojek, T. M., & Tolia, V. (1997). Adolescents with inflammatory bowel disease: The roles of negative affectivity and hostility in subjective versus objective health. *Journal of Pediatric Psychology, 22,* 723–738.

Osher, C., Goldberg, R. W., Goodman, L. A., & Rosenberg, S. D. (2003). Hepatitis C and individuals with serious mental illness. *Psychiatric Annals, 33,* 394–400.

Prugh, D. (1951). The influence of emotional factors in the clinical course of ulcerative colitis. *Gastroenterology, 18,* 339–354.

Raison, C. L., Borisov, A. S., Broadwell, S. D., Capuron, L., Woolwine, B. J., Jacobson, I. M., et al. (2005). Depression during pegylated interferon-alphaplus ribavirin therapy: Prevalence and prediction. *The Journal of Clinical Psychiatry, 66,* 41–48.

Rapoff, M. A. (1999). Adherence to pediatric medical regimens. New York: Kluwer Academic.

Rice, H. E., & Chuang, E. (1999). Current management of pediatric inflammatory bowel disease. *Seminars in Pediatric Surgery, 8*(4), 221–228.

Richardson, G., Griffiths, A. M., Miller, V., & Thomas, A. G. (2001). Quality of life in inflammatory bowel disease: A cross-cultural comparison of English and Canadian children. *Journal of Pediatric Gastroenterology and Nutrition, 32,* 573–578.

Rodrigue, J. R., & Sobel, A. B. (2003). Pediatric organ transplantation in the 21st century: Emerging clinical, ethical, and research issues. In M. C. Roberts (Ed.), *Handbook of pediatric psychology* (3rd ed., pp. 433–450). New York: Guilford.

Rosenberg, S. D., Goodman, L. A., Osher, F. C., Swartz, M. S., Essock, S. M., Butterfield, M. I., et al. (2001). Prevalence of HIV, hepatitis B, and hepatitis C in people with severe mental illness. *American Journal of Public Health, 91,* 31–37.

Schenker, S. (1984). Alcoholic liver disease: Evaluation of natural history and prognostic factors. *Hepatology, 4,* 36–43S.

Searle, A. & Bennett, P. (2001). Psychological factors and inflammatory bowel disease: A review of a decade of literature. *Psychology, Health & Medicine, 6*(2), 121–135.

Serrano-Ikkos, E., Lask, B., Whitehead, B., & Eisler, I. (1998). Incomplete adherence after pediatric heart and heart-lung transplantation. *Journal of Heart and Lung Transplantation, 17*(12), 1177–1183.

Sewitch, M. J., Abrahamowicz, M., Barkun, A., Bitton, A., Wild, G. E., Cohen, A., et al. (2003). Patient nonadherence to medication in inflammatory bowel disease. *The American Journal of Gastroenterology; 98*(7), 1535–1544.

Shaw, L. & Ehrlich, A. (1987). Relaxation training as a treatment for chronic pain caused by ulcerative colitis. *Pain, 29*(3), 287–293.

Shemesh, E., Lurie, S., Stuber, M. L., Emre, S., Patel, Y., Vohra, P., Aromando, M., & Shneider, B. L. (2000). A pilot study of posttraumatic stress and nonadherence in pediatric liver transplant recipients. *Pediatrics, 105*(2), e29.

Shepanski, M. A., Markowitz, J. E., Mamula, P., Hurd, L. B., & Baldassano, R. N. (2004). Is an abbreviated Pediatric Crohn's Disease Activity Index better than the original? *Journal of Pediatric Gastroenterology and Nutrition, 39*(1), 68–72.

Stark, L. J., Hommel, K. A., Mackner, L. M., Janicke, D. M., Davis, A. M., Pfefferkorn, M., et al. (2005). Randomized trial comparing two methods of increasing dietary calcium intake in children with inflammatory bowel disease. *Journal of Pediatric Gastroenterology and Nutrition, 40*, 501–507.

Stinson, F. S., Grant, B. F., & Dufour, M. C. (2001). The critical dimension of ethnicity in liver cirrhosis mortality statistics. *Alcoholism, Clinical and Experimental Research, 25*(8), 1181–1187.

Szajnberg, N., Krall, V., Davis, P., Treem, W., & Hyams, J. (1993). Psychopathology and relationship measures in children with inflammatory bowel disease and their parents. *Child Psychiatry and Human Development, 23*, 215–232.

Szigethy, E., Whitton, S. W., Levy-Warren, A., DeMasso, D. R., Weisz, J., & Beardslee, W. R. (2004). Cognitive-behavioral therapy for depression in adolescents with inflammatory bowel disease: A pilot study. *Journal of the American Academy of Child and Adolescent Psychniatry, 43*(12), 1469–1477.

Tojek, T. M., Lumley, M. A., Corlis, M., Ondersma, S., & Tolia, V. (2002). Maternal correlates of health status in adolescents with inflammatory bowel disease. *Journal of Psychosomatic Research, 52*, 173–179.

Trask, P. C., Esper, P., Riba, M., & Redman, B. (2000). Psychiatric side effects of interferon therapy: prevalence, proposed mechanisms, and future directions. *Journal of Clinical Oncology, 18*, 2316–2326.

Turnbull, G. K. & Vallis, T. M. (1995). Quality of life in inflammatory bowel disease: The interaction of disease activity with psychosocial function. *The American Journal of Gastroenterology, 90*(9), 1450–1454.

Vedhara, K., Cox, N. K. M., Wilcock, G. K., Perks, P., Hunt, M., Anderson, S., et al. (1999). Chronic stress in elderly carers of dementia patients and antibody response to influenza vaccination. *The Lancet, 353*, 627–631.

Wang, R. T. (2003). Is weigh reduction an effective therapy for nonalcoholic fatty liver? A systematic review. *American Journal of Medicine, 115*, 554–555.

Wood, B., Watkins, J. B., Boyle, J. T., Nogueira, J., Zimand, E., & Carroll, L. (1989). The "psychosomatic family" model: An empirical and theoretical analysis. *Family Process, 28*, 399–417.

Worthington, J., & Chapman, R. (2006). Primary sclerosing cholangitis. *Orphanet Journal of Rare Diseases, 1*(41), e1–7.

PART IV

SPECIAL TOPICS

CHAPTER 15

Chronic Pain

JOHN D. OTIS and DONNA B. PINCUS

INTRODUCTION

Although pain is typically a transient experience, for some people, pain persists past
the point where it is considered adaptive and results in emotional distress, impaired
occupational and social functioning, and increased use of health care system resources. For example, individuals who experience prolonged pain often report that
pain interferes with their ability to engage in occupational, social, or recreational activities that they previously found enjoyable. Their inability to engage in these reinforcing activities may contribute to increased social isolation, negative moods such as
feelings of worthlessness and depression, and physical deconditioning, all of which in
turn can contribute to a person's experience of pain. Over time, these types of negative
cognitive and behavioral patterns can become highly resistant to change.

Pain is currently defined as an unpleasant sensory and emotional experience associated with actual or potential tissue damage, or described in terms of such damage.
One way in which the experience of pain can be described is in terms of its duration.
Pain that is short-lived and resolves on its own over time, such as pain associated with
a minor burn, cut, or a broken bone is referred to as *acute pain*. Pain that persists for an
extended period of time (i.e., months or years), that accompanies a disease process, or
that is associated with a bodily injury that has not resolved over time may be referred
to as *chronic* pain (International Association for the Study of Pain [IASP], 1994).

PREVALENCE

Chronic pain is a major public health concern in the United States. The National Institute of Health identified chronic pain as the costliest medical problem in America, impacting nearly 100 million individuals (Byrne & Hochwarter, 2006). More recently, according to the Center for Disease Control and Prevention's annual report, one in four
adults say they suffered from a day-long episode of pain in the past month, and one in
ten adults reported pain lasting 1 year or more (CDC, 2006). Over 20% of all medical
visits and 10% of all drug sales are pain related (Max, 2003). In occupational contexts,
chronic pain is not only a significant source of absenteeism but also a major factor in
reducing productivity while at work. Indeed, approximately half of all employees experience pain while on the job, with individuals whose work involves repetitive move-

ment or heavy lifting being impacted in greater numbers (Byrne & Hochwarter). It has been estimated that pain results in $79 billion annually in lost worker productivity (Max). A recent study estimated that the total health care expenditures for back pain alone reached over $90.7 billion in 1998 (Xuemei, Pietrobon, Sun, Liu, & Hey, 2004). Overall, the total direct and indirect costs of chronic pain in the United States have been estimated to be between $150 and $260 billion annually (Byrne & Hochwarter). These statistics led the 108th U.S. Congress to formally declare the 10-year period beginning January 1, 2001, the "Decade of Pain Control and Research" (CDC).

TYPES OF PAIN

Pain can be divided into two broad categories: *nociceptive* pain and *neuropathic* pain. There are two types of nociceptive pain: somatic and visceral pain. Somatic pain is caused by the activation of pain receptors on the surface of the body, such as the skin (cutaneous tissues) or tissues that are deeper, such as muscle (musculoskeletal tissues). When pain occurs in the musculoskeletal tissues, it is called *deep somatic pain*. Deep somatic pain is usually described as "dull" or "aching" but localized. This type of pain is often expressed by people who overdo it and strain muscles when performing physical activity or exercising. Surface somatic pain is usually sharper and may have a burning or pricking quality. Common causes of surface somatic pain include postsurgical pain or pain related to a cut or burn. Viscera refers to the internal areas of the body that are enclosed within a cavity. Visceral pain is caused by activation of pain receptors resulting from infiltration, compression, extension, or stretching of the chest, abdominal, or pelvic viscera. Visceral pain is not well localized and is usually described as "pressure-like, deep squeezing." Examples of visceral pain include pain related to cancer, bone fracture, or bone cancer.

Neuropathic pain is a neurological disorder resulting from damage to nerves that carry information about pain. Neuropathic pain is reported to feel different from somatic or visceral pain and is often described using words such as "shooting," "electric," "stabbing," or "burning." It may be felt traveling along a nerve path from the spine into the arms and hands or into the buttocks or legs. Neuropathic pain has very different medication treatment options from other types of pain. For example, opioids (e.g., morphine) and nonsteroidal anti-inflammatory medications (NSAIDS; e.g., ibuprofen) are usually not effective in relieving neuropathic pain. Medication treatments for neuropathic pain also include nerve block injections and a variety of interventions generally used for chronic pain. Examples of neuropathic pain conditions include phantom limb pain, post-herpetic neuralgias, and other painful neuropathies (e.g., diabetes or alcohol related).

SPECIFIC CHRONIC PAIN CONDITIONS

Pain can occur in many parts of the body, each with its own prevalence, patterns, and presenting characteristics. However, there are a number of pain conditions that are more common than others. Chronic low back pain (CLBP) is the most common chronic pain condition, impacting 15 to 45% of adults annually and at least 70% of adults over a lifetime (Andersson, 1997). Back pain is the most common cause of job-related disability and a leading contributor to missed work. Most low back pain follows injury or trauma to the back, but pain may also be caused by degenerative conditions such as arthritis or disc disease (protruding, herniated, or ruptured disc), sciatica, osteoporosis, or other bone diseases. Chronic low back pain is often associated with affective distress and disability; however, research indicates that cognitive-behavior therapy (CBT) can be an effective treatment for chronic low back pain (Hoffman, Papas, Chatkoff, & Kerns, 2007).

Headaches represent another large category of painful conditions. The majority of headaches are so-called *primary headaches*. These include tension headache and migraine headache. Tension headaches are the most common and affect 38 to 78% of people (Rasmussen, Jensen, Schroll, & Olsen, 1991). The pain is typically located in the forehead, neck, and shoulder areas, and many people describe the feeling as having a tight band around their head. Factors that can contribute to tension headaches include stress, skipping meals, or lack of exercise. Thus, treatment often includes cognitive-behavioral stress management training and relaxation. Migraine headaches affect 18% of women and 6% of men (Lipon, Stewart, Diamond, Diamond, & Reed, 2001). They are preceded or accompanied by a sensory warning sign called an *aura*, such as flashes of light, blind spots, or tingling in the extremities. They are often accompanied by other signs and symptoms such as nausea, vomiting, and extreme sensitivity to light and sound. They may be localized behind one eye and they are associated with intense pain. Following a review of the literature, the U.S. Headache Consortium included relaxation training, thermal biofeedback combined with relaxation training, EMG biofeedback, and cognitive behavioral therapy as empirically supported treatments in the clinical practice guidelines for migraine headache (Campbell, Penzien, & Wall, 2000).

Fibromyalgia syndrome (FMS) consists of a set of unexplained physical symptoms with general pain and hypersensitivity to palpation at specific body locations called *tender points*. In addition, patients with FMS often report a range of functional limitations and psychological dysfunction, including persistent fatigue, sleep disturbance, stiffness, headaches, irritable bowel disorders, depression, anxiety, cognitive impairment, and general malaise sometimes referred to as *fibro fog* (Baumstark & Buckelew, 1992). Fibromyalgia syndrome occurs predominately in adults and has a female to male ratio of 7 to 1 in those seeking treatment. While the cause of FMS is unknown, there are many triggering events thought to precipitate its onset, including viral or bacterial infection, emotional or physical trauma, or the development of another disorder such as rheumatoid arthritis, lupus, or hypothyroidism. While studies using a CBT approach to symptom management have had some success (Turk, Okifuji, Starz, & Sinclair, 1998), more research is needed to confirm its effectiveness and to determine the best match of treatment components to particular sets of FMS symptoms.

MODELS OF PAIN

The Gate Control Theory   The Gate Control Theory, which was initially described in 1965 by Ronald Melzack and Patrick Wall (Melzack & Wall, 1965), suggested that the experience of pain was not simply the result of the interpretation of nerve impulses sent directly from sensory neurons to the brain. Rather, the theory suggested that the impulse pathway was more complex and allowed the opportunity for the impulses to be modulated by other incoming stimuli before reaching the brain. According to the theory, modulation of the signal occurs at a site in the dorsal horn of the spinal cord, where a type of "gate mechanism" exists. The gate opens and closes depending on feedback from other nerve fibers in the body, including descending neural impulses from the brain such as those related to an individual's thoughts or mood (e.g., anxiety or depression). When the gate is open, more sensory information regarding pain is allowed to be transmitted to the brain, but when the gate is closed, less information is transmitted to the brain. Thus, the theory had a significant impact on the study of pain because it recognized that psychological factors can have important roles in the experience of pain.

Several theoretical models have been proposed to describe the various factors that can impact the experience of pain. While the models differ in some respects, they all acknowledge that the experience of chronic pain is more than a phenomenon that impacts a particular body part. Chronic pain can also have a significant impact on a person's life (e.g., how they think, work, and play) and the lives of those around them.

Biopsychosocial Model   In contrast to the traditional biomedical model, which assumed that all illness was a function of biological malfunctions, the biopsychosocial model emphasizes the dynamic and reciprocal relationships between the social, biological, and psychological domains of physical health problems (Engel, 1977). Consistent with more general systems theory (von Bertanlanffy, 1968), the model notes that a change in one domain (e.g., the biological domain in the case of a chronic painful condition) necessarily results in changes in the other domains (e.g., psychological and social domains).

Biopsychosocial models suggest that pain is not just a biological process involving the transmission of sensory information about tissue damage to the brain, but is the product of the interactions among biological, psychological, and social factors. All of these factors have an impact on a person's experience of pain, including the intensity, duration, and consequences of pain. For example, when pain persists over time, a person may develop negative beliefs about his or her pain (e.g., "this is never going to get better," "I can't deal with this pain") or negative thoughts about himself or herself (e.g., "I'm worthless because I can't work," "I'm never going to get better"). As pain continues, a person may avoid participating in certain activities for fear of further injury or exacerbating the pain (e.g., work, social activities, or hobbies). As the person withdraws and becomes less active, his or her muscles may weaken, he or she may gain or lose weight, and his or her overall physical conditioning may decline.

The biopsychosocial model has been commended for emphasizing that the social domain should be attended to in terms of its impact on the experience of chronic pain (Kerns & Jacob, 1995). For example, changes such as shifting family roles, loss of income, and increased family and marital distress can have negative effects on pain and disability. However, the model's specific influence on the chronic pain field has been limited. The model has failed to contribute to specific theoretical refinements about mechanisms of transaction, particularly the potential influence of the social (and family) domain on the development and perpetuation of the chronic pain condition or its associated problems (Kerns, Otis, & Wise, 2002).

Cognitive-Behavioral Transactional Model   Building upon cognitive-social learning theory and behaviorism, a cognitive-behavioral transactional model of the role of families in the course of chronic illness has been described by Kerns, Otis, and Wise (2002). The cognitive-behavioral transactional model emphasizes the importance of social support and the family in the development and maintenance of chronic pain.

The model suggests that interactions related to pain all take place within a social and family learning environment that selectively reinforces coping attempts and outcomes in terms of optimal pain management, continued constructive activity, and emotional well-being, or, conversely, reinforces increased pain, disability, and affective distress. As such, the model has advantages over previous models by specifically identifying social and family interactions as important influences on the course of chronic pain. Consistent with a cognitive-behavioral perspective on chronic pain (Turk, Meichenbaum, & Genest, 1983), the model hypothesizes that the family plays an active role in seeking out and evaluating information about the painful condition itself and the specific challenges it poses, as well as in making judgments about the family's and its members' capacities and vulnerabilities in meeting the challenges. It is on the basis of these appraisals that the family and its members make active decisions about alternative responses, act upon their decisions, and evaluate the adequacy of the response.

Central to the transactional model is the additional notion that the family's response and its perceived effects, in turn, shape future appraisals of stress and challenge in a dynamic and reciprocal fashion. Perceptions of failed efforts to manage the painful condition will likely enhance the intensity of the perceived threat of the condition, perhaps contributing to a heightened level of perceived pain, increased disability, and affective distress. Conversely, perceptions of success in coping will likely moderate the experience of pain, increase confidence in the family's ability to respond effectively in the future, and reinforce the repeated use of similar strategies.

Cognitive-Behavioral Fear-Avoidance Model   Vlaeyen and Linton (2000) have proposed a cognitive-behavioral, fear-avoidance model of chronic pain to explain the role of fear and avoidance behaviors in the development and maintenance of chronic pain and related functional limitations. According to this model, there are two opposing responses an individual may have when experiencing pain. One response is that an individual may consider pain to be nonthreatening and consequently engage in adaptive behaviors that promote the restoration of function. In contrast, pain may be interpreted as overly threatening, a process called *catastrophizing*. Vlaeyen and Linton proposed that catastrophizing contributes to a fear of pain and may lead to avoidance of activities that may elicit pain, guarding behaviors (i.e., behaviors performed with the goal of protecting a site of pain such as bracing while walking), and hypervigilance to bodily sensations. Consistent with principles of operant reinforcement, as activities associated with pain are avoided and feelings of fear subside, avoidance behaviors are negatively reinforced. As an individual becomes more depressed and inactive, the cycle of pain is fueled even further, and fear and avoidance is further increased. Thus, avoidance has the potential to increase disability and negative mood and ultimately contribute to the experience of pain. Previous research supports a relationship between fear avoidance and chronic pain (Asmundson & Taylor, 1996; Crombez, Vlaeyen, Heuts, & Lysens, 1999).

COMORBIDITY

A substantial literature exists documenting the relationship between chronic pain and comorbid conditions such as depression (Banks & Kerns, 1996), anxiety (Asmundson, Jacobson, Allerdings, & Norton, 1996; Taylor, 2003), and addictive disorders (Brown, Patterson, Rounds, & Papasouliotis, 1996; Olsen & Alford, 2006). Depression, in particular, has been noted to be a common factor in the experience of pain, with prevalence rates estimated to be 30 to 54% in chronic pain samples (Banks & Kerns). Anxiety and heightened anxiety sensitivity (i.e., the fear of arousal-related sensations arising from beliefs that these sensations have harmful consequences) has also been found to be related to the experience of pain. For example, Asmundson and Norton (1995) found that patients with higher anxiety sensitivity were more likely to experience greater anxiety and fear of pain, more negative affect, and greater avoidance of activities. Research indicates that chronic pain affects between 24 and 67% of patients with substance use disorders; however, this group of individuals is frequently undertreated and often systematically excluded from pain treatment trials due to presumed poor compliance with treatment. Consequently, the development of treatments for individuals with comorbid pain and substance abuse represents an area where more research is needed. Additionally, some chronic pain conditions may develop secondary to injury related to traumatic life events such as motor vehicle accidents, occupational injuries, or military combat (Otis, Pincus, & Keane, 2006). For example, some studies have found that 20 to 30% of patients with posttraumatic stress disorder (PTSD) who seek outpatient treatment report a chronic pain condition (Amir et al., 1997); however, this rate has been estimated to range between 20 to 85% in military veterans or firefighters who have PTSD (Otis et al.). Importantly, interest in the relationship between chronic pain and its comorbid disorders has expanded the field of pain research, has improved our understanding of how these conditions may interact with one another, and has contributed to improvements in pain management.

PSYCHOSOCIAL FACTORS AND PAIN

Chronic pain can affect more than just a person's back or knee; it can impact every aspect of one's life including the lives of significant others. In turn, the responses of significant others and culture in which a person with pain lives can have an impact on how they experience pain. Developmental factors such as cognitive ability, prior experiences with pain, and beliefs and expectations about pain can also play a role. Therefore, it is important to consider the potential impact of these types of factors when conducting a pain assessment, conceptualizing a case, or when creating a pain treatment plan. The following section provides a brief review of these factors and their relationship to pain.

Pain and Older Adults

Research indicates that older adults with chronic pain often report similar levels of pain intensity when compared to younger adults with chronic pain (Harkins & Price, 1992). Although reductions in visual acuity, auditory sensitivity, and increases in reaction time are highly prevalent with old age, there does not appear to be a significant loss in sensitivity to painful stimuli. Although older adults experience similar sensory acuity for pain as younger adults, older adults tend to report less pain-related negative affect and suffering (Harkins & Price). One explanation for this observation may be that older adults' reaction to pain has been influenced by their socialization history (Whitbourne & Cassidy, 1996). For older adults, the presence of pain may be viewed as an expected part of growing older. In addition, the fact that a person is older may mean that they had previous exposures and more experience with painful conditions and are less affected by their presence. Given these issues, the older adult may be less likely to present with significant pain complaints during a clinical assessment or treatment, as they may assume that pain is a natural part of growing older.

In addition to sensory changes, the human body is also prone to physical changes caused by the passage of time and the effects of use, neglect, or disease, which may result in significant impairments and disability. Some of the painful conditions experienced by older adults include musculoskeletal disorders, rheumatoid and osteoarthritis, and diabetic neuropathy (Berkow & Talbott, 1995). For example, musculoskeletal injury to the low back is often accompanied by pain and disturbances in gait that may limit activities such as walking, lifting, or bending. Further, as individuals age the chances increase that they will experience persistent pain from multiple sites.

In addition to the physical changes that manifest themselves in older adulthood, there are numerous psychosocial issues that can affect the lifestyle of the older patient. Physical and financial limitations often prevent older individuals from engaging in outside activities that would provide opportunities to develop supportive emotional relationships with others. Social support networks have been found to help alleviate the effects of stress, promote effective health behaviors, and influence health outcomes (Berkman & Syme, 1979; Cohen, 1991). Older adults typically have family-linked relationships and few supports outside the family. As families become more geographically separated and spouses pass away, opportunities for social support may further decrease. For this reason, when working with older adults it may be beneficial for treatment to be held in a group format. Such a format would provide opportunities for adults to engage in positive social interactions and would promote the building of social networks that might not otherwise be available.

Many of the stressors experienced by older adults are unique to their age group. The techniques used to cope with stress, however, are not unlike those used by younger patients, and older adults use a range of strategies to cope with negative events. Overall, the literature on effective coping suggests that use of problem-focused coping strategies is more effective when dealing with relatively controllable stressors, whereas use of emotion-focused techniques are more effective when faced with relatively uncontrollable stressors (Lazarus & Folkman, 1984). Given the utility of both problem-focused and emotion-focused coping techniques, pain treatment programs could teach older adults to use both types of coping strategies and apply them where appropriate.

PAIN IN CHILDREN AND ADOLESCENTS

Brief episodes of acute pain related to routine injuries and illnesses in childhood are common, with 15% of healthy school-aged children reporting brief episodes of pain (Chambliss, Heggen, Copelan, & Pettignano, 2002). Children's typical responses to acute pain are usually short lived and normal activity is often quickly resumed, as is typically observed with adults. However, chronic pain in children, often associated with an underlying disease, a traumatic injury, or an ongoing trauma causing sustained injury can result in unnecessary suffering of the child and family, disruption of the family routine, and restriction of the child's daily activities, thereby increasing the risk of long-term disability (Caffo & Belaise, 2003). In fact, chronic pain in childhood can often result in somatic and psychiatric dysfunction, with studies showing that children experiencing chronic pain are more likely than other children to complain of anxiety, to demonstrate hypochondriacal beliefs, to engage less frequently in social activities, and to experience higher levels of generalized anxiety (Campo, DiLorengo, & Chiappetta, 2001). Chronic pain conditions in childhood may arise due to known illness (such as rheumatologic disease, sickle cell disease, or HIV infection), or to traumatic injury (due to burns, physical abuse, or motor vehicle accidents), while some chronic pain conditions in childhood may have less clear etiologies (e.g., chronic headache; Chambliss et al., 2002). Due to increased research over the past 20 years on chronic pain in children, we now understand that child pain, like adult pain, is not simply directly related to the extent of physical injury or level of tissue damage, but is influenced by many psychological factors that can modify the neural signals for pain and increase or decrease a child's distress. It has been suggested that children's pain is more plastic than that of adults, such that psychosocial factors may exert an even more powerful influence on children's pain perception than on adults' pain perception (McGrath & Hillier, 2002).

The presentation of chronic pain in children may also differ from that of adults, and there are numerous factors that may influence the child's experience of pain, including child factors (e.g., cognitive level, or temperament), cognitive factors (e.g., expectations about treatment efficacy), behavioral factors (e.g., child's distress responses, avoidance of activities), and emotional factors (e.g., anticipatory anxiety, depression; McGrath & Hillier, 2002). While some of these factors are stable for a child (e.g., temperament), other factors change progressively, (e.g., age, cognitive level, physical state, and family learning). Child factors and situational factors (e.g., level of control over situation) may interrelate to shape how children generally interpret the various sensations caused by tissue damage. For example, as children grow, they learn ways to express pain and ways to cope with pain, and their experience is certainly shaped by their family, culture, and interactions with caregivers and peers. This notion is consistent with Melzack and Wall's (1965) gate control theory, which conceptualized pain as a multidimensional experience, characterized by physiologic, affective, cognitive, behavioral, and social dimensions. Thus, even though the tissue damage for several children may be the same, certain factors specific to each child or to each child's environment can intensify pain and distress, trigger pain episodes, and prolong pain-related disability, while other factors may buffer the effects of the pain, enable the child to engage in healthy coping, and lessen distress. Thus, a thorough assessment is crucial to determine the extent to which cognitive, behavioral, emotional, or situational factors contribute to or buffer the pain experience for a child, with the understanding that these factors are likely to vary between children and may even vary over time for the same child. Children's ongoing physical growth may also play a role in their ability to recover more quickly than adults from injury.

Pain behavior in children has also been found to vary as a function of the child's developmental level. Older children will be able to describe the location, intensity, duration, and sensation of pain, whereas younger children may not be able to distinguish pain from other negative affective states (Tarnowski & Brown, 1999). Pain behavior in children has also been found to differ depending on the presence or absence of a caregiver during a painful medical procedure, with some studies finding that children whose mothers were present were more distressed, but that children prefer parents or caregivers to be present (Gonzalez et al., 1989). Parents' attitudes and expectations, their anxiety levels, and whether they are overly protective and reinforcing of dependence are variables that may affect children's ability to successfully cope. Also, some parents may inadvertently cue and reinforce their child's distress, while others may promote coping by the child (Blount, Landolf-Fritsche, Powers, & Sturges, 1991). Due to the number of parental variables that may influence child coping, there is a need to assess characteristics of the parent, child, and parent-child interactions when assessing pain in children. Given the host of factors that may influence a child's experience of pain, it is not surprising that the treatment of pain in childhood requires an integrated approach, informed by the many factors that may influence a child's pain, including the family and cultural factors that might impact the child, and the child's current methods of coping with pain. Cognitive behavioral treatments for chronic pain in children should take these factors into consideration by giving children effective strategies that will lessen their pain and distress and help them return to developmentally appropriate activities. For example, some behavioral strategies that have been utilized with child patients with pain include teaching children distraction techniques (such as counting) during painful medical procedures, or thinking about a favorite holiday. Some cognitive techniques that have shown to be helpful include teaching children to "throw away" negative thoughts about his or her ability to cope and instead utilizing positive coping thoughts such as "I can cope with anything that comes my way; I am very strong and brave." Parents can also be taught such cognitive behavioral strategies, so that children can be reminded to utilize them when participating in normal daily activities. The ultimate goal of cognitive behavioral strategies is to help children have concrete tools to cope with their experience of pain so that developmentally appropriate activities can resume.

FAMILY FACTORS AND PAIN

Interests have developed among many chronic pain researchers in exploring the ways in which family interactions can impact the experience and course of chronic pain conditions. Research supports the hypothesis that positive attention from a spouse (e.g., making the patient comfortable in a chair, or taking away duties) contingent on a patient's expressions of pain is associated with higher reported levels of pain and pain behaviors (Block, Kremer, & Gaylor, 1980; Kerns, Haythornthwaite, Southwick, & Giller, 1990), higher frequency of observed pain behaviors (Paulsen & Altmaier, 1995; Romano et al., 1992), and reports of greater disability and interference (Flor, Turk, & Rudy, 1989; Turk, Kerns, & Rosenberg, 1992). In addition, there is evidence that a high frequency of negative responding to pain from a spouse (e.g., yelling, complaining, or name calling) is reliably associated with depressive symptom severity and other demonstrations of affective distress (Kerns et al., 1990; Kerns, Southwick, et al., 1991). There is also evidence that level of global marital satisfaction and gender (Flor et al., 1989; Turk et al., 1992) and depressive symptom severity and level of pain (Romano et al., 1995) may serve to moderate these relationships. Future research in this area could examine more complex patterns of pain-relevant interactions and the role of cognitive appraisal in these interactions in an effort to improve the prediction of pain and disability.

The existing literature on the influences of the family on pain has several clinical implications. For example, it is important that clinicians assess the family's cognitions (e.g., attitudes, beliefs, and attributions) concerning the pain experience, as well as their behavioral and affective responses to the patient's pain as an important part of a comprehensive pain assessment. Clinicians can then develop a time-line of chronic pain development that examines the interactions between the pain and its associated challenges and the individual's and family's efforts to cope with them. On the basis of a comprehensive assessment, the clinician should be able to generate specific hypotheses about the nature of the problems being experienced and the factors that may be contributing to their maintenance over time. It is on the basis of this conceptualization that a multidimensional plan for treatment can be developed.

Ultimately, the health care provider, in collaboration with the family, can develop a pain management plan that targets identified problems and hypothesized factors contributing to the patient's experience of pain. For example, the treatment of one family may focus primarily on patterns of solicitous pain-relevant communication between the patient and the spouse, whereas treatment of a second family may specifically target the family's negative responses to the patient's pain verbalizations. Given the complexity of the experience of chronic pain, the intervention plan commonly incorporates multiple treatment targets and strategies. Optimally, the health care provider's treatment plan and its implementation should remain consistent with the family's treatment goals. It is important to remember that patients with chronic pain are sometimes seen only after they have had years of pain that has dramatically impacted their lives. Over time, family dynamics and roles, even those of the disabled spouse, can become highly resistant to change.

Consistent with a cognitive-behavioral approach to pain management, treatment should be time limited and problem focused. Interventions should encourage the development of an adaptive problem-solving approach to pain management, increase the effective use of available family resources, teach family members new adaptive coping skills, and help them to draw upon available external resources. Efforts to help family members reduce the stress and challenges of the painful condition and/or to reconceptualize the stress and challenges as less threatening constitute a second general goal. Reduction of the negative impact of the pain problem on the family and its members (including the individual with the chronic pain condition), and the promotion of adaptive family functioning and well-being, are the overarching or higher-order goals of the therapeutic approach.

The structure and functioning of a family system is likely to vary across individuals and over the course of time. Just as siblings, parents, and teachers can reinforce pain behaviors and disability in children, so too can spouses, adult children, and caregivers influence the experience of pain in older adults (Kerns, Otis, & Stein, 2002). Health care providers are encouraged to be flexible in their definition of "family," as they may find it necessary at times to include individuals outside of the nuclear family who possess high reinforcement potential (e.g., friends, neighbors, and health care providers). This is an especially important consideration when treating patients from different cultures who may reside with extended family members or in multifamily dwellings. For such patients, it may be clinically useful to incorporate an extended family member (e.g., aunt or grandparent) or close friend in order to maximize treatment efficacy.

CULTURE AND DIVERSITY ISSUES

Of particular importance in understanding the influence of the family on the experience of chronic pain is the cultural background and context of the family. Culture, defined as the behavioral and attitudinal norms of a group of people and the systems of meaning in which they take place, shapes a person's (or family's) beliefs and behaviors related to illness, health care practices, help-seeking behaviors, and their receptiveness to medical interventions. Culture also shapes efforts to make sense of symptoms and suffering (Kirmayer, Young, & Robbins, 1994). Cultural factors related to the experience of pain can influence pain expression, the language used to describe pain, coping responses, beliefs about pain and suffering, and perceptions of the health care system (Lasch, 2000). Culture can also influence the types of treatments that are considered acceptable. Within each cultural group, variations in symptom attribution may affect the clinical presentation, course, and outcome of many disorders, including pain disorders (Kirmayer et al.). Certainly, pain is affected by our own past experiences and the social world in which we live (Morris, 1999). Culture is defined as a shared system of values, beliefs, and learned patterns of behaviors and is not simply defined by ethnicity. Culture is also shaped by such factors as proximity, education, gender, age, and sexual preference (Low, 1984).

The prevalence of chronic pain also varies according to demographic characteristics such as race, ethnicity, gender, and class. For instance, research has shown that African American and Caucasian patients differ in the levels of pain severity and disability they report as well as in the coping strategies they employ for pain, and that some, but not all, of these differences in coping disappear when level of education is considered as a mediating variable (Cano, Mayo, & Ventimiglia, 2006).

Research also supports that an individual's beliefs can have a significant impact on his or her experience of pain (DeGood & Shutty, 1992). Especially important are beliefs about cause, control, duration, outcome, and blame (Williams & Thorn, 1989; Jensen, Turner, Romano, & Karoly, 1991). Patients who believe that they have some control over their pain, that medical services are helpful, and that they are not severely disabled from their pain, function better (Jensen & Karoly, 1992). Studies exploring the influence of cognitions on the experience of pain suggest that understanding an individual's idiosyncratic beliefs about pain can be beneficial in helping him or her to develop adaptive coping skills (Turk, 1996). An individual's pain beliefs may reflect shared cultural values and understandings that flow throughout a specific culture. How our culture instructs and guides us, overtly or covertly, in conceptualizing pain can influence our ability to adapt to a chronic pain condition (Morris, 1999).

CONDUCTING A PAIN ASSESSMENT

Whether a patient is receiving pain treatment as part of a research study or a clinical practice, they should first receive a comprehensive pain assessment in order for the therapist to develop a thorough understanding of his or her pain condition. The assessment should be repeated after treatment has been completed in order to document any changes in physical or emotional functioning that have occurred. This will allow the therapist to assess the effectiveness of the treatment intervention and is a helpful way to demonstrate progress to the patient. The data may also be of benefit when a therapist wants to demonstrate the effectiveness of their services to insurance companies or referral sources seeking pain management expertise for their patients.

The first phase of the pain assessment involves performing a clinical interview in which the patient will have the opportunity to describe his or her pain condition and how pain has impacted his or her life. When the psychologist is working as part of a multidisciplinary or interdisciplinary pain treatment team, it is also useful to include questions in the assessment that will yield information that may be of importance to other disciplines. The interview should begin by obtaining a pain history (i.e., the patient's description of the presenting pain problem), which will include details regarding the onset of the pain complaint (e.g., sudden onset associated with an event versus gradual onset), words used to describe pain (e.g., stabbing, electric, dull), and temporal patterns or cycles associated with the pain (e.g., pain that is worse in the evening versus morning). It is important to ask about past and present treatments/ medications tried for pain relief and their effectiveness (e.g., physical therapy, surgery, narcotics), and things that the patient has identified that make his or her pain increase or decrease. Note if the things identified by the patient are passive (e.g., medications and injections) versus active techniques (e.g., activity pacing). Patients should be asked about their goals for the future, since this will impact the goals set in therapy. The interview should also address areas such as mental health history and current mood, psychosocial history, and past or present substance abuse. All of this information will be useful to other pain management specialists (e.g., anesthesiologists, neurologists, physical therapists) who may consult with the therapist about the most appropriate ways to address the patient's pain.

In order to supplement information obtained in the interview, the assessment can also include self-report measures that have been validated with a chronic pain population. One of the simplest and most effective ways of assessing a person's level of pain is to ask him or her to rate their pain on a 0 to 10 scale, with 0 representing "no pain" and 10 representing "the worst pain imaginable." This type of rating is particularly useful when a therapist needs to perform a brief assessment, such as when working in a primary care setting (Jensen, Turner, Romano, & Fisher, 1999). The McGill Pain Questionnaire (MPQ; Melzack, 1975) is a self-report questionnaire consisting of 102 words separated into three major classes; the sensory, affective, and evaluative aspects of pain, and 16 subclasses. It is frequently used in studies of chronic, acute, and laboratory-induced pain, and its stability, reliability, and validity have been established (Reading, Everitt, & Sledmere, 1982). If more time is available and a more comprehensive assessment of the patient's functioning is desired, the West Haven-Yale Multidimensional Pain Inventory (WHYMPI) is recommended (Kerns, Turk, & Rudy, 1985). The WHYMPI is a 52-item self-report questionnaire that is divided into three parts. Part I includes five scales designed to measure dimensions, including (1) perceived interference of pain, (2) support or concern from spouse or significant other, (3) pain severity, (4) perceived life control, and (5) affective distress. Part II assesses patients' perceptions of the degree to which spouses or significant others display Solicitous, Distracting, or Negative responses to their pain behaviors. Part III assesses patients' report of the frequency with which they engage in four categories of common everyday activities. Its brevity, validity/reliability, self-report nature, and ease of scoring make it ideal for both clinical and research purposes. The coping strategies that individuals use in response to pain can be assessed using the Coping Strategies Questionnaire—Revised (CSQ-R; Riley, Robinson, & Geisser, 1999). Adequate internal validities for the six cognitive subscales (Diverting Attention, Reinterpreting Sensations, Catastrophizing, Ignoring Sensations, Praying and Hoping, Coping Self-statements), and a behavioral scale (Behavioral Activities) have been demonstrated (Keefe, Crisson, Urban, & Williams, 1990). Another measure of coping that has been widely used in pain research is the Pain Catastrophizing Scale (PCS; Sullivan, Bishop, & Vivek, 1995). The PCS asks patients to reflect on past painful experiences and to indicate the degree to which they experienced each of 13 thoughts or feelings when experiencing pain on a 5-point scale, from 0 (not at all) to 4 (all the time). Measures of mood, such as the Beck Depression Inventory (BDI; Beck, Steer, & Garbin, 1988) and the State Trait Anxiety Inventory (STAI; Spielberger, Gorsuch, & Luschene, 1976) are frequently used in pain research and may be considered as part of a self-report assessment battery.

COGNITIVE BEHAVIORAL THERAPY FOR PAIN

One particularly common psychological approach for treating chronic pain is cognitive-behavior therapy (CBT). This approach targets patients' maladaptive cognitive and behavioral coping and promotes the adoption of perceptions of enhanced personal control related to the pain condition and an adaptive and active problem-solving approach to pain management. Cognitive and behavioral interventions have enjoyed considerable empirical support for their efficacy in ameliorating chronic pain. Indeed, as early as 1998, cognitive-behavioral therapies were identified as efficacious treatments for several chronic pain conditions, including rheumatic diseases, chronic pain syndrome, chronic low-back pain, and irritable bowl syndrome (Compas, Haaga, Keefe, Leitenberg, & Williams, 1998). In a frequently cited meta-analysis, Morley, Eccleston, and Williams (1999) concluded from the examination of 25 randomized controlled trials that cognitive behavior therapy for chronic pain is effective, as it resulted in significantly greater improvements in pain experience, cognitive coping and appraisal, and reductions in behavioral expressions of pain when compared with alternative active treatments. As a more recent example, in a randomized controlled trial conducted by Turner, Mancl, and Aaron (2006), patients completing a four-session cognitive-behavioral intervention for temporomandibular disorder pain showed significantly greater improvements on outcome, belief, and catastrophizing measures, greater implementation of relaxation techniques to cope with pain, 35% higher rates of reporting "no pain interference" in activities at 12-month follow-up, and greater clinically meaningful improvements in pain intensity, jaw function, and depression at 12-month follow-up when compared with patients assigned to an education/attention control curriculum. This particular study has been praised for its methodological rigor and sophistication among randomized clinical trials evaluating cognitive behavioral interventions for pain (Morley, 2006). Further, in a recent meta-analysis of 22 randomized controlled trials of psychological treatments for noncancerous chronic low back pain, cognitive-behavioral and self-regulatory treatments specifically were found to be efficacious (Hoffman, Papas, Chatkoff, & Kerns, 2007). Finally, while there are few studies examining the effectiveness of psychological treatments for pain in children and adolescents, relaxation techniques as well as cognitive behavioral therapy have demonstrated the strongest positive results thus far (Eccleston, Morley, Williams, Yorke, & Mastroyannopoulou, 2002).

STRUCTURE OF COGNITIVE-BEHAVIORAL TREATMENT FOR CHRONIC PAIN

The primary goal of cognitive-behavior therapy for pain is to promote the adoption of an active problem-solving approach to tackling the many challenges associated with the experience of chronic pain. A shift from a perspective of helplessness with regard to these challenges to one of personal responsibility, self-control, and confidence is encouraged. The cognitive-behavioral approach is informed by the understanding that people generally do not stop being active because of pain, but because they have become adjusted to the idea that they are physically disabled. Thus, cognitive-behavior therapy for chronic pain involves challenging those beliefs and teaching patients ways of safely re-introducing enjoyable activities into their lives. This can be a particularly daunting task when thoughts related to disability have been in place for many years. There are several key components to cognitive-behavioral treatment for chronic pain, including cognitive restructuring (i.e., teaching patients how to recognize cognitive errors and change maladaptive thoughts related to pain into more adaptive, positive thoughts), relaxation training (i.e., teaching diaphragmatic breathing, visual imagery, progressive muscle relaxation, etc.), time-based activity pacing (i.e., teaching patients how to become more active without overdoing it), and graded homework assignments designed to decrease patients' avoidance of activity and reintroduce a healthy, more active lifestyle. Since individuals who experience chronic pain often report reduced activity levels and declines in social role functioning, CBT also focuses on promoting patients' increased activity and productive functioning using techniques such as exercise homework, activity scheduling, and graded task assignments (i.e., gradually increasing activity toward an identified goal). For example, if a patient has set an overall treatment goal of walking 1 mile per day, the patient might begin by setting the goal of walking half a mile three times per week and gradually increasing the distance walked with each visit to the therapist (see Otis, 2007 for a cognitive behavioral therapist manual and patient workbook for treating chronic pain).

CASE EXAMPLE

PRESENTING PROBLEM/CLIENT DESCRIPTION

Mr. Davis is a 62-year-old married Caucasian man who was referred to a pain psychologist after reporting back and knee pain that had been unresponsive to conservative medical treatment approaches. After receiving the consultation request and before contacting the patient, the psychologist spoke with the referring physician in order to ensure that the psychologist addressed all of the provider's concerns during the assessment. During the conversation the provider reported that he had been attempting to motivate Mr. Davis to increase his activity level; however, the patient failed to follow through with his recommendations and was becoming increasingly disabled.

Mr. Davis's assessment began with a 45-minute clinical interview, with the goal of assessing the relationship among the dimensions of pain, distress, and disability and the social context in which they occur. He arrived for the interview with his wife, by our request. Behavioral observations of Mr. Davis revealed a moderate level of pain behaviors (e.g., grimacing, bracing his back with his hand, and occasionally holding on to a wall when walking) and pain-related verbalizations such as moaning. During the interview, Mr. Davis reported that he believed the onset of his back pain was associated with a fall that occurred after climbing over a wall while performing basic training for the U.S. Marines. Following this injury he was able to return to basic training but he continued to experience intermittent pain. He indicated that pain did not impede his ability to work full time after leaving the Marines. Mr. Davis reported that approximately one year ago he fell off a ladder at home and landed on his back. He reported that as a result of the fall he experienced back pain and muscle soreness for over 3 weeks. After a period of rest, Mr. Davis returned to work with some residual pain; however, 2 months later he reinjured his back while moving a file cabinet at work. He reported that since that time he has been experiencing constant pain in his lower back and intermittent "shocking" pains down his left leg. He indicated that as a result of his back pain he has been missing days of work and spending more time at home watching television rather than spending time with friends or working in his yard, activities that he greatly enjoyed. He also reported that he enjoys watching college sports such as ice hockey and basketball. He could not identify a particular event associated with the onset of his knee pain, but indicated that the pain had gradually increased over the past 7 years.

Mr. Davis is a college graduate who served two tours of duty overseas. He and his wife have two children. Although he described his marital relationship as good, he indicated his wife "smothers" him at times, and that they have recently been having arguments related to her overly solicitous behavior. Mrs. Davis described feeling frustrated that that her husband sometimes rejects the things she tries to do for him.

Following his service in the Marines, Mr. Davis worked in construction for several years, and has been employed as an engineer for the past 10 years. He reported that he has been taking a significant amount of medical leave from his job for the past several months.

Mr. Davis reported a history of alcohol abuse but indicated that he quit drinking alcohol on his own, approximately 11 years ago. He denied current recreational drug use but admitted to using marijuana in the past. He denied a history of depression or mental health treatment; however, he reported that he feels worthless and sad almost every day for the past 4 months. During the interview, he endorsed some suicidal thoughts but expressed no intent. Mr. Davis's primary care provider had been managing his pain conservatively with recommendations of rest and light activity, and a referral to physical therapy where he received heat and massage to relax his back muscles. Given his alcohol abuse history, and current depressive symptomatology, the primary care provider decided to prescribe a non-narcotic analgesic. A recent MRI revealed a slight disc compression at L4-L5; however, a consulting neurologist documented that these findings could not fully account for Mr. Davis's current level of pain and disability. Mr. Davis's medical history was also significant for diabetes and obesity. Mr. Davis weighs 300 lbs., and much of his excess weight is carried in his abdominal region. Following the clinical interview, Mr. Davis was asked to complete several self-report questionnaires related to the experience of pain in order to supplement information gained from the interview.

Case Formulation

Assessment   The results of the assessment indicated that Mr. Davis was experiencing a moderate level of depression associated with the onset of his chronic pain condition; however, his depressive symptoms were now likely contributing to increased disability and pain. Factors contributing to his depressive symptoms included time away from his job, arguments with his wife, negative thoughts about himself as a provider (e.g., I'm worthless to my family), increased social isolation, and reduced pleasant activities. This was supported by his responses on several self-report questionnaires, which indicated that he was experiencing a moderate level of depressive symptoms and a significant level of interference in his daily activities. His responses suggested he believes his wife engages in solicitous behaviors in response to his pain complaints. While he did engage in some positive coping in response to pain (e.g., try to think pleasant thoughts), he also had a tendency to engage in catastrophic thinking (e.g., this is never going to get better).

The initial assessment enabled the psychologist to conceptualize Mr. Davis's pain experience, including factors contributing to its development and maintenance. His specific difficulties included his level of pain, increased attention from his spouse, a significant number of depressive symptoms, obesity, and decreased participation in reinforcing activities, both social and occupational.

Multidisciplinary Pain Management Team   Following the completion of the pain assessment by the psychologist, Mr. Davis's case was presented to the multidisciplinary pain management team. There appeared to be a clear etiology for his low back pain, and consultation with other members of the team supported the theory that Mr. Davis's knee pain was likely related to his years of work in construction and the fact that he was significantly overweight. Weight loss is often associated with a reduction in pain; therefore, this was considered to be an important long-term goal. A recommendation was made to the primary care provider that Mr. Davis meet with a dietician in order to help him develop a weight loss plan. No changes in his current pain medications were recommended by the neurologist; however, the physical therapist on the team recommended that Mr. Davis engage in more active, rather than passive, rehabilitation approaches to increase his strength and flexibility. All of these recommendations were communicated to the primary care provider following the meeting.

Based on the results of the assessment, it was the opinion of the pain team that Mr. Davis would benefit most from individually based pain management therapy. The results of the assessment were reviewed with Mr. Davis and his wife to highlight potential areas for intervention. Mr. Davis agreed that he could benefit from learning ways to more effectively manage his pain, so time was spent with the couple describing the therapy process and setting up a time for the first session. Expectations for active participation in the treatment process (including practice and the completion of homework assignments) were emphasized.

COURSE OF TREATMENT

Mr. Davis was seen by the psychologist for 11 sessions of weekly individual psychotherapy. Each session was approximately 50 minutes in duration and followed a manualized pain management protocol developed by Otis (Otis, 2007). Following the CBT model of pain management, the first session of treatment involved reconceptualizing pain as a manageable but not curable condition that can be influenced by a person's thoughts and behaviors. The acceptance of the idea that pain will likely always be a part of their life is important because patients who are waiting for a cure for their pain are less likely to take responsibility for managing pain or to actively participate in psychotherapy related to pain. The relationship between pain, negative thoughts, and disability was explained while drawing upon circumstances from Mr. Davis's own life to serve as examples. Mr. Davis was able to offer an example of when feelings of anger led to an increase in his pain. He was also able to articulate that pain was something that impacted all areas of his life, and was more than just a sensory experience confined to his back and his knee.

Mr. Davis worked with the psychologist to develop several overall behavioral goals that could be worked toward over the course of therapy. Rather than having goals set solely by the therapist, goals were set cooperatively with the patient so that he would be invested in their achievement. Behavioral and quantifiable goals were developed, rather than vague goals (e.g., improved quality of life or reducing pain), so that goal progress could be easily measured. Each week, small goals that successively approximated the overall behavioral goals were established and goal accomplishment was evaluated at the beginning of each subsequent session. Goals that were reachable, yet challenging, were particularly useful in encouraging goal accomplishment. Unmet goals were discussed and revised for the following week. Mr. Davis's goals included spending more time with friends and increasing time spent working in his yard. In addition, several of his goals were directly related to goals set by his physical therapist, which included walking and completing physical exercises designed to increase muscle strength and flexibility.

Over the course of therapy, Mr. Davis was taught a number of cognitive-behavioral coping skills to help him manage his pain more effectively. Each session began with an outline of major topics to be covered, and included educational information, a review of the skill to be taught and in-session practice, and homework designed to facilitate the acquisition of the skill. Initial sessions focused on teaching Mr. Davis relaxation techniques such as diaphragmatic breathing, visual imagery, and progressive muscle relaxation. Mr. Davis responded very well to these techniques and the early success provided an opportunity for the psychologist and Mrs. Davis to reinforce his efforts to manage his pain. He was taught to identify and label his thoughts and emotions and to challenge negative automatic thoughts using cognitive restructuring. Negative thoughts about himself and catastrophic ways of thinking were specifically addressed. In subsequent sessions, Mr. Davis was taught ways of gradually reintroducing pleasant activities in his life and for pacing his activity level at work and at home in order to be able to remain active yet avoid exacerbations of his pain, often associated with too much activity. Given his interest in sports, Mr. Davis responded well to an analogy that was made by the psychologist between the process of activity pacing and professional athletes who take regular breaks during a game in order to perform at their best.

The involvement of Mrs. Davis was an important factor in the success of the treatment. On occasions when she would accompany her husband to therapy appointments, Mrs. Davis was asked to be present for the last 10 minutes of the session. During that time, her husband would explain the concepts that had been covered in session and review the goals he would be working toward for the week. This also provided an opportunity for Mrs. Davis to openly express any concerns she had about the changes she had seen in her husband over the past 10 months and it allowed the therapist to observe their interactions when discussing the patient's pain problem. Although Mr. Davis reported feeling that his wife "smothers" him at times with attention, Mrs. Davis explained to her husband that she was only trying to protect him from feeling more pain. By attending portions of the therapy sessions and hearing the rationale behind some of the techniques, Mrs. Davis began to understand the importance of allowing Mr. Davis opportunities to do things for himself, and ways she could reinforce her husband for participating in daily activities even when he was in pain. Mrs. Davis's participation helped to promote reinforcement of her husband's adaptive behaviors and the coping techniques learned in treatment.

The final session included reviewing strategies for dealing with a pain flare-up or a temporary increase in pain. It was explained to Mr. Davis that even though he had completed a program to help him manage his pain, it was likely that he would experience a pain flare-up in the future. Given this, it was important to prepare for what to do when it happened so that he would not think that he had failed and abandon everything that he had learned. Mr. and Mrs. Davis were able to identify some situational and emotional factors that might trigger an increase in pain. Strategies included preparing for a pain flare-up before it occurs (becoming aware of emotional and physical cues that pain is increasing), confronting the pain flare-up by using the self-management strategies (relaxation strategies, restructuring negative thoughts), and using positive coping statements in place of negative thoughts (e.g., I've handled this much pain before, and I can do it again). Treatment goal accomplishment was assessed at the conclusion of treatment, and the self-report questionnaires were again assigned for completion.

OUTCOME AND PROGNOSIS

Mr. Davis learned a number of techniques to help him lessen the impact that his chronic pain condition has on his life. Exercises such as diaphragmatic breathing and progressive muscle relaxation helped him learn to relax his body and to identify when he was becoming tense. He recognized that prior to therapy his negative thoughts and increased isolation from other people had been causing him to become depressed, which in turn was contributing to his experience of pain. By practicing cognitive restructuring he became skilled at identifying his negative thoughts and replacing them with more adaptive ones. This, along with homework assignments designed to increase his engagement in pleasant activities, resulted in a significant decrease in his depressive symptoms. Mr. Davis indicated that he had a much better relationship with his wife by the end of treatment, which he largely attributed to having the opportunity to include his wife in sessions to openly discuss the best ways to help him with his pain. Mrs. Davis also felt that she enjoyed a more harmonious relationship with her husband, and that she now knew how to "help" without making him feel "smothered." Mr. Davis continued to report significant pain at the end of treatment; however, he indicated that he had learned ways to manage his pain without first reaching for his medication. Of particular note, Mr. Davis stated that he now had increased his enjoyment of life, and that pain was no longer a limiting factor. Of all of the skills Mr. Davis learned in treatment, Mr. Davis reported that he found that cognitive restructuring and activity pacing were most helpful. A brief follow-up assessment conducted several months after revealed that Mr. Davis had returned to work and had been doing much better at managing pain flare-ups.

CONCLUSION

In summary, research in the field of chronic pain has burgeoned in the last decade, with substantial gains being made in our understanding of the various factors that contribute to the development and maintenance of chronic pain conditions. Cognitive behavioral therapy has been demonstrated to be an effective treatment for a variety of chronic pain conditions. Such an approach helps patients to develop a healthier, active lifestyle, while improving their quality of life. Directions for future research could include tailoring cognitive behavioral treatment for pain management to the needs of individuals with specific medical conditions such as multiple sclerosis or neuropathic pain conditions, or comorbid conditions such as substance abuse, traumatic brain injury, or posttraumatic stress disorder.

REFERENCES

Amir, M., Kaplan, Z., Neumann, L., Sharabani, R., Shani, N., & Buskila, D. (1997). Posttraumatic stress disorder, tenderness and fibromyalgia. *Journal of Psychosomatic Research, 42,* 607–613.

Andersson, G. B. J. (1997). The epidemiology of spinal disorders. In J. W. Frymoyer (Ed.), *The adult spine: Principles and practices* (2nd ed., pp. 93–141). New York: Raven.

Asmundson, G. J., & Taylor, S. (1996). Role of anxiety sensitivity in pain-related fear and avoidance. *Journal of Behavioral Medicine, 19,* 577–586.

Asmundson, G. J., Jacobson, S. J., Allerdings, M., & Norton, G. R. (1996). Social phobia in disabled workers with chronic musculoskeletal pain. *Behavior Research and Therapy, 34,* 939–943.

Asmundson, G. J., & Norton, G. (1995). Anxiety sensitivity in patients with physically unexplained chronic back pain: A preliminary report. *Behaviour Research and Therapy, 33,* 771–777.

Banks, S. M., & Kerns, R. D. (1996). Explaining high rates of depression in chronic pain: A diathesis-stress framework. *Psychological Bulletin, 119*, 95–110.

Baumstark, K. E., & Buckelew, S. P. (1992). Fibromyalgia: Clinical signs, research findings, treatment implications, and future directions. *Annals of Behavioral Medicine, 14*, 282–291.

Beck, A. T., Steer, R. A., & Garbin, M. G. (1988). Psychometric properties of the Beck Depression Inventory: Twenty-five years of evaluation. *Clinical Psychology Review, 8*, 77–100.

Berkman, L. F., & Syme, S. L. (1979). Social network, host resistance, and mortality: A nine-year follow-up study of Alameda County residents. *American Journal of Epidemiology, 109*, 186–204.

Berkow, R., & Talbott, J. H. (1995). *The Merck Manual of Diagnosis and Therapy* (13th ed.). Rahway, NJ: Merck Sharp & Dohme Research Laboratories.

Block, A., Kremer, E., & Gaylor, M. (1980). Behavioral treatment of chronic pain: The spouse as a discriminative cue for pain behavior. *Pain, 9*, 243–252.

Blount, R. L., Landolf-Fritsche, B., Powers, S. W., & Sturges, J. W. (1991). Differences between high and low coping children and between parent and staff behaviors during painful medical procedures. *Journal of Pediatric Psychology, 16*, 795–809.

Brown, R. L., Patterson, J. J., Rounds, L. A., & Papasouliotis, O. (1996). Substance use among patients with chronic back pain. *Journal of Family Practice, 43*, 152–160.

Byrne, Z. S., & Hochwarter, W. A. (2006). I get by with a little help from my friends: The interaction of chronic pain and organizational support and performance. *Journal of Occupational Health Psychology, 11*(3), 215–227.

Caffo, E., & Belaise, C. (2003). Psychological aspects of traumatic injury in children and adolescents. *Child and Adolescent Psychiatric Clinics of North America, 12*, 493–535.

Campbell, J. K., Penzien, D. B., & Wall, E. M. (2000). Evidenced-based guidelines for migraine headache: Behavioral and physical treatments. U. S. Headache Consortium. Retrieved May 15, 2000, from http://www.aan.com/public/practiceguidelines/headache_gl.htm

Campo, J. V., DiLorenzo, C., & Chiappetta, L. (2001). Adult outcomes of pediatric recurrent abdominal pain: Do they just grow out of it. *Pediatrics, 108*(1), E1–7.

Cano, A., Mayo, A., & Ventimiglia, M. (2006). Coping, pain severity, interference, and disability: The potential mediating and moderating roles of race and education. *Journal of Pain, 7*, 459–468.

Center for Disease Control and Prevention, National Center for Health Statistics. (2006). *Health, United States, 2006, with chartbook on trends in the health of Americans.* Hyattsville, MD: U. S. Government Printing Office.

Chambliss, C. R., Heggen, J., Copelan, D. N., & Pettignano, R. (2002). The assessment and management of chronic pain in children. *Pediatric Drugs, 4*(11), 737–746.

Cohen S. (1991). Social supports and physical health: Symptoms, health behaviors, and infectious disease. In E. M. Cummings, A. L. Greens, & K. H. Karraker (Eds.), *Life-span developmental psychology* (pp. 213–234). Hillsdale, NJ: Erlbaum.

Compas, B. E., Haaga, D. A., Keefe, F. J., Leitenberg, H., & Williams, D. A. (1998). Sampling of empirically supported treatments from health psychology: Smoking, chronic pain, cancer, and bulimia nervosa. *Journal of Consulting and Clinical Psychology, 66*(1), 89–112.

Crombez, G., Vlaeyen, J. W. S., Heuts, P. H. T. G., & Lysens, R. (1999). Pain-related fear is more disabling than pain itself: Evidence of the role of pain-related fear in chronic back pain disability. *Pain, 80*, 329–339.

DeGood, D., & Shutty, M. (1992). Assessment of pain beliefs, coping, and self-efficacy. In D. C. Turk & R. Melzack (Eds.), *Handbook of pain assessment* (pp. 214–234). New York: Guilford.

Eccleston, C., Morley, S., Williams, A., Yoke, L., & Mastroyannopoulou, K. (2002). Systematic review of randomized controlled trials of psychological therapy for chronic pain in children and adolescents, with a sub-set meta-analysis of pain relief. *Pain, 99*, 157–165.

Engel, G. L. (1977). The need for a new medical model: A challenge for biomedical science. *Science, 196,* 129–136.

Flor, H., Turk, D. C., & Rudy, T. E. (1989). Relationship of pain impact and significant other reinforcement of pain behaviors: The mediating role of gender, marital status and marital satisfaction. *Pain, 38,* 45–50.

Gonzalez, J. C., Routh, D. K., Saab, P. G., Armstrong, F. D., Shifman, L., Guerra, E., et al. (1989). Effects of parent presence on children's reactions to injections: Behavioral, physiological, and subjective aspects. *Journal of Pediatric Psychology, 14*(3), 449–462.

Harkins, S. W., & Price, D. D. (1992). Assessment of pain in the elderly. In D. C. Turk & R. Melzack (Eds.), *Handbook of pain assessment* (pp. 315–331). New York: Guilford.

Hoffman, B. M., Papas, R. K., Chatkoff, D. K., & Kerns, R. D. (2007). Meta-analysis of psychological interventions for chronic low back pain. *Health Psychology, 26,* 1–9.

Jensen, M., & Karoly, P. (1992). Pain-specific beliefs, perceived symptom severity, and adjustment to chronic pain. *Clinical Journal of Pain, 8*(2), 123–130.

Jensen, M. P., Turner, J. A., Romano, J. M., & Fisher, L. D. (1999). Comparative reliability and validity of chronic pain intensity measures. *Pain, 83,* 157–162.

Jensen M. P., Turner J., Romano, J. M., & Karoly, P. (1991). Coping with chronic pain: A critical review of the literature. *Pain, 47*(3), 249–283.

Keefe, F. J., Crisson, J., Urban, B. J., & Williams, D. A. (1990). Analyzing chronic low back pain: The relative contribution of pain coping strategies. *Pain, 40,* 293–301.

Kerns, R. D., Haythornthwaite, J., Southwick, S., & Giller, E. L. (1990). The role of marital interaction in chronic pain and depressive symptom severity. *Journal of Psychosomatic Research, 34,* 401–408.

Kerns, R. D., & Jacob, M. C. (1995). Toward an integrative diathesis-stress model of chronic pain. In A. J. Goreczny & M. Hersen (Eds.), *Handbook of recent advances in behavioral medicine* (pp. 325–340). New York: Plenum.

Kerns, R. D., Otis, J. D., & Stein, K. (2002). Cognitive-behavioral treatment for geriatric pain: A case report. *Neuropathic Pain, 1,* 20–21.

Kerns, R. D., Otis, J. D., & Wise, E. (2002). Treating families of chronic pain patients: Application of a cognitive-behavioral transactional model. In R. J. Gatchel and D. C. Turk (Eds.), *Psychological approaches to pain management* (2nd ed., pp. 256–275). New York: Guilford.

Kerns, R. D., Southwick, S., Giller, E. L., Haythornthwaite, J., Jacob, M. C., & Rosenberg, R. (1991). The relationship between reports of pain-related social interactions and expressions of pain and affective distress. *Behavior Therapist, 22,* 101–111.

Kerns, R. D., Turk, D. C., & Rudy, T. E. (1985). The West Haven-Yale Multidimensional Pain Inventory (WHYMPI). *Pain, 23,* 345–356.

Kirmayer, L., Young, A., & Robbins, J. (1994). Symptom attribution in cultural perspective. *Canadian Journal of Psychiatry, 39,* 584–595.

Lasch, K. (2000). Culture, pain, and culturally sensitive pain care. *Pain Management Nursing, 1,* 16–22.

Lazarus, R. S., & Folkman, S. (1984). *Stress, appraisal, and coping.* New York: Springer.

Lipon, R. B., Stewart, W. F., Diamond, S., Diamond, M. L., & Reed, M. (2001). Prevalence and burden of migraine in the United States: Data from the American Migraine Study II. *Headache, 41,* 646–657.

Low, S. M. (1984). The cultural basis of health, illness and disease. *Social Work Health Care, 9,* 13–23.

Max, M. B. (2003). How to move pain research from the margin to the mainstream. *The Journal of Pain, 4*(7), 2003.

McGrath, P. A., & Hillier, L. M. (2002). A practical cognitive behavioral approach for treating children's pain. In D. C. Turk & R. J. Gatchel (Eds.), *Psychological approaches to pain management: A practitioners handbook* (2nd ed., pp. 534–552). New York: Guilford.

Melzack, R. (1975). McGill Pain Questionnaire: Major properties and scoring methods. *Pain, 1,* 277–299.

Melzack, R., & Wall, P. D. (1965). Pain mechanisms: A new theory. *Science, 50,* 971–979.

Merskey, H. (1994). Logic, truth, and language in concepts of pain. In H. Merskey & N. Bogduk (Eds.), *Classification of chronic pain* (pp. 209–214). Seattle, WA: IASP Press.

Morley, S. (2006). RCTs of psychological treatments for chronic pain: Progress and challenges. *Pain, 121,* 171–172.

Morley, S., Eccleston, C., & Williams, A. (1999). Systematic review and meta-analysis of randomized controlled trials of cognitive behaviour therapy and behaviour therapy for chronic pain in adults, excluding headache. *Pain, 80,* 1–13.

Morris, D. (1999). Sociocultural and religious meanings of pain. In R. Gatchel (Ed.), *Psychosocial factors in pain: Critical perspective* (pp. 118–131). New York: Guilford.

Olsen, Y., & Alford, D. P. (2006). Chronic pain management in patients with substance use disorders. *Advanced Studies in Medicine, 6*(3), 111–123.

Otis, J. D. (2007). *Managing chronic pain: A cognitive-behavioral therapy approach.* New York: Oxford University Press. [Therapist manual and patient workbook.]

Otis, J. D., Pincus, D. B., & Keane, T. M. (2006). Comorbid chronic pain and posttraumatic stress disorder across the lifespan: A review of theoretical models. In G. Young, A. Kane, & K. Nicholson (Eds), *Causality: Psychological knowledge and evidence in court* (pp. 242-270). New York: Kluwer Academic/ Plenum.

Paulsen, J. S., & Altmaier, E. M. (1995). The effects of perceived versus enacted social support on the discriminative cue function of spouses for pain behaviors. *Pain, 60,* 103–110.

Rasmussen, B. K., Jensen, R., Schroll, M., & Olsen, J. (1991). Epidemiology of headache in a general population: A prevalence study. *Journal of Clinical Epidemiology, 44,* 1147–1157.

Reading, A. E., Everitt, B. S., & Sledmere, C. M. (1982). The McGill Pain Questionnaire: A replication of its construction. *British Journal of Clinical Psychology, 21,* 339–349.

Riley, J., Robinson, M. E., & Geisser, M. E. (1999). Empirical subgroups of the Coping Strategies Questionnaire—Revised: A multisample study. *Clinical Journal of Pain, 15*(2), 111–116.

Romano, J. M, Turner, J. A., Friedman, L. S., Bulcroft, R. A., Jensen, M. P., Hops, H., et al. (1992). Sequential analysis of chronic pain behaviors and spouse responses. *JCCP, 60,* 777–782.

Romano, J. M., Turner, J. A., Jensen, M. P., Friedman, L. S., Bulcroft, R. A., Hops, H., et al. (1995). Chronic pain patient-spouse behavioral interactions predict patient disability. *Pain, 63,* 353–360.

Spielberger, C., Gorsuch, R., & Luschene, N. (1976). *Manual for the state-trait anxiety inventory.* Palo Alto, CA: Consulting Psychologists Press.

Sullivan, M. J. L., Bishop, S. R., & Pivik, J. (1995). The Pain Catastrophizing Scale: Development and validation. *Psychological Assessment, 7,* 524–532.

Tarnowski, K. J., & Brown, R. T. (1999). Burn injuries. In A. J. Goreczny & M. Hersen (Eds.), *Handbook of pediatric and adolescent health psychology* (pp. 115–126). Needham, MA: Allyn & Bacon.

Taylor, S. (2003). Anxiety sensitivity and its implications for understanding and treating PTSD. *Journal of Cognitive Psychotherapy: An International Quarterly, 17*(2), 179–186.

Turk, D. C. (1996). Biopsychosocial perspective on chronic pain. In R. J. Gatchel & D. C. Turk (Eds.), *Psychological approaches to pain management: A practitioner's handbook* (pp. 3–32). New York: Guilford.

Turk, D.C., Kerns, R. D., & Rosenberg, R. (1992). Effects of marital interaction on chronic pain and disability: Examining the down side of social support. *Rehabilitation Psychology, 37,* 259–274.

Turk, D. C., Meichenbaum, D., & Genest, M. (1983). *Pain and behavioral medicine: A cognitive-behavioral perspective.* New York: Guilford.

Turk, D. C., Okifuji, A., Starz, T. W., & Sinclair, J. D. (1998). Differential responses by psychosocial subgroups of fibromyalgia syndrome patients to an interdisciplinary treatment. *Arthritis Care and Research, 11,* 397–404.

Turner, J. A., Mancl, L., & Aaron, L. A. (2006). Short- and long-term efficacy of brief cognitive-behavioral therapy for patients with chronic temporomandibular disorder pain: A randomized, controlled trial. *Pain, 121,* 181–194.

Vlaeyen, J. W. S., & Linton, S. J. (2000). Fear-avoidance and its consequences in musculoskeletal pain: A state of the art. *Pain, 85,* 317–332.

Von Bertalanffy, L. (1968). *General systems theory.* New York: Braziller.

Whitbourne, S. K., & Cassidy, E. L. (1996). Adaptation. In J. Birren (Ed.), *Encyclopedia of Gerontology* (vol. 1, pp. 65–69). San Diego: Academic Press.

Williams, D. A., & Thorn, B. E. (1989). An empirical assessment of pain beliefs. *Pain, 36*(3), 351–358.

Xuemei, L., Pietrobon, R., Sun, S., Liu, G., & Hey, L. (2004). Estimates and patterns of direct health care expenditures among individuals with back pain in the United States. *Spine, 29*(1), 79–86.

CHAPTER 16

Pediatric Psychology

LAMIA P. BARAKAT and BRET A. BOYER

CHILD HEALTH PSYCHOLOGY

The field of child health psychology, or *pediatric psychology,* as it is most often termed, is a relatively recent subspecialty in psychology's history, defined in the mid-1960s and emerging as its own division of the American Psychological Association in 2000 (Barakat, Kunin-Batson, & Kazak, 2003). In its original conceptualization, child health psychology integrates clinical child and adolescent psychology with pediatrics to address issues of child development within primary care, developmental disorders, and behavioral disorders (Kagan, 1965; Routh, 1975; Wright, 1967). As a field that has a strong research and practice tradition, the scope continues to focus on children in medical settings but has now broadened to address understanding and improving the adaptation of children with chronic or acute illnesses and their families, improving adherence to treatments, and health promotion and illness and injury prevention (Brown & Peterson, 1997; Damashek & Peterson, 2002; Peterson & Gable, 1998) through applied research and psychological assessment and intervention (Elkins & Roberts, 1988).

Given the foundation of child health psychology in clinical child and adolescent psychology, the field differs substantively from health psychology focused on adults in terms of attention to developmental considerations and a focus on the social ecology of the child. On the other hand, both child and adult health psychology emphasize short-term, empirically supported treatments, consideration of health care economics, and interest in disease prevention (Harper, 1997).

SOCIAL ECOLOGY

The social ecological model of Brofenbrenner (1979) provides a framework for organizing factors that influence adaptation and has been applied to children with chronic illness (Kazak, 1989; see Figure 16.1). The model describes proximal and distal influences on the child, who is centered in a series of concentric circles that represent reciprocal influences. The child, the illness, and the child's family comprise the microsystem at the most proximal level. To illustrate, the family's beliefs about the illness and their coping approach may impact their adaptation to the demands of the illness and its treatment. Caregivers who are overwhelmed with daily disease management

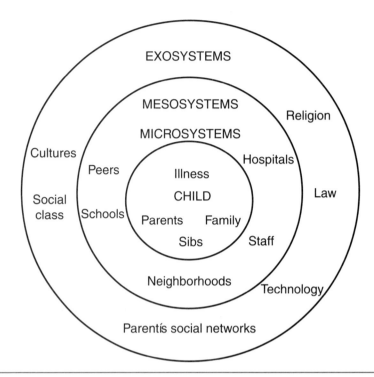

Figure 16.1 Social Ecological Model of Childhood Chronic Illness
The social ecology of pediatric illness. From Power, DuPaul, Shapiro, and Kazak (2003).
Copyright 2003 by The Guilford Press. Reprinted by permission

or who do not believe they can control their child's health may be more passive/
avoidant in their coping, resulting in distress for the child with chronic illness, the
caregiver, and potentially for healthy siblings. Conversely, children with premorbid,
difficult temperament or behavior problems will adjust more poorly to limitations imposed by the illness and may be less cooperative with medical procedures and treatments, in turn taxing caregiver coping resources.

The next level of influence, called the *mesosystem*, includes extended family, neighborhood, caregiver work, school, and hospital/medical team influences. For example,
communication with educators about a child's needs, not only through the school
nurse but by providing information to the classroom teacher and school administration allows for a responsive school environment that creates mechanisms for the child
to remain medically stable, continue to make progress at school, and feel support from
peers and teachers. Communication such as this may be essential, as educators report
that they have little training either in academic programming or continuing education
for dealing with the needs of children with chronic illness (Clay, Cortina, Harper,
Cocco, & Drotar, 2004). Meeting the educational needs of children with chronic illness
can be provided informally, such as allowing a child with sickle cell disease (SCD) to
carry water for hydration throughout the school day, or a child with Type 1 diabetes to
have a snack in the desk to eat when needed. Alternatively, existing legal mechanisms
may be utilized, such as 504 service plans or Individualized Education Plans, as outlined by the Individuals with Disabilities Education Act (IDEA), to modify educational programming to meet the child's medical, cognitive, and academic needs. In ad-

dition, communication among the child, family, and medical team plays a central role in addressing the medical and psychosocial needs of children with illness, as joint decision making and treatment alliance in the medical context may improve adherence to medical recommendations and adaptation (Gavin, Wamboldt, Sorokin, Levy, & Wamboldt, 1999; Perrin, Lewkowicz, & Young, 2000).

The *macrosystem* represents the most distal level and encompasses culture and social policy. Federal/state policies of requiring a series of immunizations prior to entry into the public school system has increased immunization rates and reduced incidence of a number of previously devastating illnesses (see Barakat, Kunin-Batson, & Kazak, 2003). Moreover, the Family Medical Leave Act of 1994 has allowed caregivers to more consistently attend to the care of their hospitalized children, with less concern about job and insurance loss. Finally, as noted previously, use of mechanisms provided through IDEA allows families and schools to modify educational programs to meet the needs of children with chronic illness.

Macrosystem influences also comprise cultural aspects, which are gaining more attention in terms of understanding beliefs about health and interaction with health care providers, reliance on particular coping mechanisms, and the psychologist's need to modify approaches to intervention in order to improve effectiveness (Clay, Mordhorst, & Lehn, 2002). For example, recent research suggests that caregivers of youth with SCD rely on religion and prayer in managing stressful aspects of this disease (Weinberger & Barakat, 2007). Religion/prayer as a coping approach may be best conceptualized as active coping, as it loaded with social support in a factor analysis and was associated with quality of life (QOL) of children with SCD. Culture also influences one's view of the health care system, health care utilization, and communication with health care providers (Clay et al., 2002).

DEVELOPMENTAL CONSIDERATIONS

Within the social ecological model, there is consideration of the passage of time. For children, passage of time requires accounting for physical, cognitive, and psychosocial development of a child at the time of diagnosis and throughout treatment, as impact of the illness and medical treatments may be mediated by these considerations (Taylor & Fletcher, 1995). At its most basic level, development determines the amount of caregiving required for youth with illnesses. Young children require significant supports, whereas adolescents may be able to take primary responsibility for home management of their illness. In addition, cognitive developmental level will influence children's understanding of their illness and treatment and directs the manner in which diagnosis and procedures are explained and how psychological interventions are delivered.

On a more complex level, developmental considerations refer to delineating disease and treatment effects on physical and cognitive functioning, and in turn, how changes or limitations in functioning may influence academic functioning, social skills and family and peer relationships, and psychological adjustment. As an illustration of this level of analysis, recent studies have attempted to identify the relative contributions of disease factors and family variables, including parent education, parenting stress, and family functioning, to neurocognitive functioning in children with illnesses that affect the brain, such as SCD (Tarazi, Barakat, Grant, & Ely, 2007) and brain tumors (Carlson-Green, Morris, & Krawiecki, 1995). Findings highlight the need to consider psychosocial factors in addition to disease parameters and their developmental influence in understanding an array of developmental outcomes.

PREVALENCE OF CHRONIC HEALTH CONDITIONS IN CHILDHOOD

Due to medical advancements in diagnosis and treatment, the prevalence of chronic health conditions in childhood is increasing, and although specific diseases remain relatively rare, the number of children affected by these conditions is substantial (Thompson & Gustafson, 1996). Estimated prevalence of chronic health conditions in childhood is between 10 and 37%, with variation depending on sample, reporters, and categorization approach (Combs-Orne, Heflinger, & Simpkins, 2002; Gortmaker & Sappenfield, 1984; Newacheck, McManus, Fox, Hung, & Halfon, 2000). Combs-Orne and colleagues, using parent report of health status in a sample of 965 Medicaid-eligible children, found that 37% of the sample had a chronic health condition. In a more conservative estimate, Newacheck and colleagues analyzed results of the 1992–1994 National Health Interview Survey on Disability and found that 18% of children met their criteria for special health care needs, which included physical, developmental, and behavioral problems that necessitated health service use. From the same survey, Newacheck and Halfon (1998) reported that childhood disability had a significant impact in restricting children's activities and resulted in missed school days and increased inpatient and outpatient health care service use. Moreover, chronic conditions follow youth into young adulthood. Henderson (1995) reported that approximately 9% of adolescents transitioning to college report chronic conditions requiring accommodations.

While prevalence rates of specific diseases have risen due to increased survival, particularly for cystic fibrosis, SCD, pediatric HIV, and cancer (Thompson & Gustafson, 1996), generally, incidence has not changed. However, asthma, Type 2 diabetes, and pediatric HIV display increased occurrence. The most common chronic childhood illness is asthma, affecting approximately five million children, with up to 10% having moderate to severe conditions (McQuaid & Walders, 2003; Thompson & Gustafson). Asthma prevalence increased dramatically over the 1980s and 1990s and is associated with a high degree of morbidity and mortality, including hospitalization, emergency room visits, and school absences. Children of lower socioeconomic status (SES), ethnic minority children, and those who reside in urban centers are at greater risk for developing asthma and its associated complications. For a comprehensive discussion of asthma, the reader is referred to Chapter 11.

The most common disorders of genetic origin (autosomal recessive) are SCD, an inherited blood disorder affecting 1 in 400–500 newborns, particularly African Americans in the United States (Lemanek, Ranalli, Green, Biega, & Lupia, 2003), and cystic fibrosis, an inherited disorder of the secretory glands, affecting primarily Caucasians, with around 30,000 youth in the United States with the disease (Stark, Mackner, Patton, & Acton, 2003). Diseases with mixed genetic and environmental etiology include diabetes and cancer. Type 1 diabetes affects 1 in 500–600 children, and Type 2 diabetes, with increasing incidence in ethnic minority youth, makes up about 10 to 20% of new diabetes cases each year (Wysocki, Greco, & Buckloh, 2003). Type 2 diabetes has been associated with the epidemic of pediatric overweight in the United States (Wysocki et al., 2003). With a current 75% survival rate, 1 in 330 children are diagnosed with cancer, and as many as 1 in 2,000 young adults are cancer survivors (Vannatta & Gerhardt, 2003), affecting all sociodemographic groups.

Pediatric HIV is transmitted either vertically (from mother to child) or horizontally (due to risky behaviors such as IV drug use and unprotected sex). The incidence of vertically transmitted HIV has been reduced substantially. In 2004, it was estimated that about 7,000 children under age 13 were living with HIV and 90% of those infections were the result of vertical transmission (Centers for Disease Control, 2004). However, rates of HIV continue to rise, due to increased cases that result from horizontal transmission. Ethnic minority youth are the most impacted by pediatric HIV—almost 20,000 youth between the ages of 15 and 24 are living with HIV/AIDS.

One final category often targeted by pediatric psychologists is childhood accidents and injuries, which account for the highest levels of morbidity and mortality across childhood and adolescence (Barakat et al., 2003). Approximately 1 in 4 children present for medical treatment each year as a result of accidents, and unintentional injuries lead to 600,000 emergency room visits per year. Moreover, traumatic brain injury resulting from accidents can have significant long-term physical and cognitive challenges.

Taken together, these statistics indicate a large proportion of children who are impacted by chronic health conditions and acute injuries through childhood and adolescence and into young adulthood. Description of the disease factors associated with these chronic conditions, which may impact developmental outcomes and adjustment over time, has taken several paths.

DISEASE FACTORS

As described in Chapter 1, the Model for Integrating Medicine and Psychology (MI-MAP) suggests that assessment of the specific stressors presented by a particular disease or health condition and the coping demands placed on children and their families by these stressors constitute the starting point of the health psychology assessment and treatment planning. A comprehensive and accurate clinical appreciation requires an understanding that (1) each disease has characteristics of its onset and disease progression that may be predictable, and (2) for individual children and their families, these characteristics may vary. For this reason, assessing categorical aspects and individual-specific (noncategorical) aspects of health conditions is imperative for the design and application of effective clinical care.

Both noncategorical and categorical approaches have been applied to delineation of disease factors and their association with adaptation (Thompson & Gustafson, 1996). The noncategorical position allows child health psychologists to identify and address characteristics common to all chronic conditions that create stressful circumstances for children and their families. These commonalities may include degree of functionality, requirements of treatment, financial obligations, and caregiver demands. On the other hand, the categorical approach has led to the identification of unique aspects of specific diseases in childhood that lead to tailored medical and psychological treatments. Although disease factors are often described and assessment of illness and treatment severity frequently included in studies, disease severity has not been consistently linked to psychosocial adaptation to illness. This lack of association is most likely due to the interaction of a number of factors in supporting resilient outcomes, as well as difficulties in measuring relevant disease factors (Barakat, Lash, Lutz, & Nicolaou, 2006; Wallander, Thompson, & Alriksson-Schmidt, 2003). Nevertheless, it remains important to understand the potential demands of illness on children and their families for assessment and intervention purposes.

A prevailing model, the family systems-illness model, describes how the psychosocial and practical demands of an illness vary over the course of the illness and depend on beliefs about illness and health care systems and on the developmental level of the child and family (Rolland, 1999). Characteristics of the disease that potentially impact functioning include onset (acute or gradual), course (progressive, constant, relapsing), outcome (terminal, life-shortening, possibility of sudden death, no impact of life span), incapacitation, and level of uncertainty about the course and outcome of an illness over time. These characteristics must be assessed within the context of delineating the phase of the illness: crisis, including diagnosis and other symptomatic periods, chronic or highs and lows of treatment, and terminal phase.

For example, in the most severe form of pediatric SCD (sickle cell anemia), diagnosis most often occurs shortly after birth, through newborn screening programs. As a result, diagnosis is acute but symptoms may not appear for some time, typically in the first year of life (National Institutes of Health [NIH], 2002). The course is considered relapsing with a number of potential complications, many of which, including painful episodes, acute chest syndrome, gallstones, splenic sequestration, and stroke, present suddenly; however, a number of symptoms such as anemia are chronic. The course is uncertain and life span is shortened. In contrast, symptoms leading to diagnosis in Type 1 diabetes mellitus are typically gradual, with a chronic course requiring daily evaluation and treatment in a complicated regimen that places ongoing demands on the child and family (Wysocki, Greco, & Buckloh, 2003). Leading to uncertainty about course and lifespan, immediate complications of Type 1 diabetes mellitus, hypo- or hyperglycemia, present acutely, while other complications occur gradually, due to long-term damage to organ systems.

Child, family, and health care provider beliefs about illness are influenced by family history and culture (Rolland, 1999). Consistent with the social ecological model, characteristics of the illness, beliefs about the illness and health care system, and family systems functioning interact over the course of the illness; the physical, cognitive, and psychosocial development of the child; and the progression in the family's stages of development to determine adaptation. In other words, age of the child and associated developmental exigencies, the family's current situation in terms of caregiver relationship and social support, and prior history with the health care system must all be reevaluated over time.

ADAPTATION TO CHRONIC ILLNESS IN CHILDHOOD

The conclusion that children with chronic illness are at risk for poor psychosocial outcomes has found its place in the literature for several decades (Pless & Roughman, 1971). More recently, in a meta-analytic review, Lavigne and Faier-Routman (1992) reported that children with chronic health conditions were at risk for development of internalizing (i.e., withdrawal, depression, anxiety) and externalizing (i.e., aggression, hyperactivity) behavior problems, although rates of disorders varied across health conditions and increase in level of risk depended on the comparison group used. Children with sensory or cognitive impairments and children with unpredictable illness courses seem to be at highest risk of adjustment problems. Other studies have documented reduced activities, social skills deficits, and problems in social functioning following diagnosis of chronic health conditions (see Barlow & Ellard [2006] for a recent review). Using a sample of children who were eligible for Medicaid, Combs-Orne and colleagues (2002) similarly found a consistent association between parent report of chronic health conditions in their children and mental health problems.

To demonstrate the nature of this research, Brown and colleagues (1993) assessed the psychosocial functioning of children with SCD compared to sibling controls

(Brown, Kaslow, Doepke, Buchanan, Eckman et al., 1993). This study is notable in its use of multiple informants (children, mothers, and teachers) and broad assessment of adaptation. They documented higher rates of internalizing behavior problems, specifically symptoms of depression, externalizing behavior problems, and limits in adaptive behavior. Moreover, the youth endorsed more negative attributional style and were ranked as less popular by classroom peers. Although a preponderance of findings support that youth with SCD are at risk (Barakat et al., 2006), it should be noted that other researchers have not reported these problems in adaptation when comparing children with sickle cell disease to controls matched on socioeconomic status (Lemanek, Moore, Gresham, Williamson, & Kelley, 1986; Midence, McManus, Fuggle, & Davies, 1996; Noll et al., 1996).

On a cautionary note, Perrin, Ayoub, and Willett (1993) noted that a number of problems with the design and methods of these studies may limit the conclusions that can be drawn, including the use of inconsistent definitions of adjustment (e.g., absence of behavior problems, adequate social functioning, high self-esteem, adaptive personality characteristics), diverse measures of adjustment (with many scales not adequately standardized for use in child samples), and variation in the chronic illness targeted. Criticism has also focused on symptom overlap of health conditions and depression and anxiety, with some researchers suggesting the omission of somatic subsets of symptoms in the report of internalizing problems in youth with chronic illness (Perrin, Stein, & Drotar, 1991).

To address a number of these limitations, Perrin and colleagues (1993) examined adjustment in five illness groups, including children with seizure disorders, children with visible disabilities, children with cerebral palsy, and a healthy control group, using standard child, parent, and teacher report measures. Their findings confirmed a number of conclusions noted in the meta-analytic and larger-scale studies, in that while healthy children were found to show better adjustment across reporters, adjustment and its correlates differed depending on chronic illness group.

As another approach to outcome assessment, many are turning to evaluation of quality of life, in that it provides consideration for the interplay of physical functioning with self, social, and behavioral adjustment, and therefore is considered more sensitive to variations in disease status and treatment demands. Quality-of-life scales may be disease specific; however, a number of forms have been developed that are designed for use across illness categories, such as the Children's Health Questionnaire (Landgraf, Abertz, & Ware, 1996), the PedsQL Pediatric Quality of Life Inventory (Varni, Seid, & Kurtin, 2001), and the Miami Pediatric Quality of Life Questionnaire (Armstrong et al., 1999). Quality of life of chronic illness groups is limited. For instance, Nicolaou and Barakat (2007) noted caregiver and child report of quality of life for child survivors of brain tumors was significantly lower than that reported for children with SCD, possibly reflecting differences in ongoing disease complications such as deficits in cognitive functioning and timing of diagnosis (birth for SCD versus childhood for brain tumor survivors).

RISK AND RESISTANCE MODELS FOR EXPLAINING ADAPTATION

Because of significant variability in adaptation across and within illness groups, different models have been put forth to explain outcomes and guide interventions. The most commonly used models conceptualize illnesses and their associated complications and treatments as acute and chronic stressors to which children and their fami-

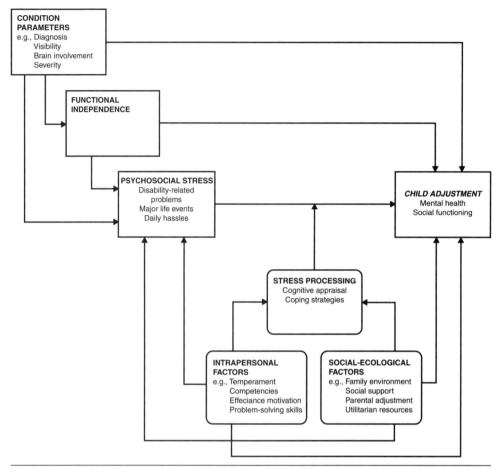

Figure 16.2 Risk-Resistance-Adaptation Model
Wallander and Varni's disability-stress-coping model of adjustment. Square corner boxes
indicate risk factors; round-corner boxes indicate resilience factors. Adapted from Wallander
and Varni (1992). Copyright 1992 by the Guildford Press.

lies must respond over long periods of time. Risk factors, such as sociodemographic
factors and disease variables, including functional limitations, cognitive effects, and
severity, which increase the likelihood of problems in psychosocial adaptation are outlined (see Figure 16.2; Wallander et al., 2003). In addition, resistance factors—including appraisals and coping, intrapersonal resources, and family functioning and social
support—are suggested as promoting adaptation in children and their caregivers. A
substantial literature has arisen establishing these models, by documenting the association of these risk and resistance factors with adaptation among a number of chronic
illness groups, with the strongest support for resistance factors (Lavigne & Faier-
Routman, 1993). Recent critiques have suggested that direct effects may not fully explain the role of these variables in outcomes; indirect effects may be more explanatory
(Holmbeck, 1997).

Brown, Doepke, and Kaslow (1993) applied a risk-and-resistance model to understanding adaptation of children and adolescents with SCD. In their literature review,
they found support for the role of disease severity as a risk factor and coping strate-

gies and family functioning as resistance factors for psychological adjustment. Burlew, Telfair, Colangelo, and Wright (2000) examined the relative strength of disease factors and psychosocial variables (self-esteem, social assertiveness, social support, family functioning) in explaining the symptoms of anxiety and depression in adolescents with SCD. Findings suggested that psychosocial variables accounted for more variance in adaptation than disease factors, with the intrapersonal factors of self-esteem and social assertiveness showing the strongest predictive power. However, psychosocial variables were not found to moderate the association of disease factors with adaptation. Similarly, Lutz, Barakat, Smith-Whitley, and Ohene-Frempong (2004) did not find support for indirect effects in their examination of the associations of disease severity, functional disability, coping strategies and psychological adjustment in children with SCD.

In an application of risk-resistance models, Barakat, Smith-Whitley, and Ohene-Frempong (2002) identified risk and resistance factors that influence adherence to prescribed treatment following admission to an acute care unit designed to provide intensive education and treatment for families of children with SCD. Seventy-three primary caregivers and their children (age 8 or older) completed forms assessing coping, family functioning, and child and parent adaptation. Treatment adherence variables (medical staff rating, SCD-related care activities, percentage of agreement between treatment recommendations made and care activities, and problems with adherence, noted in chart) indicated low to moderate adherence. Disease complications, family flexibility, and less parental reliance on passive coping accounted for significant proportions of the variance in treatment adherence (medical staff rating, SCD-related care activities, percentage of agreement between treatment recommendations made and care activities, and problems with adherence as noted in chart).

INTERVENTIONS

Early descriptions of pediatric interventions outlined psychoeducational approaches targeting adherence to medical procedures and psychological adjustment by providing illness information, supporting coping skills, and fostering social support and improved family functioning (Cofer & Nir, 1976; Gaudet & Powers, 1989). More recently, in conjunction with the conclusion that empirical research on pediatric interventions was undertaken much less frequently than descriptive studies (Drotar, 1997), emphasis was placed on testing and utilizing empirically supported treatments, as evidenced in the dedication of several issues of the *Journal of Pediatric Psychology* to reviewing treatment research for particular pediatric conditions such as pediatric overweight, procedure-related pain, pediatric headache, and enuresis (Barakat et al., 2003). In terms of future directions and consistent with the recommendations of the American Psychological Association's task force recommendations on evidence-based practice (Levant, 2005), applied research in pediatric psychology is expanding to improve external validity by furthering our understanding of what aspects of treatment work for whom, under what conditions, and in what contexts. In addition to attempts to reach underserved groups, to provide interventions in community-based and practice settings, and to examine cost/effectiveness of our interventions (Drotar), Clay and colleagues (2002) pointed out the need to pay particular attention to the role of ethnicity and culture in development, implementation, and evaluation of pediatric interventions. These authors highlight, for example, how cultural beliefs about diseases, coping, and health care utilization may limit the acceptability of some interventions.

In a meta-analytic review of 42 studies, Kibby, Tyc, and Mulhern (1998) reported that pediatric interventions effectively improve adjustment and reduce disease-related problems (effect sizes of 1.03 and 1.20, respectively) and that treatment gains are maintained up to 12-month follow-up. Particularly strong findings were noted for cognitive-behavioral interventions and for interventions targeting older females, while disease parameters were not associated with treatment outcome. The authors suggested that future research consider developing noncategorical treatment approaches for issues that affect all children with chronic illness, interventions be developed or modified with consideration of age and gender of participants, and follow-up assessments be incorporated into research methods (Kibby et al.).

Pediatric interventions may be grouped into those that support emotional/behavioral adaptation to chronic childhood illness and those that target disease management by addressing symptoms of the condition, such as treatments to reduce disease-related pain or interventions to improve adherence (Kibby et al., 1998). There are other targets for intervention and modes of intervention that are beyond the scope of this chapter, such as efforts aimed at health promotion, prevention of unintentional injury, and cognitive remediation for traumatic brain injury.

Although detailed descriptions or an exhaustive list of childhood health conditions is not possible within this chapter, an overview of several are provided. These are examples of diseases and health issues that have substantially developed literatures and serve as models to highlight the application of health psychology care to pediatric treatment. Overviewed here are *childhood cancer, pain* in the pediatric context, and *diabetes* management.

CANCER SURVIVAL

Pediatric cancer diagnosis is traumatic, as it presents significant illness, threat to bodily integrity, and possible death, and it is most frequently followed by invasive treatments, risk for relapse, and the potential for medical late effects as children move off treatment (Meister & Meadows, 1993). The literature suggests that while children and their families experience high levels of distress upon diagnosis and initial treatment, only a subset of children and their mothers and fathers are at risk for depression and anxiety symptoms into the survival phase (Kupst et al., 1995; Sahler et al., 2002; Vannatta & Gerhardt, 2003). Educational, occupational, and social functioning may also be limited (Meadows, McKee, & Kazak, 1989). Working within a trauma framework, Kazak and her colleagues have documented significant posttraumatic stress symptoms in adolescent survivors of cancer, young adult survivors of cancer, their mothers and fathers, and siblings (Alderfer, Labay, & Kazak, 2003; Barakat et al. 1997; Hobbie et al. 2001). Between 5 and 21% of childhood cancer survivors and their family members meet criteria for posttraumatic stress disorder (PTSD), with the majority meeting criteria for at least one symptom cluster, particularly reexperiencing and arousal (Kazak, 2001; Landolt, Vollrath, Ribi, Gnehm, & Sennhauser, 2003; Smith, Redd, Peyser, & Vogl, 1999).

Interventions for children on treatment for cancer target procedural pain, parental distress and coping, and/or school reintegration and associated social functioning. Based on findings of a strong association of maternal coping and adjustment with child and family adaptation to cancer over time (Kupst et al., 1995), Sahler and colleagues (2002) described a randomized, controlled evaluation of a problem-solving skills training with 92 mothers of children who were recently diagnosed with cancer.

The intervention was modeled after cognitive-behavioral interventions in which stressors are identified and patients are taught a five-step process for coping, including adjusting one's appraisal of the problem and increasing motivation to address it successfully, operationalization of the problem, generating solutions and making decisions about how to move forward, and implementing solutions (D'Zurilla & Nezu, 1999). Problem-solving skills were provided through individual, weekly sessions over an 8-week period in which mothers identified problems and implemented a plan after generating and evaluating possible solutions. Problems were cancer related and covered other issues, including parenting stressors and emotional reactions. The authors reported improved problem-solving abilities (in particular, constructive problem solving) and decreased distress for mothers, who received the training immediately after the intervention with continued but reduced improvements at 3-month follow-up. Reduced dysfunctional problem solving served as a mediator for decreased distress more than constructive problem solving.

Varni and colleagues (1993) provided children on treatment for newly diagnosed cancer an individual intervention targeting school reintegration by supporting social skills, assertiveness, and social problem-solving (Varni, Katz, Colegrove, & Dolgin, 1993). This intervention was compared to a standard school reintegration program, which included education of school personnel, improving communication among the family, medical team, and school, and presentations to classes about cancer. Both groups showed improvements at short- and long-term follow-up on measures of anxiety, social support, and behavior problems, with the individual social skills training group showing the most substantial change from baseline assessment. In a group social skills training for 18 survivors of brain tumors, Barakat and colleagues (2003) provided specific training in nonverbal social skills, starting, maintaining, and ending conversations, accepting compliments, cooperation and conflict-resolution in six group sessions with four to six participants (Barakat et al. 2003). The intervention comprised instruction in the targeted social skills, modeling and rehearsal, feedback, and homework, to encourage generalization in the home and school settings. Parents participated in a parallel parent group to review the social skills, learn how to support their maintenance and generalization, and to address other issues related to social functioning. The authors reported improved social skills, social functioning, and quality of life across child, parent, and teacher reporters from baseline assessment to 6-month follow-up.

Recent interventions have targeted posttraumatic stress symptoms and family communication in the survivors of childhood cancer and their family members. In the Surviving Cancer Competently Intervention Program, Kazak and colleagues (2004) combined cognitive-behavioral treatment of posttraumatic stress symptoms for mothers, fathers, teen survivors, and siblings in separate groups with a multiple family group format (Gonzalez, Steinglass, & Reiss, 1989). In the groups, the families discussed how cancer-related posttraumatic stress symptoms affect the family and how the family might "put cancer in its place" by communicating and supporting each other in the future (Kazak et al., 2004). The intervention was provided in a 1-day workshop, in which groups of four to six families addressed changing belief systems in the first two sessions and joined as families in the afternoon to integrate modified beliefs into family communication and cohesion in the last two sessions. Using baseline and 9–month follow-up assessments, the authors reported that posttraumatic stress symptoms were reduced most for fathers and teen survivors, and that family functioning improved for the intervention group compared to a waitlist control group.

These cancer-related PTSD intervention studies exemplify situations in which the health psychology literature has assessed and identified disease-specific clinical issues, then designed, applied, and evaluated therapies to ameliorate these difficulties.

DISEASE-RELATED PAIN

Pain had been documented to occur in children with surprising frequency, with older children reporting more pain and associated disability (Eccleston, Morley, Williams, Yorke, & Mastroyannopoulou, 2002). For example, Perquin and colleagues (2000) documented pain reports in 25% of their large sample of school-age children, with pain located in the head, limb, and gut (Perquin, et al.). Moreover, pain, both chronic and acute, is a central complication of a number of chronic conditions in childhood—pain management is central to the treatment of SCD, juvenile rheumatoid arthritis, cancer, and headache. Additionally, pediatric psychologists are consulted for distress associated with procedure-related pain, or that associated with venipuncture, needle sticks, burn treatment, or other procedures that are frightening and/or painful. Disease-related pain is differentiated from procedure-related pain and is discussed separately. This section primarily addresses disease-related pain.

Assessment and treatment are closely intertwined, and efforts are being made to improve the reliability of pain assessment through the use of daily paper-and-pencil pain diaries, self- and parent-report retrospective measures of pain, and refinement of Likert-type ratings of current pain. For example, the use of pager systems has been implemented for parents' report of pain in their preschool children with sickle cell disease, and hand-held computers have been piloted as a way to gain daily self-reports of pain in a mixed illness sample (Ely, Dampier, Gilday, O'Neal, & Brodecki, 2002; Palermo, Valenzuela, & Stork, 2004). However, problems with communication about pain by children to health care providers, and health care providers' underestimation of children's pain experience persist and may result in under-treatment of pain in pediatric populations (Varni et al., 1996).

Recent reviews of the literature highlight effective approaches to disease-related pain, pointing to cognitive-behavioral strategies as the treatment of choice (Eccleston et al., 2002; Walco, Sterling, Conte, & Engel, 1999). Walco examined studies that targeted pain associated with cancer, rheumatoid arthritis, and SCD. Although there were few well-controlled studies, promising findings were noted for a cognitive-behavioral intervention conducted by Gil, Carson, Redding-Lallinger, Daeschner, and Ware (1997), and Gil et al. (2001). In this trial, efficacy of a coping skills intervention was compared with standard care to address painful episodes in 46 children with sickle cell disease. The one-session intervention provided face-to-face instruction in relaxation, imagery, and self-talk that was followed by daily practice at home, supported by an audiotape. Results at the end of the intervention suggested that the coping skills training reduced pain sensitivity and negative thinking. However, at one-month follow-up, only effects for increased coping attempts remained, and there were no between-group differences on measures of pain and health care contact.

In an extension of this work (Schwartz, Radcliffe, & Barakat, 2007), a cognitive-behavioral intervention including deep breathing, relaxation, guided imagery, and positive coping self-statements is being compared to a disease-education control intervention and provided to adolescents with SCD along with a support person in the home. Modifications have been implemented to increase acceptability of the pain intervention by this primarily African American sample. For example, guided imagery content is selected by the teen to ensure interest in the scenes, multiple family members are included as support persons when indicated, and coping self-statements have been changed from the "standard" statements to those that are more consistent with African American adolescent terminology. Preliminary findings indicate decreased pain, high acceptability, and moderate retention for the pain intervention group.

Eccleston and colleagues' (2002) meta-analytic review summarized findings across studies, primarily targeting headache pain using a variety of cognitive-behavioral strategies, conducted in clinic or school settings, and provided individually, with a parent, or in a group. Outcome measures varied widely and included pain diary reports of frequency, intensity, and duration of pain, medication use, and school attendance. Results indicated that cognitive-behavioral interventions were effective in reducing pain when compared to controls. The authors emphasized the need for more controlled trials of cognitive-behavioral interventions for disease-related pain, in order to address pain in additional illness groups (beyond pediatric headache), delineate effective components, and better assess associated distress and functional limitations as outcomes.

PROCEDURE-RELATED PAIN

Pain and distress associated with medical procedures have received considerable research and intervention attention, especially when these procedures constitute a repeated, ongoing aspect of treatment, such as lumbar punctures and bone marrow aspirations for children with leukemia. Similar to findings for disease-related pain, recent reviews have described that nonpharmacologic interventions such as hypnotic interventions (Richardson, Smith, McCall, & Pilkington, 2006), and cognitive-behavioral interventions targeting distraction, counter-conditioning, and relaxation of anxious arousal (Kazak, 2006; Slifer, Tucker, & Dahlquist, 2002) are strongly supported by empirical evidence. Boyer (1998) provided a model for conducting cognitive-behavioral interventions for procedural pain with children of varied ages, emphasizing the individualization of intervention techniques to the needs of each child and family. By distinguishing the medium of intervention (e.g., imagery, play) to target particular factors (e.g., distraction of attention, reduction of sympathetic nervous system arousal, dissociation of painful sensation), the intervention can be tailored to children of differing ages, coping disposition, and anticipatory expectations.

DIABETES MANAGEMENT

Because Type 1 diabetes is a chronic and, at present, incurable condition, it requires intensive and ongoing disease self-management and places considerable demands on children and their families. In addition to the general issues covered in Chapter 8, several research and clinical issues are particularly relevant to children and are briefly reviewed here. Among these are developmental factors, family factors, and diagnostic levels of psychopathology among youth. Since the onset of diabetes may occur at any age throughout childhood and adolescence (as well as early to mid-adulthood), the child's age and cognitive development are crucial factors in his or her acquisition and maintenance of knowledge regarding self-management (Johnson, 1995: Wysocki, Meinhold, et al., 1996), consistency of self-management activities (Band, 1990; Thomas, Peterson, & Goldstein, 1997), and independence in self-management (Drotar & Levers, 1994; La Greca, Follansbee, & Skyler, 1990; Palmer et al., 2004; Wysocki, Taylor, et al., 1996) . Despite the fact that adolescents show greater knowledge about diabetes management (Johnson; Wysocki, Meinhold, et al., 1996) and greater resources for coping and problem solving than younger children, they often exhibit poorer self-management and poorer metabolic control (Band; Thomas et al.). Research attempting to clarify why adherence to diabetes self-care may suffer as cognitive and social maturity advance has identified at least two factors: effect of social peer pressures, and changes in parental support and responsibility for the diabetes management.

Peer pressure may exert a negative influence on disease management in Type 1 diabetes, while peer support may provide positive influence. For example, peers relationships have been found to impede adolescents' self-management behaviors, such as eating in public contexts (Delamater, Smith, Kurtz, & White, 1988). Research has also found that children with diabetes may be bullied more than healthy children (Storch et al., 2004) and that peer victimization relates to poorer self-management and metabolic control (Storch et al., 2006). In contrast, adolescents with diabetes highly value peer support (Greco et al., 1991), and peer support may assist teens in more successfully performing self-management activities (La Greca et al., 1995).

In addition, better adherence to diabetes self-care and improved metabolic control have been found when patients are in supportive family contexts (Greco et al, 1991; La Greca et al., 1995; La Greca & Bearman, 2002; Lewin et al., 2006; Skinner, John, & Hampson, 2000), particularly when family functioning involves effective communication, problem solving, and conflict resolution (Wysocki, Greco, & Buckloh, 1993); when parental involvement is perceived as collaborative rather than controlling (Wiebe et al., 2005); and when the type and amount of parental assistance is age and developmentally appropriate (La Greca, Follansbee, & Skyler, 1990; Palmer et al., 2004). Furthermore, there is evidence that adherence mediates the relationship between family factors and glycemic control (Lewin et al.), indicating that family factors impact the consistency of self-management activities, and the difference in self-management activities, in turn, impacts the important medical outcomes.

While many parents cope successfully with the multifactorial self-management regimen for diabetes (Lowes, Lyne, & Gregory, 2004), parents report that providing the necessary diabetes care to their children generates considerable parenting stress. Diabetes-related parenting stress is greater for caregivers with younger children, with lower socioeconomic resources, and in single-parent families (Streisand, Swift, Wickmark, Chen, & Holmes, 2005). Indeed, two studies have reported posttraumatic stress disorder among 16 to 24% of mothers and 8 to 22% of fathers of children newly diagnosed with Type 1 diabetes (Landolt et al., 2002; Landolt, Vollrath, Laimbacher, Gnehm, & Sennhauser, 2005). Such findings are concerning, because parental anxiety may disrupt family functioning and, thereby, interfere with optimal diabetes management. Moreover, mothers' sense of empowerment relates to both adherence and metabolic control for their children with diabetes (Florian & Elad, 1998), and the avoidance and anxiety of PTSD may interfere with parental empowerment and other important parenting factors.

Children with diabetes exhibit an increased risk of psychological difficulties, including depression, anxiety, and eating disorders. A prospective study indicated that, among individuals with childhood onset of diabetes, 27% experienced a major depressive episode and 13% experienced an anxiety disorder in the 10 years following their diabetes diagnosis (Kovacs, Goldston, Obrosky, & Bonar, 1997). Although some studies have found rates of depression among individuals with Type 1 diabetes that were similar to individuals without diabetes, with 14% reporting mild depression symptoms and 8.6% reporting moderate to severe symptoms, those with depression often show poorer adherence (Lustman, Griffith, & Clouse, 1996), poorer metabolic control (Lawrence et al., 2006; Lustman et al.), and more visits to the emergency room (Lawrence et al.). Effective treatment of depression symptoms also improves medical outcomes (Lustman et al.), making it an imperative consideration in overall disease management. In addition, children with diabetes are at risk for disordered eating, which may be more prevalent among adolescents than adults, and may result in persistently elevated blood glucose (Pollock-BarZiv & Davis, 2005; Takii et al., 1999). A type of purging specific to young women with diabetes involves the intentional omission of insulin administration in order to prevent blood glucose from being metabolized (Polonsky et al. 1994; Takii et al.). Eating disorders in Type 1 diabetes are also associated with the strategic focus on food (Antisdel & Chrisler, 2000), high body dissatisfaction (Colton, Rodin, Olmsted, & Daneman, 1999), self-blame and avoidant coping (Grylli, Wagner, et al., 2005), family eating patterns (Mellin, Neumark-Sztainer, Patterson, & Sockalosky, 2004), and personality factors (Grylli, Hafferel-Gattermayer, et al., 2005) including borderline personality characteristics (Pollock-BarZiv & Davis).

Extrapolating from these studies, younger children with diabetes require much more parental guidance and care, thereby increasing parenting stress. As children reach adolescence, parents may wish to transition from a "parent-care" to a "self-care" process and facilitate the adolescent taking greater responsibility for his or her diabetes management. If this is attempted too early, before children are well prepared in terms of knowledge and skills and before they are cognitively mature enough to handle problem solving, metabolic control often worsens. Parents who are able to change the way in which they assist their child yet continue their involvement throughout the transition (e.g., providing reminders but allowing the child to independently do the management activity, fading prompts for disease management over time, and engaging in collaborative problem solving with reduced authoritarian guidance) may have greater success relinquishing the primary responsibility while maintaining glycemic control. Importantly, peer relations become central to the success of this transition, and adolescents may avoid disclosure of their diabetes to peers (Jacobson et al., 1986). Assertive social skills may allow the adolescent to effectively negotiate these social contexts (Citrin, La Greca, & Skyler, 1985; Gross, 1987; Kaplan, Chadwick, & Schimmel, 1985). Families may benefit from assistance in diabetes-related problem solving and communication, and the difficult changes in parenting as children age and develop. Furthermore, clinicians need to assess for diagnostic and subclinical levels of anxiety, depression, and eating disorders in both patients and their parents.

In short, family functioning, peer-relations, and difficulties adjusting to and applying diabetes self-management all play a significant role in the patient's and family's quality of life and medical outcomes; all are amenable to psychological interventions. Empirical studies have documented the effectiveness of stress management and coping skills training, diabetes-specific problem solving therapies, family therapies, and cognitive-behavioral therapies for depression and anxiety for children and adolescents and should be considered a primary resource to ameliorate the impact of these factors on both adjustment and medical outcomes in diabetes treatment (see Drotar, 2006 for review). Although Drotar offers a comprehensive review of these various therapies, we here offer an example of such interventions, to highlight effective health psychology therapies for families facing Type 1 diabetes.

Anderson and colleagues (1999) compared three groups, one receiving a family teamwork intervention, one receiving an attention-control condition, and one receiving standard care in their outpatient appointments over a 12–month period. Families in the teamwork condition received four brief, focused training sessions during their outpatient visits, regarding (1) the changes in needs for adolescents' parental involvement in diabetes care, (2) coping with conflicts around blood glucose monitoring and (3) conflicts around food, and (4) parental support for exercise. In the year following the therapy, patients in the family teamwork condition displayed less parent-child conflict, consistency in parental involvement in blood glucose monitoring (compared to a decrease in parental involvement for the other groups), and more improvements in glycemic control. This study highlights the positive impact of a brief family-focused intervention, provided in the context of routine diabetes-care outpatient visits, on family conflict and, most importantly, upon primary medical outcomes.

CASE EXAMPLE

This case was chosen because it highlights several important aspects of pediatric psychology assessment and interventions: Development considerations, disease course, demands of disease management, and the role of family support and child psychosocial adjustment. The patient, here referred to by a fictitious nickname, "Skip," was diagnosed with Type 1 diabetes when he was 8 years old. He lived with his two parents, a married heterosexual couple, and his older sister, age 11. Skip's family was well educated, and his mother was currently not working, intending to return to her previous career when her children were older. Skip's father was employed, and the family was financially stable, with health insurance supplied by the father's workplace.

Skip began managing his blood glucose using a multiple daily injection regimen, in a basal/bolus format (See Chapter 8 for more details of the treatment regimen). After success with this regimen, Skip was transitioned to using a continuous subcutaneous insulin infusion pump. Since he was using a basal/bolus format of insulin regimen from the outset, he did not have to restrict his eating regarding types or amounts of food, but did need to take the appropriate amount of insulin for the types and amounts of food he was eating at any given time.

Skip and his family were referred for psychological intervention when Skip was 9 years old by his certified diabetes educator (CDE) due to difficulty with inserting the infusion sets for his pump. Placing the infusion set involves a needle insertion (described in Chapter 8) that Skip found more distressing than the use of the small-gauge insulin needles. Skip was tremendously avoidant of changing the infusion sets, which needed to be done every 3 days. He did not report that he was frightened, but behaved as if he was, engaged in extensive and very creative stalling techniques, and usually required 30 minutes to an hour to accomplish the task (which should require a few minutes). Put simply, Skip was frightened and avoidant of the procedure. He attempted to assert some control by delaying the initiation of the procedure, making requests that his mother do particular things as she replaced the infusion set, but found that these attempts to postpone and control did little to quell his anxiety and, in the end, failed to avert the task. His mother was trying desperately to accommodate these requests, but realized that the course of events had become a sequence of bargaining, followed by her eventually insisting on initiating the placement, and Skip becoming unresponsive to her reassurances. With each subsequent episode, this pattern appeared to escalate.

During the initial assessment by the health psychologist, it became apparent that Skip was relatively well behaved in most domains of his life and that his mother seldom needed to exert strategic contingencies to manage his behavior. His mother was comfortable taking responsibility for managing the timing and execution of his diabetes care, which appeared appropriate for someone his age, but Skip was now resisting her activities. This resistance was worsening over time, and his mother felt too guilty to set limits regarding his cooperation with these needle insertion procedures and was somewhat too solicitous with Skip. Her reason for pursuing therapy was that she felt unable to manage the situation and was concerned that he might begin resisting the other diabetes-management activities, like his finger sticks.

After a brief interaction in the second session, by which to establish further familiarity with Skip, attain his trust, and ascertain his interests, the clinician offered to help develop a plan to make the infusion set placements easier and less scary or painful. Using guided imagery, the clinician assisted Skip in creating and focusing on a covert imagery experience that both focused his attention away from the distressing aspect of the needle insertion and reduced his anticipatory sympathetic nervous system arousal (Boyer, 1998). Because Skip recounted with pride that, while on a recent vacation, he had learned to water ski for the first time, the clinician guided Skip through imagery in which he recalled vividly the experience of skiing behind the boat, of letting go of the towline, and the sensation of slowly and smoothly sinking into the water as his speed slowed on the skis. Skip would narrate what he was imaging, and his mother would tell him when to "let go of the line" at the moment she was ready to place the set. Skip would narrate the sensation of concluding his successful round of skiing by slowly drifting down into the water. As he did so, his mother would execute the needle placement. The imagery utilized a recent experience of accomplishment and control and served to distract Skip's attention, concluding in a brief relaxation of his anticipatory anxiety as the needle was quickly inserted. Skip's mother's cue to "let go of the line" prevented Skip from extending the imagery into another delay tactic.

The imagery was first employed during a session, under the clinician's guidance. The actual imagery was audiotaped and given to the family. The mother was coached in guiding the imagery, and the family felt confident enough to try it at home. After the first several successful uses of the imagery, the audiotape was no longer required, Skip and his mother developed an effective rhythm for the procedure, and there was little to no report of pain, distress, or avoidance. After a few appointments to evaluate the effectiveness of this means to cope with the procedure, support its use, address his mother's discomfort with setting behavioral contingencies, and assess for any other difficulties, it was observed that Skip loved his new pump (as he was fond of computer games and gadgets), and was having little to no difficulties. The imagery intervention was then altered, to induce Skip to replace the infusion set himself while doing the imagery. Therapy was concluded.

After the passage of 5 years, the family recontacted the health psychologist. With assistance from his parents, Skip had become more and more independent in his self-management activities. However, at the age of 14, he was diagnosed with celiac disease, an intolerance for gluten that is present in about 3 to 7% of individuals with diabetes (Murray, 2005), about 20 times higher prevalence than in the general population (Barera et al., 2002). Skip now had to adhere to a dietary restriction that excluded gluten (in wheat, oats, barley, etc.), which was far more intrusive upon his eating than the diabetes regimen. He was angry and depressed, and initially responded by ignoring a number of his diabetes self-management activities. Treatment involved referral to a nutritionist and cognitive-behavioral individual and family psychological intervention to (1) assist in Skip's problem solving regarding maintenance of both satisfying quality of life *and* his gluten-free eating and (2) reduce anger and depression. After 7 months of this weekly combination of family therapy and individual therapy, sessions were faded, and therapy concluded after 11 months of treatment. Skip, at this point, had resumed all of his academic, social, and recreational activities, and experienced greater ease with his regimen.

REFERENCES

Alderfer, M., Labay, L., & Kazak, A. E. (2003). Brief report: Does posttraumatic stress apply to siblings of childhood cancer survivors? *Journal of Pediatric Psychology, 28,* 281–286.

Anderson, B. J., Brackett, J., Ho, J., & Laffel, L. M. B. (1999). An office-based intervention to maintain parent-adolescent teamwork in diabetes management. *Diabetes Care, 22,* 713–731.

Antisdel, J. E., & Chrisler, J. C. (2000). Comparison of eating attitudes and behaviors among adolescents and young women with Type I diabetes mellitus and phenylketonuria. *Journal of Developmental and Behavioral Pediatrics, 21,* 81–86.

Armstrong, D. A., Toledano, S. R., Miloslavish, K., Lackman-Zeman, L., Levy, J. D., Gay, C. L., et al. (1999). The Miami Pediatric Quality of Life Questionnaire: Parent scale. *International Journal of Cancer, 83,* 11–17.

Band, E. B. (1990). Children's coping with diabetes: Understanding the role of cognitive development. *Journal of Pediatric Psychology, 15,* 27–41.

Barakat, L. P., Hetzke, J., Foley, B., Carey, M., Gyato, K., & Phillips, P. (2003). Evaluation of a social skills training group intervention with children treated for brain tumors: A pilot study. *Journal of Pediatric Psychology, 28,* 299–307.

Barakat, L. P., Kazak, A. E., Meadows, A. T., Casey, R., Meeske, K., & Stuber, M. L. (1997). Families surviving childhood cancer: A comparison of posttraumatic stress symptoms with families of healthy children. *Journal of Pediatric Psychology, 22,* 843–859.

Barakat, L. P., Kunin-Batson, A., & Kazak, A. E. (2003). Child health psychology. In A. Nezu, C. Nezu, & P. Geller (Eds.), *Handbook of psychology: Health psychology* (vol. 9, pp. 439–464). New York: Wiley.

Barakat, L. P., Lash, L., Lutz, M. J., & Nicolaou, D. C. (2006). Psychosocial adaptation of children and adolescents with sickle cell disease. In R. T. Brown (Ed.), *Pediatric hematology/oncology: A biopsychosocial approach.* New York: Oxford.

Barakat, L. P., Smith-Whitley, K., & Ohene-Frempong, K. (2002). Treatment adherence in pediatric sickle cell disease: Disease-related risk and psychosocial resistance factors. *Journal of Clinical Psychology in Medical Settings, 9,* 201–209.

Barlow, J. H., & Ellard, D. R. (2006). The psychosocial well-being of children with chronic disease, their parents and siblings: An overview of the research evidence base. *Child: Care, Health & Development, 32*(1), 19–31.

Barera, G., Bonfanti, R., Viscardi, M., Bazzigaluppi, E., Calori, G., Meschi, F., et al. (2002). Occurrence of celiac disease after onset of Type 1 diabetes: A 6–year prospective longitudinal study. *Pediatrics, 109,* 833–838.

Boyer, B. A. (1998). A clinical model for procedural pain interventions: Practice guidelines for comprehensive and individualized application. *Families, Systems & Health, 16,* 103–126.

Brofenbrenner, U. (1979). *The ecology of human development.* Cambridge, MA: Harvard University Press.

Brown, R. T., Doepke, K. J., & Kaslow, N. J. (1993). Risk-resistance-adaptation for pediatric chronic illness: Sickle cell syndrome as an example. *Clinical Psychology Review, 13,* 119–132.

Brown, R. T., Kaslow, N. J., Doepke, K., Buchanan, I., Eckman, J., Baldwin, K., et al. (1993). Psychosocial and family functioning in children with sickle cell syndrome and their mothers. *Journal of the American Academy of Child and Adolescent Psychiatry, 32,* 545–553.

Brown, D., & Peterson, L. (1997). Unintentional injury and child abuse and neglect. In R. T. Ammerman & M. Hersen (Eds.). *Handbook of prevention and treatment with children and adolescents: Intevention in the real world context* (pp. 332–356). Hoboken, NJ: Wiley.

Burlew, K., Telfair, J., Colangelo, L, & Wright, E. C. (2000). Factors that influence adolescent adaptation to sickle cell disease. *Journal of Pediatric Psychology, 25,* 287–299.

Carlson-Green, B., Morris, R. D., & Krawiecki, N. (1995). Family and illness predictors of outcome in pediatric brain tumors. *Journal of Pediatric Psychology, 20,* 769–784.

Centers for Disease Control. (2004). *HIV/AIDS Surveillance Report* (vol.16). Retrieved from www.cdc.gov/hiv/stats/2004SurveillanceReport.pdf

Citrin, W., La Greca, A. M., & Skyler, J. S. (1985). Group intervention in Type I diabetes mellitus. In P. I. Ahmed & N. Ahmed (Eds.), *Coping with juvenile diabetes* (pp. 181–204). Springfield, IL: Thomas.

Clay, D. L., Cortina, S., Harper, D. C., Cocco, K. M., & Drotar, D. (2004). Schoolteachers' experiences with childhood chronic illness. *Children's Health Care, 33,* 227–239.

Clay, D. L., Mordhorst, M. J., & Lehn, L. (2002). Empirically supported treatment in pediatric psychology: Where is the diversity? *Journal of Pediatric Psychology, 27,* 325–337.

Cofer, D. H., & Nir, Y. (1976). Theme-focused group therapy on a pediatric ward. *International Journal of Psychiatry in Medicine, 6,* 541–550.

Colton, P. A., Rodin, G. M., Olmsted, M. P., & Daneman, D. (1999). Eating disturbances in women with Type I diabetes mellitus: Mechanisms and consequences. *Psychiatric Annals, 29,* 213–218.

Combs-Orne, T., Heflinger, C. A., & Simpkins, C. G. (2002). Comorbidity of mental health problems and chronic health conditions in children. *Journal of Emotional and Behavioral Disorders, 10,* 116–126.

Damashek, A. & Peterson, L. (2002). Unintentional injury prevention efforts for young children: Levels, methods, types, and targets. *Journal of Developmental & Behavioral Pediatrics, 23,* 443–455.

Delamater, A. M., Smith, J. A., Kurtz, S. M., & White, N. H. (1988). Dietary skills and adherence in children with Type 1 diabetes mellitus. *Diabetes Educator, 14,* 33–36.

Drotar, D. (1997). Intervention research: Pushing back the frontiers of pediatric psychology. *Journal of Pediatric Psychology, 22,* 593–606.

Drotar, D. (2006). Psychological interventions: Diabetes. In D. Drotar (Ed.), *Psychological interventions in childhood chronic illness* (pp. 139–155). Washington, DC: American Psychological Association.

Drotar, D. & Levers, C. (1994). Age differences in parent and child responsibilities for management of cystic fibrosis and insulin-dependent diabetes mellitus. *Journal of Developmental & Behavioral Pediatrics, 15,* 265–272.

D'Zurilla, T. J., & Nezu, A. M. (1999). *Problem-solving therapy: A social competence approach to clinical intervention.* New York: Springer-Verlag.

Eccleston, C., Morley, S., Williams, A., Yorke, L., & Mastroyannopoulou, K. (2002). Systematic review of randomized controlled trials of psychological therapy for chronic pain in children and adolescents, with a subset meta-analysis of pain relief. *Pain, 99,* 157–165.

Elkins, P. D., & Roberts, M. C. (1988). *Journal of Pediatric Psychology:* A content analysis of articles over its first 10 years. *Journal of Pediatric Psychology, 13,* 575–594.

Ely, B., Dampier, C., Gilday, M., O'Neal, P., & Brodecki, D. (2002). Caregiver report of pain in infants and toddlers with sickle cell disease: Reliability and validity of a daily diary. *The Journal of Pain, 3,* 50–57.

Florian, V., & Elad, D. (1998). The impact of mothers' sense of empowerment on the metabolic control of their children with juvenile diabetes. *Journal of Pediatric Psychology, 23*, 239–247.

Gaudet, L. M., & Powars, G. M. (1989). Systems treatment in pediatric chronic illness: A parent group program. *Family Systems Medicine, 7*, 90–99.

Gavin, L. A., Wamboldt, M. Z., Sorokin, N., Levy, S. Y., & Wamboldt, F. S. (1999). Treatment alliance and its association with family functioning, adherence, and medical outcome in adolescents with severe, chronic asthma. *Journal of Pediatric Psychology, 24*, 355–365.

Gil, K. M., Carson, A. K. K., Redding-Lallinger, J. W., Daeschner, C. W., & Ware, R. E. (2001). Coping skills training in children with sickle cell disease: Daily coping practice predicts treatment effects. *Journal of Pediatric Psychology, 26*, 163–173.

Gil, K. M., Wilson, J. J., Edens, J. L., Workman, E., Ready, J., Sedway, J., et al. (1997). Cognitive coping skills training in children with sickle cell disease pain. *International Journal of Behavioral Medicine, 4*, 247–264.

Gonzalez, S., Steinglass, P., & Reiss, D. (1989). Putting the illness in its place: Discussion groups for families with chronic medical illnesses. *Family Process, 28*, 69–87.

Gortmaker, S. L., & Sappenfield, W. (1984). Chronic childhood disorders: Prevalence and impact. *Pediatric Clinics of North America, 31*, 3–18.

Greco, P., La Greca, A. M., Auslander, W. F., Spetter, D., Skyler, J. S., Fisher, E.B., et al. (1991). Family and peer support of diabetes care among adolescents (Abstract). *Diabetes, 40*, (Suppl. 1), 537A.

Gross, A. M. (1987). A behavioral approach to the compliance problems of young diabetics. *Journal of Compliance in Health Care, 2*, 7–21.

Grylli, V., Hafferl-Gattermayer, A., Wagner, G., & Schober, E. (2005). Eating disorders and eating problems among adolescents with Type 1 diabetes: Exploring relationships with temperament and character. *Journal of Pediatric Psychology, 30*, 197–206.

Grylli, V., Wagner, G., Hafferl-Gattermayer, A., Schober, E., & Karwautz, A. (2005). Disturbed eating attitudes, coping styles, and subjective quality of life in adolescents with Type 1 diabetes. *Journal of Psychosomatic Research, 59*, 65–72.

Harper, D. C. (1997). Pediatric psychology: Child psychological health in the next century. *Journal of Clinical Psychology in Medical Settings, 4*, 181–192.

Henderson, C. (1995). *College freshman with disabilities: A statistical profile*. Washington, DC: HEATH Resource Center.

Hobbie, W. L., Stuber, M. L., Meeske, K., Wissler, K., Rourke, M. T., Ruccione, K., et al. (2002). Symptoms of posttraumatic stress in young adult survivors of childhood cancer. *Journal of Clinical Oncology, 18*, 4060–4066.

Holmbeck, G. N. (1997). Toward terminological, conceptual, and statistical clarity in the study of mediators and moderators: Examples from the child-clinical and pediatric psychology literatures. *Journal of Consulting and Clinical Psychology, 65*, 599–610.

Jacobson, A. M., Hauser, S. T., Wertlieb, D., Wolfsdorf, J., Orelans, J., & Vieyra, M. (1986). Psychological adjustment of children with recently diagnosed diabetes mellitus. *Diabetes Care, 9*, 323–329.

Johnson, S. B. (1995). Insulin-dependent diabetes mellitus in childhood. In M.C. Roberts (Ed.), *Handbook of pediatric psychology* (2nd ed., pp. 263–285). New York: Guilford.

Kagan, J. (1965). The new marriage: Pediatrics and psychology. *American Journal of Diseases of Childhood, 110*, 272–278.

Kaplan, R. M., Chadwick, M. W., & Schimmel, L. E. (1985). Social learning intervention to improve metabolic control in Type I diabetes mellitus. *Diabetes Care, 8*, 152–155.

Kazak, A. E. (1989). Families of chronically ill children: A systems and social-ecological model of adaptation and challenge. *Journal of Consulting and Clinical Psychology, 57*, 25–30.

Kazak, A. E. (2001). Posttraumatic stress disorder in childhood cancer survivors: How common is it? *Journal of the National Cancer Institute, 93*(4), 262–263.

Kazak, A. E. (2006). Evidence-based interventions for survivors of childhood cancer and their families. *Journal of Pediatric Psychology, 30,* 29–39.

Kazak, A. E., Alderfer, M., Streisand, R., Simms, S., Rourke, M., Barakat, L. P., et al. (2004). Treatment of posttraumatic stress symptoms in adolescent survivors of childhood cancer and their families: A randomized clinical trial. *Journal of Family Psychology, 18,* 493–504.

Kibby, M. Y., Tyc, V. L., & Mulhern, R. K. (1998). Effectiveness of psychological intervention for children and adolescents with chronic medical illness: A meta-analysis. *Clinical Psychology Review, 18,* 103–111.

Kovacs, M., Goldston, D., Obrosky, D. S., & Bonar, L. K. (1997). Psychiatric disorders in youths with IDDM: Rates and risk factors. *Diabetes Care, 20,* 36–44.

Kupst, M. J., Natta, M. B., Richardson, C. C., Schulman, J. L., Lavigne, J. V., & Das, L. (1995). Family coping with pediatric leukemia: Ten years after treatment. *Journal of Pediatric Psychology, 20,* 601–617.

La Greca, A. M., Auslander, W. F., Greco, P., Spetter, D., Fisher, E. B., & Santiago, J. V. (1995). I get by with a little help from my family and friends: Adolescents' support for diabetes care. *Journal of Pediatric Psychology, 21,* 449–476.

La Greca, A. M., & Bearman, K. J. (2002). The Diabetes Social Support Questionnaire-Family Version: Evaluating adolescents' diabetes-specific support from family members. *Journal of Pediatric Psychology, 27,* 665–676.

La Greca, A. M., Follansbee, D. M., & Skyler, J. S. (1990). Developmental and behavioral aspects of diabetes management in youngsters. *Children's Health Care, 19,* 132–139.

Landgraf, J. M., Abertz, L., & Ware, J. E. (1996). *The CHQ User's Manual* (second printing). Boston, MA: HealthAct.

Landolt, M. A., Vollrath, M., Laimbacher, J., Gnehm, H. E., & Sennhauser, F. H. (2005). Prospective study of posttraumatic stress disorder in parents of children with newly diagnosed Type 1 diabetes. *Journal of the American Academy of Child & Adolescent Psychiatry, 44,* 682–689.

Landolt, M. A., Ribi, K., Laimbacher, J., Vollrath, M., Gnehm, H. E., & Sennhauser, F. H. (2002). Posttraumatic stress disorder in parents of children with newly diagnosed Type 1 diabetes. *Journal of Pediatric Psychology, 27,* 647–652.

Landolt, M. A., Vollrath, M., Ribi, K., Gnehm, H. E., & Sennhauser, F. H. (2003). Incidence and associations of parental and child posttraumatic stress symptoms in pediatric patients. *Journal of Child Psychology and Psychiatry, 44,* 1199–1207.

Lavigne, J. V., & Faier-Routman, J. (1992). Psychological adjustment to pediatric physical disorders: A meta-analytic review. *Journal of Pediatric Psychology, 17,* 133–157.

Lavigne, J. V., & Faier-Routman, J. (1993). Correlates of psychological adjustment to pediatric physical disorders: A meta-analytic review and comparison with existing models. *Journal of Developmental and Behavioral Pediatrics, 14,* 117–123.

Lawrence, J. M., Standiford, D. A., Loots, B., Klingensmith, G. J., Williams, D. E., Ruggiero, A., et al., (2006). Prevalence and correlates of depressed mood among youth with diabetes: The SEARCH for Diabetes in Youth study. *Pediatrics, 117,* 1348–1358.

Lemanek, K. L., Moore, S. L., Gresham, F. M., Williamson, D. A., & Kelley, M. L. (1986). Psychosocial adjustment of children with sickle cell anemia. *Journal of Pediatric Psychology, 11,* 397–410.

Lemanek, K. L., Ranalli, M. A., Green, K., Biega, C., & Lupia, C. (2003). Diseases of the blood: Sickle cell disease and hemophilia. In M. C. Roberts (Ed.), *Handbook of pediatric psychology* (3rd ed., pp. 321–341). New York: Guilford.

Levant, R. F. (2005). President's column: Evidence-based practice in psychology. *APA Monitor, 36,* 5.

Lewin, A. B., Heidgerken, A. D., Geffken, G. R., Williams, L. B., Storch, E. A., Gelfand, K.M., et al. (2006). The relation between family factors and metabolic control: The role of diabetes adherence. *Journal of Pediatric Psychology, 31*, 174–183.

Lowes, L., Lyne, P., & Gregory, J. W. (2004). Childhood diabetes: Parents' experience of home management and the first year following diagnosis. *Diabetic Medicine, 21*, 531–538.

Lustman, P. J., Griffith, L. S., & Clouse, R. E. (1996). Recognizing and managing depression in patients with diabetes. In B. J. Anderson & R. R. Rubin (Eds.), *Practical psychology for diabetes clinicians* (pp. 143–152). Alexandria, VA: American Diabetes Association.

Lutz, M. J., Barakat, L. P., Smith-Whitley, K., & Ohene-Frempong, K. (2004). Psychological adjustment of children with sickle cell disease treated in an acute care unit: The role of family functioning and coping. *Rehabilitation Psychology, 49*, 224–232.

McQuaid, E. L., & Walders, N. (2003). Pediatric asthma. In M. C. Roberts (Ed.), *Handbook of pediatric psychology* (3rd ed., pp. 269–285). New York: Guilford.

Meadows, A. T., McKee, L., & Kazak, A. E. (1989). Psychosocial status of young adult survivors of childhood cancer: A survey. *Medical and Pediatric Oncology, 17*, 466–470.

Meister, L. A., & Meadows, A. T. (1993). Late effects of childhood cancer therapy. *Current Problems in Pediatrics, 23*, 102–131.

Mellin, A. E., Neumark-Sztainer, D., Patterson, J., & Sockalosky, J. (2004). Unhealthy weight management behavior among adolescent girls with Type 1 diabetes mellitus: The role of familial eating patterns and weight-related concerns. *Journal of Adolescent Health, 35*, 278–289.

Midence, K., McManus, C., Fuggle, P., & Davies, S. (1996). Psychological adjustment and family functioning in a group of British children with sickle cell disease: Preliminary empirical findings and a meta-analyses. *British Journal of Clinical Psychology, 35*, 439–450.

Murray, J. A. (2005). Celiac disease in patients with an affected member, type 1 diabetes, iron-deficiency, or osteoporosis? 128(4 Suppl. 1), S52–S56.

National Institutes of Health. (2002). *The management of sickle cell disease.* NIH Publication no. 02-2117. Washington, DC: Author.

Newacheck, P. W., & Halfon, N. (1998). Prevalence and impact of disabling chronic conditions in childhood. *American Journal of Public Health, 88*, 610–617.

Newacheck, P. W., McManus, M., Fox, H. B., Hung, Y., & Halfon, N. (2000). Access to health care for children with special health care needs. *Pediatrics, 105*, 760–766.

Nicolaou, D. C., & Barakat, L. P. (2007). *Pediatric quality of life assessment in two chronic illness groups: Sickle cell disease and brain tumor survivors.* Unpublished manuscript.

Noll, R. B., Nannatta, K., Koontz, K., Kalinyak, K., Bukowski, W. M., & Davies, W. H. (1996). Peer relationships and emotional well-being of youngsters with sickle cell disease. *Child Development, 67*, 423–436.

Palermo, T. M., Valenzuela, D., & Stork, P. P. (2003). A randomized trial of electronic versus paper pain diaries in children: Impact on compliance, accuracy, and acceptability. *Pain, 107*, 213–219.

Palmer, D. L., Berg, C. A., Wiebe, D., Beveridge, R. M., Korbal, C. D., Upchurch, R., et al. (2004). The role of autonomy and pubertal status in understanding age differences in maternal involvement in diabetes responsibility across adolescence. *Journal of Pediatric Psychology, 29*, 35–46.

Perquin, C. W., Hazebroek-Kampscheur, A. A. J. M., Hunfeld, J. A. M., Bohnene, A. M., van Suijlekom-Smit, L. W. A., Passchier, J., et al. (2000). Pain in children and adolescents: A common experience. *Pain, 87*, 51–58.

Perrin, E. C., Ayoub, C. C., & Willett, J. B. (1993). In the eyes of the beholder: Family and maternal influences on perceptions of adjustment of children with chronic illness. *Journal of Developmental and Behavioral Pediatrics, 14*, 94–105.

Perrin, E. C., Lewkowicz, C., & Young, M. H. (2000). Shared vision: Concordance among fathers, mothers and pediatricians about unmet needs of children with chronic health conditions. *Pediatrics, 105,* 277–285.

Perrin, E. C., Stein, R., & Drotar, D. (1991). Assessing the adjustment of children with a chronic illness: Cautions in using the Child Behavior Checklist (CBCL). *Journal of Pediatric Psychology, 16,* 411–421.

Peterson, L., & Gable, S. (1998). Holistic injury prevention. In J. R. Lutzker (Ed.), *Handbook of child abuse research and treatment* (pp. 291–318). New York: Plenum.

Pless, I. B., & Roughman, K. (1971). Chronic illness and its consequences: Some observations based on three epidemiological surveys. *Journal of Pediatrics, 79,* 351–359.

Pollock-BarZiv, S. M., & Davis, C. (2005). Personality factors and disordered eating in young women with Type 1 diabetes mellitus. *Psychosomatics, 46,* 11–18.

Polonsky, W. H., Anderson, B. J., Lohrer, P. A., Aponte, J. E., Jacobson, A. M., & Cole, C. E. (1994). Insulin omission in women with IDDM. *Diabetes Care, 17,* 1178–1185.

Richardson, J., Smith, J. E., McCall, G., & Pilkington, K. (2006). Hypnosis for procedure-related pain and distress in pediatric cancer patients: A systematic review of effectiveness and methodology related to hypnotic interventions. *Journal of Pain and Symptom Management, 31,* 70–84.

Rolland, J. S. (1999). Parental illness and disability: A family systems framework. *Journal of Family Therapy, 21,* 242–266.

Routh, D. K. (1975). The short history of pediatric psychology. *Journal of Clinical Child Psychology,* (Fall), 6–8.

Sahler, O. Z. J., Varni, J. W., Fairclough, D. L., Butler, R. W., Noll, R. B., Dolgin, M. J., et al. (2002). Problem-solving skills training for mothers of children with newly diagnosed cancer: A randomized trial. *Journal of Developmental and Behavioral Pediatrics, 23,* 77–87.

Schwartz, L., Radcliffe, J., & Barakat, L. P. (2007). The development of a culturally sensitive pediatric pain management intervention for African-American adolescents: Sickle cell disease as an example. *Children's Health Care.* In press.

Skinner, T. C., John, M., & Hampson, S. E. (2000). Social support and personal models of diabetes as predictors of self-care and well-being: A longitudinal study of adolescents with diabetes. *Journal of Pediatric Psychology, 25,* 256–267.

Slifer, K. J., Tucker, C. L., & Dahlquist, L. M. (2002). Helping children and care-givers with repeated invasive procedures: How are we doing? *Journal of Clinical Psychology in Medical Settings, 9,* 131–152.

Smith, M. Y., Redd, W. H., Peyser, C., & Vogl, D (2001). Post-traumatic stress disorder in cancer: A review. *Psycho-Oncology, 8,* 521–537.

Stark, L. J., Mackner, L. M., Patton, S. R., & Acton, J. D. (2003). Cystic fibrosis. In M. C. Roberts (Ed.), *Handbook of pediatric psychology* (3rd ed., pp. 286–303). New York: Guilford.

Storch, E. A., Heidgerken, A. D., Geffken, G. R., Lewin, A., Ohleyer, V., Freddo, M., et al. (2006). Bullying, regimen self-management, and metabolic control in youth with type 1 diabetes. *The Journal of Pediatrics, 148,* 784–787.

Storch, E. A., Lewin, A., Silversein, J. H., Heidgerken, A. D., Strawser, M. S., Baumeister, A., et al. (2004). Peer victimization and psychosocial adjustment in children with type 1 diabetes. *Clinical Pediatrics, 43,* 467–471.

Streisand, R., Swift, E., Wickmark, T., Chen, R., & Holmes, C. S. (2005). Pediatric parenting stress among parents of children with Type 1 diabetes: The role of self-efficacy, responsibility, and fear. *Journal of Pediatric Psychology, 30,* 513–521.

Takii, M., Komaki, G., Uchigata, Y., Maeda, M., Omori, Y., & Kubo, C. (1999). Differences between bulimia nervosa and binge-eating disorder in females with Type I diabetes: The important role of insulin omission. *Journal of Psychosomatic Research, 47,* 221–231.

Tarazi, R. A., Barakat, L. P., Grant, M., & Ely, E. (2007). Neuropsychological functioning of preschool children with sickle cell disease. *Journal of Child Neuropsychology, 13*, 155–172.

Taylor, H. G., & Fletcher, J. M. (1995). Editorial: Progress in pediatric neuropsychology. *Journal of Pediatric Psychology, 20*, 695–701.

Thomas, A. M., Peterson, L., & Goldstein, D. (1997). Problem solving and diabetes regimen adherence by children and adolescents with IDDM in social pressure situations: A reflection of normal development. *Journal of Pediatric Psychology, 22*, 541–561.

Thompson, R. J., Jr., & Gustafson, K. E. (1996). *Adaptation to chronic childhood illness.* Washington, DC: American Psychological Association.

Vannatta, K., & Gerhardt, C. A. (2003). Pediatric oncology: Psychosocial outcomes for children and families. In M. C. Roberts (Ed.), *Handbook of pediatric psychology* (3rd ed., pp. 342–357). New York: Guilford.

Varni, J. W., Katz, E. R., Colegrove, R., & Dolgin, M. (1993). The impact of social skills training on the adjustment of children with newly diagnosed cancer. *Journal of Pediatric Psychology, 18*, 751–767.

Varni, J. W., Rapoff, M. A., Waldron, S. A., Gragg, R. A., Bernstein, B. H., & Lidsley, C. B. (1996). Chronic pain and emotional distress in children and adolescents. *Journal of Developmental and Behavioral Pediatrics, 17*, 154–161.

Varni, J. W., Seid, M., & Kurtin, P. S. (2001). The PedsQL4.0: Reliability and validity of the Pediatric Quality of Life Inventory Version 4.0 Generic Core Scales in healthy and patient populations. *Medical Care, 39*, 800–812.

Walco, G., Sterling, C., Conte, P., & Engel, R. (1999). Empirically supported treatments in pediatric psychology: Disease-related pain. *Journal of Pediatric Psychology, 24*, 155–167.

Wallander, J. L., Thompson, R. J., Jr., & Alriksson-Schmidt, A. (2003). Psychosocial adjustment of children with chronic physical conditions. In M. C. Roberts (Ed.), *Handbook of pediatric psychology* (3rd ed., pp. 141–158). New York: Guilford.

Weinberger, B. S., & Barakat, L. P. (2007). *Coping in adolescents with sickle cell disease and their caregivers: An engagement-disengagement perspective.* Unpublished manuscript.

Wiebe, D. J., Berg, C. A., Korbel, C. D., Palmer, D. L., Beveridge, R. M., Upchurch, R., et al. (2005). Children's appraisals of maternal involvement in coping with diabetes: Enhancing our understanding of adherence, metabolic control, and quality of life across adolescence. *Journal of Pediatric Psychology, 30*, 167–178.

Wysocki, T., Meinhold, P., Taylor, A., Hough, B. S., Barnard, M. U., Clarke, W. L., et al. (1996). Psychometric properties and normative data for the parent version of the Diabetes Independence Survey. *Diabetes Educator, 22*, 587–591.

Wysocki, T., Greco, P., & Buckloh, L. M. (2003). Childhood diabetes in psychological context. In M. C. Roberts (Ed.), *Handbook of pediatric psychology* (3rd ed., pp. 304–320). New York: Guilford.

Wysocki, T., Taylor, A., Hough, B. S., Linscheid, T. R., Yeates, K. O., & Naglieri, J. A. (1996). Deviation from developmentally appropriate self-care autonomy: Association with diabetes outcomes. *Diabetes Care, 19*, 119–125.

Wright, L. (1967). The pediatric psychologist: A role model. *American Psychologist, 22*, 323–325.

CHAPTER 17

Substance Abuse in Medical Settings

ALLISON DORLEN PASTOR, APARNA KALBAG-BUDDHIKOT,
and ADAM C. BROOKS

INTRODUCTION

Mr. X, a divorced 54-year-old Caucasian male, presents to your primary care clinic with blood sugar levels that have consistently remained elevated for the past year despite vigorous treatment with oral hypoglycemic agents. Though he presents as alert and oriented this morning, you detect a faint odor of alcohol on his breath, and you suspect that excessive alcohol intake might be exacerbating his condition. In prior visits he has denied any alcohol use, let alone problematic use. You would like to address this issue in a direct but sensitive way so as to maximize the likelihood that Mr. X will follow up with appropriate treatment and ultimately improve his blood sugar and overall health. However, you are unclear about what strategies would be most successful in accomplishing this goal, and furthermore, you are unsure how to assess the extent of his problem and to ascertain the most appropriate treatment. How should you proceed with Mr. X?

A thorough substance abuse assessment along with an understanding of treatment options is an important component of comprehensive treatment in primary care and other medical settings. However, as this scenario suggests, many factors can hinder a practitioner attempting to make a sensitive and effective assessment. These may include the brevity of patient appointments, the lack of training about the prevalence and clinical manifestations of alcohol and drug abuse, and limited information about substance abuse treatment settings and systems. In addition, patients may present barriers to assessment and intervention, such as a lack of awareness of the risks of alcohol or drug use, or reluctance to discuss issues that may be personal, feel stigmatizing, or seem unrelated to physical health.

Drug and alcohol problems are prevalent in the United States. According to the Substance Abuse and Mental Health Services Administration's 2005 National Survey on Drug Use and Health (SAMHSA, 2005), 22.8% of the U.S. population (55 million people) binged on alcohol at least once, consuming five or more drinks in one sitting during the month prior to the survey. Another 6.6% of the population, or 16 million people, reported binge drinking on at least five occasions in the month prior to the survey. An estimated 9.1% of the population (22.2 million people) was classified with substance dependence or abuse in the past year, based on criteria specified in the *Diag-*

nostic and Statistical Manual of Mental Disorders, 4th edition (DSM-IV; APA, 1994). Of these, 15.4 million were dependent on or abused only alcohol, 3.6 million were dependent on or abused only illicit drugs, and 3.3 million were classified with dependence or abuse of both alcohol and illicit drugs.

The need for improved detection of substance abuse in the medical setting, particularly in primary care clinics, is significant. Health problems resulting from prolonged or acute alcohol and substance use are widely documented in the medical literature. Patients who engage in excessive drinking and drug use have been found to have heightened prevalence of several medical conditions, including injuries, pneumonia, and hypertension (Mertens, Weisner, Ray, Fireman, & Walsh, 2005). Less quantifiable is the negative effect that a loved one's substance abuse can have on the lives of family members and friends, such as emotional strain, financial burden, fatigue, and anxiety and depression.

Practitioners in a primary care setting are uniquely positioned to assist patients with substance abuse problems. They are the professionals most likely to see patients on an ongoing and regular basis for routine medical visits or specific medical problems, and therefore can be the first to identify, intervene, and follow up with a patient's substance-related problems. Furthermore, research has demonstrated that brief interventions—counseling delivered by primary care providers and other health professionals in the context of several standard office visits—can reduce patients' consumption levels by 10 to 30% (Kahan, Wilson, & Becker, 1995; Wilk, Jensen, & Havighurst, 1997). However, despite the opportunities for screening and intervention in primary care settings, research suggests that practitioners may miss indicators of substance abuse. In one study, 45% of persons presenting for addiction treatment in the public system reported that their primary care physician was unaware of their substance abuse (Saitz, Mulvey, Plough, & Samet, 1997). Saitz and colleagues found that the patients most likely to have reported physician unawareness were those without health insurance, without a history of medical illness, and with no prior substance abuse or mental health treatment. Often, practitioners ask patients about consumption, but few go beyond an initial inquiry, thereby missing potential diagnostic opportunities (Bradley, Curry, Koepsell, & Larson, 1995; Wenrich, Paauw, Carline, Curtis, & Ramsey, 1995). One survey found that among practitioners, greater confidence in drug/alcohol assessment skills, greater familiarity with expert substance abuse recommendations, and the belief that patients will not be offended by substance use questions all contributed to better screening and intervention practices (Friedmann, McCullough, Chin, & Saitz, 2000). These findings highlight the importance of integrating consistent alcohol and drug screening into routine medical care.

This chapter is written predominantly for physicians, nurses, physician assistants, health psychologists, and other clinicians working in medical settings (social workers, occupational and physical therapists). It is up to the individual practitioner to determine what techniques and approaches are realistic, given interdisciplinary staffing considerations and environmental constraints. While some of the in-depth counseling approaches discussed in this chapter may be more appropriate for health psychologists or other counselors, these techniques can be useful for practitioners of all disciplines to understand in the course of assessment. After reading this chapter, health care practitioners should be able to do the following:

1. Recognize the clinical presentation of acute and chronic alcohol use and the use of the most commonly abused drug.

2. Identify patients at risk for developing alcohol or drug problems who may benefit from primary prevention interventions such as patient education.
3. Identify whether a patient's alcohol or drug use is problematic.
4. Interview a patient about his or her use of substances in a manner that will maintain rapport and increase the probability of follow-up on treatment recommendations.
5. Gain awareness of one's own preconceived notions, biases, or assumptions about substance abusing patients.
6. Increase familiarity with treatment resources in order to make appropriate referrals and effect smoother transitions to substance abuse treatment facilities.

DEFINITIONS

Before discussing the assessment and treatment of drug and alcohol problems, it is important to define and classify the various problem behaviors. It is also useful to be aware of the risk factors associated with their development. A brief discussion of these areas follows.

An important task of the primary care practitioner is to determine the level of concern that is warranted, based on a patient's reported use of alcohol or drugs. Fortunately, there are some established practice guidelines to assist the practitioner in this decision making. According to the U.S. Preventive Services Task Force (1996), there are three main categories of substance use: risky, harmful, and dependent/addicted. *Risky* alcohol/drug use means that there is the potential for problematic health, legal, or social consequences with continued or escalating use. *Harmful* alcohol/drug use refers to patients who have already experienced negative substance-related consequences. Finally, *dependent* or *addicted* alcohol/drug use is associated with loss of control and drug-seeking behavior that may require referral for specialized treatment. One prevalence study conducted in primary care settings found that 20% of male patients and 10% of female patients who came to see their physicians met the criteria for at-risk, problem, or dependent alcohol use (Manwell, Fleming, Johnson, & Barry, 1998). These categories and associated guidelines are illustrated in the following alcohol section.

Alcohol   "Risky" drinking is defined as having more than 7 drinks per week or more than 3 drinks per occasion for women, and more than 14 drinks per week or more than 4 drinks per occasion for men. Special consideration is necessary when assessing alcohol use among adolescents, pregnant women, the elderly, those medically compromised, and those taking prescription medications for which alcohol use is contraindicated. For some of these patients, depending upon their specific medical issues, any amount of alcohol use can be deemed risky.

"Harmful" drinking is defined as experiencing physical, social, or psychological harm from alcohol use. These patients may already be encountering marital discord, problems at work, alienation from social circles, or financial or legal problems related to episodes of drinking. Anecdotally, clinicians observe that harmful drinking can present itself in more subtle ways, such as i1mpaired productivity the day after a night of drinking, weight gain related to drinking binges, sudden changes in mood, increased irritability, or fluctuations in energy level and/or motivation.

"Dependent" drinking manifests as continued drinking despite significant alcohol-related problems. The criteria for alcohol dependence are listed in the following assessment section. Dependence involves repeated, compulsive drinking, a feeling of loss of control over alcohol intake, a desire to quit or cut down, and frequent (often unsuccessful) efforts to limit or cease drinking. A dependent alcohol user may choose to use alcohol to the exclusion of other activities, such as spending time with loved ones, working, attending school, or pursuing hobbies. Often, but not necessarily, an individual can develop a tolerance for alcohol, whereby an increased amount is required to derive the same effect from the substance. Additionally, alcohol-dependent individuals can experience a withdrawal syndrome that leads them to seek alcohol to alleviate associated symptoms. These withdrawal symptoms will be discussed in greater detail in the Medical Interventions section.

An important caveat about alcohol abuse or dependence diagnoses is that these categories are *qualitatively* different from normal drinking rather than *quantitatively* different. Some practitioners may give a diagnosis of abuse or dependence based largely on the amount of alcohol a patient is consuming. Though the quantity of alcohol intake is a key variable in an assessment, it is the consequences and the subjective experience of the intake (e.g., craving, loss of control) that should be primary in formulating the diagnosis.

Prescription Drugs   "Non-medical use" is a term used to describe nonprescribed use of a medication. It is defined as using a psychotherapeutic drug "even once, that was not prescribed for you, or that you took only for the experience or feeling it caused" (SAMHSA, 2002, p. 53). Commonly abused classes of prescription drugs include opioids, which are often prescribed to treat pain (e.g., OxyContin, Darvon, Vicodin), central nervous system depressants, often prescribed to treat anxiety and sleep disorders (e.g., barbiturates such as Nembutal, benzodiazepines such as Valium, Xanax), and stimulants, often prescribed to treat narcolepsy, ADHD, and obesity (e.g., Dexedrine, Ritalin). In detecting possible prescription drug abuse, providers should note any dramatic increases in the amount of a medication needed or frequent requests for refills before the quantity prescribed should have been used, which can indicate the development of tolerance or diversion of medications (e.g., selling or giving medications to a third party). Additionally, one must be keen to a patient's report of lost pills or prescriptions. Practitioners should also be alert to the fact that those addicted to prescription medications often engage in "doctor shopping," moving from provider to provider in an effort to get multiple prescriptions for the drugs they abuse. Some strategies that can help prevent misuse of prescriptions include: (a) frequent doctor visits and prescribing smaller amounts of medication between visits, (b) asking patients to bring pill bottles to appointments, and counting the number of pills left, (c) prescribing pills with less abuse potential (e.g., sedating antidepressant versus sedative/hypnotic), and (d) ordering random urine toxicology tests during doctor's visits.

Illicit Street Drugs Generally, any use of street drugs is considered to be high risk. Merely obtaining illicit drugs can be dangerous, and their use carries risks of exposure to toxic additives and possible overdose. Illicit drugs will be discussed in more detail in the Associated Features of Substance Disorders section.

Risk Factors

Risk factors for the development of alcohol and substance abuse are generally recognized to be a function of a complex interaction between biological/genetic factors and psychological/contextual factors. A comprehensive review of all related factors is beyond the scope of this chapter. However, key findings are highlighted in the following section, with an emphasis on practical information for practitioners working in a primary care setting.

Biological Risk Factors   Anecdotally, many practitioners tend to notice a clustering of alcoholism and/or drug abuse within families while taking patient histories. Decades of research on familial patterns lend credence to these observations. For example, children of alcoholics are four to five times more likely to develop alcoholism than individuals in the general population (Bohman, Sigvardsson, & Cloninger, 1981). There are multiple explanations in the research literature for the clustering of substance-related problems in families. These explanations include differences in physiological sensitivity and responsiveness to alcohol and other drugs, neurotransmitter variations among individuals that affect physiological response, prenatal exposure to alcohol and other drugs, and differences in prefrontal EEG patterns (Deckel, Bauer, & Hesselbrock, 1995). Other research points to two different subtypes of alcohol users, where Subtype I is associated with later onset and less antisocial behavior, while Subtype II is purported to have an earlier onset, a greater genetic influence and more risk of antisocial behavior and violence (Cloninger, Sigvardsson, Reich, & Bohman, 1986). There is also some evidence supporting the role of temperament, which is found to be in large part heritable, in the development of substance abuse problems. For instance, there is a body of research linking impulsivity and sensation-seeking traits to increased substance abuse (Ball, Carroll, & Rounsaville, 1994).

Psychological/Contextual Risk Factors   In addition to biological influences, a substance abuse problem is also composed of a set of learned behaviors. This concept can provide another explanation for clustering of alcohol and drug use in families: a psychological term called *social learning* or *modeling* (Bandura, 1985). Social learning posits that the behavior of important developmental role models influences the development of our own behavior. Therefore, alcohol/drug-using family members, peers, and spouses can affect an individual's own alcohol/drug-related behavior. Further, the emotional climate in families of persons abusing substances (e.g., conflict, volatility, and/or instability), may enhance vulnerability to substance-related problems in offspring and significant others (Andreas, O'Farrell, & Fals-Stewart, 2006). Finally, Opponent Process Theory is another approach to explaining the development and maintenance of substance use behavior. According to this theory, substances are initially used to derive both psychological and physiological pleasure. However, over time they provide diminishing returns after prolonged use, while the effects of withdrawal become increasingly intensified and unpleasant. Eventually, substances are often used primarily to ward off negative withdrawal symptoms (Ettenberg, 2004; Ettenberg, Raven, Danluck, & Necessary, 1999).

There are additional important red flags that the practitioner should keep in mind while assessing substance abuse. First, the biggest risk factor for an individual's future use of alcohol and other drugs is a personal past history of drug or alcohol abuse. Certainly, not every person with a history of substance abuse will necessarily relapse in the future, but these individuals are at greater risk than the general population. Second, research has indicated that another important marker for risk of drug/alcohol dependence is age at the time of first use. Research has shown that first use of alcohol between the ages of 11 to 14 greatly heightens the risk of progression to the development of alcohol disorders (DeWit, Adlaf, Offord, & Ogborne, 2000). The same has been found to be true for drugs; teens that use drugs before age 15 have 6 to 10 times greater rates of drug dependency than the general population (Higgins, 1988; Robins & Przybeck, 1987). Finally, as will be discussed further, psychopathology is another risk factor for the development of substance-related problems.

ASSESSMENT ISSUES

This section provides a guide for the assessment of substance use that has proven both effective and expedient. Examples of helpful clinical interviewing strategies are provided and specific clinical signs and symptoms of drug and alcohol intoxication and abuse are reviewed. Specific assessment questionnaires that can be used in their entirety or adapted for specific situations are also discussed. Finally, associated medical sequelae are briefly described.

The Clinical Interview

In any clinical examination, routine questions inquiring about the amount and frequency of alcohol and drug use are necessary to avoid missing possible substance abuse problems. When initially detecting a possible substance disorder, it is critical that the interviewer not become judgmental when asking questions but remain neutral and supportive. It is believed that feelings of shame or guilt about one's drug use actually hinder future treatment entry and success (Thom, 1987). This has been further supported by the authors' clinical experience. An open, conversational manner can help patients admit to using alcohol and/or drugs and also identify ways in which the use is interfering or causing problems in daily life. In certain situations, knowing ahead of time that a urine sample will be requested for toxicology tests can motivate some patients to admit their most recent drug use during the interview. Correctly identifying alcohol and/or drug use is important to determine whether medical conditions/treatments are being adversely affected by such use and for accurately identifying the best treatment options.

Alcohol and drug abuse/dependence as defined by the *DSM-IV* (APA, 1994) are included in figures 17.1 and 17.2.

In the vignette described at the beginning of the chapter, Mr. X's resistance to admitting a problem with alcohol confounds the interviewer. In previous appointments, Mr. X has denied using alcohol. Here is one way in which to address this resistance.

PRACTITIONER: Mr. X, good to see you today. How are you feeling?

Mr. X: I'm okay, just feeling tired, I guess.

PRACTITIONER: Well, I have the results of your most recent blood test and your blood glucose has not gone down since your last visit 3 months ago. Why do you think this is?

Mr. X: I don't know, doc, you're the expert.

PRACTITIONER: Well, I am an expert in my field, but you are an expert on yourself. We need to work together to determine what is going on with your lab tests. Mind if I ask you some more questions?

Mr. X: Nope, go right ahead.

After asking routine questions about diet, exercise, and medication adherence, the practitioner begins his questions about alcohol and drug use.

Substance abuse is defined as a maladaptive pattern of substance use leading to clinically significant impairment or distress as manifested by one (or more) of the following, occurring within a 12–month period.

1. Recurrent substance use resulting in a failure to fulfill major role obligations at work, school, or home (such as repeated absences or poor work performance related to substance use, substance-related absences, suspensions, or expulsions from school, or neglect of children or household).
2. Recurrent substance use in situations in which it is physically hazardous (such as driving an automobile or operating a machine when impaired by substance use).
3. Recurrent substance-related legal problems (such as arrests for substance-related disorderly conduct).
4. Continued substance use despite having persistent or recurrent social or interpersonal problems caused or exacerbated by the effects of the substance (for example, arguments with spouse about consequences of intoxication and physical fights).

Note: The symptoms for abuse have never met the criteria for dependence for this class of substance. According to the *DSM-IV*, a person can be abusing a substance or dependent on a substance but not both at the same time.

Figure 17.1 *DSM-IV* Criteria for Substance Abuse
Source: Adapted from American Psychiatric Association. 1994. *Diagnostic and Statistical Manual of Mental Disorders: DSM-IV.* Washington DC: Author.

PRACTITIONER: Have you used any alcohol in the past 3 months?

MR. X: No.

PRACTITIONER: It is important that you think and try to remember, because alcohol can increase your blood sugar levels and make your medications less effective.

MR. X: Well, I think I drank a glass or two of wine with dinner on my birthday.

PRACTITIONER: How about last night or this morning?

MR. X: Ummm, no, not really.

PRACTITIONER (non-critical manner): Well, Mr. X, I am concerned that you are drinking. I can smell alcohol on your breath this morning.

MR. X (irritated): Are you saying I am lying to you?

PRACTITIONER: No, I am not saying that. I am asking about your drinking habits because it can have severe effects on your physical health and I would be negligent if I didn't ask you about your use. I want you to know that drinking doesn't make you a bad person. I am asking because I need your help in determining what could be causing those glucose levels to stay so high. (pauses).

MR. X: Well, I do drink every night, but it has never gotten in the way of my work or family.

By using a nonconfrontational style and making the patient a partner, the practitioner is more likely to uncover underlying substance use problems. Once the practitioner has successfully addressed the resistance, it is much easier to proceed with determining severity and duration of use. In some cases, asking for collateral information from friends and family members, especially those who live with the patient, can provide information regarding frequency of use and effects of use on functioning. Also, use the results of urine and/or blood tests to strengthen your diagnosis.

Substance dependence is defined as a maladaptive pattern of substance use leading to clinically significant impairment or distress, as manifested by three (or more) of the following, occurring any time in the same 12–month period:

1. Tolerance, as defined by either of the following: (a) a need for markedly increased amounts of the substance to achieve intoxication or the desired effect or (b) markedly diminished effect with continued use of the same amount of the substance.
2. Withdrawal, as manifested by either of the following: (a) the characteristic withdrawal syndrome for the substance or (b) the same (or closely related) substance is taken to relieve or avoid withdrawal symptoms.
3. The substance is often taken in larger amounts or over a longer period than intended.
4. There is a persistent desire or unsuccessful efforts to cut down or control substance use.
5. A great deal of time is spent in activities necessary to obtain the substance, use the substance, or recover from its effects.
6. Important social, occupational, or recreational activities are given up or reduced because of substance use.
7. The substance use is continued despite knowledge of having a persistent physical or psychological problem that is likely to have been caused or exacerbated by the substance (for example, current cocaine use despite recognition of cocaine-induced depression or continued drinking despite recognition that an ulcer was made worse by alcohol consumption).

Figure 17.2 DSM-IV Criteria for Substance Dependence
Source: Adapted from American Psychiatric Association. 1994. *Diagnostic and Statistical Manual of Mental Disorders: DSM-IV.* Washington, DC: Author.

ASSESSMENT MEASURES

One of the most widely used alcohol screening questionnaires to date is the CAGE (Mayfield, McLeod, & Hall, 1974). The term CAGE is an acronym for four specific questions asked of a patient by an interviewer (see Table 17.1). A positive answer on the test can be an indicator of covert problem drinking. Strengths of the CAGE questionnaire include its brevity and its ease of administration, and the acronym "CAGE" serves as a mnemonic to aid practitioners' recall of the individual test items.

The Alcohol Use Disorder Identification Test (AUDIT; Saunders, Aasland, Babor, de la Fuente, & Grant, 1993) was developed by the World Health Organization and is a recommended screening questionnaire for problematic alcohol use. The AUDIT consists of three questions on consumption, three questions on dependence symptoms, and three questions on harmful use of alcohol, with a cutoff score of 8 indicating problem drinking. It can be administered during a clinical interview or by pencil and paper format, such as during the patient's time in the waiting room. The questionnaire in its entirety can be found on the World Health Organization web site. Some studies have suggested that computer or pencil and paper tests may elicit more candid responses (Chan-Pensley, 1999). While there are a number of excellent assessment measures (e.g, the Michigan Alcoholism Screening Test [MAST; Selzer, 1971]), the AUDIT is the only instrument specifically designed to identify hazardous and harmful drinking (Reid, Fiellin, & O'Connor, 1999).

Table 17.1

The CAGE Questionnaire*

C	Have you ever felt you ought to **C**ut down on your drinking?
A	Have people **A**nnoyed you by criticizing your drinking?
G	Have you ever felt bad or **G**uilty about your drinking?
E	Have you ever had a drink first thing in the morning to steady your nerves or to get rid of a hangover (**E**ye-opener)?"

*One or more positive responses can be an indicator of problem drinking.
Source: Adapted from Mayfield, D., McLeod, G., & Hall, P. (1974). The CAGE questionnaire: Validation of a new alcoholism screening instrument *The American Journal of Psychiatry, 131*(10), 1121–1123.

The medical community generally recommends the "5 As" as a framework for assessing a behavioral health behavior: **A**sk about the behavior; **A**ssess the extent of the problem and the patient's willingness to change; **A**dvise the patient about risks, benefits, and options; **A**ssist and offer to help with a health behavior change, including goal setting or a referral; and **A**rrange follow-up (e.g., set up a date or time frame to assess progress and reassess goals). This is a helpful framework to consider; however, since this framework does not take into consideration specific techniques to use with patients, or how to understand the patient's problem or his or her willingness to change, we will address these issues in the Treatment section.

A detailed assessment of alcohol and drug use is important in determining a patient's risk and/or treatment needs. As shown here, asking specific questions about quantity and frequency of substance use will elicit more useful information regarding drinking and drug use.

PRACTITIONER: So, you mentioned drinking alcohol regularly. I'd like to ask you some more questions about your drinking.

MR. X: Uh, ok.

PRACTITIONER: How many days in the past week did you drink alcohol?

MR. X: I usually have a glass of vodka when I get home from work—every night except Tuesday, when I had to work late.

PRACTITIONER: How many glasses do you tend to drink?

MR. X: One.

PRACTITIONER: How big is the glass?

MR. X: About this big *(motions the height of a tall glass—about 12 or more ounces*)*. On the weekends I sometimes have two.

PRACTITIONER: How long have you been drinking at this level?

MR. X: Since I got fired from my last job . . . about 6 months ago. I got kind of down, and even since I got my new job I haven't really snapped out of it.

PRACTITIONER: What's the longest you have gone without drinking in the past 6 months?

MR. X: About a week, 2 months ago, when we went on vacation. I guess it was fine, but I did feel kinda lousy the first few days.

PRACTITIONER: Have you used any other drugs in the past month? Or any prescription medications, even if they weren't prescribed for you?

---

*Note that in this scenario Mr. X's "one glass" of vodka is likely to be the equivalent of up to 3 standard drinks of liquor.

MR. X: No. I tried pot once and cocaine once in college, but I've always just liked alcohol.

ASSOCIATED FEATURES OF SUBSTANCE DISORDERS

Although the *DSM-IV* provides specific criteria to determine substance dependence disorders, it is also useful for practitioners to learn the associated medical and contextual features for each class of substance. Note that these features can get blurred in the presence of multiple substance disorders and/or concomitant psychiatric or medical disorders.

Alcohol Disorders   Of concern for an alcohol-addicted patient is withdrawal. During withdrawal, physical symptoms such as sweating, nausea/vomiting, insomnia, tachycardia, dilated pupils, hand tremors, or memory difficulties may be present. Patients may also report irritability, anxiety, or fatigue. For patients with severe dependence (e.g., drinking at least a pint of alcohol a day for months), delirium tremens (DTs) are possible upon cessation of use. DTs are a cluster of mental symptoms, including psychosis (i.e., auditory, visual, or tactile hallucinations) and neurological symptoms (i.e., seizures) that are triggered by an abrupt cessation of alcohol. DTs are often accompanied by high blood pressure, increased pulse rate, elevated temperature, and agitation. Therefore, it is advisable that practitioners suggest cessation of alcohol use for these patients only in a supervised medical setting, such as an inpatient detoxification facility, where DTs can be clinically managed. In addition to physical and neurological evidence, elevated liver function tests (i.e., Gamma-glutamyl transpeptidase [GGT], Aspartate aminotransferase [AST], Alanine aminotransferase [ALT]; indicative of alcoholic hepatitis) and elevated triglyceride levels can provide concomitant evidence of an alcohol disorder. Testing and treatment for other medical problems associated with use of alcohol is necessary. This may include disorders such as hepatitis, blood clotting disorders, alcoholic neuropathy, heart disorders, chronic neurologic syndromes (such as Wernicke-Korsakoff syndrome), and malnutrition.

Cocaine disorders   Cocaine is often used recreationally by so-called "weekend warriors" who will binge on the drug throughout the weekend and still maintain work and social responsibilities. Cocaine can be inhaled intranasally, injected intravenously, and smoked (free-base, or more commonly, "crack"). Over time, cocaine can become psychologically addicting. Like marijuana users, cocaine users rarely endorse physical withdrawal symptoms but may report sleep disturbances if specifically asked. Educating patients during the interview about psychological withdrawal symptoms such as depressed mood and anxiety can also help elicit endorsement of withdrawal. Prolonged intranasal use of cocaine often results in septal perforation, which is a hole in the nasal septum, the tissue that separates the nostrils (Slavin & Goldwyn, 1990). A history of hypertension, seizures, transient ischemic attacks, and myocardial infarctions may be present (Kloner & Rezkalla, 2003).

Marijuana Disorders   Marijuana is most often smoked, although it may be also added to food and drink. Research has demonstrated that chronic use can result in sleep difficulty, marijuana craving, aggression, and irritability (Budney, Hughes, Moore, & Novy, 2001). In addition, male patients may suffer from depressed testosterone levels and low sperm count. In female users, abnormal menstruation and failure to ovulate have been documented. It is important not to jump to conclusions regarding frequency of use when examining urine toxicology reports, since even a single use may show a positive result for up to 3 weeks, depending on body fat composition. Chronic users may take up to 6 weeks to provide a clean urine sample.

Heroin (Opiate) Disorders   Heroin is most commonly used intranasally or intravenously, although opiate pill use is on the rise, especially the use of Oxycontin and Vicodin among young adults. Recent reports indicate that 2.4 million people over age 12 used analgesics for nonmedical purposes (Office of Applied Studies & RTI International, 2006). Risk of overdosing is very high in opiate users, and immediate cessation of use can lead to serious physical withdrawal symptoms, including sweating, tremors, and vomiting. Intraveneous users often try to mask needle "track" marks on their arms and legs with full-length clothing, but a physical exam should provide evidence of such use. Chronic heroin users who experience decreased effects of heroin will often use sedatives, including benzodiazepines and alcohol, to enhance the effects of heroin. Others will use cocaine or amphetamines mixed with heroin (i.e., speedballs), or immediately use cocaine afterward to counter the sedative effects of the opiates. Oftentimes, chronic pill users arrive at clinics seeking medication to alleviate complaints of physical pain. In order to reduce the chance that a person who is legitimately experiencing pain does not end up addicted to the analgesic, the prescribing physician must balance the need for pain management with risk of dependence. Clinicians should explain the dangers of recreational opiate use, including the side effects from taking the medication with other medications or drugs. It is important to note that the development of tolerance and withdrawal can occur in patients legitimately prescribed opiates for chronic pain. In other words, physiological tolerance is not synonymous with addiction. However, the phenomenon of tolerance and withdrawal that can accompany more chronic use of opiates is neither necessary nor sufficient in properly identifying addiction. Addiction involves cognitive, behavioral, and psychological symptoms that indicate an individual continues to use a drug despite significant substance-related consequences (APA, 1994). Other psychological aspects of addiction can include the subjective experience of craving a drug, losing control of drug use, and compulsive drug taking.

Benzodiazepine Use Disorders   Frequently, benzodiazepines are used in combination with alcohol, heroin, or other depressants to increase the effect of the drugs. As with the other depressants, patients report both physical and psychiatric withdrawal symptoms, including insomnia, increased perspiration, anxiety, tachychardia, loss of appetite, depression, delusions, and the possible risk of seizure activity in severe cases. It is critical that patients using benzodiazepines be counseled regarding the negative consequences of abruptly halting their use and that patients provide accurate information regarding the amount used. It is often necessary to refer these patients to an addiction psychiatrist who can medically supervise an outpatient taper over a period of several weeks. Quantitative urine toxicology can provide additional evidence of recent use and amount used. Patients who complain of withdrawal effects, including increased anxiety, can be managed using antidepressants that also have anxiolytic properties (e.g., Paxil).

Crystal Methamphetamines/Club Drug Use Disorders   Crystal methamphetamine ("crystal," "crank") and other chemical drugs, such as ketamine, also known as "Special K," and ecstasy (MDMA) pills, also known as "X" or "E," are usually used for their hallu-cinogenic and stimulant properties. Methamphetamine and ketamine can be used in pill form, intravenously, or inhaled, and the crystal form of methamphetamine ("ice") can be smoked. This class of drugs, often used by young adults who frequent night clubs, have become popular for their stimulant properties, which allow users to dance or have sex for many hours. Use of these stimulants causes an increase in body tem-perature, pulse, and blood pressure. This class of drug can also lead to hallucinations, paranoia, and bizarre, aggressive, and psychotic behavior.

MEDICAL CONSEQUENCES OF CHRONIC ALCOHOL AND DRUG USE

Because of the many and varied effects of repeated alcohol or drug use on multiple body systems, substance use assessments often require more complex assessment procedures than many other medical problems. This assessment might require a sep-arate office visit, not unlike assessments for other chronic problems like hypertension or asthma. A significant medical condition associated with alcohol abuse is Wernicke's encephalopathy, caused by thiamine deficiency and associated with acute mental con-fusion, ataxia, and ophthalmoplegia, which is a paralysis or weakness of one or more eye muscles. Additionally, Korsakoff amnestic syndrome is a late neuropsychiatric manifestation of Wernicke's encephalopathy, marked by memory loss and confabula-tion, the confusion of true memories with false memories. This condition is commonly known as Wernicke-Korsakoff syndrome or psychosis.

In addition, chronic alcohol users also face the risk of liver disease, including alco-holic hepatitis and cirrhosis. Alcoholic hepatitis is an inflammation of the liver tissue that can lead to morbidity if left untreated but is largely reversible after prolonged ab-stinence. It is marked by loss of appetite, nausea, jaundice, fever, dry mouth, fatigue and ascites (fluid retention in the abdomen). Abnormal alkaline phosphatase (ALP) and iron levels on blood and liver enzyme tests require follow-up, including a liver biopsy to confirm hepatitis. Cirrhosis, a more severe form of liver disease, is marked by scarring of the liver tissue and cell death. As cells die, the liver becomes less effi-cient at metabolizing fats, proteins, and carbohydrates. In addition to the symptoms of hepatitis, cirrhosis is also associated with portal hypertension (high blood pressure develops as the portal vein in the liver becomes blocked from reduced liver function-ing), liver cancer, kidney dysfunction, and Type 2 diabetes. Although medications to slow the progress of liver disease are available and liver transplants have become more common, cirrhosis is irreversible.

Alcohol consumption and Type 2 diabetes, another metabolic disorder, have a U-shaped relationship. A moderate amount of alcohol consumption (1–3 drinks per day) has been found to reduce diabetes and coronary disease by more than 50% com-pared to not drinking at all. But those who drink more than three drinks per day have more than a 43% increased risk for diabetes compared to moderate drinkers (Howard, Arnsten, & Gourevitch, 2004). In the case of Mr. X, his daily use of at least three drinks of vodka is most likely reducing his control over his blood sugars.

A well-established body of literature has examined the risk factors for contracting HIV infection in persons abusing intravenous drugs. The national Centers for Disease Control and Prevention (CDC) report that approximately 36% of the total AIDS cases in the United States occurred as a result of exposure to the HIV virus during injection drug use (CDC, 2002). Knowledge of HIV status in persons abusing substances can help facilitate appropriate referrals to both medical care (i.e., starting antiretroviral treatment for HIV) and substance abuse treatment in a timely fashion.

BARRIERS TO ASSESSMENT

There are a number of factors that can make assessment of a substance disorder challenging. As in the case of Mr. X, patients who have recently used alcohol or drugs can present with withdrawal-related irritability or dysphoria. Eliciting detailed and accurate information about past episodes of use and past treatment may be difficult while the patient is in an altered cognitive state. Therefore, plan to complete the clinical interview on a future visit to follow up on ambiguous answers, if possible.

Upon receiving feedback about alcohol or drug problems, patients can have a variety of reactions. Mr. X's comment above stating, "you are the expert" is an example of someone who is verbally acquiescing but in essence demonstrating a distrust of authority. Developing trust with the patient is paramount to help him or her (a) understand what the diagnosis means and why it is being made, (b) learn what treatment options are available, and (c) feel reassured that the practitioner will not inform the police or other authorities about illegal drug use.

When working with people from different cultures, a number of additional factors need to be addressed. Western medicine and diagnostic systems value individuality and freedom. Alternatively, many non-Western cultures may value a familial or societal focus. Therefore, when interviewing someone from a non-U.S. cultural background, it is vital that the practitioner understand family and community dynamics. For example, a Puerto Rican woman whom one of the authors interviewed would not agree to enter treatment until she had spoken to her husband, who essentially made all of the important decisions in the family. By immediately labeling this woman resistant to treatment, the practitioner would have demonstrated cultural insensitivity. It is important to learn who else in the patient's familial and/or social milieu makes medical decisions, and to include those individuals during the clinical interview and explanation of the diagnosis and treatment options. It is also important to note that immigrant families may have two or three generations of individuals with conflicting values (e.g., an adult grandson wants to enter treatment but his grandmother does not support treatment recommendations). In this case, addressing the concerns of other family members is just as critical as overcoming individual resistance.

As a practitioner, understanding one's own preconceived biases about certain patient characteristics can help reduce the chances of providing a misdiagnosis. A patient's socioeconomic status, race, age, gender, disability status, and/or sexual orientation may play a role in the kind of questions asked during the clinical interview. Practitioners bring their own individual life and professional experiences to each interview they conduct. For example, if a practitioner would never imagine that an elderly widow might misuse her prescription anxiolytic medications, or that the highly visible power broker from Wall Street smokes marijuana daily, he or she would never think to ask and therefore would not discover this problem. Each of the authors has been surprised on many instances by a patient's unexpected disclosure about drug- or alcohol-related problems. Practitioners sometimes assume that persons abusing substances will present as homeless, unshaven, and having a severe mental illness. They may assume that the individual will show up to the emergency room when they have hit rock bottom. In reality, keen clinical judgment is necessary to identify persons abusing substances, because most will present with subtle symptoms. As clinical investigation begins, be sensitive to the fact that an initial impression may be wrong and that current users will often admit past use but are more reluctant to endorse current use.

SPECIAL POPULATIONS

While practitioners should be sensitive to substance-related clues and concerns in all patients, some warrant special attention because of unique risk status. The following discussion outlines populations that, for a variety of reasons, may be overlooked in primary care settings or who experience heightened sensitivity to the negative effects of substances.

Women   Studies have found that women can become intoxicated after drinking half as much as men, metabolize alcohol differently, and have a greater risk of dying from alcohol-related accidents and illnesses (Grant et al., 1994). Further, the onset and course of alcohol problems and their medical sequelae (e.g., progression to addiction, cirrhosis, hypertension, and malnutrition) are accelerated in women. This phenomenon has been referred to in the literature as *telescoping* (Fillmore, 1987). Additionally, studies suggest that women are much more likely than men to be prescribed an abusable prescription drug, particularly narcotics and antianxiety drugs. Finally, no discussion of women and substance abuse is complete without a mention of the risk of prenatal alcohol or drug exposure to the fetus in women of childbearing age. All women who are considering becoming pregnant, or who use alcohol and/or drugs and do not use a reliable method of birth control, must be advised about the risks, which include fetal alcohol syndrome (FAS), alcohol-related birth defects (ARBD), alcohol-related neurological disorders (ARND) and fetal alcohol effects (FAE). Children born to mothers who drank during pregnancy have a higher incidence of dropping out of school, attention deficits, learning disabilities, trouble with the law, and preventable mental retardation (Streissguth, Barr, Kogan, & Bookstein, 1996).

Adolescents   On average, first alcohol use in adolescents occurs at about 13 years of age (SAMHSA, 1999). However, among those who begin to drink on a regular basis, the consequences can be lethal. Nearly 40% of surveyed students in grades 9 through 12 reported riding in a car with a driver who had been drinking (CDC, 1995). This is of particular concern, as motor vehicle crashes are the leading cause of death among young people, and a significant proportion are directly related to the use of alcohol. One study suggests that alcohol abuse is associated with other risky behaviors, such as unsafe sexual activity leading to pregnancy and sexually transmitted diseases (Strunin & Hingson, 1992). Adolescents who use alcohol are more likely to have sexual intercourse, with a greater number of partners than their nondrinking peers (Valois, Oeltmann, Waller, & Hussey, 1999). Given these consequences, all adolescents need to be carefully assessed for alcohol and drug-related behavior at each visit.

According to current guidelines for health supervision, every adolescent should routinely be asked questions such as "Have you drunk alcohol in the past month? How much? What is the most you ever had to drink? Have you ever tried other drugs? How often have you taken them in the past month?" (Green, 1994). When affirmative answers are given, further assessment is needed. The American Academy of Pediatrics recommends the use of the following questionnaire, called the CRAFFT (**C**ar, **R**elax, **A**lone, **F**orget, **F**riends, **T**rouble; Knight et al., 1999). The questions are shown

Table 17.2
The CRAFFT Questionnaire*

C	Have you ever ridden in a **C**AR driven by someone (including yourself) who was high or had been using alcohol or drugs?
R	Do you ever use alcohol or drugs to **R**ELAX, feel better about yourself, or fit in?
A	Do you ever use alcohol or drugs while you are by yourself, or **A**LONE?
F	Do you ever **F**ORGET things you did while using alcohol or drugs?
F	Do your family or **F**RIENDS ever tell you that you should cut down on your drinking or drug use?
T	Have you ever gotten into **T**ROUBLE while you were using alcohol or drugs?

*Two or more yes answers warrant referral to a mental health specialist.
Source: Adapted from Knight, J. R., Shrier, L. A., Bravender, T. D., Farrell, M., VanderBilt, J., & Shaffer, H. J. (1999). A new brief screen for adolescent substance abuse. *Archives of Pediatrics & Adolescent Medicine, 153*, 591–596.

in Table 17.2, and two or more positive answers on this questionnaire warrant referral to a mental health specialist.

Elderly   Some researchers estimate the prevalence of substance use disorders to be 2 to 3% among older women and perhaps 10% among older men, (Schuckit, 2000). Elderly alcohol abusers have been divided into two general types: the late onset group, comprising 40% of alcohol dependent patients who begin drinking at the age of 45 to 50, and the early onset group, the other 60% who have been abusing alcohol for many years (American Medical Association, 1996). The late onset alcoholics generally have fewer health problems, more social supports, and an overall better prognosis than the early-onset alcoholics (Rigler, 2000).

Alcohol or drug abuse in older adults can be triggered by changes in life such as retirement, death or separation from a friend or loved one, health concerns, impairment of sleep, and/or familial conflict. Furthermore, increased exposure to prescription medications among older adults may also increase the risk for abuse: 27% of all anti-anxiety prescriptions and 38% of hypnotic prescriptions in 1991 were written for older adults (Center for Substance Abuse Treatment, 1998). Finally, age-associated changes in physiological functioning, combined with concurrent medical problems, can affect how these drugs are metabolized. When working with depressed older adults, clinicians should consider whether any sleep impairment, decreased appetite, moodiness, sadness, and/or cognitive impairment they observe could be related to the patient's use of alcohol, depressants, or stimulants.

Another subset of individuals who require thorough assessment and appropriate treatment recommendations are persons abusing substances who also suffer from co-occurring psychiatric symptoms. What follows is a review of some of these disorders and an illustration of how to assess for psychiatric comorbidity using the example of Mr. X.

PSYCHIATRIC COMORBIDITY

It is estimated that 30 to 60% of persons abusing substances suffer from comorbid psychiatric conditions (Leshner, 1999). The self-medicating hypothesis states that individuals use drugs to reduce co-occurring anxious, depressive, and/or psychotic symptoms (Khantzian, 1985; 1997). Another theoretical camp suggests that a subset of individuals with comorbid conditions induced their psychiatric symptoms by chronically using drugs and/or alcohol (Tjepkema, 2004). When assessing comorbidity, the practitioner must discern if psychiatric symptoms are present and whether symptoms occurred before, during, or after a period of substance use. Our practitioner will interview Mr. X and ask about co-occurring psychiatric disorders.

PRACTITIONER: So, you mentioned earlier that you've been feeling tired lately?

MR. X: I'm okay, but I feel tired all the time.

PRACTITIONER: How about your mood when you are tired? Do you feel sad or depressed?

MR. X: Oh yeah, I feel sad all the time. Day and night. I end up sleeping 11 to 12 hours.

PRACTITIONER: How is your appetite? What do you eat in a day?

MR. X: I eat maybe one meal a day. When I get up I don't eat breakfast, then have a sandwich for lunch then will finish a bag of chips with salsa in the evening.

PRACTITIONER: How about having difficulty concentrating?

MR. X: No, I don't think so.

PRACTITIONER: Do you still do things that you enjoy? Like I know you used to go fishing.

MR. X: No, I don't even talk to my fishing buddies anymore. It's probably been a year since I have seen them.

PRACTITIONER: Do you have thoughts about dying?

MR. X: Sometimes, but I would never do anything about it.

PRACTITIONER: How long has this period gone on that you have felt depressed?

MR. X: Since I lost my job in November.

PRACTITIONER: So let's see, that was about 5 months ago. That is about the same time that you started drinking more, right?

MR. X: Yeah. I probably started drinking a month or so before I got fired.

PRACTITIONER: Were you feeling depressed before you started drinking?

MR. X: No, I mean I did go through a pretty bad depression when I got divorced 5 years ago. But then I was doing okay until now.

After completing more questions regarding manic, anxious, and psychotic symptoms, this practitioner is able to provide a diagnosis of Alcohol-Induced Mood Disorder, depressive type.

Mood Disorders   Depression is one of the most common comorbid psychiatric disorders and can occur both as an antecedent to and as a consequence of substance use (e.g., Mr. X), especially during withdrawal from alcohol, cocaine, heroin, or marijuana. Substance abuse can easily mask an underlying mood disorder that can remain unidentified and untreated. The long-term risk of not identifying a mood disorder is that the substance use often does not remit until mood symptoms are treated. Researchers have found that a staggering 50 to 60% of persons abusing substances suffer from a mood disorder (Regier et al., 1990), although these are not easily diagnosed. Bipolar disorder, for example, may be under-diagnosed, or misdiagnosed as unipolar depression, in substance-abusing populations by as much as 50% (Albanese, Clodfelter, Pardo, & Ghaemi, 2006). This may lead to inadequate treatment (e.g., prescribing an antidepressant instead of a mood stabilizer) of the underlying mood disorder and ultimately a relapse of the substance use. A determination of the exact chronology of depressive symptoms (i.e., before the onset of a substance disorder, during use, during abstinence) and whether a person has manic symptoms can have significant treatment implications and must be addressed thoroughly in the initial clinical interview. The Timeline Follow-Back Interview (TLFB; Sobell et al., 1980), which provides a reliable method of assessing days of alcohol use versus abstinence, can be modified for use with other drugs and to document periods of manic and depressive episodes. The interview generally provides an easy and methodical way to document both days of using substances and periods of mood symptoms, even during a short clinical interview. Depending on how extensive the person's history and how forthcoming a patient is about these periods, a follow-up interview may be required to complete the interview.

Anxiety Disorders   One third of alcoholics may experience some form of anxiety disorder including agoraphobia and social anxiety (Cox, Norton, Swinson, & Endler, 1990). In fact, 20% of those with social anxiety have a co-occurring alcohol disorder versus 10% of those in the general population (Cox et al.). Anxiety disorders (e.g., panic disorder, panic attacks) may also be present in marijuana and cocaine users, often as a result of using high quantities of the drug (Cox et al.). Additionally, posttraumatic stress disorder (PTSD) is a common comorbid disorder with substance abuse. Overall, research has shown that individuals exposed to stressful events are more likely to abuse alcohol and other drugs or undergo relapse (Dawes et al., 2000), and PTSD comorbidity rates reflect this finding. In a general population study, the overall lifetime rate of PTSD was 7.8%. Among men with a lifetime history of PTSD, 34.5% reported drug abuse or dependence at some point in their lives versus 15.1% of men without PTSD. For women, 26.9% with a lifetime history of PTSD reported drug abuse or dependence during their lives versus 7.6% of women without PTSD (Kessler, Sonnega, Bromet, Hughes, & Nelson, 1995). Several studies have suggested that substance abuse may develop after the onset of PTSD as the individual attempts to self-medicate symptoms of the disorder. For example, in a longitudinal study of young adults, Chilcoat and Breslau (1998) found a more than four-fold increased risk of drug abuse and dependence among individuals with PTSD. The risk for abuse or dependence was highest for prescribed psychoactive drugs.

Attention-Deficit/Hyperactivity Disorder   Prevalence rates for adult ADHD in persons abusing substances range from 11 to 20% (Levin, Evans, & Kleber, 1998; Clure et al., 1999; King, Brooner, Kidorf, Stoller, & Mirsky, 1999). ADHD may worsen the symptoms of substance abuse, making it more difficult for addicted patients to comply with requirements of treatment programs and remain abstinent. Some theorists suggest that hyperactive or inattentive patients use substances such as cocaine and other amphetamines to help themselves temporarily calm down and focus (Cocores, Davies, Mueller, & Gold, 1987). Others posit that patients with ADHD are more likely than their non-ADHD peers to try substances because of their increased impulsivity and novelty-seeking behavior, especially during adolescence (Ernst et al., 2006).

Schizophrenia   Similar to other psychiatric disorders, the presence of substance use is higher in schizophrenics than the general population (50% versus 16%; Kendler, Gallagher, Abelson, & Kessler, 1996; Regier et al., 1990). Schizophrenics with substance use problems are more likely to be nonadherent to treatment and have higher incidences of suicide attempts, hospitalizations, and an increased chance of negative physical health consequences, including hepatitis and HIV (Brunette, Noordsky, Buckley, & Green, 2005).

Personality Disorders   Individuals with cluster B personality disorders (narcissistic, histrionic, borderline, and antisocial) have the highest incidence of co-occurring substance abuse disorders of the three *DSM-IV* personality disorder clusters (Nace, 1990). Within cluster B, borderline personality disorder and antisocial personality disorder have the highest comorbidity rates—30 to 50% (Trull, Sher, Minks-Brown, Durbin, & Burr, 2000) and 84% (Regier et al., 1990), respectively. Personality theorists suggest that individuals with cluster B personality disorder traits are more vulnerable to drug and/or alcohol disorder because substances at least temporarily allow a person to experience feelings of dominance over others (Benjamin, 1996), to soothe tensions created by hypersensitivity to criticisms or evaluation (Beck & Freeman, 1990), to provide novel stimuli (Millon & Davis, 1996), and to provide dissociation from one's own emotional experience (Richards, 1993).

Given the wide variety of substance use disorders, associated features, and concomitant medical and psychiatric conditions, a thorough assessment of substance use and the effect it has on a patient's day-to-day life is necessary. Sound clinical judgment regarding the severity of use and the potential harm the use has on vocational, family, and social functioning can lead to the most parsimonious but effective treatment recommendation. While such a thorough assessment may be beyond the scope of the primary care office visit, a health psychologist can collaborate with the primary care physician to ascertain a more comprehensive clinical picture. The next section provides a basic introduction to treatment options and how to find appropriate referrals.

TREATMENT OF SUBSTANCE USE DISORDERS

Treatment will be outlined in three sections. First, the various types of treatments, both medical and psychosocial, are described. Second, a theoretical framework for practitioners to help patients develop and maintain motivation to stop using substances, along with suggestions for brief interventions, is presented. Third, a summary of considerations when making a referral is provided.

MEDICAL INTERVENTIONS

With certain substances such as alcohol, opiates, and benzodiazepines, physical dependence may contribute to severe withdrawal symptoms upon cessation that must be medically managed. This can call for outpatient detoxification, inpatient detoxification, or, in the case of opiate addiction, replacement/maintenance treatment.

In general, detoxification includes the use of supportive medications and/or agonist therapies to manage the patient's physical withdrawal symptoms. The process of detoxification can be uncomfortable and in certain cases hazardous to the patient. Therefore, it is recommended that these interventions be handled by specialists or other experienced personnel. In the following paragraphs are some important considerations for detoxification from alcohol, opiates, and benzodiazepines.

Alcohol   Alcohol withdrawal may range from a mild and uncomfortable disorder to a serious, life-threatening condition. Symptoms usually begin within 12 hours of the last drink, peak within 48 to 72 hours, and may persist for a week or more (Bayard, McIntyre, Hill, & Woodside, 2004). Symptoms such as sleep changes, rapid changes in mood, and fatigue may last for several months after cessation of use (Eickelberg & Mayo-Smith, 1998). Chlordiazepoxide (Librium) is the most widely used medication for alcohol detoxification, and can provide immediate relief for symptoms such as shaking, elevated pulse, increased blood pressure, agitation, and anxiety (Miller, 1995). After detoxification, a variety of maintenance medications can be employed to prevent relapse in alcohol-dependent patients, such as naltrexone (Revia) or disulfiram (Antabuse). These medications act by either blocking the pleasurable effects of alcohol (naltrexone), or inducing illness if patients use alcohol while taking the medication (disulfiram). When combined with psychosocial treatment, these medications bode well for patient recovery (McCaul & Petry, 2003). In order for these medications to be effective, patients must understand that consistent compliance with medication regimens is essential. Health psychologists can provide support and interventions to increase adherence to complex or aversive prescription regimens.

Opiates   Treatment of opiate withdrawal symptoms can include supportive care and medications, including methadone or buprenorphine to slow onset of withdrawal and clonidine to reduce physical symptoms of withdrawal (Van den Brink & Haasen, 2006). In some circumstances a replacement/maintenance treatment is indicated. These circumstances include patients who have attempted detoxification multiple times with little success as well as patients with chronic pain conditions that might be exacerbated by abstinence from opiates. Maintenance treatments require patients to register with a clinic or physician to receive a legal, synthetic opiate, which is safely regulated. The purpose of maintenance treatment is to help patients stabilize their lives over a period of time before attempting to function without opiates. For maintenance of opiate-dependent patients, methadone is the most widely used medication (Kreek & Vocci, 2002). Buprenorphine, a newer maintenance medication, has been demonstrated to have significant potential to block the effects of opiates and has a lesser withdrawal syndrome. When combined with the opiate antagonist naloxone, withdrawal symptoms are attenuated to create a maintenance agent with less abuse potential without causing unpleasant withdrawal (Vocci, Acri, & Elkashef, 2005). It can be made available in an office-based setting several times per week. To find a local credentialed physician who can administer buprenorphine, visit the SAMHSA web site for the buprenorphine physician locator.

Benzodiazepines   Rapid cessation of benzodiazepines in a dependent person can result in seizures and other medical complications (Vicens et al., 2006). In general, addiction psychiatrists will attempt an office-based detoxification if the period of abuse is not long, if physical withdrawal symptoms are tolerable, and in the absence of other concomitant major medical conditions. In addition to detoxification, the patient may find relief of anxiety and/or sleep difficulties through the use of nonpharmacological interventions (Khong, Sim, & Hulse, 2004). A health psychologist can help coordinate various treatment options, including biofeedback for sleep disorders and relaxation training for anxiety symptoms. If outpatient treatment is not possible, a referral to an inpatient detoxification facility is required.

Psychosocial Treatment

In addition to medical approaches, psychosocial and/or behavioral approaches are helpful in treating substance abuse. The following section will discuss the various psychosocial approaches, ordered from the least intensive to most intensive. In psychosocial approaches, the person abusing substances learns helpful information about his or her drug-using patterns, establishes and maintains abstinence, and learns to resist drug craving and to avoid triggers for drug use.

Twelve-step treatment includes support groups such as Alcoholics Anonymous and Narcotics Anonymous, which view addiction as an illness that is treatable through a commitment to abstinence and support from other addicts (Alcoholics Anonymous World Services, 1972). Twelve-step groups encourage attendance at meetings on a regular or daily basis. Members are encouraged to "work the steps," usually with the guidance of a voluntary sponsor (Alcoholics Anonymous World Services). The only requirement for membership in an Alcoholics Anonymous Group is "the desire to stop drinking" (Alcoholics Anonymous World Services). For individuals who prefer to attend a less religious/spiritual program, with fewer references to God and a "higher power" than in Alcoholics Anonymous, there are other self-help programs available, such as Rational Recovery and Smart Recovery.

Professional outpatient treatment normally involves attending two to three group psychotherapy and psychoeducational meetings per week, and may include individual counseling as well. This approach emphasizes intensity of intervention, such that patients can be requested to attend group meetings frequently, even daily, especially during the early phase of recovery. These approaches are typically geared toward more severe users, and may include vocational and social rehabilitation efforts.

In the most severe cases, practitioners may want to consider referring a patient for inpatient detoxification, followed by a 14, 21, or 28-day rehabilitation facility. These referrals are normally made when substance use has impaired the patient's functioning to the extent that intensive rehabilitation and time away from the environment where use is occurring are required. If a severely dependent patient has no vocational prospects and/or pending legal consequences of drug use, he or she may choose or be referred to live in a high-commitment therapeutic community. A therapeutic community is a highly structured residential environment where the patient receives constant rehabilitation and feedback on behaviors that might lead to relapse (De Leon, 2000). A typical length of stay in a therapeutic community can range from six months to two years, and during this time, treatment staff focus rehabilitative efforts across a broad array of patient functioning, such as vocational, social, and legal (De Leon, 2000).

MOTIVATION TO CHANGE AND INTERVENTION STRATEGIES

Quite often, medical professionals are the first to detect a patient's substance use problems and raise the awareness of its health-related consequences. Therefore, a medical practitioner may be the first professional to engage the patient in a discussion about treatment options. These initial conversations with a patient about treatment options are critical. During these discussions, the patient begins to consider the importance of and need for treatment, weigh the costs versus the benefits of treatment, and learn about treatment options and efficacy. In order to discuss treatment referrals, the practitioner often needs to appreciate and overcome patients' various objections and concerns about treatment. Here is a framework for understanding these objections and proceeding with an appropriate course of action.

The Stages of Change When considering a referral for treatment, it is important to maintain the same level of sensitivity and nonjudgmental outlook on the patient's

Table 17.3

Prochaska and DiClemente's Transtheoretical Stages of Change

---

1. *Precontemplation:* The patient does not see that a behavior problem exists, and may resent the implication that he or she needs to do something about his or her substance use.

2. *Contemplation:* The patient becomes aware of some of the negative consequences of his or her use and begins engaging in a cost-benefit decision to determine whether quitting/cutting down feels necessary.

3. *Preparation:* The patient has decided to change his or her behavior and seeks strategies and resources to begin the change process.

4. *Action:* The patient settles on a plan to begin behavior change, and begins following the steps of the plan.

5. *Maintenance:* The patient makes changes and consolidates his or her lifestyle gains for a period of time.

6. *Relapse:* Assumes that more than one effort to make permanent change will be necessary for the patient, and that he or she may experience setbacks in his or her efforts and cycle back into using substances and an earlier stage of change. Educating the patient about this stage is an important feature of managing realistic expectations.

Source: Adapted from Prochaska, J. O., & DiClemente, C. C. (1984). *The transtheoretical approach: Crossing the traditional boundaries of therapy.* Malabar, FL: Krieger.

problem that was employed in assessing the problem. An understanding of Prochaska and DiClemente's (1984) transtheoretical model of behavior change can help a practitioner maximize the likelihood that a patient will follow through on the referral. The transtheoretical model posits that when faced with a possible behavior change, patients transition through universal stages of processing information about change, of the importance of and need for treatment. These stages, outlined in Table 17.3, include deciding whether to change, what to change, and how to implement changes. For a full review of the transtheoretical model, please see Chapter 3.

It is important to remember that the transtheoretical model is dynamic, meaning that patients may not progress through the stages in an orderly fashion. A patient may cycle back and forth between stages, or may fail at a change attempt when in the *action* stage, and cycle back to *contemplation*. Also, because the transtheoretical model applies to many types of negative, health-related behaviors, patients may simultaneously be at multiple stages of the change cycle for different health-related behaviors. The following clinical exchange illustrates this principle.

PRACTITIONER: I really appreciate you sharing so much about your diet with me, and being so honest about your struggle to monitor your blood sugar. I hope what I've shared with you will help you make some changes that might get you back on track and get your sugar under control.

MR. X: You know, doc, I had been thinking about trying to check my sugar more, but it just seemed too hard (*contemplation*). But you've got me thinking I've gotta do it. I'm going to attend that class on Tuesday where they help you work that glucose-testing machine (*preparation/action*).

PRACTITIONER: That's a great first step! I'll let the teacher know you'll be there. Regular monitoring, with dietary changes, will help you. Speaking of dietary changes, I know we disagree a bit about your drinking, but how do you feel at this point about the information I've given you on the connection between drinking and elevated sugar?

MR. X: I keep telling you, my drinking is no problem! I'm going to cut back on sweets, but you can stop nagging me. I'm not an alcoholic (*precontemplation*).

While this patient is clearly in the *action* stage of learning to monitor his blood sugar, he still needs more time and information to decide to change his drinking. His use of the term "alcoholic" may indicate a defensive attitude about his drinking, and the physician's attempt to make a referral to substance treatment at this point would be premature and likely counterproductive. The issue of drinking should be addressed again with the patient at the next visit, but will probably require the practitioner to understand where a patient is located in the stages of change for that behavior. For example, with a "precontemplating" patient like Mr. X, the practitioner could ask about the concerns his family members might have about his drinking, or the ways his depression might be related to his current and past alcohol use.

Intervention Strategies   The practitioner has a number of counseling approaches available that both can communicate concern about problematic substance use and help a patient make a decision to enter substance treatment. One such approach is motivational interviewing (Miller & Rollnick, 2002), a counseling style that helps patients resolve their ambivalence about behavior change and begin to initiate positive change. For a full review of motivational interviewing, see Chapter 3. A motivational interviewing style uses a variety of techniques to build empathy with patients and help them talk about the possibilities of change. These techniques are used with several core assumptions about change: (1) practitioners avoid taking an expert role in the process, but rather view patients as *collaborators* in setting a treatment plan; (2) practitioners respect the patient's *autonomy* regarding a decision to change, and (3) practitioners try to evoke the patient's own reasons for change rather than imposing external motivators on him or her. In the style of motivational interviewing, here are some guidelines for intervening with a substance abusing patient.

1. Use open ended questions. Unlike assessment of drinking and drug use, which requires asking very specific questions about amount and frequency of intake, counseling patients about substance problems involves asking open-ended questions. Unlike "yes/no" questions, which tend to direct the conversation, open-ended questions allow patients to voice their concerns about their behavior. Initially, questions can be related to general health and how alcohol or drugs relate to it. For example, "How have you been feeling lately?" and "How do you think your alcohol/drug use may affect your health and fitness?"
2. Support patients' efforts. Often patients feel stymied or demoralized in their efforts to cut down use, or pressured by family or friends to stop using. Patients can feel encouraged when practitioners genuinely point out their positive efforts (regardless of how small) to take responsibility for their problem. Examples of supportive communication from practitioners can include, "It's not easy to open up and talk about this like you have," or "Your concern about this problem shows how committed you are to taking care of yourself and your family."
3. Help patients talk about the positives and negatives of their drinking/drug use in a nonjudgmental way. Practitioners can help patients gain awareness of their

feelings about their use by asking them "What do you like about alcohol? What don't you like?" "What do other people—friends, family—say about your use?" "What are your goals, professionally and personally? How does alcohol/drug use interfere with them?"

4. Ask patients about short- and long-term consequences of use. Prompting patients to visualize future consequences can be helpful in shifting motivation to different stages of change. For example, asking patients, "What would be different in your life if you were not using drugs?" or "What might happen to you if you continue drinking this way for the next year? Next 5 or 10 years?" and "What concerns do you have about your current drinking?"

5. Encourage patients to talk about change. After discussing these issues, the practitioner might ask the patient what he or she would like to do about his or her drinking. For example, "Have you thought about making some changes?" "What do you think you might do?" If a patient's motivation seems to fluctuate, this should be viewed as normal; as discussed, change is a dynamic process.

REFERRAL CONSIDERATIONS

There are many factors to consider in making a referral to substance treatment. To help guide the practitioner through the referral process, questions to consider are listed in Table 17.4. These questions are intended as a starting point, to identify and clarify these factors and tailor an appropriate referral for a particular patient.

Table 17.4
Factors to Consider when Selecting a Referral for a Substance-Abusing Patient

1. *Severity of problem:* Is the problem acute, chronic, or both? How long has the patient been using the substances? Has he or she had significant amounts of time (e.g., months or years) abstinent, either recently or in the remote past?

2. *Necessity of medical intervention:* What drugs are involved? Are drug/alcohol withdrawal symptoms currently present, and if so, will an inpatient detoxification be required? Are co-occurring medical problems present that could complicate an outpatient detoxification?

3. *Patient resources:* What resources are available to the patient? Does this patient have friends and family to help support treatment efforts? Does he or she have insurance, or the ability to afford inpatient or outpatient treatment? Is he or she a sole caretaker of children or elderly relatives? Can he or she reasonably take a leave of absence from work for treatment if necessary?

4. *Patient characteristics:* Are there co-occurring psychiatric problems (e.g., dual diagnosis) or concurrent medical problems that need attention? Is this patient willing to participate in treatment at the time? What goals does the patient have for himself or herself and his or her drug/alcohol use? What stage of change is the patient currently in?

5. *Patient-specific treatment issues:* Is the treatment limited to substance use cessation, or does the drug/alcohol problem also cause or exacerbate other problems? Is the patient in need of (a) family counseling, (b) simultaneous vocational rehabilitation, and/or (c) concurrent psychiatric treatment?

6. *Flexibility of treatment:* Is the facility or treatment center flexible enough to provide needed treatment at a level appropriate to the patient's level of severity? Does the program need to be organized around a patient's work schedule (e.g., evenings and weekends)?

When making a referral to treatment, a practitioner may want to consider less intensive approaches for users of lesser severity. For patients whose use patterns would be considered no more serious than "risky," self-directed education can suffice. There are numerous Internet resources that can be used to educate patients about risky use, allowing them to interact with educational software to evaluate their own level of use. For patients with more severe drug use, a referral to an office-based addiction specialist for evaluation or treatment could be appropriate, based on patient preference or limited impact of the problematic use.

Finding a Referral   Given the variety and complexity of the problems of typical persons abusing substances, it may seem daunting to find the most appropriate treatment referral for a patient. In our experience, it is better to take the time to network and develop knowledge of treatment resources in one's own professional community rather than casting about for a referral when an intoxicated patient is waiting in one's office. A strategy to expand one's knowledge is to identify services offered within one's own clinical setting and/or affiliated hospital(s), find out who handles admissions, and then contact these individuals directly to discuss which facilities they like to refer to when patients are not appropriate for their own program. Another strategy is to call local referral services, such as city hotlines or community referral networks, and ask them to send you a directory of facilities that they use. The Substance Abuse and Mental Health Services Administration of the U.S. Department of Health and Human Services offers a web site that will assist practitioners in finding appropriate referrals by allowing practitioners to search for types of facilities based on zip code and proximity. This web site also includes the option of searching for settings that treat dual-diagnosis patients. Additionally, many substance treatment facilities include units or subprograms for such patients who have co-occurring psychiatric disorders.

Addressing the multiple problems of persons abusing substances can seem overwhelming. However, recent long-term follow-up studies of persons abusing substances have demonstrated that community treatment does have a beneficial effect on patient outcome (Hubbard, Craddock, & Anderson, 2003). While many patients do require more than one episode of treatment to regain their health, there is compelling evidence that even one episode of treatment lasting 3 months or more predicts significant improvement and reduction in substance use 5 years after treatment (Hubbard, Craddock, & Anderson).

In their everyday practice with patients, nurses, physician assistants, physicians, health psychologists, and other clinicians working in medical settings (social workers, occupational and physical therapists) have significant opportunities to recognize substance abuse, an oft-concealed but persistent psychiatric disorder. They can also provide brief but powerful in-office interventions that can facilitate entry into focused, longer-term substance abuse treatment. Patient and practitioner characteristics, considerations of health care settings, and comorbidity with other psychiatric disorders make early identification of the disorder challenging. However, even small, subtle efforts toward increased screening and follow-up can make an important difference in altering the course of substance abuse in a patient's life. With knowledge about the presentation of substance use problems, the processes that effect change in substance use behaviors, and the options for treatment, practitioners can intervene appropriately to help patients adopt more healthful behaviors.

REFERENCES

Albanese, M. J., Clodfelter, R. C. Jr., Pardo, T. B., & Ghaemi, S. N. (2006). Underdiagnosis of bipolar disorder in men with substance use disorder. *Journal of Psychiatric Practice.* 12(2),124–127.

Alcoholics Anonymous World Services, Inc. (1972). *A brief guide to alcoholics anonymous.* New York: The A. A. Grapevine.

Andreas, J. B., O 'Farrell, T. J., & Fals-Stewart, W. (2006). Does individual treatment for alcoholic fathers benefit their children? A longitudinal assessment. *Journal of Consulting and Clinical Psychology,* 74(1),191–198.

American Medical Association, Council on Scientific Affairs. (1996). Alcoholism in the elderly. *Journal of the American Medical Association,* 275, 797–801.

American Psychiatric Association. (1994). *Diagnostic and Statistical Manual of Mental Disorders* (4th ed.). Washington, D.C.: Author.

Ball, S. A., Carroll, K. M., & Rounsaville, B. J. (1994). Sensation seeking, substance abuse, and psychopathology in treatment-seeking and community cocaine abusers. *Journal of Consulting and Clinical Psychology,* 62(5), 1053–1057.

Bandura, A. (1985). *Social foundations of thought and action.* Englewood Cliffs, NJ: Prentice Hall.

Bayard, M., McIntyre, J., Hill, K. R., & Woodside, J., Jr. (2004). Alcohol withdrawal syndrome. *American Family Physician,* 69(6), 1443–1450.

Beck, A. T., & Freeman, A. (1990). *Cognitive therapy of personality disorders.* New York: Guilford.

Benjamin, L. S. (1996). An interpersonal theory of personality disorders. In J. F. Clarkin & M. F. Lenzenweger (Eds.), *Major theories of personality disorder* (pp. 141–220). New York: Guilford.

Bohman, M., Sigvardsson, S., & Cloninger, C. R. (1981). Maternal inheritance of alcohol abuse: Cross fostering analysis of adopted women. *Archives of General Psychiatry,* 38, 965–969.

Bradley, K. A., Curry, S. J., Koepsell, T. D., & Larson, E. B. (1995). Primary and secondary prevention of alcohol problems: U.S. internist attitudes and practice. *Journal of General Internal Medicine,* 10, 67–72.

Brunette, M. B., Noordsy, D. L., Buckley, P., & Green, A. I. (2005). Pharmacologic treatments for co-occurring substance use disorders in patients with schizophrenia: A research review. *Journal of Dual Diagnosis,* 1, 41–55.

Budney, A. J., Hughes, J. R., Moore B. A., & Novy P. L. (2001). Marijuana abstinence effects in marijuana smokers maintained in their home environment. *Archives of General Psychiatry,* 58(10), 917–924.

Centers for Disease Control and Prevention (CDC). (1995). *Youth Risk Behavior Surveillance System (YRBSS) Summary.* Atlanta, GA: Author.

Centers for Disease Control and Prevention (CDC). (2002). *HIV/AIDS Surveillance Report,* 14. Atlanta, GA: Author.

Center for Substance Abuse Treatment (1998). Substance abuse among older adults. *Treatment Improvement Protocol (TIP) Series 26.* DHHS Publication no. (SMA) 98-3179. Rockville, MD.: Substance Abuse and Mental Health Services Administration.

Chan-Pensley, E. (1999). Alcohol-use disorders identification test: A comparison between paper and pencil and computerized versions. *Alcohol and Alcoholism,* 34(6), 882–885.

Chilcoat, H. D., & Breslau, N. (1998). Posttraumatic stress disorder and drug disorders. *Archives of General Psychiatry,* 55, 913–917.

Clure, C., Brady, K. T., Saladin, M. E., Johnson, D., Waid, R., & Rittenbury, M. (1999). Attention-deficit/hyperactivity disorder and substance use: Symptom pattern and drug choice. *American Journal of Drug and Alcohol Abuse* 25(3), 441–448.

Cloninger, C. R., Sigvardsson, S., Reich, T., & Bohman, M. (1986). Inheritance of risk to develop alcoholism. *NIDA Research Monographs,* 66, 86–96.

Cocores, J. A., Davies, R. K., Mueller, P. S., & Gold, M. S. (1987). Cocaine abuse and adult attention disorder. *Journal of Clinical Psychiatry, 48,* 376–377.

Cox, B. J., Norton, G. R., Swinson, R. P., & Endler, N. S. (1990). Substance abuse and panic-related anxiety: A critical review. *Behaviour Research and Therapy, 28*(5), 385–393

Dawes, M. A., Antelman, S. M., Vanyukov, M. M., Giancola, P., Tarter, R. E., Susman, E. J., et al. (2000). Developmental sources of variation in liability to adolescent substance use disorders. *Drug and Alcohol Dependence; 61*(1), 3–14.

Deckel, A. W., Bauer, L., & Hesselbrock, V. (1995) Anterior brain dysfunctioning as a risk factor in alcoholic behaviors. *Addiction, 90*(10), 1323–1334.

De Leon, G. (2000). *The therapeutic community: Theory, model, and method.* New York: Springer.

DeWit, D. J., Adlaf, E. M., Offord, D. R., & Ogborne, A. C. (2000). Age at first alcohol use: A risk factor for the development of alcohol disorders. *American Journal of Psychiatry, 157,* 745–750.

Eickelberg, S. J., & Mayo-Smith, M. F. (1998). Management of sedative-hypnotic intoxication and withdrawal. In A. W. Graham & T. K. Schultz (Eds.), *Principles of addiction medicine* (2nd ed., pp. 452–453). Chevy Chase, MD: American Society of Addiction Medicine.

Ernst, M., Luckenbaugh, D. A., Moolchan, E. T., Leff, M. K., Allen, R., Eshel, N., et al. (2006). Behavioral predictors of substance-use initiation in adolescents with and without Attention-Deficit/Hyperactivity Disorder. *Pediatrics, 117*(6), 2030–2039.

Ettenberg, A. (2004). Opponent process properties of self-administered cocaine. *Neuroscience and Biobehavioral Reviews, 27*(8), 721–728.

Ettenberg, A., Raven, M. A., Danluck, D. A., & Necessary, B. D. (1999). Evidence for opponent-process actions of intravenous cocaine. *Pharmacology, Biochemistry, and Behavior, 64*(3), 507–512.

Fillmore, K. M. (1987). Women's drinking across the adult life course as compared to men's. *British Journal of the Addictions, 82,* 801–811.

Friedmann, P. D., McCullough, D., Chin, M. H., & Saitz, R. (2000). Screening and intervention for alcohol problems. *Journal of General Internal Medicine, 15*(2), 84–91.

Grant, B. F., Harford, T. C., Dawson, D. A., Chou, S. P., Dufour, M., & Pickering, R. P. (1994). Prevalence of *DSM-IV* alcohol abuse and dependence: United States, 1992. *Alcohol Health and Research World, 18,* 243–248.

Green, M. (1994). *Bright futures: Guidelines for health supervision of infants, children, and adolescents.* Arlington, VA: National Center for Education in Maternal and Child Health.

Higgins, P. S. (1988). *The prevention of drug abuse among teenagers: A literature review.* St. Paul, MN: Amherst H. Wilder Foundation.

Howard, A. A., Arnsten, J. H., & Gourevitch, M. N. (2004). Effect of alcohol consumption on diabetes mellitus: A systematic review. *Annals of Internal Medicine,* 211–219.

Hubbard, R. L., Craddock, S. G., & Anderson, J. (2003). Overview of 5-year follow-up outcomes in the drug abuse treatment outcome studies (DATOS). *Journal of Substance Abuse Treatment, 25,* 125–134.

Kahan, M., Wilson, L., & Becker, L. (1995). Effectiveness of physician-based interventions with problem drinkers: A review. *Canadian Medical Association Journal, 15,* 851–859.

Kendler K. S., Gallagher T. J., Abelson J. M., & Kessler, R. C. (1996). Lifetime prevalence, demographic risk factors, and diagnostic validity of nonaffective psychosis as assessed in a U.S. community sample. The National Comorbidity Survey. *Archives of General Psychiatry, 53*(11), 1022–1031.

Kessler, R. C., Sonnega, A., Bromet, E., Hughes, M., & Nelson, C. B. (1995). Posttraumatic stress disorder in the National Comorbidity Survey. *Archives of General Psychiatry, 52,* 1048–1060.

Khantzian, E. J. (1985). The self-medication hypothesis of addictive disorders: Focus on heroin and cocaine dependence. *American Journal of Psychiatry, 142*(11), 1259–1264.

Khantzian, E. J. (1997). The self-medication hypothesis of substance use disorders: A reconsideration and recent applications. *Harvard Review of Psychiatry, 4*(5), 231–244.

Khong, E., Sim, M., & Hulse, G. (2004). Benzodiazepine dependence. *Australian Family Physician, 33*(11), 923–926.

King, V. L., Brooner, R. K., Kidorf, M. S., Stoller, K. B., & Mirsky, A. F. (1999). Attention deficit hyperactivity disorder and treatment outcome in opioid abusers entering treatment. *The Journal of Nervous and Mental Diseases, 187*(8), 487–495.

Kloner, R. A., & Rezwalla, S. H. (2003). Cocaine and the heart. Comment in *New England Journal of Medicine, 348,* 487–488.

Knight, J. R., Shrier, L. A., Bravender, T. D., Farrell, M., VanderBilt, J., & Shaffer, H. J. (1999). A new brief screen for adolescent substance abuse. *Archives of Pediatrics & Adolescent Medicine, 153,* 591–596.

Kreek, M. J., & Vocci, F. J. (2002). History and current status of opioid maintenance treatments: Blending conference session. *Journal of Substance Abuse Treatment, 23,* 93–105.

Leshner, A. I. (1999). Drug abuse and mental disorders: Comorbidity is reality. Director's column. *NIDA Notes, 14* (4).

Levin, F. R., Evans, S. M., & Kleber, H. D. (1998). Prevalence of adult attention deficit hyperactivity disorder among cocaine abusers seeking treatment. *Drug and Alcohol Dependence 52*(1), 15–25.

Manwell, L. B., Fleming, M. F., Johnson, K., & Barry, K. L. (1998). Tobacco, alcohol, and drug use in a primary care sample: 90–day prevalence and associated factors. *Journal of Addictive Diseases, 17,* 67–81.

Mayfield D., McLeod, G., & Hall, P. (1974). The CAGE questionnaire: Validation of a new alcoholism screening instrument. *The American Journal of Psychiatry, 131*(10), 1121–1123.

Mayo-Smith, M. F. (1997). Pharmacologic management of alcohol withdrawal. A meta-analysis and evidence-based practice guideline. *Journal of the American Medical Association, 278,* 144–151.

McCaul, M. E., & Petry, N. M., (2003). The role of psychosocial treatments in pharmacotherapy for alcoholism. *The American Journal on Addictions, 12,* S41–S52.

Mertens, J. R., Weisner, C., Ray, G. T., Fireman, B., & Walsh, K. (2005). Hazardous drinkers and drug users in HMO primary care: Prevalence, medical conditions, and costs. *Alcoholism: Clinical & Experimental Research, 29*(6), 989–998.

Miller, N. S. (1995). Pharmacotherapy in alcoholism. *Journal of Addictive Diseases, 14,* 23–46.

Miller, W. R., & Rollnick, S. (2002). *Motivational interviewing: Preparing people for change* (2nd ed.). New York: Guilford.

Millon, T., & Davis, R. (1996). An evolutionary theory of personality disorders. In J. F. Clarkin & M. F. Lenzenweger (Eds.), *Major theories of personality disorder* (pp. 221–346). New York: Guilford.

Nace, E. P. (1990). Substance abuse and personality disorder. *Journal of Chemical Dependency Treatment, 3,* 183–198.

Office of Applied Studies & RTI International. (2006). *The National Survey of Drug Use and Health Report (NSDUH), 26.* Rockville, MD: Substance Abuse and Mental Health Services Administration.

Prochaska, J. O., & DiClemente, C. C. (1984). *The transtheoretical approach: Crossing the traditional boundaries of therapy.* Malabar, FL: Krieger.

Regier, D. A., Farmer, M. E., Rae, D. S., Locke, B. Z., Keith, S. J., Judd, L. L., et al. (1990). Comorbidity of mental disorders with alcohol and other drug abuse: Results from the epidemiologic catchment area (ECA) study. *Journal of the American Medical Association, 264,* 2511–2518.

Reid, M. C., Fiellin, D. A., & O'Connor, P. G. (1999). Hazardous and harmful alcohol consumption in primary care. *Archives of Internal Medicine, 159,* 1681–1689.

Richards, H. J. (1993). *Therapy of the substance abuse syndromes.* Northvale, NJ: Jason Aronson.

Rigler, S. K. (2000). Alcoholism in the elderly. *American Family Physician 61*(6), 1710–1716.

Robins, L. N., & Przybeck, T. R. (1987). *Age of onset of drug use as a factor in drug and other disorders.* National Institute on Drug Abuse Monograph 56 (pp.178–192). (DHHS Publication no. ADM 87-1335). Washington, DC: U. S. Government Printing Office.

Saitz, R., Mulvey, K. P., Plough, A., & Samet, J. H. (1997). Physician unawareness of serious substance abuse. *American Journal of Drug and Alcohol Abuse, 23*(3), 343–354.

Saunders, J. B., Aasland, O. G., Babor, T. F., de la Fuente, J. R., & Grant, M. (1993). Development of the Alcohol Use Disorders Identification Test (AUDIT): WHO collaborative project on early detection of persons with harmful alcohol consumption. II. *Addiction, 88,* 791–804.

Schuckit, M. A. (2000). *Drug and alcohol abuse: A clinical guide to diagnosis and treatment* (5th ed.) New York: Kluwer Academic.

Selzer, M. L. (1971). The Michigan Alcoholism Screening Test: The quest for a new diagnostic instrument. *American Journal of Psychiatry, 127,* 1653–1658.

Slavin, S. A., & Goldwyn, R. M.(1990). The cocaine user: The potential problem patient for rhinoplasty. *Plastic and Reconstructive Surgery, 86*(3), 436–442.

Sobell, M. B., Maisto, S. A., Sobell, L. C., Cooper, A. M., Cooper, T., & Sanders, B. (1980). Developing a prototype for evaluating alcohol treatment effectiveness. In L. C. Sobell, M. B. Sobell, and E. Ward (Eds.), *Evaluating alcohol and drug abuse treatment effectiveness: Recent advances* (pp. 129–150). New York: Pergamon.

Streissguth, A. P., Barr, H. M., Kogan, J., & Bookstein, F. L., (1996). Understanding the occurrence of secondary disabilities in clients with fetal alcohol syndrome (FAS) and fetal alcohol effects (FAE). Tech. Rep. no. 96-06. *Final report to the Centers for Disease Control and Prevention (CDC).* Seattle: University of Washington, Fetal Alcohol & Drug Unit.

Strunin, L., & Hingson, R. (1992). Alcohol, drugs, and adolescent sexual behaviors. *International Journal of Addictions, 27,* 129–146.

Substance Abuse and Mental Health Services Administration. 1999. *National household survey on drug abuse: Main findings 1997.* Rockville, MD: Author.

Substance Abuse and Mental Health Services Administration. (2002). *Results from the 2001 National Household Survey on Drug Abuse: Volume II.* Technical Appendices and Selected Data Tables. (Office of Applied Studies, NHSDA Series H-18, DHHS Publication no. SMA 02-3759). Rockville, MD: Author.

Substance Abuse and Mental Health Services Administration. (2005). *Results from the 2004 National Survey on Drug Use and Health: National Findings* (Office of Applied Studies, NSDUH Series H-28, DHHS Publication No. SMA 05–4062). Rockville, MD: Author.

Thom, B. (1987). Sex differences in help-seeking for alcohol problems—2. Entry into treatment. *British Journal of Addiction, 82*(9), 989–997.

Tjepkema, M. (2004). Alcohol and illicit drug dependence. *Health Reports, 15,* (Suppl.), 9–19.

Trull T. J., Sher, K. J., Minks-Brown, C., Durbin, J., & Burr, R. (2000). Borderline personality disorder and substance use disorders: A review and integration. *Clinical Psychology Review, 20*(2), 235–253.

U.S. Preventive Services Taskforce. (1996). Screening for problem drinking. In *Guide to clinical preventive services* (pp. 567–582). Baltimore: Williams & Wilkins.

Valois, R. F., Oeltmann, J. E., Waller, J., & Hussey, J. R. (1999). Relationship between number of sexual intercourse partners and selected health risk behaviors among public high school adolescents. *The Journal of Adolescent Health, 25*(5), 328–335.

Van den Brink, W., & Haasen, C. (2006). Evidenced-based treatment of opioid-dependent patients. *The Canadian Journal of Psychiatry, 51*(10), 635–646.

Vicens, C., Fiol, F., Llobera, J., Campoamor, F., Mateu, C., Alegret, S., et al. (2006). Withdrawal from long-term benzodiazepine use: Randomised trial in family practice. *British Journal of General Practice, 56*(533), 958–963.

Vocci, F. J., Acri, J., & Elkashef, A. (2005). Medication development for addictive disorders: The state of the science. *American Journal of Psychiatry, 162,* 1432–1440.

Wenrich, M. D., Paauw, D. S., Carline, J. D., Curtis, J. R., & Ramsey, P. G. (1995). Do primary care physicians screen patients about alcohol intake using the CAGE questions? *The Journal of General Internal Medicine, 10,* 631–634.

Wilk, A. I., Jensen, N. M., & Havighurst, T. C. (1997). Meta-analysis of randomized control trials addressing brief interventions in heavy alcohol drinkers. *Journal of General Internal Medicine 12,* 274–283.

CHAPTER 18

Sexuality and Reproductive Health of Men and Women

WILLIAM R. STAYTON, DEBRA W. HAFFNER, and SUSAN S. MCNIFF

INTRODUCTION

- Sexuality is a natural and healthy part of living.
- Sexuality involves more than sex, and sex involves more than intercourse.
- Sexual feelings and sexual behaviors are integral aspects of reproductive health.
- A client's sexual attitudes, behaviors, and relationships all influence how effective a particular contraceptive method will be.
- Understanding sexual behavior is critical for designing interventions that will reduce unintended pregnancies and sexually transmitted infections (STIs), including infection with the human immunodeficiency virus (HIV).*

Sexuality and reproductive health care are interdependent. Reproductive health care providers help people manage their sexual lives. Although contraceptive services have traditionally helped plan the number and spacing of children, most clients seek contraception primarily to separate procreation from the recreational aspects of sexual intercourse.

Sexuality, however, is about much more than sexual intercourse. It encompasses the sexual knowledge, beliefs, attitudes, values, and behaviors of individuals. It includes not only anatomy, physiology, and biochemistry of the sexual response system, but also identity, orientation, roles, personality, thoughts, feelings, and relationships. The expression of sexuality is influenced by ethical, spiritual, cultural, and moral concerns (Barback, 1976).

Men's and women's sexual attitudes and behaviors influence their choice of contraception and their ability to use the methods effectively. On a very fundamental level, individuals' reproductive health care decisions rest on their ability to make informed

---

* Portions of this chapter have been adapted with permission from the following source: Hatcher, Robert A. (ed). (2004). *Contraceptive Technology*, 18th rev. ed. New York: Ardent Media. 2004. While this chapter is directed primarily to heterosexual couples needing contraception, the authors believe sexuality is an important part of most adults' lives: gay men, lesbians, postreproductive-age women, the physically or mentally challenged, and so on.

and healthy choices about their sexuality. The decision to become sexually involved—whether the relationship is consensual, whether it is monogamous, whether it is protected against unplanned pregnancy and sexually transmitted infections (STIs), or whether sexuality is a pleasurable or painful part of life—is related to the ability to make responsible sexual choices.

Many reproductive health care clinicians have treated an individual's sexuality needs as separate and distinct from contraceptive and other reproductive health needs. Practitioners may not have been trained in addressing sexual health concerns. The pressure to reach the largest number of people in an efficient manner may limit counseling to method instruction and preclude time for helping clients manage their sexual lives in a way consistent with their own values and goals.

The 1994 International Conference on Population and Development directly recognized the relationship of sexuality to reproductive health, acknowledging that sexuality issues must be addressed in reproductive health care settings: "Reproductive health therefore implies that people are able to have a satisfying and safe sex life and that they have the capability to reproduce and the freedom to decide if, when, and how often to do so. . . . Reproductive health . . . also includes sexual health, the purpose of which is the enhancement of life and personal relations, and not merely counseling and care related to reproduction and sexually transmitted diseases." (United Nations, 1994, section 7, 2:43). The report was endorsed by more than 200 countries.

Practitioners have a unique opportunity to provide information, education, and counseling to clients who might otherwise have no readily available resource for help. As important, addressing sexual concerns directly with clients as they choose their method may improve how effectively they use contraception.

SEXUAL BEHAVIOR IN THE UNITED STATES

Human sexual interaction is surely the least understood and least investigated behavior in daily life, so reproductive health care practitioners are placed at a serious disadvantage. Solid information on contraceptive use during penile-vaginal intercourse yields knowledge about contraceptive failure and pregnancy risk taking. Solid information on heterosexual and same-gender sexual practices (anal, vaginal, and oral intercourse) and partner networks (who does what with whom and when) yields knowledge about the transmission of STIs, including infection with the human immunodeficiency virus (HIV). Understanding the psychological and social reasons for sexual behaviors is necessary for designing effective interventions to reduce risk taking with regard to pregnancy and infection. Understanding and combating STI transmission can be even more difficult than understanding and combating unintended pregnancy—the sexual behaviors that result in an STI are more varied, and the sexual networks extend beyond the present into the past. Until recently, information about sexual behaviors was limited to questions included in surveys primarily devoted to other topics, such as general social, family, or fertility surveys or nongeneralizable surveys of college students or the readers of magazines. In 1994, the National Opinion Research Center (NORC) at the University of Chicago completed the largest, most current study of sexual behaviors in the United States. The study was based on interviews with a national probability household sample of more than 3,400 men and women age 18 to 59 years (Laumann, Gagnon, Michael, & Michaels, 1994).

In general, Americans are having less sex than was generally believed. Eighty-three percent of American adults age 18 to 59 had one partner or no partner in the last year

Table 18.1

Survey of sexual behaviors in the United States, 1994

- 83% of Americans had one partner or no partner in the last year.
- Most married couples have sexual intercourse a few times a month.
- The most frequent and most enjoyed sexual behavior for heterosexual adults is penile-vaginal intercourse.
- One-fourth of adults have oral sex regularly.
- 10% of married women and 25% of married men have had an affair.
- More than 4 in 10 adults have had five or more sexual partners in their lifetime.
- One in five Americans had a new sexual partner in the past 12 months.
- The median number of lifetime sexual partners by age 60 is two for women and six for men.

Source: Laumann et al, (1994).

of the study, and most people had sexual relations a few times a month. American adults were about equally divided among those who have sexual relations with a partner at least twice a week, a few times a month, a few times a year, or not at all (Table 18.1; Laumann et al, 1994).

Younger Americans behave significantly differently than older Americans. Younger people begin having intercourse earlier, marry later, and have more lifetime partners. One of the surprises of the study is that marriage is a great leveler. Married adults share remarkably similar patterns of sexual behavior, regardless of attitudes, premarital experience, religious or ethnic background, or geography. The vast majority of married people report that they are monogamous, engage in sex a few times a month, and focus on penile-vaginal intercourse as their primary sexual behavior (see Table 18.1).

Gender differences clearly exist when it comes to sexual attitudes and behaviors. Men are much more likely than women to report recreational sex, a greater number of partners, a greater interest in a variety of sexual activities, and less monogamy. Women are much more likely to say their first intercourse was as a result of peer pressure, they do not consistently have orgasms, and they have never masturbated. Men also reported greater access to sexual partners, particularly as they age; although almost 6 in 10 single men age 45 to 59 had a partner in the last year, only one third of women did. In fact, 6 in 10 single women in this age group had no partner during the last 12 months of the study (Laumann et al., 1994). This was the last major national survey of this type in the United States and is still considered the standard for today (Carroll, 2007).

ADOLESCENT SEXUAL BEHAVIOR

Young people today, in sharp contrast to their predecessors, experience the onset of puberty and reach maturity early on in adolescence. Consequently, their reported sexual behavior and attitudes are quite different from the data collected and recounted a generation or two ago. Because research designed to examine the subject of adolescent sexuality is most often controversial, a limited amount of scientific data is readily available. It appears that adults seem to falsely fear that if young people are encouraged to participate in open dialogue about sexual attitudes and beliefs, it is tantamount to giving them ideas and encouragement to engage in sexual behavior.

Nonetheless, information regarding adolescents' sexual behavior—*attitudes, decisions, and activities*—is considered to be a valuable resource to help parents begin the conversation with their children. Additionally, school counselors and educators use the data to design sexual health programs and academic curricula for middle and high schools.

SEXUAL BEHAVIOR

The Youth Risk Behavior Surveillance System (YRBS), which is published by the United States Centers for Disease Control and Prevention, measures sexual behaviors, alcohol and other drug use, and tobacco use, as well as behaviors that contribute to unintentional injuries and violence. Considered by experts in the field to offer the most current information about adolescent sexual behavior, the YRBS is conducted with students in grades 9 through 12 at high schools across the United States. In the YRBS (2001) and Grunbaum et al. (2002) reported the following regarding the adolescent sexual behavior of high school students:

- 45.6% of high school students (48.5% of males and 42.9% of females) reported having had sexual intercourse
- 60.5% of twelfth graders, 51.9% of eleventh graders, 40.8% of tenth graders, and 34.4% of ninth graders reported having had sexual intercourse
- 60.8% of Black students, 48.4% of Hispanic students, and 43.2% of White students reported having had sexual intercourse
- 33.4% of students reported they were currently sexually active (defined as having had sexual intercourse in the 3 months preceding the study)
- 6.6% of students reported initiating sexual intercourse before age 13
- 16.3% of Black students, 7.6% of Hispanic students, and 4.7% of White students reported having had sexual intercourse before age 13

Related alcohol and drug use during last intercourse was reported by 25.6% of sexually active high school students. Surprisingly, little variance exists between the percentages of students in grades nine through 12—25.4% of twelfth graders, 24.7% of eleventh graders, 27.7% of tenth graders, and 24% of ninth graders claim to have used alcohol during their last intercourse. Additionally, the practice of multiple sexual partners, *having had sex with four or more partners,* was reported by 14.2% of the students surveyed.

ORAL SEX VERSUS "SEX"

Pop literature and the media suggest that adolescents are engaging in oral sex at an alarming rate. The supposition that adolescents do not consider oral sex to be "sex" continues to expand. Aside from avoiding the risk of pregnancy and some sexually transmitted diseases, speculation has suggested that oral sex is a means to preserve one's virginity. Specifically, one survey (Sex Smarts, 2000) of 510 adolescents ages 12 to 17 concluded that 44% of male participants "strongly agree" or "agree" *that oral sex is not as big a deal as sexual intercourse.* To further buttress the notion of "sex" versus oral sex, 24% of respondents in a survey of 505 adolescents reported that oral sex is an activity that is "almost always" or "most of the time" part of a casual relationship.

CONTRACEPTIVE USE

Various studies have been conducted to determine contraceptive use among adolescents. They include the YRBS, the *National Survey of Adolescents and Young Adults: Sexual Health Knowledge, Attitudes, and Experiences,* and the United States Department of Health and Human Services' National Center for Health Statistics, which collects data for the National Survey of Family Growth. Condom use and birth control pills were the two most commonly surveyed methods. The 2001 YRBS found that among currently sexually active students:

- 70% of adolescents ages 15 to 17 who engaged in sexual intercourse reported using birth control or protection *all* of the time; 21% *most of the time,* 5% some of the time, and 4% *never*
- 57.9% (65.1% of males and 51.3% of females) reported using condoms during last intercourse
- 18.2% (21.1% of females and 14.9% of males) reported that either they or their partner used birth control pills before last intercourse

TEEN PREGNANCY

Despite reports of a decrease in teen pregnancy and birth rates in the United States, 13% of all births are to teens. Furthermore, the United States has the highest adolescent pregnancy, abortion, and birth rates in the developed world. Succinctly, nearly one million teenage girls, according to the United States Accounting Office, become pregnant every year and more than half of them give birth.

Because teen pregnancy is a complex issue that requires multifaceted initiatives, the Child Welfare League of America has developed and published *Standards of Excellence for Services for Adolescent Pregnancy Prevention, Pregnant Adolescents, and Young Parents.* In an effort to continue the decline in teen pregnancy and birth rates, counselors and educators must stay informed of best practices. A sampling of these best practices include:

- Assertiveness and decision-making training
- Inclusion of males in adolescent pregnancy prevention programming
- Increasing access to family planning
- Mentoring and role model programs

SEXUALITY EDUCATION

Building a strong foundation for sexual health is the gestalt of sexuality education. It is a life-long experiential process that occurs in homes, schools, faith-based institutions, health care professionals, and undoubtedly through the media and Internet, concludes the Henry J. Kaiser Family Foundation. Unfortunately, a misunderstanding of the complexities of sexuality education can detract from the recognition of its importance. Furthermore, research has shown that the frequency, topics, and comfort levels of parents and children with regard to sexuality discussions vary greatly. Nonetheless, adolescents have consistently ranked their parents as one of their primary sources of information on sexuality issues. Moreover, studies conducted by Whitaker and Miller (2000) endorse the belief that adult-child communication can decrease sexual risk behaviors.

The emergence of school-based sexuality education designed to complement and augment what adolescents learn from their families, religious, and community groups has increased in recent years. In particular, the National Guidelines Task Force has identified four main goals that comprehensive sexuality education programs provide:

- Accurate information about human sexuality
- An opportunity for young people to develop and understand their values, attitudes, and beliefs about sexuality
- Help to young people with relationship development and interpersonal skills
- Help for young people in exercising responsibility regarding sexual relationships, including addressing abstinence, pressures to become prematurely involved in sexual intercourse, and the use of contraception and other sexual health measures

Summarily, sexuality education aims to address the biological, sociocultural, physiological, and spiritual dimensions of sexuality from the affective, behavioral, and cognitive domains.

SAME-GENDER SEXUAL BEHAVIOR

Reproductive health care practitioners have long understood that presuming heterosexuality can compromise care. Many clinic counselors report that they see lesbian clients who prefer the reproductive health care they receive at contraceptive clinics. Many lesbians reluctantly take condoms and foam as a method in exchange for their annual Papanicolaou smears and pelvic exams. However, there are little reliable data on same-gender sexual practices of men and almost none on women who have sex with other women.

In 1948, Alfred Kinsey, in his landmark report on the sexual behaviors of American men, reported that 37% of the total male population had an overt homosexual experience (that did not include orgasm) between adolescence and old age, that 10% of males are more or less exclusively homosexual for at least 3 years between the ages of 16 and 65, and that 4% of white males are exclusively homosexual throughout their lives (Kinsey, Pomeroy, & Martin, 1948). Kinsey never published comparable figures for women. These findings about men, which were not based on random samples, led to the widely quoted figure that 10% of American adults are homosexual.

The NORC3 study used a range of questions to elicit information on same-gender sexual attraction, behavior, and identification. Unfortunately, the small numbers in this study do not reveal a great deal about self-identified gays and lesbians. Respondents were asked, "Do you consider yourself heterosexual, homosexual, bisexual, or something else?" Few women (1.4%) reported themselves as homosexual or bisexual; 2.8% of men did. This finding was very similar to other recent studies in the United States, England, and France that found 2 to 4% of adults self-identified as gay or lesbian. However, in the NORC study, 10% of the men and 9% of the women reported feeling same-gender sexual attraction, having had sex with someone of the same sex, or self-identifying as gay or lesbian. Forty-four percent of these men and 59% of these women reported desire only (Laumann et al., 1994).

WHAT DO PEOPLE DO?

The media often give the impression that everybody in America is having more sex, hotter sex, and better sex than they really are. In fact, most Americans are fairly conservative in their sexual practices. When the Kinsey studies were first published, Americans were surprised to find a significant minority of people had visited prostitutes, many people had at least one same-gender sexual experience, and there was a substantial rate of extramarital affairs (Kinsey et al., 1948; Kinsey, Pomeroy, & Martin, 1953). These data, with all their limitations, suggest that changes in sexual behaviors probably began around the turn of the century, and the so-called sexual revolution of the 1960s and 1970s was really just a continuation, and perhaps an acceleration, of those trends (Schwartz, Gillmore, & Civic, 1996).

Several factors have been offered as explanations for these trends. During the mid-1900s, larger numbers of young Americans began to go to college and the age of marriage was delayed as a result. More women entered the labor force and became financially independent. Marrying later and divorcing more, adults who were single and sexually available increased in number.

Kinsey found that by age 25, three-fourths of men but only one third of women had had sexual intercourse (Kinsey et al., 1948, 1953). By 1992, 89% of men and 94% of women age 18 to 24 had had vaginal intercourse. Only 5% of American adults were virgins. The vast majority of Americans first have intercourse by their twentieth birthday, and almost all adults, regardless of marital status, are sexually experienced by their mid-twenties (Laumann et al., 1994).

The NORC3 study found that the most frequent, and most enjoyed, sexual behavior for heterosexual adults is penile-vaginal intercourse. About two-thirds of men and 60% of women have had oral sex, although only about a fourth do so regularly. Oral sex is more common in short-term relationships and more likely among whites compared with blacks. Older adults (over age 50) are less likely to engage in oral sex. About one-fourth of men and one-fifth of women report having ever had anal sex, and about 10% of single men and women have had heterosexual anal sex. Rates of anal sex are higher among Hispanics.

Frequency of sexual interactions is a factor of age, relationship duration, and marital status. In general, cohabiting couples have more sex than married couples; married people have more sex than singles. Due to increased age of marriage and the high divorce levels, there are now significantly more heterosexual adults who are not married but are nevertheless sexually involved (Schwartz et al., 1996).

Ten percent of women and 25% of men report they have had an extramarital sexual relationship (Laumann et al., 1994). Since more men are involved in affairs, presumably without their wives' knowledge, more women may be at risk of STIs than they expect. Research is not available on what proportion of men have same-gender relationships outside of marriage. "These findings suggest not only that the clinician would be wise to ask about behavior rather than sexual orientation, but also that some married persons will perceive themselves to be at no (or low) risk of STIs when in fact their spouse's extramarital sexual activities may place them at risk" (Schwartz et al., 1996).

RISK OF HIV AND OTHER STIS

The authors of the NORC3 study convincingly argue that the 83% of American adults age 18 to 59 years who had either one partner or no partner last year faced little risk of exposure to HIV, unless one or both partners are exposed by sharing injecting-drug equipment. Indeed, they found most American adults have sexual relationships with people very much like themselves; this fact, coupled with the limited infectivity of HIV, is part of the reason that HIV infection has not exploded among heterosexuals in the United States.

However, both the HIV and STI epidemics have clearly affected large numbers of people attending reproductive health clinics. Many people's behaviors place them at risk of infections, and clinics must now address how clients are protecting themselves against these risks. The NORC3 study found risky behaviors.

- More than 4 in 10 Americans age 18 to 59 years have had five or more partners. An estimated 13 million Americans have had 21 or more partners since the age of 18.
- One in six Americans report they have had an STI.
- One in five Americans have had a new sexual partner in the past 12 months— 25% of the men and 15% of the women. Of these, 8.5% had a one-encounter sexual relationship and 12% had a sexual relationship that lasted less than 2 months. The more partners one has had, the less likely they are to be known well, the less likely they are to be from the same social networks, and the less exclusive the relationships are likely to be.
- Condom use is still very low. Only 20% of people who had three or more partners in the past 3 years always used condoms with their primary partner. Although knowledge of AIDS is very high, less than half of those surveyed said using a condom is a very effective way to prevent HIV.

NONVOLUNTARY SEXUAL ACTIVITY

Not all sexual behavior is voluntary, and a history of sexual abuse and sexual assault may severely compromise one's ability to have safe, satisfying sexual relationships. It is important for clinicians to ask questions about prior sexual assault and abuse. It is not uncommon for young adolescent women to reveal they are being forced into sexual relationships with older men, some of whom live in the same household.

Almost one-fourth of women report they have been forced to have sexual relations during their adult lives, most often by their committed partner. In the NORC study, (Laumann et al., 1994) 2% of women report they had been forced by their partners to have sexual relations, while only 3% of men report they had ever forced a woman. Just under one in five men and women report having been sexually abused as children. At least 683,000 adult American women are raped each year (National Victims Center, 1992). Between 1992–2002, the annual average of attempted and completed rapes reported was 366,460. This is believed to be about one half of all rapes committed (Carroll, 2007). A history of sexual abuse seems to have especially pernicious effects. Women with histories of sexual abuse are more likely than other women to be unhappy, have more than 10 lifetime sex partners, lack interest in sex, be unable to have orgasms, feel sex was not pleasurable in the past year, and report other sexual problems.

Adolescents are particularly vulnerable to sexual abuse, and 6% of boys and 15% of girls are sexually assaulted prior to their sixteenth birthday. In a study of adolescent girls in foster care, 43% reported experiencing some type of sexual abuse. The most prevalent type of abuse was being touched or fondled by an adult, against her wishes. One in six reported being forced to have intercourse with an adult. One third of young women had been sexually abused before their tenth birthday (Polit, White, & Morton, 1990). In fact, nearly one third of rapes are committed against women 11 to 17 years of age (National Victims Center, 1992). Nearly three-fourths of young women who had intercourse before age 14 report the experience was involuntary (Child Welfare League of America, 1994). These studies are considered to be the most comprehensive studies ever undertaken in the United States and are still considered scientifically accurate (Carroll, 2007).

A disproportionate number of young women who become pregnant during adolescence are victims of childhood sexual abuse. In one study of adolescents who were pregnant or were parents, 70% of whites, 42% of blacks, and 37% of Hispanics had been sexually abused as a child (Boyer & Fine, 1992). In another study, 64% of parenting and pregnant adolescents reported they had at least one unwanted sexual experience (Child Welfare League of America, 1994).

SEXUAL ANATOMY

MALE SEXUAL ANATOMY

Men tend to be conditioned to focus on genital sexual stimulation rather than whole-body touch arousal. Retraining to be comfortable and to accept and enjoy whole-body stimulation may be a desirable sexual goal for some men. Except for those men who do not respond to nipple caresses and those who deny their sensitivity because of the fear of being unmasculine, the remainder of men are likely to be pleased and excited by nipple stimulation. The sexual sensitivity of male genitalia varies strikingly according to anatomic area. The sites of highly pleasurable sensitivity (in order of decreasing response to touch) are as follows:

- Area of frenular attachment on ventral surface of penis, just behind the glans
- Coronal ridge of glans
- Urethral meatus
- Shaft of the penis
- Penile base located within the perineal area between the area of scrotal attachment and the anus
- Scrotum and testicles
- Perianal skin, the skin surrounding the anus

FEMALE SEXUAL ANATOMY

Virtually any portion of a woman's skin may give pleasurable and exciting sensations when caressed, providing she is willing and not distracted by extraneous thoughts or events. Women tend to be whole-body oriented for sexual touching rather than genitally oriented, as men are trained to be. Breast and nipple sensitivity tends to be high in most women, but some women do not find breast caressing particularly arousing.

For most women, the glans and shaft of the clitoris, the inner surfaces of the labia minora, and the first inch and a half of the vagina are the most sexually sensitive areas of all. Indeed, the clitoral head (glans) may be so exceedingly sensitive that direct touch is sometimes or always uncomfortable. Many women enjoy indirect clitoral touch by caressing the clitoral shaft rather than the glans. Women, as well as men, have (or may acquire) high levels of sexual responsiveness to anal penetration. The frequency, sensation, intensity, and duration of orgasm are highly variable in women. Women also vary greatly in what stimuli induce orgasm for them (dream, fantasy, breast stimulation, masturbation, a partner's hand, a partner's mouth, intercourse, or other stimulation). It is common for healthy, normal women not to be orgasmic through penile-vaginal thrusting alone.

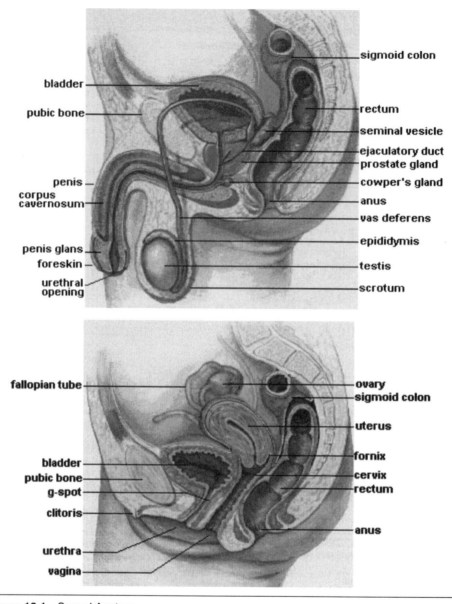

Figure 18.1   Sexual Anatomy

Researchers suggest that women may have three different types of orgasm (Singer & Singer, 1983; Ladas, Whipple, & Perry, 2005). First is a vulvar, or tenting, orgasm, where the clitoris or some outside stimuli such as fantasy or breast stimulation is the main focus of the orgasmic experience. Second, a uterine or A-frame orgasm is felt deeper inside the abdomen and may be triggered by stimulation of the G-spot, or Grafenberg spot, an area in the anterior vaginal wall that is sensitive to sexual stimulation. Some women report ejaculating a milky-white fluid from the urethra when they reach orgasm through this stimulation. The ejaculate is described as different from urine, differing in color, clarity, and odor, and does not stain. It should be regarded as a normal variant of the female sexual response and not as a symptom of urinary incontinence. The third type of orgasm is a blended orgasm, which is a combination of the first two.

SEXUAL RESPONSE

In the past 40 years, the medical and behavioral sciences have yielded information about healthy sexual functioning. Sexual arousal and response are natural to everyone from birth to death. They are not experiences that begin at adolescence and end with menopause, but rather occur to be enjoyed and experienced throughout the life cycle. Reproductive health care providers can incorporate the information that is now available into clinical practice. There have been three major contributions to the overall understanding and knowledge of adult sexual response.

Four Phases of Response

William Masters and Virginia Johnson can be credited with beginning the modern movement toward our understanding of the sexual response cycle. They divided the sexual response cycle into four phases: excitement (or arousal), plateau, orgasm, and resolution. In their seminal book, *Human Sexual Response* (Masters & Johnson, 1966), they detail these phases of the response cycle for both men and women.

Triphasic Model

Another major contribution to our understanding of sexual function comes from Helen Singer Kaplan (1981, 1983, 1987). She described sexual response in a triphasic model consisting of desire, excitement, and orgasm. In discussing her differences with the Masters and Johnson model, she combined their excitement and plateau stages as describing different degrees of the vasodilatory excitement phase. She believed the resolution stage of the Masters and Johnson model merely refers to the absence of sexual arousal.

Kaplan (1979) stressed that it is natural to have sexual desire. She discussed all the factors that contribute to the inhibition of sexual desire: medication, relational problems, sexual abuse, and the effects of illness and disease. Among the major psychological contributors to sexual desire disorders are childhood sexual abuse, rape, negative attitudes toward sexuality, low self-esteem, religious orthodoxy, and relational problems.

EROTIC STIMULUS PATHWAY

A most important contribution to the knowledge base in clinical sexology comes from the Erotic Stimulus Pathway (ESP) theory of David M. Reed (Stayton, 1989). The ESP theory enhances our understanding and ability to treat sexual dysfunctions. Reed divides the sexual response cycle into four phases that correspond to those of Kaplan and Masters and Johnson. For many people, these phases are learned developmentally. In the *seduction phase*, a person learns how to get aroused sexually and how to attract someone else sexually. Seduction translates into memories and rituals.

For example, adolescents may spend much time on personal appearance, choice of clothes, and mannerisms. These can enhance positive self-esteem if the adolescents like the way they feel. If the adolescents feel good about the way they look and feel, then attracting another person will be much easier. As the adolescents get older, these positive feelings are translated into sexual desire and arousal. These seductive techniques are stored in the memory and can be activated later on in life.

In the *sensations phase,* the different senses can enhance sexual excitement and ideally prolong the plateau phase. The early experiences of touch (holding hands, putting arms around a loved one) become very important. The sense of vision (staring at a loved one, holding an image of him or her when absent) is a way of maintaining interest and arousal. Hearing the loved one in intimate conversation or over the telephone becomes very important. Hearing the sounds of a partner responding to sexual stimulation can be titillating. The smell of the loved one, either a particular scent he or she wears or the sexual smell brings additional excitement. Finally, the taste of a food or drink or the taste of the loved one become important to memory and fantasy. All these senses extend the excitement into a plateau phase, which makes one want to continue the pleasurable moment over a longer period of time. These seduction and sensation experiences are the psychological input to the physiology of sexual response. They are the precursors to sexual climax and orgasm.

In the *surrender phase,* orgasm is a "psycho-physiological surprise." The issues surrounding orgasm include power and control. Persons with orgasmic dysfunction may be in a power struggle with themselves or with their partners or with the messages received about sex. Over-control or under-control can affect orgasmic potential and the ability to allow all of one's passion to be expressed.

Finally, the *reflection phase* is central to the sexual experience, especially for the person having intercourse for the first time. How does the person feel immediately after the experience? If the person feels it was a positive experience, the reflection will create positive feedback that will affect future desire. If it is negative, it will diminish future desire, at least for that specific partner, if not for sex itself. It is important that the first sexual experience not be traumatic, otherwise it can have a negative effect on future sexual encounters. For example, in a case of sexual abuse or rape, it can take years for the victim to be able to experience sex in a positive way. The effects of early negative sexual experiences can manifest in lack of sexual desire, vaginismus or dyspareunia, orgasmic disorders, sexual orientation confusion, gender dysphoria, low self-esteem, and erotophobia.

CONTRACEPTIVE CHOICE AND SEXUALITY

Attitudes about sexuality and the characteristics of sexual relationships influence choice of a contraceptive method, how effectively the method is used, and satisfaction with the method. Ambivalence about sexuality contributes to unintended pregnancies and STIs. For example, a 1996 study of women found "women who think planning ahead for birth control can spoil the fun of sex are no more or less likely to use contraceptives, but they are less likely to be satisfied with their method, and, if they use the pill, less likely to use it consistently" (Forrest & Frost, 1996, pp. 246–255, 277).

There is no perfect, 100% effective, 100% easy-to-use, pleasurable contraceptive. Clients can be advised to consider comfort with their body, desire to keep contraception independent of intercourse, the degree of cooperation they can expect from their partner, and whether they also need protection against STIs.

FEAR OF INFECTION

Worry about HIV, genital warts, and other incurable viral STIs often clouds the sexual experience for couples. It can be discouraging to realize that assuring protection from unwanted pregnancy is only half the battle for couples with any possible STI risk. Some people give up on sex altogether, some manage excellent safer sex techniques, but many more give up on safety. The clinician's task is to help at-risk patients in their efforts to keep sex pleasurable and infection-free, tailoring advice to fit an individual patient's sexual patterns.

FEAR OF PREGNANCY AND INFERTILITY

Fear or hope for pregnancy may powerfully affect sexual desire and performance. For men, the subject of pregnancy may cause concerns, but their level of concern tends to be lower than women's. Even among perimenopausal, postmenopausal, contracepting, or sterilized women, the fantasy, memory, hope, fear, anticipation, dread, joy, or desperation and despondency of pregnancy have an impact on identity that men generally do not feel. A woman who has more children than she wants may feel she literally risks the further destruction of her life every time she has penile-vaginal intercourse. An infertile woman may put her feminine identity on the line every month she tries to conceive and is likely to feel emotionally intimidated by the typical infertility workup.

Instructions to time intercourse around ovulation can be particularly stressful for both partners. Even among well-adjusted couples, such instructions are likely to precipitate performance anxiety as well as power and control conflicts. After couples begin timed intercourse, the man may experience an inability to achieve or maintain erections and the couple may have major conflicts. The spontaneity and romantic parts of lovemaking disappear, and couples often panic. Couples trying timed intercourse often need counseling and a break from the pressure of trying to conceive.

Options for assisted reproduction include (Carroll, 2007):

1. Artificial insemination or artificially inserting sperm into the woman's reproductive tract.
2. In vitro fertilization (IVF) by means of removing the woman's ova and fertilizing it with sperm, then placing it back into her uterus.
3. Gamete intrafallopian tube transfer (GIFT) or collecting the sperm and the ova and injecting them both into the fallopian tube before fertilization.
4. Intracytoplasmic sperm injection (ICSI) or injecting sperm into the center of the ova.
5. Sperm, embryo, or ova cryopreservation or freezing of these for later use.

INFLUENCE OF CONTRACEPTIVE CHOICE

Hormonal Contraceptives

The primary sexual advantage of oral contraceptive pills, progestin-only pills, Nuva-Ring, Evra patch, injectables, and implants is that their use is entirely independent of coitus—they do not interrupt lovemaking. Further, women can adopt these methods without the cooperation, or even the knowledge, of their partners. For some couples, assurance of safety from pregnancy leads to increased frequency and satisfaction with sex. There are no timing issues, no stopping to use the method, and virtually no fear of pregnancy. Some women experience increased sexual desire when taking hormones.

Conversely, one of the occasional side effects of some hormonal contraceptives is diminution or loss of sexual desire. A woman whose usual sexual response pattern is well established over time is likely to immediately recognize any loss of desire that closely follows the initiation of a new hormonal method as an undesirable effect of the method. Such patients will usually report their symptom. A different hormonal method may alleviate the problem.

VAGINAL BARRIERS AND SPERMICIDES

Diaphragms, cervical caps, films, suppositories, and foam may either increase sexual pleasure or impair sexual functioning. Clients must be comfortable touching and handling their genitals to use these methods successfully. Using these methods often requires women to plan for intercourse in advance or to interrupt lovemaking. Some couples include inserting the method as part of their sexual play. The extra lubrication is a plus for some couples and a messy interference for others.

For some women, inserting a vaginal barrier before the beginning of a sexual interaction may increase excitement about the upcoming behavior. For others, carrying the equipment when going out for a date may feel uncomfortable and can alter the negotiation between partners. Inserting the vaginal barrier during precoital play carries the risk of interrupting a tender and romantic interlude with a purely mechanical task. One possible negative sexual outcome of diaphragm use for some women is an increased risk of cystitis infections, toxic shock syndrome, or postcoital drip, thereby making intercourse painful if not impossible. This is particularly true for couples having very frequent or particularly rigorous intercourse because it may move and become less reliable (Carroll, 2007).

The female condom offers particular challenges related to sexual functioning. Although some women users report that it increased their pleasure during intercourse, others report it as awkward to place and use. The external ring requires that oral sex take place before insertion or after removal.

CONDOMS

For many couples, condoms are a sexual boon, while for others, their use dampens sexual experience. Condom use requires that the couple communicate about their decision to have intercourse, which is likely to benefit both the sexual interaction and the relationship as a whole. Condoms can help men maintain their erection longer, perhaps increasing the likelihood that women will achieve orgasm during intercourse.

Yet, some men feel constricted by condom use. Couples need careful encouragement on how to integrate putting on the condom as part of foreplay prior to intercourse. Men need to be encouraged to practice condom use when they are not with a partner so they increase their condom skills; women can experiment with erotic techniques for putting condoms on their partners. Some men report they lose their erections when faced with an unrolled condom; practice in private should help alleviate this problem. Young women may need to discuss how to bring up and negotiate condom use with their male partners. Because so many women have older partners, power issues related to condom use are very real. The clinician can help the patient role-play discussing condom use with her partner and develop strategies with a resistant partner. Clinicians can also encourage clients to bring their male partners to the clinic for education and counseling.

Some men lose their erection rapidly after ejaculation, whereas others maintain a relatively erect penis for some time, perhaps as long as 15 to 20 minutes. Because even a few minutes of rest and relaxation while the penis is still inside the partner may result in spillage of semen, men should hold the rim of the male condom at the base of the penis as they withdraw. Doing so prevents the condom from slipping off.

Coitus Interruptus

Withdrawal requires the man to pull out and move away from his partner when his desire is to push deeper and hold more firmly. For some heterosexual couples, this contraceptive method may leave the woman in a state of high excitement without orgasmic relief. Couples using withdrawal should make a special effort to reinstitute sexual play after withdrawal to make sure both partners have achieved gratification and relief of sexual tension. The method can encourage attention on performance rather than pleasure.

Rapid Reinsertion   When seminal fluid is still in the urethra as well as on the glans and shaft of the penis, insemination can still occur if the penis is reinserted. Therefore, if the penis is reinserted immediately after ejaculation, withdrawal is not a satisfactory technique for contraception. Reinsertion should not take place without cleansing the male genitalia (washcloth and warm water with or without soap) and urinating to flush the urethra.

Abstinence

It is likely all adults will go through periods of abstinence. In some cases, single people choose abstinence because of their conviction that sexual intercourse should occur only in marriage. Some single people remain abstinent because they lack a desirable partner. Some couples experience periods of abstinence because of illness, physical separation, or relationship conflicts. There is no uniformly accepted definition of abstinence. Some people have defined abstinence as no genital contact of any kind outside of a monogamous marriage. Others have defined abstinence as not engaging in penetrative behaviors.

Young people need support for choosing abstinence until they are physically, emotionally, and cognitively ready for a mature sexual relationship. Adolescents need to know that "not everybody is doing it": although many American adolescents have had sexual intercourse, many have not. Adolescents need to understand that sexual intercourse is not a way to achieve adulthood, that adolescents in romantic relationships can express sexual feelings without engaging in intercourse, and that there are many ways to give and receive sexual pleasure without the risks associated with penetrative behaviors (National Guidelines Task Force, 1996). Clinicians should spend ample time with adolescent clients to address their decision to be sexually involved.

Adult couples may achieve satisfaction with sexual abstinence providing both select this alternative as the one that most closely meets their individual needs. A relationship can be almost anything so long as both partners agree on what it is to be. When one partner does not agree to abstinence but does not wish to give up the relationship, then a continuing conflict arises that will have emotional consequences for each individual and for the couple. One or both partner(s) may choose abstinence for contraception, for protection from an STI, as part of sexual aversion, or as a symptom of alcoholism or other addiction, depression, or distraction. The person who feels abandoned because of a partner's decision to abstain may use masturbation as an alternative, may reluctantly accept abstinence also, or may choose to seek another partner outside of the primary relationship.

The couple practicing sexual abstinence may lose a major method of nonverbal communication in their relationship and may find it difficult to compensate by communicating in less intimate ways. They must make special efforts to maintain or strengthen other forms of communication.

FERTILITY AWARENESS

Couples using fertility awareness methods must carefully assess their impact on their sexual relationship. Both partners must be committed to fertility awareness as the primary contraceptive method for it to be effective. Couples must negotiate in advance what the use of this method will mean during the fertile days: will they abstain from all sexual behaviors, will they abstain only from penile-vaginal intercourse, or will they use a barrier method? How sure are they that they will be able to maintain sexual limits once sexual activity is in progress? It is even possible that abstaining from sexual intercourse may enhance the experience when it does occur.

INTRAUTERINE DEVICES

The primary advantage of the intrauterine device (IUD) regarding sexual functioning, is that, like the pill, its use is completely separate from coitus and it is highly effective. Intrauterine device users do not need cooperation from their partner. However, women who experience severe or frequent bleeding with the IUD may find it affects their own and their partner's aesthetic experience during intercourse.

VOLUNTARY SURGICAL CONTRACEPTION

Sterilization could improve or hinder sexual functioning. Men considering vasectomy (or getting one's vas deferens tied in order to block sperm from being ejaculated) need careful counseling that a vasectomy will not affect or impair their ability to have an erection. As many men are not familiar with their reproductive anatomy, beyond their penis and scrotum, clinicians may begin with basic anatomy education, including the sexual function of different organs. Clinicians can further help men understand that vasectomy does not affect their erectile or orgasmic potential.

For many women, sterilization (or getting one's fallopian tubes tied so the ovum cannot be fertilized) removes the fear of pregnancy and leads to an increase in desire and frequency of intercourse. For others, reproductive capacity is intimately connected with sexual desire, and sterilization may have the opposite effect.

BRIEF INTRODUCTION TO SEXUAL COUNSELING

Few patients who have a sexual problem or dysfunction are beyond help, if they want to change and if the counselor is willing to help. By simply allowing them a place to ventilate or by providing basic information, counselors can often help patients solve their problems. A brief sexual history is a good place to start (Table 18.2).

Table 18.2

Taking a sexual history

The following questions may be helpful in encouraging clients to talk about their sexual lives or to choose a contraceptive method:

1. Tell me about your earliest sexual experience.
2. Briefly give me a history of your sexual experiences to date.
3. Did you agree to these experiences?
4. How has contraception fit into your sexual behaviors?
5. Are you willing to use a contraceptive method at the time of intercourse?
6. Does your partner actively support your use of contraception?
7. Are you looking for a method you can integrate into lovemaking?
8. How likely is it that you will have more than one sexual partner?
9. Do you have any questions or concerns that you would like to discuss about your present sexual response or your relationship?

The PLISSIT counseling model was developed for health care providers not trained in sex therapy who wish to address the sexual needs and concerns of their patients and make appropriate referrals when necessary (Annon, 1974). PLISSIT is an acronym for four stages of counseling: Permission giving, Limited Information giving, Specific Suggestions, and Intensive Therapy.

Permission-giving is not the same as telling the patient what to do. Permission is usually for thoughts, feelings, or behaviors and may be expressed as permission to do or not to do. Permission-giving from a knowledgeable professional figure is quite powerful. Counselors are not required to give permission for thoughts, feelings, or behaviors that violate their professional value system; however, they are required by professional honesty to indicate to the patient when this is the case and to be frank about differing beliefs and values among professionals.

Limited information-giving usually involves discussing anatomy and physiology as well as dispelling myths about sex. This task is often easy for health care providers because of knowledge about anatomy and physiology. Sexual myths are common, but trained health workers can usually dispel them easily.

Specific suggestions involve skill-building, such as changing position for sexual activities, using lubricants (for dyspareunia), considering Viagra for erectile dysfunction, or using a squeeze or stop-start technique (for rapid ejaculation).

Intensive therapy will probably prove too time-consuming and involved for all but those who are specially trained and wish to devote considerable time to such work. Intensive therapy may be necessary for body-image problems, relationship problems, identity issues, depression, personality disorders, or psychoses.

Patients are rarely hesitant to provide sexual information if the clinician is professional, concerned, self-confident, and nonjudgmental. Even though the patient may offer no data on the first visit, the experience demonstrates willingness to deal with these special subjects, and, often on subsequent visits, patients will offer additional significant and useful data.

If the patient has beliefs or practices that may be harmful or dysfunctional, such as masturbating while asphyxiating oneself or having unprotected sex while being HIV+, it is important to talk about the consequences of those beliefs and practices and discuss alternatives. If a clinician is unwilling to offer care because of personal values or professional ethics, he or she can recommend an alternative source of reputable help. Family planning clinicians should have a referral list of certified sex counselors and therapists.

COMMONLY ASKED QUESTIONS

A client's questions about sexuality often indirectly approach personal worries and concerns:

- How often do most couples my age have sex?
- Is it normal to have times in your marriage when you do not want to have sex?
- How often is it okay to masturbate?

The client with these questions is often asking "Am I normal?" Factual information about frequency may help assure the client, but he or she may also need time to process his or her own feelings about sexual behavior. Clients can be reassured there is no "right" answer to these questions; people must decide, alone or with their partner, what frequency is acceptable. Assure married clients that sexual drives fluctuate during different periods of life, so communication is essential. The questioner on masturbation needs to know that "once is too much if you don't like it," and that too much is when it interferes with your life, relationship, and work.

- My partner wants to (fill in behavior) and I do not. What can I do?
- My partner wants less sex than I do. What can I do?
- What can I do to improve my sex life?

These clients are seeking assistance with couple issues. For example, they may need permission to discuss this issue with their partner. They may need encouragement to say "no" to sexual behaviors or to ask for more control and input over sexual encounters. These clients and partners may need to be referred for counseling.

- How can I tell if my partner has an STI?
- How do I know if my partner is being honest with me?

The reality is that no one can ever know for sure if a partner is being completely honest about past or current sexual history. Unfortunately, some people do lie to their partners, and in some cases, some people may not be aware themselves of their past exposure to STIs and even HIV. To eliminate transmission risk, condoms must be used with each and every act of vaginal, oral, and anal intercourse when a partner's health history is unknown. Of course, if the partner has obvious genital sores, lesions, or secretions, all sexual contact is best avoided until medical advice has been sought and the condition diagnosed and treated.

- Intercourse is painful for me.
- My partner cannot maintain an erection.
- I have never had an orgasm.

These clients may be helped by simple information. The clinician needs to elicit additional information from the client: How often does this happen? Under what conditions does it happen? The information given in the next section may be helpful.

INTRODUCTION TO COMMON SEXUAL DYSFUNCTIONS

Sexual dysfunctions are indeed common. Among the 3,400 National Health and So-cial Life Survey respondents age 18–59, 43% of women and 31% of men confronted such problems in the past year (Laumann, Paik, & Rosen, 2001).

Sex therapy in its beginnings was framed in relational terms. In their book, *Human Sexual Inadequacy*, Masters and Johnson said "there is no such thing as an uninvolved partner in any marriage in which there is some form of sexual inadequacy" (Masters & Johnson, 1970, p.2). Even though some sexual dysfunctions, such as female orgas-mic disorder, can be treated on an individual basis, it is still important to offer to in-clude her partner so she can become orgasmic with her partner as well as alone.

The effects of a sexual dysfunction on a relationship cannot be overstated. Perfor-mance fears, anxiety, and low self-esteem often are direct results of a person feeling like a failure in the bedroom. Depression is common in either or both partners if they can-not get aroused or feel they cannot satisfy their partner. On the other hand, improving sexual functioning can help the entire relationship blossom, just as resolving some of the marital discord can promote a more relaxed and satisfying sexual interaction.

Since 1970, not only has much more been learned about sexual function and dys-function, but the field of sex therapy has expanded to include a wider range of sexual issues such as sex therapy with persons with a disability, both physical and mental, and gender identity issues. While we are all born sexual and with the capacity for sex-ual response, most people were not taught to be good lovers. In America's sexually re-pressive and sex-negative culture, being a good lover is a matter of learning new atti-tudes and skills; sex instruction with adults can provide the "how to" of being a lover. Overcoming a sexual dysfunction can be a by-product of learning and practicing the techniques of being a considerate and passionate lover.

While most clinics do not provide sex therapy, it is important to know when to re-fer a client to a competent sex therapist. Clinicians should refer clients who require more than information and education to a qualified gynecologist, sex counselor, or therapist. To find a certified sex counselor or therapist, clinicians can contact the American Association of Sex Educators, Counselors and Therapists (AASECT), PO Box 1960, Ashland, VA 23005-1960 or via their web site at www.aasect.org. In this sec-tion are simple suggestions for assessing when to refer a client for sex or relationship therapy.

ETIOLOGY OF SEXUAL DYSFUNCTION

Human sexual response consists of a complex orchestration of emotional and hor-monal influences, via the autonomic nervous system, to trigger basic reflexes. Any agent that alters metabolism, stimulates or depresses the central nervous system, or locally influences anatomy or physiology is likely to affect sexual functioning (Satter-field & Stayton, 1980). Stress, emotional well-being, relational issues, and general health affect sexual intimacy and functioning.

Organic factors   Any possibility of organic, physiological, or chemical factors in the sexual dysfunction should be ruled out. Emotional and physiological illness, neuro-logical disorders, use of illicit drugs or medications, or psychotropic drugs can raise or lower sexual desire or function. Couples need a complete physical examination when beginning treatment.

Some of the more common diseases associated with lowered sexual desire, physiological functioning or both are heart disease and stroke, cancer, chronic illness, chronic pain, chronic obstructive pulmonary disease (COPD), diabetes, multiple sclerosis, alcoholism, spinal cord injuries, and HIV/AIDS.

When Masters and Johnson (1970) first presented their material on sexual inadequacy, it was believed that more than 90% of sexual dysfunction was caused by psychological factors. Performance anxiety was believed to be the chief factor. Other causes of sexual dysfunction were thought to be borderline personality disorder, obsessive-compulsive personality disorders, anxiety disorders, and depression. While it is true that all of these can affect sexual function, they are not the only factors to be evaluated. Effective evaluation of sexual dysfunctions must investigate physiological factors, psychological disorders, as well as psychological factors that do represent other psychological diagnoses.

Relationship   It is common for therapists to believe from their own clinical experience and from familiarity with the sex therapy literature that most sexual problems are due to significant relationship problems. Hostility, battles for power and control, poor communications, and excessive dependency are incompatible with sexual intimacy and good functioning. For sex therapy to be successful, problems with the relationship need to be resolved. Otherwise, the behavioral suggestions recommended later in this section will not work and can even increase marital discord. Many clients will need to be referred for couples counseling.

Sociocultural and Religious Factors   The United States is one of the most sexually repressive cultures in history when compared to both ancient and other contemporary societies. Kaplan as well as Masters and Johnson held that religious orthodoxy has played a major part in the widespread sexual dysfunction of our day. Guilt, fear, and the denial of sex as pleasure have led to sexual inhibition. In recent decades, widely held gender-role stereotypes (males as aggressive, females as passive, and so on) have been challenged. Cultural imprinting or conditioning (males pressured to perform quickly; females conditioned to not stimulate the male directly) can create sexual dysfunctions.

SEXUAL DESIRE DISORDERS

The desire disorders (Kaplan, 1979) are associated with Reed's seduction phase. In any given case, it must be determined when seduction takes place: in the present or the past? These disorders must create enough distress and interpersonal difficulty for both partners to be motivated to change.

Lack of desire may be lifelong or acquired; that is, desire may have once been there, but then have diminished for some reason. A lack of desire may be generalized; that is, experienced in every situation, or it may be situational, occurring only in certain situations. For example, one may have desire on vacation but not at home in familiar surroundings, or one may lack lustful feelings with a long-term partner but feel aroused by others. The dysfunction may be due only to psychological factors or to a combination of psychological and organic disease or chemical factors. Sexual desire disorders should be referred to a trained sex therapist.

In hypoactive sexual desire disorder, there is a lack of desire for sexual activity and often an inability to experience sexual fantasies. In a sexual aversion disorder, there is an aversion or avoidance to kissing, touching, and genital sexual contact. A picture or genital model can be used to discuss the client's feelings about observing or touching the model.

SEXUAL AROUSAL DISORDERS

An arousal disorder has an impact on a couple's emotional well-being, whether the disorder affects a woman or a man, and whether medical intervention is successful or not. Clinicians should consider whether medical interventions should be linked to psychotherapeutic support for the couple, either in the clinical setting or by referral. For example, it is common for the nondysfunctional partner to feel he or she is no longer attractive, or to worry that the partner is attracted to someone else. People experiencing a dysfunction may lose self-confidence and may believe that their desire for the partner is permanently lost. Both may feel powerless and fearful. Even if a medical intervention is technically successful, sexual desire may still be affected if interpersonal issues are not addressed and treated.

Female Sexual Arousal Disorder   Women who have difficulty becoming aroused will have difficulty lubricating and feeling erotic genital sensations. There is little or no genital swelling. It is important to evaluate the couple's foreplay patterns to assess whether there has been enough attention paid to the woman's arousal. If her partner is anxious about his potential loss of erection, he may initiate intercourse before she is physically and/or emotionally prepared.

The first step is a thorough medical evaluation, looking especially for drug therapies such as selective serotonin reuptake inhibitors (SSRIs), neurologic disorders, and chronic conditions such as diabetes that can impair sexual function. Then, interventions to consider are over-the counter lubricants such as Astroglide, Replens, and K-Y Jelly, and, for perimenopausal women, hormonal creams or other hormonal treatment to diminish vaginal dryness. A prescription-only mechanical intervention to increase genital blood flow, a clitoral pump known as the Eros-CTD Treatment (Clitoral Therapy Device), is available through UroMetrics, Inc. A number of testosterone and other hormonal products and vasodilators, such as oral phentolomine, herbal treatments like Zestra, Avlimil, viacreme, and yohimbine are under study as treatments for female arousal disorders (Rae, 2001; Carroll, 2007), and while not FDA approved, the results of current studies are promising. These pharmacotherapeutic agents are meant to enhance the desire for sex, increase arousal response, and/or improve blood flow to the genitals.

While product labeling states that Viagra and now Levitra are indicated only for the treatment of erectile dysfunction (*Physician's Desk Reference*, 2002), these drugs have been used to treat women, and women often ask their reproductive health care providers about Viagra. It has not proven to be effective in treating sexual dysfunction in women as it has in men, with the exception of SSRI-associated dysfunction (Boyce & Umland, 2001; Carroll, 2007). The risk of long-term use has not been tested. Wellbutrin, an antidepressant, may increase sexual interest in women who are not depressed (Carroll).

Male Erectile Disorder   If a man has difficulty gaining or maintaining an adequate erection suitable for sexual activity, he suffers from erectile disorder. The first step is a thorough medical evaluation (most often conducted by a urologist), looking especially for ischemic heart disease, diabetes, prostate cancer treatment, neurological disorders, and use of SSRIs. Then, a mechanical intervention to consider that is available by prescription is the vacuum pump to draw blood into the penis. When an erection is attained, a rubber band or similar device is placed over the base of the penis to hold the blood in.

Topical medications such as minoxidil are effective for some men. Other topical products that show promise contain glyceryltrinitrate, nitroglycerine, alprostadil, or papavarine. Little is known about potential adverse effects of vaginal absorption of these products during intercourse (Rowland & Burnett, 2000).

Oral medications such as Viagra, Levitra, and Cialis are effective for many men. These medications have demonstrated effectiveness in men whose erectile dysfunction is associated with prostatectomy, radiation therapy, diabetes, certain neurologic disorders, and drug therapies such as SSRIs (Boyce, 2001). Contraindications include the use of organic nitrate therapy, and the manufacturer warns that Viagra should not be generally used in men for whom sexual activity is inadvisable because of underlying cardiovascular status (*Physician's Desk Reference*, 2002).

Yohimbine, another oral product made from the bark of the yohimbe tree, is available in health food stores or by prescription as Yocon. Other oral products hold promise for the future, and oral agents have emerged as a first line option for many patients (Rowland & Burnett, 2000).

Intraurethral suppositories containing the vasoactive drug alprostadil (Prostaglandin E1), such as Muse and Alibra, have been successful for some men. Intracavernosal injection is one of the most effective ways to obtain and maintain erection, and alprostadil products Caverject and Edex are among the most commonly used. Penile injections are considered safe, but the idea of giving oneself a shot in this area may be hard for some men (Rowland & Burnett, 2000).

Sensate Focus for Male and Female Arousal Disorders

Simple pleasuring exercises can increase or enhance the arousal process. Masters and Johnson called these exercises *sensate focus*. First, the couple sensually touch each other over their entire bodies, except for the genital and breast areas. This is often difficult, because when the couple is experiencing sexual difficulties, one or both often take on spectator roles and try to think about what is going on in their partner's head. They lose the focus on their own pleasure as participants.

Once partners have been able to focus on their own pleasurable experiences, they can explore the breasts and genitals and determine which touches are pleasurable, threatening, or irritating. What many couples do not realize is that different areas on the breasts and genitals can be more erotic and sensitive than other spots. Next, the couple caresses the breasts and genitals to produce arousal. If either of the partners experiences arousal, they may go on to noncoital orgasm, unless the dysfunction is directly related to orgasm.

Before trying intercourse, when he is able to gain an erection consistently, the man should deliberately lose his erection by having his partner stop stimulating him. Once his erection has gone down, his partner should then restimulate him until he has another erection. The important lesson here is that if there has been no orgasm, he can lose his erection several times and regain it with further erotic stimulation. Too often a man incorrectly believes that if he loses his erection once, the experience is over for him. After the man has accomplished losing and regaining an erection, his partner can stimulate him while he is lying on his back and then mount him and just hold his penis near her labia and clitoris. When she does this and he holds the erection, she can then insert the penis into her vagina without doing any thrusting, so he can experience being contained in her vagina without stimulation. He will then lose his erection and she can restimulate him. When he gets an erection again, she can put his penis into her vagina and begin slowly thrusting. They can continue this exercise until they are having satisfying intercourse.

If these exercises do not help, it could be because there are self-defeating thoughts of failure, performance anxiety that persists, or some underlying dynamic that undermines success. Occasionally, for example, a person or their partner fears success because it may lead the man to go outside their relationship for sex. Maintaining the dysfunction is a protective mechanism against infidelity. It is important to discuss the possibilities of why the therapy is not working.

ORGASMIC DISORDERS

The psychological issues involved in orgasmic disorders usually involve issues of power and control. Other issues include an inability to relax, let go, and let the tension of the sexual response take over. Being vulnerable, fearing failure, or fearing success can affect orgasmic potential.

Female Orgasmic Disorder   A woman who has never been orgasmic should begin with self-exploration and stimulation to experience her sexual response cycle without having to perform in front of her partner. The books *For Yourself, Sex for One: The Joys of Self-loving*, (Dodson, 1987) or *Becoming Orgasmic: A Sexual and Personal Growth Program for Women* (Heiman & LoPiccolo, 1988) are helpful resources for clients to learn about masturbation and orgasm. A vibrator also can be a useful aid in helping the woman experience her orgasmic potential. Once she has become orgasmic, it is easier for her to share with her partner the type of touch that helps her reach an orgasm. As she develops her orgasm response, she can then introduce the experience into intercourse by touching herself or by using a vibrator while her partner's penis is inside her. Women should not get discouraged if orgasm does not occur during the first few lovemaking encounters. It takes time, practice, patience, and comfort. Many women are not orgasmic through intercourse alone.

Male Orgasmic Disorder   A man who cannot have an orgasm with intercourse is relatively rare. There has been little research or science regarding this phenomenon. The first concern would be if the person is on antidepressants or drugs that might be inhibiting his ability to ejaculate. Psychologically, it is important to investigate whether there has been any history of relational emotional trauma. Some believe that a causal factor could be repressive religious training. Another factor to investigate is whether the individual can get himself excited when alone, but blocks that excitement when with a partner (Joannides, 2006). Another possibility is that the male orgasm is inhibited because of a fear of an unwanted pregnancy or STI. These men need information about contraception and safer sex methods. Feeling safe can enhance his orgasmic release. After exploring these possibilities, suggest that he masturbate with his partner so she can experience him having an orgasm. During intercourse, when either partner is ready for orgasm, he should withdraw and masturbate until he feels himself on the brink of orgasm and then again insert his penis in the vagina. The goal is to have him experience having an orgasm. Once this occurs it may be easier for him to get to the point of orgasm through intercourse. A lot of patience and practice are needed for this dysfunction.

Premature Ejaculation While it is true that premature ejaculation is the most common sexual problem experienced by men, one should not get caught up with the concept that there is one cause, one treatment or one cure (Metz & McCarthy, 2003). The most common treatments suggested are the "stop-start" method and the "squeeze" technique. The "stop-start" method is often the easier and preferred procedure. After the man is aroused, his partner should stimulate (masturbate) him until he is almost ready to ejaculate. He should signal his partner, who then stops any further stimulation until the feeling of ejaculatory inevitability subsides. His partner then resumes stimulation until he again feels he is going to ejaculate, and then the partner stops. After stopping three or four times, he should go ahead and have an ejaculation. This process should be repeated several times a week until the client is able to hold back ejaculation for as long as he likes. Next, he can try intercourse, using the female superior position, going through the same process. When his penis is in her vagina, she should begin moving up and down on the penis, until he feels he is going to ejaculate. She should stop until he loses that feeling, and when he does, start moving up and down again. After repeating this exercise several times, the couple can proceed to have an orgasm.

It is also possible to treat premature ejaculation with antidepressants, such as small doses of Prozac, Paxil, or Zoloft. Combining the use of one of these medicines with the preceding exercises can bring about more rapid results (Crenshaw & Goldberg, 1996).

If these suggestions do not work, then the couple needs to see a sex therapist and explore their relationship dynamics (Metz & McCarthy, 2003).

SEXUAL PAIN DISORDERS

When a client suffers from dyspareunia (painful intercourse), vaginismus (inability to insert the penis into the vagina because of spasms), or vulvodynia (sensitive or painful areas in the vagina), it may be best to refer the client to a certified sex therapist or to a specialist, such as a gynecologist who is trained to help with these dysfunctions.

CASE EXAMPLE

John Smith, aged 49, came into treatment with the presenting problem of difficulty with achieving and maintaining erections. He had been married 25 years and has three teen-aged children. He claimed that, for the past year, he had been having increasing difficulty achieving a full erection. While apparently overweight, he claimed to be in good health. He said that he has had no affairs and that he is still attracted to his wife. The problem has created tension in his marriage. His wife said that he does not even try to make love anymore and that she fears that he is no longer attracted to her.

First, the therapist had Mr. Smith see his primary physician for a general checkup, and see a urologist to rule out any urologic problem. It was learned that Mr. Smith had been on medication for high blood pressure. His physician adjusted the medication so that the side effects would not affect his erectile ability. The physicians ruled out diabetes, any penile neuropathy, or a venous leakage (or increased outflow of blood from the erect penis due to a leakage in the valve that holds the blood in the penis).

Following the change in medication, Mr. Smith continued to have performance anxiety, believing that he could not maintain an erection. The physician recommended that he try Viagra, Levitra, or Cialis, but he was reluctant to use these medications.

In taking a sex history, the therapist discovered that Mr. and Mrs. Smith's love-making style had become routine, without any variation or experimentation. The routine love-making may have been contributing to his difficulty getting sufficiently aroused. As persons grow older, it is important to have both increased physical and mental stimulation. It was suggested that the couple try a series of sensate focus exercises to increase body arousal, decrease performance focus, and help bring some excitement back to their love-making. It became apparent that Mr. Smith had not gotten much communication from his wife regarding what she found physically and sexually exciting and pleasurable, and had not communicated well with her regarding his own pleasure. Mr. Smith had been "goal oriented" in love-making—that is, once they decided to make love, the couple would go to bed, start with kissing, then progress to caressing, including genital touching, then to some oral sex, followed by intercourse with him on top (male superior position). The problem that developed was that he would gain an erection, but when he was about to insert for intercourse, he would lose his erection.

The sensate focus exercises are a graduated set of exercises that help the couple to discover that the entire body has erotic potential and each exercise can be an end in itself. The sensate focus exercises are based on a concept of "pleasure-directed" experiences, starting with a head and face caress, followed by nongenital pleasuring, then genital exploration and stimulation, erotic foreplay, including the use of toys, and finally introducing various positions for intercourse. The therapist discussed with Mr. Smith whether it would be helpful to use visual aids to help him and his wife understand anatomy, the sexual and erotic response cycle, and the graduated series of exercises. The exercises used by this therapist can be found on the following website: www.hsab.org. Link to "A Guide to Sexual Pleasure." There is a therapist series and a client series. There is a DVD for heterosexual couples, gay male couples, and lesbian couples. Over the course of several weeks, in which Mr. Smith and his wife practiced the graduated steps of the sensate focus, he found that he was attaining an erection during the nongenital focused touching, and maintaining the erection for extended periods of their activity. Although he reported becoming more anxious when they did progress to engaging in intercourse, he successfully maintained an erection, and felt relieved. Across the subsequent weeks, his apprehension regarding his erectile function faded, and he became less anxious in anticipation and more able to relax into the pleasure of their erotic activities. The therapist worked with the couple for a slightly longer time, in order to help facilitate continuing the enhanced communication and feedback with each other during sex.

REFERENCES

Annon, J. S. (1974). *The behavioral treatment of sexual problems. Vol. 1, brief therapy.* (pp. 100–105). Honolulu: Mercantile.

Barbach, L. (1976). *For yourself: The fulfillment of female sexuality.* Garden City, NY: Doubleday.

Boyce, E. G., & Umland, E. M. (2001). Sildenafil citrate: A therapeutic update. (Review). *Clinical Therapeutics, 23,* 2–23.

Boyer, D., & Fine, D. (1992). Sexual abuse as a factor in adolescent pregnancy and child mal-treatment. *Family Planning Perspectives, 24,* 4–11.

Carroll, J. (2007). *Sexuality now: Embracing diversity* (2nd ed.) Belmont, CA: Thomson/Wadsworth.

Child Welfare League of America. (1988). *CWLA standards of excellence for services for adolescent pregnancy prevention, pregnant adolescents, and young parents.* (Revised edition). Washington, DC: Author.

Child Welfare League of America. (1994). *A survey of 17 Florence Crittenton agencies serving minor mothers.* Washington, DC: Author.

Crenshaw, T. L., & Goldberg, J. P. (1996). *Sexual pharmacology.* New York: W.W. Norton.

Dodson, B. (1987). *Sex for one: The joys of self-loving.* New York: Harmony Books.

Forrest, J. D., & Frost, J. J. (1996). The family planning attitudes and experiences of low-income women. *Family Planning Perspectives, 28,* 246– 255.

Grunbaum, J. A., Kann, L., Kinchen, S. A., Ross, J. G., Gowda, V. R., Collins, J. L., et al. (2002, June 28).Youth risk behavior surveillance (YRBS)—United States, 2001. *Morbidity and mortality weekly report,* vol. 51, no. SS-4, 1–64.

Hatcher, R. A. (2004). *Contraceptive technology* (18th ed.) New York: Ardent Media.

Heiman, J., & LoPiccolo, J. (1988). *Becoming orgasmic: A sexual and personal growth program for women.* Englewood Cliffs, NJ: Prentice-Hall.

Hoff, T., et al. (2003). *National survey of adolescents and young adults: Sexual health knowledge, attitudes, and experiences.* Menlo Park, CA: Henry Kaiser Family Foundation.

The Henry Kaiser Family Foundation and *Seventeen Magazine.* (September 2000). *Sex smarts: Decision-making.* Menlo Park, CA: Author.

The Henry Kaiser Family Foundation and *Seventeen Magazine. Sex smarts: Relationships.* (October 2002). Menlo Park, CA: Author.

The Henry Kaiser Family Foundation. (2007). *Talking with kids about tough issues: A national survey of parents and kids, questionnaire and detailed results.* Menlo Park, CA: Author.

Joannides, P. (2006). *Guide to getting it on* (5th ed.). Waldport, OR: Goofy Foot.

Kaplan, H. S. (1979). *Disorders of sexual desire: And other new concepts and techniques in sex therapy.* New York: Brunner/Mazel.

Kaplan, H. S. (1981). *Active treatment of sexual dysfunctions.* New York: Brunner/Mazel.

Kaplan, H. S. (1983). *The evaluation of sexual disorders: Psychological and medical aspects.* New York: Brunner/Mazel.

Kaplan, H. S. (1987). *Sex aversion, sex phobias and panic disorders.* New York: Brunner/Mazel.

Kinsey, A. C., Pomeroy, W. B., & Martin, C. E. (1948). *Sexual behavior in the human male.* Philadelphia: W.B. Saunders.

Kinsey, A. C., Pomeroy, W. B., & Martin, C. E. (1953). *Sexual behavior in the human female.* Philadelphia: W.B. Saunders.

Ladas, A. K., Whipple, B., & Perry, J. D. (2005) *The G spot: And other recent discoveries about human sexuality.* New York: Holt, Rinehart and Winston.

Laumann, E. O., Gagnon, J. H., Michael, R. T., & Michael, S. (1994). *The social organization of sexuality-sexual practices in the United States.* Chicago: University of Chicago Press.

Laumann, E. O., Paik, A., & Rosen, R. C. (2001). Sexual dysfunction in the United States: Prevalence and predictors. In E. O. Laumann, & R. T. Michael (Eds.), *Sex, love, and health in America* (pp. 352–376). Chicago: University of Chicago Press..

Masters, W., & Johnson, V. (1966). *Human sexual response.* Boston: Little, Brown & Company.

Masters, W., & Johnson, V. (1970). *Human sexual inadequacy.* Boston: Little, Brown & Company.

Metz, M. E., & McCarthy, B. W. (2003). *Coping with premature ejaculation.* Oakland, CA: New Harbinger Publications.

National Guidelines Task Force. (1996). *Guidelines for comprehensive sexuality education* (2nd edition, kindergarten–12th grade. New York: Sexuality Information and Education Council of the United States.

National Victims Center. (1992). *Rape in America: A report to the nation.* Arlington, VA: Author.

Physicians' Desk Reference (56th ed.). (2002). Montvale, NJ: Medical Economics Company.

Polit, D. F., White, C. M., & Morton, T. D. (1990). *Child sexual abuse and premarital intercourse among high risk adolescents. JAHC, 11,* 231–234.

Rae, S. (2001, March/April). Rx: Desire: There's new hope for women with a loss of libido—and it's NOT Viagra. *Modern maturity.*

Rowland, D. L. & Burnett, A. L. (2000). Pharmacotherapy in the treatment of male sexual dysfunction. *Journal of Sex Research, 37,* 226–243.

Satterfield, S., & Stayton, W. (1980). Understanding sexual function and dysfunction. In W. Stayton, (Ed.), *Topics in Clinical Nursing, 1,* 21–32.

Schwartz, P., Gillmore, M., & Civic, D. (1996). The social context of sexuality. In W. Cates et al. (Eds.), *Sexually transmitted diseases.* New York: McGraw Hill.

Singer, J., & Singer, I. (1983). Types of female orgasm. In J. LoPiccolo & L. LoPiccolo (Eds.), *Handbook of sex therapy.* New York: Plenum.

Stayton, W. R. (1989). A theology of sexual pleasure. *American Baptist Quarterly, 8,* 94–108.

United Nations. (1994). *Programme of action.* Reproductive rights and reproductive health. Proceedings of the International Conference on Population and Development, September 5–13, 1994; Cairo, Egypt. Section 7, 2:43.

United States General Accounting Office. (1998, November). *Teen pregnancy: Sate and federal efforts to implement prevention programs and measure their effectiveness.* GAO/HEHS-99-4. Washington, DC: Author.

Whitaker, D., & Miller, K. S. (2000, March). Parent-adolescent discussions about sex and condoms: Impact on peer influences of sexual risk behaviors. *Journal of Adolescent Research, 15,*(2), 251–273.

Author Index

Subject Index

Page numbers in *italics* indicate tables/figures.